SIKH SOLDIER
VOLUME TWO
Gallantry Awards

Shaheed Baba Deep Singh Ji (1684-1757).

NARINDAR SINGH DHESI

With the assistance of:
GRAHAM WATKINS B.Sc. (Hons)

Published by

The Naval & Military Press Ltd
Unit 10 Ridgewood Industrial Park,
Uckfield, East Sussex,
TN22 5QE England

Tel: +44 (0) 1825 749494
Fax: +44 (0) 1825 765701

www.naval-military-press.com
www.military-genealogy.com
www.militarymaproom.com

Copyright © Narindar Singh Dhesi, 2010.

ACKNOWLEDGEMENTS

The sources of the research have included the British Library, the National Army Museum and the Ministry of Defence Library, London. Books I found particularly useful were:

- *Battle Honours of The Indian Army* by Major Sarbans Singh
- *The Battle Honours of the British and Indian Armies* by Colonel H. C. B. Cook

My warmest thanks to darling daughter Surindar for her encouragement and bearing the brunt of daddy's "Sikh Attacks".

In closing, this book would not have seen the light of the day without the contributions of the long-suffering Hon. Prof. Graham Watkins, who helped not only to edit and proof-read most of the manuscript but also made it ready for publication.

ACKNOWLEDGEMENTS

I would like to thank the following people for their assistance in getting this book to press: the Web Master/Indian Army for sending me the Ashok Chakra citation of Naib Subedar Gurnam Singh; to Mr. Rakesh Koshy of the Bharat Rakshak Website for permission to reproduce the Saragarhi article by Mr. L. N. Subramaniam; to Sardar Amolak Singh for permission to publish Baba Deep Singh's painting; the staff of the National Archives of the United Kingdom, The British Library and The National Army Musuem.

Valuable data was sourced from the *London Gazette* and *Roll of Honour, Indian Army 1914 – 1921*.and the most comprehensive book on the Indian Order of Merit by Peter Duckers *Reward of Valour* published by Jade Publishing Ltd.

I have extensively consulted the outstanding collection of Mr. S. S. Gandhi on the Indian gallantry awards:

Portraits of Valour: India's Highest Gallantry Awards and their recipients
Edited by Mr. S. S. Gandhi

This book can be ordered directly from the publisher by emailing them at defrev@nda.vsnl.net.in or by phone/fax;

The Defence Review
1605, B-1, Vasant Kunj
New Delhi - 110 070
Tel: 2689-1598
Fax: 2613-2906

My warmest thanks to darling daughter Surindar for her encouragement and bearing the brunt of daddy's "Sikh Attacks". Sincere thanks to the Sikh websites: sikhnet.com and allaboutsikhs.com

In closing, this book would not have seen the light of the day without the contributions of the long-suffering Hon. Prof. Graham Watkins, who helped not only to edit and proofread most of the manuscript but also made it ready for publication.

FOREWORD

The art of appreciating the brave and gallant is not new. They form one of the most important constituents of a nation's stability. History defines gallantry as commanded respect and appreciation. Whether being the appointed head of a clan, raised memorials in honour of the martyrs-brave souls or granted titles, robe of honour, cash awards or medals etc., recognition of bravery has always been a very prestigious affair. Since ancient times soldiers have been honoured for gallantry in battle. Over the years and in different societies such honours have taken many forms but since the 1850s specific acts of bravery 'in the face of the enemy' by British and Imperial forces have been recognised by the award of a range of wearable decorations. These provide a visible indication both of the bravery of the recipient and of its recognition by the government and nation. All the members of the Indian Defence Force were eligible for, and granted, the British Empire's decorations for gallantry. The Indian Order of Merit (I.O.M.) was the highest gallantry award available to Indian soldiers between 1837 and 1911, when the eligibility for the Victoria Cross was extended to Indian officers and men. Consequently the highest decorations an Indian could get were the Victoria Cross, followed by the Indian Order of Merit, the Military Cross, Indian Distinguished Service Medal, Military Medal, George Cross, etc.

The Indian Order of Merit ranks high among the oldest and most venerable of decorations for bravery, pre-dating the Victoria Cross by nineteen years and the United State's. Medal of Honour by twenty-four years. The order was removed when India became independent in 1947.

India instituted its own gallantry awards following the British pattern of awards, when it turned Republic in 1950. Foremost in precedence were the wartime gallantry awards: the Param Vir Chakra, followed by the Mahavir Chakra and the Vir Chakra. At the same time there were peacetime bravery awards: the Ashoka Chakra and Kirti Chakra. These awards can be made to any member of the armed forces as well as civilians in the war effort.

The annals of Sikh history are replete with examples of gallantry on the battlefield, but the gallantry awards earned by the Sikh soldier have never before been collated and documented in one volume.

This volume, which Mr. Dhesi has written with such loving labour, speaks for itself. The following pages will preserve forever the memory of the Sikh soldiers who have fought and died in declaration of their faith.

DEDICATION

When Guru Gobind Singh created the Order of the Khalsa, he laid the foundations of the Sikh military might by setting up a tradition of reckless valour, which became the distinguishing feature of Sikh soldiery. They came to believe in the triumph of their cause as an article of faith, and asked for no nobler end than a death on the battlefield:

> With clasped hands this boon I crave
> When time comes to end my life
> Let me fall in mighty strife.

> What Guru Gobind Singh succeeded in doing was to
> "Teach the sparrow to hunt the hawk and one man fight a legion."
> (Sardar Khushwant: Singh *The Sikhs Today*)

The Sikh soldier went through two holocausts in his epic struggle for survival: against the organized forces of the Afghans and against the Imperial Forces of the Mughal Empire.

"The Sikhs, it was thought, had been hammered out of existence. But the hammering did not reduce them to pulp, but hardened the remnants to tempered steel." *(V. Smith, History of India)*

The Sikh soldier went on to dominate his enemies and establish a Sikh Kingdom in Northern India. At the fall of the Sikh Kingdom, he went soldiering to the far corners of the British Empire. Now he stands tall as a Sentinel of his Motherland. This is a token dedication to the Sikh soldier for his unflinching courage on the field of battle, with his battle cry:

Jo Bole So Nihal, Sat Sri Akal.

CONTENTS

Acknowledgements	iii
Foreword	iv
Dedication	v
Introduction	1
Nishan Sahib and the Khanda	2
Indian Military Ranks and their British Equivalents	3
Victoria Cross	4
Indian Order of Merit	10
Military Cross	117
Indian Distinguished Service Medal, 1914 - 1921	190
Indian Distinguished Service Medal, 1922 – 1947	255
Military Medal	282
Distinguished Flying Cross	294
Medaille Militaire (France)	295
The Legion of Honour	296
The Purple Heart	297
Silver Star	298
Bronze Star	299
Burma Gallantry Medal	300
The George Cross	301
The Empire Gallantry Medal	302
George Medal	304
Al Valore Militare (Italy)	304
Distinguished Service Order	305
British Empire Medal	309
Order of the British Empire	314
Croix de Guerre (France)	319
Croix de Guerre (Belgium)	320
Cross of St. George (Russia)	321
The Guides	322
Division of Army after Independence	325
Param Vir Chakra	328
Ashoka Chakra	333
Mahavir Chakra	338
Vir Chakra	361
Kirti Chakra	423
Shaurya Chakra	435

INTRODUCTION

The annals of Sikh history are replete with examples of gallantry on the battlefield. One is always tempted to ask why this tiny community has made such disproportionate sacrifices. The Sikh soldier by nature seeks action, and the Punjabi tradition of the Saint-soldier began right from the very inception of the Sikh ethos.

The Punjabi soldier is imbued with the discipline of deeds - a primary concept for the path of virtuous deeds is the only discipline acceptable to God. He is inextricably tied to the world by the sword. This is the distinction that the Ten Masters deliberately and clearly demarcated as a departure from other Indian traditions.

For the Sikh soldier there is no other path than that which considers the good of all. For service for God is synonymous with service for man. Altruistic activities have the highest priority in the discipline of the Sikhs. The demands of moral life invite the greatest of sacrifices, even of life itself.

From this stems the Sikh battle anthem, "Oh God, grant me such a boon that I may never cease from doing righteous deeds. When time comes to end my life let me fall in mighty strife"

The Sikh soldier has fought on every major battlefield in the world: he fought and defeated the traditional conquerors of India – the Afghans and the Mughals - and established a Sikh Empire in northern India. At the fall of the Sikh Kingdom he became a "Motor Muscle" of the British Empire, and fought from the trenches of France and Flanders to the sands of the African Sahara, from the deserts of Middle East to the steaming jungles of Burma, and the frozen tundra of China. After Independence in 1947 he was first in the field, and has the honour of having participated in all the battles to defend his Motherland since that time, including the liberation of Bangladesh.

In conclusion, let me add that the gallantry awards earned by the Sikh soldier have never before been collated and documented in one volume, and if this brief survey inspires someone to take up an exhaustive treatment of the subject, I shall consider the effort well rewarded.

NISHAN SAHIB

The origin of the Nishan Sahib is traced to the time of Guru Hargobind Singh the tenth Master, who hoisted it over the Akal Takhat at Amritsar in 1606. Nishan Sahib in the Sikh tradition means the holy flag or exalted ensign - a symbol representing the values of the Sikh faith, as it is, indeed, the symbol of the freedom of the Khalsa The Sikhs ask in their prayers everyday to forever keep the Nishan Sahib fluttering high; representing their sovereignty, and the principles of fighting against injustice

THE KHANDA

The Khanda is one of most important symbols of Sikhism and is emphasized by the fact that all the Sikh flags have the Khanda on them. It is a collection of four weapons commonly used by Sikhs at the time of Guru Gobind Singh.

The weapons are: a double-edged sword, called a Khanda, which sits in the middle, Chakkar a circular weapon that surrounds the Khanda which indicates that God and eternal life is without end and is perfect. Two single-edged swords, or Kirpans, are crossed at the bottom and sit on either side of the Khanda and Chakkar. They represent the dual nature and duties of the Gurus, Miri and Piri.

The weapons have symbolic meanings. The Khanda symbolises knowledge of God, the Chakkar symbolizes the oneness of God, Miri means political sovereignty and Piri means spiritual sovereignty.

INDIAN MILITARY RANKS AND THEIR BRITISH EQUIVALENTS

ARMY

Viceroy's Commissioned Officers

Indian Infantry	Indian Cavalry	British
Subedar Major	Risaldar Major	Major
Subedar	Risaldar	Captain
Jemadar	Jemadar	Lieutenant

Non-Commissioned Officers

Indian Infantry	Indian Cavalry	British
Havildar Major	Kot Daffadar	Sergeant Major
Havildar	Daffadar	Sergeant
Naik	Lance Daffadar	Corporal
Lance Naik	Acting Lance Daffadar	Lance Corporal
Sepoy	Sowar	Private

Ressaidar

A rank of cavalry officer between Jemadar and Risaldar. In 1921 the rank was abolished and all Ressaidars became Risaldars.

Naib Subedar

Prior to 1965 the rank of Naib Subedar was known as Jemadar.

Other specialised titles are self-explanatory, examples being Bugler, Trumpeter, Drummer, Gunner, Driver, Assistant Surgeon, Signalman, Rifleman and so on.

NAVY and AIR FORCE

The ranks are the same as and equivalent to the British.

VICTORIA CROSS

The Victoria Cross (VC) is the highest recognition for valour "in the face of the enemy" that can be awarded to members of the British and some Commonwealth armed forces (British Empire personnel prior to the Commonwealth). In 1911 King George V extended this to include officers and men of the Indian Army. Previously the equivalent award for which these soldiers were eligible was the Indian Order of Merit.

Victoria Cross (cont.)

NAIK (LATER JEMADAR) NAND SINGH VC

The Japanese had taken Burma and were poised for the invasion of India. 1ST Battalion, 11TH Sikh Regiment became part of 7TH Indian Division formed for the re-conquest of Burma and the destruction of the Japanese forces. The Japanese would not surrender; and had to be killed one by one. On the night of March 11TH/12TH, 1944, a Japanese platoon about 40 strong, with medium and light machine-guns and a grenade discharger, infiltrated into the battalion's position covering the main Maungdaw-Buthidaung road. They occupied a dominating position where they dug foxholes and trenches on the precipitous sides of the hill, threatening to hold up the main advance. A platoon was ordered to capture the position at all costs. Naik Nand Singh, a section commander, led his men on a narrow path up to the top of a very steep knife-edged ridge. This necessitated proceeding in single file under heavy machine-gun and rifle fire. Shouting the famous Sikh battle cry "Sat Siri Akal". Nand Singh led the attack. Although wounded in the thigh, he rushed ahead of his section and captured the first enemy trench. He then crawled forward alone under heavy fire. Although wounded again in the face and shoulder by a grenade that burst one yard in front of him, he took the second trench at the point of his bayonet. Shortly afterwards, when all his section had been either killed or wounded, Naik Nand Singh dragged himself out of the trench and captured a third trench, killing all the occupants with his bayonet. Due to the capture of these three trenches the remainder of the platoon were able to seize the top of the hill and deal with the remaining Japanese. During these operations Nand Singh personally killed seven of the enemy.

Owing to his determination, outstanding spirit, and magnificent courage, the dominating position was won back from the enemy and he was awarded the Victoria Cross.

In the 1947 conflict over Kashmir, Nand Singh was mortally wounded while leading a bayonet attack on the enemy. For his supreme sacrifice in this action Nand Singh was awarded MVC (Mahavir Chakra), the second highest military award for valour in India. Nand Singh is the only Indian soldier to have been awarded both the VC and MVC.

Born at Bahadurhur Village, Patiala State, Punjab, India, in 1914.
Killed at Uri, Kashmir, 12TH December 1947, aged 33.

Victoria Cross (cont.)

SEPOY (LATER CAPTAIN) ISHAR SINGH VC

In 1922, Sepoy Ishar Singh earned a unique 'peacetime' Victoria Cross, making him an even more exclusive soldier than his peers, who earned theirs in the heat of overseas campaigns during wartime.

Along the rugged, barren, mountainous Northwest Frontier of India lived truculent peoples of various clans who were a law unto themselves. Fanatically religious and incited by their Mullahs, they often declared 'holy war' on the infidel. These well armed, blood thirsty marauders, ready to kill, torture and mutilate, constantly raided the British territories and attacked the military posts and their supply convoys of camels laden with food, weapons and ammunition. On the 10TH April 1921, near Haidari Kach (Waziristan), when his convoy protection troop was attacked, Ishar Singh was leading a Lewis-gun section. Early in the action he had received a very severe gunshot wound in the chest, and had fallen beside his Lewis-gun. During the ensuing hand-to-hand fighting, the British and Indian officers of his company were either killed or wounded, and Ishar Singh's Lewis-gun was captured. Calling up two other men, he got up, charged the attackers, killing two of them and chasing away a third, and recovered the Lewis-gun. Although bleeding profusely, he again got the gun into action.

His Jemadar took the gun from Ishar Singh and ordered him to go back and have his wounds dressed. Instead of doing this Ishar Singh went to the medical officer and was of great assistance in pointing out where the wounded were and in carrying water to them. He made innumerable journeys to the river and back for this purpose. On one occasion he stood in front of the medical officer who was dressing a wounded man, thus shielding him from the gunfire with his own body. It was over three hours before he finally submitted to be evacuated, being then too weak from loss of blood to object. His gallantry and devotion to duty were beyond praise. His conduct inspired all that saw him and earned him the Victoria Cross.

In 1947 Ishar Singh was transferred to The Sikh Regiment and retired with the rank of Captain.

Born at Newwan, Hoshiarpur District, and 13TH December 1895.
Died at Newwan, Hoshiarpur District, 2ND December 1963, aged 68 Years.

Victoria Cross (cont.)

HAVILDAR (LATER MAJOR) PARKASH SINGH VC

In Burma on January 6TH, 1943, near the Japanese-occupied village of Donbaik, the enemy hurled a salvo of grenades at the leading armoured troop carrier. Havildar Parkash Singh's superior officer, Captain Bert Causey, was immediately wounded. Parkash took command while Causey retired. He saw that further forward two other carriers were bogged down and under heavy fire from the advancing Japanese. With his Bren gunner wounded, he drove forward with one hand, firing the Bren with the other. He charged into the ranks of the astonished Japanese, scattering them and continued into their fixed positions causing such consternation that they fled. He then returned to pick up the stranded men. Despite a hail of fire from a fresh Japanese attack, all eight men embarked and crouched, shaking, on the floor with rifle and machine-gun fire hammering against the casing all the way back to the British/Indian lines.

On January 19TH the carriers were ordered to advance along the beach and draw the enemy's fire. They were greeted by a burst of anti-tank gunfire against the lightly armoured carriers. Several were wrecked, including Causey's, whose driver had both legs shot off. Dragging his terrified driver out of a trench, Parkash guided his carrier down to the beach again, through a hail of small and large calibre gunfire. He discovered that Causey and his driver were too badly injured to be moved. Ignoring Causey's pleas to retreat and save himself, Parkash rigged up a makeshift tow-chain, exposing himself to enemy fire as he scuttled between the two vehicles. Causey was too weak from his wounds to put his vehicle in neutral and Parkash vaulted from one vehicle to the other to free the jammed lever. One of the more hair-raising tows in vehicular history then took place; over rough ground with anti-tank rounds ripping through the hulls of both carriers. For the last hundred yards, in a gesture of admirable bravado, Parkash sat on top of his vehicle, a splendid, be-turbaned figure with arms folded, impassively ignoring the Japanese bullets whistling around his ears. As they came into their own lines one observer said presciently "There's a fellow winning a VC."

In 1947 Parkash Singh was transferred to the Sikh Regiment, retiring with the rank of Major in 1968.

Born at Sharikar, Lyallpur District, Punjab, India, 31ST March 1913.
Died in London, 23RD March 1991 aged 78.

Victoria Cross (cont.)

LIEUTENANT KARAMJEET SINGH JUDGE VC

In Burma on the 18TH March 1945, Lieutenant Karamjeet Singh Judge was ordered to capture the Cotton Mill area on the outskirts of Myingyan.

Up to the last moment Lieut. Karamjeet Singh Judge dominated the entire battlefield by his numerous and successive acts of superb gallantry. Although cover around the tanks was non-existent, Lieutenant Karamjeet Singh Judge remained with the tanks, regardless not only of heavy small-arms fire directed at him but also of extremely heavy shelling directed at the tanks. Lieut. Karamjeet Singh Judge succeeded in recalling the tanks and personally indicated the bunkers for the tanks to deal with, thus allowing the infantry to advance. In every case Lieutenant Karamjeet Singh Judge personally led the infantry charges against the bunkers and was invariably the first to arrive. In this way, this brilliant and courageous officer eliminated ten bunkers. On one occasion, as he was going into attack, two Japanese with fixed bayonets suddenly rushed at him from a small nullah at a distance of only ten yards. He killed both. About fifteen minutes before the battle finished, a last nest of three bunkers was located in a position that was difficult for the tanks to approach. An enemy light machine-gun was firing from one of them and holding the advance of the infantry. Undaunted and at great personal risk, Lieutenant Karamjeet Singh Judge directed one tank to within 20 yards of the bunkers, and then threw a smoke grenade as a marker. After some minutes firing from the tank, he asked the commander to cease firing whilst he went in with a few men to mop up. He then went forward and got within 10 yards of the bunker, when the machine-gun opened fire again, mortally wounding him in the chest. By this time, however, the remaining men of the section were able to storm this strong point and so complete the long and arduous task. During this battle, Lieutenant Karamjeet Singh Judge was an example of cool and calculated bravery. In three previous and similar actions, this young officer had already proved himself an outstanding leader of matchless courage. In his last action, Lieut. Karamjeet Singh Judge gave a superb demonstration of inspiring leadership and outstanding courage.

Born at Kapurthala, Kapurthala State, Punjab, India, and 25TH May 1923.
Killed in action at Myingyan, Burma, 18TH March 1945 aged 22.

Victoria Cross (cont.)

NAIK (LATER SUBEDAR MAJOR) GIAN SINGH VC

In Burma, on March 2ND 1945, the Japanese were holding a strong position astride the Kamye-Myingyan road. As all water supply points were within the enemy's position, it was vital that he should be dislodged. The attack on the first objective was successful and one platoon was ordered to attack a village to the right. This platoon's attack, with the aid of tanks, advanced very slowly under very heavy enemy fire. Naik Gian Singh was in command of the leading section. The enemy was well concealed along the cacti hedges but Naik Gian Singh soon observed enemy foxholes some 20 yards ahead. Ordering his light machine-gunner to cover him, he rushed the enemy foxholes alone, firing his Tommy gun. He was met by a hail of fire and wounded in the arm. In spite of this he continued his advance alone, hurling grenades. He killed several Japanese including four in one of the enemy main weapon pits. By this time a troop of British tanks moved in support and came under fire from a cleverly concealed enemy anti-tank gun. Naik Gian Singh quickly saw the threat to the tanks, and ignoring the danger to himself and in spite of his wounds, he again rushed forward, capturing the gun and killing the crew single-handed. His section followed him, and he then led them down a lane of cacti hedges, clearing all enemy positions, which were being firmly held. Some 20 enemy bodies were found in this area, the majority of which fell to Naik Gian Singh and his section. After this action, Naik Gian Singh was ordered to the Regimental First-Aid Post but, in spite of his wounds, requested permission to lead his section until the whole action had been completed. This was granted. There is no doubt that many casualties to Naik Gian Singh's platoon were prevented by his acts of supreme gallantry, they enabled the whole operation to be carried out successfully with severe losses to the enemy. Although wounded, the magnificent gallantry, devotion to duty and leadership of Gian Singh throughout this action could not have been surpassed.

At the division of the Indian Army in 1947 Gian Singh was posted to The Sikh Regiment. During the Indo-China War of 1962, Subedar Major Gian Singh was again decorated, on this occasion with the Indian MC.

Born at Shahbazpur Village, Julluner District, Punjab, India, 5TH October 1920. Died in peaceful retirement at Jullunder, 6TH October 1996 aged 76.

INDIAN ORDER OF MERIT

The East India Company first introduced this medal in 1837 and it was proposed for "conspicuous gallantry in the field". The Indian Order of Merit was the highest gallantry award available to Indian soldiers between 1837 and 1911, when the eligibility for the Victoria Cross was extended to Indian officers and men. The Indian Order of Merit ranks high among the oldest and most venerable of decorations for bravery, pre-dating the Victoria Cross by nineteen years and the United State's. Medal of Honour by twenty-four years. The order was removed when India became independent in 1947.

At the fall of the Sikh kingdom and the annexation of the Punjab to the British Empire, the British had to police the turbulent tribes of the North West Frontier of India. To provide military backing for the administrators, a special force, The Punjab Frontier Force, was formed and consisted of regiments of cavalry, battalions of infantry and mountain batteries. The bulks of volunteers for the Frontier Force were veterans of the Khalsa Armies of Maharajah Ranjit Singh, and they had some 700 miles of frontier to guard.

The following Sikh officers and men were awarded the Indian Order of Merit in consideration of their conspicuous gallantry against the Afridi tribe on the North West Frontier of India.

ACTION AGAINST AFRIDIS 1853

CORPS OF GUIDES

SUBEDAR	KOR SINGH	1853	BORER VALLEY
SOWAR	DUL SINGH	1853	BORER VALLEY

BOZDAR 1857

In 1857, the 2ND Punjab Infantry had to force the Khan Band defile in North West Frontier of India to take action against the Bozdar tribe. It had been the scene of combat in which the Bozdars some years before had suffered very severely at the hands of the Khalsa Army of the Sikh Kingdom. The following Sikh soldiers were awarded the Indian Order of Merit in consideration of their conspicuous gallantry against the Bozdar tribe.

2ND PUNJAB INFANTRY

SEPOY	BUX SINGH	1857	KHAN BAND
SEPOY	JAWHIR SINGH	1857	KHAN BAND

Indian Order of Merit (cont.)
THE SEPOY MUTINY 1857

The Bengal Army mutinied at the Meerut cantonment near Delhi on 10TH May 1857. The Mutiny spread to Delhi, Agra, Cawnpore and Lucknow, starting a yearlong insurrection against the British. The Pathans of the N.W. Frontier, the Gurkhas of Nepal, the Sikhs of the Punjab, and the Rajputs of Rajasthan supported the British. The Mutineers finally surrendered on June 20TH 1858.

During the Mutiny, one of the most extraordinary actions on record, The Defence of a house at Arrah, was made by a detachment of sixty men of the Sikh Military Police Battalion in defending a house for ten days against three disciplined regiments of the Mutineers. In 1864 the Battalion became a regular army unit: the famous 45TH Rattray's Sikhs. 231 Indian Order of Merit medals were awarded to Sikh soldiers during the Mutiny. All belonged to the teeth arms of the Indian Army.

BHUTAN DEWANGIRI 1865

As a result of continuing Bhutanese raids into Indian Territory, the government decided on a punitive action against them. The raiders were met and overcame at Dhalimkote, Bhumsong and Charmoorchee. A detachment captured Dewanigiri on 2ND April 1865, after which the Bhutanese accepted defeat. The following Sikh officers and men were awarded the Indian Order of Merit in consideration of their conspicuous gallantry against the Bhutanese raiders.

14TH BENGAL CAVALRY

RISALDAR	CHOORMUN SINGH	1865	BHUTAN
SOWAR	DOORJUN SINGH	1865	BHUTAN
SOWAR	BHURT SINGH	1865	BHUTAN

19TH PUNJABIS

HAVILDAR	PREM SINGH	1865	BHUTAN
NAIK	HEERA SINGH	1865	BHUTAN

THE MUNNIPORE VALLEY 1866

By the 1820s the Burmese had overrun Manipur and Assam, and it was a constant threat to the Eastern Frontiers of British-India. Thus an alliance was formed between the Munnipuris and the British to drive off the Burmese. In 1866, the British cooperated with the Munnipuris to stem the Burmese incursions in Munnipore Valley.

5TH REGIMENT NATIVE INFANTRY

Sepoy Narian Singh was awarded the Indian Order of Merit for conspicuous gallantry in action at Bishenpur in the Munnipore Valley. He was the only soldier to be awarded a gallantry award in these operations.

Indian Order of Merit (cont.)
SULLIMAN KHELS 1866 - 67

The following Sikh officers were awarded the Indian Order of Merit for their conspicuous gallantry in actions against the Sulliman Khel marauders from across the borders of the North West Frontier of India.

4TH PUNJAB CAVALRY

| JEMADAR | KISHAN SINGH | 1866 | KUROTI |

5TH PUNJAB CAVALRY

| DAFFADAR | OOJAGAR SINGH | 1867 | HURRUND |

ABYSSINIA EXPEDITION 1868

In 1868, a combined British and Indian force invaded Abyssinia to secure the release of captives held hostage by King Theodore. The decisive action was fought at Apogee, near the capital. A detachment of 23RD Sikh Pioneers charged forward and met the enemy in close combat. The Abyssinian courage could not stand up to the Sikh bayonets and they were beaten off with very heavy losses. The following Sikh officers and men of the 23RD Sikh Pioneers were awarded the Indian Order of Merit in consideration of their conspicuous gallantry. They were the only gallantry awards made to Indian soldiers in this expedition.

23RD SIKH PIONEERS

SUBEDAR MAJOR	NATHA SINGH	1868	APOGEE
SUBEDAR	KHARAK SINGH	1868	APOGEE
SEPOY	FUTTEH SINGH	1868	APOGEE
SEPOY	JOWALA SINGH	1868	APOGEE
BUGLER	KHUSHAL SINGH	1868	APOGEE

LOOSHAI EXPEDITION 1871
(North East Frontier of India)

A spate of significant Lushai raids into Manipur, Tripura and Sylhet, in which six-year old English girl was seized, culminated in a 17-hour attack on a fortified tea plantation, defended by about 80 Frontier Police and Sepoys. This resulted in a punitive expedition lasting from November 1871 to February 1872, involving 4,000 Indian troops. Twenty Lushai villages were destroyed and the English girl rescued. There were no major Lushai raids for the next decade.

44TH REGIMENT OF LIGHT INFANTRY

NAIK BUGHET SINGH

Naik Bughet Singh was awarded the Indian Order of Merit for conspicuous gallantry in action at Khollel in the Looshai Expedition of 1871. Naik Bughet Singh was the only soldier to be awarded a gallantry award in these operations.

Indian Order of Merit (cont.)
JOWAKI EXPEDITION 1877

The Jowaki Afridis occupied territory between Peshawar and the Kohat Pass on the North West Frontier of India. After continuous attacks by them upon neighbouring tribes in Boris Valley, forces were sent to suppress them in 1877.

14TH REGIMENT OF FEROZEPORE SIKHS
HAVILDAR DHARUM SINGH
Havildar Dharum Singh was awarded the Indian Order of Merit for conspicuous gallantry in action against the Afridis. He was the only soldier to be awarded a gallantry award in these operations.

SUAKIN 1885

After the British intervention in Egypt in 1882, there was trouble in the neighbouring Sudan in 1885. British-backed Egyptian regime in the Sudan was threatened by an indigenous rebellion under the leadership of Muhammed Ahmed, known to his followers as the Mahdi. An Indian force was dispatched for the operations against the Dervish followers of the Mahdi. The 9TH Bengal Cavalry were highly praised for their operations around Suakin. The following Sikh officers and men were awarded the Indian Order of Merit in consideration of their conspicuous gallantry during these operations.

9TH BENGAL CAVALRY

RESSAIDAR	HOOKUM SINGH	1885	SUAKIN
L. DAFFADAR	INDHUR SINGH	1885	SUAKIN
L. DAFFADAR	POOURN SINGH	1885	SUAKIN
TRUMPETER	KAISER SINGH	1885	SUAKIN

THE SECOND AFGHAN WAR 1878-1880

British Government in 1878 were anxious to counter Russian influence in Afghanistan and demanded the Afghans to receive a British military mission to Kabul. When the Afghan ruler Sher Ali refused, Britain mounted an expedition to compel his submission The Battle of Ali Masjid was the opening battle between the British forces and the Afghan army. The following soldiers were awarded collective Indian Order of Merit for their conspicuous gallantry in action on the 21ST November 1878 in the attack on the Afghan fort at Ali Masjid.

14TH FEROZEPORE SIKHS

HAVILDAR	DEWAH SINGH	1878	ALI MASJID
HAVILDAR	MAUN SINGH	1878	ALI MASJID
SEPOY	HEERAH SINGH	1878	ALI MASJID
SEPOY	BUDH SINGH	1878	ALI MASJID
SEPOY	UTTER SINGH	1878	ALI MASJID
SEPOY	DHAN SINGH	1878	ALI MASJID

Indian Order of Merit (cont.)
THE SECOND AFGHAN WAR 1878-1880 (cont.)

24TH PUNJABIS

SEPOY KAPUR SINGH

Sepoy Kapur Singh was awarded Indian Order of Merit for conspicuous gallantry in action in Choora Valley on 31ST January 1878.

NAIK DHURM SINGH
NAIK SOOBAH SINGH

The above soldiers were awarded Indian Order of Merit for their great coolness, under heavy fire of artillery and musketry, in saving the reserve ammunition and entrenching tools from falling into enemy hands.

27TH PUNJABIS

HAVILDAR GOORDIT SINGH
SEPOY ASA SINGH

The above soldiers were awarded Indian Order of Merit for conspicuous gallantry in action on the 21ST November 1878 at Ali Masjid, in advancing to occupy a Sangar close to the enemy's position.

HAVILDAR DYAL SINGH

Havildar Dyal Singh was awarded the Indian Order of Merit for conspicuous gallantry in action on the 21ST November 1878 at Ali Masjid, in carrying Sepoy Jowahir Singh, when wounded, out of heavy fire.

29TH PUNJABIS

HAVILDAR GOORMUKH SINGH
SEPOY HEERA SINGH

The above soldiers were awarded Indian Order of Merit for conspicuous gallantry in the action of 28TH November 1878 at the Turai Glen near Peiwar Kotal.

SUBADAR MAJOR JUGGET
HAVILDAR NUTHA SINGH

The above soldiers were awarded Indian Order of Merit for conspicuous gallantry in action at the assault of the Spin Gawai Kotal on the 2ND December 1878.

LANCE NAIK SHER SINGH

Lance Naik Sher Singh was awarded the Indian Order of Merit for conspicuous gallantry in the action with the enemy at the capture of the Peiwar Kotal on the 2ND December 1878.

Indian Order of Merit (cont.)
THE SECOND AFGHAN WAR 1878-1880 (cont.)

5TH PUNJAB CAVALRY, FRONTIER FORCE

SOWAR JHANDA SINGH

Sowar Jhanda Singh was awarded the Indian Order of Merit for conspicuous gallantry in heading the charge of his troop against a force may times its number and under heavy fire, in the fight against the Mangals on the 7TH January 1879.

The following Sikh officers and men were awarded a collective Indian Order of Merit for their conspicuous gallantry in action at Latabad Pass on the 2ND April 1879.

SOWAR	BUSSAWA SINGH	1879	LATABAD
K. DAFFADAR	HARSA SINGH	1879	LATABAD
DAFFADAR	KESAR SINGH	1879	LATABAD
DAFFADAR	MAIAH SINGH	1879	LATABAD
SOWAR	NUTHA SINGH	1879	LATABAD

GUIDES CAVALRY, PUNJAB FRONTIER FORCE

The following Sikh officers and men were awarded a collective Indian Order of Merit for their conspicuous gallantry in a cavalry charge against a large body of fanatical Khugiani Ghazis near Fatehbad on the 2ND April 1879.

SOWAR	DEWAN SINGH	1879	FATTEHBAD
SOWAR	KARDOO SINGH	1879	FATTEHBAD
DAFFADAR	JEWAN SINGH	1879	FATTEHBAD
RESSAIDAR	NAND SINGH	1879	FATTEHBAD
SOWAR	PREM SINGH	1879	FATTEHBAD
SOWAR	YAKUB SINGH	1879	FATTEHBAD

2ND SIKH INFANTRY, PUNJAB FRONTIER FORCE

SUBEDAR MAJOR GURBAX SINGH

Subadar Major Gurbax Singh was awarded the Indian Order of Merit for conspicuous gallantry in leading and encouraging the men during the advance on the enemy's position, and charging a band of Ghazis while under continuous enemy rifle fire.

SEPOY ALA SINGH

Sepoy Ala Singh was awarded the Indian Order of Merit for conspicuous gallantry in single handedly attacking several Ghazis and killing two of them, while receiving severe wound in the encounter.

Indian Order of Merit (cont.)
THE SECOND AFGHAN WAR 1878-1880 (cont.)

14TH BENGAL LANCERS

JEMADAR GOPAL SINGH

Jemadar Gopal Singh was awarded the Indian Order of Merit for conspicuous gallantry in action at Churdeh Valley on the 11TH December 1879.

23RD SIKH PIONEERS

SUBEDAR MEHTAB SINGH
HAVILDAR GULAB SINGH

The above soldiers were awarded the Indian Order of Merit for conspicuous gallantry in action at Latabad on 16TH December 1879.

SEPOY CHATTAR SINGH

Sepoy Chattar Singh was awarded the Indian Order of Merit for leaping across a wet ditch in the face of some forty of the enemy, and bayoneting several of them on 1ST September 1880.

SEPOY GUNDA SINGH

Sepoy Gunda Singh was awarded the Indian Order of Merit for bayoneting two of the enemy, in a charge at their Sangars, in which he was particularly forward, and saving the life of Subadar Dewa Singh, whom these men at attacked on 1ST September 1880.

SUBEDAR DEWA SINGH

Subedar Dewa Singh was awarded the Indian Order of Merit for conspicuous gallantry in action near Kandahar on the 1ST September 1879, on which occasion he led the way in charge on one of enemy's Sangars, which he was the first to enter, and in which two guns were captured.

CHARASIA

Charasia, situated about six miles from Kabul, was where in October 1879, the Kabul Field Force, advancing to exact retribution for massacre of the British Mission, routed the Afghan field army. The following Sikh officers and men were awarded the Indian Order of Merit in consideration of their conspicuous gallantry during these operations.

JEMADAR	BOOR SINGH	1879	CHARASIA
SEPOY	CHUNDA SINGH	1879	CHARASIA
SUBEDAR	DEWA SINGH	1879	CHARASIA
HAVILDAR	GOORDIAL SINGH	1879	CHARASIA
SEPOY	JHUNDA SINGH	1879	CHARASIA
SEPOY	HURDIT SINGH	1879	CHARASIA
SUBEDAR	MEHTAB SINGH	1879	CHARASIA
NAIK	OOTUM SINGH	1879	CHARASIA

Indian Order of Merit (cont.)
THE SECOND AFGHAN WAR 1878-1880 (cont.)

The battle of Maiwand was one of the principal battles of the Second Afghan War. The battle ended in defeat for the British Brigade. Following Sikh officers and men were awarded the Indian Order of Merit in consideration of their conspicuous gallantry in keeping off parties of the enemy's cavalry, who were in pursuit, thus saving the lives of many wounded and exhausted men.

3RD SIND HORSE

SOWAR	BEER SINGH	1880	MAIWAND
LANCE NAIK	BISHUN SINGH	1880	MAIWAND
LANCE NAIK	JOWALA SINGH	1880	MAIWAND
SOWAR	LEHNA SINGH	1880	MAIWAND
SOWAR	SOONDAR SINGH	1880	MAIWAND

10TH BENGAL LANCERS

SOWAR BHAGWAN SINGH
Sowar Bhagwan Singh was awarded Indian Order of Merit for conspicuous gallantry in Afghanistan on the 19TH April 1880.

19TH BENGAL LANCERS

RESSAIDAR JOWAHIR SINGH
Ressaidar Jowahir Singh was awarded the Indian Order of Merit for conspicuous gallantry in action at Ahmed Khel on the 19TH April 1880, on which occasion, at the head of three dismounted men, he dashed through some fifteen or twenty of the enemy, who were resisting their passage, killing two of them with his own hands and receiving a wound in the encounter.

KOT DAFFADAR HOOKUM SINGH
Kot Daffadar Hookum Singh was awarded the Indian Order of Merit for conspicuous gallantry in action at Patkao Shana on the 1ST July 1880, in charging single handedly five of the enemy, and killing two of them.

SOWAR GULAB SINGH
Sowar Gulab Singh was awarded Indian Order of Merit for conspicuous gallantry in action at Ahmed Khel on the 19TH April 1880, in dismounting and leading an attack under a heavy fire, on a number of the enemy who had posted themselves in a ditch, killing more than one of them and setting an excellent example to the other men with him.

DAFFADAR NAURUNG SINGH
Daffadar Naurung Singh was awarded the Indian Order of Merit for conspicuous gallantry in action at Patkao Shana on the 1ST July 1880, on which occasion he led the charge against the enemy and killed several of the enemy himself.

Indian Order of Merit (cont.)
THE SECOND AFGHAN WAR 1878-1880 (cont.)
19TH BENGAL LANCERS (cont.)

DAFFADAR HARDIT SINGH
Daffadar Hardit Singh was awarded the Indian Order of Merit for conspicuous gallantry in action at Ahmed Khel on 19TH April 1880, on which occasion, although severely wounded; he engaged and cut down two of the enemy, who were attacking a fellow cavalryman, Sowar Boota Singh.

LANCE DAFFADAR KEHAR SINGH
Lance Daffadar Singh was awarded the Indian Order of Merit for conspicuous gallantry in action at Ahmed Khel on 19TH April 1880, in saving the life of Ressaidar Ganda Singh, when the later was attacked by two of the enemy, also, on the same occasion, single handedly charging a group of eight or ten Ghazis and killing two of them.

LANCE DAFFADAR SARDAR SINGH
Lance Daffadar Sardar Singh was awarded the Indian Order of Merit for conspicuous gallantry in action at Ahmed Khel on 19TH April 1880, in charging, with Kot Daffadar Hubboob Singh, a superior number of the enemy who had suddenly attacked the flank of the squadron to which he belonged, killing two of them.

SOWAR KHUSHAL SINGH
Sowar Khushal Singh was awarded the Indian Order of Merit for conspicuous gallantry in action at Ahmed Khel on 19TH April 1880, in rescuing Kot Daffadar Kurram Singh who was severely wounded and nearly overcome in a conflict with two Ghazis.

SOWAR RAM SINGH
Sowar Ram Singh was awarded the Indian Order of Merit for conspicuous gallantry in action at Ahmed Khel on 19TH April 1880, in charging three of the enemy's horsemen who were rushing on Surgeon Murphy, killing one of them and saving that officer's life.

SOWAR UTTAR SINGH
Sowar Uttar Singh was awarded the Indian Order of Merit for conspicuous gallantry in action at Ahmed Khel on 19TH April 1880, on which occasion, although wounded in two places, he charged two Ghazis, killing one of them, and saved the life of Daffadar Narain Singh, whom they had beset.

Indian Order of Merit (cont.)
THE SECOND AFGHAN WAR 1878-1880 (cont.)

45TH RATTRAY'S SIKHS

SEPOY LAL SINGH
SEPOY NUND SINGH
SEPOY THERAJ SINGH

The above soldiers were awarded the Indian Order of Merit for conspicuous gallantry on the 7TH March near Maidan Neck, when on escort duty with a survey party.

1ST PUNJAB CAVALRY, FRONTIER FORCE

SOWAR BOOTAH SINGH

Sowar Bootah Singh was awarded the Indian Order of Merit for conspicuous gallantry in action at Arzu on the 23RD April 1880, in singly engaging and cutting down in hand-to- hand fight two of the enemy.

DAFFADAR CHAIT SINGH

Was awarded the Indian Order of Merit for conspicuous gallantry in action at Patkao Shana on 1ST July 1880, on which occasion he killed three of the enemy, one of them being a deserter, who had gone over to the enemy.

SOWAR JOWAHIR SINGH

Sowar Jowahir Singh was awarded the Indian Order of Merit for conspicuous gallantry in action at Ahmed Khel on 19TH April 1880, on which occasion he dismounted and attacked two of the enemy who had taken refuge in a Nullah, killing one in hand-to-hand encounter.

LANCE DAFFADAR GUJAR SINGH

Lance Daffadar Gujar Singh was awarded the Indian Order of Merit for conspicuous gallantry on the 24TH October 1880, in aiding Ressaidar Lahrasaf Khan and Sowar Sawan Singh of the same corps, when attacked by superior numbers of the enemy, several of whom he cut down and killed.

4TH PUNJAB CAVALRY, FRONTIER FORCE

SOWAR KISHEN SINGH

Sowar Kishen Singh was awarded the Indian Order of Merit for conspicuous gallantry during the attack made on the Sulaiman Khel village in the Gomal Valley on the 5TH January 1879.

GUIDES INFANTRY, PUNJAB FRONTIER FORCE

The following Sikh officers and men were awarded Indian Order of Merit for their conspicuous gallantry in the capture of the Afghan capital Kabul.

HAVILDAR	JOWALLA SINGH	1880	KABUL
HAVILDAR	JEWUND SINGH	1880	KABUL
HAVILDAR	UTTER SINGH	1880	KABUL
HAVILDAR	WURRIAM SINGH	1880	KABUL

Indian Order of Merit (cont.)
THE SECOND AFGHAN WAR 1878-1880 (cont.)

2ND SIKH INFANTRY, PUNJAB FRONTIER FORCE (cont.)

SEPOY JAI SINGH

Sepoy Jai Singh was awarded the Indian Order of Merit for conspicuous gallantry in singly attacking several ghazis and killing two of them, while receiving a severe wound in the encounter.

SEPOY HIRA SINGH
SEPOY PERTAB SINGH

The above Sepoys were awarded the Indian Order of Merit for conspicuous gallantry in exhibiting great coolness and intrepidity under continuous rifle fire from the enemy. They were both severely wounded while prominently leading their platoon during the advance on an Afghan position.

3RD SIKH INFANTRY, PUNJAB FRONTIER FORCE

HAVILDAR GURDIT SINGH

Havildar Gurdit Singh was awarded the Indian Order of Merit for conspicuous gallantry in action near Kabul on the 14TH December 1879, on which occasion, when a detachment of the regiment was retiring from the Conical Hill near the Alibad Kotal, he ran back under heavy fire and rescued a wounded man, who would otherwise have been killed by the enemy.

SEPOY PUNJAB SINGH

Sepoy Punjab Singh was awarded the Indian Order of Merit for conspicuous gallantry in action at the Takht I Shah Hill near Kabul on the 12TH December 1879, in proceeding, under heavy fire, to the assistance of an officer, who was severely wounded, remaining with him and eventually carrying him out of fire.

NAIK SHAM SINGH

Naik Sham Singh was awarded the Indian Order of Merit for conspicuous gallantry in action at Mir Karez on the 10TH December 1879, on which occasion he was most forward in the attack on the enemy's position and set a brilliant example to the men of the regiment.

4TH SIKH INFANTRY, PUNJAB FRONTIER FORCE

HAVILDAR DAVI SINGH

Havildar Davi Singh was awarded the Indian Order of Merit for conspicuous gallantry in action at Gumal on the 6TH April 1880, on which occasion, with a detachment of eighteen men, he attacked and drove off a large body of Waziri raiders and saved the village from destruction.

Indian Order of Merit (cont.)

THE SECOND AFGHAN WAR 1878-1880 (cont.)

5TH PUNJAB INFANTRY, PUNJAB FRONTIER FORCE

SUBEDAR BUDH SINGH

Subedar Budh Singh was awarded the Indian Order of Merit for conspicuous gallantry in action at Charasia on the 6TH October 1880.

The following Sikh officers and men were awarded Indian Order of Merit for their conspicuous gallantry in the capture of the Afghan capital Kabul.

SEPOY	MAN SINGH	1880	KABUL
HAVILDAR	SHAM SINGH	1880	KABUL
NAIK	SURWAN SINGH	1880	KABUL

4TH ROYAL ARTILLERY

| LASCAR | CHUREN SINGH | 1880 | KANDHAHAR |

BURMA 1885

King Thebaw of Burma's reign of misgovernment ended with his interfering with the British trading companies. He rejected an ultimatum demanding protection for British subjects, so war was declared on him on the 8TH November 1885. Burmese opposition soon collapsed and the country was annexed to the British Empire. The following Sikh soldiers were awarded Indian Order of Merit for their conspicuous gallantry in various actions fought against the Burmese during 1885 and 1886.

4TH BENGAL INFANTRY

| HAVILDAR | SRIPAL SINGH | 1885 | POOTHA |
| HAVILDAR | MOHAN SINGH | 1885 | TUMMOO |

BENGAL SAPPERS AND MINERS

| SAPPER | KALA SINGH | 1885 | MAWLU |

27TH BENGAL INFANTRY

| HAVILDAR | MANGAL SINGH | 1886 | MAUNGWET |

NORTH WEST FRONTIER 1888

4TH PUNJAB INFANTRY

NAIK MEHTAB SINGH

Was awarded Indian Order of Merit for conspicuous gallantry in a punitive expedition against the Black Mountain tribes of North West Frontier of India at Garhi in 1888.

Indian Order of Merit (cont.)
BURMA 1889

The renewal of Chin and Lushai raids on the British territories, prompted the British on the Chin-Lushai expedition of 1889. The expedition involved 7,400 men in three columns, one operating from Chittagong against the Lushais, the other two from Burma against the Chins. The British defeated the raiders and went on to annex all Naga territory west of the Dikhu River to the British Empire. The following Sikh officers were awarded the Indian Order of Merit for their conspicuous gallantry in various actions fought against the Chins and Lushais.

8TH BENGAL INFANTRY

SUBEDAR	RATAN SINGH	1889	MOWNIN
SUBEDAR	AMAR SINGH	1889	SINYIN

21ST BENGAL INFANTRY

JEMADAR	MANGAL SINGH	1889	YNATHA

5TH PUNJAB CAVALRY

HAVILDAR	KIRPAL SINGH	1889	MGOUNG
JEMADAR	KAHAN SINGH	1889	MGOUNG

SOMALILAND 1890

The British administered the Protectorate of Somaliland from India. The Mahdi 'The Mad Mullah' a militant reformist of a puritanical sect, the Salihaya Order, organized a religious war against the British. The British responded by dispatching Zaila Field Force against him. The force which included 17TH Regiment Bombay Infantry, embarked at Aden and landed at Zaila in Somaliland on the 13TH January 1890. They carried out punitive raids against the Somali clans, the followers of the Mahdi. One hundred camels and large flock of sheep were captured, while some of the enemies were killed and others taken prisoners. On the 29TH January the force halted and established a camp at Hussain. A party of the enemy rushed the camp. They were driven out with a loss of eight killed, not before they had killed four of the 17TH Regiment Bombay Infantry. Subedar Jaimal Singh served with the detachment of Sikh soldiers that had been sent to Somaliland to stiffen up the Bombay Infantry.

17TH REGIMENT BOMBAY INFANTRY

SUBEDAR JAIMAL SINGH

Subedar Jaimal Singh was awarded Indian Order of Merit for conspicuous gallantry in the repulse of the enemy at Hussain on the 29TH January 1890.

Indian Order of Merit (cont.)
BURMA 1891

A coup in Manipur in September 1890 resulted in the death of the British Chief Minister with his senior staff. This resulted in the Anglo-Manipur War. The British forces finally defeated the Manipur forces and captured Imphal on 27Th April 1891. This ended the independent status of the Kingdom of Manipur, and was the last kingdom to be incorporated into British India.

YEU BATTALIONNN

SUBEDAR AMAR SINGH
Was awarded Indian Order of Merit for conspicuous gallantry in action at Mona on 27TH April 1891 at overcoming Manipur resistance.

HAZARA 1891
4TH REGIMENT SIKH INFANTRY, PUNJAB FRONTIER FORCE

On 18 June 1888, on the North West Frontier of India a patrol engaged in survey work in Hazara was ambushed and wiped out. The Hazara Field Force was assembled and leashed against the tribes throughout the Black Mountains.

NAIK GIAN SINGH
Was awarded Indian Order of Merit for conspicuous gallantry in the operations in Hazara.

GULISTAN

A short but fierce action was fought against the Orakzais tribe at Gulistan on the North West Frontier of India on the 20TH April 1891, resulting in British victory with one man killed and four wounded. The Orakzais lost about 200 men. The following Sikh soldiers were awarded Indian Order of Merit for their conspicuous gallantry at Gulistan.

29TH PUNJABIS

SEPOY	DIWAN SINGH	1891	GULISTAN
SEPOY	JAIMAL SINGH	1891	GULISTAN

HUNZA

On 2ND December 1891, during the assault on Nilt Fort in Hunza, on the North West Frontier of India, Sapper Hazara Singh, with a storming party, blew open the inner gate with gun cotton which he had placed and ignited. This point was under heavy fire from the towers flanking the gateway and from loopholes in the gate itself. Sapper Hazara Singh was awarded the Indian Order of Merit for conspicuous gallantry in this action. However his comrade in the same action, Captain Aylmer was awarded the Victoria Cross.

BENGAL SAPPERS AND MINERS

SAPPER	HAZARA SINGH	1891	NILT FORT

Indian Order of Merit (cont.)
BRITISH CENTRAL AFRICA 1891

The Arab and African slave traders dominated Central Africa in 1890. To contain them the British administration sought to borrow Sikh soldiers from the Indian Army to form the Central African Rifles. These Sikh soldiers were handpicked cream of the Indian Army. They were the first regular army troops ever to operate in East and Central Africa. These Sikh soldiers formed the nucleus and the backbone of the Central African Rifles.

MAKANJIRA

An expedition was mounted against the slaver Makanjira on lake Nyassa on November 1891. After hard fighting the Sikhs took all Makanjira's defences and destroyed his town and dhows. The following Sikh soldiers were awarded the Indian Order of Merit for their conspicuous gallantry in storming Makanjira's defences.

NAIK	BADHAWA SINGH	1891	MAKANJIRA
SEPOY	BACHAN SINGH	1891	MAKANJIRA
SEPOY	HAKIM SINGH	1891	MAKANJIRA

CHIKALA

A punitive expedition was made against the Yao Chief Kawinga in November 1891. The Chief's stronghold on the Chikala Mountains was attacked. The attack was beaten off but Kawinga was compelled to sue for peace and made to release captive slaves. The Sikhs suffered several casualties. The following Sikh soldiers were awarded the Indian Order of Merit for their conspicuous gallantry in defeating Kawinga.

SEPOY	JAGAT SINGH	1891	CHIKALA
SEPOY	PREM SINGH	1891	CHIKALA
SEPOY	LAL SINGH	1891	CHIKALA

SS DOMIRA

The following Sikh soldiers were awarded the Indian Order of Merit for their conspicuous gallantry in the actions against slavers at Kisungale on Lake Nyassa. They defended and eventually floated Dumbarton built steamer *SS Domira*, which for seven days had lain aground. They served as 'Marines' under heavy and continues fire from the stronghold of the Gao Chief Makanjira.

The Sikhs earned widespread acclaim for their adaptability to soldiering in tropical Africa.

AVILDAR	NAND SINGH	1891	*SS DOMIRA
NAIK	ISHAR SINGH	1891	*SS DOMIRA
HAVILDAR	JHANDA SINGH	1891	*SS DOMIRA

Indian Order of Merit (cont.)
BURMA

The Kachins have been the object of many police operations and two regular expeditions of 1892-93. The Burma Military Police carried out constant punitive measures against them. The Kachins, who simultaneously raided the town of Myitkyina, heavily attacked a police column, proceeding to establish a post at Sima. A force of 1200 troops was sent to put down the rising. The enemy received their final blow at Palap, but not before three officers were killed, three wounded, and 102 Sepoys and followers killed and wounded.

3RD BENGAL INFANTRY

Jemadar Hira Singh was awarded the Indian Order of Merit for conspicuous gallantry in action at Chingjaroj in 1892.

BURMA MILITARY POLICE

In 1886 the Government of India sanctioned the raising of the Military Police to facilitate the withdrawal of the main part of the regular forces from Burma. The Military Police Battalions were organized like regular army regiments and their duties were entirely military. The Military Police at the end of 1888 included 3,937 Sikhs.

The following Sikh officers were awarded the Indian Order of Merit for their conspicuous gallantry in the defence of Sima Post at Palap.

JEMADAR	HARI SINGH	1893	PALAP
SUBEDAR	MEHTAB SINGH	1893	PALAP
SEPOY	KISHAN SINGH	1893	PALAP
SEPOY	LEHNA SINGH	1893	PALAP
SEPOY	GYAN SINGH	1893	PALAP
SEPOY	UTTAM SINGH	1893	PALAP
SEPOY	GANDA SINGH	1893	PALAP
BUGLER	PURAN SINGH	1893	PALAP
JEMADAR	SAWAN SINGH	1893	PALAP

When 1ST Burma Division was at Taungoo to hand over to the Chinese, there occurred a historic incident, *a last charge of the Indian horsed cavalry*. On 22ND March 1942, a mounted squadron of Sikhs, yelling their war cries with the trumpeter sounding the charge, galloped straight at the Japanese. None reached the enemy: most were killed. (Quoted from :*Indian Army* by Charles W. Trench)

Indian Order of Merit (cont.)
BRITISH CENTRAL AFRICA 1893-1894
FORT McGUIRE

The slaver Makanjira had attacked Fort McGuire in great force, and was defeated with heavy loss, by the soldiers of 45TH Rattray's Sikhs. Havildar Bulaku Singh was awarded the Indian Order of Merit for conspicuous gallantry during this action.

45TH RATTRAY'S SIKHS

| HAVILDAR | BULAKU SINGH | 1894 | FORT McGUIRE |

FORT JOHNSTON

The following Sikh soldiers were awarded the Indian Order of Merit for their conspicuous gallantry in the operations against the slavers around Fort Johnston in January 1894.

15TH LUDHIANA SIKHS

| NAIK | KARAM SINGH | 1894 | FORT JOHNSTON |

24TH SIKH PIONEERS

| SEPOY | SUNDAR SINGH | 1894 | FORT JOHNSTON |

ASSAM

In 1894 the Bor Abors of Bomjur from Burma ambushed and killed four Sepoys on patrol in Assam, seized three boats and carried them off. A British expedition was despatched against them, during which their villages were burned and quantities of their crops were destroyed.

LAKHIMPUR MILITARY POLICE BATTALION

HAVILDAR BUTA SINGH
Havildar Buta Singh was awarded the Indian Order of Merit for conspicuous gallantry in action at Abor in 1894.

WAZIRISTAN

The operations were necessary owing to the continual attacks by the Waziris on the Afghan Frontier Delimitation party, on the North West Frontier of India. The tribesmen suffered heavy casualties from the party's escort. The following Sikh officer and Sowars were awarded the Indian Order of Merit for their conspicuous gallantry in the operations against the Waziris around Wanu in January 1894.

1ST PUNJAB CAVALRY

DAFFADAR	THAKUR SINGH	1894	WANU
SOWAR	MAN SINGH	1894	WANU
SOWAR	KHANDA SINGH	1894	WANU

Indian Order of Merit (cont.)
MALAKAND

In 1895, a coup d'etat in Chitral cost the life of the ruling chief, and the victors attempted to drive out the British representative, which necessitated the dispatch of a 16,000 strong British expedition to reduce the rebels. At the Malakand Pass, on April 3RD, 1895, the invading troops overwhelmed some 12,000 Chitralis, who lost more than 500 men before giving up control of the pass. At a dramatic charge by 50 Sabres of Guides Cavalry on 2,000 threatening Swati tribesmen, the tribesmen broke and fled to the safety of the hills. The following Sikh officers were awarded the Indian Order of Merit for their conspicuous gallantry in the operations at Khar.

CORPS OF GUIDES CAVALRY

DAFFADAR	TOTA SINGH	1895	KHAR
DAFFADAR	SOBA SINGH	1895	KHAR

DEFENCE OF CHITRAL

In early 1895, following the death of a chieftain and conflict over the succession, a British force ended up besieged in Chitral fort, in the shadow of the Hindu Kush in what is now north-west Pakistan. The small British garrison of the fort, which included a detachment of 88 men of the 14TH Ferozepore Sikhs, was responsible for the defence of the fort for 46 days. Captain Townsend, in his report on the siege, wrote: "The spirit of the 14TH Sikhs was our admiration; the longer the siege lasted the more eager they became to teach the enemy a lesson. There could not be finer soldiers than these men of the 14TH Sikhs and they were our sheet anchor in the siege". The garrison at Chitral Fort held out until the approach of a small force from Gilgit under Colonel Kelly, which caused Chitralis to withdraw. The following Sikh officers and men were awarded Indian Order of Merit for their conspicuous gallantry, and all the men in the fort were given six months pay as bonus.

14TH FEROZEPORE SIKHS

SUB. MAJOR	ATAR SINGH	1895	CHITRAL FORT
SUBEDAR	PERTAB SINGH	1895	CHITRAL FORT
NAIK	ATAR SINGH	1895	CHITRAL FORT
SEPOY	BHOLA SINGH	1895	CHITRAL FORT
SEPOY	PARTAB SINGH	1895	CHITRAL FORT
SEPOY	MAL SINGH	1895	CHITRAL FORT

Indian Order of Merit (cont.)
RELIEF OF CHITRAL 1895 (cont.)

The following Sikh officers of 32ND Sikh Pioneers were awarded the Indian Order of Merit for their conspicuous gallantry in the relief of the Chitral Fort. They set out from Gilgit to cover 220 miles of very poor road to Chitral. The importance of the Sikh Pioneer's epic march was never fully recognized, most of the publicity and fame for the relief being lavished on the well-known British regiments like the 60TH Rifles and Gordon Highlanders.

32ND SIKH PIONEERS

JEMADAR	SHER SINGH	1895	CHITRAL FORT
HAVILDAR	WADHAWA SINGH	1895	CHITRAL FORT
SUBEDAR	BHAG SINGH	1895	CHITRAL FORT
SUBEDAR	PREM SINGH	1895	CHITRAL FORT
JEMADAR	SHER SINGH	1895	CHITRAL FORT
HAVILDAR	WASAWA SINGH	1895	CHITRAL FORT

KORAGH

The under mentioned non-commissioned officers and men were granted the Indian Order of Merit in recognition of the gallantry and devotion exhibited by them in the action at Koragh, in Chitral, on the 10TH March 1895. These men were the sole survivors of the sixty soldiers who were entrapped in the Koragh defile and had to cut their way out against overwhelming odds.

14TH FEROZEPORE SIKHS

SUBEDAR	SUNDAR SINGH	1895	KORAGH
HAVILDAR	BUR SINGH	1895	KORAGH
SEPOY	JAIMAL SINGH	1895	KORAGH
HAVILDAR	BHAG SINGH	1895	KORAGH
SEPOY	GANGA SINGH	1895	KORAGH
SEPOY	DYAL SINGH	1895	KORAGH
SEPOY	BUKAN SINGH	1895	KORAGH
SEPOY	DASONDA SINGH	1895	KORAGH
SEPOY	JODH SINGH	1895	KORAGH
SEPOY	MAL SINGH	1895	KORAGH
SEPOY	SAHIB SINGH	1895	KORAGH
SEPOY	PREM SINGH	1895	KORAGH
SEPOY	SADAH SINGH	1895	KORAGH
SEPOY	SANT SINGH	1895	KORAGH
SEPOY	THAMAN SINGH	1895	KORAGH
SEPOY	SHAM SINGH	1895	KORAGH
SEPOY	MAHTAB SINGH	1895	KORAGH
HAVILDAR	SANTOKH SINGH	1895	KORAGH

Indian Order of Merit (cont.)
CHITRAL 1895 (cont.)

The following non-commissioned officer and men of the Bengal Sappers and Miners and 6TH Punjab Infantry were awarded Indian Order of Merit in recognition of the gallantry and devotion exhibited by them in the action at Reshun in Chitral, on the 10TH March 1895.

BENGAL SAPPERS AND MINERS

SAPPER	CHANDA SINGH	1895	RESHUN
NAIK	KALA SINGH	1895	RESHUN

6TH PUNJAB INFANTRY

SEPOY	BAL SINGH	1895	RESHUN

CENTRAL AFRICA

A. J. Swann, a contemporary writer, describes on the extent and evils of the slave trade in Central Africa thus: 'Besides those actually captured, thousands are killed or die of their wounds and famine, driven from their homes by the slave raider. Thousands perish in internecine wars, waged for slaves with their own clansmen or neighbours, slain by the lust for gain, which is stimulated by the slave purchasers. The many skeletons we have seen amongst the rocks and woods testify to the awful sacrifice of human life which must be attributed directly or indirectly to this trade of hell.'

In 1891, British Protectorate was proclaimed over Nyasaland and the authorities commenced series of campaigns against the slavers. The campaigns continued until the final battle against the Sultan of Nkonde in 1895.

A British officer describes the battle against Mlozi the Sultan of Nkonde. ' The champions of freedom were at death – grips with the slavers of the most ruthless type. The fierce onslaught of our Indian troops was met with stubborn defence worthy of a better cause, for these people fight like demons behind entrenchments." As they rushed out to attack their besiegers, the Sikhs repulsed them and counter attacked, swarming over the walls to capture the town and Mlozi. Mlozi was tried, condemned and hanged. The following Sikh officers and men were awarded the Indian Order of Merit for their conspicuous gallantry at Nkonde.

NIAK	ATMA SINGH	1895	NKONDE
SEPOY	PERTAB SINGH	1895	NKONDE
SEPOY	SUNDAR SINGH	1895	NKONDE
SEPOY	NARYAN SINGH	1895	NKONDE
SEPOY	SHAM SINGH	1895	NKONDE
SOWAR	JOWALA SINGH	1895	NKONDE

Indian Order of Merit (cont.)
MAIZAR

A political agent with a military escort of British officers and Indian Sepoys rode out to Maizar, on the North West Frontier of India, to settle a dispute between the tribal Maliks. As the escort rested under some trees, the tribals suddenly attacked them. All of the British officers were soon wounded but the Sikh officers nobly rose to the occasion. Subedars Naryan Singh and Sundar Singh gallantly covered their retreat, in the course of which the latter and ten of his Sepoys sacrificed their lives to enable the remainder to get clear of the village. The following Sikh officers and men were awarded the Indian Order of Merit for their conspicuous gallantry in these operations.

6TH, 8TH MOUNTAIN BATTERIES

LANCE NAIK	ACHAR SINGH	1897	MAIZAR
LANCE NAIK	ATAR SINGH	1897	MAIZAR
LANCE NAIK	KESAR SINGH	1897	MAIZAR
SUBEDAR	NARYAN SINGH	1897	MAIZAR
LANCE NAIK	UTTAM SINGH	1897	MAIZAR
HAVILDAR	NIHAL SINGH	1897	MAIZAR
HAVILDAR	BUR SINGH	1897	MAIZAR
GUNNER	JOWALA SINGH	1897	MAIZAR
GUNNER	DIWAN SINGH	1897	MAIZAR
GUNNER	MAGH SINGH	1895	DABAR

THE FOLLOWING SIKH SOLDIERS, WHO HAD SACRIFICED THEIER LIVES, WERE AWARDED THE POSTHUMOUS INDIAN ORDER OF MERIT AND THEIR WIDOWS GRANTED PENSIONS.

1ST REGIMENT SIKH INFANTRY, PUNJAB FRONTIER FORCE

SUBEDAR	SUNDAR SINGH	1897	MAIZAR
NAIK	BUR SINGH	1897	MAIZAR
LANCE NAIK	KANAIYA SINGH	1897	MAIZAR
SEPOY	INDAR SINGH	1897	MAIZAR
BUGLER	ISHAR SINGH	1897	MAIZAR
LANCE NAIK	BELA SINGH	1897	MAIZAR
NAIK	ASSA SINGH	1897	MAIZAR

51ST SIKHS

H. CAPTAIN	NARYAN SINGH	1897	MAIZAR
JEMADAR	SHIB SINGH	1897	MAIZAR

55TH RIFLES

HAVILDAR	ISHAR SINGH	1897	MAIZAR
HAVILDAR	BELA SINGH	1897	MAIZAR

Indian Order of Merit (cont.)
MALAKAND

In July 1897 the garrison in Malakand was alerted to a mass attack led by the 'Mad Mullah'. Although there was a fort at Malakand, many of the men were in camps outside the fort. When the alarm sounded the British officers McRae and Taylor ran out with some Sikhs and engaged the attackers in a narrow defile, in which Taylor was killed. This action prevented the enemy from encircling the camp and cutting it off from the fort. The Sikhs held the right of the position against repeated day and night attacks between 26TH and 30TH July. A detachment of the 45TH Rattray's Sikhs clashed with a fanatical tribal horde advancing on the garrison. Outnumbered by swarms of tribesmen, the Sikhs disputed every yard as they retreated back to the rest of their regiment. They were required to make a desperate bayonet charge during the storm-laden night of 30TH, which scattered the tribesmen. It was all over by the time reinforcements arrived the next day; the tribesmen had fled back to the hills. The following Sikh officers and men were awarded the Indian Order of Merit for their conspicuous gallantry in these operations.

24TH PUNJABIS

HAVILDAR	WADHAWA SINGH	1897	MALAKAND
SUBEDAR	FATEH SINGH	1897	MALAKAND
LANCE NAIK	SAWAN SINGH	1897	MALAKAND

35TH SIKHS

HAVILDAR	KURM SINGH	1897	MALAKAND
JEMADAR	WARYAM SINGH	1897	MALAKAND

45TH RATTRAY'S SIKHS

HAVILDAR	JAWALA SINGH	1897	MALAKAND
LANCE NAIK	SANT SINGH	1897	MALAKAND
JEMADAR	NATHA SINGH	1897	MALAKAND
NAIK	JEEWA SINGH	1897	MALAKAND
NAIK	PREM SINGH	1897	MALAKAND
JEMADAR	NAND SINGH	1897	MALAKAND
HAVILDAR	MEHTAB SINGH	1897	MALAKAND
HAVILDAR	MANGAL SINGH	1897	MALAKAND
H. MAJOR	TEJA SINGH	1897	MALAKAND
HAVILDAR	VIR SINGH	1897	MALAKAND
LANCE NAIK	BOLA SINGH	1897	MALAKAND
SEPOY	BOLA SINGH	1897	MALAKAND

Indian Order of Merit (cont.)

MALAKAND 1897(cont.)

GUIDES CAVALRY AND INFANTRY

SOWAR	GURDIT SINGH	1897	MALAKAND
DAFFADAR	SHAM SINGH	1897	MALAKAND
JEMADAR	BAHADUR SINGH	1897	MALAKAND
SEPOY	JOWAHIR SINGH	1897	MALAKAND
SEPOY	BISHAN SINGH	1897	MALAKAND

CHAKDARA FORT

Defence of Chakdara Fort by six British officers and 240 Indian soldiers of the 45TH Sikhs and 11TH Bengal Lancers against 14,000 Pathan tribesmen, must rank as one of the greatest feat of arms in military history. Eventually there was tremendous execution of the tribals at Chakdara Fort. The following Sikh soldiers were awarded Indian Order of Merit for their conspicuous gallantry at the Chakdara Fort.

45TH Sikhs

NAIK	CHANNAN SINGH	1897	CHAKDARA

11TH BENGAL LANCERS

NAIK	ARJAN SINGH	1897	CHAKDARA

SAMANA

At the time of the Afridi incursion into the Khyber and Samana ranges, Major Des Voeux was in command of Fort Cavagnari at Gulistan. 165 men of the 36TH Sikh Regiment occupied the Fort. After the enemy had captured the small post at Saragarhi, and annihilated the gallant Sikh garrison of 21 men, they proceeded to attack Fort Cavagnari, which was closely besieged for three days. The Sikhs conducted the defence with great gallantry. On one occasion a sortie was made with great daring by two havildars and 28 Sepoys from the walls. Though over half were killed or wounded, they captured three of the enemy's standards and succeeded in driving the enemy away. The little garrison was cut off from water and its ammunition had to be closely husbanded. The garrison had been under continuous fire for 52 hours, suffering 44 men killed or wounded. For their stout hearted defence of these posts the 36TH Sikhs were later awarded the battle-honour 'Samana' distinction held by no other regiment, British or Indian.

The following Sikh officers and men were awarded the Indian Order of Merit for their conspicuous gallantry at Ft.Cavagnari.

Continued on next page.

Indian Order of Merit (cont.)

SAMANA 1897(cont.)

36TH SIKH REGIMENT OF BENGAL INFANTRY

SUBEDAR	PHUMAN SINGH	1897	FT. CAVAGNARI
HAVILDAR	KAKA SINGH	1897	FT. CAVAGNARI
HAVILDAR	SHER SINGH	1897	FT. CAVAGNARI
HAVILDAR	MEHPAL SINGH	1897	FT. CAVAGNARI
HAVILDAR	SUNDAR SINGH	1897	FT.CAVAGNARI
LANCE NAIK	DEWA SINGH	1897	FT. CAVAGNARI
LANCE NAIK	BHOLA SINGH	1897	FT. CAVAGNARI
NAIK	ATTAR SINGH	1897	FT. CAVAGNARI
NAIK	SUJAN SINGH	1897	FT. CAVAGNARI
SEPOY	BADAN SINGH	1897	FT. CAVAGNARI
SEPOY	BASSAWA SINGH	1897	FT. CAVAGNARI
SEPOY	BHAGWAN SINGH	1897	FT. CAVAGNARI
SEPOY	GHULA SINGH	1897	FT. CAVAGNARI
SEPOY	GURMUKH SINGH	1897	FT. CAVAGNARI
SEPOY	HARNAM SINGH	1897	FT. CAVAGNARI
SEPOY	HIRA SINGH	1897	FT. CAVAGNARI
SEPOY	KALA SINGH	1897	FT. CAVAGNARI
SEPOY	NATHA SINGH	1897	FT. CAVAGNARI
SEPOY	SAWAN SINGH	1897	FT. CAVAGNARI
SEPOY	SUBHA SINGH	1897	FT. CAVAGNARI
SEPOY	THAMAN SINGH	1897	FT. CAVAGNARI
SEPOY	WARIAM SINGH	1897	FT. CAVAGNARI
SEPOY	CHAJJA SINGH	1897	FT. CAVAGNARI
SEPOY	RUR SINGH	1897	FT. CAVAGNARI
SEPOY	HANSA SINGH	1897	FT. CAVAGNARI
SEPOY	JIWAN SINGH	1897	FT. CAVAGNARI
SEPOY	MIHAN SINGH	1897	FT. CAVAGNARI
SEPOY	MEHMA SINGH	1897	FT. CAVAGNARI
SEPOY	BELA SINGH	1897	FT. CAVAGNARI

KURRAM VALLEY 1897

3RD BENGAL CALVALRY

On August 1897, 3RD Bengal Cavalry was moved to Kohat as part of the Kohat Kurram Force to chastise the Orakzais Afridis for their attacks on the British forts.

SOWAR DIWAN SINGH

Sowar Diwan Singh was awarded Indian Order of Merit for conspicuous gallantry in the operations against Orakzais Afridis and for bringing wounded comrades out of an Afridi ambush.

Indian Order of Merit (cont.)
BAJAUR 1897

Afghanistan's Kunar Province borders the district of Bajaur on the North West Frontier of India. The district was of strategic importance to British India. The army constantly patrolled the district to stem cross-border raids by the tribals at Badmani, Bilot, Inyat Killa, and Darbur. The following Sikh officers and men were awarded Indian Order of Merit for their conspicuous gallantry against the raiders.

11th BENGAL LANCERS

L. DAFFADAR	SANT SINGH	1897	BADMANI PASS
SOWAR	WADHAWA SINGH	1897	BADMANI PASS
SOWAR	INDAR SINGH	1897	BILOT

8th MOUNTAIN BATTERY

JEMADAR	ISHAR SINGH	1897	BILOT
GUNNER	MAGH SINGH	1897	BILOT

BENGAL SAPPER AND MINERS

NAIK	NATHA SINGH	1897	BILOT

35th SIKHS

SUBEDAR	MANGAL SINGH	1897	INYAT KILLA
LANCE NAIK	BARYAM SINGH	1897	INYAT KILLA
NAIK	KARAM SINGH	1897	DARBUR

SHABKADR 1897

In August 1897, the Mohmands, inspired by Mullah of Hadda, Najib-ud-din, attacked the village of Shankargarh some 18 miles north of Peshawar, on the North West Frontier of India. Most of the villagers had taken refuge in the Shabkadr fort and the Mohmands who numbered about four to five thousand made a planned assault on the fort. The fort stood on a mound and had 50 ft. high walls. It was held by a detachment of Border Police, who managed to repel that first attack. The 13th Bengal Lancers went to the relief of Shabkadr fort and chased the Mohmands back to the hills. The following Sikh soldiers were awarded the Indian Order of Merit for their conspicuous gallantry against the Mohmands.

13th BENGAL LANCERS

DAFFADAR	SEWA SINGH	1897	SHABKADR
SOWAR	HIRA SINGH	1897	SHABKADR

Indian Order of Merit (cont.)
TIRAH 1897-98

During the summer of 1897, along the Northwest Frontier of India, various tribes fielded a force of close to fifty thousand men to harass and destroy British forts and villages. When they captured Khyber Pass in August, the British Government decided they must be removed. The Army immediately fielded two Divisions to engage them. The campaign in Tirah employed by far the largest force in a Frontier Expedition. There was some hard fighting at the Khaibar Pass, Tseri Kando, Maidan, and Arhanga Pass. Particularly at the storming of the Dargai Heights, where the Sikhs, rushed at the open and murderous fire and won the heights in forty minutes. The following Sikh officers and men were awarded the Indian Order of Merit for their conspicuous gallantry in the Tirah campaign of 1897- 98.

2ND MOUNTAIN BATTERY

NAIK	GUNGA SINGH	1897	TIRAH
GUNNER	HIRA SINGH	1897	TIRAH
DRIVER	MEHTAB SINGH	1897	TIRAH

30TH PUNJAB INFANTRY

HAVILDAR	KESAR SINGH	1898	KHAIBAR PASS

14TH FEROZEPORE SIKHS

HAVILDAR	BOGGA SINGH	1897	DARGAI
JEMADAR	KAKA SINGH	1897	DARGAI

15TH LUDHIANA SIKHS

SUBEDAR	GURDIT SINGH	1897	TSERI KANDAO
HAVILDAR	HIRA SINGH	1897	TSERI KANDAO
SUBEDAR	BHAGAT SINGH	1897	TSERI KANDAO
SUBEDAR	GURDUT SINGH	1897	TSERI KANDAO
SEPOY	BHOLA SINGH	1897	DARGAI
JEMADAR	WARYAM SINGH	1897	DARGAI
SEPOY	KISHUN SINGH	1897	DARGAI
SEPOY	AMAR SINGH	1897	DARGAI
SEPOY	BISHAN SINGH	1897	DARGAI
HAVILDAR	BELA SINGH	1897	DARGAI

Indian Order of Merit (cont.)
TIRAH 1897-98(cont.)
15TH LUDHIANA SIKHS (cont.)

SUBEDAR	HIRA SINGH	1897	TIRAH
SEPOY	SAHIB SINGH	1897	TIRAH
HON. LT.	PHUMAN SINGH	1897	TIRAH
NAIK	GULAB SINGH	1897	TIRAH
NAIK	KIRPAL SINGH	1897	TIRAH

TSERI KANDAO

At Tseri Kandao, the Sikhs, who numbered perhaps 60, were hard pressed and commenced to move forward towards the enemy, shouting their war cries. It was a supreme moment. The Sikh muskets and bayonets met the Pathan rush, shooting them down with savage energy. The Pathans were repulsed with terrible slaughter. Havildar Wariam Singh was awarded Indian Order of Merit for conspicuous gallantry at Tseri Kandao.

36TH SIKHS

| HAVILDAR | WARIAM SINGH | 1897 | TSERI KANDAO |

DARGAI

There were some 12,000 Afridis on the heights of Dargai in strongly built Sangars, their standards bravely mocking the troops far below. Covered by the divisional artillery and despite heroic efforts the attackers had to take cover in dead ground. Then occurred one of the most famous attacks on the Frontier. The Gordon Highlanders and the Sikhs stormed the Dargai Heights. With bayonets glinting in the bright sunlight, they charged across the glacis, pass the trapped Gurkhas, and on, up the narrow twisting path, scrambling ever higher towards the muzzle flashes in the Sangars, while all the way, above the shouts and yells, the crash and the rattle of musketry, the pipes screamed their ancient rant with the Sikh cries of "Khalsa! Khalsa! Sat Siri Akal" The Afridis knew it was time to go and everywhere gave way and ran. Soon the Highlanders and the Sikhs crowned the heights and Dargai was won. The following Sikh officers and men were awarded the Indian Order of Merit for their conspicuous gallantry in storming and taking the Dargai Heights.

3RD SIKH INFANTRY

SUBEDAR	LEHNA SINGH	1897	DARGAI
SEPOY	DAVI SINGH	1897	DARGAI
SEPOY	MAGAR SINGH	1897	DARGAI
LANCE NAIK	JAI SINGH	1897	DARGAI
JEMADAR	MIT SINGH	1897	DARGAI

Indian Order of Merit (cont.)
EAST AFRICA 1897 – 98

A mutiny in 1897 of the Sudanese troops used by the colonial government led Britain to take a more active interest in the Uganda Protectorate. A party consisting of Lieutenant Macdonald, Jemadar Bhagwan Singh and thirty N.C.O.'s and men of the 14TH and 15TH Sikh Regiments with half trained Swahilis soldiers proceeded to British East Africa and joined an expedition formed under Major J R. L. Macdonald, to fight mutineers and other hostile elements in Uganda. A small force under Major J R. L. Macdonald arrived at Lubwa Fort on Lake Victoria on the 18TH October 1897, where they found it occupied by mutinous Sudanese troops. On the following day the mutineers attacked Major MacDonald's force for five hours, but were defeated, and driven back into the fort. This was a remarkable feat by the Sikhs and the half trained Swahilis and by the fact the mutineers were led by experienced native officers. On the 11TH December, Lieutenant Macdonald and his small party were covering the activities of men delegated to destroy the rebel's plantations and gardens, when the enemy made a desperate flank attack on the working parties. Lieutenant Macdonald was shot and mortally wounded. Sepoy Sahib Singh, with the help of Sepoy Phuman Singh, defended Macdonald against overwhelming odds and carried him to a more secure position. Another force crossing a swamp supposed to be impassable, attacked the rebel stockade at Kabagambi, and carried it with great gallantry.

The officer in charge of the expedition, Major Macdonald, writing about the party, stated:
"This detachment fully maintained the great reputation of the Sikhs, and fought with such gallantry that they secured the admiration of all."
The following Sikh soldiers were awarded the Indian Order of Merit for continuous conspicuous gallantry in action, and

14TH FEROZEPORE SIKHS

JEMADAR	B. SINGH	1897	LUBWA FORT
NAIK	SHAM SINGH	1898	LUBWA FORT
SEPOY	KAKA SINGH	1898	KABAGAMBI
SEPOY	BAGHA SINGH	1898	KABAGAMBI

15TH LUDHIANA SIKHS

SEPOY	SAHIB SINGH	1897	LUBWA FORT
SEPOY	PHUMAN SINGH	1898	KABAGAMBI
SEPOY	GOLAB SINGH	1898	KABAGAMBI
SEPOY	BISHAN SINGH	1898	KABAGAMBI
SEPOY	KIRPAL SINGH	1898	KABAGAMBI
HAVILDAR	AVTAR SINGH	1898	KABAGAMBI

Indian Order of Merit (cont.)

SEPOY BUTTA SINGH - IOM

Won for gallantry against the Ogadan Somalis in East Africa 1898

For some years the Ogadan Somalis had been causing trouble, which culminated in an extensive slave raid in Jubaland. It was decided to take punitive measures to bring the Somalis to order. On 22ND of June 1898 a patrol of 41 Sikhs, including Rifleman Butta Singh, under Jemadar Radha Singh, was sent out on reconnaissance from Helishid. They were ambushed by a large force of Somalis and suffered very heavy losses, with 27 killed, including the Jemadar, and 4 wounded. Apparently the party was caught by surprise and the enemy got among them before they had time to fix bayonets. In this action Rifleman Butta Singh, though twice wounded, showed great gallantry in carrying Rifleman Maya Singh, who was severally wounded to safety and executed a very skilful retirement with his comrades, two of whom were also wounded. There is no doubt that these men were only able to return to Helishid due to Rifleman Butta Singh's quick and effective actions. He was at once promoted to Naik and subsequently received the Indian Order of Merit for his gallantry. The official citation for this award reads:

"Naik Butta Singh, 4TH Bombay Rifles, was granted the Indian Order of Merit for conspicuous gallantry in action near Helishid, on lake Wama, East Africa, on 22ND June 1898, on which occasion, though twice severely wounded himself, he went to the assistance of Sepoy Maya Singh, who was mortally wounded, and after driving off several parties of the enemy, finally brought Maya Singh into camp with the assistance of two other Sepoys."

Butta Singh's richly deserved award was the only gallantry decoration granted for this campaign. It is not known how long Butta Singh had served with the 4TH Bombay Rifles, but it is certainly a significant feat of arms that, as a rifleman, he had the composure, the leadership skills, and enough understanding of field tactics to execute this withdrawal against such overwhelming odds with such few men.

Indian Order of Merit (cont.)
CHINA 1900

In 1900, the Boxers, a xenophobic movement in China, carried out series of attacks on foreign missionaries, merchants and property. The Chinese government did little to remedy the situation, and in June 1900 issued an edict, which amounted to support for the Boxers. The foreign legations in the Imperial capital Pekin (Beijing) were besieged by the Boxers, and held out for three months despite having a small garrison. An international relief force was organised by seven nations, and in June 1900 the Taku Forts were captured. The force then moved on Pekin, which was captured in August. Eventually peace was concluded in January 1901. The following Sikh soldiers were awarded the Indian Order of Merit for their conspicuous gallantry against the Boxers.

4TH PUNJAB INFANTRY

| LANCE NAIK | LEHNA SINGH | 1901 | TAITO |
| NAIK | DIAL SINGH | 1901 | TAITO |

ASHANTI (GHANA) 1900

After the deposition of King Prempeh I of the Ashanti by the British in 1896, led to a decision to capture the Golden Stool, which symbolised Ashanti royal power. The Ashanti chiefs thwarted this attempt, and their people promptly rose against the British, besieging the Governor in Kumasi, the capital of Ghana. The rising was finally suppressed in December 1900. The Sikhs of the Central African Rifles were most forward in their attacks. "All ranks, especially those fine soldiers the Sikhs, behaved admirably,' wrote Colonel J. Wilcocks in his official despatch,' and if it were not for this impossible forest we should soon wipe out most of the Ashantis". One this occasion Ashanti war camp was captured and destroyed.

12TH BURMA INFANTRY

NAIK HIRA SINGH

Naik Hira Singh, a volunteer from the Burma Infantry attached to the Central African Rifles, was awarded the Indian Order of Merit for conspicuous gallantry in action. He was foremost in the attack as the Ashanti fled to the bush.

Ashanti Chief

Indian Order of Merit (cont.)
MAHSUD WAZIRI

To stem the continues marauding raids of the Waziri tribes across the North West Frontier of India in Waziristan, British were compelled to mount expeditions against the various sections of the Waziri tribes. There was some hard fighting at Tiarza, Hmedwan, and Umar Raghza. The following Sikh soldiers were awarded the Indian Order of Merit for their conspicuous gallantry in action.

23RD SIKH PIONEERS

SEPOY	SUNDAR SINGH	1901	TIARZA
SEPOY	JHANDA SINGH	1901	TIARZA

45TH RATTRAY'S SIKHS

SUBEDAR	ALA SINGH	1902	AHMED WAN
HAVILDAR	WASAWA SINGH	1901	UMAR RAGHZA
SEPOY	RHODA SINGH	1901	UMAR RAGHZA

KOT SHINGI

In a punitive expedition Across the North West Frontier of India in 1901, 1ST Punjab Infantry advanced on Kot Shingi, after they had destroyed some small villages en route. They encountered and overcame heavy opposition as they destroyed Kot Shingi. Sepoy Badan Singh was most forward in the attacks and was awarded the Indian Order of Merit for his conspicuous gallantry.

1ST PUNJAB INFANTRY

SEPOY	BADAN SINGH	1901	KOT SHINGHI

GUMATI

The tribal raiders continued to commit numerous crimes across the North West Frontier of India. In 1902; the British decided to send a punitive expedition into the district. On arrival at Gumati the column found itself confronted by a strong fortified enclosure, thickly surrounded by trees, and strongly held by the tribals. Two attempts at breaching the walls were unsuccessful and it was at last decided to carry the place by escalade. A party of the 4TH Sikhs stormed and took the place, killing all in the fortified enclosure.

4TH SIKHS

The following Sikh soldiers were awarded the Indian Order of Merit for conspicuous gallantry in action at Gumati.

SUBEDAR	MIT SINGH	1902	GUMATI
LANCE NAIK	BHOLA SINGH	1902	GUMATI

Indian Order of Merit (cont.)
TIBET 1904

In December 1903 the British marched over the Himalayas to Tibet to counter a non-existent Russian threat. A medieval Tibetan army confronted them. It was a clash between the mightiest political power in the world at that time, armed with Maxim guns and Lee Enfield rifles, and one of the weakest. 23RD Sikh Pioneers regiment supplied the main fighting force, supported by units of the 32ND Sikh Pioneers. Both regiments were veterans of frontier warfare but unusual in that they fought with a pick- axe in one hand and a rifle in the other, a dual role combining the duties of a pioneer regiment with that of fighting infantry. The Sikh Pioneers endured terrible weather conditions, including crossing the Kangra-La Mountain at 17,500 feet. The world record of high altitude warfare established by the Sikh Pioneers at the battles of Karo lasted for the best part for ninety years. It has certainly been broken by the 15TH Punjab (Patiala) battalion, at the unique, high altitude battle of Zojila, against Pakistan.

The following Sikh soldiers were awarded the Indian Order of Merit for their conspicuous gallantry in action in the invasion of Tibet.

SUBEDAR WASAWA SINGH (POSTHUMOUS)
32ND SIKH PIONEERS

On the 18TH May 1904, the Tibetans occupied a building at Lhasa, from where the fire from Martinis was most disconcerting. It was decided to storm that building. A party of Sikh Pioneers under Subedar Wasawa Singh was detailed for the storming. As an entrance could not be forced, the Sikh Pioneers blew open the gates and slaughtered the garrison. The Pioneers then moved out against the Tibetans at the village garrisons of Karola, Chilra and Tagu. They captured the first two garrisons, but the third garrison was obstinately held. As Havildar Wasawa Singh laid a successful charge to blow a breach, he was shot through the head. The Pioneers in their fury stormed through the breach and killed all the Tibetans in the garrison. A posthumous Indian Order of Merit was bestowed on gallant Wasawa Singh; this was a Bar to the Indian Order of Merit he was awarded for the relief of Chitral Fort in 1895.

SEPOY PREM SINGH
32ND SIKH PIONEERS

Sepoy Prem Singh was awarded the Indian Order of Merit for his conspicuous gallantry in the attack and destruction of the Tibetan garrisons at Tagu and Karola in 1904. This was a Bar to the Indian Order of Merit he was awarded for the relief of Chitral Fort in 1895.

Indian Order of Merit (cont.)
TIBET 1904 (cont.)
SEPOY SAHIB SINGH
32ND SIKH PIONEERS

In January 1904, the invading force in Tibet commenced their hard marching from Phari to Gyantse. A highly disciplined and equipped force of the Sikh Pioneers proceeded towards Tibetan camp at Changra and was ordered to disarm the men in the camp. During the disarming of the armed men, a Tibetan general drew his pistol and blew off the jaw of the Sikh Sepoy, who was taking their arms. That started the conflagration. The Sikhs charged and pursued the Tibetans to the village of Guru, where the Tibetans were either killed or taken prisoners at the point of the bayonet. The total Tibetan loss was 620 killed and 222 taken prisoners. Then the Sikhs advanced against the gorge of the Red Idol, where the Tibetans were entrenched behind the boulders and hiding in the caves. The Sikhs charged and captured the Tibetans at gorge of the Red Idol. Sepoy Sahib Singh was awarded the Indian Order of Merit for conspicuous gallantry at Red Idol; he had entered the caves alone and bayoneted the occupants.

SUBEDAR WASANT SINGH
32ND SIKH PIONEERS

On 7TH May the attacking force had covered forty-five miles to Karola in three marches, much of it on foot and in single file. 'A tremendous exertion walking let alone climbing'. The Tibetans had built their wall about a mile and half beyond the pass and put up series of Sangars in front of and above the wall at both ends, both flanks of the wall were unapproachable, and the only method of attack was in front. The attack was launched with two companies of the 32ND Pioneers and half a company of Gurkhas. They were to ascend the cliff against Sangars high up the hillside. Both the Sikhs and the Gurkhas were pinned down by the Tibetans fire and could not make any headway. ' There was a deadlock, and no means could be found to drive the enemy from the advanced defences which they were holding so gallantly. There seemed a little chance of doing anything more until nightfall. It was an anxious moment.' A party of dozen men led by Subadar Wasant Singh scaled the ' almost perpendicular face of the 1,500-foot southern scarp'. Subadar Wasant Singh's gallant section poured down deadly rifle fire on the Sangar. The defenders lost their nerve and bolted! And the Pioneers carried the position. It was a notable victory; the Tibetans numbered 3,000 and lost 270 killed and many taken prisoners. Subadar Wasant Singh was awarded the Indian Order of Merit for conspicuous gallantry in a unique action, having been fought 16,500 feet above the sea level.

Indian Order of Merit (cont.)
TIBET 1904 (cont.)
SEPOY BHAGWAN SINGH
32ND SIKH PIONEERS

Sepoy Bhagwan Singh accompanied Subedar Wasant Singh in scaling the 1,500-foot escarpment was most forward in carrying the Tibetan position. He was awarded the Indian Order of Merit for his conspicuous gallantry in a unique action, having been fought 16,500 feet above the sea level. This was a Bar to the Indian Order of Merit he was awarded for the relief of Chitral Fort in 1895.

HAVILDAR LABH SINGH
32ND SIKH PIONEERS

As per Sepoy Sahib Singh, page 42.

In January 1904, the invading force in Tibet commenced their hard marching from Phari to Gyantse. A highly disciplined and equipped force of the Sikh Pioneers proceeded towards Tibetan camp at Changra and was ordered to disarm the men around. During the disarming of the armed men, a Tibetan general drew his pistol and blew off the jaw of the Sikh Sepoy who was taking their arms. That started the conflagration. The Tibetans were pursued to the village of Guru, which was taken at the point of the bayonet. The total Tibetan loss was 620 killed and 222 taken prisoners. Havildar Labh Singh was awarded the Indian Order of Merit for his conspicuous gallantry and leadership

NAIK JHANDA SINGH
32ND SIKH PIONEERS

Naik Jhanda Singh was awarded the Indian Order of Merit for his conspicuous gallantry in the attack and destruction of the Tibetan garrisons at Tagu and Karola.

PALLA

The Tibetans heavily reinforced a complex of buildings that made Palla Manor. On the 28TH May, the Sikhs and the Gurkhas took the buildings, one by one at the point of the bayonet. "The occupants to their everlasting credit, fought magnificently." They lost four hundred of their numbers, killed or wounded. Another hundred and fifty were taken prisoners. The following Sikh soldiers were awarded the Indian Order of Merit for their conspicuous gallantry at Palla Manor.

| SUBEDAR | KESAR SINGH | 1904 | PALLA |
| SEPOY | SAHIB SINGH | 1904 | PALLA |

Indian Order of Merit (cont.)
TIBET 1904 (cont.)

23RD SIKH PIONEERS

The 32ND Sikh Pioneers took a prominent part in the Tibetan campaign. However, the 23RD Sikh pioneers were involved in the original advance to Gyants and then proceeded to work as far as Kangma, next post below Chumbi, which they garrisoned. A wing of the regiment formed part of the reinforcing column, which reached Chumbi in June 1904. After severe fighting at Chumbi they took part in the advance on Lhasa.

The following Sikh soldiers were awarded the Indian Order of Merit for their conspicuous gallantry in the severe fighting at Chumbi.

SEPOY	TILOK SINGH	1904	CHUMBI
SEPOY	JOWALA SINGH	1904	CHUMBI
SELPOY	ROLLA SINGH	1904	CHUMBI

NORTH WEST FRONTIER 1908

In 1908, the Zakha Khel Afridis began raiding from the Bazar Valley in the Tribal areas across the North West Frontier of India. This encouraged raids by the Mohmands, who threatened Shabkadr Fort. By using surprise and rapid movement, the Indian soldiers subdued the Afridis and the Mohmands within a fortnight in February 1908. The following Sikh officers and men were awarded the Indian Order of Merit for their conspicuous gallantry in action.

22ND PUNJABIS

HAVILDAR	SADHU SINGH	1908	KASAI
NAIK	RAM SINGH	1908	KASAI

28TH PUNJABIS

HAVILDAR	HARI SINGH	1908	BAZAR
NAIK	GURDIT SINGH	1908	BAZAR

53RD SIKHS

SEPOY	HIRA SINGH	1908	N. W. FRONTIER
NAIK	TEJA SINGH	1908	GOMAL PASS
SEPOY	BASANT SINGH	1908	GOMAL PASS

54TH SIKHS

SEPOY	BISHAN SINGH	1908	BAZAR

34TH SIKH PIONEERS

SEPOY	BHULA SINGH	1908	ZANAWAR
SEPOY	PAKHAR SINGH	1908	ZANAWAR

Indian Order of Merit (cont.)
FIRST WORLD WAR

In World War One, the Indian Army saw extensive service on the Western Front ,Battle of Gallipoli, Sinai, Palestine, Mesopotamian, Siege of Kut, and East Africa.

About 43,000 Indian soldiers were killed and 65,000 wounded during World War One.

Also serving during the World War One, were the "Imperial Service troops," provided by the semi-autonomous Princely States. About 21,000 men were raised, mainly consisting of Sikhs of Punjab and Rajputs from Rajputana.These forces played a prominent fighting role in the Sinai, Palestine and East African Campaigns. The Sikhs soldiers for their fighting qualities were over recruited in all the teeth arms of the Army.

4TH CAVALRY

LANCE DAFFADAR PURAN SINGH

Lance Daffadar Puran Singh was awarded the Indian Order of Merit for conspicuous gallantry in action on the 6TH January 1916. He carried out messages to a very exposed position under heavy continuous fire, about three miles from the village of Shaikh Saad in Mesopotamia.

DAFFADAR HAKIM SINGH

Daffadar Hakim Singh was awarded the Indian Order of Merit for conspicuous gallantry and devotion to duty in France in 1917.

5TH KEVO LANCERS (PROBYN'S HORSE)

DAFADAR PARTAB SINGH

Daffadar Partab Singh was awarded the Indian Order of Merit for conspicuous gallantry and devotion to duty on 7th February 1916 during retirement from Butaniyeh in Mesopotamia. He voluntarily gave up his horse to and officer when the latter's horse was shot during a charge on the enemy.

6TH KEO CAVALRY

LANCE DAFFADAR KARAM SINGH

Lance Daffadar Karam Singh was awarded the Indian Order of Merit for conspicuous gallantry and devotion to duty on the night of the 4TH–5TH February 1918 in France. This non-commissioned officer showed great coolness and ability in command of the signallers. During the heavy barrage all the telephone communication with Brigade Headquarters were cut. Lance Daffadar Karam Singh quickly organised visual communication by lamp and then led a patrol to discover where the line was cut, which he mended and thus restored telephonic communication. His courage, coolness and devotion to duty were a fine example to all ranks.

Indian Order of Merit (cont.)
FIRST WORLD WAR (cont.)

7TH HARIANA LANCERS

JEMADAR SUDHAN SINGH (POSTHUMOUS)
Was awarded posthumous Indian Order of Merit for conspicuous gallantry near Shaiba in Mesopotamia, on the 13TH April 1915, in charging the enemy's trenches under very heavy fire form all sides. In doing so he showed remarkable bravery and set a fine example to the men. He was unfortunately killed a few yards in front of the enemy's position.

DAFADAR PIARA SINGH (POSTHUMOUS)
Was awarded posthumous Indian Order of Merit for handling his section in the firing line with conspicuous gallantry and ability on the 22ND November 1915 in Mesopotamia. He set a very fine example to his men and died from wounds during the action.

DAFFADAR SEWA SINGH (POSTHUMOUS)
Was awarded posthumous Indian Order of Merit for conspicuous gallantry and devotion to duty at Kut al Amara on the 28TH September 1915, when 25 Kurdish cavalry ambushed his patrol. He endeavoured to save the lives of two of his men who were wounded and was killed in the attempt.

KOT DAFFADAR LAL SINGH
Was awarded the Indian Order of Merit for conspicuous gallantry and devotion to duty at Kut al Amara on the 28TH September 1915. He successfully withdrew his troop under heavy enfilade of fire from Turkish positions.

JEMADAR PANJAB SINGH (POSTHUMOUS)
Was awarded posthumous Indian Order of Merit for conspicuous gallantry in Mesopotamia on the 22ND November 1915 in carrying messages under heavy fire. Twice he endeavoured to take a message through to two squadrons on the left of the line and was killed on the third attempt.

DAFFADAR KEHAR SINGH
Was awarded the Indian Order of Merit for conspicuous gallantry and devotion to duty in Mesopotamia on 22ND November 1915.While under very high fire form the enemy trenches, he dismounted of his own accord, picked up a wounded Sowar who had fallen from his horse and carried him over 100 yards to a safe position, then mounted and rejoined his troop.

DAFFADAR TILOK SINGH
Was awarded the Indian Order of Merit for conspicuous gallantry and devotion to duty in Mesopotamia on 11TH September 1917. He made a daring and successful reconnaissance of a ford across a river, which was close to the enemy trenches.

Indian Order of Merit (cont.)
FIRST WORLD WAR (cont.)

11TH KEO LANCERS

JEMADAR BHAGWAN SINGH
Was awarded the Indian Order of Merit for conspicuous gallantry and devotion to duty on the night of 22nd – 23rd May 1918, in a raid on the enemy trenches in Egypt. He led the attack on a post with the greatest dash and resolution. Though leading a troop, he did not hesitate to attack a post estimated to contain fifty of the enemy, under heavy machine-gun and rifle fire at point blank range.

L. DAFFADAR JIT SINGH
Was awarded the Indian Order of Merit for conspicuous gallantry and devotion to duty whilst serving with the Indian Army Corps, in France and Flanders in 1915.

LANCE DAFFADAR GANGA SINGH
Was awarded the Indian Order of Merit for conspicuous gallantry and devotion to duty whilst serving with the Indian Army Corps, in France and Flanders in 1915.

RESSAIDAR BHAGGA SINGH
Was awarded the Indian Order of Merit for conspicuous gallantry and devotion to duty whilst serving in Mesopotamia in 1920.

L. DAFFADAR RHODA SINGH
Was awarded the Indian Order of Merit for conspicuous gallantry and devotion to duty whilst serving in Mesopotamia in 1920.

12TH CAVALRY

LANCE DAFFADAR NARANG SINGH
Was awarded the Indian Order of Merit for conspicuous bravery during the retirement from Butaniyeh in Mesopotamia, on the 7TH February 1916, when he went back under heavy fire at close range to bring in a wounded man.

JEMADAR PERTAB SINGH
Was awarded the Indian Order of Merit for courage and devotion to duty during the retirement from Butaniyeh in Mesopotamia, on the 7TH February 1916.

Subadar Swaran Singh I.O.M., 1917.

Indian Order of Merit (cont.)
FIRST WORLD WAR (cont.)

14TH CAVALRY (SCINDE HORSE)

SOWAR HUKAM SINGH *See also SOWAR BALWANT SINGH page 56*
Was awarded the Indian Order of Merit for conspicuous gallantry and devotion to duty in Egypt on the morning of the 23^R September 1918. When his squadron, with a troop from 29TH Lancers, was attacking an enemy position, the objective of his troop was two houses, from the top of which heavy machine-gun fire was being directed on the troop. Sowar Hukam Singh and two other Sowars, without the slightest hesitation and with the greatest gallantry, charged through to the enemy under heavy machine-gun fire. By their dash and gallantry, these men helped to capture 7 machine-guns and 500 infantry.

SOWAR DHAN SINGH
Was awarded the Indian Order of Merit for conspicuous in gallantry in the action at Hafiz Khor in the North West Frontier of India on the 15TH September 1915. When retiring from the hills, he saw a comrade whose horse was killed and he was stranded in the direction of the rapidly advancing enemy. Sowar Dhan Singh galloped back and rescued the man under heavy enemy fire.

RISALDAR HARGYAN SINGH
Was awarded the Indian Order of Merit for conspicuous gallantry and devotion to duty whilst serving in Mesopotamia in 1917.

DAFFADAR DHARAM SINGH
Was awarded the Indian Order of Merit for conspicuous gallantry and devotion to duty whilst serving with the Indian Army Corps in France and Flanders in 1916.

16TH CAVALRY

RISALDAR PREM SINGH (POSTHUMOUS)
Was awarded posthumous Indian Order of Merit for conspicuous gallantry at Bushire in Persia, on the 9TH September 1915. He courageously led an attack by his troop into the middle of some 400 of the advancing enemy, where he was killed.

DAFFADAR AMRIK SINGH
Was awarded the Indian Order of Merit for conspicuous gallantry and devotion to duty on 22ND November 1915 in Mesopotamia. He brought up, under very heavy shell and rifle fire, an army transport cart within 200 yards of the firing line trench in which eight wounded men were lying. He made four journeys from the cart to the trench, carrying back a wounded man on each occasion. He eventually brought all the party back to the field ambulance.

Indian Order of Merit (cont.)
FIRST WORLD WAR (cont.)

16TH CAVALRY (cont.)

SOWAR SHER SINGH
Was awarded the Indian Order of Merit for conspicuous gallantry and devotion to duty on 22ND November 1915 in Mesopotamia. He went to the assistance of another Sowar who was lying in the open severely wounded and carried him some distance until he was severely wounded himself.

HON. CAPT.   BHARAT SINGH   1919   L/GAZETTE
(NO CITATION AVAILABLE)

HON.LT. BALWANT SINGH
Was awarded the Indian Order of Merit for conspicuous gallantry and devotion to duty at Bushire, Persia in 1917.

17TH CAVALRY PAGE

DAFFADAR NIHAL SINGH
Was awarded the Indian Order of Merit for gallantry and devotion to duty whilst serving with the Indian Corps in France and Flanders.

18TH KEVO CAVALRY

DAFFADAR BISHAN SINGH
Was awarded the Indian Order of Merit for conspicuous bravery and devotion to duty near Shaiba in Mesopotamia, on the 3rd March 1915. Daffadar Bishan Singh charged through a body of Arab horsemen to the assistance of an officer who was surrounded on all sides by the enemy.

19TH LANCERS

JEMADAR BISHAN SINGH
Was awarded the Indian Order of Merit for gallantry and devotion to duty while serving with the Indian Army Corps in France and Flanders. 18TH January 1917.

DAFFADAR MEHAR SINGH
Was awarded the Indian Order of Merit for gallantry and devotion to duty under an intense enemy bombardment on the 14TH February 1918 in France and Flanders. Daffadar Mehar Singh went out to mend the telephone line which was broken in places, mended it and re-established communication, showing complete disregard for personal danger. This was done on his own initiative and without orders being given him.

Indian Order of Merit (cont.)
FIRST WORLD WAR (cont.)

20TH DECCAN HORSE

DAFFADAR SARDAR SINGH
Was awarded the Indian Order of Merit for gallantry and devotion to duty whilst serving with the Indian Corps in France and Flanders in 1914.

21ST PAVO CAVALRY (FRONTIER FORCE)

SOWAR CHANNAN SINGH
Was awarded the Indian Order of Merit for conspicuous gallantry in Mesopotamia on the 27TH April 1918. He showed great courage and coolness under heavy fire. When his British officer's horse was shot during a charge on the enemy, Sowar Channan Singh turned back and took the officer upon his own horse and brought him to safety. He then rallied a number of his comrades and made a second charge on the enemy.

LANCE DAFFADAR BAKSHISH SINGH
Was awarded the Indian Order of Merit for gallantry and devotion to duty while serving in Mesopotamia in 1917.

LANCE DAFFADAR KIRPAL SINGH
Was awarded the Indian Order of Merit for gallantry and devotion to duty in Mesopotamia on the 5TH November 1917. During the reconnaissance of the enemy's position he led his patrol with remarkable coolness in the face of heavy fire, within few hundred yards of the enemy's trenches. Throughout the day he kept his patrol in observing the enemy in and advanced and critical position, sending back most useful information.

22ND SAM BROWN'S CAVALRY (FRONTIER FORCE)

RISALDAR AVTAR SINGH
Was awarded the Indian Order of Merit for gallantry and devotion to duty while serving in Mesopotamia in 1917.

23RD CAVALRY

RISALDAR SANT SINGH
Was awarded the Indian Order of Merit for conspicuous gallantry and devotion to duty in Mesopotamia on to 27TH October 1918. When his squadron commander was killed, Risaldar Sant Singh took command of the Squadron and led them with marked skill and coolness under heavy enemy fire until all the ammunition was expended. He then conducted a well-ordered and successful withdrawal. Later he called for volunteers and, accompanied by four men, went back for his squadron commander's body, which he eventually succeeded in bringing back with him in spite of the intensity of the enemy's fire. Throughout the action he behaved with consummate coolness and displayed power of command of a high order.

Indian Order of Merit (cont.)
FIRST WORLD WAR (cont.)

27TH LIGHT CAVALRY

RESSAIDAR BALWANT SINGH
Was awarded the Indian Order of Merit for gallantry and devotion to duty whilst serving with the Indian Corps in France and Flanders in 1916.

29TH LANCERS (DECCAN HORSE)

DAFFADAR PURAN SINGH
Was awarded the Indian Order of Merit for conspicuous gallantry whilst serving with the British forces in France and Flanders in 1916.

SOWAR CHANDAN SINGH
Was awarded the Indian Order of Merit for gallantry and devotion to duty in the fields of France and Flanders in 1917.

SOWAR INDAR SINGH
Was awarded the Indian Order of Merit for gallantry and devotion to duty in the fields of France and Flanders in 1917.

SOWAR BALWANT SINGH *See also SOWAR HUKAM SINGH page 53*
Was awarded the Indian Order of Merit for conspicuous gallantry and devotion to duty in Egypt on the morning of the 23^R September 1918. When his squadron with a troop form 14TH Cavalry, was attacking an enemy position, the objective of his troop was two houses, from the top of which heavy machine-gun fire was being directed on the troop. Sowar Hukam Singh and two other Sowars, without the slightest hesitation and with the greatest gallantry, charged through to the enemy under heavy machine-gun fire. By their dash and gallantry, these men helped to capture 7 machine-guns and 500 infantry.

31ST DCO LANCERS

RISALDAR KABUL SINGH
Was awarded the Indian Order of Merit for gallantry and devotion to duty in the fields of France and Flanders in 1917.

RESSAIDAR INDAR SINGH
Was awarded the Indian Order of Merit for gallantry and devotion to duty whilst serving in Waziristan in 1919.

LANCE DAFFADAR GULAB SINGH
Was awarded the Indian Order of Merit for gallantry and devotion to duty whilst serving in Waziristan in 1919.

Indian Order of Merit (cont.)
FIRST WORLD WAR (cont.)

33RD QVO LIGHT CAVALRY

DAFFADAR NIHAL SINGH
Was awarded the Indian Order of Merit for gallantry and devotion to duty whilst serving with the Indian Army Corps in France and Flanders in 1917.

LANCE DAFADAR ARJAN SINGH
Was awarded the Indian Order of Merit for conspicuous gallantry at Shaiba in Mesopotamia, on the 9TH February 1915. During a reconnaissance, assisted by Sowars Buta Singh and Mangal Singh, he succeeded under the close fire of the enemy, in hoisting onto the front of his saddle the dead body of a comrade and bringing it back to the main body, and subsequently conveying it to Shaiba.

| RISALDAR | SANTA SINGH | 1915 | MESOPOTAMIA |
| SOWAR | BUDA SINGH | 1915 | MESOPOTAMIA |

The above soldiers were awarded the Indian Order of Merit for conspicuous bravery and devotion to duty near Shaiba in Mesopotamia, on the 3rd March 1915, in charging through a body of Arab horsemen, to the assistance of an officer who was surrounded on all sides by the enemies.

34TH PAVO POONA HORSE

JEMADAR PREM SINGH (POSTHUMOUS)
Was awarded posthumous Indian Order of Merit for conspicuous gallantry and devotion to duty in Egypt on the 28Th July 1918. Jemadar Prem Singh organised and carried out a successful attack, with his troop, on a hostile party. Owing to his dash and perseverance, 15 of the enemy were killed, one officer and four men being made prisoners. He personally killed two of the enemy. The example of fearlessness, which he set, was magnificent. Jemadar Prem Singh was killed in the action.

36TH JACOB'S HORSE

JEMADAR WAZIR SINGH
Was awarded the Indian Order of Merit for conspicuous gallantry in France and Flanders on the night of the 17TH – 18TH November 1917. Jemadar Wazir Singh led a patrol of six men across No Man's Land and clashed with a party of 20 of the enemy who bombed them, killing one of the patrol and wounding the Jemadar. Having now only four men, one having strayed from the patrol, Jemadar Wazir Singh kept the patrol well in hand and succeeded in routing the greatly superior number of the enemy by bombing and rifle fire.

Indian Order of Merit (cont.)
FIRST WORLD WAR (cont.)

6TH JACOB'S HORSE (cont.)

DAFFADAR HARDITT SINGH
Was awarded the Indian Order of Merit for gallantry and devotion to duty whilst serving with the Indian Army Corps in France and Flanders in 1917.

JEMADAR AMAR SINGH
Was awarded the Indian Order of Merit for conspicuous gallantry on 23RD September 1918 in Egypt. During an action with the enemy, Jemadar Amar Singh was sent out with a troop to endeavour to get round the enemy's flank, as the regiment was being held up frontally. He located six machine-guns which he promptly charged and captured taking several prisoners, thus enabling the regiment to advance.

JEMADAR KABIR SINGH
Was awarded the Indian Order of Merit for gallantry and devotion to duty in the fields of France and Flanders in 1917.

38TH KGO CENTRAL INDIA HORSE

RESSAIDAR DAYAL SINGH
Was awarded the Indian Order of Merit for conspicuous gallantry on the night of 21ST – 22ND September 1918 in Egypt. The regimental outpost line was attacked by and unknown number of the enemy. Ressaidar Dayal Singh was sent with his troop to reinforce the advance squadron. On arrival at the outpost he immediately led a charge on the enemy. With great dash Ressaidar Dayal Singh and his troop killed a number of the enemy and captured over 150 prisoners.

RESSAIDAR JEWAND SINGH
Was awarded the Indian Order of Merit for gallantry and devotion to duty in the fields of France and Flanders in 1918.

39TH KGO CENTRAL INDIA HORSE

SOWAR DALIP SINGH
Was awarded the Indian Order of Merit for conspicuous gallantry on the 30TH August 1917 in France. Sowar Dalip Singh saved the lives of two comrades who were beset by the German soldiers.

SOWAR INDAR SINGH
Was awarded the Indian Order of Merit for gallantry and devotion to duty in the fields of France and Flanders in 1917.

HON.LT. JAWANA SINGH
Was awarded the Indian Order of Merit for gallantry and devotion to duty in the fields of France and Flanders in 1919.

Indian Order of Merit (cont.)
FIRST WORLD WAR (cont.)

QVO CORPS OF GUIDES (FRONTIER FORCE)

HAVILDAR KISHAN SINGH
Was awarded the Indian Order of Merit for conspicuous bravery in an action, which took place in the vicinity of Rustam, North West Frontier of India, on the 17TH August 1915. During the retirement of the Guides Infantry from the foothills east of Rustam, three Ghazis suddenly attacked Havildar Kishan Singh while he was carrying out the retirement of his section across a Nullah. Havildar Kishan Singh immediately turned about and closed in with attackers; he bayoneted two and although severely wounded by sword cuts in four places, succeeded in killing the third Ghazi by clubbing him on the head with his rifle, breaking his rifle in the act.

21ST KOHAT MOUNTAIN BATTERY

LANCE NAIK KARAM SINGH
Was awarded the Indian Order of Merit for conspicuous gallantry on the 19TH May 1915, during operations near Gaba Tepe (Gallipoli, Turkey). Although Lance Naik Karam Singh was rendered absolutely blind by a bullet, which had passed, behind his eyes, he continued to pass orders, and so enabled the fire of his section to proceed without interruption. He remained on duty until forcibly removed.

26TH JACOB'S MOUNTAIN BATTERY

HAVILDAR GURDIT SINGH
Was awarded the Indian Order of Merit for gallantry and distinguished service with Indian Expeditionary Force at the Dardanelle in Turkey in 1915.

GUNNER NAIK BIR SINGH
Was awarded the Indian Order of Merit Indian Order of Merit for conspicuous gallantry on the 9TH May 1915, during operations near Gaba Tepe (Gallipoli, Turkey).

HAVILDAR INDAR SINGH
Was awarded the Indian Order of Merit in 1917 for gallantry and devotion to duty in the Egypt.

27TH MOUNTAIN BATTERY

HAVILDAR BHAN SINGH
Was awarded the Indian Order of Merit for gallantry and devotion to duty in East Africa in 1916.

LANCE NAIK NATHA SINGH
Was awarded the Indian Order of Merit for gallantry and devotion to duty in East Africa in 1916.

Indian Order of Merit (cont.)
FIRST WORLD WAR (cont.)

30TH MOUNTAIN BATTERY

GUNNER HAVILDAR WARYAM SINGH

Was awarded the Indian Order of Merit for conspicuous gallantry during the operations at Butaniyeh in Mesopotamia, on the 7TH February 1916. Gunner Havildar Waryam Singh very ably covered the retirement of the other gun of his section and then extricated his own gun. The Arabs by this time having approached to 50 yards of his position. He then carried back to safety a wounded non-commissioned officer of the 44TH Merwara Infantry.

DRIVER MAYA SINGH

Was awarded the Indian Order of Merit for bravery and devotion to duty during the retirement from Butaniyeh in Mesopotamia, on the 7TH February 1916. Driver Maya Singh went forward with another man from his section to help a section that was under attack. He assisted in distribution of ammunition to the threatened section and afterwards remained to cover their retirement. He was previously commended for his gallantry during the operations of the 14TH January 1916.

1ST KGO SAPPERS AND MINERS

JEMADAR HARDIT SINGH

Was awarded the Indian Order of Merit for conspicuous gallantry and devotion to duty during the forcing of the passage up a river in Mesopotamia on the 20TH December 1916. Jemadar Hardit Singh volunteered to take charge of a party required to launch a pontoon and row it across the river under heavy fire in full view of the enemy. It was chiefly due to his splendid personal example and his constant encouragement to his men that they kept cool and steady and succeeded in launching the pontoon in spite of heavy casualties.

JEMADAR RAMRUP SINGH

Was awarded the Indian Order of Merit for conspicuous initiative and gallantry on the 12TH November 1914 in France. Having received a message that four men who had gone to blow up a house lay wounded, he led a party to their assistance and brought them back to the safety of their own lines.

NAIK SAWAN SINGH

Was awarded the Indian Order of Merit for conspicuous gallantry and coolness in Mesopotamia on the night of the 4TH April 1916. Naik Sawan Singh was in charge of parties Sappers in the front line. He and two other non–commissioned officers freely exposed themselves under heavy rifle and machine gun fire to bring back injured Sappers to their own lines. It was mainly due to his action that the line was successfully consolidated. He had previously rendered good service by the energy with which he had led the Sappers against the enemy's positions.

Indian Order of Merit (cont.)
FIRST WORLD WAR (cont.)
1ST KGO SAPPERS AND MINERS (cont.)

HAVILDAR WAZIR SINGH
Was awarded the Indian Order of Merit for conspicuous gallantry and devotion to duty in Egypt during the operations of September and October 1918. Especially on the 19TH September 1918, when in charge of party of Sappers advancing with the infantry against the enemy's trenches. He was particularly noticeable for his dash and courage and set a fine example to his men. He had previously done good work and behaved with great bravery, particularly on the night of the 28TH–29TH May, when in charge of a party erecting a wire entanglement, he was wounded but refused to leave his party until he personally saw the work was completed.

3RD SAPPERS AND MINERS

NAIK DALIP SINGH
Was awarded the Indian Order of Merit for his conspicuous gallantry during the action at Sahil in Mesopotamia, on 17TH November 1914. Naik Dalip Singh with a party of Sappers was always well forward in action and led his squad with great determination into the enemy's trenches. Naik Dalip Singh was also awarded **Cross Of St. George,** being Imperial Russia's highest military award for gallantry in the face of enemy; it held the same value and honour as the British Victoria Cross, US Medal of Honour, and the French Legion of Honor.

SUBEDAR BIR SINGH
Was awarded the Indian Order of Merit for conspicuous gallantry and devotion to duty in Mesopotamia on 17TH March 1916. During the enemy's attack, the Sappers were driven back, but did not cease in the work of making a block until four men of the party had been killed and wounded by rifle fires and bombs at ten yards range. Subedar Bir Singh then assisted in checking the enemy's advance at the block and completed the work with the survivors of his party. Subedar Bir Singh was also awarded **Cross Of St. George** being Imperial Russia's highest military award for gallantry in the face of enemy.

SAPPER INDAR SINGH (POSTHUMOUS)
Was awarded posthumous Indian Order of Merit for conspicuous gallantry and devotion to duty in Mesopotamia on the 7TH December 1915. He died of wounds whilst engaged in the demolition of an enemy bridge under heavy fire.

SUBEDAR MALLA SINGH M.C.
Was awarded the Indian Order of Merit for gallantry and devotion to duty with the British Expeditionary Force in the fields of France and Flanders in 1917.

Indian Order of Merit (cont.)
FIRST WORLD WAR (cont.)
3RD SAPPERS AND MINERS (cont.)

NAIK SON SINGH
Was awarded the Indian Order of Merit for conspicuous gallantry on the 9TH December 1915 in Mesopotamia. He was one of the parties who assisted to demolish an enemy bridge under heavy fire.

SAPPER SON SINGH
Was awarded the Indian Order of Merit for conspicuous gallantry and ability at Kut al Amara on the 28TH September 1915. When his Jemadar and Havildar had been wounded, Sapper Son Singh assumed command of the troop, and led them to the final assault with great coolness and determination.

JEMADAR UTTAM SINGH
Was awarded the Indian Order of Merit for gallantry and devotion to duty in the fields of France and Flanders in 1914.

JEMADAR GURMUKH SINGH
Was awarded the Indian Order of Merit twice, for gallantry and devotion to duty in the fields of France and Flanders in 1914 and for gallantry in Mesopotamia in 1916. Jemadar Gurmukh Singh was also awarded **Cross Of St. George** being Imperial Russia's highest military award for gallantry in the face of enemy for his gallant services in the First Worl War.

SIGNAL COMAPANY

SAPPER BHAG SINGH
Was awarded the Indian Order of Merit for conspicuous gallantry and devotion to duty on the 17TH April 1916 in France. While performing the duty of linesman, together with another Sapper, Sapper Bhag Singh went out under heavy rifle fire to repair a cable. On approaching to within 200 yards of a trench, which they thought was still occupied by our troops, they came under very heavy fire from two machine-guns and a number of rifles from the trench. Bhag Singh's companion was killed instantly while three bullets hit him. He flung himself down and continued to crawl for a distance of 200 yards and delivered a priority message and brought back the receipt to Brigade Headquarters, again under machine–gun and rifle fire when exposure meant instant death. Sapper, Sapper Bhag Singh has been with his company since the beginning of the war and was present at all the battles in France, and has invariably behaved with utmost gallantry.

Indian Order of Merit (cont.)
FIRST WORLD WAR (cont.)

12TH PIONEERS, KELAT-I-GHILZAI REGIMENT

SUBEDAR MAINGHA SINGH OBI
Was awarded the Indian Order of Merit for gallantry and devotion to duty whilst serving with the Indian Army Corps in France and Flanders during the First World War.

14TH KGO FEROZEPORE SIKHS

LANCE NAIK HAZARA SINGH
Was awarded the Indian Order of Merit for conspicuous gallantry in Turkey on the 9TH August 1915. Lance Naik Hazara Singh carried ammunition to the firing line under heavy fire, the only route being commanded by a Turkish machine-gun. He was also brought to notice on other occasions, particularly on the 19TH August 1915, when he helped a wounded man to safety and then returned to work of pulling down a Turkish barricade, for which he had volunteered.

JEMADAR MEWA SINGH
Was awarded the Indian Order of Merit for gallantry and devotion to duty Mesopotamia on the 26TH October 1918. Jemadar Mewa Singh commanded his platoon in the foremost position with marked courage and initiative. Though wounded he refused to be evacuated and remained at duty, doing all in his power to consolidate the successes gained until ordered to hospital the next day. His conduct throughout the action was magnificent.

JEMADAR PARTAB SINGH
Was awarded the Indian Order of Merit for conspicuous gallantry and devotion to duty in Mesopotamia on 26TH October 1918. He led his platoon with the greatest coolness in the front line of an attack. Later, on the 29TH October 1918, he joined in another attack and although wounded at an early stage, he continued the advance at a critical time.

15TH LUDHIANA SIKHS

HAVILDAR MAHAN SINGH
Was awarded the Indian Order of Merit for gallantry and devotion to duty in the fields of France and Flanders in 1916.

LANCE NAIK MANGAL SINGH
Was awarded the Indian Order of Merit for gallantry and devotion to duty whilst serving in France in 1916. Lance Naik Mangal Singh was one of a party of ten men under Lieut. Smyth who carried a consignment of bombs over 250 yards of open ground under shrapnel fire, having already watched two other groups fails in the attempt. Only two of the party reached the trench unhurt. Lance Naik Mangal Singh was awarded Indian Order of Merit while Lieut. Smyth was awarded the Victoria Cross.

Indian Order of Merit (cont.)
FIRST WORLD WAR (cont)

15TH LUDHIANA SIKHS (cont)

LANCE NAIK BAKSHI SINGH
Was awarded the Indian Order of Merit for gallantry and devotion to duty in the fields of France and Flanders in 1915.

HAVILDAR BISHAN SINGH
Was awarded the Indian Order of Merit for gallantry and devotion to duty in the fields of France and Flanders in 1915.

JEMADAR BAKHI SINGH
Was awarded the Indian Order of Merit for gallantry and devotion to duty in the fields of France and Flanders in 1915.

JEMADAR BISHAN SINGH IDSM
Was awarded the Indian Order of Merit for gallantry and devotion to duty on the North West Frontier of India in 1917.

SEPOY MEHR SINGH
Was awarded the Indian Order of Merit for gallantry and devotion to duty on the North West Frontier of India in 1917.

SUBEDAR NARAIN SINGH
Was awarded the Indian Order of Merit for gallantry and devotion to duty on the North West Frontier of India in 1917.

SEPOY BATTAN SINGH
Was awarded the Indian Order of Merit for conspicuous gallantry and ability in action on the 1ST February 1917 in Mesopotamia. In an action a Lewis gun had jammed at a critical moment and bombers were called and none being available. Sepoy Battan Singh immediately organised a bombing attack under heavy fire and kept the enemy at bay until the Lewis gun was ready for action. He had displayed marked courage throughout the Mesopotamia campaign.

JEMADAR BASANT SINGH
Was awarded the Indian Order of Merit for conspicuous gallantry during the Senussi campaign in Egypt in 1916.

19TH PUNJABIS

SUBEDAR BAL SINGH
Was awarded the Indian Order of Merit for conspicuous gallantry in fighting against the Bolsheviks in Trans–Caspia on the 14TH October 1918. In an attack on the enemy, Subedar Bal Singh led his platoon with great dash and bravery under very heavy machine-gun fire. He took command of the company when the British Officer had been wounded and by his coolness and power of command ensured the retirement being conducted in an orderly manner.

Indian Order of Merit (cont.)
FIRST WORLD WAR (cont)

19TH PUNJABIS (cont)

SUBEDAR HUKAM SINGH (POSTHUMOUS)
Was awarded the Indian Order of Merit for conspicuous gallantry in against the Bolsheviks in Trans–Caspia. This Sikh officer led his platoon into action on the 19TH January 1919 with the greatest gallantry and inspired all his men by his fearlessness. He was killed while encouraging and leading his men.

SEPOY DALEL SINGH
Was awarded the Indian Order of Merit for conspicuous gallantry in fighting against the Bolsheviks in Trans–Caspia on the 14TH October 1918. Sepoy Dalel Singh carried messages throughout the day for his company commander regardless of personal safety and finally delivered an important message after being severely wounded.

20TH DCO INFANTRY (BROWNLOW'S PUNJABIS)

BUGLE MAJOR SURAIN SINGH
Was awarded the Indian Order of Merit for conspicuous gallantry at Saihan on the 13TH November 1914 in going forward in the face if heavy fire and climbing on and setting fire to building held by the enemy.

HAVILDAR MEWA SINGH
Was awarded the Indian Order of Merit for conspicuous gallantry and devotion to duty at Kut al Amara on the 28TH September 1915. Havildar Mewa Singh carried and fired a machine gun 1,000 yards from position to position under heavy fire though the gun was so hot that it blistered his shoulder through coat and shirt.

SEPOY HAZARA SINGH (POSTHUMOUS)
Was awarded posthumous Indian Order of Merit for conspicuous gallantry and initiative in action in Mesopotamia on 21ST April 1917. His skilled handling when in charge of a Lewis gun was to a great extent responsible for retaking a portion of the enemy's line from which some of the troops had been driven out. He then mounted his gun in the recaptured position and materially assisted in keeping down the fire of the enemy's machine-guns, maintaining his position for the greater part of the day in spite of heavy fire until he was killed.

21ST PUNJABIS

LANCE NAIK BAWA SINGH
Was awarded the Indian Order of Merit for conspicuous gallantry and initiative in Mesopotamia on 8TH February 1917. When his company had occupied a captured trench, ammunition ran short and more was urgently required to repel a counter-attack, which had commenced. Lance Naik Bawa Singh gallantly left the trench and collected ammunition from the dead and wounded that were lying in the open. This was carried out under heavy shell and machine-gun fire.

Indian Order of Merit (cont.)
FIRST WORLD WAR (cont)

22ND PUNJABIS

HAVILDAR LAL SINGH

Was awarded the Indian Order of Merit for conspicuous gallantry and devotion to duty on the 22ND November 1915 in Mesopotamia. He was with the leading line of infantry, which reached a very exposed position without support. When the two Indian officers senior to him were killed, and the company on the left retired, he was left with only a few men but held his position until ordered to retire.

23RD SIKH PIONEERS

SEPOY SOHAN SINGH

Was awarded Indian Order of Merit for conspicuous gallantry and devotion to duty in Aden on the 4th July 1915. He also showed the greatest pluck and determination when he escaped from captivity. He made his way through 350 miles of strange country and after undergoing many privations due to lack food and water and a bad climate, rejoined the British forces.

NAIK PHAGA SINGH

Was awarded the Indian Order of Merit in Egypt for conspicuous gallantry on the 9TH September 1917. On the night of 8TH September Naik Phaga Singh was in command of a section of a raiding party. On finding that a wounded man had been left behind, Naik Phaga Singh immediately led out men in the moonlight in the face of heavy machine-gun fire to rescue the wounded man. In the process of safely bringing the soldier back to the line he himself was wounded.

HAVILDAR MANGAL SINGH

Was awarded the Indian Order of Merit for conspicuous gallantry whilst serving with the British forces in Egypt in 1917.

NAIK SHER SINGH

Was awarded the Indian Order of Merit for conspicuous gallantry in action on the 4TH February 1915 at Shimber Berris, in Somaliland. While placing a charge against the door of a fort, he was knocked over and rendered practically insensible by the discharge of the Dervish rifles through the door. After getting up and joined by Havildar Teja Singh, he returned and placed the charge in the correct place and thus blew the gate enabling the Sikh Pioneers to attack and capture the fort.

HAVILDAR TEJA SNGH

Was awarded the Indian Order of Merit for conspicuous gallantry in action on the 4TH February 1915 at Shimber Berris, Somaliland. He followed Naik Sher Singh to the door of a fort and coolly placed a charge of gun cotton, arranged fuses correctly, fired the charge and enabled the demolition to be carried out successfully.

Indian Order of Merit (cont.)
FIRST WORLD WAR (cont.)

23RD SIKH PIONEERS (cont)

SUBEDAR BINDA SINGH
Was awarded the Indian Order of Merit for conspicuous gallantry and coolness on action on the 9th January 1917 in Mesopotamia. He was in command of a platoon and did sterling work in assisting a British Infantry regiment to hold on the captured portion of the enemy's first line trenches. He set a fine example of coolness and courage in circumstances of extreme danger. He has on several other occasions shown the same fine qualities of dogged determination and leadership.

24TH PUNJABIS

HAVILDAR SUNDAR SINGH (POSTHUMOUS)
Was awarded posthumous Indian Order of Merit for conspicuous gallantry and devotion to duty during the battle of Ctesiphon in Mesopotamia, on the 22nd November 1915. After the British officer had been mortally wounded, Havildar Sundar Singh led the way through the wire attacking the trenches and capturing the surviving Turkish soldiers. He was killed in action.

LANCE NAIK KEHR SINGH
Was awarded the Indian Order of Merit for conspicuous gallantry and devotion to duty on the 15th June 1920 with the Army of the Black Sea. Although severely wounded, Lance Naik Kehr Singh continued to fire his Lewis gun under heavy enemy machine-gun fire from three directions. He was injured and carried back, but retained his Lewis gun, which he brought into action in another position.

LANCE NAIK LAL SINGH
Was awarded the Indian Order of Merit for conspicuous gallantry at Barjisiya in Mesopotamia, on the 14th April 1915. He carried his machine gun into action and fired it for nearly two hours under devastating enemy fire. He was subsequently wounded.

LANCE NAIK PARMODH SINGH
Was awarded the Indian Order of Merit for conspicuous gallantry and devotion to duty near Nasiriyah in Mesopotamia, on the 14th April 1915. Under heavy enemy fire Parmodh Singh rescued a wounded Havildar and Sepoy. Arabs constantly attacked them but Parmodh Singh kept the Arabs at bay and eventually brought the two wounded men to safety.

SUBEDAR SOHAN SINGH
Was awarded the Indian Order of Merit for most conspicuous gallantry near Nasiriyah, Mesopotamia, on the 14th April 1915 in bringing up reinforcements under heavy fire to the companies attacking the enemy at Sand hills. He displayed great courage and coolness.

Indian Order of Merit (cont.)
FIRST WORLD WAR (cont.)

24TH PUNJABIS (cont.)

JEMADAR MANGAL SINGH
Was awarded the Indian Order of Merit for marked gallantry and devotion to duty near Nasiriyah, Mesopotamia, on the 14TH April 1915. Jemadar Mangal Singh remained behind to protect a British officer who was wounded, until sent back by him for ammunition. On his return be remained in the firing line, keeping the Turks at bay until rescued by a bellum party.

JEMADAR LACHMAN SINGH
Was awarded the Indian Order of Merit for marked gallantry and devotion to duty near Nasiriyah, Mesopotamia, on the 14TH April 1915, in making several efforts after the withdrawal had begun to go back under heavy fire and search for wounded officers.

LANCE NAIK PAL SINGH (POSTHUMOUS)
Was awarded posthumous Indian Order of Merit in Mesopotamia for conspicuous gallantry and devotion to duty on the 22ND November 1915. He assisted in saving a machine-gun falling into enemy hands, and throughout the day behaved in a most gallant manner, setting a very fine example to all around him. He was killed in action.

SUBEDAR UJAGAR SINGH
Was awarded the Indian Order of Merit for conspicuous gallantry on several occasions with the Salonika Force. Subedar Ujagar Singh showed himself a most able platoon leader, courageous and resourceful, and inspired his men on all occasions by his gallantry and fine example.

NAIK LABH SINGH IDSM
Was awarded the Indian Order of Merit for conspicuous gallantry and devotion to duty in the battle of Ctesiphon in Mesopotamia, on the 22ND November 1915. He rescued a British officer under very heavy fire and carried him to safety. Later he assisted the Signal Section in sending messages under continuous hostile shellfire.

NAIK BHAG SINGH
Was awarded the Indian Order of Merit for conspicuous gallantry and devotion to duty on the 15TH June 1920 with the Army of the Black Sea. Although severely wounded, he continued to lead his section and direct the fire of his guns under heavy machine-gun fire. He set a splendid example to his men.

27TH PUNJABIS

SUBEDAR BHAGAT SINGH MC
Was awarded the Indian Order of Merit for conspicuous gallantry and good leadership during operations on the 17TH April 1916, in Mesopotamia. He was well to the front during the attack after his Company Commander, Company Officer and Havildar in his company were either killed or wounded.

Indian Order of Merit (cont.)
FIRST WORLD WAR (cont.)

27TH PUNJABIS (cont.)

SUBEDAR KAHN SINGH
Was awarded the Indian Order of Merit for conspicuous gallantry on the 17TH April 1916 in Mesopotamia. He was the first Indian Officer in the enemy's trenches before the bombardment had lifted. Subedar Kahn Singh was conspicuous for gallantry and calmness during the retirement and in his endeavour to reform parties of various units until he was wounded and incapacitated.

HAVILDAR PARTAB SINGH
Was awarded the Indian Order of Merit for conspicuous gallantry and good leadership in the action on the 19TH September 1918 in Egypt. After his platoon commander has been wounded, he took charge of the platoon and very ably led the men when the order was given to charge a battery of four guns firing at point blank range. He was the first to come forward, and charging a few yards ahead of his men, assisted in the capture of the whole battery.

JEMADAR NAND SINGH (POSTHUMOUS)
Was awarded posthumous Indian Order of Merit in Mesopotamia for conspicuous gallantry in action on the 9TH March 1917. When his platoon was under heavy fire and was suffering severe casualties, Jemadar Nand Singh showed marked coolness in controlling his men. By fine example and personal courage he succeeded in taking them absolutely unshaken to the most advanced firing position within close range of the enemy. This gallant officer was afterwards killed in action.

30TH PUNJABIS

SUBADAR LABH SINGH
Was awarded the Indian Order of Merit for conspicuous bravery and initiative in action on the 18TH October 1917 in East Africa. Subadar Labh Singh's skilful control of fire and fearless example enabled determined enemy counter-attacks to be repulsed by the company commanded.

JEMADAR SUNDAR SINGH
Was awarded the Indian Order of Merit for conspicuous gallantry and skill in handling machine-gun section on the 3RD August 1917 in East Africa. The enemy was attacking from both flanks and the front at very close quarters and the Machine Gun Officer was severely wounded. Jemadar Sundar Singh took command of the Machine Gun Section and succeeded in withdrawing the entire machine–guns except one and brought them safely back.

Indian Order of Merit (cont.)

FIRST WORLD WAR (cont.)

32ND SIKH PIONEERS

JEMADAR KHARAK SINGH
Was awarded the Indian Order of Merit for gallantry and devotion to duty in the fields of France and Flanders in 1915.

HAVILDAR MANGAL SINGH
Was awarded the Indian Order of Merit in Mesopotamia for conspicuous gallantry and devotion to duty on the 21ST September 1917. Havildar Mangal Singh was sent out on a patrol in No Man's land with the object of searching the ground and to place surrender literature as closer as possible to the enemy's lines. To do this he had to crawl over and exposed skyline 100 yards from the enemy's trenches, when one of his men was mortally wounded. He made arrangements to send this man back to the lines, having first bandaged him. With the remaining six men he advanced to within 50 yards to the enemy's trenches under sharp fire from their listening posts. He set up the surrender literature tied to a stick and rested it against an enemy corpse. He then withdrew his patrol without further casualties.

34TH SIKH PIONEERS

SUBEDAR MAGHAR SINGH
Was awarded the Indian Order of Merit in Mesopotamia for conspicuous gallantry and devotion to duty in action on the 23RD March 1917. His company commander having become casualty early in the day, Subedar Maghar Singh although wounded, took command and it was due to his fine leadership and example that his company did so well. Although it had suffered heavy casualties it was one of the last units to withdraw. After withdrawing, although wounded in five places, he helped to reorganize his company and get the wounded under cover.

HAVILDAR NIKKA SINGH
Was awarded the Indian Order of Merit for gallantry and devotion to duty in France and Flanders on 24TH November 1914. All the men of his section having been killed or wounded he carried his machine-gun to the support trenches alone.

SUBADAR NATHA SINGH
Was awarded the Indian Order of Merit for gallantry and devotion to duty at Festubert, France, on 23RD November 1914. All the men having been killed or wounded Natha Singh kept his machine-gun in action for some time against the enemy who had broken to their trenches.

HAVILDAR PALA SINGH
Was awarded the Indian Order of Merit for gallantry and devotion to duty at Festubert, France, on 23RD November 1914 when he helped to remove all the wounded from the Regimental Aid Post when a section of trenches had been overwhelmed.

Indian Order of Merit (cont.)
FIRST WORLD WAR (cont.)

34TH SIKH PIONEERS (cont.)

LANCE NAIK TOTA SINGH (POSTHUMOUS)
Was awarded posthumous Indian Order of Merit for gallantry and devotion to duty in France and Flanders, on 23RD November 1914, when a German attack broke through the trenches. Tota Singh remained firing from behind a barricade until he was killed.

NAIK BIR SINGH
Was awarded the Indian Order of Merit for gallantry and devotion to duty at Festubert in France, on 23RD November 1914, while fighting against a German attack, which had broken through the trenches.

SEPOY MASTAN SINGH
Was awarded the Indian Order of Merit for gallantry and devotion to duty in the fields of France and Flanders in 1915.

SUB. MAJOR JAWALA SINGH
Was awarded the Indian Order of Merit for gallantry and devotion to duty in the fields of France and Flanders in 1915.

NAIK GUJAR SINGH
Was awarded the Indian Order of Merit for gallantry and devotion to duty in the fields of France and Flanders in 1915.

35TH SIKHS

SEPOY BIR SINGH
Was awarded the Indian Order of Merit for conspicuous gallantry during the attack on the 5TH November 1917 in Mesopotamia. When his company had occupied the enemy's second line, he repeatedly went with messages over ground swept by fire. Although wounded he continued to carry on his duties as runner as all the other company runners had become casualties.

Subadar 35TH Sikhs

Indian Order of Merit (cont.)
FIRST WORLD WAR (cont.)

35TH SIKHS (cont.)

SUBEDAR ARJAN SINGH
Was awarded the Indian Order of Merit for gallantry and devotion to duty in the North West Frontier of India in 1919.

HAVILDAR BIR SINGH
Was awarded the Indian Order of Merit in Mesopotamia for conspicuous gallantry and skill on the 15TH April 1916, when in command of a piquet of 14TH Rifles. Havildar Bir Singh organised an attack on a hostile piquet over 200 yards of open ground in broad daylight The attack was made by a dash over the open to bombing distance of the enemy. Havildar Bir Singh led the charge himself and threw the first bomb. The enemy were bombed into surrender. The enemy piquet consisted of one officer and 21 other ranks of which the officer and 17 other ranks were captured, two killed and two escaped. The attack was made under flanking fire from the remainder of the enemy's piquet. Havildar Bir Singh was also awarded '**Cross Of St. George**' being Imperial Russia's highest military award for gallantry in the face of enemy.

SEPOY NATHA SINGH - *also Harnam Singh, 47th Sikhs.*
Was awarded the Indian Order of Merit in Mesopotamia for gallantry and devotion to duty in an action on the 23RD March 1917, when forming a part of a patrol. On reaching a point 600 yards from the enemy's position, they came under heavy fire and having obtained the required information withdrew. On reaching cover, however, it was found that a Sepoy of the patrol was missing. They both went back and found the Sepoy lying wounded. Between them they succeeded in carrying him back to safety in spite of the fact that the enemy's fire was concentrated on them from front and flank and that the enemy mounted troops were advancing to try to cut off the wounded man.

36TH SIKHS

NAIK FAKIR SINGH
Was awarded the Indian Order of Merit in Mesopotamia for conspicuous gallantry and coolness in action on the 1ST February 1917. On arrival in the enemy's second line in the attack, he found none of his section had survived, so he collected remnants of other sections and rallied them; he then collected bombs in the open and commanded his newly formed section with great ability.

SEPOY BHAGWAN SINGH
Was awarded the Indian Order of Merit for conspicuous gallantry and devotion to duty in the fields of France and Flanders in 1915.

Indian Order of Merit (cont.)
FIRST WORLD WAR (cont)

36TH SIKHS (cont)

SUBEDAR SUNDAR SINGH

Was awarded the Indian Order of Merit in Mesopotamia for conspicuous gallantry during the operations on the 12TH April 1916. He was severely wounded leading two sections forward under heavy rifle and machine-gun fire, and although in great pain from a shattered thigh, he continued to encourage and hold together his remaining men, who had been severely tried by heavy losses and were still subjected to a heavy fire.

NAIK KARTAR SINGH

Was awarded the Indian Order of Merit in Mesopotamia for conspicuous gallantry and initiative in action on 16TH February 1917. He commanded a Lewis gun team and on seeing that a team of another Lewis gun all had been either killed or wounded, he took over the other gun and worked them both until forced to withdraw, bringing away both guns back with him.

JEMADAR MASSA SINGH

Was awarded the Indian Order of Merit in Mesopotamia for conspicuous gallantry and devotion to duty during the operations on the 12TH April 1916. He commanded his Company with coolness and skill during the action. His Company Commander was killed while going forward under heavy fire to the assistance of a wounded British Officer; seeing this Jemadar Massa Singh at once went out and was severely wounded while bandaging him.

NAIK HARI SINGH

Was awarded the Indian Order of Merit in Mesopotamia for conspicuous gallantry at the action on the 15TH April 1916 when he gallantly seconded his leader and assisted in the bombing party and very materially helped in making it a success.

NAIK PRITAM SINGH
LANCE NAIK PREM SINGH

The above soldiers were awarded the Indian Order of Merit in Mesopotamia for conspicuous gallantry during the operations on the 12TH April 1916. These non - commissioned officers of the Machine-Gun Section kept their gun in action after the rest of the detachment were either killed or wounded. They finally succeeded in bringing away their gun when the retirement was ordered.

JEMADAR SEWA SINGH

Was awarded the Indian Order of Merit in Mesopotamia for conspicuous gallantry and coolness in action on the 1ST February 1917. In the attack on the enemy's position, finding that nearly all the British officer were casualties, he rallied the men in the enemy's front line, exposing himself most fearlessly, After the withdrawal he brought in wounded men both by daylight and after dark. He had been brought to notice for conspicuous gallantry on a previous occasion.

Indian Order of Merit (cont.)
FIRST WORLD WAR (cont

36TH SIKHS (cont)

SEPOY SARDARA SINGH
Was awarded the Indian Order of Merit in Mesopotamia for conspicuous gallantry and conspicuous gallantry and devotion to duty on the 5TH November 1917. When all the section of his Lewis gun had become casualties, he succeeded in bringing his gun into action and kept it in action single handedly throughout the whole day, leaving the trench many times under heavy fire to collect ammunition from the wounded. By his determined and skilful handling of the gun he contributed largely to the repulse of a counter-attack.

45TH RATTRAY'S SIKHS

SUBEDAR MAJOR SUNDAR SINGH
Was awarded the Indian Order of Merit in Mesopotamia for conspicuous gallantry and conspicuous gallantry and dash in action on the 29TH and 30TH January 1917. Leading his platoon he cleared the front line of one of the objectives with great gallantry and leadership. He has always displayed the greatest coolness and courage in action and has set a splendid example to al ranks of the Regiment.

NAIK BAGGA SINGH
Was awarded the Indian Order of Merit in Mesopotamia for conspicuous gallantry and determination in action on the 29TH and 30TH January 1917. He behaved with great courage and coolness when in charge of bombing party, holding off a much larger number of the enemy's bombers, although wounded early in the action. He has displayed gallantry on previous occasions.

JEMADAR HARNAM SIINGH –*also Natha Singh, 35TH Sikhs*
Was awarded the Indian Order of Merit in Mesopotamia for conspicuous gallantry in an action on the 23RD March 1917 when forming a part of a patrol. On reaching a point 600 yards from the enemy's position, they came under heavy fire and having obtained the required information withdrew. On reaching cover, however, it was found that a Sepoy of the patrol was missing. They both went back and found the Sepoy lying wounded. Between them they succeeded in carrying him back to safety in spite of the fact that the enemy's fire was concentrated on them from front and flank and that the enemy mounted troops were advancing to try to cut off the wounded man.

LANCE NAIK MALL SINGH
Was awarded the Indian Order of Merit in Mesopotamia for conspicuous gallantry and ability in action on the 1ST February 1917. A Lewis gun jammed at a critical moment and bombers were called for; none being available, he immediately organised a bombing attack under heavy fire and kept the enemy off until the Lewis gun was ready for action. He displayed marked courage throughout the day.

Indian Order of Merit (cont.)
FIRST WORLD WAR (cont.)
45TH RATTRAY'S SIKHS (cont.)

SUBEDAR NARAIN SINGH
Was awarded the Indian Order of Merit in Mesopotamia for conspicuous gallantry on the 1ST February 1917. He led his platoon with great courage and although his British officer was killed, he stemmed several counter-attacks. He was eventually cut off from his regiment but succeeded in regaining the regimental lines in the evening although severely wounded. He brought in five other severely wounded men with him.

HAVILDAR TARA SINGH
Was awarded the Indian Order of Merit in Mesopotamia for conspicuous gallantry and devotion to duty on the afternoon of the 29TH October 1918. During an attack he was in charge of the regimental signallers and displayed the greatest coolness under fire. Later during an evening counter–attack he rushed forward on his own initiative with his men and took up a commanding position in a part of the line, which was very thinly held. By his prompt action he rendered valuable assistance in repelling the counter-attack. He had on previous occasions shown similar courage and resource.

LANCE NAIK CHANNAN SINGH
Was awarded the Indian Order of Merit in Mesopotamia for conspicuous gallantry and devotion to duty on 16TH February 1917. During an enemy counter-attack, two men firing a Lewis gun in and exposed position were killed. Lance Naik Channan Singh rushed forward 30 yards under hot fire, seized the Lewis gun, brought into line with his own gun and continued to fire it. But for his action the gun would certainly have been lost to the enemy.

SEPOY HARNAM SINGH
Was awarded the Indian Order of Merit in Mesopotamia for conspicuous gallantry and devotion to duty on the 29TH October 1918. At a moment when an enemy counter-attack on the left flank was maturing, he led his platoon with great dash against it and broke it up. Afterwards he seized and held an advanced position although most of his ammunition was expended. His conspicuously gallant conduct and skilful dispositions had the result of securing the right flank.

Sepoy 45TH Sikhs

Indian Order of Merit (cont.)
FIRST WORLD WAR (cont)

45TH RATTRAY'S SIKHS (cont.)

LANCE NAIK UJAGAR SINGH
Was awarded the Indian Order of Merit for conspicuous gallantry and devotion to duty in Mesopotamia on the afternoon of the 29TH October 1918. Lance Naik Ujagar Singh was sent forward with his Lewis gun section to cover the advance of his platoon. While advancing under heavy fire he lost three men killed before reaching the position and the remainder within 15 minutes of reaching it. However, he held on to his position alone and although exposed to heavy fire from front and flank, kept his gun in action until all his ammunition had been expended. By his brave and determined action he rendered valuable assistance to two platoons, which were advancing to repel a counter-attack. His behaviour throughout was magnificent.

47TH SIKHS

In a collective action the following soldiers had overrun a section of the enemy trenches, bayoneting all the occupants before them.

SUBEDAR BAKSHI SINGH
Was awarded the Indian Order of Merit for gallantry and devotion to duty with the British Expeditionary Force in France in 1915.

SUBEDAR HARNAM SINGH
Was awarded the Indian Order of Merit for gallantry and devotion to duty with the British Expeditionary Force in France in 1915.

HAVILDAR NARAIN SINGH
Was awarded the Indian Order of Merit for gallantry and devotion to duty with the British Expeditionary Force in France in 1915.

HAVILDAR LACHMAN SINGH
Was awarded the Indian Order of Merit for gallantry and devotion to duty with the British Expeditionary Force in France in 1915.

HAVILDAR GAJJAN SINGH
Was awarded the Indian Order of Merit for gallantry and devotion to duty with the British Expeditionary Force in France in 1915.

SEPOY RUR SINGH
Was awarded the Indian Order of Merit for gallantry and devotion to duty with the British Expeditionary Force in France in 1915.

JEMADAR SUCHA SINGH
Was awarded the Indian Order of Merit for gallantry and devotion to duty with the British Expeditionary Force in France in 1915.

Indian Order of Merit (cont.)
FIRST WORLD WAR (cont)

47TH SIKHS (cont)

SUBEDAR SUCHA SINGH
Was awarded Indian Order of Merit in France and Flanders for conspicuous gallantry on the 26TH and 27TH December 1916. He went out by day in front of the line and located three enemy piquets. On the following night he displayed marked ability in assisting to drive back the enemy and occupying their piquets. His coolness and courage during the operations and his constant eagerness in volunteering for patrol work are worth of the highest praise.

SUBEDAR MOTA SINGH
Was awarded the Indian Order of Merit for conspicuous gallantry and devotion to duty in the fields of France and Flanders in 1915. He was also awarded '**Cross Of St. George**' being Imperial Russia's highest military award for gallantry in the face of enemy.

HAVILDAR MASTAN SINGH
Was awarded the Indian Order of Merit in Mesopotamia for conspicuous gallantry in the action on the 5TH November 1917. He took command of a platoon and attacked and drove out enemy entrenched piquets. During the subsequent attacks on the enemy he showed great bravery, skill and determination.

LANCE NAIK THAMAN SINGH
Was awarded the Indian Order of Merit in Egypt for conspicuous gallantry during the attack on the 19TH September 1918. Although wounded in two places, he carried his Company Commander, who was seriously wounded, back to the shelter under heavy machine-gunfire. He then rejoined his company and carried further operations, setting fine example of endurance.

SUBEDAR MEHAR SINGH
Was awarded the Indian Order of Merit Egypt for conspicuous gallantry and devotion to duty in the operations on the 19TH and 20TH September 1918. On 19TH with skilful handling of his company, he greatly contributed to the successes of the operations. On the 20TH September, he collected a few men at a critical time and rushed the enemy automatic rifle, which was enfilading the advance of the rest of the company, and destroyed it.

HAVILDAR WAZIR SINGH
Was awarded the Indian Order of Merit in Egypt for conspicuous gallantry and devotion to duty in the operations on the 19TH and 20TH September 1918. On the 19TH September he took command of his platoon when the commander was wounded and showed great ability and judgment. On the 20TH September when the company was held up by heavy rifle fire, with a few men he rushed the enemy automatic rifle which was enfilading the advance and caused the enemy to abandon two other automatic rifles by his skilful use of the captured weapon.

Indian Order of Merit (cont.)
FIRST WORLD WAR (cont.)

48TH PIONEERS

HAVILDAR BHAG SINGH
Was awarded the Indian Order of Merit for very conspicuous gallantry and ability near Nasiriyah in Mesopotamia, on the 14th July. He assumed command of the Pioneer bridging parties after both Indian officers were wounded and carried through the work of bridging the Mejenineh Creek with great coolness and courage.

HAVILDAR DAYAL SINGH
Was awarded the Indian Order of Merit for conspicuous gallantry and devotion to duty on the 22nd November 1915 when in command of the regimental stretcher-bearers at the battle of Ctesiphon in Mesopotamia.

51ST SIKHS (FRONTIER FORCE)

NAIK PREM SINGH
Was awarded the Indian Order of Merit for display of great personal gallantry and for cheerful execution of duty under great hardships in Mesopotamia. While with the Brigade Signal Section though wounded early on the 6th January 1916, he continued to carry out his duties imparting cheerfulness amongst his men.

NAIK JEWAND SINGH
Was awarded the Indian Order of Merit in Mesopotamia for conspicuous gallantry and perseverance when in command of a cable-laying party on the night of the 6th and 7th January 1916. For two hours he searched for the regiment forming the right flank to link up to headquarters, working under heavy enemy fire and fully knowing that he was likely to meet enemy position en route. This eventually occurred when in his efforts to remove one of his parties, who was wounded, he was hit. However, he sent back word that the line must be laid on a bearing, which was eventually realised.

SUBEDAR CHANDA SINGH
Was awarded the Indian Order of Merit for display of great courage and endurance throughout the engagements of the 7th, 13th and 21st January 1916, when he exhibited indifference to personal dangers, and his ability and thoroughness in the execution of his duties. He was slightly wounded on the 13th January but made no mention of the fact and when left in charge of a portion of the line, collected scattered details strengthened his position and submitted a report on the situation to Brigade Head Quarters. On the 21st he was severally wounded while leading his men with very conspicuous gallantry but refused to be evacuated, until all the wounded officers had been evacuated. His conduct throughout had the special effect of taking successive trenches in the action at Sheikh Saad in Mesopotamia on the 7th January 1916.

Indian Order of Merit (cont.)
FIRST WORLD WAR (cont.)

51ST SIKHS (FRONTIER FORCE) (cont.)

HAVILDAR SUHEL SINGH
Was awarded the Indian Order of Merit in Mesopotamia for conspicuous gallantry and devotion to duty on the 6TH January 1916. He showed an example of coolness and bravery in the advance on the Turkish trenches under very heavy fire. The zeal with which his section followed his example was in a great measure responsible for the successful advance of his Company. On the following day he led assault with fixed bayonets on the enemy's position. He was also brought to notice for conspicuous gallantry and devotion to duty during the action of the 8TH March 1916 in bringing up ammunition to the regiments in the firing line.

SUBEDAR ARJAN SINGH
Was awarded the Indian Order of Merit for conspicuous gallantry in action on the 22ND April 1917 in Mesopotamia. With a detachment of a British regiment, he led a small party of his men against the enemy and reached one of their batteries. He fought with the greatest determination; only the smallness of his numbers and the lack of reinforcements prevented the capture of the guns. He finally withdrew after the officer in command had insisted on his doing and brought back all the wounded with him. He has previously been brought to notice for gallantry in the field.

HAVILDAR NIKKA SINGH
Was awarded the Indian Order of Merit in Mesopotamia for conspicuous gallantry and initiative in action on the 22ND April 1917, in bringing his Lewis gun into action at close range under heavy fire. He exposed himself recklessly so as to obtain better fire position and checked an attempted enemy counter–attack. He has also distinguished himself on previous occasions and has done consistently well in every action.

53RD SIKHS

SUBEDAR MOLAR SINGH
Was awarded the Indian Order of Merit on the 21st July 1915. This Sikh officer led a platoon in action at Shaikh Othman in Aden, with great coolness and conspicuous gallantry and gave a excellent example to his men at a time when they had several casualties in space of few minutes.

JEMADAR CHANAN SINGH
Was awarded the Indian Order of Merit in Mesopotamia for all the actions in January 1916 in which the 28TH Frontier Force Brigade was engaged. This Machine Gun Jemadar behaved with the greatest dash and gallantry and though wounded, continued directing the fire of his guns wit skill and coolness.

Indian Order of Merit (cont.)

FIRST WORLD WAR (cont.)

53RD SIKHS (cont.)

HAVILDAR SHINGAR SINGH

Was awarded the Indian Order of Merit in Mesopotamia for the action at Fort Cbibibat on the 13TH January 1916. He led his section with very conspicuous gallantry during the advance. After being very severely wounded and being unable to move, he sat up encouraging his men and directing their movements until the regimental first aid post removed him.

SEPOY SHINGAR SINGH

Was awarded the Indian Order of Merit in Mesopotamia for conspicuous gallantry on the 8TH March 1916. Three times he went to the rear and brought ammunition to the firing line and distributed it with great coolness under heavy fire.

SUBEDAR BUTA SINGH

Was awarded the Indian Order of Merit in Mesopotamia for conspicuous gallantry on 7TH April 1916. He applied first aid to a wounded British Officer who was lying in an exposed position under heavy shell, machine-gun and rifle fire. He then assisted in removing him to a less exposed position and attended to him until it was possible to remove him after dark.

NAIK KEHAR SINGH

Was awarded the Indian Order of Merit in Mesopotamia for conspicuous gallantry. Naik Kehar Singh was placed in charge of a party of the Brigade Signalling Section in what was almost a forlorn hope at Sheikh Saad on the 16TH and 7TH January 1916. It was essential to get a line out to a flank position but the enemy's fire was so hot that two attempts had failed. Naik Kehar Singh was chosen to lead the third attempt and though wounded, he succeeded in getting the line to its destination by sheer pluck and ingenuity.

LANCE NAIK DALEL SINGH

Was awarded the Indian Order of Merit in Egypt for conspicuous gallantry and initiative on the night of the 6TH and 7TH May 1918. Lance Naik Dalel Singh accompanied a patrol of two platoons, which was surprised by a large body of the enemy and came under fire of rifle and machine-guns at close range. He repulsed the attacks and systematically withdrew his platoons. He had previously done excellent work and obtained accurate and valuable information.

Indian Order of Merit (cont.)
FIRST WORLD WAR (cont.)

55TH COKE'S RIFLES

The following Sikh soldiers were awarded a collective gallantry award for their outstanding performance in Waziristan.

LANCE NAIK ISHAR SINGH
Was awarded the Indian Order of Merit for continuous conspicuous gallantry against the Mahsuds in Waziristan in 1916.

JEMADAR KISHAN SINGH
Was awarded the Indian Order of Merit for continuous conspicuous gallantry against the Mahsuds in Waziristan in 1916.

SEPOY RAM SNGH
Was awarded the Indian Order of Merit for continuous conspicuous gallantry against the Mahsuds in Waziristan in 1916.

JEMADAR KEHAR SINGH
Was awarded the Indian Order of Merit for continuous conspicuous gallantry against the Mahsuds in Waziristan in 1916.

56TH PUNJABI RIFLES (FRONTIER FORCE)

HAVILDAR SUBA SINGH
Was awarded the Indian Order of Merit for conspicuous gallantry and devotion to duty when in command of a patrol of nine men on the Suez Canal on 22nd March 1915. Havildar Suba Singh surprised and engaged a strong raiding party of Turks estimated at 400, under German officers, in the fight that ensued, he showed a determined front and fought with great gallantry. Although severely wounded Havildar Suba Singh continued to lead and encourage his men and extricated his patrol from a very difficult situation with a loss of two killed and three wounded, whilst the losses to the enemy were estimated at 12 killed and 15 wounded.

JEMADAR SAPURAN SINGH
Was awarded the Indian Order of Merit for conspicuous gallantry for both at Sheikh Saad and at Fort Cbibibat in Mesopotamia on the 12TH January 1916, this Machine Gun Havildar showed the greatest bravery in the handling of his guns. He commanded the detachment when the Machine Gun Officer was killed on the 13TH January and brought his guns forward another 500 yards into the firing line under heavy fire.

SEPOY JETHA SINGH
Was awarded the Indian Order of Merit for conspicuous gallantry in the action at Sheikh Saad in Mesopotamia on the 6TH and 7TH January 1916. During the advance. Sepoy Jetha Singh was severely wounded in the arm. After his wound had been bound up, he refused to wait for the stretcher-bearers but took his place again in the next rush and continued in the firing line until fainted.

Indian Order of Merit (cont.)
FIRST WORLD WAR (cont.)

56TH PUNJABI RIFLES (FRONTIER FORCE) (cont.)

HAVILDAR JAGAT SINGH

Was awarded the Indian Order of Merit for the action at Fort Cbibibat on the 13TH January 1916, Havildar Jagat Singh displayed very conspicuous personal bravery, when in the foremost line overlooking the Wadi, though only 30 yards from the enemy and under constant fire, he continued firing until hit in the shoulder. He then raised himself on his knees, took a long drink from his bottle in full view of the enemy, removed his accoutrements to ease his wound and then walked back to cover some 50 yards away, showing and inspiring greatest contempt for the enemy's fire throughout.

SUBEDAR MAJOR HARNAM SINGH

Was awarded the Indian Order of Merit for conspicuous gallantry during operations on the 8TH March 1916 in Mesopotamia. Subedar Major Harnam Singh commanded and led the Company with great ability and courage after the Company Commander had been wounded.

LANCE NAIK BISHUN SINGH

Was awarded the Indian Order of Merit in Mesopotamia for conspicuous gallantry in the action on the 22ND April 1917. Shortly after the first line was taken a strong counter-attack was made by the enemy and Lance Naik Bishun Singh with his Lewis gun team and a few other men in an advanced post held out until all except three were hit and he himself wounded. Finding himself isolated owing to his right flank having been forced back by the counter-attack, he managed to get his gun back to the main line and re-opened fire. He has always behaved with the greatest gallantry and has been present in every action, in which his regiment has been engaged since 1914. Whenever volunteers for any dangerous exploit have been called for, he has always been the first to step forward.

57TH WILDE'S RIFLES (FRONTIER FORCE)

JEMADAR MANGAL SINGH

Was awarded the Indian Order of Merit for conspicuous gallantry and devotion to duty in France and Flanders in 1915. On 26TH April 1915 during the 2ND Battle of Ypres on recovering consciousness after being gassed, and in spite of intense suffering, he went out time after time and helped to bring in the wounded under fire.

SEPOY ATMA SINGH

Was awarded the Indian Order of Merit for conspicuous gallantry and devotion to duty in France and Flanders in 1915. Atma Singh was one of a machine–gun detachment, and helped to bring a gun up to near the firing line and into firing position under a hot fire. Here he held on until the front line was driven out by gas but he himself declined to budge until ordered to retire.

Indian Order of Merit (cont.)
FIRST WORLD WAR (cont.)
58TH VAUGHAN'S RIFLES (FRONTIER FORCE)

SEPOY DEWAN SINGH
Was awarded the Indian Order of Merit for gallantry and devotion to duty with the British Expeditionary Force in France and Flanders in 1915.

SUBEDAR KARAM SINGH
Was awarded the Indian Order of Merit for gallantry and devotion to duty with the British Expeditionary Force in the fields of France and Flanders in 1914. On 31ST October 1914 he continued to command his men though dangerously wounded and showing most excellent spirit until removed at night.

SUBEDAR SUHEL SINGH (POSTHUMOUS)
Was awarded posthumous Indian Order of Merit for gallantry and devotion to duty with the British Expeditionary Force in France and Flanders in 1915. He was killed in action on 25TH September 1915 in the attack on Aubers Ridge.

JEMADAR SIHEL SINGH (POSTHUMOUS)
Was awarded posthumous Indian Order of Merit for gallantry and devotion to duty with the British Expeditionary Force in France and Flanders in 1915. He was killed in action on the first day of the Battle of Loos, 25TH September 1915.

SUBEDAR HARCHAND SINGH
Was awarded the Indian Order of Merit for gallantry and devotion to duty with the British Expeditionary Force in France and Flanders in 1915.

SEPOY ISAR SINGH
Was awarded the Indian Order of Merit for gallantry and devotion to duty with the British Expeditionary Force in France and Flanders in 1915.

HAVILDAR SANTA SINGH
Was awarded the Indian Order of Merit for gallantry and devotion to duty with the British Expeditionary Force in France and Flanders in 1915.

LANCE NAIK PHANGAN SINGH
Was awarded the Indian Order of Merit for gallantry and devotion to duty with the British Expeditionary Force in France and Flanders in 1915.

French woman pinning a flower to honour Sikh soldiers arriving in France 1914

Indian Order of Merit (cont.)
FIRST WORLD WAR (cont.)

59TH SCINDE RIFLES (FRONTIER FORCE)

SUBEDAR TOLA SINGH

Was awarded the Indian Order of Merit in Mesopotamia for conspicuous gallantry on the 8TH March 1916. Both British officers being wounded, he took command of the Company and during the withdrawal from the redoubt he held his men well in hand. He placed himself under the orders of the Officer Commanding 47TH Sikhs and rendered invaluable service in rallying the men of his regiment as they reached the line of the 47TH Sikhs. He collected and led parties of men to recover wounded from the ground under very heavy fire. Eventually he retired with the 47TH Sikhs and was wounded during the movement. He has been in every action with his regiment since October 1914 and has always been conspicuous for his work.

HAVILDAR BUTA SINGH

Was awarded the Indian Order of Merit for gallantry and devotion to duty with the British Expeditionary Force in France and Flanders in 1915.

62ND PUNJABIS

SEPOY NIHAL SINGH

Was awarded the Indian Order of Merit for gallantry and devotion to duty whilst serving with the British Expeditionary Force in France and Flanders in 1915.

66TH PUNJABIS

SEPOY DHIR SINGH

Was awarded the Indian Order of Merit in Mesopotamia for conspicuous gallantry and devotion to duty on the 22ND November 1915. Sepoy Dhir Singh was attached to the Maxim Battery. When the machine-guns were running short of ammunition and a number of the men of his section had been killed or wounded, he carried up ammunition and kept the guns supplied at a critical time until he himself was severally wounded.

SEPOY MUGH SINGH

Was awarded the Indian Order of Merit in Mesopotamia for conspicuous gallantry and devotion to duty during the battle of Ctesiphon on 22ND November 1915, when under heavy fire he carried two British Officers who were wounded and helpless to a place of safety.

SUBEDAR MAJOR BISHAN SINGH

Was awarded the Indian Order of Merit in recognition of his conspicuous gallantry in action at Ctesiphon on the 22ND November 1915. Subedar Major Bishan Singh showed a splendid example of coolness to his men and led them through each advance with courage and resolution.

Indian Order of Merit (cont.)
FIRST WORLD WAR (cont

69TH PUNJABIS

SUBEDAR MAJOR JOGINDAR SINGH
Was awarded the Indian Order of Merit for conspicuous gallantry and devotion to duty when fighting in a holding action near Neuve Chapelle whilst serving in the Indian Army Corps in France and Flanders in 1915.

LANCE NAIK NIDHAM SINGH
Was awarded the Indian Order of Merit for conspicuous gallantry and devotion to duty when fighting in a holding action near Neuve Chapelle whilst serving in the Indian Army Corps in France and Flanders in 1915.

72ND PUNJABIS

JEMADAR PHUMAN SINGH
Was awarded the Indian Order of Merit for conspicuous bravery during the raid on enemy Sangars on the 16TH August 1918 in Egypt. The British officers and two Indian officers of the assaulting and clearing parties had become casualties and Jemadar Phuman Singh, under heavy shell-fire, reorganized the few remaining men and attempted with great gallantry to penetrate the enemy Sangar. The order to retire at this time had already been given, but did not reach Jemadar Phuman Singh, who was on the right of the clearing party. This gallant officer managed to get within twenty yards of the enemy Sangars but his party having become too small to be any avail and he ordered a retirement, which was successfully carried out under heavy enemy machine-gun and high explosive shell fire.

LANCE NAIK JAGAT SINGH
Was awarded the Indian Order of Merit for conspicuous gallantry and devotion to duty in the raid on enemy Sangars on the 16TH August 1918 in Egypt. Although himself wounded, he remained with his British officer who wounded with a broken leg was left about one hundred yards from the enemy Sangars when the assaulting party had to withdraw owing to heavy casualties. Lance Naik Jagat Singh under heavy fire attended to the British officer and dressed his wounds. He then, under orders from his officer, returned to the Regimental Post and gave the information, which led to his officer being brought in.

SEPOY KISHEN SINGH
Was awarded the Indian Order of Merit in Egypt for conspicuous bravery and devotion to duty. In the raid on enemy Sangars on the 16TH August 1918, when and Indian officer was wounded in the leg within a few yards from the enemy Sangar, and the party had been compelled by casualties to withdraw, Sepoy Kishen Singh remained with the officer and although under fire managed to drag him back under cover of rocks some two hundred yards away.

Indian Order of Merit (cont.)
FIRST WORLD WAR (cont

76TH PUNJABIS

NAIK SUNDAR SINGH (POSTHUMOUS)
Was awarded posthumous Indian Order of Merit for conspicuous bravery at Gurmah Safhah in Mesopotamia, on the 5TH July 1915. After his entire gun teams had been killed, Naik Sundar Singh made repeated attempts to bring some Maxim guns out under heavy fire at a distance of only 50 yards from the enemy, so they did not fall into enemy hands. He was killed in the attempt.

HAVILDAR GANDA SINGH
Was awarded the Indian Order of Merit for marked gallantry near Nasiriyah in Mesopotamia on the 14TH and 24TH July 1915. He was always well to the front and set a fine example of coolness and courage under heavy enemy fire.

HAVILDAR KESAR SINGH
Was awarded the Indian Order of Merit for very conspicuous gallantry at Khafajiyah in Mesopotamia on the 15TH May 1915, in courageously swimming the Kharkeh river, a rapid stream 150 yards wide, supported by a covering fire but in the face of a heavy fire from the enemy on the opposite bank.

NAIK RAM SINGH (POSTHUMOUS)
Was awarded posthumous Indian Order of Merit for very conspicuous gallantry at Gurmah Safhah in Mesopotamia on 5TH July 1915 when with Hukam Singh attempted to move machine–guns under heavy fire out of an impossible position. Naik Ram Singh was killed in the attempt.

LANCE NAIK HUKAM SINGH
Was awarded the Indian Order of Merit for very conspicuous gallantry at Gurmah Safhah in Mesopotamia on 5TH July 1915 when with Ram Singh attempted to move machine–guns under heavy fire out of an impossible position.

SEPOY BATTAN SINGH
Was awarded the Indian Order of Merit for conspicuous gallantry and devotion to duty during the battle of Ctesiphon in Mesopotamia on the 22ND November 1915, when over the ground absolutely devoid of cover and under heavy fire, he drove up to the firing line to distribute ammunition, thus greatly relieving the situation.

82ND PUNJABIS

SEPOY KESAR SINGH
Was awarded the Indian Order of Merit in Mesopotamia for conspicuous gallantry on the 8TH March 1916. Sepoy Kesar Singh took command of his section when his officer was killed and led it forward under heavy fire. He shot ten of the enemy and although wounded himself he assisted to withdraw the only two remaining men of his section.

Indian Order of Merit (cont.)
FIRST WORLD WAR (cont

89TH PUNJABIS

SEPOY DASUNDA SINGH

Was awarded the Indian Order of Merit for conspicuous gallantry in the operations on the Suez Canal on the 3RD February 1915. Sepoy Dasunda Singh brought up ammunition to his comrades under a heavy fire and each time on the return journey carried back a wounded man to the ambulance, which was about 800 to 1,000 yards in rear. He also carried Sepoy Hakim Singh, who was killed and Sepoy Sucha Singh, who was wounded, from the firing line, removing his boots in order to perform the journey quicker.

SEPOY INDAR SINGH

Was awarded the Indian Order of Merit for gallantry and devotion to duty with the British Expeditionary Force in France and Flanders in 1915

90TH PUNJABIS

SEPOY PARTAB SINGH

Was awarded the Indian Order of Merit for very gallant conduct and devotion to duty near Nasiriyah in Mesopotamia, on the 24TH July 1915. Sepoy Partab Singh had two bullet wounds through the upper part of his right arm, but did not pause to bind up his wounds and refused to go back to have them dressed. He continued to join the attack, when he was again wounded. He had two fingers cut off and was unable to handle his rifle. He again refused to go back and busied himself helping bind up the other wounded soldiers and generally assisted them. He had only one and a half year's service.

LANCE NAIK KUNDA SINGH (POSTHUMOUS)

Was awarded posthumous Indian Order of Merit for very conspicuous gallantry and devotion to duty near Nasiriyah in Mesopotamia, on the 24TH July 1915. Lance Naik Kunda Singh was killed while carrying on his back Havildar Sarayan Singh who had been disabled, from an exposed position 100 yards from the enemy, into cover.

SEPOY GANDA SINGH (POSTHUMOUS)

Was awarded posthumous Indian Order of Merit for very conspicuous gallantry and devotion to duty in sending messages by heliography under heavy fire throughout the action, from the firing line, on the 11TH September 1916 in Mesopotamia. He was killed in the act of signalling.

SEPOY BALWANT SINGH

Was awarded the Indian Order of Merit for conspicuous gallantry and devotion to duty on the 28TH September 1917 in Mesopotamia. When a portion of his line was driven back 250 yards by and enemy counter-attack, he, supported by heavy artillery fire, remained behind on his own imitative with a non–commissioned officer and kept up rapid fire till the line was re-established.

Indian Order of Merit (cont.)
FIRST WORLD WAR (cont

91ST PUNJABIS

SEPOY NARD SINGH

Was awarded the Indian Order of Merit for very conspicuous gallantry and coolness on the 4TH July 1919, with the Egyptian Expeditionary Force. A party of 15 signallers and an escort under a British officer were attacked by about 40 of the enemy in the hills and British officer was severally wounded in the leg. Sepoy Nard Singh immediately went to the assistance of the British officer and dragged him under cover, remaining with him while the enemy searched the ground in the vicinity and killed a wounded Sepoy lying close to their hiding place.

92ND PUNJABIS

NAIK NIHAN SINGH

Was awarded the Indian Order of Merit for conspicuous gallantry at Tussum during operations on the Suez Canal on the 3RD February 1915. As his company moved out to counter–attack the enemy. Naik Nihan Singh worked his way to a point from where he shot and killed one of the enemies, while the remainder of the group rushed back to their trench. He kept firing on the enemy in the trench and enabled his company to get to a point from which they could infiltrate the enemy trench. This they did and compelled the enemy to surrender. During the remainder of the day's fighting, Naik Nihan Singh led his squad with coolness and pluck.

SUBEDAR HAZARA SINGH

Was awarded the Indian Order of Merit for conspicuous gallantry at Orah in Mesopotamia on the 20TH January 1916. When ordered to advance to ascertain the enemy's strength, he led his men forward with great daring in face of a terrific fire. He persisted in his advance till ordered to retire. He was severely wounded in the action.

SUBEDAR SHER SINGH

Was awarded the Indian Order of Merit for conspicuous gallantry and initiative in action on the 22ND February 1917 in Mesopotamia. When all the British officers of his company had become casualties, he continued to consolidate and command his company under intense fire in a manner deserving of the highest praise.

Indian Order of Merit (cont.)
FIRST WORLD WAR (cont

SUBEDAR PARTAB SINGH

Was awarded the Indian Order of Merit for conspicuous gallantry, and coolness during action on 22ND April 1916. As the British officer fell mortally wounded at an early stage of the attack, Subedar Partab Singh had promptly taken command of the Company, which was the leading company, and carried on attacking the enemy. He commanded his company with ability and coolness until he had only nine men left and only withdrew when ordered to by his commander. He has shown the same coolness, competence and disregard of danger when in the firing line in the all the actions. He is the only Indian officer of the regiment who has been present in all actions, which the Regiment had fought in Mesopotamia and on Suez Canal in 1915. He has never been off duty and has frequently commanded his Double Company in action.

93RD BURMA INFANTRY

SUBEDAR INDAR SINGH

Was awarded the Indian Order of Merit in Mesopotamia for conspicuous gallantry on 18TH April 1916. During a Turkish counter-attack, Subedar Indar Singh controlled and reformed scattered parties of all units under a heavy enemy fire during a critical time. Several times he formed firing lines on his own initiative, which drove the enemy off.

SUBEDAR LACHMAN SINGH

Was awarded the Indian Order of Merit for conspicuous gallantry, ability and leadership when commanding a platoon in an action on the 9TH January 1917 in Mesopotamia. He succeeded in stopping and rallying men of another regiment who were momentarily withdrawing under heavy fire. He has proved himself an exceptional officer in all actions.

96TH BERAR INFANTRY

SEPOY MEHAR SINGH

Was awarded the Indian Order of Merit for very conspicuous gallantry and devotion to duty at Bushire, Persia, on the 9TH September 1915. Sepoy Mehar Singh continued to fight after being twice wounded. He stopped fighting when he received three more wounds and was ordered to fall out of the firing line.

SUBEDAR DHAN SINGH

Was awarded the Indian Order of Merit for very conspicuous gallantry for the attack on Dilwar Fort near Bushire, Persia, on 13TH August 1915.

Indian Order of Merit (cont.)
FIRST WORLD WAR (cont.)

97th INFANTRY

HAVILDAR RACHPAL SINGH

Was awarded the Indian Order of Merit in Mesopotamia for conspicuous bravery in the action of Orah on the 21st January 1916, in charging the enemy's trench, bayoneting four of the enemy and killing an officer with a bomb. He only retired after losing his rifle and being twice wounded.

104th RIFLES

SUBEDAR SABAL SINGH
NAIK NET SINGH

The above soldiers were awarded the Indian Order of Merit for very conspicuous gallantry during the action at Sahil in Mesopotamia on the 17th November 1914. While under fire from and old fort and a wall perpendicular to it on the edge of a palm grove on the enemy's left flank, they charged the wall at the head of some 20 or 30 men of various units. They were the first in this part of the line to enter the enemy's position and capture it. Subsequently, on the 7th December at Qurnah, Subedar Sabal Singh showed special gallantry in leading his company against the enemy's trenches under fire.

107th PIONEERS

BUGLER NATHA SINGH

Was awarded the Indian Order of Merit for gallantry and devotion to duty with the British Expeditionary Force in France and Flanders in 1915.

119th INFANTRY

HAVILDAR CHAMAN SINGH

Was awarded the Indian Order of Merit for gallantry and devotion to duty at Kut al Amara on the 24th December 1915, when he was in command of the regimental machine–gun section. He worked two guns with great coolness and materially assisted in beating off the attacks of the enemy. During hand-to-hand fighting, which took place later though wounded he displayed great gallantry against the enemy.

124th INFANTRY

SEPOY HARNAM SINGH

Was awarded the Indian Order of Merit in Mesopotamia for conspicuous gallantry and devotion to duty on the 5th November 1917. When his company was temporarily held up by heavy machine-gun fire from a flank, he rose and advanced on the enemy alone. Stimulated by his fine example, his platoon at once followed him and carried through the attack without further check.

Indian Order of Merit (cont.)
FIRST WORLD WAR (cont

125^(TH) RIFLES

RIFLEMAN SUKH SINGH

Was awarded the Indian Order of Merit for conspicuous gallantry and initiative on the 19^(TH) September 1918 in Palestine. During the attack on the enemy position, Rifleman Sukh Singh and a British officer had got some distance ahead of the rest of the company. While so advancing, Rifleman Sukh Singh managed to capture two enemy horses, of which he gave one to his officer and mounted the other himself. Continuing to press forward in this manner, they caught sight of an enemy battery in retreat. Without the slightest hesitation, they galloped in pursuit and on coming up on the guns; Rifleman Sukh Singh held ten of the enemy, whilst the officer compelled the surrender of the battery officers and the guns.

WAZIRISTAN

The Waziristan Campaign was a series of operations conducted in Waziristan by British forces between 1917and 1920. Whilst British Forces were engaged elsewhere in the First World War, Waziris took advantage and launched raids against British garrisons The fighting lasted for 12 months with aircraft being used to suppress tribesmen in some raids. The British Forces eventually restored order in Waziristan.

The following Sikh soldiers were awarded the Indian Order of Merit for conspicuous gallantry and devotion to duty in the Waziristan operations.

151^(ST) PUNJABI RIFLES

SEPOY	HARPAL SINGH	1917	WAZIRISTAN
HAVILDAR	SARDAR SINGH	1917	WAZIRISTAN
SEPOY	BATTAN SINGH	1917	WAZIRISTAN

Waziris Tribesmen

Indian Order of Merit (cont.)
FIRST WORLD WAR (cont

152ND PUNJABIS

HAVILDAR WASAKHA SINGH
Was awarded the Indian Order of Merit in Egypt for conspicuous gallantry during the operations in September and October 1918. Particularly on the 19TH September 1918, during an attack when his company commander fell wounded in the open, Havildar Wasakha Singh with another man at once advanced from a captured enemy position to bring the officer into cover under heavy machine-gun fire. Whilst doing so, the other man was severely wounded but Havildar Wasakha Singh succeeded in bringing the officer and the other man under cover of rocks.

SEPOY KARTAR SINGH (POSTHUMOUS)
Was awarded posthumous Indian Order of Merit in Egypt for conspicuous gallantry on the 19TH September 1918. After the first attempt to take the enemy trenches had failed, and the men were falling back to their original position, Sepoy Kartar Singh rushed forward under heavy fire from second line, throwing bombs until the supply was exhausted and he was killed. He displayed great courage and devotion to duty.

INDIAN SUBORDINATE MEDICAL DEPARTMENT

SUB ASSISTANT HARNAM SINGH
Was awarded the Indian Order of Merit for conspicuous gallantry and initiative on the 23RD and 24TH November 1914 in France and Flanders.

SUB ASSISTANT RAM SINGH
Was awarded the Indian Order of Merit for gallantry and devotion to duty with the British Expeditionary Force in France and Flanders in 1915.

SUB ASSISTANT PARGAN SINGH I.O.M. & BAR
Was awarded the Indian Order of Merit for gallantry and devotion to duty in attending wounded of his own and other regiments, both Indian and British, under heavy fire in the action of Shaikh Saad in Mesopotamia on the 7TH and 8TH January 1916. (He was also awarded the Indian Order of Merit for gallantry in France.)

SUB ASSISTANT BHAGWAN SINGH
Was awarded the Indian Order of Merit for gallantry and devotion to duty on 28TH June at Gallipoli, Turkey. He carried on medical duties with the battalion single-handed for sometime. At Anzac he attended to casualties from other units in addition to those of his own unit.

Indian Order of Merit (cont.)

FIRST WORLD WAR (cont)

INDIAN MEDICAL DEPARTMENT (cont)

SUB ASSISTANT ISHAR SINGH
Was awarded the Indian Order of Merit for gallantry and devotion to duty in Gallipoli, Turkey in 1916.

SUB ASSISTANT LAL SINGH
Was awarded the Indian Order of Merit for conspicuous gallantry and devotion to duty during the action of the 17TH and 18TH April 1916, in Mesopotamia. At the approach of the enemy, he supervised the evacuation of the Regimental Aid Post during the absence of the Medical Officer. On the way, he found and abandoned machine-gun and carried himself about 400 yards to a safe position in the rear while under heavy fire. He also displayed great devotion to duty in tending the wounded. During the action of the 8TH March 1916,

SUB ASSISTANT HUKAM SINGH
SUB ASSISTANT MULA SINGH
The above soldiers were awarded the Indian Order of Merit for conspicuous gallantry and devotion to duty in East Africa in 1917. Hukam Singh also served with the King's African Rifles.

SUB ASSISTANT DAULAT SINGH
Was awarded the Indian Order of Merit for conspicuous gallantry and devotion to duty at Gallipoli in Turkey in 1917.

SUB ASSISTANT MUL SINGH
Was awarded the Indian Order of Merit for conspicuous gallantry and initiative in action on the 17TH February 1917 in Mesopotamia. Sub Assistant Mul Singh remained in the front line trenches under heavy fire. At night he more than once went over the parapet into No Man's Land to supervise the bringing in of the wounded when he would have been perfectly justified in staying in the Aid Post. His cheerful spirit in all weathers, his moral and gallant example and his untiring energy has been a pattern of soldierly conduct on every occasion.

BURMA MILITARY POLICE

SOWAR KALA SINGH
Was awarded the Indian Order of Merit for conspicuous gallantry, on the 24TH February 1915 in the Kachin Hills of Burma, when carrying dispatches with a comrade through jungle country infested by the enemy. During the journey, they were fired on from an ambuscade and Sowar Kala Singh's comrade was, severely wounded and rendered unconscious. Kala Singh saved the soldiers life by dragging him to safety

Indian Order of Merit (cont.)

FIRST WORLD WAR (cont)

BURMA MILITARY POLICE (cont)

LANCE NAIK KAHAN SINGH

Was awarded the Indian Order of Merit for conspicuous gallantry on 9TH January 1917 during an attack on Turkish trenches in Mesopotamia. The attack along the main trench met with such strenuous resistance that it resolved itself in to a bombing duel until Sepoy Kahan Singh, on his own initiative, climbed out of the trench with his Lewis gun, which he shouldered, and opened fire on the enemy on the trench below. He drove the enemy out of the trench and continued to fire his Lewis gun at the enemy until a bomb attack broke the stock of his gun, severely wounding him in the shoulder. For this splendid act of gallantry, he was given an immediate award of the Indian Order of Merit.

JEMADAR MIT SINGH

Was awarded the Indian Order of Merit for conspicuous gallantry and continuous devotion to duty in Egypt 1917.

RISALDAR NAND SINGH
SOWAR ARJAN SINGH

The above soldiers were awarded the Indian Order of Merit for conspicuous gallantry and continuous devotion to duty on the North West Frontier of India in 1919.

SEPOY JAI SINGH

Was awarded the Indian Order of Merit for conspicuous gallantry in action at Khan Abu Malul, Egypt, and 19TH September 1918. Several times Sepoy Jai Singh was forced to withdraw with his Lewis gun by the grenade attacks by the enemy. He displayed great determination and courage in coming into action in different places.

KACHIN HILLS

In 1931 there was an uprising by the peasantry against the British rule, as they demanded independence for Burma. British authorities ruthlessly subdued the peasantry.

The following Sikh soldiers were awarded Indian Order of Merit for their conspicuous and continuous gallantry in action at Kachin Hills in Burma.

SUBEDAR	CHANAN SINGH	1931	KACHIN HILLS
LANCE NAIK	TAHAL SINGH	1931	KACHIN HILLS
JEMADAR	DHYAN SINGH	1932	KACHIN HILLS

Indian Order of Merit (cont.)

FIRST WORLD WAR (cont.)

The Russian revolution opened the way for Turkish forces and German spies via Russia into Afghanistan. In order to counter the Turkish threat the British joined with the Russian Mensheviks and decided to drive the Russian Bolsheviks out of Trans Caspia. The British troops were therefore, concentrated on the borders and fought continuous action against the Bolsheviks.

BURMA MOUNTED RIFLES

RISALDAR GULZAR SINGH
Was awarded the Indian Order of Merit for conspicuous gallantry on the 25TH May 1918 in South Persia. He extricated his squadron from a very difficult situation in excellent order. Having done so returned to the open to help bring in the bodies of an officer and wound men, under heavy enemy fire. He was conspicuous for his skilful leadership in every action in which he was engaged.

JEMADAR KISHEN SINGH
Was awarded the Indian Order of Merit for conspicuous gallantry on the 23RD October 1918 in South Persia, in an action in which two of his troopers were wounded about three hundred yards from the enemy's position. Jemadar Kishen Singh gallantly led his troop to their rescue and brought them in. In another action Jemadar Kishen and two troopers were severely wounded and lay out exposed to the enemy fire from 4.15 pm till dusk, when it became possible to rescue them.

SOWAR UTTAM SINGH
Was awarded the Indian Order of Merit for conspicuous gallantry on the 23RD October 1918 in South Persia.

FARIDKOT SAPPERS AND MINERS

CAPTAIN NAND SINGH
Was awarded the Indian Order of Merit for conspicuous gallantry and devotion to duty in the field. He served in East Africa from 1914 to 1918, and ended the campaign as Lieutenant Colonel.

The Jind Infantry, a Sikh Princely states unit, was in Africa from October 1914 to December 1917. They earned the highest opinions from all the generals under whom they served, especially their fighting at Jassin in East Africa in 1915.

JIND INFANTRY

SUBEDAR HARNAM SINGH
Was awarded the Indian Order of Merit for his gallant conduct at Jasin in East Africa, on the 18TH January 1915. He rallied a small party to cover a retirement and held the enemy in check until all in his party were killed, he himself severely wounded and taken prisoner.

Indian Order of Merit (cont.)

FIRST WORLD WAR (cont)

JIND INFANTRY (cont)

NAIK KEHAR SINGH
Was awarded the Indian Order of Merit for the exemplary cool manner in which he worked his machine gun under heavy fire on the 16TH and 17TH December near Masanga, while serving with the Indian Expeditionary Force in East Africa.

SUBEDAR BHAGWAN SINGH
Was awarded the Indian Order of Merit for his gallant conduct in East Africa on the 18TH January 1916.

SEPOY SADDA SINGH (POSTHUMOUS)
Was awarded posthumous Indian Order of Merit for conspicuous gallantry in action on the 9TH October 1916 in East Africa. He proceeded forward under a hot fire along a communication trench and removed a number of dead bodies, which were impeding the advance. He has since died of wounds.

PATIALA INFANTRY

The Patiala Infantry reached Ismailia in November 1914, doing arduous reconnaissance in the canal area and defending the Suez Canal. They took part in actions against the Turks at El Arish, Rafa, Kabar Majahid and the attack on Es-Salt. They left Suez for Patiala on 9TH October 1919. A Double Company of the Patiala Infantry was attached to the 14TH Sikhs and fought with them in the Gallipoli campaign and went on to serve in Egypt, Persia and Mesopotamia.

CAPTAIN BHAGWAN SINGH
Was awarded the Indian Order of Merit in Egypt for gallantry and devotion to duty on the night of 29TH–30TH April 1918, when in the command of the advance guard, which was subsequently held up by the party of the enemy with machine-guns concealed in thick scrub. Captain Bhagwan Singh led his men in such a prompt and fearless manner that the enemy were forced to retire hastily.

SUBEDAR KALA SINGH
Was awarded the Indian Order of Merit for conspicuous gallantry in action at Gallipoli in 1916. Subedar Kala Singh served with the 14TH Sikhs. A Double Company of the Patiala Infantry was attached to the 14TH Sikhs and stayed with them after the Gallipoli campaign and served in Egypt, Persia and Mesopotamia.

SUBEDAR DHARM SINGH
Was awarded the Indian Order of Merit for gallantry and devotion to duty on the 30TH April 1918 in Egypt. His platoon came under very heavy shell and machine–gunfire. An order was issued for the company to withdraw to a more sheltered position but Subedar Dharm Singh remained where he was as he had two seriously wounded soldiers with him whom he could not remove. He remained there for over two hours until stretcher–bearers could go out and bring them in.

Indian Order of Merit (cont.)

FIRST WORLD WAR (cont.)

MALAY STATES GUIDES

The Malay States Guides, Infantry and Artillery were raised in 1875 from Sikhs and Punjabi Mussulmans, being ex-Indian Army soldiers. They had been more or less on continuous service within the states. The Sikh contingent went on to serve in Aden during the First World War and was disbanded at the end of the war.

JEMADAR GURDIT SINGH

Was awarded the Indian Order of Merit for conspicuous gallantry in action on the night of 15TH and 16TH February 1918, in Aden. This Sikh officer commanded a platoon in an attack against an enemy piquet. He personally volunteered to go forward and exactly locate the piquet and by doing so materially assisted the success of the operation. Subsequently in the attacks, he led his platoon with great gallantry and determination.

HAVILDAR KEHAR SINGH
SEPOY SARWAN SINGH

The above soldiers were awarded the Indian Order of Merit in Aden for conspicuous gallantry on the 5TH August 1916, in dashing out to within 400 yards of the enemy's position and bringing in a wounded Indian officer under heavy shell and rifle fire.

NAIK SAWAN SINGH

Was awarded the Indian Order of Merit gallantry and devotion to duty in Aden in 1915.

BOMBAY PIONEERS

HAVILDAR NATHA SINGH

Was awarded the Indian Order of Merit gallantry and devotion to duty with the British Expeditionary Force in France and Flanders in 1915.

JEMADAR MAINGHA SINGH

Was awarded the Indian Order of Merit gallantry and devotion to duty with the British Expeditionary Force in France and Flanders in 1915.

JEMADAR INDAR SINGH
HAVILDAR GAND A SINGH

The above soldiers were awarded the Indian Order of Merit for conspicuous gallantry and good work at Tussum, in the operations on the Suez Canal on the 3RD February 1915. When the platoon commander was killed, the command of the platoon devolved upon Jemadar Indar Singh who continued the fight until relieved by the 2ND Rajputs. Jemadar Indar Singh and Havildar Ganda Singh behaved gallantly in charging a number of the enemy, who had landed with fixed bayonets.

Indian Order of Merit (cont.)

BATTLE OF SARAGARHI

The Battle of Saragarhi is the incredible story of 21 men of the 36TH Sikhs (currently the 4TH Battalion, Sikh Regiment) who gave up their lives in devotion to their duty. In keeping with the tradition of the Indian Army, they fought to the death rather than surrender. The Battle at Saragarhi is one of eight stories of collective bravery published by UNESCO (United Nations Educational, Scientific and Cultural Organization). It has been mentioned as one of the five most significant events of its kind in the world, which includes the Saga of Thermoplyae associated with the heroic stand of a small Greek force against the mighty Persian Xerxes in 480 B.C.

The British colonial rulers had constructed a series of forts to control the North West Frontier Province (NWFP - today a state in Pakistan) and to provide security to troops against marauding tribesmen and their *lashkars* (large body of troops). Most of these forts had initially been built by Maharaja Ranjit Singh as part of the consolidation of the Sikh Empire in Punjab, and the British added more. The British had only partially succeeded in gaining control over this region, and consequently skirmishes and sometimes-serious fights with the tribals were a frequent occurrence. However, the NWFP was a good training ground for the Indian Army to hone its skills and techniques.

Two such forts on the Samana ridge of the Hindukush and Sulaiman ranges, that is, Fort Lockhart and Fort Gulistan, were a few miles apart. Since these forts were not inter-visible, a signalling relay post called Saragarhi was located mid-way on a bluff to provide heliographic communications between them. This post or picket had been fortified to provide safety and protection to the signalling detachment.

In 1897 there was a general uprising in the NWFP engineered by Afghans as part of their policy, which came to be known as the 'prickly heat policy' to direct the wrath of the tribals against the British. In this uprising, *Mullahs* (Muslim religious leaders) played a prominent role. It was the duty of the 36TH Sikhs to occupy Gulistan and Lockhart forts. On 3RD and 9TH September 1897, Orakazai and Afridi *lahars* attacked Fort Gulistan. On both occasion the attacks were beaten back. A relief column was sent from the fort to assist in beating back these attacks.

The relief column from Lockhart on the return trip reinforced the signalling detachment at Saragarhi making its strength to one Non-Commissioned Officer (NCO) and 20 Other Ranks (ORs). In a renewed effort, on 12TH September 1897, hordes of tribesmen laid siege to Fort Lockhart and Saragarhi, with the aim of overrunning the latter and at the same time preventing any help from the former.

Indian Order of Merit (cont.)

BATTLE OF SARAGARHI (cont.)

The Commanding Officer of 36TH Sikhs, Lt. Col. Haughton, was at Fort Lockhart and in communication with the Saragarhi post through helicograph. The defenders of Saragarhi, under the indomitable and inspiring leadership of their detachment Commander, Havildar Ishar Singh, resolved to defend their post in the best tradition of their race and Regiment. They were not there to hand over the post to the enemy and seek safety elsewhere. Havildar Singh and his men knew well that the post would fall, because a handful of men in that make-shift fort of stones and mud walls with a wooden door could not stand the onslaught of thousands of tribesmen. These plucky men knew that they would go down but they had resolved to do so fighting to the last.

From Fort Lockhart, troops and the Commanding Officer could count at least 14 standards and that gave an idea of the number of tribes and their massed strength against the Saragarhi relay post (estimated at between 10,000 to 12,000 tribals). From early morning the tribals started battering the fort. The Sikhs fought back valiantly. The men of the 36TH Sikhs repulsed charge after charge. The tribal leaders started to make tempting promises so that the Sikhs would surrender. But Havildar Singh and his men ignored them. For quite some time, the troops held their own against the determined and repeated attacks by the wild and ferocious hordes. A few attempts were made to send a relief column from Fort Lockhart but the tribals foiled these.

At Saragarhi, the enemy made two determined attempts to rush the gate of the post and on both occasions the defenders repulsed the assault. While the enemy suffered heavy casualties, the ranks of the defenders too kept dwindling as the fire from the attackers took its toll and their ammunition stocks were depleting. Unmindful of his safety, Sepoy Gurmukh Singh kept signalling a minute-to-minute account of the battle from the signal tower in the post to Battalion HQs. The battle lasted the better part of the day. When repeated attacks failed, the enemy set fire to the surrounding bushes and shrubs and two of the tribesmen under cover of smoke, managed to close in with the post's boundary wall in an area blind to the defenders' observation and rifle fire from the post holes. They succeeded in making a breach in the wall. This development could be seen from Fort Lockhart and was flashed to the post.

A few men from those defending the approaches to the gate were dispatched to deal with the breach in the wall. This diversion by the enemy and the defenders' reaction resulted in weakening of the fire covering the gate. The enemy now rushed the gate as well as the breach. Thereafter, one of the fiercest hand-to-hand fights followed.

Indian Order of Merit (cont.)

BATTLE OF SARAGARHI (cont.)

One of the Havildar Singh's men, who was seriously wounded was profusely bleeding, had taken charge of the Guardroom and shot four of the enemy as they tried to approach his charge. All this time, Sepoy Gurmukh Singh continued flashing details of the action at the post. Beside this the Commanding Officer of 36TH Sikhs and others at Lockhart Fort also saw this unique saga of heroism and valour unfold at Saragarhi. The battle had come too close for Sepoy Gurmukh Singh's comfort, so he asked Battalion HQs for permission to shut down the heliograph and take up his rifle. Permission was flashed back. He dismounted his heliograph equipment, packed it in a leather bag, fixed bayonet on his rifle and joined the fight. From his vantage point in the tower he wrought havoc on the intruders in the post. He died fighting, but took 20 of the enemy with him. The tribals set fire to the post, while the brave garrison lay dead or dying with their ammunition exhausted. Next morning the relief column reached the post and the tell tale marks of the epic fight were there for all to see. The tribals later admitted to a figure of 180 dead and many more wounded. This episode, when narrated in the British Parliament, drew from the members a standing ovation in the memory of the defenders of Saragarhi. The story of the heroic deeds of these men was also placed before Queen Victoria. The account was received all over the world with awe and admiration. All the 21 valiant men of this epic battle were awarded the Indian Order of Merit (posthumously) which at the time was one of the highest gallantry awards given to Indian troops and is considered equivalent to the present-day Mahavir Chakra. The dependants of the Saragarhi heroes were awarded 50 acres of land and 500 Rupees. Never before or since has a body of troops that is all of them, won gallantry awards in a single action. It is indeed a singularly unique action in the annals of Indian military history. A tablet was erected in the memory of these brave men. The tablet reads:

"The Government of India have caused this tablet to be erected to the memory of the twenty one non-commissioned officers and men of the 36TH Sikh Regiment of the Bengal Infantry whose names are engraved below as a perpetual record of the heroism shown by these gallant soldiers who died at their posts in the Defence of the fort of Saragarhi, on the 12TH September 1897, fighting against overwhelming numbers, thus proving their loyalty and devotion to their sovereign, the Queen Empress of India, and gloriously maintaining the reputation of the Sikhs for unflinching courage on the field of battle."

(http://www.bharat-rakshak.com)

Indian Order of Merit (cont.)

THE SARAGARHI HEROES

Havildar Ishar Singh

Naik Lal Singh	Sepoy Narayan Singh
Lance Naik Chanda Singh	Sepoy Gurmukh Singh
Sepoy Sundar Singh	Sepoy Jivan Singh
Sepoy Ram Singh	Sepoy Gurmukh Singh
Sepoy Uttar Singh	Sepoy Ram Singh
Sepoy Sahib Singh	Sepoy Bhagwan Singh
Sepoy Hira Singh	Sepoy Bhagwan Singh
Sepoy Daya Singh	Sepoy Buta Singh
Sepoy Jivan Singh	Sepoy Jivan Singh
Sepoy Bhola Singh	Sepoy Nand Singh

Ruins of Saragarhi Fort after its recapure with Sikhs lining the wall.

"On Saragarhi's ramparts died the
bravest of the brave,
Neath Saragarhi's ruined walls they
Found a fitting grave,
For Saragarhi bears the fame,
They gave their lives to save"

Indian Order of Merit (cont.)

THE THIRD AFGHAN WAR 1919

Sensing post-First World War British fatigue, the frailty of British positions along the Afghan border, Amanullah, the new ruler of Afghanistan, suddenly attacked the British in May 1919 in two thrusts. The British were taken by surprise, and Afghan forces achieved some success in the early days of the war, as Pashtun tribesmen from both sides of the border joined forces with them. The military skirmishes ranged along much of the border area. Fighting occurred in Chitral, in the Khyber Pass, through the Kurram Valley, in the Tochi Valley, in Waziristan, and Baluchistan. The war did not last long, however, because both sides were soon ready to sue for peace. The Afghans were unwilling to sustain continued British air attacks on Kabul and Jalalabad, and the British were unwilling to take on an Afghan land war so soon after the bloodletting of First World War. Amanullah sued for peace on 31ST May, and peace was restored by the treaty of Rawalpindi on the 8TH August 1919. Although an armistice ended the fighting in Afghanistan, the North West Frontier Campaigns on the borders continued until 1937. The Afghan war ended but this did not improve the situation in Waziristan.

A British officer wrote: " At no time in their history had the Mahsuds and Wazirs been so well armed as at this juncture, since in additon to their normal armament, considerable quantities of government rifle and ammunition had fallen recently into their hands. To supplement their stocks the tribesmen had received large supplies of ammunition throutgh the agency of anti-British Afghan officials in Khost. These tribesmen have long been remarkable for their courage, activity and hardihood, and when the mountanious and difficult nature of their country in considered, together with the fact that their numbners included about 1,800 army deserters and so highly trained in our tactics and methods of fighting, it will be realized that they constituted a formidable enemy."

BHISTI GURDIT SINGH
66TH PUNJABIS

More than 6,000 Mahsuds and Bhittanis surrounded Jandola fort in tribal area of South Waziristan, on May 28TH. The tribesmen cut off the water supply, a mile distant from the fort, on the first day of the siege, and water was rationed to one water-bottle a man a day. The weather was extremely hot, and discipline was severely tested by this scarcity of water. On the 7TH June a sortie party rushed out to obtain water, bringing back with them three day's supply. It was during this operation that *Bihishti* (water carrier) Gurdit Singh earned the Indian Order of Merit. He went backwards and forwards continually to carry water. Even after he was wounded he went out again. On his final trip, his *mashk* (leather water-container) being punctured by bullets in two places, he plugged the holes with his hands, although he was again wounded on his way back. Fortunately, his wounds did not prove fatal and he lived to serve the Battalion for many years.

Indian Order of Merit (cont.)

THE THIRD AFGHAN WAR 1919 (cont.)
HAVILDAR ISHAR SINGH, I.D.S.M.
76TH PUNJABIS

It is a little epic, the day of 76TH Punjabis on Flathead. They were a very, very young second-line battalion, and they bumped into a fight such, as the oldest of veteran Frontier Force battalions had never dreamt of. Nevertheless, they attacked with go, when bidden, and when told to hang on, hung on to what they had got. They grimly stuck to their ground the whole of that weary hard fought day. Five separate times did the Mahsud counter-attack, and five separate times with bullet and butt, bayonet and bomb, did the 76TH hurl him back down the slopes. Havildar Ishar Singh was awarded the Indian Order of Merit for conspicuous bravery and leadership after one of the heaviest fights of the Frontier.

'Sepoy Ishar Singh, had been hitherto been employed in the Mess soda-water 'factory' and had been chaffed about this by his companions. 'We go and fight while you make *sod- pani'*. This was too much for Ishar Singh, who went and made an *arz* (petition) to be allowed to join his company in action. He displayed marked gallantry and was one of the very first into the enemy trenches, and in this, his first battle, earned I.D.S.M. Later he was to earn three more 'mentions in despatches', stop a bullet, and win the Indian Order of Merit on the North-West Frontier and get promoted in the field for still further gallantry.' (Qureshi: *The First Punjabis*).

JEMADAR MAGHAR SINGH
34TH SIKH PIONEERS

On December 18TH 1919, a military column moved out to take Spinkai Ghash on the North West Frontier of India, with the idea of covering the occupation of a camp on Palosina plain, three miles north of Jandola. A Mahsud lashkar about 2,000 strong and about 1,000 Wana Waziris were on their way to oppose the advance of the column. On the 19TH and the 20TH two abortive but costly attempts were made to establish a permanent piquet on Mandanna Hill, which was rushed and captured by the Mahsuds. That evening it was decided to establish a permanent piquet on Black Hill. The units detailed for the task were the 82ND Punjabis, 109TH Infantry and 34TH Sikh Pioneers, supported by some artillery. On the 21ST as the units occupied Black Hill unopposed, the Mahsuds rushed the hill from three directions. They drove in the companies of 109TH Infantry and 82ND Punjabis and killed the Company Commander and the Havildar. At this juncture Havildar Maghar Singh took charge and the Sikh Pioneers beat off four attacks and forced the Mahsuds to retire. The casualties on both sides were heavy. For his gallant part and leadership in this attack Havildar Maghar Singh was awarded the Indian Order of Merit.

Indian Order of Merit (cont.)

THE THIRD AFGHAN WAR 1919 (cont.)
SUBEDAR KARAM SINGH
36TH MOUNTAIN BATTERY

At Abadeh fort in South Persia, about 180 miles from Isfahan, a small garrison of British and Indian troops had been beleaguered since 28TH June 1918 by Qashqais tribesmen and mutineer levies. The garrison had held out against enormous odds, and was relieved on 17TH July by a section of Mountain Artillery and Burma Mounted Rifles, which had made a forced march of 180 miles in seven days in intense heat. Subedar Karam Singh was awarded the Indian Order of Merit for conspicuous gallantry during the siege.

23RD SIKH PIONEERS

In 1920, The 23RD Sikh Pioneers returned from Palestine, then proceeded to Waziristan to join the force that carried out punitive operations against the Mahsuds. During these operations, the following Sikh officers were awarded the Indian Order of Merit for conspicuous gallantry in action.

SUBEDAR	SANT SINGH	1920	WAZIRISTAN
SUBEDAR	SAPURAN SINGH	1921	WAZIRISTAN

9TH INFANTRY BRIGADE

The following units of the 9TH Infantry Brigade carried out punitive operations in Waziristan for several weeks and the following Sikh officers and men were awarded the Indian Order of Merit for conspicuous gallantry in action.

11TH LANCERS

RESSAIDAR	BHAGA SINGH	1920	WAZIRISTAN
DAFADAR	HAZARA SINGH	1921	WAZIRISTAN

13TH LANCERS

HON CAPTAIN	INDAR SINGH	1920	WAZIRISTAN

ROYAL MOUNTAIN ARTILLERY

HAVILDAR	MOTA SINGH	1921	WAZIRISTAN

151ST INFANTRY

SEPOY	HARPAL SINGH	1920	WAZIRISTAN

152ND PUNJABIS

JEMADAR	LEHNA SINGH	1920	WAZIRISTAN

2ND PUNJAB REGIMENT

SUBEDAR	HARI SINGH	1935	WAZIRISTAN

Indian Order of Merit (cont.)

THE THIRD AFGHAN WAR 1919 (cont.)

13TH FRONTIER FORCE RIFLES

SEPOY	RAM SINGH	1920	WAZIRISTAN
JEMADAR	JIWAN SINGH	1921	WAZIRISTAN
JEMADAR	TARA SINGH	1937	WAZIRISTAN

11TH SIKH REGIMENT

LANCE NAIK	SARWAN SINGH	1919	WAZIRISTAN
HAVILDAR	TARA SINGH	1921	WAZIRISTAN
HAVILDAR	GANGA SINGH	1921	WAZIRISTAN
HAVILDAR	HARDIT SINGH	1921	WAZIRISTAN
SEPOY	MAHA SINGH	1921	WAZIRISTAN
SUBEDAR	UTTAR SINGH	1921	WAZIRISTAN
SUBEDAR	ARJAN SINGH	1932	WAZIRISTAN
SEPOY	THAMAN SINGH	1932	WAZIRISTAN
NAIK	SANTA SINGH	1937	WAZIRISTAN
SUBEDAR	HAZARA SINGH	1937	WAZIRISTAN
SUBEDAR	MILKHA SINGH	1938	WAZIRISTAN

14TH PUNJAB REGIMENT

NAIK	BHAG SINGH	1920	WAZIRISTAN
LANCE NAIK	KEHAR SINGH	1920	WAZIRISTAN
SUBEDAR	BALWANT SINGH	1936	WAZIRISTAN

15TH PUNJAB REGIMENT

JEMADAR	JAGAT SINGH	1921	WAZIRISTAN
JEMADAR	BALWANT SINGH	1931	WAZIRISTAN

BURMA MOUNTED RIFLES

SOWAR	ARJAN SINGH	1919	WAZIRISTAN
RISALDAR	NANDA SINGH	1919	WAZIRISTAN
SUBEDAR	CHANAN SINGH	1931	WAZIRISTAN
LANCE NAIK	TAHAL SINGH	1931	WAZIRISTAN
JEMADAR	DHYAN SINGH	1934	WAZIRISTAN

Indian Order of Merit (cont.)

SECOND WORLD WAR
JEMADAR AMAN SINGH
INDIAN ARMOURED CORPS, MIDDLE EAST

"During the night of 15TH and 26TH July 1941, Jemadar Aman Singh led a successful raid against an enemy machine-gun post and three other successive positions. All were attacked and stormed with hand grenades and bayonets and the defenders killed. Aman Singh showed the highest qualities of leadership and personal bravery, setting a splendid example to those serving under him. At the conclusion of his task, he brought all his men safely back in spite of heavy mortar and machine-gun fire. The raiding party suffered only a single causality, one man being slightly wounded. The success of this raid was not only due to his courageous leadership, but also to the zeal, energy and skill, which he had shown during the preliminary reconnaissance of the enemy position."

HAVILDAR JAGIR SINGH (POSTHUMOUS)
INDIAN ENGINEERS, BURMA

"On 26TH February 1944, Jagir Singh was Platoon Havildar of a Sapper Platoon detailed to support and help in the mopping-up of a strong enemy bunker position. The Sappers were ordered to attack a large enemy bunker, which was holding up the advance, and one section was detailed for the job. Havildar Jagir Singh begged to be allowed to accompany this section as he pointed out that the platoon commander was new and the section had no Havildar. He was finally allowed to go. As the section advanced the light machine-gunner was hit and seriously wounded. Havildar Jagir Singh, realizing the situation and not being able to give any assistance from his position, at once sprang out of his trench, and standing on a mound in full view of several enemy positions, fired the Bren from the hip at an enemy party about 10 yards distant. Shouting taunts and insults at the enemy, and firing heavily at them, he was seen to kill three of them for certain. When ordered to climb down from the mound he reluctantly obeyed but protested that he could not see from lower down. As the advance was still being held up, he resumed his old position. Cheering on his own men he kept up a heavy fire on the enemy. He appeared to have a charmed life as hand grenades and bullets directed at him all missed, but finally a sniper firing out of a large bunker killed him. His magnificent example of courage and spirit inspired his men to such and extent that they successfully attacked and destroyed the Japanese held bunker. He left a standard of conduct and bravery to his platoon which is already legend."

Indian Order of Merit (cont.)

SECOND WORLD WAR (cont.)
LANCE NAIK RATTAN SINGH
INDIAN SIGNALS, ITALY

"Lance Naik Rattan Singh displayed outstanding bravery when in charge of a cable-laying party during the fighting at Cassino on 15TH and 17TH March 1944. His first task was to lay a line behind the battalion moving to attack Hangman's Hill on the night of 16TH March. Owing to the dark night and weather conditions, he was unable to keep his cable laying in pace with the infantry battalion, and on reaching Cassino, could not locate the Battalion Headquarters. Heavy fighting was still in progress in the town, but with complete disregard for his own personal safety he spent the remainder of the night looking for the Headquarters. When morning came, he became the target for close-range sniper fire but continued his search, and eventually found the infantry, who had taken over the buildings on the edge of the town. While still under constant and intense fire of all description, he collected his signal party and completed the laying of the cable, although his party suffered heavy casualties in the process. Under the shelling and mortaring, which was continuous, this was almost an impossible task; but Lance Naik Rattan Singh persevered at it all day, and such communication as was possible with the battalion was entirely due to his magnificent effort. On the night $16^{TH}/17^{TH}$ the battalion continued its advance to its objective on Hangman's Hill and again Lance Naik Rattan Singh made the most determined and gallant effort to lay a line through behind advancing infantry. Owing to the natural difficulties and enemy opposition, this proved an impossible task, but Rattan Singh would not desist from his efforts until personally ordered to do so by his commander. Throughout the rest of battle, until 28TH March, he continued to display outstanding courage and devotion, without thought of personal risk in maintaining line communication with forward units. The great bravery and devotion displayed by Lance Naik Rattan Singh are worthy of the highest praise, and were a magnificent inspiration and example to the party of which he was in charge."

Sikh Signallers laying telephone wires in Mesopotamia.

Indian Order of Merit (cont.)

SECOND WORLD WAR (cont.)
JEMADAR KARTAR SINGH, (POSTHUMOUS)
14TH PUNJAB REGIMENT, MDDLE EAST

"On 23RD July 1942 Jemadar Kartar Singh led his platoon forward in the face of intense medium machine-gun and shellfire. He was wounded and blown over by a shell-burst but rose and continued to lead and encourage his men. Soon after he was again hit in the head by a bullet but he still attempted to rise but was unable to do so. Nevertheless, he encouraged his platoon from where he lay until he finally died from his head wound."

SUBEDAR FATEH SINGH (POSTHUMOUS)
1ST PUNJAB REGIMENT, MIDDLE EAST

"Subedar Fateh Singh was a veritable pillar of strength in his Company. His courage and leadership were outstanding and it is no exaggeration to say that whenever he led, no man ever hesitated to follow. His Battalion took part in many attacks and Subedar Fateh Singh was present at them all. He was always with his men encouraging them on and praising them in every way, doing his utmost to see that the Company did the job thoroughly. During a night march on 19TH June 1941 one platoon lost its way. Subedar Fateh Singh himself went in search of this platoon and managed to find it. He did not hesitate to go alone in the darkness of the night although fully aware that he may himself have run into enemy posts. Having found the platoon, he formed part of the reinforcements, which were being rushed to the aid of the others who were surrounded, and while on the way up he brilliantly led the platoon against a nest of machine-guns, completely routing the enemy. On 30TH November 1941 the Battalion was up against very stiff opposition. Subedar Fateh Singh's company was pinned down by extremely heavy machine-gun fire and was also being heavily shelled, but seeing the necessity of immediate action, he stood up and cheered his men on and it was then that he was killed by a burst of machine-gun fire. His action was a tonic to the men; they no longer hesitated in going forward to their objective in spite of heavy losses."

Naik, Punjab Regiment

Indian Order of Merit (cont.)

SECOND WORLD WAR (cont.)

JEMADAR DHERA SINGH
2ND PUNJAB REGIMENT, MIDDLE EAST

"The success of the attack of 'B' Company on an enemy strong point on 25TH November 1941 was very largely due to the courageous and cool-headed leadership of Jemadar Dhera Singh. Directing the centre and the right-hand platoons in broad daylight, in full view of the enemy and under considerable fire, he co-ordinated their attack, and by his example of coolness and daring, led them into the final charge with such dash and determination that the position was taken, resulting in the capture of two Italian Officers, 42 other ranks, a 20 mm gun and other weapons and war materials. There is no doubt that, by risking his life so that his men could see him was a great factor in preventing any hesitation, which at that point might have been fatal. On many previous occasions, Jemadar Dhera Singh has led his platoon successfully against enemy positions showing utter disregard for his own personal safety. For continuous good work and exhibition of sterling qualities of leadership throughout the Eritrean campaign and the operations in the Western Desert, Jemadar Dhera Singh was awarded the Indian Order of Merit."

SUBEDAR ARJAN SINGH
1ST PUNJAB REGIMENT, BURMA

"At Ahkaungbaukywa, Arakan, on the 25TH January 1944, Subedar Arjan Singh personally led an assault of ten men up the western slope of Four Tree Hill, in the face of intense machine-gun and grenade fire, and took an enemy post consisting of a bunker covered by wire and flanked by foxholes. He pushed on to the second post where he was seriously wounded. He was carried down the hill, where he recovered consciousness, and although unable to stand, he directed and organized the evacuation of the wounded. He refused to leave until all the serious cases had been removed. Subedar Arjan Singh showed the highest degree of courage during the assault, and his dash and leadership was inspiration to all."

Subedar, Punjab Regiment

Indian Order of Merit (cont.)

SECOND WORLD WAR (cont.)

JEMADAR AMAR SINGH
2ND PUNJAB REGIMENT, MIDDLE EAST

"On 25TH March 1941, Jemadar Amar Singh led his platoon against an enemy machine gun holding up the attack, and captured the gun and the crew. A few minutes later, his platoon was heavily counter-attacked and had to withdraw. He immediately re-organized his platoon, advanced and re-captured the position. Later he led a party against enemy hiding in some rocks and captured them. Throughout the night, though repeatedly counter-attacked, he maintained his position by personal example and encouragement. The bravery and coolness displayed by him under fire was of a very high order and an inspiration to his men."

HAVILDAR SARDHARA SINGH (POSTHUMOUS)
2ND PUNJAB REGIMENT, SOUTH EAST ASIA

"On 4TH March 1946 two platoons of Havildar Sardhara Singh's company, returning from patrol, were ambushed about 400 yards from the company position by 150 enemy, who had closed on them during the advance. The patrol was quickly surrounded and pinned down by heavy light and medium machine-gun fire at close range. Havildar Sardhara Singh and his platoon had manned the defences and, recognizing the danger, he took his Bren gun and doubled out to a listening post 200 yards outside the position. He knew unless a gap was quickly made the patrol could not reach the perimeter without suffering heavy loss. He therefore rapidly organized his men and opened fire on the enemy's rear, temporarily confusing them and opening the vital gap. The enemy now turned heavy fire on him and began a determined advance on his position. Knowing the patrol was still in danger and that much still depended on him, he decided he must attract the attention to himself. Ordering his men to stay under cover, he seized the Bren gun and, coolly standing up in full view amid a hail of bullets, opened further fire on the enemy, shouting encouragement to the patrol who were now in sight. Amid this heavy fire the end was inevitable, almost at once he was hit in the side, but kept up his fire until he was mortally wounded by a further burst in the chest. This gallant NCO's quick grasp of the situation, prompt action, and outstanding leadership undoubtedly saved the lives of many of his comrades. His magnificent bravery and devotion to highest ideals of a soldier were an example of supreme sacrifice beyond all praise."

Indian Order of Merit (cont.)

SECOND WORLD WAR (cont.)

NAIK JAGAT SINGH
2ND PUNJAB REGIMENT, MIDDLE EAST

"Whilst on patrol on 15TH June 1942, Naik Jagat Singh showed outstanding leadership. As Section Commander, he attacked an enemy armoured tractor mounted with an 88 mm gun, destroying the tractor and the gun with a stick bomb, and captured a prisoner. Later, on the night of 16TH/17TH June, Naik Jagat Singh, together with some of his section, were captured and placed in a truck under guard. Before the enemy had been able to totally disarm the party, this NCO knocked out his guard with a spare light machine-gun barrel, enabling thereby not only himself but also others of his section to escape. During the same incident he also helped to carry a wounded comrade."

JEMADAR GURBAKSH SINGH (POSTHUMOUS)
11TH SIKH REGIMENT, MIDDLE EAST

"During the attack on the 27TH November 1941, Jemadar Gurbaksh Singh displayed outstanding gallantry and leadership. He was in command of 12TH Platoon, and personally led his platoon during the initial advance. Very heavy fire from all weapons caused the attack to waver somewhat. Jemadar Gurbaksh Singh, however, rallied his men and took them forward over open ground in the face of heavy fire to within 150 yards of the enemy position. There the fire was so intense that the platoon had momentarily to go to ground. Gurbaksh Singh was still not content and got up from cover to lead the platoon in the final assault on the enemy position. He had no sooner left cover than he was hit with a burst of machine-gun fire and a mortar bomb and was killed on the spot. The outstanding courage and leadership of Jemadar Gurbaksh Singh are worthy of the highest praise."

HAVILDAR NATHA SINGH (POSTHUMOUS)
13TH FRONTIER FORCE RIFLES, MIDDLE EAST

"During the night of 25TH/26TH March 1941, Havildar Natha Singh was commanding a forward platoon, which twice repulsed determined attacks. After the first attack, the platoon suffered casualties from our own artillery fire. After the second attack had been repulsed, the artillery fire again came down very heavily on the platoon's position. Havildar Natha Singh ordered his platoon back to another position about 100 yards in the rear and he remained in the original position. He was last seen alive throwing grenades at the enemy who were lying up in broken ground some thirty yards away. On the artillery fire ceasing, the platoon occupied its original position and found him dead. His very gallant conduct kept the enemy at bay and undoubtedly saved many lives in his platoon."

Indian Order of Merit (cont.)

SECOND WORLD WAR (cont.)

HAVILDAR SADHU SINGH
16TH PUNJAB REGIMENT, MIDDLE EAST

"Between the 20TH and 22ND April 1943 the battalion had captured its objectives on the Djebel Garci feature. The adjutant had been wounded and relieved by the Signal Officer. The responsibility for all communications thus devolved on to Sadhu Singh as the Signal Havildar. Shelling and mortaring was continuous throughout the day and night, and communications by line were continually being cut. Sadhu Singh, showing the utmost resourcefulness and complete disregard for his personal safety, organized repair parties throughout the day and night. Casualties then became very heavy among the signallers and it became incumbent upon Havildar Sadhu Singh, apart from his other responsibilities, to carry out repairs himself, working over extremely difficult terrain and under enemy machine-gun and shellfire. This work he carried out again and again, showing unequalled example of devotion to duty. It was through his efforts that communications remained of a high standard throughout, resulting in the quick anticipation and neutralization of enemy counter attacks. Havildar Sadhu Singh showed extraordinary fortitude and courage, working unrelieved and unceasingly for 72 hours."

JEMADAR MUNSHA SINGH (POSTHUMOUS)
11TH SIKH REGIMENT, NORTH WEST FRONTIER

"Jemadar Munsha Singh was in command of a platoon posted on the right flank of the position to prevent sniping at the Baggage train as it joined the main road from Anzatalai Camp. Strong parties of the enemy, which had crept up close to them in the thick bushes, which covered the hillside, heavily engaged his platoon and the two platoons on his left. He led an attack on a party of some 15 of the enemy who were occupying a Sangar about 200 yards to his front and which was outflanking the piquet on his left. He displayed the utmost gallantry in the attack. The fighting occurred in the Sangar occupied by the enemy, but they could not stand up to the platoon's bayonet charge and withdrew down the forward slopes of the position. Jemadar Munsha Singh led his platoon after them and inflicted some more casualties and then withdrew to the Sangar. Whilst he was advancing down the forward slopes he saw four enemy rifles, which had been abandoned. He therefore reorganized his platoon in the Sangar and arranged for covering fire under which he attempted to collect these rifles, but was killed in the attempt. His gallantry and leadership were most conspicuous."

Indian Order of Merit (cont.)

SECOND WORLD WAR (cont.)
JEMADAR DIDAR SINGH, (POSTHUMOUS)
11TH SIKH REGIMENT, BURMA

"On the night of 24TH/25TH March 1944, east of the Ngakyedauk Pass in Arakan, a party of the enemy, estimated about one company, infiltrated behind the forward positions and occupied a ridge overlooking the East Gate of the Administrative Base. It was of vital importance that this ridge should be captured without delay, in order that the road to the Administrative Base could be opened. Jemadar Didar Singh was ordered to take his platoon and attack and capture the end of the ridge overlooking the main road. The leading section of the Jemadar's platoon came under heavy enemy fire as it approached the top of the ridge and was held up. He dashed forward and led the section on under heavy fire to capture the forward line of trenches of his objective. The platoon was again held up on this line by heavy fire from the second line of enemy trenches. In spite of this fire at point blank range, Jemadar Didar Singh got up and bombarded the enemy with hand grenades. This forced the enemy to withdraw further along the ridge to their main positions and enabled the Jemadar to capture and secure the whole of his objective. Twelve of the enemy was killed while withdrawing along the ridge. The enemy main position was to be attacked from the other end of the ridge to that which Jemadar Didar Singh had captured. In this attack Didar Singh was instructed to give covering fire to the attacking platoons and to destroy any enemy trying to make their escape. Although these attacks made considerable initial progress, they were held up before reaching their final objective by four light machine-guns located some 100 yards in front of his position. As soon as Jemadar Didar Singh saw that the covering fire had not silenced these machine-guns and the attack could make no further progress, he personally took forward a patrol to try and destroy the machine-guns with grenades. This involved a difficult advance along a knife-edge ridge under considerable fire. Jemadar Didar Singh got his patrol forward with great skill and dash, and succeeded in throwing a number of grenades on the enemy guns. He was, however, hit by enemy grenades in the chest and killed while in the act of throwing a further grenade on the enemy. Jemadar Didar Singh showed outstanding initiative, determination and bravery under heavy enemy fire and his leadership, devotion to duty, and complete disregard of his own safety were an example to all."

Indian Order of Merit (cont.)

SECOND WORLD WAR (cont.)

JEMADAR MEHAR SINGH
11TH SIKH REGIMENT, BURMA

"On the night of 6TH/7TH May 1944 Jemadar Mehar Singh was commanding the leading platoon in an attack on an important hill feature in Kalalpanzin Valley. He led his platoon under the heavy artillery barrage with such dash and determination that the enemy was forced to make a hasty retreat from their covering positions. On the 12TH March 1944, Jemadar Mehar Singh's platoon was ordered to recapture a hill feature overlooking the Maungdaw-Buthidaung road, on to which the enemy had infiltrated during the night. The enemy had constructed deep foxholes and trenches along the top of the knife-edged ridge of the feature. The Jemadar personally led his Platoon on the steep slope of the hill with great determination and dash, under heavy enemy grenade and machine-gun fire. He was wounded early on and his platoon temporarily held up. With complete disregard for his own safety he reorganized his platoon and led them forward to capture the objective and completely annihilate the enemy platoon. Jemadar Mehar Singh's brilliant leadership and great bravery enabled his men to kill thirty-three of the enemy and capture all their arms and equipment. The recapture of this hill feature was of vital importance and was held by a very determined enemy."

SEPOY DARSHAN SINGH
13TH FRONTIER FORCE RIFLES, ITALY

"On the 18TH December 1943 during an attack south of Villa Grande, Sepoy Darshan Singh was commanding a section. He was one of the three volunteers to go forward and silence an enemy machine-gun. Whilst advancing with his objective in view, another enemy machine-gun opened up on his company position. Realizing that it must be dealt with first, Sepoy Darshan Singh immediately advanced on it single-handed across a very difficult ground covered with wire and under heavy enemy fire. In doing so he was wounded in the shoulder but continued on his objective, killing one of the enemy machine-gunners and wounding the other. This Sepoy showed great valour, which, combined with his initiative and perseverance, was largely instrumental in enabling his company to advance and secure their objective."

Indian Order of Merit (cont.)

SECOND WORLD WAR (cont.)

HAVILDAR KULDIP SINGH IDSM
8TH PUNJAB REGIMENT, ITALY

"On the night of 18TH/19TH February 1944 Havildar Kuldip Singh was second-in-command of a fighting patrol of 22 men sent to inflict casualties and to take prisoners from the village of Orsogna. The patrol arrived at the outskirts of the village without incident and attacked the first house found to be occupied by the enemy. Havildar Kuldip Singh dashed into the house with two men and surprised the enemy; they captured one prisoner and injured the remainder as they fled. The rest of the patrol then advanced, but just before reaching the house about six mines exploded, wounding ten of the men, including the officer in command of the patrol who was very seriously wounded. Havildar Kuldip Singh at once took charge and, as the main objective of the patrol had been achieved, decided to withdraw. He organized the evacuation of the casualties to the rear. The route was now under heavy fire but Havildar Kuldip Singh remained behind alone and covered the withdrawal by throwing grenades collected from the wounded. Two more men were wounded and, accompanied by one man; he twice went back over the open snow-covered ground and brought them back. A third man was heard calling for help near to the house, and the gallant Havildar went back again, this time alone. Many of the wounded had to be carried back 1,500 yards. The coolness, initiative and determination shown by this Havildar under most difficult circumstances were outstanding."

SUBEDAR MAJOR SOHAN SINGH OBI
13TH FRONTIER FORCE RIFLES, MIDDLE EAST

"During an action on 28TH June 1942 when the Battalion's position was over-run by enemy tanks, Subadar Major Sohan Singh was instrumental in getting all the Battalion transport away to a place of safety. Later in the afternoon when he heard that his Commanding Officer had been captured, he proceeded alone in a truck to the scene of the capture in order to effect rescue. He was captured in the process. It was only through a ruse arranged by his Commanding Officer that he subsequently escaped, and it had been only with the greatest difficulty that he was persuaded to fall in with the plan, as he demanded to stay prisoner with the rest. His courage and demeanour during this episode was most praiseworthy. On this and many other occasions Subadar Major Sohan Singh, by cheerfulness and courage, set a high example to all ranks in the Battalion."

Indian Order of Merit (cont.)

SECOND WORLD WAR (cont.)
JEMADAR BACHINT SINGH
14TH PUNJAB REGIMENT, BURMA

"On the 5TH February 1944, Jemadar Bachint Singh worked his patrol up to a Japanese bunker to observe and report on the enemy's position. His patrol was detected and fired on from three sides and one man wounded. Jemadar Bachint Singh waited till he had obtained the information which he had been sent to get, and then withdrew his patrol with great skill, bringing away the wounded man. During the withdrawal a Sepoy became missing. Jemadar Bachint Singh went back with one man and recovered the missing man who had got separated and had hidden in a nullah near the enemy position. On 9TH February during the attack on an enemy position, Jemadar Bachint Singh's platoon was the leading platoon of the company. As they approached the Japanese position, heavy and sustained fire broke from a hitherto unlocated bunker. The Jemadar, however, immediately rallied his men and led his platoon through the fire-swept area and reached the foot of the bunker. By that time he had only eight men left unwounded. He remained here organizing the final assault and inspiring the attacking parties. Not until the entire enemy had been silenced, and he had orders to pull out, did he finally withdraw having organized the collection of all wounded and arms of his company."

HAVILDAR ARJAN SINGH (POSTHUMOUS)
14TH PUNJAB REGIMENT, BURMA

"Havildar Arjan Singh was Platoon Havildar of the leading platoon of a Company in its attack on the enemy positions on 15TH January 1944. In the preliminary advance the leading Section Commander was killed and the Company Commander of the flank of the platoon was seriously wounded. Realizing that there was only one feasible quick approach to the enemy's position in the jungle, Arjan Singh, although badly wounded in the arm, led the remainder of the section up a steep track to the final assault. When still short of the enemy position he was killed by a grenade, but by then his leadership had taken the section into the assault and the enemy was routed. He showed complete disregard for his personal safety and by his example the section captured the enemy position without suffering further loss."

Indian Order of Merit (cont.)

SECOND WORLD WAR (cont.)

SUBEDAR SANTA SINGH
13TH FRONTIER FORCE RIFLES, BURMA

"On 14TH February 1944 near Ngangyaung, the company of which Subedar Santa Singh was second-in-command attacked a ridge under cover of artillery fire. Two days previously the company had reconnoitred this position and it was found to be covered by crossfire from concealed medium machine-guns and under close range small-arms fire. Everyone in the Company was aware of the fact that if the artillery failed to neutralize the machine-guns they would have to face heavy fire. Subadar Santa Singh was present when orders were given out and agreed with the Company Commander that whatever happened they would continue to charge over the bodies of their own killed and wounded. This they did, with the greatest dash and gallantry, in the face of heavy fire. When the Company Commander was killed, Subadar Santa Singh took over the command of the survivors and prepared to hold the position gained, under close enemy fire. When ordered to move, he skilfully extricated the survivors and took up a new position, which he held until relieved. The personal bravery, coolness and military skill shown by Subedar Santa Singh were of the highest order."

SEPOY SAUDAGAR SINGH (POSTHUMOUS)
13TH FRONTIER FORCE RIFLES, MIDDLE EAST

"During the attack on 8TH May 1941 on a hill, a high and difficult feature strongly held by the well-entrenched enemy, Sepoy Saudagar Singh was a member of the leading section. On nearing the summit, a heavy shower of hand grenades checked the advance of the section and Sepoy Saudagar Singh was wounded. In spite of his wound and utterly regardless of the very heavy rifle and machine-gun fire encountered, he led his section over most precipitous ground. He reached the enemy's trench, bayoneted two of the defenders and was killed as he bayoneted the third. The remainder of the enemy then fled. His very gallant conduct in the face of heavy odds inspired his section to continue the advance and capture the position."

Indian Order of Merit (cont.)

SECOND WORLD WAR (cont.)

JEMADAR BAHADUR SINGH
13TH FRONTIER FORCE RIFLES, BURMA

"At Nat Taung, Kabaw Valley, on the 11TH March 1944, Jemadar Bahadur Singh was in command of a platoon, which furnished observations and listening posts in the area. Bahadur Singh's orders were to give early information of any enemy move and to delay an advance as much as possible. On the morning of 11TH March, he reported by wireless that there had been considerable vehicle movement northwards up the valley during the night, and that enemy patrols were active some 400 yards from his position. Later that night, two runners reported to the patrol base that they had got separated from the platoon, and that the Platoon had been surrounded by the enemy, and that Jemadar Bahadur Singh was fighting on. These enemy attacks were all broken up with heavy losses, but as mortar fire was becoming increasingly accurate, Jemadar Bahadur Singh decided to move his position to a feature further north. On arrival there, he again found himself under fire from the south and from a spur overlooking his position from the north. One enemy attack was beaten off but again mortar fire became heavy, and Jemadar Bahadur Singh commenced to move to a ridge some 400 yards to the west. About one third of the way to the new position, some 20 to 30 enemy were met in a Chaung, and confused fighting went on for some minutes. The enemy in the Chaung suffered heavy casualties from grenades, but the situation was made serious by the advance of an enemy section from the spur to the north, which got within about 10 yards. Jemadar Bahadur rallied his platoon and led a bayonet charge, which carried his now depleted platoon through the remaining enemy in the Chaung, with 16 men, including two wounded. He continued to repulse every attempt by the enemy to turn him off the hill. These attacks continued until about 1700 hrs. when Jemadar Bahadur Singh again moved, first south then west, in order to cover the Holkhom track. The enemy was severely mauled during these actions on the 11TH March. From the report of one of the missing men who spent two nights hidden in the centre of the Japanese position, the enemy was fully occupied evacuating his casualties. Throughout these engagements Jemadar Bahadur Singh displayed skill, judgment and courage of the highest order, and his personal bravery and determination earned him the respect and admiration of all ranks and classes of the battalion."

Indian Order of Merit (cont.)

SECOND WORLD WAR (cont.)
SUBEDAR BASANT SINGH
SIKH LIGHT INFANTRY, BURMA

"On 21ST March Subedar Basant Singh was commanding his platoon of the Sikh Light Infantry in the area of Okshithon near Meiktila, Central Burma, when enemy were seen in scrubland on their flank. Subadar Basant Singh immediately organized and led an attack against the enemy who were discovered to be in a dug-out position with light machine-guns and grenade dischargers. The enemy strength was 56, which was considerably larger than Subadar Basant Singh's platoon. In a series of sharp encounters and section charges, all led personally by this very gallant officer, forty enemies were killed in hand-to-hand fighting. The Japanese who fled were quickly killed by reinforcements, who had by then arrived. This officer's leadership, bravery and personal example were undoubtedly the cause of such a fine victory. He further distinguished himself in many patrol actions between March 20TH and April 2ND while the battalion was on a detached ambush role. On 6TH April 1945, when the battalion was preparing their night camp under heavy sniping fire after the successful attack on Thabebyn village, Subadar Basant Singh was wounded in the left thigh at the same time as his Company Commander was mortally wounded. Subadar Basant Singh paid no attention to his own wound and at once assumed command of his company and organized them on the perimeter for the night. The next morning this intrepid officer led out a fighting patrol and routed out and killed five Japanese snipers. On 9TH April, in the attack on Hmingladon Monastery, when Subadar Basant Singh's company commander was wounded, this officer again assumed command of the company and led the successful final assault, which resulted in the capture of the Monastery. On 8TH May 1945 Subadar Basant Singh took out a small patrol of two sections to search a village near Penwagon in South Burma where Japanese had been reported. The patrol found approximately 100 Japanese in a nullah near the village. Instead of keeping them under observation and reporting back, this gallant leader at once decided to attack the enemy himself. This he did to such good effect that seven enemy were killed, fifteen wounded, and the remainder fled in confusion. This extremely fine officer acted throughout the South Burma campaign with great distinction, and his personal bravery and coolness under fire was a by-word in the Regiment. His keen desire to engage and kill without the slightest regard for disparity in strength is an inspiring example to all ranks in the finest tradition of the fighting classes of the Indian Army."

Indian Order of Merit (cont.)

SECOND WORLD WAR (cont.)

JEMADAR BHAGAT SINGH (POSTHUMOUS)
1ST PUNJAB REGIMENT, MIDDLE EAST

"Jemadar Bhagat Singh led his platoon during an attack launched by a company on the night of 18TH/19TH June 1941. The company was under heavy machine-gun and rifle fire and casualties were fairly heavy, but he inspired his men to advance, keeping up their spirit and maintaining the momentum of the attack. After about three hours of heavy fighting and rapid advance, the company came up against three strongly held machine-gun pillboxes. The fire was very heavy; the men were tired, and their number considerably depleted; nevertheless this officer led them forward with confidence and determination. His attack caused the enemy to run. In the very final stages, a fourth pillbox opened up rapid fire and Jemadar Bhagat Singh was killed."

HAVILDAR JAGIR SINGH (POSTHUMOUS)
11TH SIKH REGIMENT, WAZIRISTAN

"At Tappi, on the 16TH August 1940, an advance was held up by four hostiles firing from the tower. After first boring a hole in the tower by means of light machine-gun fire, Havildar Jagir Singh rushed forward and dropped a grenade in the hole, killing the hostiles and enabling the advance to continue. Later the same day Havildar Jagir Singh was commanding his platoon when they came under very heavy fire from hostiles in a walled orchard, and were immediately pinned to the ground. Covered by the advance of a platoon on his right, he immediately collected his own platoon and led a bayonet charge on the orchard from a flank. After hand-to-hand fighting he succeeded in clearing the orchard before he himself was killed at the head of his platoon. Throughout the day this Havildar displayed exceptional gallantry and leadership."

CHM SAPURAN SINGH (POSTHUMOUS)
11TH SIKH REGIMENT, BURMA

"15TH May 1944 Burma, CHM Sapuran Singh repeatedly crept forward close to the enemy and engaged them with grenades. He led his men despite enemy fire at point blank range. Later CHM Sapuran Singh, showing great dash and determination, led a counter-attack and succeeded, with a bayonet charge, in throwing the enemy off the position with very heavy casualties. CHM Sapuran Singh was killed whilst charging the retreating enemy. It was due to this NCO's outstanding bravery and leadership that the enemy attack failed and was driven off in disorder. Throughout these two actions, one of which was fiercely fought in close contact with the enemy for over nine hours, CHM Sapuran Singh set a fine example to the whole company and displayed superb leadership."

Indian Order of Merit (cont.)

SECOND WORLD WAR (cont.)

HAVILDAR BABU SINGH (POSTHUMOUS)
INDIAN ENGINEERS, MIDDLE EAST

"Havildar Babu Singh was Section Havildar to a Sikh section that was ordered to build a crossing over the Wadi Zigzao on the night of 22ND/23RD March 1943. The approaches to, and the Wadi itself, were subject to intense enemy shellfire and heavy machine-gun fire. During the night this Havildar supervised the ramps on both sides of the Wadi to the stores area, finally driving down two lorry loads of stores to the site himself. His courage and leadership were beyond all praise and his magnificent example of personal bravery, a source of great inspiration to all his men. Towards the end of the operation, while manoeuvring a lorry-load of stores into position, an anti-tank shell killed him."

LANCE NAIK KERNAIL SINGH (POSTHUMOUS)
11TH SIKH REGIMENT, BURMA

"On the 5TH February 1944 Lance Naik Kernail Singh was a Section Commander in a platoon ordered to attack the enemy in a position in a hill feature near Linbali in the Kalalpanzin Valley. The platoon penetrated into the enemy position and preparatory to making the final assault, had reached a point about 50 yards from the top of the feature, when they came under extremely heavy light machine-gun, grenade and rifle fire. Very soon only nine men were left unwounded. The Company Commander, who was present and wounded, decided that the platoon was insufficiently strong to overcome the enemy's resistance and ordered a withdrawal. The Company Havildar Major, with Lance Naik Kernail Singh and one Sepoy, continued to advance with the intention of covering the withdrawal of the platoon, which was hampered by the presence of many wounded men. The Company Havildar Major was killed almost immediately and the Sepoy wounded, whereupon, Lance Naik Kernail Singh, his Tommy gun out of action, seized an light machine-gun and continued alone. He was last seen advancing on the enemy position firing the machine-gun from the hip. This act of gallantry and self-sacrifice on the part of Lance Naik Kernail Singh caused a diversion sufficient to enable the remainder of the platoon, with its casualties, to withdraw without further loss. His body was found lying across a trench in which there were three dead Japanese, in the heart of the enemy position."

MILITARY CROSS

The Military Cross is awarded to commissioned officers of the substantive rank of Captain or below or Warrant Officers for distinguished and meritorious services in battle. "…gallantry during active operations against the enemy."

FIRST WORLD WAR

SAM BROWN'S CAVALRY

RISALDAR	KISHAN SINGH	1919	EGYPT

RISALDAR MUKAND SINGH
2ND LANCERS GARDNER'S HORSE

During the Second battle of Cambrai in France in 1917: "Risaldar Mukand Singh led his troops at gallop through the damaged wire of the enemy position, and engaged the retreating enemy with the lance, killing several of the enemy himself. Later, he assisted in organizing the defence of the captured position, displaying great skill and energy, and showing a fine example to his men for which he was awarded the Military Cross."

SUBEDAR MALLA SINGH
3RD SAPPERS AND MINERS

"In the attack on Neuve Chapelle, in France, on the 28th October 1914; after all the British Officers of his Company had become casualties, and the Company had suffered very heavy losses Subedar Malla Singh led the Company with distinction under most trying circumstances. He did invaluable work in both re-organizing the Company, and directing its work in the trenches during the winter of 1914. Subedar Malla Singh fought with supreme disregard of danger, and when retreat was inevitable, he conducted his small party with the greatest skill and coolness. For his gallantry and leadership throughout the action he was awarded the Military Cross."

Military Cross (cont.)
FIRST WORLD WAR (cont.)

SUB ASSISTANT SURGEON BHAGWAN SINGH
INDIAN ARMY MEDICAL CORPS

Surgeon Bhagwan Singh was awarded the Military Cross "For conspicuous gallantry and devotion to duty at Sharqat, in Mesopotamia, on 29TH October 1918. When the Regimental Aid Post came under heavy fire, he displayed the utmost coolness in appeasing the wounded and alleviating their sufferings. Throughout this action his conduct was a fine example to his subordinates."

CAPTAIN INDARJIT SINGH
INDIAN ARMY MEDICAL CORPS

The 57TH Rifles and 129TH Baluchis suffered a great loss on the 23RD November by the death of their Medical Officers, Captain Indarjit Singh and Major Atal. The combined dressing stations had been established at about 1500 yards behind the fire trench at Festubert, in France. In the afternoon the enemy put several large shells in the house, which was entirely demolished killing the both medical officers.

"The loss of Captain Indarjit Singh was a severe blow to the regiment, as he had endeared himself to all ranks by his unfailing cheerfulness, wonderful stamina, and complete devotion to the common task. His courage and skill in attending to wounded men were above all praise, and he well deserved the Military Cross, which was bestowed on him for services at Mytschaete. Messines and Levantine, The notification did no arrive until after his death, and he therefore did not know the honour he had gained, although he had full assurance of the regiment's appreciation of the service he had done".

Charging on foot with the lance: Bengal Lancers attack German Trenches.
From the painting by R. Caton Woodville.

Military Cross (cont.)

FIRST WORLD WAR (cont.)

11TH SIKH REGIMENT

| SUBEDAR | BHOG SINGH | 1915 | L/GAZETTE |

14TH FEROZEPORE SIKHS

| SUBEDAR | NARIAN SINGH | 1919 | MESOPOTAMIA |
| SUBEDAR | JAIMAL SINGH | 1919 | MESOPOTAMIA |

15TH LUDHIANA SIKHS

| S. MAJOR | BUDH SINGH | 1924 | L/GAZETTE |

RESSAIDAR BUR SINGH
16TH CAVALRY

Ressaidar Bur Singh was awarded the Military Cross in France in 1918. "On the night of 22ND–23RD May 1918, in a raid on enemy trenches, he led the attack on the right hand post with great dash and resolution. Though only leading a troop, he did not hesitate to attack a post estimated to contain 75 or more of the enemy, under heavy machine-gun and rifle fire at point blank range. His troop killed and wounded a large number of the enemy."

21ST CAVALRY

| RISALDAR MAJ. | SUNDAR SINGH | 1919 | EGYPT |

24TH PUNJABIS

| JEMADAR | SOHAN SINGH | 1918 | MESOPOTAMIA |

27TH PUNJABIS

| SUBEDAR | BHAGAT SINGH | 1919 | EGYPT |

28TH PUNJABIS

| JEMADAR | TARA SINGH | 1916 | MESOPOTAMIA |

29TH PUNJABIS

| HON. CAPTAIN. | MAN SINGH | 1916 | EGYPT |

Military Cross (cont.)

FIRST WORLD WAR (cont.)
SUBEDAR SANT SINGH
34TH SIKH PIONEERS

"At Festubert in France, on 23RD November 1914, severe and desperate fighting occurred when a German attack broke through the trenches of the 34TH Sikh Pioneers. The Sikhs fought valiantly, and the following soldiers were awarded gallantry awards in this action. Sepoys Ishar Singh, Bachittar Singh, Katha Singh, Naik Bir Singh and Havildars Naryan Singh, Harnam Singh and Pala Singh. The 34TH were overpowered by numbers and by bombs. Subedar Sant Singh rallied his half company and held them in position when the enemy broke in. Subedar Sant Singh behaved with great courage in our subsequent counter attack, in which he was wounded. He was awarded an immediate the Military Cross for his gallantry and leadership."

36TH SIKHS

S. MAJOR	THAKUR SINGH	1918	MESOPOTAMIA

45TH SIKHS

SUBEDAR	KEHAR SINGH	1918	MESOPOTAMIA

SUBEDAR MAJOR THAKUR SINGH
36TH SIKHS

Both the 36TH and 45TH Sikhs were in Mesopotamia, and participated in the Battle of Hai River in early 1917. About 1,200 Turks held this position in very well prepared entrenchments. Both Regiments assaulted this position shoulder to shoulder in the face of heavy machine-gun fire. Although the first three lines were captured, casualties were very heavy during the course of the day. At one time, the 45TH was more or less isolated as an enveloping counter attacks were launched by the Turks. These were eventually pushed back. The fierceness of the fighting can be judged by the fact, that at the end of the day, the 45TH was left with just three British and three Indian officers and 200 men. The 36TH Sikhs also suffered heavily. During the period 28TH January 1917 to 1ST February 1917 the Regiment sustained a total of 620 casualties or 83 per cent of the total strength. Subedar Major Thakur Singh led the Regiment out of battle; he alone (of the British and Indian officers who had taken part in the battle) had survived. Subedar Major Thakur Singh was awarded the Military Cross for conspicuous gallantry and leadership. He led the Company with distinction under most trying circumstances.

Military Cross (cont.)

FIRST WORLD WAR (cont.)

SUBEDAR MIT SINGH, MBE, OBI, IDSM and BAR.
47TH SIKHS

"On the 5th November 1917, at Tekrit, Mesopotamia, the British Officer commanding the Company being wounded, Subedar Mit Singh at once took Command, and led the Company throughout the attacks with great skill. By his coolness and fine handling his men and Lewis guns, he was largely instrumental in repelling a counter attack and in maintaining the ground won. His name had previously been brought to notice and he was awarded the Military Cross for gallantry and marked initiative in action."

SUBEDAR THAKUR SINGH, FRANCE 1915
47TH SIKHS

"At Neuve Chapelle, France, on 27TH October 1915, the attack over about 200 yards of open ground, took place under heavy fire from rifles, machine- guns and howitzers, but the advance was carried steadily carried out and the Germans driven back. The British officer was severely wounded directly he came into the open, and Subedar Thakur Singh took command of the Company and led it with skill and gallantry till he was also hit. He subsequently received the Military Cross for his conduct in this action. This was the first Military Cross awarded during the First World War."

54TH SIKHS

JEMADAR	BIKHAM SINGH	1919	EGYPT

HAVILDAR INDAR SINGH
58TH FRONTIER FORCE RIFLES

On November 23RD, 1914, in France and Flanders, the enemy pushed up his sap to within five yards of the Indian Corps line and then commenced a very violent attack, whereby the 9TH Bhopal Infantry and 34TH Pioneers were driven out of their trenches. While early on the morning of the 24TH some of the 58TH Rifles on the left of the right section of the defence were forced out of their trench and affairs began to look critical, all the British officers had been killed. Havildar Indar Singh then took command of the Company and held the position against heavy attacks until relieved next morning for which he was promoted to Jemadar and awarded the Military Cross.

Military Cross (cont.)

FIRST WORLD WAR (cont.)

72ND PUNJABIS

| SUBEDAR | ATMA SINGH | 1918 | EGYPT |

93RD BURMA INFANTRY

| SUBEDAR | HARNAM SINGH | 1918 | EGYPT |

10TH PIONEERS

| SUBEDAR | ALA SINGH | 1919 | EGYPT |

150TH INFANTRY

| SUBEDAR | NARIAN SINGH | 1919 | N. W. FRONTIER |

LIEUTENANT.MOHINDER SINGH
THE SIKH REGIMENT

"At the outbreak of the Second World War, 5TH Battalion, 11TH Sikh Regiment was stationed at Razmak, in Waziristan. The Afghan tribals were asserting their authority in the area, often including sniping at the troops and raiding piquets. With pressure on the Indian Army to send troops for the Allied Forces in Africa, Europe and against aggressive Japan, the British Empire did not want to face another war on the Afghan front. Thus, the battalion was tasked to fight off the raiding Afghans. The battalion distinguished itself on the front, particularly in the Shahwali and Tochi valley columns. On 25TH October 1939 the Razcol (" Razmak Column") moved from Anztalai to Shahwali, through an extremely hostile belt, on a punitive expedition against rebellious tribesmen. The 5TH Battalion platoon commanded by 2ND Lieutenant Mohinder Singh was given the task of capturing and holding the last route picket of the day, before the Brigade camped for the night. However, the tribals who had fought the Razmak Brigade all day now concentrated on this platoon's position and launched a major attack on the picquets. While coming down, Mohinder Singh discovered two badly wounded men had been left behind in the screening piquet. He immediately wheeled right and occupied an alternative position, which could still provide protection to the brigade column. Simultaneously, the platoon fixed bayonets and charged the hostiles, killing ten and wounding forty while incurring no casualties whatsoever. The earlier wounded men were brought back plus the abandoned tribal weapons as well. On joining the rear guard, the platoon got busy constructing Sangar but the brigade commander called the Commanding Officer of the battalion informing him that 2ND Lieutenant Mohinder Singh was recommended for and immediate award of the Military Cross. This was, in fact, the first Military Cross warded to the Indian Army in the 2ND World War. As in First World War, the first Military Cross awarded during the Second World War, was also conferred on and officer of the 5TH Battalion, 11TH Sikh Regiment."

Military Cross (cont.)

SECOND WORLD WAR
MAJOR HARWANT SINGH,
THE SIKH REGIMENT

"The 2nd Battalion, The Sikh Regiment in the van of the 4TH Indian Division, had reached Urbino, 15 miles from the Adriatic coast and due east of Florence. This was on the 30TH August 1944. During the next few days it moved slowly westwards behind the enemy rearguards. On the 4TH September, it watched the 4TH Battalion advancing in great style with the 5TH Indian Infantry Brigade of the 4TH Indian Division to the capture of Tavaletto. A few hours the same day, the 2ND Battalion itself was in action, some 3,000 yards to the West, in an attack on the village of Poggio San Giovanni. For this attack, 'A' and 'D' companies under Major Harwant Singh and Major Anson respectively moved for some distance up the mined bed of the river Foglia, and then swung north into the hills in which Poggio San Giovanni lay. The village was on a commanding position in the enemy defence lines, which lay along a high razor-backed feature above the valley of the Conca, and was strongly held. Late in the evening, concentrations from the Divisional artillery were called for, and were effectively inflicted heavy causalities on the Germans. The village fell at last light, after brisk fighting, and the establishment of the troops there did much to relieve pressure on right flank of the Gurkhas, who were meeting strong resistance in the hills.

Major Harwant Singh. Commanding the 'A', forward company in the attack, accurately set the tone when his Company was held up by three concealed Machine-guns, which were sweeping the ridges and gullies across which his men were attacking. Moving about in the open among his forward troops, encouraging the men, locating the enemy machine–guns, and coolly making his plan to silence them. Major Harwant Singh drew heavy artillery and machine-gun fire, and in one burst of machine-gun fire, he was wounded in the chest, while every other member of his Company Headquarters was either killed or wounded. However, having made his plan and sent vital information back to Battalion Headquarters, Major Harwant Singh advanced with his right leading platoons, as soon as his left forward platoon which had moved higher up the ridge to turn the enemy right flank, had silenced the machine-guns, capturing a Spandau and killing its crew. During this phase of the attack Major Harwant Singh was wounded in the arm by shellfire. Later he was hit again, and wounded in the leg, but continued to command his company with complete disregard for his own personal safety, for a total of 4 and half hours after he was first hit. It was only when the position was firmly established, and direct order had been given by Lieut.Col.Mitheson, commanding the Battalion, to hand over his company and come back for treatment that he consented to be removed to the Regimental Aid Post. For the fine courageous example he set Major Harwant Singh was properly awarded an immediate Military Cross."

Military Cross (cont.)

SECOND WORLD WAR (cont.)

LIEUTENANT AVTAR SINGH
THE SIKH REGEMENT

"On 2nd March 45 in the Field Lieutenant Avtar Singh was detailed as Field Operations Officer with the leading company "A" of the 4TH Battalion, The Sikh Regiment during the operations, which led to the capture of Meiktila in Burma. The enemy had mined the town very thoroughly and numerous snipers were active. An enemy gun opened fire as they neared the railway crossing and knocked out one Sherman tank. Lieutenant Avtar Singh brought down a concentration of fire, which temporarily neutralized the gun. When, later, the gun opened fire again, in spite of the heavy sniping, Light Machine Gun and Maxi Machine Gun fire and bursting mines, Lieutenant Avtar Singh climbed up into an adjoining house and brought down another concentration of fire on the area where the gun flash was seen. This enabled the Tank Squadron Commander who was near him, to move to a position from which the gun could be engaged directly with fire from the Tank's 75mm gun, and the enemy gun was finally silenced. By his initiative, disregard of danger, appreciation of the urgency of the situation and accurate shooting he definitely aided the "Cleaning up" operation and very materially speeded up the conclusion of the battle of Meiktila."

Lieutenant Avtar Singh was recommended for the Military Cross. This was approved and details were published in the London Gazette of 13TH July 1945.

Lieutenant General Rajinder Singh Sujlana, AVSM, VSM
Commandant and Colonel of The Sikh Regiment

Military Cross (cont.)

SECOND WORLD WAR (cont.)

JEMADAR BHAG SINGH
THE SIKH REGIMENT

"On the night of 3/5 July Jemadar Bhag Singh was in command of an isolated platoon in the village of Satthagyen in Burma, some 3 miles away from the Battalions position. The total strength of the platoon numbered 22 men. At about 2100 hours approximately 150 Japanese heavily attacked the platoon. The telephone line was cut and owing to the heavy rain the wireless ceased to function and all the communication with the Battalion was lost, so that no defensive fire could be given from supporting arms. A determined enemy under cover of heavy Mortar, Grenade Discharger and Automatic fire, heavily attacked the platoon throughout the night. Jemadar Bhag Singh moved continuously from trench to trench cheering and encouraging his men and by his inspired leadership the platoon succeeded in beating off all enemy attacks. On the morning of 4TH July an attack was launched to relieve the platoon, but it was not until 1000 hours that the contact was established. When relieved the platoon had less than 5 rounds of ammunition per man and 29 enemy bodies were found on the wire surrounding the position. The inability of the enemy to take the village largely contributed to holding off the offensive by Jemadar Bhag Singh. Again at Abya on the night of 6/7 July Jemadar Bhag Singh was commanding his platoon in an attack on a very strongly fortified Japanese position and was severely wounded in the arm. Despite his wounds he continued to lead his platoon with the greatest gallantry and resolution. After the attack owing to the shortage of Viceroy's commissioned officers, Jemadar Bhag Singh refused to be evacuated. In the five days hard, bitter fighting the conduct of Jemadar Bhag Singh was beyond praise. His gallantry and tenacity were an inspiration to all ranks of the Battalion and he richly deserved the award of the Military Cross."

JEMADAR SARWAN SINGH
BURMA REGIMENT

"On the night 11/12 May 1946, Jemadar Sarwan Singh, The Burma Regiment, was in command of a platoon, which was in action against a desperate gang of dacoits at Butt Erfly Bend, near Ma-Urin, in the Delta. The fire of the Dacoits was very accurate and caused the death of two Sepoys, which in turn caused the troops to hold back. However, Jemadar Sarwan Singh rallied his men and retrieved the situation with a gallant charge, which resulted in the rout of the dacoits of whom a number were killed, wounded and captured." Jemadar Sarwan Singh was awarded the Military Cross on 26TH August 1946.

Military Cross (cont.)

SECOND WORLD WAR (cont.)
SUBEDAR BISHAN SINGH
THE SIKH REGIMENT

"Subedar Bishan Singh has been present with the Battalion throughout the Burma campaign from 1942 to 1945, and he has at all time displayed outstanding leadership and gallantry. He has been in the forefront of some of the fiercest fighting seen by the Battalion and has been wounded no less than four different occasions when leading his men against the Japanese. In June 1944 he displayed exceptional courage and devotion to duty, when operating behind the enemy lines north of Kanglatongbi. On one occasion in these operations over seventy Japanese, launched a fanatical attack against his platoon, and overran his leading section. Subedar Bishan Singh was wounded early in the action, but her refused to be evacuated and remained with his platoon. There is no doubt that his great courage and leadership so inspired his men that they successfully beat off superior Japanese Forces in some fierce close-in fighting. Again at Pagn in February 1945, he displayed outstanding bravery and leadership on two occasions against superior numbers of Japanese. It was due again to his leadership and bravery that considerable losses were inflicted on the enemy. Finally in the closing stages of the war, he displayed courage beyond the call of duty in several attacks in the fighting in the Sittang bend, where he was seriously wounded for the fourth time leading his men against strong Japanese positions to relieve the troops encircled at Naungkashe. It was partly due to this officer's leadership and determination that the operation was successfully accomplished" He was strongly recommended for and awarded the Military Cross on 20TH March 1946.

JEMADAR DIDAR SINGH
BURMA REGIMENT

"In Kohima area in Burma on 28TH May 1944, Jemadar Didar Singh led his platoon in a counter–attack on a position recently captured by the enemy and succeeded in capturing his objective, destroying 2 Light Machine Gun Posts and 2 other Automatic Gun Posts, inflicting several casualties on the enemy. He showed great coolness and clever leadership, being responsible for leading the Company to the objective through thick jungle. On all Operations he has shown courage and initiative, and is very strongly recommended for the Military Cross." Jemadar Didar Singh was awarded the Military Cross on 15TH October 1944.

Military Cross (cont.)

SECOND WORLD WAR (cont.)
SUBEDAR MAJOR BADAN SINGH
THE SIKH REGIMENT

"Subedar Badan Singh was captured at Mersa Matruh in June 1942 and eventually sent to Italy, and was in camp 91 in September 1943. During the proceeding time of his captivity he had made constant efforts to escape, notably two tunnelling schemes, both of which were unfortunately discovered. On 13TH September 1943, Subedar Badan Singh was in charge of a party of VCO'S near the main gate of the camp. They had arranged to break open this gate and someone had to climb the wire and overpower the sentry. Subedar Badan Singh successfully carried out this part of the programme, and he himself made off towards Cassino, hoping to rejoin the British Indian forces. For nine months, with insufficient clothing and very little to eat he evaded recapture, living through the harsh Italian winter in the mountains, and losing no opportunity for sabotage. In this work he induced number of Italian deserters to assist him until June 1944 when he succeeded in rejoining the British forces. Subedar Badan Singh had a fine record while a prisoner of war for cheerfulness and unconquered will to escape. After his own escape he was not content to merely evade recapture but did excellent work cutting enemy communications etc. whenever possible, and this inspite the fact that at that time he was 47 years old and living under conditions that might have daunted a far younger man." Subedar Badan Singh was awarded the Military Cross on 10TH March 1946.

SUBEDAR GURCHARAN SINGH
THE SIKH REGIMENT

"On the 21ST May 1945, Subedar Gurcharan Singh was commanding the right forward Platoon of the Company in Burma. He was ordered to capture the village of Kabaing, which was held by a strong party of the Japanese. The assaulting troops had to cross 500 yards of open country, which included a wide Chaung with precipitous sides and deep running water, and during this phase the Platoon came under very heavy small arms fire. The men were tired after a long gruelling march. Subedar Gurcharan Singh personally led his leading section to the assault; he dashed at the first Light Machine Gun post and bayoneted two of the enemy. With great dash, courage and determination he continued to lead the assault on to each succeeding enemy post. His Platoon killed thirty-nine of the enemy with bayonet and grenade with small loss to themselves. It was largely due to the inspired leadership of Subedar Gurcharan Singh that the Company achieved such overwhelming success; sixty-seven of the enemy was killed and much valuable equipment captured." Subedar Gurcharan Singh was awarded the Military Cross on 20TH June 1945.

Military Cross (cont.)

SECOND WORLD WAR (cont.)
SUBEDAR JOGINDAR SINGH
THE SIKH REGIMENT

"At Pagan, Burma, in 1945, Subedar Jogindar Singh was 2ND I/C of the 'B' company which with tank support was attacking an enemy position. A party of the enemy about 150 strong slipped behind the company cutting them off from their base. The company was pinned down to the ground by very heavy fire in open country and was in a critical position. The Company Commander was seriously wounded. Subedar Jogindar Singh took command of the Company and under heavy machine gun fire, with complete disregard for his own personal safety, rapidly reorganized his company, moving from one Platoon to another encouraging his men. He then moved to the tanks, which had been singled out a special target by the enemy and coolly directed their fire on the enemy concentrations and strong points. Only due to his great gallantry, coolness and initiative a very critical situation was converted to an overwhelming victory. Thereafter having inflicted heavy casualties on the enemy he successfully withdrew his Company together with all the wounded back to the Battalion position. He was slightly wounded during this engagement but refused attention at that time until the time of evacuation. On the night of $18/19^{TH}$ February, his company was heavily attacked. Subedar Jogindar Singh again showed great coolness, initiative and gallantry, moving from position to position under very heavy Grenade Discharger and Medium Machine Gun fire, he located the enemy concentrations and assembly areas, and directed mortar fire onto these concentrations. He was instrumental in beating off this attack with heavy losses to the enemy. He has shown a devotion to duty of a higher order than that normally expected of a VCO". Subedar Jogindar Singh was awarded an immediate Military Cross on 25TH May 1945.

Sikh soldiers in Burma 1943

Military Cross (cont.)

SECOND WORLD WAR (cont.)
JEMADAR MEWA SINGH
THE SIKH REGIMENT

"On the night of 12TH September 1944, Jemadar Mewa Singh's Company was ordered to carry out a night attack on the village of Onverno, Italy. The country was low lying and closely scrub covered and was subsequently found to be firmly held by the enemy. The attack was prematurely discovered and from the outset the Company and especially Jemadar Mewa Singh's Platoon came under very heavy shell, mortar and small arms fire. Jemadar Mewa Singh's Platoon formed the right flank of the Company's advance and was quickly engaged in close fighting, by no less than five enemy posts which were well dug in and concealed in the scrub covered foothills. Further advance being impossible Jemadar Mewa Singh ordered the Platoon to dig in and face the enemy on all fronts. While these positions were being taken up he fearlessly moved from section to section in the face of considerable small arms fire, encouraging all ranks, and creating a feeling of great confidence. When the day broke, the Platoon was heavily mortared, and counter attacked by the enemy. Jemadar Mewa Singh moved to an exposed position from which he could see how each section was progressing, and inspite of heavy mortaring and small arms fire he coolly directed the fire fight. The enemy attack was driven off; seven enemy dead being accounted for, and at least an equal number known to have been evacuated either killed or wounded. Touch with the remainder of the company having been lost during the night Jemadar Mewa Singh then decided to continue alone on to his objective and most skilfully and courageously conducted this advance. Onverno was reached and found to be strongly held by the enemy. Inspite of this Jemadar Mewa Singh launched two attacks on the village and only when these had failed with considerable loss, brought his Platoon with nine casualties safely back through the enemy lines. His courageous leadership throughout the night and day and his resourcefulness and initiative when separated from remainder of his Company, were an inspiration of the highest order to the Platoon he commanded, and a magnificent example of fighting spirit to the regiment as a whole". Jemadar Mewa Singh was awarded an immediate Military Cross.

Sikh soldiers at Cassino, Italy

Military Cross (cont.)

SECOND WORLD WAR
JEMADAR KAKA SINGH (cont.)
THE SIKH REGIMENT

"During the Company attack on the village of Poggio San Giovanni in Italy, on 4TH September 1944. Jemadar Kaka Singh was commanding the left leading Platoon of 'A' Company. The advance was held up by fire from three well-concealed enemy Medium Machine Guns, which were sweeping down the ridges and gullies across which the Company was moving for the attack. Jemadar Kaka Singh leaving one section in position to engage the enemy's attention, and to disguise his own intention, moved round under cover with his remaining two sections, in order to achieve a position further up the ridge from which he could outflank the enemy's right. While doing so, he was suddenly engaged at a range of 50 Yards by a Spandau fire, which had remained silent and unlocated up to this time. Taking immediate action, he turned on this new danger, collected his two sections, and charged up the hill throwing Grenades as he went, killing the German gunners and capturing their Machine Gun. He quickly consolidated his position and brought his Bren Guns into action silencing the three enemy Machine Guns that had been holding up the advance of the remainder of his Company. This inspite of the fact that German Artillery, endeavouring to deal with this new threat to their right flank, had brought fire down on his position, on which he had no time to dig in. Jemadar Kaka Singh showed to the full his qualities of leadership in keeping his guns in action and enabling the advance to go forward, inspite of being exposed in the open and subjected to accurate enemy shellfire. His skill in use of the ground, his presence of mind in charging the enemy position which suddenly opened up on him, and the speed with which he reorganized his sections and silenced the concealed German Machine Guns was an inspiration to all those under his command." Jemadar Kaka Singh was awarded an immediate Military Cross on 4TH September 1944.

Sikh raiders in Italy 1945

Military Cross (cont.)

SECOND WORLD WAR (cont.)
SUBEDAR GULCHARAN SINGH
THE SIKH REGIMENT

"On 20TH February 1944, in Burma, Subedar Gulcharan Singh commanded No 10 Platoon, which had been ordered to carry out an attack on an enemy position. At 1330 hours his platoon had reached their rendezvous in the Nullah. Shortly afterwards two of his men were wounded by enemy Mortar fire (one fatally) and the Platoon came under Light Machine Gun fire from the hill feature. Disregarding these mishaps, Subedar Gulcharan Singh carried on, and led his platoon forward immediately below the feature called Sikh Hill. The success of the attack very largely depended on keeping in close to the tanks, and strictly adhering to the timetable arranged. When the covering fire ceased the attacking Platoon was within 50 yards of the enemy's positions. Shower of Grenades and Light Machine Gun fire some 20 yards from the enemy halted Subedar Gulcharan Singh's forward section, three men having been wounded and one killed. Covered by few Mortar bombs from the rear and Grenades from the leading section, he now attacked from the right. This attack was also checked when three men were wounded. A third attack was then made on the left, again being halted after one man had been killed and one wounded. So far the Platoon had suffered two men killed and seven wounded. Subedar Gulcharan Singh's platoon was now in a semi circle about 15 yards from the enemy, who was in a strong entrenched position. Headquarters had now reinforced the platoon with three sections, two of which were covering the right flank. A general attack was then made, during which some of the enemy left their trenches and ran away. Other Japanese stuck it out; Jemadar Gulcharan Singh personally shot one and bayoneted another. The remainder were bombed out. He now took a patrol forward to search the Southern and Western slopes of Sikh Hill. He moved two parties along two parallel spurs. About 30 yards from the main position he saw a party of 7 Japanese in a Nullah between the two spurs and were immediately attacked. Three were killed from burst by a Light Machine Gun and as the other four were trying to escape, Jemadar Gulcharan Singh ordered the rest of his patrol on the other side to get forward. This they did, sighting the Japs and killing them all with rifle and Light Machine Gun fire. From the moment that the orders for the attack were issued until the last Japanese was killed, Jemadar Gulcharan Singh was an inspiration to his men and to the whole Company. He displayed outstanding tactical ability, remaining cool and level headed throughout the action. He was with his leading men during the whole attack, cheering and leading them on. He proved himself to be a leader in every sense of the word." Jemadar Gulcharan Singh was strongly recommended for and awarded the Military Cross on 22ND February 1944.

Military Cross (cont.)

SECOND WORLD WAR (cont.)
LIEUTENANT PRITAM SINGH
THE SIKH REGIMENT

"Lieutenant Pritam Singh has shown gallantry and leadership of a very high order while in command of the Mortar Platoon during recent operations in Burma. During a prolonged enemy attack throughout the whole of a night in May, his cool courage and example inspired his men to maintain their Mortars in action in spite of Artillery, Mortar, Grenade and Medium Machine Gun fire at very close range both on the Mortar position and Observation Point. Although the enemy was threatening the mortar position on several occasions the mortar Platoon fired continuously throughout the action and assisted in no small way in repulsing the enemy with great loss. Lieutenant Pritam Singh has carried out difficult patrols behind the enemy lines with great courage and determination. He has on several occasions set an example to the men by his complete disregard for his own safety and his determination to support rifle companies under all conditions and at any cost. Lieutenant Pritam Singh gave a fine example of this on 30TH May when the enemy commenced shelling his Observation Post while covering an attack near the village of Modhung. He continued to direct the fire of his Mortars inspite of shells falling all around him. He brought down such accurate and effective concentrations on the enemy that the leading Platoon was able to get on to its first objective with little loss. He stayed at his Observation Post directing fire of his Mortars until he was badly wounded and became too weak to observe fire." He was strongly recommended for and awarded the Military Cross on 6TH October 1944.

Sikh Soldiers in Burma, 1944

Military Cross (cont.)

SECOND WORLD WAR (cont.)
SUBEDAR NARANJAN SINGH
THE SIKH REGIMENT

"Subedar Naranjan Singh has shown himself to be an outstanding Platoon Commander during all the Burma Campaigns from 1942 to 1945, having seen great deal of heavy fighting. In particular on 3RD of May 1945, he was detailed to contact and destroy an enemy party of 40 in the village of Mondaing in Burma. To reach this village entailed a march of four miles over very open country in daylight. With great skill and leadership he led his men to Mondaing where he made contact with the enemy, killing a Japanese officer and three men without loss to his Platoon. In addition he captured and destroyed an enemy truck with much ammunition. On the night of 10TH May Subedar Naranjan Singh was in command of an ambush party, which while returning to the Battalion area came on to the 'B' Echelon transport of a large enemy force attacking the Battalion position. Without hesitation he led his Platoon to attack and inflicted great number of casualties on the enemy and damage to his transport. He continued to harass the enemy from the rear until the Japanese force stopped its attacks and retreated from the front of the Battalion position. He had been slightly wounded during the last two months but on both occasions refused evacuation. The leadership and skill of Subedar Naranjan Singh has throughout been of the highest order and he has in great measure contributed to the successes obtained by his Company." He was strongly recommended for and awarded the Military Cross on 19TH July 1946.

SUBEDAR ISHAR SINGH IDSM
THE SIKH REGIMENT

"Subedar Ishar Singh has shown gallantry and devotion to duty of the highest order. His steadfastness and leadership have maintained the morale, determination and fighting spirit of his men throughout a long and arduous campaign in Burma. On numerous occasions under fire, Subedar Ishar Singh set an example to his company; an example which has always been and inspiration to his men. He has been wounded in four different actions and each time refused to go back to have his wounds dressed until the end of the action; and when all other casualties had been evacuated to safety. On one occasion during a Japanese attack on his Company Subedar Ishar Singh crawled round under heavy fire to each Platoon to give them encouragement. While at another time when his Company was severely shelled and mortared prior to an attack he so encouraged his men that they moved forward and captured the objective according to plan inspite of number of casualties in the forming up area. Subedar Ishar Singh has displayed great courage and shown that he is fearless in action." Subedar Ishar Singh was strongly recommended for and awarded the Military Cross on 5TH April 1945.

Military Cross (cont.)

SECOND WORLD WAR (cont.)
SUBEDAR GURBACHAN SINGH
THE SIKH REGIMENT

"On the 6TH July 1945 at Atya in Burma, Subedar Gurbachan Singh was the senior officer of 'A' Company, which was detailed to attack a strongly fortified Japanese position, situated in a n isolated Pagoda in the centre on flooded paddy fields. The attack was across 300 yards of open flooded paddy fields often waist deep in water and swept by shell and Machine Gun fire. The Company Commander was seriously wounded and the Company Officer Lieut. Jogindar Singh was killed while moving forward to take over command of the Company. Subedar Gurbachan Singh at once took command and endeavoured to lead two Platoons round in a flank attack under the covering fire of the leading Platoon, which was already pinned to the ground by the enemy fire. Heavy casualties were suffered and to save further loss of life the Company was ordered to withdraw. With complete disregard for his own safety Subedar Gurbachan Singh moved from section to section passing orders and cheering and encouraging his men. It took Subedar Gurbachan Singh twenty four hours to extricate his Company together with all their wounded, arms and ammunition and throughout this time he was always to be seen where the fire was hottest and the situation most critical. With gallantry, resolution and complete disregard for his own safety Subedar Gurbachan Singh was an inspiration to all ranks and entirely responsible for the successful extrication of his Company from an untenable position." Subedar Gurbachan Singh was awarded an immediate Military Cross on 6TH July 1945.

LIEUTENANT UJAGAR SINGH
THE SIKH REGIMENT

"At Aronyaung, Mayo Peninsula in Burma on the night of 20TH April, Lieutenant Ujagar Singh was Second–in–Command of the Company holding a high ridge on the right of the Battalion's position. At about 2000 hours Lieutenant Ujagar Singh, who was in a position at the foot of the ridge, received an urgent message from his Company Commander to come to his assistance on the ridge top. By the time Lieutenant Ujagar Singh with his Platoon had reached the top, the Japanese had attacked, the Company Commander and two men were missing, and the rest of the men were out of the trenches and disorganised. Lieutenant Ujagar Singh at once got all his men back in their trenches, and going from position to position encouraged his men to such good effect that they held on to their hill in spite of being attacked twice more in the night, and heavily mortared and grenaded the next morning". For his leadership and stout resistance Lieutenant Ujagar Singh was strongly recommended for and awarded the Military Cross on 16TH December 1943.

Military Cross (cont.)

SECOND WORLD WAR (cont.)
SUBEDAR BACHAN SINGH
THE SIKH REGIMENT

"At Skanemtkyi in Burma on the 6TH May 1945, Subedar Bachan Singh was the senior officer of the advance guard companies, who spotted a party of fifteen Japanese bathing in the Pani Chaung by Kaemgngegy. They were immediately attacked, some were killed and the remainder chased across the nullah into the village. Once reaching the village the Platoon came under very heavy rifle and Medium Machine Gun fire. The Japanese held the village in great strength and the attackers suffered a numbers of casualties. Subedar Bachan Singh realised that, owing to the close proximity of several wounded men to the enemy trenches, any further advance would be impossible until these men had been evacuated. With complete disregard for his own safety he therefore led three men forward in and endeavour to silence the enemy trench, which was preventing the collection of the wounded. Under heavy fire this party crawled forward to within ten yards of the enemy trench where it was stopped by six-foot bamboo fence. They endeavoured to throw grenades over this fence into the enemy trench, they became an easy target for the enemy and the three men were rapidly killed leaving Subedar Bachan Singh as the sole survivor. He crawled back collected another section and again endeavoured to close in with the enemy strong point from another direction, but the party was again stopped from closing in with the enemy by another bamboo fence and further casualties were suffered. Subedar Bachan Singh realizing that further attacks on this strong point would only result in further casualties, ordered two men to give covering fire while he crawled forward and dragged six wounded men back into the cover of nearby trench, then under cover of Mortar fire he led the third and successful attack which succeeded in capturing the village and liquidating the enemy. The gallantry, tenacity and complete disregard for his own safety of Subedar Bachan Singh were an inspiration to the whole Company and resulted in nearly 30 of the enemy killed, and many more wounded and a large amount of equipment being captured and destroyed. The enemy was approximately a 100 strong and after their first surprise fought with dogged courage. The courage, self sacrifice and devotion to duty of Subedar Bachan Singh was of the highest order and far succeeded the call of duty." Subedar Bachan Singh was awarded an immediate Military Cross 6TH May 1945.

Military Cross (cont.)

SECOND WORLD WAR (cont.)
SUBEDAR MOHINDER SINGH
SIKH LIGHT INFANTRY

"On 18TH March 1945, Subedar Mohinder Singh was Second-in-Command of 'B' Company, Sikh Light Infantry. The Company was ordered to capture the village of Kandaingbauk in Meiktila area of Central Burma. Within the first five minutes of the advance, the Company Commander was killed and all the Platoon Commanders wounded. Subedar Mohinder Singh was severely wounded in the leg. Despite his wound he took command of the Company and continued the advancer until the Company was pinned down, by accurate Medium Machine Gun, Light Machine Gun and Mortar fire. Subedar Mohinder Singh re-organised the Company under fire and withdrew them to a more favourable position. He was the last man to withdraw and refused to have his wound dressed until all his men had been treated. The Company had suffered heavy casualties; 25 killed and 53 wounded including all officers and Platoon Havildars, yet this young officer though in considerable pain showed his powers of leadership and command and extricated his Company skilfully. When his wound had been dressed, he asked permission to attack again. Throughout the action Subedar Mohinder Singh displayed outstanding instigative, drive and courage in the best traditions of the Sikhs." Subedar Mohinder Singh was awarded the Military Cross on the 2ND March 1945.

Sikh Light Infantry soldiers advancing using cover at Pyawbwe in Burma, 1945.

Military Cross (cont.)

SECOND WORLD WAR (cont.)
JEMADAR GURDIAL SINGH
NABHA AKAL INFANTRY

"On 5TH October 1944, 'C' Company of the Nabha Akal Infantry was ordered to take the high feature of Finnachio in Italy. Jemadar Gurdial Singh's platoon took part in the first wave of the assault. Jemadar Gurdial Singh led the charge up the steep side of the feature in a magnificent manner taking his place at the head of his assaulting party and shouting encouragement to his men under very heavy Spandau, grenade and mortar fire. On nearing the objective he came upon an enemy trench whose occupants had been giving the advancing troops a great deal of trouble. Seeing that unless this batch of the enemy was quickly neutralized they would cause many more casualties among the assaulting section. Jemadar Gurdial Singh rushed up to them alone and firing his pistol into their midst and showing outstanding courage under heavy fire, succeeded in killing and wounding all the occupants. Inspired by his brilliant leadership, his assaulting sections stormed and took their objective, causing many casualties to the enemy. On the same day his Company was again employed in another attack in which Jemadar Gurdial Singh again led his men into assault with outstanding bravery, which encouraged his men to carry through the attack with success." Jemadar Gurdial Singh was awarded an immediate Military Cross on 5TH October 1944.

MAJOR INDER SINGH
NABHA AKAL INFANTRY

"On 30TH November 1944, Major Inder Singh was in command of 'D' Company of the Nabha Akal Infantry during the attack on Alberto in Italy. Ten minutes before the starting time fresh information compelled him to make urgent alterations to his plan. At the outset of the advance the Company came under heavy enemy Artillery and small arms fire halting the Company. Casualties were heavy including all three Platoon Commanders. Without the slightest hesitation and with complete disregard for his own safety Major Inder Singh immediately ran forward to carry out a recce. He then moved form Platoon to Platoon still under very heavy fire encouraging his men and giving orders to continue the advance. The coolness, courage and leadership displayed by Major Inder Singh were outstanding and undoubtedly ensured the capture of his objective. He displayed a devotion to duty of a very high order and his personal example was an inspiration to the rest of his Company." Major Inder Singh was awarded an immediate Military Cross on 30TH November 1944.

Military Cross (cont.)

SECOND WORLD WAR (cont.)

JEMADAR SHAM SINGH
NABHA AKAL INFANTRY

"On 13TH October 1944, 'A' Company of the Nabha Akal Infantry was ordered to attack Pt. 598 during the 8TH Army's advance through Italy. They reached this point but were severely shelled and mortared by the enemy that the Company was given the order to withdraw after the Company Commander and two Platoon Commanders had been seriously wounded. Then the Commanding Officer ordered the 'B' Company to reoccupy the feature and Jemadar Sham Singh's Platoon was dispatched to do so whilst the remaining two Platoons of 'B' Company stayed in reserve. During the assault Jemadar Sham Singh placed himself at the head of the assaulting troops. The whole Platoon came under heavy small arms fire coupled with Artillery and Mortar fire, but Jemadar Sham Singh undaunted by this terrific fire led his men in a magnificent charge onto the objective, shouting encouragement to them and having not the slightest regard for his personal safety. It was entirely due to the effort of Jemadar Sham Singh that the assault, which was directed at an extremely strong enemy position, was a success. Again on the same day the enemy put in a very heavy counter attack, which was strongly supported by Artillery, Mortar and Spandau fire. Jemadar Sham Singh conducted himself magnificent manner during the whole of the enemy attack, exposing himself to the enemy fire many times in his efforts to encourage his Platoon. Owing to Jemadar Sham Singh's gallantry under very heavy fire, his Platoon was able to beat off the enemy counter attack and inflict heavy casualties on him. His courageous behaviour has been an example to the entire Company." Jemadar Sham Singh was awarded an immediate Military Cross on 13TH October 1944.

CAPTAIN PRITAM SINGH
16TH PUNJAB REGIMENT

Captain Pritam Singh was a Prisoner of War in Japanese hands in Singapore, and escaped from captivity to India. He was awarded the Military Cross on 26TH March 1943. The submission for the Military Cross included the following passage: "For security reasons, the accompanying submission which contains the names of five officers who escaped from enemy captivity in Singapore, gives no details of the actions for which the awards are recommended." So the citation for the awards read: "The King has been graciously pleased to approve the following awards in recognition for the distinguished service in the field."

Military Cross (cont.)

SECOND WORLD WAR (cont.)
LIEUTENANT BALDEV SINGH
1ST PATIALA INFANTRY

"On the night of 18TH April 1944, when the Company under the command of Lieutenant Baldev Singh was occupying an isolated position in Burma; a superior enemy force took up a position close to the Company. On the morning of the 19TH April, Lieutenant Baldev Singh was ordered to keep this enemy force occupied in order to prevent it digging in before the main force arrived to attack the position in the afternoon. Lieutenant Baldev Singh therefore organised constant "Jitter" parties around the enemy position, he himself leading one of these parties in order to raise the moral and self-confidence of his Company. By his bold action and personal example he successfully prevented the enemy digging more than one foot in ten hours. This greatly assisted the main force in capturing the position and saved many casualties. Subsequently on the 28TH April he led a party of twenty strong on a special mission lasting four days. This party operated at a radius of ten miles from the main base, behind the strong enemy position at Sanjing. In carrying out this mission Lieutenant Baldev Singh's party was for seventy-two hours on the main Japanese line of control, during which time he laid three successful ambushes against superior enemy forces. As a result of these ambushes, 29 of the enemy were killed; three of them by Lieutenant Baldev Singh, and in addition much valuable information were obtained. His casualties were one man wounded. The success of this mission was due to the personal gallantry and leadership of Lieutenant Baldev Singh. Lieutenant Baldev Singh's determination, devotion to duty and disregard of personal safety has been noticeable in previous operations to which he had taken part." Lieutenant Baldev Singh was strongly recommended for and awarded the Military Cross on 15TH August 1944.

1ST Patiala Infantry parading captured Japanese flags at Patiala, 1946.

Military Cross (cont.)

SECOND WORLD WAR (cont.)

JEMADAR AMIR SINGH
1ST PATIALA INFANTRY

"On the 19TH April 1944, a strong enemy force occupied a position between Jemadar Amir Singh's Company and the Imphal-Ukhrul road in Burma. Jemadar Amir Singh was therefore given the task of harassing this enemy force in order to prevent him from digging in before the arrival of the rest of the Battalion. Jemadar Amir Singh led a section, which operated on the enemy's flank and continuously harassed the enemy to great effect. When he was due to be relieved he again volunteered to lead another section as he considered that his knowledge of the area would be of great assistance. He was eventually recalled for further operations. During the whole of the period he successfully kept the enemy occupied and inflicted a number of casualties on them. Later in the same day Jemadar Amir Singh was commanding a leading Platoon in and attack on a hill feature covering the main enemy position. Under heavy enemy fire, he led his Platoon with such dash and determination that the enemy was forced to beat a hasty retreat. Subsequently another Platoon passed through his position, he then repulsed the enemy counter attack on the flank of the other Platoon, inflicting heavy casualties. Again on the 29TH April he commanded a party of 20, which was sent out, with the task of conducting Guerrilla operations on the enemy in the Samshak area. His party operated continuously for 18 hours on the Japanese line of control, and laid several successful ambushes, with the result that at least 12 Japanese were killed, and valuable identifications obtained, without any loss to his party. Throughout these operations Jemadar Amir Singh led his Platoon with skill and determination". Jemadar Amir Singh was strongly recommended for and awarded the Military Cross on 16TH August 1944.

JEMADAR RAKHA SINGH
1ST PATIALA INFANTRY

"On 19TH April 1944, during attack on Sakpao in Burma, Jemadar Rakha Singh's Platoon was ordered to capture a steep hill overlooking Sakpao. Enemy had established himself o this hill, but Jemadar Rakha Singh by skilful use of the ground completely surprised the enemy and carried the position at the point of the bayonet making the enemy withdraw hurriedly and in disorder. Later, when his Company Commander was killed and he was severely wounded, he with great determination and disregard of his own safety took over the command of the company and reorganized his defences and met a second counter attack successfully. He refused to be evacuated and remained in command till the arrival of the Company Commander. He showed leadership, determination and gallantry under fire of the highest order". Jemadar Rakha Singh was awarded the Military Cross on 21ST May 1944.

Military Cross (cont.)

SECOND WORLD WAR (cont.)

SUBEDAR AJMER SINGH
1ST PATIALA INFANTRY

"On 24TH July 1944, Subedar Ajmer Singh was commanding the forward platoon, when his Company was ordered to capture Ralph Hill, a prominent feature covering enemy line of control on Tamu road in Burma. His forward Sections were held up by heavy enemy fire. His Platoon was now in a position overlooked by the enemy. There was no other approach to the enemy's position. Subedar Ajmer Singh at once went forward encouraging his men and with complete disregard for his own safety, he personally led his Platoon up the steep slopes of the hill with great determination and dash completely annihilating the enemy platoon. Subedar Ajmer Singh's brilliant leadership and bravery enabled his men to kill 17 of the enemy and capture all their arms and equipment. On 27TH July 1944, he led a very successful fighting patrol at Lockhao River, killing many Japanese who wanted to escape that way. And from 27TH July to 31ST July, when the Company had succeeded in establishing himself in the rear of the enemy's position, he successfully led many small Jittering parties the whole day, to stop the enemy form strengthening their positions before the final attack. Throughout the bitter fighting at Sakpao, and subsequent operations Subedar Ajmer Singh set a magnificent example and was inspiration to all ranks of the Battalion." Subedar Ajmer Singh was strongly recommended for and awarded the Military Cross on 12TH October 1944."

SUBEDAR DARBARA SINGH
1ST PATIALA INFANTRY

"On 25TH July 1944, at Ralph Hill, after capture of enemy position, a platoon under the command of Subedar Darbara Singh was sent to clear a road to the 1ST Seaforths Highlander's position about two miles away. His scouts saw an enemy party in position in their front, covering a gun withdrawal, which was escorted by one company. Subedar Darbara Singh, who was moving with the leading section, at once led the charge, without waiting for the rest of the platoon to come up. He succeeded in capturing the position after killing all seven Japanese occupants. He then advanced further and with his whole platoon captured a feature overlooking the road. He again inflicted heavy casualties on the enemy's main party including two gun mules. Later, when the enemy counter attacked in superior force to regain the feature, he repulsed the attack with heavy losses to the enemy, with the result that the enemy had to leave all gun ammunition and vital parts of the gun on the spot. Subedar Darbara Singh's dauntless courage, self sacrifice and bold leadership was of a very high order, which was responsible for loss of a gun and heavy casualties to the enemy." Subedar Darbara Singh was strongly recommended for and awarded the Military Cross on 16TH November 1944.

Military Cross (cont.)

SECOND WORLD WAR (cont.)
JEMADAR SARWAN SINGH
1ST PATIALA INFANTRY

"During an advance o enemy positions in Chamol area in Burma, on 34TH July 1944, Jemadar Sarwan Singh was commander of forward Platoon and established himself on the bound after pushing back small enemy party to a hill beyond. Another Platoon ordered to leapfrog through, had not yet arrived, when Jemadar Sarwan Singh saw two enemy platoons advancing towards the targeted position. Realizing that the enemy position would become very strong on arrival of the reinforcements, Jemadar Sarwan Singh, at once without waiting for orders, led a charge on the advancing enemy. When his forward section was held up by heavy Light Machine Gun fire from front and bunker position on his right, he put his 2 inch Mortar and reserve section to neutralize the right position and without hesitation, and shouting at the top of his voice" Patiala Will Not Be Held Up By The Japanese" and with complete disregard for his safety personally led the forward sections into uphill charges. After a stiff fight in which many enemy soldiers were killed, he succeeded in capturing both enemy positions before the arrival of his reinforcements. Enemy soon put up a counter attack on their lost positions. Again quite regardless of his own safety, he moved between his three sections, first to ensure that fire was held until enemy were within forty yards and later to exhort the men under his command during the actual attack. The enemy was forced to retreat in disorder abandoning four of their dead comrades on the field. From the noise in the Nullah nearby it appeared that considerable damage was done to the enemy. By his very fine personal example, and leadership, under almost intolerable weather conditions he captured, the position, which if allowed to be reinforced would have resulted in a major operation and many casualties. Earlier when in occupation of defensive position near Chamsol, he exhibited remarkable qualities of leadership and personal gallantry in beating off all enemy attacks. Although wounded during the four attacks, he refused to be evacuated until ordered by his Company Commander next morning. On 25TH July 1944, when his Company was boxing-in the enemy position in Chamsol area, he again proved himself most resourceful in preventing all his efforts to escape. Jemadar Sarwan Singh's dash throughout these operations has been of a very high order, he showed most outstanding power of leadership under most difficult conditions, while his personal bravery and relentless determination to close with the enemy can seldom have been surpassed." Jemadar Sarwan Singh was strongly recommended for and awarded the Military Cross on 12TH October 1944.

Military Cross (cont.)

SECOND WORLD WAR (cont.)

SUBEDAR CHAIJU SINGH
1ST PUNJAB REGIMENT

Officers and men of the 1ST Punjab Regiment in Burma on their race for Rangoon performed many daring and gallant deeds. On May 16TH, Subedar Chaiju Singh's fighting patrol contacted a party of thirty Japanese dug in on a small feature. Despite his numerical inferiority, the Subedar led a direct attack against the Japanese machine-gun post and personally killed a Japanese officer in close combat, while his patrol accounted for ten others; the remaining Japanese took to their heels. Subedar Chaiju Singh was awarded the Military Cross for his conspicuous gallantry and leadership.

SEPOY SEWA SINGH
1ST PUNJAB REGIMENT

"On May 16TH 1945, 'A' company on its dash for Rangoon had to mop up many Japanese companies on the way and their advance was held up by heavy automatic fire from concealed positions. Subadar Sewa Singh took a reconnaissance patrol forward through dense jungle, directed artillery fire on the Japanese bunker holding up the advance and personally led a small party, drove the Japanese from their positions, killing three of them". For his gallantry and leadership Subedar Sewa Singh was awarded the Military Cross on 17TH August 1945.

SUBEDAR GURBACHAN SINGH
1ST PUNJAB REGIMENT

"During the Second Arakan Campaign in Burma, 1ST Punjab Regiment had commenced its epic struggle to clear the Ngakyedauk Pass of the enemy. Various tactical positions were occupied on the western slopes of the Mayu Range. On February 10TH while advancing to its objective, which was held up by the Japanese in a strongly entrenched position, the Commanding Officer was killed almost immediately. Subedar Gurbachan Singh carried on and silenced the post by courageously crawling forward and throwing grenades at the post. As no further progress could be made, the company with its dead and wounded withdrew on the following morning. The commanding officer and five other ranks were killed and Jemadar Lall Singh and seven other ranks wounded." For his gallant conduct and leadership Subedar Gurbachan Singh was awarded the Military Cross.

Military Cross (cont.)

SECOND WORLD WAR (cont.)
CAPTAIN BUDH SINGH
1ST PUNJAB REGIMENT

"On the Donbaik front in Burma, the 'D' company, 1ST Punjab Regiment had advanced with great gallantry on the right. As it reached the start-line it found the two companies of the Inniskilling Fusiliers were not quite up on the start-line. Not wishing to lose the effect of the artillery barrage, the company, under the command of Captain Budh Singh, advanced over the open and bullet-swept country and captured its objective. At that moment both its flanks lay open owing to the Japanese–occupied position on its left and the momentarily absence of the Inniskilling Fusiliers on the right. Terrific fire on the front and flanks took a heavy toll on the attackers. Captain Budh Singh realized that all that he could do now was to withdraw across the open to his original position. This he did with cool courage, collecting as many of the wounded men as he could on his way back. The company strength was reduced to forty-four through casualties including Jemadar Surjan Singh and Havildar Major Indar Singh." For his gallantry during this engagement Captain Budh Singh was awarded the Military Cross on 4TH March 1943.

CAPTAIN BUDH SINGH, MC and BAR
1ST PUNJAB REGIMENT

"During the night of 12TH / 15TH March 1943, at Hitzwe in Burma, Captain Budh Singh's Company was attacked six times by strong determined Japanese forces. All the attacks were driven off with heavy losses to the enemy. Captain Budh Singh throughout the night was an inspiration to his men and it was largely due to his magnificent example that the attacks were so successfully defeated. At the dawn on The 14TH March, a force of approx. 300 Japanese attacked a platoon of Captain Budh Singh's Company holding a hill guarding Battalion Headquarters. Captain Budh Singh went with reinforcements to his platoon and took charge of the situation. The attack was driven off leaving 73 dead Japanese around the position. Captain Budh Singh on both these occasion displayed courage and leader ship of a very high order." For his valiant leadership, Captain Budh Singh was awarded a bar to his Military Cross on 4TH March 1943.

Military Cross (cont.)

SECOND WORLD WAR (cont.)

SUBEDAR JASWANT SINGH
1ST PUNJAB REGIMENT

"On the morning of 11TH February 1942 in the action on Reformatory Road on Singapore Island where the Battalion held the forward position of the Brigade, Subedar Jaswant Singh took over command of the Company after the Company Commander was severely wounded. The company was being subjected to heavy shelling; continuous mortar and Light Machine Gun fire, sustaining heavy casualties to its forward platoons. Subedar Jaswant Singh immediately commenced to rally the Company, got up reinforcements, reorganized the position, and had casualties removed. His gallant action in face of the enemy re-established confidence and enabled the Company to hold on to the Right Forward position of the Battalion until later in the afternoon, when other plans were evolved. Again in the operations, which succeeded this action, as second - in - Command of the Company, Subedar Jaswant Singh continually encouraged and heightened the morale of his Company by his gallant behaviour and disregard of personal danger." Subedar Jaswant Singh was strongly recommended for and awarded the Military Cross on 19TH December 1942.

SUBEDAR MANGAL SINGH
1ST PUNJAB REGIMENT

"Subedar Mangal Singh commanded No. 6 Platoon of 'D' Company, 1ST Punjab Regiment on the Mayu Rane front in Burma. On 19TH February 1944, this company was ordered to attack and capture the feature 391523, the only approach to which was over very narrow knife-edge, covered the whole way by enemy Medium Machine Guns. Subedar Mangal Singh successfully captured the enemy's forward post, destroyed a Medium Machine Gun, and section of seven enemies at very small loss to himself. Soon afterwards another pocket of enemy was spotted about 30 yards away, and Subedar Mangal Singh charged at them with his two sections, but unfortunately came under a shower of grenades from two previously undiscovered enemy positions, and half the force became casualties, he himself being wounded in the left arm. He successfully brought all his casualties back and to reach the seriously wounded, he had to creep right forward, while doing so another grenade blew most of his right toe off but this did not deter this daring and fearless leader, who really loved his men, carried the wounded man back to his trenches and continued to command his platoon until relieved later. Subedar Mangal Singh, during this action and throughout the previous and present campaign has shown the finest example of gallantry, daring and leadership and has earned the praise of all ranks." Subedar Jaswant Singh was strongly recommended for and awarded the Military Cross on 25TH February 1944.

Military Cross (cont.)

SECOND WORLD WAR (cont.)
SUBEDAR SUKHMANDAR SINGH
1ST PUNJAB REGIMENT

"On the 12TH February 1944, Subedar Sukhmandar Singh was commanding No.8 Platoon of 'A' Company on Cresta Run in the Naguebaik Pass in Burma. He was ordered by his Company Commander to take point 1070 with his platoon. After stiff climb the platoon reached its objective and started to dig in, but before much progress had been made it was attacked from the North end of the feature. This was beaten off successfully and the Japanese party driven off the feature with the loss of four, apparently wounded men. Twice parties of about 15 to 20 Japanese again attacked the platoon both of which were successfully driven off. In the second attack a Bren gun jammed at a critical moment and Subedar Sukhmandar Singh personally held the enemy off with a Tommy gun until the stoppage was rectified. The platoon held the feature for another 24 hours when a Company of another regiment relieved it. Subedar Sukhmandar Singh, a Sikh, was commanding a platoon of young Jat Sepoys inexperienced in war, and the fact that his platoon put up such a stout hearted defence reflects the greatest credit on this officer. In addition he displayed personal courage, determination and leadership of a very high order" Subedar Sukhmandar Singh was awarded the Military Cross 22ND June 1944.

SUBEDAR SARJIT SINGH
1ST PUNJAB REGIMENT

"Subedar Sarjit Singh came up with the Battalion to the Burma front in 1942 and had fought with it throughout. He was second in command of the Mortar Section. Early in March 1943, when the Battalion Headquarters position was attacked most violently by enemy at Hitzwe, most of his men were casualties, but with only two other men he manned both the three inch mortars and kept on engaging enemy Medium Machine Gun for about one hour until enough men were raised to attack and drive the enemy away. He proved himself to be a perfect example of a gallant leader of men. Owing to Subedar Sarjit Singh's steadiness, courage and power of leadership, he was given accelerated promotion and given command of the only Sikh Company of the Battalion, soon to be followed by the position of senior V.C.O. in the Company. As the other two platoons of the Company were composed of very young and raw men, all the difficult tasks in the Company's role were invariably given to Subedar Sarjit Singh. His patrol actions during the Ngakyedauk and Sialamum operations contributed largely to the success of the forthcoming Battalion Operations. The constant outstanding work done by Subedar Sarjit Singh throughout the war and cool headedness and gallantry that he has shown on all occasions has earned him the respect from all ranks of the Battalion." Subedar Sarjit Singh was strongly recommended for and awarded the Military Cross on 19TH March 1945.

Military Cross (cont.)

SECOND WORLD WAR (cont.)
SUBEDAR MUNSHA SINGH
1ST PUNJAB REGIMENT

"Subedar Munsha Singh, has been commanding the Sikh platoon in 'A' Company throughout the Burma campaign. He was wounded during the fighting in the Litan area of Arakan and Imphal front. He first distinguished himself in the operations in the Ngakyedauk pass when his platoon led the successful attack on Pt.1070. Next day in the attack on Sugar Loaf; he led the final assault, which cleared the feature of Japanese soldiers. In this attack he displayed great qualities of determination and leadership, and personally led the bayonet charge, which drove the enemy from his positions. Again fighting in the Litan area he and his platoon were conspicuous for their excellent work. He was severely wounded leading a counter attack on a strongly held Japanese position. Subedar Munsha Singh has always displayed military qualities of a very high order. A natural leader, his courage and determination are outstanding and an example to all ranks of his Company." Subedar Munsha Singh was strongly recommended for and awarded the Military Cross on 12TH March 1944.

SUBEDAR KARTAR SINGH
2ND PUNJAB REGIMENT

"On 23RD November 1945, during and attack in Ngemplak area of Sourabaya in Burma, two sections of the leading platoon of Subedar Kartar Singh's company, of which he was second in command, were pinned down to the ground by enemy automatic fire from two strong concrete bunkers. Subedar Kartar Singh dashed forward from Company Headquarters under very heavy fire to take charge of he situation. He then at very great risk to himself, carried out a personal reconnaissance before leading the third section of the platoon in an outflanking movement, which culminated in a magnificent charge onto enemy position. While leading this extremely gallant charge Subedar Kartar Singh fell severely wounded in the stomach. From where he lay, he continued to shout words of encouragement to his men until they had over-run the position. He refused to be evacuated until he was certain the platoon could continue its advance without him. Subedar Kartar Singh's outstanding leadership and utter disregard for his own safety were superb examples of courage and devotion to duty and inspiration to all." Subedar Kartar Singh was awarded an immediate Military Cross on 23RD November 1945.

Military Cross (cont.)

SECOND WORLD WAR (cont)
MAJOR BHAG SINGH
2ND PUNJAB REGIMENT

"On 16TH September 1944, at the commencement of the operation against Japanese rear guard at Tongzang in Burma, Major Bhag Singh was sent with his Company to cut the Imphal-Tiddim road in the area of Tutee. Owing to the necessity for speed he had no opportunity to recce the route nor was information available as to enemy dispositions in that area. By skilful navigation mostly at night over 3 miles and a 4,000 feet descent and climb, Major Bhag Singh led his Company through thick jungle over and unrecced Nullah crossing to the appointed position. There he positioned his men on the escape route of approximately 100 enemies, whom he had located on the heights dominating the crossing of the Manipur River. The following night the enemy forced to withdraw ran into the Company position and finding their way blocked prepared to attack it. Their determined attack was repulsed, and the enemy left behind twelve dead including two officers and much material. A Japanese Sergeant Major was captured who gave information of vital importance about their future operations. Throughout this and the following night Major Bhag Singh and his men held on to their position and carried out aggressive patrolling often under considerable fire and heavy sniping from numerous enemy in the vicinity. The aim of this skilful and difficult operation was to separate two portions of the enemy rear guard, and finally to force the withdrawal of some 200 disorganised Japanese soldiers, which was successfully carried out." Major Bhag Singh was strongly recommended for and awarded the Military Cross on 16TH December 1944.

SUBEDAR SUDHA SINGH
2ND PUNJAB REGIMENT

"On 30TH November 1944 in La Podesta area in Italy, Subedar Sudha Singh was in command of a rifle Company that was ordered to capture Caterina. Subedar Sudha Singh formed up his Company and personally led them in an extremely difficult advance to the assault over mine-strewn and shell swept country in pitch darkness. After contact, Subedar Sudha Singh so directed his platoons that the enemy was taken by surprise and a large number of prisoners and booty was captured. Not content with this, Subedar Sudha Singh after contacting all his platoons, ordered a platoon to the right, by which tactics he succeeding in trapping another few Germans who were running away. Despite intense shelling, Subedar Sudha Singh never ceased to visit his platoon including the forward sections, and personally organised the consolidating of the positions. It was largely through the gallantry and skill of Subedar Sudha Singh that this Company's attacks were so completely successful." Subedar Sudha Singh was awarded an immediate Military Cross on 30TH November 1944.

Military Cross (cont.)

SECOND WORLD WAR (cont.)
JEMADAR PRITAM SINGH
2ND PUNJAB REGIMENT

"On the night of 19/20 May 1944, on the Ortgna front in Italy, Jemadar Pritam Singh displayed personal courage of a high order and showed a capacity for determined leadership of and exceptional standard. When leading his platoon on a night raid he found the initial objectives empty. Without hesitation he chose new objectives and attacked, although he knew that there was a possibility that the supporting fire might not conform. As a result of his initiative 12 Germans were killed, many others severely handled, and a very valuable prisoner of war taken. He is acknowledged to have killed three Germans in the course of a savage close quarter fighting. He engaged the enemy until the wounded got clear and then withdrew his force in full control. Jemadar Pritam Singh's leadership and personal gallantry was an inspiration to his men and a source of strength to all ranks of the unit." Jemadar Pritam Singh was awarded an immediate Military Cross.

SUBEDAR MAJOR DAULAT SINGH
2ND PUNJAB REGIMENT

"On the 20TH April 1945, the Battalion attacked a strong enemy position on the R. Idice south of Mezzo Lara in Italy, and suffered very heavy casualties. Subedar Major Daulat Singh after replenishing ammunition visited Regimental Aid Post and reassured the wounded. He then went forward and visited the leading companies, which by then were established on the near bank, but still under heavy Artillery and small arms fire. Subedar Daulat Singh visited each Company, encouraging and inspiring all ranks. The sight of this fine officer moving through heavy fire with coolness and confidence, regardless of danger had great effect on the morale of the men who had undergone very trying conditions and were still under fire. Subedar Major Daulat Singh's courage, devotion to duty, and cheerfulness were of the highest order. His presence in the forward area at critical period had a marked effect on the course of battle." Subedar Major Daulat Singh was awarded an immediate Military Cross on 12TH July 1945.

Military Cross (cont.)

SECOND WORLD WAR (cont.)
CAPTAIN NARANJAN SINGH
2ND PUNJAB REGIMENT

"Captain Naranjan Singh has carried out the duties of the battle adjutant in Tactical Headquarters, throughout the period from September 1943 to May 1945. During these operations the personal gallantry, initiative and unswerving devotion to duty of Captain Naranjan Singh have been outstanding, particularly during the operations in Po Valley at the Quaderna and Idice rivers in Italy during April 1945. During these operations Tactical Headquarters frequently came under severe and accurate enemy shelling. Despite this, Captain Naranjan Singh, with complete disregard for his own safety, organised and kept in operation the Tactical Headquarters. Without Captain Naranjan Singh's devotion to duty and personal courage during these periods of strain, the smoothness and efficiency with which Tactical Headquarters operated would have been absent. He was frequently called upon to make decisions of a grave tactical nature, in the absence of his Commanding Officer, and not content in merely giving his decision he went forward to the companies under fire to see the situation for himself and ensure that the decision was carried out. At Modina, Captain Naranjan Singh went forward on his own initiative, through intense enemy shelling and personally took command of a rifle company whose commander had been killed. He remained with the Company throughout the grave period, and only returned to Tactical Headquarters after three days when the situation had become easier. The personal courage and gallantry of Captain Naranjan Singh throughout the operations has always been of the highest order and beyond the normal call of duty. His initiative in making decisions in the absence of the Commanding Officer and his total disregard for his own safety in organising the Tactical Headquarters under heavy shellfire had far-reaching effects upon the course of the battle". Captain Naranjan Singh was awarded an immediate Military Cross.

SUBEDAR RAM SINGH
2ND PUNJAB REGIMENT

On 16TH May 1944, at Kangla Tonbi in Burma, the Punjabis clashed with the Japanese. Both Companies engaged suffered considerable losses. Among the killed was Subedar Dhera Singh, having twice been awarded the I.O.M. in the Western Desert. In another contact with the Japanese on 14TH September, resulted in a short but fierce action, cost the Punjabis six killed and six wounded. The killed included then the Company Commander, Ram Singh. Also Subedar Pritam Singh, whose gallant conduct on that day was followed by a posthumous award of Indian Order of Merit, for his gallantry in these actions Subedar Ram Singh, was awarded the Military Cross.

Military Cross (cont.)

SECOND WORLD WAR (cont.)

MAJOR RAWIND SINGH GREWAL
8TH PUNJAB REGIMENT

"At Sindangrapong in Java on 17TH December 1945, Major Rawind Singh Grewal's company was carrying out a reconnaissance with a troop of tanks in support. He was suddenly confronted with a roadblock manned by 400 enemies whom he immediately attacked killing 80, for the loss of one killed and three wounded. When he came to withdraw, another large body had worked round behind him and laid an ambush in a cutting. By his intrepid bravery and exemplary leadership, Major Grewal withdrew his company with the loss of two killed and twenty one wounded after inflicting extremely heavy casualties on the enemy." Major Rawind Singh was awarded the Military Cross on 6TH February 1946. Major Rawind Singh eventually attained the rank of Major General in the Indian Army.

JEMADAR WIR SINGH
8TH PUNJAB REGIMENT

"Jemadar Wir Singh displayed very high qualities of leadership until severely wounded at Kampar in Malaya in 1942. Throughout the earlier battles he showed great courage. In the successful counter-attack by his Company at Kampar he was the sole officer surviving, both British officers being killed early in the engagement. His handling of the Company was exemplary. By the end of fighting at Kampar his Company had lost 75 percent killed and wounded. Jemadar Wir Singh was largely responsible for the high morale of the survivors." Jemadar Wir Singh was strongly recommended for and awarded the Military Cross.

SUBEDAR JOGINDAR SINGH
8TH PUNJAB REGIMENT

"On 11TH May 1944, during the crossing of River Gari, Subedar Jogindar Singh was detailed as Assistant Beach Master. He crossed the river under very heavy shelling and Mortar fire with the foremost platoon of the assaulting troops and as three of his staff were wounded during the crossing he single-handed prepared the crossing places for the Companies under heavy fire and encouraged and helped the various platoons as they crossed. He also organised the collection and despatch of the wounded back across the river moving almost in the open under shell, Mortar and Medium Machine Gun fire with complete disregard for his personal safety. A short while later in the action his Company Commander was killed, remainder of the Company having suffered heavy casualties. Subedar Jogindar Singh was ordered to take over command and re-organise the Company. (Continued on next page)

Military Cross (cont.)

SECOND WORLD WAR (cont.)
SUBEDAR JOGINDAR SINGH (cont.)

Having done this the Company was moved forward to occupy a prominent feature of the objective. This feature was subjected to heavy enemy counter attack, as a result of which Subedar Jogindar Singh and 30 men of the original Company remained. Throughout the action the courage and cool bravery of Subedar Jogindar Singh in addition to the assistance given by him, proved and inspiration to all and greatly assisted in the Battalion crossing." Subedar Jogindar Singh was awarded an immediate Military Cross.

SUBEDAR KARAM SINGH
12TH FRONTIER FORCE REGIMENT

"Subedar Karam Singh has commanded a Machine Gun platoon for eighteen months in the forward area of the Arakan front in Burma. During this period he has shown outstanding qualities of leadership and devotion to duty. On 9TH October 1944, in the area south of Maungdaw, one his sections was preparing to take up position on the Sausage feature when it came under concentrated artillery fire from a Japanese 75m.m. gun. One of his Sepoys was badly wounded, and Subedar Karam Singh, regardless of his personal safety, ran out into the open and brought him back into a trench. In the afternoon of the same day, one of his Sections was giving a supporting fire on to Point 305 feature, and shortly after opening fire; its guns came under direct fire from an enemy 75m.m. gun, but encouraged by Jemadar Karam Singh's presence and coolness under fire the Section maintained its concentrated fire. The platoon thus neutralized the enemy's small arms fire and enabled the operation to be carried out successfully with few casualties. For a further month until its withdrawal in November, Subedar Karam Singh commanded his Platoon with great courage under constant enemy shellfire. He was at all times an inspiration and example to his men and was responsible for the many successful attacks carried out by his Platoon against the enemy." Subedar Karam Singh was awarded the Military Cross on 26TH December 1944.

Military Cross (cont.)

SECOND WORLD WAR (cont.)

MAJOR HARBANS SINGH VIRK
12TH FRONTIER FORCE REGIMENT

"On the 8TH March 1945, Major Virk was in command of "C" Company and with Royal Deccan Horse in support, was ordered to attack and capture the village of Sadaung, in Burma, which was known to contain a strong force of the enemy with 75mm guns, Medium Machine guns and Mortars. He went in from the North at 1315 hours, and inspite of heavy enemy fire, secured a firm base well inside the village. At 1430 hours, however, his company was held up by heavy mortar fire from South of the village, and very accurate Medium Machine Gun fire from the front and a pagoda to the left flank. Discharger Grenades were also being showered in to his position. Nothing daunted, this gallant officer, filled with determination to exterminate the enemy, he left the platoon in what cover was available, and extricated his other two platoons, with the object of putting in and attack from the Eastern Flank. The country here was very boggy, and two tanks at once sank into the mud, but relying on swift and decisive action to achieve success he ordered the tanks away to high ground on the left to give covering fire, and formed his men for the attack. At 1600 hrs, he rose, and with great shout to his men dashed into the centre of the enemy position, which was quickly overrun. He then led his men in a further magnificent charge, to clear the southern portion of the village, and finally reported at 1700 hrs that the enemy was beaten and running. The tanks then came to they're own and demoralized the running Japanese. The enemy killed by Major Virk and his company on this afternoon, amounted to over one hundred and the booty included two 75mm guns, five Medium Machine Guns, two 81 mm Mortars and quantities of small arms and equipment, at the cost of comparatively light casualties to the Company. This victory was solely due to the high courage and initiative of this lion-hearted officer. Throughout the action, under extremely heavy fire, he was ubiquitous, climbing on to the tanks to give orders under hail of bullets. He so inspired his men with his indomitable spirit, that when he gave the order for the charge, they followed him with the utmost dash, and the battle was won. This officer has shown highest qualities of courage and leadership throughout the present operations, and has led and inspired his men on the victory on several previous occasions. It was the faith in their leader, inspired and bred from previous actions that gave the great impetus to the company to achieve what they did on this day. His personal count of dead Japanese had been considerable." Major Harbans Singh Virk was awarded an immediate Military Cross followed by the DSO on 27TH May 1945

Military Cross (cont.)

SECOND WORLD WAR (cont.)
JEMADAR PHAGA SINGH
12TH FRONTIER FORCE REGIMENT

"On the 2ND March 1945, Jemadar Phaga Singh was a Platoon Commander in 'A' Company, which was part of an attacking force ordered to capture and clear the area of Meiktila town in Burma. The attack was supported b a troop of tanks. Shortly after crossing the starting line, Jemadar Phaga Singh's platoon came under very heavy automatic, mortar, and grenade and rifle fire, and was pinned to the ground, suffering casualties. The whole area was a mass of bunkers and foxholes, and infested with cunningly concealed snipers. Without hesitation Jemadar Phaga Singh ran forward to his leading Sections, pin-pointed the opposition in front of each, and then rushed back to the tanks, giving them instructions, led them up to positions from which they could bring fire to bear on the enemy. Throughout the action he was under heavy fire, and his complete disregard for his own life, and the devotion with which he calmly directed the fire of the tanks, thus enabling his men to advance and mop up, was beyond praise, and an inspiration not only to his own men, but to the tank crews in addition. He was greatly to the fore in the evacuation of his casualties. His indomitable courage and determination to exterminate every Japanese soldier, throughout eight gruelling hours of stiff hand-to-hand fighting was worthy of the highest standards of the Indian Army, and his personal count of enemy dead was considerable. As part of the same operations, Jemadar Phaga Singh's platoon was ordered to form part of Road Block on the Mandalay Road. On the morning of the 14TH March the enemy attacked the position, but was driven off with heavy casualties. Thereafter supported by armoured cars, Jemadar Phaga Singh's platoon was ordered to go forward and capture a Japanese gun that had been located the previous day. When hearing the advance the enemy opened up with concentrated fire, and made determined attempts to destroy the armoured cars with magnetic mines. In this they were frustrated, but the cars were forced to withdraw to a safer distance. Jemadar Phaga Singh then went in to the attack, and under his inspiring leadership the Frontiersmen overran the enemy position, killing 20 Japanese in hand-to-hand fighting and completely routed the enemy force, considerably superior in numbers to their own. In the two actions detailed above Jemadar Phaga Singh showed the highest qualities of courage and true leadership, and the great success achieved against determined enemy are due to the outstanding qualities as a great leader in the Field." Jemadar Phaga Singh was awarded an immediate Military Cross at the conclusion of the above fighting.

Military Cross (cont.)

SECOND WORLD WAR (cont.)
JEMADAR UDHAM SINGH
12TH FRONTIER FORCE REGIMENT

"On 10TH March 1945, Jemadar Udham Singh was the platoon commander of No.3 Platoon, 'A' Company, detailed to attack and clear up an enemy position astride the road Meiktila-Mahlaing in Burma. A troop of tanks was operating in support of his platoon. The platoon deployed and went into action with the tanks on the left of the road and at once came up against fanatical Japanese resistance. The country here was broken, and covered with thick scrub, and a network of defences and foxholes, which proved more than usually difficult to locate. Jemadar Udham Singh, however, resolved to deal harshly with the enemy, and led his section in with great dash and vigour. He led his men in this close and difficult country, in the most exemplary manner, without thought of personal danger, being always to the fore and quick to expose himself whenever it became necessary to direct the fire of the tanks. He took his platoon into action at 25 strong and after magnificent fighting on the part of all, he had only 12 men left, the remainder either being killed or wounded. The troop of tanks then went off leaving his small force to carry on without them, and surrounded by snipers on all sides. This situation, however, merely goaded this gallant leader to redouble his efforts, rallying his men he went forward again, clearing up trench after trench, and inflicting great slaughter amongst the enemy. It was not until 1400 hours that a fresh company supported by tanks could be sent forward to relieve him on the ground to carry on the fight. Jemadar Udham Singh had killed many Japanese both with grenades and Sten gun, and it was his gallantry and inspiring leadership that spurred on the remnants of his gallant band of men to fight with frenzy, until finally ordered to withdraw and reorganize. Jemadar Udham Singh's conduct in the evacuation of all his casualties under heavy fire, both small arms and artillery, was of the highest order, and his bravery and inspiring leadership was an example to all members of the Battalion." Jemadar Udham Singh was awarded an immediate Military Cross on 10TH March 1945.

Sikh scout Burma 1944

Military Cross (cont.)

SECOND WORLD WAR (cont.)
JEMADAR NARAIN SINGH
12TH FRONTIER FORCE REGIMENT

"On the 10TH April 1945, Jemadar Narain Singh was a platoon commander of 'B' Company, when the Battalion was ordered to attack and consolidate the Frontier Force lines area of the main Pyawbwe-Meiktila road in Burma, as there was a strong enemy presence there. The 'B' Company had to advance across 1000 yards of bullet-swept, open country. Jemadar Narain Singh was in the vanguard of the advance, which was an inspiration to the remainder of the Battalion, who were privileged to witness his determined progress. Jemadar Narain Singh kept the platoon under perfect control inspite of casualties from the enemy's Light Machine Guns. On arrival it was found that contrary to reports, the Frontier Force lines area was very strongly held by the enemy. The attack went in on a two Company front, with 'B' Company on the right. Jemadar Narain Singh's platoon at once came under heavy mortar and automatic fire, and the platoon suffered casualties. Holding his ground, however, Jemadar Narain Singh arranged, at great personal risk to himself, the evacuation of his wounded and then personally directed the artillery fire, preliminary to his further advance. He then led his platoon forward, but the enemy once again replied with every thing he had and the attacking platoon suffered more casualties. Time was precious however, and without further ado, Jemadar Narain Singh led the charge, and rushed in at their head to capture the first objective. Inspired by his leadership his men fought magnificently, and the area was soon under control. There remained the wooded area, round the church and up to the railway line to be captured. Again 'B' Company was on the right, and Jemadar Narain Singh urgently requested that his platoon lead the attack. His request was granted and the men went in at the head of the tanks. The enemy fought back bravely and tenaciously, as the platoon cleared the whole area yard-by-yard. Throughout this day, Jemadar Narain Singh led his men with utmost gallantry. His fierce cries of 'Sat Siri Akal', and the encouragement he gave his men, going from section to section and personally directing the attack, were an inspiration to all, and his imperturbability under heaviest fire was beyond praise. On this day, Jemadar Narain Singh personally killed six Japs and his platoon added another 133 to very substantial Battalion total. Within Company has earned for himself the name of 'Sher' (Lion)" Jemadar Narain Singh was awarded an immediate Military Cross on the 10TH April 1945.

Military Cross (cont.)
SECOND WORLD WAR (cont.)
MAJOR HIMMAT SINGH SANDHU
12TH FRONTIER FORCE REGIMENT

"Major Himmat Singh Sandhu was in command of the Company supplying boatmen for ferrying across personnel during the crossing of the River Gari in Italy on the night of 11/12TH May 1944, where his men were exposed to machine gun and mortar fire from enemy posts. On completion of their task the Company proceeded towards the enemy positions and ran into three machine gun posts. On each occasion, in spite of the continuous fire from the posts, Major Sandhu personally organised and led a series of charges against the posts. Visibility being such that their exact positions could not be located and Major Sandhu, was forced to shout his commands and drew much of the fire on himself. His relentless attack on these posts under almost continuous fire from grenades and machine guns and smoke resulted in two enemy posts being withdrawn and the third destroyed. Throughout the action Major Sandhu was conspicuous in his complete indifference to danger and his fearless leadership. His personal example was outstanding." Major Himmat Singh Sandhu was awarded an immediate Military Cross on 12TH May 1944.

MAJOR AMAR SINGH
12TH FRONTIER FORCE REGIMENT

"On 17TH March 1944, the Company commanded by Major Amar Singh took over the left forward Company position of 'B' sector of the 8TH Indian Division front, very close to strong German position in Orso area in Italy. The enemy was very aggressive with shelling, mortar fire and Machine Gun fire and his strong fighting patrols were very active. The Company's forward platoon, situated in a very exposed position in a cave and completely isolated, was particularly an enemy objective. By day no movement was possible and by night it was very difficult. The night after the Company's arrival, the enemy launched an attack on the platoon in the caves, supported by heavy covering fire. All communications were quickly cut. Major Amar Singh went forward immediately under heavy fire to control the situation, taking an NCO and three soldiers with him. After encouraging his isolated platoon and taking necessary measures to meet the situation, he returned to his Headquarters and directed the fire of his mortars so successfully that the attack was repulsed with loss. He was the only survivor of the party he took forward with him and had he not acted as he did, his platoon would have been overrun. During his Company's tenure of this exposed forward position, in close contact throughout with and aggressive enemy, Major Amar Singh set a magnificent example of courage and coolness under fire and of cheerful acceptance of the hardships involved in the appalling winter weather conditions. His offensive spirit and sound leadership quickly resulted in his Company dominating the caves area, a complete reversal of the previous position." Major Amar Singh was awarded an immediate Military Cross.

Military Cross (cont.)
SECOND WORLD WAR (cont.)
JEMADAR DHANA SINGH
12TH FRONTIER FORCE REGIMENT

"Jemadar Dhana Singh has commanded the Pioneer Platoon of the 1ST Battalion 12TH Frontier Force Regiment throughout the Italian campaign. During this period well over two thousand mines have been lifted by the Platoon, a large proportion by Jemadar Dhana Singh himself. He performed outstanding work during the winter of 1944/45 in the appalling weather and precipitous country of the Northern Apennines where the enemy were using mines in very large numbers. During the assault crossing point of Santerno River, regardless of the heavy shelling and small arms fire, he cleared and marked a track for personnel and vehicles through the extensive minefields, lifting over one hundred mines, many of which were booby trapped, and thus played a very large part in the success of the operation. By his constant searching for and neutralizing enemy mines, by skill and fearless example in dealing with new types and by his sustained courage throughout the campaign, Jemadar Dhana Singh has inspired his platoon to a state of keenness and efficiency, which saved the Battalion many casualties." Jemadar Dhana Singh was strongly recommended for and awarded the Military Cross on 14TH June 1945.

JEMADAR MOHINDER SINGH
12TH FRONTIER FORCE REGIMENT

"On the 11TH April 1945, during the assault across the River Santerno in the area of Ca Lugo in Italy, Jemadar Mohinder Singh commanded a platoon of 'D' Company, and had the task of securing the houses beyond the West Flood bank. His first attempt to cross the Flood bank was met with heavy Spandau fire from the left flank and the houses in front, three men being killed instantly and others wounded. Jemadar Mohinder Singh immediately reorganized his platoon and detailing his gunner to engage the enemy in the houses and another party to cover the left flank, he himself led the remainder of the platoon through the enemy fire and over the bank. With speed and determination he attacked and captured three houses and went on to mop up two further enemies occupied houses. During this period the platoon suffered further casualties but captured between twenty and thirty prisoners. Jemadar Mohinder Singh secured the important bridgehead, which enabled the rest of the Company to fan out behind the enemy positions and capture twenty more prisoners. Jemadar Mohinder Singh then quickly organised a defensive position and passed on all necessary information to the reserve Company Commander, who by now was ready to go through. The magnificent skill and quick thinking and aggressive leadership of Jemadar Mohinder Singh and his complete disregard for danger were and inspiration to his platoon and a major factor in the establishment of a bridgehead over the River Santerno." Jemadar Mohinder Singh was awarded an immediate Military Cross.

Military Cross (cont.)
SECOND WORLD WAR (cont.)

SUBEDAR KARTAR SINGH
12TH FRONTIER FORCE REGIMENT

"Throughout the period from May to August 1944, Subedar Kartar Singh was employed as senior Viceroy's Commissioned Officer in the Sikh Company of the Battalion in Burma. In this capacity he was also Company's Second in Command. During this period the Company took part in many engagements against the Japanese and Subedar Kartar Singh was with the Company on each of these actions. When in action, he has conducted himself in every respect with the highest traditions of the Indian Army. Subedar Kartar Singh has always been at the head of his Company, shouting words of encouragement and inspiration to the men. His utter fearlessness and complete disregard of personal danger has been invaluable steadying influence upon men of the Sikh Company, large proportion of who were young and without experience of war. His personality and vitality have been most pronounced in battle, and he proved to be as steadfast and courageous in adversity as in success. He has been a dashing leader in close hand-to-hand fighting. During periods of rest, Subedar Kartar Singh's knowledge and control of the men of his Company was of great value to the Company Commander in his work of reorganisation and rehabilitation. Subedar Kartar Singh is an excellent administrator and under his charge the internal administration of the Company, so essential to success in operations, has worked with great smoothness. He has constantly displayed gallantry, leadership and initiative of a very high order and has at all times been and example to the Company of offensive spirit and desire to close in with and destroy the enemy. He is a fine officer, with a fine influence in the area of a difficult command." Subedar Kartar Singh was awarded an immediate Military Cross in August 1944.

JEMADAR UJAGAR SINGH
14TH PUNJAB REGIMENT

"On 14TH October 1944, Jemadar Ujagar Singh in command of a fighting patrols of 25 men, which had arrived on the Mamgheng ridge in the Chin Hills in Burma. Early in the morning the patrol encountered an enemy force of over 500 armed with 31 Light Machine Guns and Mortars. The battle, which ensued, lasted for over three hours and many casualties were inflicted upon the enemy. During these operations Jemadar Ujagar Singh commanded his patrol with marked ability and courage and though opposed by overwhelming odds kept up the battle until casualties and lack of ammunition compelled him to disengage". Jemadar Ujagar Singh was strongly recommended for and awarded the Military Cross on 28TH February 1945.

Military Cross (cont.)
SECOND WORLD WAR (cont.)
JEMADAR SANTA SINGH
12TH FRONTIER FORCE REGIMENT

"During the battle for the Castelnuovo feature North of Tavaletto in Italy, Jemadar Santa Singh was commanding the leading platoon of 'A' Company. During the night of 5/6TH September 1944, his platoon took part in an attack, which eventually had to be abandoned because the original line of approach was found to be impassable. On the morning of 6TH September his platoon assisted the tanks in their advance over an exposed ground, which was under heavy mortar and machine gun fire. On the afternoon of 6TH September Jemadar Santa Singh was ordered to cooperate with 'D' Company in their attack on Point 419. The approaches to this objective were over open ground, which was under fire from enemy mortars and machine guns. Jemadar Santa Singh placed himself at the head of his men and led them forward on the left of 'D' Company within hundred yards of the objective where a low bank offered them some cover. From here he observed that the enemy fire from some houses on the left of Point 4198 were holding up 'D' Company's advance. He made an extensive reconnaissance during which he was under constant fire and eventually found a small drain, which gave cover of advance. Posting two of his sections to give covering fire from the low bank, he then led the third section up this drain and rushed an enemy machine gun post in a surprise attack and captured four of the gun crew with their gun. The enemy from the second post panicked and fled leaving their gun behind them, while the assaulting section suffered no casualties at all. 'D' Company was then able to capture Point 419 without further trouble. That night 6/7 September the enemy counter attacked the whole Battalion position with great determination Jemadar Santa Singh rallied his exhausted platoon, he ran from one section to another shouting words of encouragement and praise to his me, many of whom were raw recruits and were in battle for the first time, and had been continuously in action for twenty-four hours. Later the same night the platoon ran short of ammunition, Jemadar Santa Singh distributed the captured German machine guns to them and kept his men firing them until reserve ammunition was brought forward the next morning. The Company had lost their Commander on the first night of the operations, but through bold initiative, resourcefulness and above all magnificent example of personal courage, Jemadar Santa Singh was able very materially to contribute to the success of the whole battle." Jemadar Santa Singh was awarded an immediate Military Cross.

Military Cross (cont.)
SECOND WORLD WAR (cont.)
CAPTAIN BUTA SINGH BAJWA
12TH FRONTIER FORCE REGIMENT

"On Arezzo sector during the Battalion attack on the Campriano feature in Italy on 25TH July 1944, 'C' Company under the command of Captain Bajwa was ordered to advance in rear of 'B' Company and capture Point 584. Soon after crossing the start line the Company came under intense mortar and shellfire. Captain Bajwa infiltrated the Company forward through the enemy defensive fire to a nullah. Soon the Company again came under heavy fire at close range from enemy light automatics, mortars and small arms fire. Despite the intense fire and increasing casualties Captain Bajwa made no less than three attempts to take his Company forward on to the high ground. He tried first one flank and then another, and on each occasion pressed home the attack with great determination. However owing to mounting casualties his Company was withdrawn and amalgamated with 'B' Company. During the remainder of the night the amalgamated Company was subjected to intense shelling and mortaring. Early in the morning the enemy were preparing to counter attack from the right flank. Captain Bajwa realizing the seriousness of the situation reinforced his right platoon and directed accurate fire on the enemy and completely smashed the impending attack. Throughout this long and difficult action Captain Bajwa with his unflinching determination to get forward at all costs, his bravery and the skill with which he handled his Company in the dark, he set an inspiring example to all, and was in keeping with the finest traditions of the Sikhs." Captain Bajwa was awarded an immediate Military Cross.

JEMADAR KARNAIL SINGH
13TH FRONTIER FORCE RIFLES

"During the advance on to the Gothic Line, in Italy, on the 13TH September 1944, Jemadar Karnail Singh led his platoon forward in skilful and daring manner to take a wooded feature strongly held by the enemy. While passing through a clearing, the platoon was suddenly fired on at point–blank range by an enemy Machine Gun. Without hesitation Jemadar Karnail Singh, immediately rushed forward single handedly to attack the post, only to fall with a bullet wound through the knee. Crawling forward he continued to direct and encourage his men until the enemy post was outflanked and two Machine Guns and forty Germans soldiers captured. It was only when the action was over that he allowed himself to be carried to the rear. A courageous officer with plenty of initiative whose determination after he was wounded did much to aid the success of the operations." Jemadar Karnail Singh was awarded an immediate Military Cross.

Military Cross (cont.)
SECOND WORLD WAR (cont.)
MAJOR KEHAR SINGH RAI
12TH FRONTIER FORCE REGIMENT

"On 8TH July 1944, a Japanese force of some 500 strong, supported by Artillery, Mortars and Medium Machine Guns, attacked positions in the village of Chepu in Burma, held by a Battalion of the 12TH Frontier Force Regiment. The Japanese managed to occupy the North and higher end of a hill feature overlooking the village, thus dominating the positions below with Medium Machine Guns. The troops in the lower positions were very exposed, but it was essential to the success of the operations that these positions should continue to be held. Major Kehar Singh Rai was ordered to take his company forward into these positions to reinforce the Company already there. On arrival in the positions, Major Rai found that both the Company Commander and the Company Officer of this Company had been killed and that the Company had suffered heavy casualties. He at once rallied the men and reorganized the defence of the area. Later in the afternoon, two platoons of another Company were despatched to strengthen Major Rai's position. The Company Commander was seriously wounded immediately after arrival in the position. Major Rai at once took command of these men and personally led them to their positions, despite heavy fire from Medium Machine Guns. Throughout the many attacks made upon his position by the Japanese during the day and despite heavy Mortar, Artillery and Medium Machine Gun fire, Major Rai remained completely unperturbed and was always in complete control of the situation. His personal gallantry and determination in the hand-to-hand fighting which accompanied these attacks was a great source of inspiration and encouragement to his men. Major Rai displayed complete contempt for personal safety at all times and was always in the thick of the fight, encouraging his men by both word and deed to even greater efforts. Major Rai's sustained offensive spirit and refusal at any time to permit the initiative to remain in the hands of the attacking Japanese largely contributed to the success of the defence of that day, and the infliction of very heavy casualties upon the Japanese." Major Kehar Singh Rai was strongly recommended for and awarded the Military Cross on 7TH August 1944.

Military Cross (cont.)
SECOND WORLD WAR (cont.)
MAJOR AMRIK SINGH
12TH FRONTIER FORCE REGIMENT

"During the period Major Amrik Singh has been in command he has proved himself to be a brave and skilful commander. He fought and led his Company with great distinction at Meiktila in Burma. On the second day of the attack on the town, and though wounded himself, in the shoulder, he refused to be evacuated, and by evening had cleared the enemy from whole of the built-up area from North to South. In the process his Company suffered heavy casualties, but his determination to defeat the enemy, and his fine personal example, inspired his men to win through bitter and difficult hand-to-hand fighting. A few days later he organised a most successful roadblock on the Mandalay Road, when his Company killed 40 Japanese and captured several guns. Again on the Meiktila–Mahlaing road he led his Company in to attack and capture the high ground against numerically superior enemy forces over most difficult and broken country thickly entrenched and bunkered. In two days fighting the infantry with the Tanks in support, and despite their own heavy casualties killed over 200 of the enemy. Major Amrik Singh distinguished himself again at Kandaung and at the battle of Pyawbwe, numerous Japanese being killed and much equipment captured on both occasions. Finally it was Major Amrik Singh and his Company, which after a day and night of tough, close quarter fighting, secured the bridgehead over the Pegu river, thus enabling the Division to continue its advance Southwards. This gallant and capable officer has been an inspiration and example to his men, throughout these operations, and has shown a high standard of personal skill and bravery. Despite very heavy casualties amongst his command, he has maintained a magnificent fighting spirit in his Company. The Company bears the proud record of never having failed to win all objectives given to them. No praise can be high enough for the way Major Amrik Singh has led and commanded his Company throughout these operations." Major Amrik Singh was strongly recommended for and awarded the Military Cross on 15TH May 1945.

Military Cross (cont.)
SECOND WORLD WAR (cont.)
JEMADAR BALWANT SINGH
13TH FRONTIER FORCE RIFLES

"Jemadar Balwant Singh's platoon assaulted and captured against heavy opposition, a prominent rocky feature during the night of 10/11TH December 1945, in Italy. On 12TH December, in thick fog the enemy launched a determined attack on the platoon's position up the spur from the South East and was repulsed. For the next three hours, bitter fighting continued, the enemy repeatedly attempting to work their way on to the top. Owing to the pressure elsewhere it was not possible for relief to reach them until 0950 hours. By this time two men in the platoon remained unwounded. The platoon had lost 6 killed and 13 wounded. Jemadar Balwant Singh himself was wounded in both hands but continued to command his platoon skilfully and very gallantly, thereby retaining a valuable Artillery Observation Post. Jemadar Balwant Singh undoubtedly inflicted heavy losses on the enemy. Three enemies were killed in the platoons position with his Light Machine Gun. An enemy prisoner later stated that his Company Commander had been ordered to capture the position at all costs." For his leadership and gallantry Jemadar Balwant Singh was awarded an immediate Military Cross.

JEMADAR SANTA SINGH
13TH FRONTIER FORCE RIFLES

"On 6TH April 1945, 'A' Company was in position on the summit of a high steep feature, East of Taungup Road in Burma. The summit was divided into two knolls of equal height separated from each other by a bare narrow ridge about hundred yards long and five yards wide. The sides of the ridge were almost precipitous. The enemy about thirty to forty strong, with medium Machine Gun and two Light Machine Guns, were dug in on the Eastern Knoll. Jemadar Santa Singh led his platoon along the ridge with supporting fire from tanks and Medium Machine Guns on the South and North flanks respectively. When supporting fire ceased he led his platoon straight in on the enemy positions. Although wounded in the first rush he charged on, inflicting heavy casualties on the enemy with his Sten gun. The attack and subsequent consolidation were successful, the enemy Medium Machine Gun was captured, and heavy casualties inflicted on the enemy, sixteen bodies being recovered including that of an officer. With this attack the enemy resistance on Point 370, which had been the scene of bitter fighting for two days ceased. Throughout, the great personal courage and skill shown by Jemadar Santa Singh, allied to his complete disregard of personal risk, was an inspiration to his platoon, which under his command nothing would have stopped, and vital factor in the complete capture of the feature." Jemadar Santa Singh was awarded an immediate Military Cross.

Military Cross (cont.)
SECOND WORLD WAR (cont.)
JEMADAR CHANAN SINGH
13TH FRONTIER FORCE RIFLES

"Jemadar Chanan Singh, as senior Indian Officer of his Company, has displayed first class qualities as a sagacious leader during the advance through the Gothic Line in Italy, for the period ending 12TH October 1944. On several occasions he has volunteered to go out on patrol, bringing back useful information. Once, during an attack on a high wooded feature, when the situation was particularly serious since all Light Machine Gun ammunition had run short, and German Patrols were calling on the men to surrender, Jemadar Chanan Singh seized a rifle and standing up in and exposed position with complete disregard for his own safety called on his Sikhs to remember 'Saragarhi', and fight to the finish with their hands. Later on he personally led a bombing attack, which successfully dealt with a German patrol, which had infiltrated into the Company position. Jemadar Chanan Singh has at all times set a very high example, and has been a tower of strength to Company Commander throughout the operations." Jemadar Chanan Singh was awarded the Military Cross on 28TH June 1945.

SUBEDAR GURBUX SINGH
14TH PUNJAB REGIMENT

"Subedar Gurbux Singh was second in command of 'A' Company, when the Company carried out an attack on the enemy position on the Windwin feature 5648 0n 15TH January 1944. Early in the action the Company Commander, with two platoons, carried out an encircling attack on the enemy and was seriously wounded. On receiving the information Subedar Gurbux Singh went forward from the covering platoon and on arrival he found that with the Company Commander the Leading Platoon Commander was also wounded and the Platoon Havildar killed. He reorganized these two platoons, under heavy grenade fire, and pressed home the attack. This was carried out with great dash, largely through Subedar Gurbux Singh's leadership, and the position was taken. On 17TH January 1944, the Company was attacked from the rear by approximately one platoon of the enemy. The attack lasted for two hours and was repulsed. Subedar Gurbux Singh again showed great coolness in the control of his Company. During these actions Subedar Gurbux Singh has shown personal courage and powers leadership of high order." Subedar Gurbux Singh was awarded and an immediate Military Cross on 19TH January 1944.

Military Cross (cont.)
SECOND WORLD WAR (cont.)
LIEUTENANT SUCHA SINGH
15TH PUNJAB REGIMENT

"Lieutenant Sucha Singh was commanding "D" Company, 15TH Punjab Regiment during the Kama Bridgehead operations near Prome in Burma. On the 27TH May 1945, the Company was ordered to move its position to the right in order to close up with the next Company and block a possible escape route of the Japanese in the Bridgehead. Owing to late receipt of the orders only two platoons of the Company had reached the new position and were not dug in when the Japanese put in their first attack. This was repulsed with heavy loss to the enemy. The third platoon came up before dusk and the defensive position was dug, but not wired, as none could be brought up. A further attack by the Japanese was also beaten off. During the night and altogether seven attacks were put in by the Japanese on this position, which proved that it lay across and important Japanese escape route. Twice during these attacks, the direction of which was from three sides, the Japs penetrated the position but were driven out by grenades and the bayonet. Throughout the engagement Lieutenant Sucha Singh directed the defence with utmost coolness and determination, encouraging the Company with cheering remarks. During one attack he killed a Japanese soldier who was creeping up unnoticed along a covered approach. His communications throughout the night was only by 48 set to the next Company, and his N.C.O.'s set did not work. Nevertheless he passed all orders through his set with complete coolness and caused most accurate artillery defensive fire to be brought down in front of his position. The Company counted forty-eight dead Japanese bodies' around the position the next morning and the Company had suffered four killed and seven wounded. The leadership of Lieutenant Sucha Singh throughout the whole engagement was of the highest order and contributed very largely to the successful defence of the position and the blocking of one important Jap escape route. In view of the fact that the officer was a subaltern commanding a Company for the first time in action, his performance is considered especially outstanding." Lieutenant Sucha Singh was awarded and immediate Military Cross.

Military Cross (cont.)

SECOND WORLD WAR (cont.)
JEMADAR KESAR SINGH
15TH PUNJAB REGIMENT

"On 11TH May at Seitpudaung in Burma, Jemadar Kesar Singh was in command of a fighting Patrol, which suddenly encountered the Japanese in considerably great strength. The Patrol came under heavy fire from Japanese automatic fire and four of the platoon was wounded immediately, including Jemadar Kesar Singh. As a large party of enemy move round the right flank, ignoring his own wounds Jemadar Kesar Singh fought back inflicting losses on them, and by skilful disposition and his own example of steadiness under fire, extricated his platoon, taking his casualties to Paddaukon Village. The Japanese in greatly superior numbers again attacked and attempted to surround him, but Jemadar Kesar Singh again fought back hard inflicting casualties and skilfully extricating his platoon again. He made repeated contact with the enemy and finding all routes blocked by superior numbers of the enemy took up a defensive position for the night. Next day he continued to encounter superior numbers of Japanese and continued to fight back stoutly, inflicting more casualties on the enemy and succeeding in safeguarding his own increasing casualties. By ignoring his own wounds and by his cheerfulness and personal example, the Jemadar heartened the wounded that they too made light of their wounds. On the third day Jemadar Kesar Singh although in pain so inspired his platoon that they continued in excellent fighting spirit, fought their way back to their Company line and brought in all their wounded and identifications of enemy killed. The platoon had been out for 56 hours surrounded by enemy, and, though short of food, had covered many miles in thick jungle and fought with conspicuous success, inflicting many casualties on the enemy. It was Jemadar Kesar Singh's high standard of military skill and leadership, his complete disregard of personal safety, his steadiness, determination and example that inspired his men to such heights of endurance." Jemadar Kesar Singh was awarded an immediate Military Cross.

Military Cross (cont.)

SECOND WORLD WAR (cont.)

JEMADAR CHATTAR SINGH MM
15TH PUNJAB REGIMENT

"On the night of 14/15TH September 1944, Jemadar Chattar Singh was commanding a Platoon of "B" Company, which had been ordered to capture A di Vitiglano in Italy. While the Company was forming up for the attack on a narrow ridge the enemy brought down heavy artillery fire on the forming up area, causing casualties and considerable confusion in the darkness. In spite of the heavy fire Jemadar Chattar Singh made no attempt to take cover but moved about the area rallying the men till control was restored and the men were in position. He then personally led the assault up an exceptionally steep hillside, covered with thick scrub, and in pitch darkness against strongly prepared enemy positions on the crest of the ridge 350 feet above the forming up place. During this very difficult climb, under frequent enemy fire, Jemadar Chattar Singh's platoon was unable to fire its weapons or throw grenades on account of the steepness of the hill but Jemadar Chattar Singh's determination, personal leadership and disregard for danger brought hi men to the top. On reaching the crest, Jemadar Chattar Singh himself led the assault on the enemy trenches. During this assault he saw that one of the enemy, who had been captured, was about to throw a stick grenade; he himself at once attacked the man, and after a hand-to-hand struggle, overcame and dis-armed him. Throughout the action Jemadar Chattar Singh's gallantry and leadership was exceptionally fine and an inspiration to the whole of his Company." Jemadar Chattar Singh was awarded an immediate Military Cross.

CAPTAIN PIARA SINGH
16TH PUNJAB REGIMENT

"On 9TH April, 1944, at Wilugyaung in Burma, Captain Piara Singh was sent to the aid of and recover three Patrols that were cut off by the enemy. After seven days without food and most his ammunition exhausted, Captain Piara Singh returned through the enemy lines with these Patrols. On 21ST April 1944, at Khomwei a superior Japanese force attacked his position. He drove them back and chased them some two miles across a plain inflicting severe casualties on them. On 27TH April, at Laukai, where identification of the enemy was required he captured two Japanese soldiers as a result of a skilful ambush. The leadership, the high standard of courage and devotion to duty shown by this officer was an example of the highest degree to all his men." Captain Piara Singh was strongly recommend for and awarded the Military Cross on 1ST August 1944.

Military Cross (cont.)

SECOND WORLD WAR (cont.)
JEMADAR DHARAM SINGH
15TH PUNJAB REGIMENT

"On the night of 17/18TH October 1944, during the attack on Groce Daneie in Italy, Jemadar Dharam Singh was commanding a platoon of "B" Company. While waiting in a assembly position to cross the start line the enemy brought down heavy and accurate artillery and mortar fire which compelled the Company to disperse and take cover. Shortly before the Company was to cross the start line the Company Commander was wounded and his runner killed by the shelling. Jemadar Dharam Singh was then ordered to collect the Company and take it back via the Battalion Headquarters to Finnachio, as the proposed cross-country route was considered impracticable. In spite of the heavy shelling and darkness Jemadar Dharam Singh collected the Company and got on the move in remarkably short space of time and without any loss of a single man or mule. As the Company moved forward heavy and concentrated fire was again experienced and most of the Company was thrown into confusion. Jemadar Dharam Singh showed complete disregard for danger and by his coolness and personal example retained control of his platoon and kept up the morale of his men. When eventually "B" Company made contact with "D" Company the situation was extremely critical, as heavy casualties had been suffered, they had no artillery support, and the advance was held up by heavy Machine Gun fire. Jemadar Dharam Singh's coolness and confidence and his immediate offer to lead the advance restored morale and put new life into all ranks. Finally, after additional artillery support had been arranged, Jemadar Dharam Singh led his platoon with the greatest confidence and boldness, so inspiring his men that all enemy resistance was over-run and the objective captured just before the dawn. Jemadar Dharam Singh in this operation showed himself to be a very cool, brave and inspiring leader and won the confidence of all he led into battle." Jemadar Dharam Singh was awarded an immediate Military Cross.

Military Cross (cont.)

SECOND WORLD WAR (cont.)
SUBEDAR HARI SINGH
15TH PUNJAB REGIMENT

"During the period 16TH November 1944 to 15TH February 1945, Subedar Hari Singh, a Platoon Commander of "A" Company, has shown initiative and personal courage of the highest order on several occasions. On 25TH January at the Ngapyin Bridgehead, in Burma, "A" Company was sent out to investigate the result of and air strike, which had been made about 200 yards outside the Brigade perimeter. Subedar Hari Singh's platoon was leading and had completed its first bound. Subedar Hari Singh was between the two leading sections and had signalled his right hand section Bren gun to move forward slightly. As the Bren gun section moved forward the enemy opened fire and the No 1of the Bren gun was killed. At the same time fire was opened on the Subedar from his right and front. With great coolness Hari Singh ordered his Platoon Havildar to man the right hand Bren gun and engage the enemy's Light Machine Guns. Four enemies were killed but the Light Machine Guns were not silenced. Simultaneously a party of about 20 Japanese charged the Platoon position and was engaged by the left hand section, 7 enemies being killed. The Platoon was then was ordered to withdraw and Subedar Hari Singh carried out the withdrawal with exceptional ability. Under cover of 2-inch Mortar and Light Machine Gun fire he withdrew the Platoon group by group without suffering further casualties and bringing back his dead. On several previous occasions Subedar Hari Singh's Platoon had borne the brunt of strong enemy attacks during the establishment of the Bridgeheads. The excellent control and personal example displayed by Subedar Hari Singh enabled the Platoon to inflict many casualties on the enemy, with little loss to the platoon. At all times Subedar Hari Singh has been an outstanding example to his fellow Viceroy's Commissioned Officers". Subedar Hari Singh was strongly recommend for and awarded the Military Cross on 25TH June 1945.

JEMADAR DIDAR SINGH
BURMA REGIMENT

"In Kohima area in Burma on 28TH May 1944, Jemadar Didar Singh led his platoon in a counter–attack on a position recently captured by the enemy and succeeded in capturing his objective destroying 2 Light Machine Gun Posts and 2 other automatic rifle posts, inflicting several casualties on the enemy. He showed great coolness and leadership, being responsible for leading the Company to the objective through thick jungle. On all Operations he has shown courage and initiative, and is very strongly recommended for the Military Cross." Jemadar Didar Singh was awarded the Military Cross on 15TH October 1944.

Military Cross (cont.)

SECOND WORLD WAR (cont.)
JEMADAR KAPUR SINGH
15TH PUNJAB REGIMENT

"During 16TH November to 15TH February 1945, Jemadar Kapur Singh has been an outstanding example to his fellow Viceroy Commissioned Officers for his courage and initiative. On several occasions his Platoon was heavily attacked by the enemy and in particular on the night of 22/23 January 1945 in the Ngapyin Bridgehead. Attacks started at 1230 hours and immediately his Platoon suffered casualties. One section was completely disabled having 4 men killed and 2 wounded, leaving a dangerous gap. With a composite section drawn from his Platoon Headquarters, and remaining two sections he continued to deny the ground to the enemy until he was reinforced. The attacks continued throughout the night and Jemadar Kapur Singh, under heavy fire moved amongst his section posts, exhorting his men with complete disregard for his own safety. In a later action a few days later Jemadar Kapur Singh was wounded while leading his Platoon. Throughout the operations Jemadar Kapur Singh has set a high example of courage and determination." Jemadar Kapur Singh was awarded the Military Cross on 28TH August 1945.

SUBEDAR GURDAS SINGH
16TH PUNJAB REGIMENT

"At the Imphal Area in Burma, on 28TH May 1944, Subedar Gurdas Singh was second in command of his company. The Japanese shelled the Battalion position for some three hours, particularly concentrating on his company's position. The fire was extremely accurate and came mainly from 105 mm guns. These shells in many cases pierced the head cover of the bunkers and the company suffered heavy casualties. Subedar Gurdas Singh moved from bunker to bunker while the shells were exploding. He bandaged up the wounded in bunkers and encouraged the remainder to stand firm. While moving from bunker to bunker, he was wounded by a bursting shell. Unable to move he refused to leave the company position until the Company Commander ordered his stretcher-bearers to carry him out. The fearless example displayed by Subedar Gurdas Singh inspired the whole company with the resolution to hold on at all costs, and undoubtedly contributed to the firmness with which his company beat off subsequent Japanese attacks." Subedar Gurdas Singh was awarded the Military Cross on 3RD July 1944.

Military Cross (cont.)

SECOND WORLD WAR (cont.)
JEMADAR SARDARA SIGNH
16TH PUNJAB REGIMENT

"From 9TH March to 23RD March, Jemadar Sardara Singh commanded a platoon, which flanked pt 593 and overlooked Monte Cassino Monastery in Italy. The enemy had excellent observation over the routes, between this platoon, the next platoon and the Company Headquarters. Accurate sniping made movement from Company Headquarters to either platoon impossible by day. Jemadar Sardara Singh, as a senior Viceroys Commissioned Officer commanded both forward platoons and controlled the defence of this locality, which was of vital importance to the whole Brigade sector. He frequently visited not only his own section posts but also the other Platoon Headquarters to pass them orders and instructions and properly coordinate the defence. This he did by crawling behind bushes and rocks and taking advantage of all- available cover. Enemy shelling, mortaring and accurate sniping was often concentrated along the area over which he had to pass and to get through unwounded seemed impossible, but he managed to pass through many times to pass his orders. By night the enemy would become more active and in addition to heavy mortaring and shelling, small arms fire and grenades were directed onto the forward positions. Jemadar Sardara Singh showed complete disregard for his own personal safety and moved from post to post encouraging and fostering offensive spirit of his men. The daily casualties reduced the strength of his platoon severely but Jemadar Sardara Singh appeared to become even more cheerful and confident. Cold nights and rain added to the discomfort of the men but by his personal example and presence whenever the enemy became aggressive his men were inspired to still greater endurance. Thus throughout a period of a fortnight of great strain Jemadar Sardara Singh was responsible for the successful defence of this essential position. Completely undisturbed by the heaviest enemy fire he was able to send back most valuable and accurate information of enemy dispositions and movements. He was responsible for locating hostile batteries and his reports were always prompt and to the point. By his gallantry and devotion to duty he showed leadership of a high order under conditions, which could hardly have been more unpleasant and dangerous. His conduct is in the best traditions of the Indian Army." Jemadar Sardara Singh was awarded an immediate Military Cross.

Military Cross (cont.)

SECOND WORLD WAR (cont.)
SUBEDAR NARINJAN SINGH
16TH PUNJAB REGIMENT

"Shortly after dark on 27TH July 1944, "A" Company after long and arduous flank march of fourteen hours through thick jungle reached the road Palel-Taku, in Burma, four miles in the front of advanced positions occupied by the Battalion. The Company had been ordered to lay an ambush astride the road in this area. The road at this point was completely overlooked by Hill 87, which a patrol of Subedar Narinjan Singh's platoon reported to be occupied by the enemy in great strength. Subedar Narinjan Singh was ordered to attack the hill and drive off the enemy. The ground, over which the attack was to be made, and the exact positions and the strength of the enemy were unknown. Despite this and all the other difficulties inherent in a night attack over un-reconnoitred ground, Subedar Narinjan Singh resolutely led his platoon towards the enemy position. When advancing some distance the platoon came under fire from automatic rifles. Making an accurate and rapid appreciation of the situation, Subedar Narinjan Singh ordered his platoon to attack. He led the attack to capture the position at the point of the bayonet, driving out the enemy, who fled, leaving a quantity of automatic weapons, rifles and other equipment. By his resolution, courage and skilful handling of his platoon Subedar Narinjan Singh was responsible for capturing, under very difficult conditions a feature, which was essential for the further advance of the Brigade. Subedar Narinjan Singh has constantly shown great personal courage and outstanding leadership, and was an inspiration to his Company throughout the operation." Subedar Narinjan Singh was awarded the Military Cross on 11TH August 1944.

JEMADAR MEHAR SINGH
INDIAN ENGINEERS

"From 30TH March 1944, Jemadar Mehar Singh was in charge of a working party of men, on Mt. Cairo in Italy. On the night of April 4TH, six shells fell in the region where his men were mustering to collect the supplies to carry forward. He immediately made arrangements to evacuate his casualties, rallied the remainder of his men and with complete disregard for personal danger led them, continuously under shell fire, up the steep mountain-side and delivered the supplies to the Infantry. He then conducted the party back to Camp through heavy shell and mortar fire. His excellent presence of mind and outstanding leadership were in no doubt responsible for the supplies getting through." Jemadar Mehar Singh was awarded an immediate Military Cross.

Military Cross (cont.)

SECOND WORLD WAR (cont.)
SUBEDAR SHAM SINGH
16TH PUNJAB REGIMENT

"On 1ST April 1944, when his Company was on a position southwest of Buthidaung in Burma, Subedar Sham Singh was in command of a recce patrol, which was ambushed and encircled by jungle set on fire by the enemy. Subedar Sham Singh kept complete control of his patrol and fought his way out of the ambush wiping out an enemy Light Machine Gun and killing at least four of the enemy. In this action the Patrol lost one man killed. Subedar Sham Singh having withdrawn his Patrol went back, recovered the body, searched the Japanese position and reported the area clear. In this action Subedar Sham Singh was wounded but refused to leave his Company. On the following day Subedar Sham Singh led another patrol against the enemy. After personal recce of a route used by the enemy, he set up an ambush in which 25 Japanese were killed and injuries inflicted on the ones fleeing the ambush. Again on 3RD April Subedar Sham Singh lead a patrol of two sections to the South of Comma position where they encountered the enemy in superior strength. With great dash and gallantry the Subedar personally lead his Patrol in a charge. In the ensuing hand-to-hand fighting six of the enemy was killed with the bayonet, ten by rifle fire and at least fifteen more badly wounded with the loss of only two killed to the patrol. Then Subedar Sham Singh skilfully extricated his patrol under heavy Mortar and Light Machine Gun fire bringing back an enemy body and enemy weapons for identification. He was the last to withdraw after ensuring that his own dead were recovered. In all these actions the Platoons casualties were extremely light. The success obtained by the patrols in these actions was entirely due to the cool-headedness, clear planning and complete disregard for his own safety of Subedar Sham Singh, who throughout by his leadership, example and determination to close with the enemy was an inspiration to his men." Subedar Sham Singh was awarded an immediate Military Cross.

JEMADAR AMAR SINGH
HONG KONG AND SINGAPORE ARTILLERY

"At police Barracks, Mount Pleasant, on the 13TH February 1942 Jemadar Amar Singh was in command of a 40 mm gun. This particular position was subjected to persistent and repeated bombing and machine gun attacks by low flying aircraft throughout the day. Jemadar Amar Singh fought his gun in the coolest possible manner. Never failing to engage a suitable target a bringing down at least one enemy aircraft and certainly damaging others. This action was an inspiration to neighbouring units and was an outstanding feature of days fighting." For his outstanding courage and tenacity Jemadar Amar Singh was awarded the Military Cross in 1942.

Military Cross (cont.)

SECOND WORLD WAR (cont.)
JEMADAR LAL SINGH
INDIAN ARMOURED CORPS

"At Singu in Burma on 11TH February 1945, Jemadar Lal Singh was Commander of one of the leading tanks, which came under heavy and accurate automatic and close range anti tank gunfire. His tank received multiple hits and the petrol tank began to leak. In spite of the grave risk of fire, Jemadar Lall Singh remained in action returning the fire of the guns and making calm and accurate reports to his troop leader. Later while still engaging the gun, which had not yet been silenced, his tank was again penetrated frontally. Jemadar Lall Singh unperturbed reported the position of the flash, which he could now see and with the help of other tanks silenced it. Although his tank had received 13 direct hits of which 3 penetrated, he kept his tank in action until assaulting troops reached the objective, only then halted when all his petrol had expired. His skill, dogged determination and splendid courage were an inspiration to the remainder of the Squadron." Jemadar Lal Singh was strongly recommended for and awarded the Military Cross on 24TH April 1945.

JEMADAR LAL SINGH MC and BAR
INDIAN ARMOURED CORPS

"At Pozut in Burma, on 25TH April 1945, Jemadar Lall Singh encountered a party of Japanese in strongly defended positions. As he was unable to depress the guns of his tank sufficiently to fire at the enemy, he threw grenades from the turret of his tank. The enemy returned fire and wounded him in the shoulder. Undeterred, he dismounted from his tank and by throwing more grenades killed four of the enemy. Unable to dislodge the remainder he returned to the Squadron Commander, to report the situation, and although suffering from his wound led a section of attached Infantry back to the position, where under his leadership the remaining enemy was completely destroyed. Jemadar Lall Singh set a very high example of gallantry and his leadership, and disregard for his personal safety was an inspiration to all ranks." For outstanding services and continuous gallantry in action, Jemadar Lall Singh was awarded an immediate Bar to his Military Cross.

Military Cross (cont.)

SECOND WORLD WAR (cont.)
JEMADAR GURBACHAN SINGH
INDIAN ARMOURED CORPS

"During the attack of Pyawbwe in Burma, on 10TH April 1945, Jemadar Gurbachan Singh was commanding a troop of tanks leading the attack. With superlative dash and vigour, and in order to give the maximum support to the attacking infantry, he led his troop unscathed through a heavily mined area onto the enemy position where he found himself almost on top of two enemy Light Machine Gun posts. Disdaining to reverse his tank, and leaning far out of his turret, he succeeded in throwing grenades into and destroying both positions. He then engaged and destroyed a 70 mm gun, a 37 mm gun, and a Light Machine Gun position, and forced a 75 mm gun to be pulled out of action that was later found abandoned. The alert, fearless, and dashing leadership of Jemadar Gurbachan Singh was commented on by all ranks taking part in the attack and was of great assistance in the capture of the position, which caused the enemy to withdraw that night. Jemadar Gurbachan Singh was strongly recommended for and awarded the Military Cross on 24TH May 1945"

JEMADAR PRITAM SINGH
INDIAN ARMOURED CORPS

"Jemadar Pritam Singh has fought in all the actions in which "A" Squadron had been engaged, from the period between crossing the Irrawaddy until the capture of Pegu in Burma. Throughout this campaign he has commanded his tank with extreme competence and effect, and his conduct has been deserving of very high praise. He has twice been wounded, and once burnt, when his tank was destroyed by an enemy action on 28TH April 1945. He has always shown tremendous keenness to close with the enemy, and has fought his tank with an efficiency and relish for action, which called for the highest praise. His conduct throughout has been a constant source of inspiration to the men under his command, and the object of confidence and admiration of his Squadron Commander." Jemadar Pritam Singh was awarded the Military Cross on 5TH November 1945."

Military Cross (cont.)

SECOND WORLD WAR (cont.)
RISALDAR WARYAM SINGH
INDIAN ARMOURED CORPS

"On 16TH May 1944 Lieutenant Bishops troop of which Risaldar Waryam Singh was the senior Tank Commander was in support of a Company of 2ND Punjab Regiment carrying out an attack on the enemy position at Kanglatongbi in Burma. Early on in the action Lieutenant Bishop was killed and Risaldar Waryam Singh took over the command of the troop. He showed great power of leadership and displayed outstanding dash and initiative. At one time be went forward with one tank ahead of the infantry clearing up small parties of enemy and was ordered to withdraw. Later he received orders to go forward with one tank and rescue the crew of the ditched tank. The tank was extremely difficult to locate, and this operation took an hour to accomplish. During which time he showed great skill and initiative and by his fine example of coolness and imperturbability on the wireless, reassured the trapped crew until he was able to come alongside the tank and take the crew aboard. After this, Risaldar Waryam Singh commanded his troop until the Squadron finally came out of the action at the end of June. Again on 7TH June, the Squadron was in support of 2ND West Yorkshire Regiment. Risaldar Waryam Singh's troop with one Platoon of the Yorkshires was detailed as right flank protection. Here, a considerable amount of enemy opposition was encountered including a 75 mm gun. Throughout this action Risaldar Waryam Singh gave the utmost support to the Infantry and personally knocked out the enemy gun. He maintained his troop in action for 7 hours showing great coolness and resourcefulness during the whole of the action." Risaldar Waryam Singh was strongly recommended for and awarded the Military Cross on 5TH April 1945."

JEMADAR KARTAR SINGH
INDIAN ARTILLERY

"From the 7TH to the 10TH February 1944, between Kreingyaug and east of Ngakyedauk Pass in Burma, during repeated attacks on the gun position, Jemadar Kartar Singh showed great initiative and complete disregard for his own safety. His cheerfulness and calmness under fire served as an inspiring example to all ranks serving under him. He continually moved about from post to post, directing and encouraging the defence, exposing himself thereby to Light Machine Gun fire and grenades at short range." Jemadar Kartar Singh was awarded an immediate Military Cross on the 10TH February 1944.

Military Cross (cont.)

SECOND WORLD WAR (cont.)
RISALDAR HAZARA SINGH
INDIAN ARMOURED CORPS

"At Chaukggyin in Burma on 26TH November 1944, Risaldar Hazara Singh was in command of a troop of tanks leading the advance. The enemy permitted the troop and its escorting infantry platoon to advance right up to his positions before opening heavy automatic and grenade fire on the Infantry and Mortars and Artillery fire on the tanks. The tanks quickly neutralized, the enemy fire then switched accurate fire on to the other enemy positions enabling the infantry platoon to assault the forward enemy posts. Throughout the action, which lasted some two hours, Risaldar Hazara Singh displayed great coolness; skill and initiative in engaging enemy positions, maintaining contact with his Infantry platoon and in sending back clear and accurate information by wireless. He withdrew only on orders from the Infantry Brigade Commander. The success of this action, during which considerable casualties were inflicted on the enemy, was very largely due to the skill, leadership and courage of Risaldar Hazara Singh." Risaldar Hazara Singh was strongly recommended for and awarded the Military Cross on 22ND March 1945.

JEMADAR HAZURA SINGH
INDIAN ARMOURED CORPS

"Between 30TH May and 2ND June 1944 the Division fought its way from Auce to Alatal. Jemadar Hazura Singh was in almost continuous contact with the enemy, and the advance was greatly accelerated by his gallantry, tactical skill and energy. On 31ST May his was the leading troop of the Squadron when it encountered a strong enemy rearguard. Here his gallant and skilful leadership enabled his troop to advance two miles against stiff opposition, capturing many prisoners. At Verlolion, 1ST June, the leading element of the Squadron became pinned by heavy shell and Machine Gun fire. An enemy counter attack from a flank threatened to overrun them. Jemadar Hazura Singh rapidly appreciated the situation, and on his own initiative, led his troop to a position from which it neutralized this threat although he was greatly outnumbered. Throughout the heavy fighting during the second half of June, this officer was always conspicuous for his gallantry. He reorganized parties who had lost their commanders, and greatly helped supporting tanks by collecting information and directing their fire, often from exposed position. Throughout the campaign in Italy, this officer has shown initiative, outstanding leadership and sound tactical judgment, while his devotion to duty and personal gallantry have been a fine example to his men." Jemadar Hazura Singh was awarded the Military Cross on 19TH April 1945.

Military Cross (cont.)

SECOND WORLD WAR (cont.)
RISALDAR JAGIR SINGH
INDIAN ARMOURED CORPS

"On 31ST December 1944, Risaldar Jagir Singh was ordered to take a daylight patrol to the commanding village of Molazzana in Italy, and find out whether it was held, and if possible, obtain identification. While still a mile short of the objective the patrol was heavily fired on from two enemy positions and pinned down. By skilful leadership and clever use of ground, Risaldar Jagir Singh avoided casualties and continued his advance. The patrol reached the outskirts of Molazzana, capturing a prisoner on the way. Valuable information was gained of enemy mortar and defensive positions. Risaldar Jagir Singh appreciated that he must return by another route, but soon after leaving, the village was again heavily fired on. At the same time an Observation Post was located. The patrol attacked the Post and two enemy gunners were captured. Shortly after this the Patrol was engaged from several enemy Posts by small arms, mortar and grenades and a fire fight ensued in which two other ranks were wounded and the prisoners attempted to escape. These were however were recaptured and Risaldar Jagir Singh brought his patrol back complete. The information and identifications gained were of great value and obtained in the face of considerable opposition. Risaldar Jagir Singh showed great gallantry, skill and leadership, throughout, and his initiative and determination were fine example to his men." Risaldar Jagir Singh awarded an immediate Military Cross.

MAJOR MOHINDER SINGH
INDIAN ARTILLERY

"During May, June and July 1944, Major Mohinder Singh commanded his Battery with conspicuous success throughout the operations on the Assam-Burma borders. His technical efficiency, disregard of his own safety under fire, personal encouragement to his subordinates were responsible for the success of such artillery support that was asked for by the Infantry at Kohima, Kidena and Ukhrul. During the arduous march to Ukhrul his initiative, energy and the example he set to men played a major part in the surmounting by his Battery of obstacles of the utmost severity. Throughout these operations Major Mohinder Singh has on all occasions displayed the highest qualities of leadership, devotion to duty, and courage, setting thereby an example, which has been an inspiration to all with whom be, came in contact." Major Mohinder Singh, Singh was strongly recommended for and awarded the Military Cross on 5TH April 1945.

Military Cross (cont.)

SECOND WORLD WAR (cont.)
JEMADAR BABU SINGH
INDIAN ARTILLERY

"On 18TH May 1945, at Zalon, a few miles north of Prome in Burma, Jemadar Babu Singh was the artillery observation officer in an isolated position near the bank of the Irrawaddy. At 0445 hours the Company was heavily attacked and the Company Commander, was badly wounded, and later died. Jemadar Babu Singh took command and moved boldly about encouraging all ranks and for a time himself engaged the enemy with a Bren gun. Later on getting in touch with his guns, he brought down most effective fire on the enemy. At 0900 hours as all communications failed, and the ammunition was running low Jemadar Babu Singh volunteered to try to get out for help in spite of the obvious great risk involved in getting through the enemy ring. But before going far he had attracted the attention of one of our light aircraft. Jemadar Babu Singh recognized it as a plane being used for artillery observation, by improvising various signals, made the pilot understand something of the situation. Shortly after the Jemadar got through a message by wireless for help. At 1015 hours Royal Air Force began to attack the enemy position and then attacked the Company itself with bombs and machine guns, causing several casualties. With complete disregard for his own safety Jemadar Babu Singh at once left his trench, and stood up waving and firing Very Lights in an attempt to show the aircraft that they were friendly. At 1530 hours boats arrived to take away casualties, and he helped the success of their evacuation effectively neutralizing the enemy near the riverbank. During the night the Company was subjected to grenade and gunfire, which caused several casualties. Before dawn the enemy again opened up with automatics, once again Jemadar Babu Singh neutralized the enemy threat. Early on 19TH May after assisting in the making of a fire plan to cover the withdrawal. Jemadar Babu Singh executed the withdrawal most skilfully without further trouble. Throughout, Jemadar Babu Singh displayed exceptional initiative doing much more than his normal duty. His example of courage and coolness was magnificent and inspired many. His skill in directing the fire of his guns and in so successfully covering the Company's final withdrawal earned the praise of all ranks". Jemadar Babu Singh was awarded an immediate Military Cross.

Sikh Gunners

Military Cross (cont.)

SECOND WORLD WAR (cont.)

LIEUTENANT MEHAR SINGH JAWANDA
INDIAN ARTILLERY

"At Sirurukhong in Burma on 14TH June 1944, Lieutenant Mehar Singh was Forward Observation Officer with a Company, which was attacking the village. Owing to the conformation of the ground and to the number of buildings in the village, observation was very limited; clear fields of view of over thirty yards were rarely available. Lieutenant Mehar Singh accompanied the leading platoon of the company in the initial assault onto the forward edge of the village. Immediately entering the village the platoon was held up by heavy rifle and Light Machine Gun fire to their front. From the platoon's position Lieutenant Mehar Singh was unable to pin point accurately the position of the Japanese. Accordingly, he crawled forward until, from a distance of thirty yards, he was able to see the enemy weapon pits. Giving his fire orders from behind a very shallow bund, he brought down fire from the Mountain Battery onto these positions and eliminated them. The platoon advanced and Lieutenant Mehar Singh accompanied it, moving with the leading section. He was constantly on the alert for targets, and once sighted, engaged them without hesitation, and with great accuracy. Lieutenant Mehar Singh displayed complete contempt for personal safety and on several occasions carried out reconnaissance of his targets from forty or fifty yards distance, under persistent and heavy, light and medium machine gun fire. His personal bravery and keenness were exceptional and throughout this action he displayed initiative and dash of a high order in engaging surprise targets. The successes of the attacks were in a large measure due to the excellent control of the Mountain Battery by Lieutenant Mehar Singh." Lieutenant Mehar Singh was awarded the Military Cross on 12TH August 1944.

MAJOR GURBAKSH SINGH
INDIAN MEDICAL SERVICE

"During the attack of M Di Buffalo in Italy, on the 6TH and 7TH October 1944, the Regimental Aid Post in which Major Gurbaksh Singh was tending his wounded came under heavy enemy shelling on many occasions. Twice the Regimental Aid Post was hit, but this unit Medical Officer continued on imperturbably, with complete disregard of his own personal danger. His only thought was to attend to the casualties and he only moved his Regimental Aid Post on the order of the Commanding Officer. Throughout this action Major Gurbaksh Singh, inspite of 47 years of age, with his courage and determination was instrumental in maintaining a very high standard of morale. Major Gurbaksh Singh was awarded an immediate Military Cross followed by the DSO on 21ST November 1944."

Military Cross (cont.)

SECOND WORLD WAR (cont.)

JEMADAR BUDH SINGH
INDIAN ARTILLERY

"On 7TH July 1944, at Chepu in Burma, the 3RD Mountain Battery were across the lines of withdrawal of a large party of Japanese, who attacked desperately all day in an effort to breakthrough. Jemadar Budh Singh with about twenty men of his battery took over a sector of the position just below a ridge whence the main strength of the enemy attacks developed. When a party on his flank was driven back, Jemadar Budh Singh's party held their ground and continued successfully to engage the enemy at a range of few yards though their flank was temporarily left open. Jemadar Budh Singh acted with conspicuous gallantry and his determination to hold his ground and to beat the enemy off was an inspiration to his men. Though wounded, he continued to carry out his duties and set a fine example of leadership and courage." Jemadar Budh Singh was awarded an immediate Military Cross.

MAJOR UTTAM SINGH SIDHU
INDIAN MEDICAL SERVICE

"Major Uttam Singh was Officer Commanding 4TH Bearer Company during the fighting beyond Tiddim, in Burma Throughout this period he was responsible for their devoted and arduous work in extremely difficult country. In and attack on 16TH December 1943, in particular, his leadership and example were outstanding. Often under heavy fire, he organised his men forward of the Regiment Aid Post and evacuated casualties from behind the heaviest fighting. He was later second-in-command of 37TH Field Ambulance and in the absence of his Commanding Officer an officiating A.D.M.S., had been thrust upon him. During the withdrawal of the Division, the heavy responsibility not only of collecting casualties from delaying actions but of safely conveying them some 160 miles to Imphal, the casualties and sick gradually mounting to 1000. He carried out this unexpected and difficult task with great initiative and determination. When they came under enemy shellfire, his fine example of courage, devotion to duty and disregard of his own safety inspired confidence in both wounded and medical personnel and was largely responsible for their safe conduct. His behaviour was worthy of the highest traditions of the Indian Army." Major Uttam Singh was strongly recommended for and awarded the Military Cross on 1ST August 1945.

Military Cross (cont.)

SECOND WORLD WAR (cont)

HARBANS SINGH
INDIAN MEDICAL SERVICE

"On 11TH April 1945, during the assault across the River Santerno in the CA DI Lugo area in Italy, Lieutenant Harbans Singh was Regimental Medical Officer of Frontier Force Regiment, Having treated and evacuated men wounded in the early stages of the operation, and not satisfied with the speed at which casualties were reaching the Regimental Aid Post, he moved forward to the river bank. There he showed outstanding courage in collecting groups of casualties, dressing them and evacuating them by Jeep. Regardless of heavy shelling and the risk of walking into minefields, which were known to be thickly laid in the area and had not yet been marked, he continued this splendid work throughout the night and into the following day. In this period a hundred and twenty casualties from the Battalion and supporting arms passed through his hands, His outstanding work, far beyond the call of duty, he was and inspiration to all who saw him, and maintained the high morale of the forward Companies, under the most difficult conditions." Lieutenant Harbans Singh was awarded an immediate Military Cross.

CAPTAIN RATTAN SINGH SAHI
INDIAN MEDICAL SERVICE

"During the operations on the Mareth Line on the night 27/28 March 1943, five platoons of the Battalion had advanced t seize the "Delhi" feature. The night was very dark and the route not only precipitous but strewn with Anti Personnel Mines. After the two platoons had reached their objective, the carrying party signalled they were held up by an "S" minefield and booby traps and had suffered five casualties. They were then 300 feet from the top of the feature. Captain Sahi without hesitation and without guide climbed some 1500 feet through minefields and, under fire, with his stretcher bearers and reached the carrying party, still held up with essential weapons and ammunition, he went forward and reconnoitred a safe route through the Anti Personnel minefields to the summit for the party. By his courage and devotion to duty he was able to evacuate the wounded and extricate the carrying party from a difficult situation. During the operations in the Wadi Akarit area in North Africa, on 6TH April 1943, Captain Sahi invariably proceeded immediately to the area where casualties were the heaviest. On many occasions he attended wounded under heavy concentrated enemy fire. This officer has all times set a splendid example to all ranks by his coolness under fire and, by his devotion to duty, has undoubtedly saved many lives." Captain Rattan Singh Sahi was awarded the Military Cross on 10TH April 1943.

Military Cross (cont.)

SECOND WORLD WAR (cont.)

CAPTAIN HARDIT SINGH AHLUWALIA
INDIAN MEDICAL SERVICE

"During the fighting at Keren in Eritrea, on 15TH to 27TH March 1941, Captain Ahluwalia did outstanding work. He commanded the A.D.S. behind the 11TH Indian Infantry Brigade and organised the evacuation of wounded with such skill that in one day alone 860 passed through. The line of evacuation lay along a track winding down the precipitous hillside. This necessitated bearer posts at intervals along it. The whole area was under close and accurate artillery and mortar fire. The A.D.S. itself was hit. The track was, of course, a special target. Captain Ahluwalia was indefatigable and ubiquitous. He was constantly up and down the hill supervising the work of evacuation, and encouraging his stretcher-bearers. His cheerful disregard of fire, and cool devotion to duty in addition to his capacity for organization, won the admiration of all and were undoubtedly responsible for the smooth evacuation of casualties in circumstances of the greatest difficulty. His gallantry and efficiency under fire and in conditions imposing great physical effort and fatigue over a prolonged period of heavy fighting are worthy of recognition." Captain Ahluwalia was awarded an immediate Military Cross.

BANTA SINGH
ROYAL INDIAN ARMY SERVICE CORPS

"In Letmauk Area in Burma from 20TH to 28TH March, Risaldar Banta Singh was commanding a party of 58 AT Company detached form its parent unit and under command of 2ND Infantry Brigade. The later operations of this Brigade lay through trackless and dense bamboo jungle and culminated in their being surrounded by the enemy and forced to remain in a defended locality for over three weeks until extricated. The terrain embraced by this defended area was most unsuitable for any pack animals and ponies in particular. The area was repeatedly attacked, jittered and subjected to harassing fire by the Japanese. In spite of all these adverse conditions and the fact that he spoke no English and the West Africans knew no Urdu, Risaldar Banta Singh displayed outstanding qualities of initiative, leadership, calmness and devotion to duty, Throughout he cheerfully rendered the maximum assistance to his Brigade and all officers who came in contact with him have nothing but the highest praise for his actions, which were an example and inspiration to British, Indians and Africans. His animal management during this most arduous and trying period was of such high order that casualties to men and animals were remarkably slight. The behavior and example of Risaldar Banta Singh were throughout those of highly courageous and devoted soldier." Risaldar Banta Singh was strongly recommended for and awarded the Military Cross on 17TH January 1946.

Military Cross (cont.)

SECOND WORLD WAR (cont.)

JEMADAR JAGIT SINGH
ROYAL INDIAN ARMY SERVICE CORPS

"During May 1944, Jemadar Jagit Singh was a troop commander and took part in the operations before Orsogna in Italy. He was responsible for the maintenance of forward and isolated Infantry companies. His troop headquarters was often shelled by day and the tracks he had to use by night were known to the enemy and strongly patrolled. On several occasions his mule train clashed with the enemy but his bold and efficient leadership never failed to ensure the arrival of the mules and their loads. In August 1944, he was made acting Indian Adjutant just before the assault crossing of the River Arno began. His increased responsibilities took him into contact with all lower sections of the Company. One many occasions he fearlessly rendered first aid to the wounded drivers, he evacuated wounded animals and organised the salvage of saddlery under most severe conditions. Day after day he walked over the exposed hillsides frequently in full view of the enemy, under mortar and artillery fire, in order to visit forward sections where he inspired the men by his personal bravery and contempt for danger, at the same time he encouraged the muleteers, in spite of fatigue, discomfort, and danger, to take all necessary steps to maintain the condition of their animals and efficiency of their equipment. Throughout this period, under great strain and hazardous circumstances, he maintained the utmost cheerfulness. His was in complete control of every situation, from holding off enemy patrol to organising a grooming parade, after exhausting night under fire. He was an inspiration to the whole unit". Jemadar Jagit Singh was awarded the Military Cross on 24TH February 1945.

JEMADAR SARWAN SINGH
BURMA REGIMENT

"On the night 11/12 May 1946, Jemadar Sarwan Singh, The Burma Regiment, was in command of a platoon, which was in action against a desperate gang of Decoits at Butt Erfly Bend, near MA-URIN, in the Delta. The fire of the Dacoits was accurate and caused the death of two Sepoys, which in turn caused the troops to hold back. However, Jemadar Sarwan Singh rallied his men and retrieved the situation with a gallant charge, which resulted in the rout of the dacoits of whom a number were killed, wounded and captured." Jemadar Sarwan Singh was awarded the Military Cross on 26TH August 1946.

Military Cross (cont.)

SECOND WORLD WAR (cont.)

CAPTAIN INDERJIT SINGH GILL
ROYAL ENGINEERS

This Citation was marked "Most Secret" and it was requested that no details should be made public or communicated to the Press.

"On 30TH May 1943, instructions were sent to Brigadier Myers to arrange for the cutting of all the main North to South communications in Greece between the end of June and the first week in July. Plans had already been prepared for this eventuality and Brigadier Myers issued instructions for all the main roads and the railway and all telephone lines to be cut on 21ST June 1943, and to be kept out of order by further demolitions up to 7TH July, with a view to making them unusable for a further seven days i.e., up to 14TH July. This series of operations was known an Operation "Animals". During the period 21ST June to 10TH July, the British personnel of Brigadier Myers's mission were employed night after night on different operations throughout Greece cutting road and railway. Owing to the greater reliability of British personnel, only small proportion of the total Andarti (Greek Partisans) strength was made use of. The success of Operation "Animals" was due to the magnificent way in which the British personnel acted under the command of the four senior Liaison officers under whom Brigadier Myers had decentralized responsibility for areas throughout Greece. Captain Gill proceeded in mufti with Major Barker on reconnaissance of the railway on the South side edge of the Thessaly Plath between 14TH and 18TH June. This reconnaissance necessitated a night's journey across the Plain on horseback, and, due to enemy patrolling, the reconnaissance itself to be carried out in mufti. Four days later he returned with explosives and one Andarti assistant and successfully demolished a bridge to the South of Proerna. During the reconnaissance and during the actual operations he showed greatest coolness and courage and complete disregard for personal danger. Due to the proximity of German patrols on the railway, he was at all times in grave risk of being discovered. The successful achievement of this operation was entirely due to his personal gallantry. During the past three months Captain Gill's work has been of the very highest order. He has constantly worked unsparingly and his work has been an inspiration to the Andarti with him." Captain Inderjit Singh Gill was awarded an immediate Military Cross on 23RD December 1943. Captain Gill transferred to the Indian Army in 1945 and eventually achieved the rank of Lieutenant General.

Military Cross (cont.)

SECOND WORLD WAR (cont.)

SUBEDAR SUKH SINGH
INDIAN ARTILLERY

"As senior Subedar of the Regiment, Subedar Sukh Singh was specially attached to Scindia Battery. His tact and powers of leadership were most striking. But more than this his complete coolness under shellfire and courageous example, which steadied the soldiers, exposed to fire for the first time, were admired by every man in the Battery and transcended all considerations of different castes. Notably at Kyigon in Burma on March 15TH he assisted in evacuating casualties to the Regimental Aid Post when a gun pit received a direct hit from a shell, and shells continued to fall the troop position. Again he displayed courage of the highest order when at Meiktila Dropping Zone. A serious ammunition fire had broken out, ignoring the danger from exploding mortar bombs he personally led a party of his own men in an attempt to drag valuable stores and ammunition to safety. A parachute ignited a mortar bomb close to him and he was severely wounded in the leg, but continued to encourage the only organised party, until he fainted from his wound. His courage and leadership on this occasion were beyond praise." Subedar Sukh Singh was strongly recommended for and awarded the Military Cross on 16TH November 1945.

JEMADAR MEWA SINGH
INDIAN ENGINEERS

"Jemadar Mewa Singh has shown outstanding leadership since joining this unit. He has the full confidence of his men who will follow him into any danger. This was particularly shown on 3RD September 1944, at Montetrini in Italy, when his platoon was consistently shelled for two hours whilst they were making road diversion. After each concentration of shells had landed he collected his men and quickly led them back to their task and thus finished the work in the quickest possible time. Again between 1ST and 6TH November 1944, he was in charge of a detachment in support of 5TH RGR in Tredo Zio in Italy, and carried out a series of bold reconnaissance for jeep tracks. He always carried on until held up by accurate enemy small arms or mortar fire.

Again on the East road in the Serchio Valley on 30TH December 1944, whilst acting in support of the 6TH Lancers, he led a reconnaissance party ahead of the armoured cars to the blown bridge. His party came under mortar fire but he completed the recce until just short of Castelvecchio where he came under close range small arms fire. His report provided valuable information for forward planning." Jemadar Mewa Singh was strongly recommended for and awarded the Military Cross on 16TH April 1945.

Military Cross (cont.)

SECOND WORLD WAR (cont.)

JEMADAR NAND SINGH
INDIAN ENGINEERS

"In Arakan, Burma, whilst engaged on operations for the capture of the Westraji Tunnel on the Maungdaw-Buthidaung road on 26th March 1944, Jemadar Nand Singh was in charge of his section erecting S.B.G. bridge over a bridge, which had been demolished by the enemy. The work was carried out under fire from enemy snipers. He organised the whole of this task, which was not finished until the following morning. During the night there were Japanese in close proximity and the Section was sniped and mortared. As soon as the bridge was finished, this enabled tanks to get up to the mouth of the Tunnel and to clear the enemy. Later in the operations in the Eastern Tunnel with some of his section he lifted enemy mines laid on the road near the Tunnel and carried out a reconnaissance into the enemy territory. During the whole period his keenness, and of danger from enemy action set high example to his men which inspired them with confidence, and by his leadership enabled them to carry out their duties of a highly efficient manner. "Jemadar Nand Singh was strongly recommended for and awarded the Military Cross on 26TH October 1944.

SUBEDAR BHAGAT SINGH
INDIAN ENGINEERS

"Over a long period as Subedar of 69TH Indian Field Company and especially since 8TH Indian Division came to Italy in September 1943, Subedar Bhagat Singh has shown himself to be an outstanding officer in leadership, efficiency and devotion to duty, and disregard of personal danger. His qualities as a leader were particularly outstanding during the operations in the Serchio Valley in January 1945; when his Company was called upon to perform series of bridging operations under accurate enemy fire. The most noteworthy were at L192005 and L83002. Subedar Bhagat Singh was present at all these operations and gave continuous encouragement to his men both by word and by his reassuring presence. In this manner be ensured the earliest construction of the bridges and contribute greatly to the success of ensuing operations. A senior officer in the Divisional Engineers Subedar Bhagat Singh had frequently acted as an advisor in the matters of personnel. By his sound judgment and advice he has thus also contributed largely to the smooth running and general efficiency in battle of the whole Division of Sappers." Subedar Bhagat Singh was awarded the Military Cross on 13TH September 1945.

Military Cross (cont.)

SECOND WORLD WAR

MILITARY CROSS AND BAR

During the Second World War the following Indian officers were awarded a Bar to their Military Cross, that is, they won the MC again.

11TH SIKH REGIMENT

| SUBEDAR | GURCHARAN SINGH | 1945 | BURMA |

1ST PUNJAB REGIMENT

| LT. | BUDH SINGH | 1943 | BURMA |

8TH PUNJAB REGIMENT

| CAPTAIN | GIRDHARI SINGH | 1944 | ITALY |

INDIAN ARMOURED CORPS

| JEMADAR | LALL SINGH | 1945 | BURMA |

ROYAL INDIAN ARTILLARY

| HAVILDAR | SINGH | 1944 | BURMA |

INDIAN DISTINGUISHED SERVICE MEDAL
1914 – 1921

Instituted in 1907, the Indian Distinguished Service Medal was awarded for distinguished services in the field for Indian commissioned and non-commissioned officers and men of the Indian regular forces. The order was removed when India became independent in 1947.

During the First World War the Indian Cavalry in France consisted of the 1st Indian Cavalry Division and 2nd Indian Cavalry Division. A total of fourteen regiments of the Indian cavalry went to France in 1914.There were two regiments each in the three cavalry brigades in each of the two cavalry divisions and one regiment in each of the two infantry division as divisional reconnaissance regiments. The Indian Cavalry endured the severest test of trench warfare in a totally unfamiliar climate and stood up to undreamed of artillery bombardments with cheerful fortitude. Field Marshal Sir Douglas Haig sent the following farewell message: "As the Indian Cavalry regiments are now leaving France, I wish to record my very great appreciation of the valour, determination and devotion to duty shown by all ranks in the field. Indian officers, non-commissioned officers and men have been absent for more than three years in a foreign country, thousands of kilometres from their home and families, in a climate to which they are totally unaccustomed, and have by their gallant deeds added even greater lustre to the already glorious names of their respective regiments."

2ND LANCERS (GARDNER'S HORSE)

During the First World War, the 2ND Lancers were sent to France as part of the Mhow Cavalry Brigade, 2ND Indian Cavalry Division. Once in France, when called upon, they served in the trenches as infantry. During their time in France, the regiment was involved in the Battles of the Somme, Bazentin, Flers Courcelette, the advance to the Hindenburg Line and the Battle of Cambrai. The Regiment's only Victoria Cross during the First World War was awarded to Lance-Daffadar Gobind Singh. The following Sikh officers and sowars were awarded the Indian Distinguished Service Medal for their gallantry in France.
(Continued on next page)

Indian Distinguished Service Medal, 1914 - 1921 (cont.)

2ND LANCERS (GARDNER'S HORSE) (cont.)

JEMADAR	DHARA SINGH	1917	FRANCE
KOT DAFFADAR	DHARAM SINGH	1918	FRANCE
SOWAR	MOHAN SINGH	1918	FRANCE
LANCE DAFFADAR	SOBHA SINGH	1918	FRANCE
SOWAR	AMAR SINGH	1918	FRANCE
SOWAR	SOHAN SINGH	1918	FRANCE
SOWAR	KEHAR SINGH	1918	FRANCE
DAFFADAR	RAM SINGH	1918	FRANCE
SOWAR	LAHORA SINGH	1918	FRANCE
SOWAR	HARNAM SINGH	1919	LEBANON
LANCE DAFFADAR	NAND SINGH	1919	LEBANON
SOWAR	DULEEP SINGH	1919	LEBANON
SOWAR	ARJAN SINGH	1919	LEBANON

9TH HODSON'S HORSE

The 9TH Hodson's Horse sailed for France in October 1914 and returned to India on 1ST January 1921. During their time on the Western Front the regiment fought at the Battles of Somme and Cambrai. It still recalls Cambrai as the regiment's most splendid battle, and celebrates Cambrai Day every year. The following Sikh officers and sowars were awarded the Indian Distinguished Service Medal for their gallantry in France and Flanders.

LANCE DAFFADAR	PAREETAM SINGH	1917	FRANCE
SOWAR	SUJJAN SINGH	1917	FRANCE
SOWAR	SARAIN SINGH	1918	FRANCE
RESSAIDAR	HARDIT SINGH	1918	FRANCE
SOWAR	KAPUR SINGH	1918	FRANCE
LANCE DAFFADAR	RATTAN SINGH	1918	FRANCE

Indian Distinguished Service Medal, 1914 – 1921 (cont

10TH DCO LANCERS (HODSON'S HORSE)

The 10TH Lancers were not to serve in France during the First World War but went to Mesopotamia, where they took part in the capture of Baghdad, Khan Baghdadi and finally Mosul. The regiment had played a major part in defeating the Turks in Mesopotamia. The following Sikh officers and Sowars were awarded the Indian Distinguished Service Medal for their gallantry in Mesopotamia.

RISALDAR	LABH SINGH	1919	MESOPOTAMIA
DAFFADAR MAJOR	KIRPAL SINGH	1920	MESOPOTAMIA
SOWAR	SUNDAR SINGH	1920	MESOPOTAMIA
SOWAR	BAHAL SINGH	1920	MESOPOTAMIA
SOWAR	SARWAN SINGH	1920	MESOPOTAMIA
DAFFADAR	MAHTAB SINGH	1920	MESOPOTAMIA

11TH KEO LANCERS (PROBYN'S HORSE)

During the First World War, the regiment sent drafts to other units fighting in France, Egypt, and East Africa and served in the Black Mountain Expedition in Waziristan. However their main engagements were fought in Mesopotamia. The following Sikh officers and Sowars were awarded the Indian Distinguished Service Medal for their gallantry.

LANCE NAIK	RAM SINGH	1917	EAST AFRICA
L / DAFFADAR	LASHKAR SINGH	1917	EAST AFRICA
RISALDAR	RAM SINGH	1917	WAZIRISTAN
DAFFADAR	DALIP SINGH	1918	EGYPT
DAFFADAR	RAM SINGH	1918	EGYPT
SOWAR	MOHAN SINGH	1918	FRANCE
SOWAR	RAM SINGH	1918	FRANCE
SOWAR	FAUJA SINGH	1918	FRANCE
SOWAR	BHAG SINGH	1920	MESOPOTAMIA
SOWAR	LAKHA SINGH	1921	MESOPOTAMIA
LANCE DAFFADAR	ARJAN SINGH	1921	MESOPOTAMIA
SOWAR	AMAR SINGH	1921	MESOPOTAMIA

Indian Distinguished Service Medal, 1914 – 1921 (cont.)

12TH CAVALRY

Like its sister regiment 11TH Keo Lancers, the 12TH Cavalry did not serve in France but went to Mesopotamia in 1918. The 12TH distinguished itself in the second battle of Kut. The regiment then commenced the pursuit to Baghdad and kept up constant pressure on the withdrawing Turks. The regiment was present at the final defeat of the Turks in Mesopotamia. The following Sikh soldiers were awarded the Indian Distinguished Service Medal for their gallantry during the Mesopotamian campaign.

DAFFADAR	WARYAM SINGH	1918	MESOPOTAMIA
LANCE DAFFADAR	MEHR SINGH	1918	MESOPOTAMIA
LANCE DAFFADAR	PASHAORA SINGH	1919	MESOPOTAMIA
LANCE DAFFADAR	CHANAN SINGH	1919	MESOPOTAMIA
LANCE DAFFADAR	SANTA SINGH	1919	MESOPOTAMIA
LANCE DAFFADAR	JAGAT SINGH	1919	MESOPOTAMIA
DAFFADAR	KARTAR SINGH	1919	MESOPOTAMIA
LANCE DAFFADAR	INDAR SINGH	1919	MESOPOTAMIA
LANCE DAFFADAR	NARAIN SINGH	1919	MESOPOTAMIA
LANCE DAFFADAR	BHAN SINGH	1917	MESOPOTAMIA

13TH DOC LANCERS (WATSON'S HORSE)

During the First World War the regiment remained on the North West Frontier of India until July 1916, when the regiment was moved to Mesopotamia for the relief of Kut al Amara. The regiment proceeded to attack the Turks at Ctesiplhon, Tigris, Sharqat and finally at the capture of Baghdad. The following Sikh soldiers were awarded the Indian Distinguished Service Medal for their conspicuous gallantry in Mesopotamia.

SOWAR	UJAGAR SINGH	1917	MESOPOTAMIA
JEMADAR	JAGPAL SINGH	1918	MESOPOTAMIA
SOWAR	PURAN SINGH	1918	MESOPOTAMIA
RISALDAR	AJIT SINGH	1919	MESOPOTAMIA
RESSAIDAR	NARAIN SINGH	1919	MESOPOTAMIA
DAFFADAR	PREM SINGH	1919	MESOPOTAMIA
DAFFADAR	INDAR SINGH	1919	MESOPOTAMIA

Indian Distinguished Service Medal, 1914 – 1921 (cont.)

16TH CAVALRY

During the First World War the regiment remained in India but sent detachments to serve in Egypt, Mesopotamia and Persia. The following Sikh soldiers were awarded Indian Distinguished Service Medal for their gallantry in these theatres of war.

LANCE DAFFADAR	KALA SINGH	1915	MESOPOTAMIA
LANCE DAFFADAR	PHUMAN SINGH	1915	MESOPOTAMIA
SOWAR	PHUMAN SINGH	1915	MESOPOTAMIA
SOWAR	NIKKA SINGH	1915	MESOPOTAMIA
SOWAR	KIRPAL SINGH	1916	BUSHIRE
SOWAR	ATMA SINGH	1916	BUSHIRE
LANCE DAFFADAR	GUJAR SINGH	1918	EGYPT
SOWAR	HAZARA SINGH	1918	EGYPT

19TH LANCERS (FANE'S HORSE)

During the First World War, 19TH Lancers were sent to France and fought in the Battles of Ypres, Somme, Cayeux, Arras, Cambrai; and pursued the Germans to the Hindenburg Line. In 1918 they moved to Egypt for the Palestine Campaign, where they were attached to the 4TH Cavalry Division and fought at the Battles of Tel el Kebir, Aleppo, and advancing to the Jordan Valley where they were involved in the capture of Damascus. The following Sikh soldiers were awarded the Indian Distinguished Service Medal for their gallantry and leadership.

DAFFADAR	SANT SINGH	1917	FRANCE
LANCE DAFFADAR	BHAGAT SINGH	1917	FRANCE
RISALDAR MAJOR	HIRA SINGH	1918	FRANCE
RISALDAR	MOTI SINGH	1918	FRANCE
SOWAR	SUNDAR SINGH	1918	FRANCE
SOWAR	KISHEN SINGH	1918	FRANCE
SOWAR	BISHAN SINGH	1918	FRANCE
RESSAIDAR	DIDAN SINGH	1919	EGYPT
RESSAIDAR	INDAR SINGH	1919	EGYPT

Indian Distinguished Service Medal, 1914 – 1921 (cont.)

20TH DECCAN HORSE

The 20TH Deccan Horse was sent to France for service on the Western Front and was part of the 9TH Cavalry Brigade of the 2nd Indian Cavalry Division. They would at times serve as infantry in the trenches. The regiment was involved in the Battles of Givenchy, Somme, Bazentin, Devil Wood, Flers Courcelettes and Cambrai, before being withdrawn for service in Palestine. The following Sikh soldiers were awarded the Indian Distinguished Service Medal for their gallantry and leadership in battle.

SOWAR	SIRDAR SINGH	1917	FRANCE
RESSAIDAR	DALIP SINGH	1917	FRANCE
KOT DAFFADAR	HIRA SINGH	1917	FRANCE
JEMADAR	DALIP SINGH	1918	FRANCE
RISALDAR	BACHANT SINGH	1919	EGYPT

21ST PAVO CAVALRY (FRONTIER FORCE)

During the First World War the regiment had arrived in Mesopotamia and was to take part in the advance to Baghdad and finally capture Mosul. The 21ST Cavalry joined Cassel's column in Baghdad and took part in the action at Shatt-el-Adheim. In the course of the long pursuit after capturing 800 prisoners, the regiment charged a Turkish column and captured another 1,000 prisoners. The following Sikh soldiers were awarded the Indian Distinguished Service Medal for their outstanding feat of arms in Mesopotamia.

DAFFADAR	SANTOKH SINGH	1918	MESOPOTAMIA
SOWAR	AVTAR SINGH	1918	MESOPOTAMIA
SOWAR	KISHEN SINGH	1918	MESOPOTAMIA

22ND SAM BROWN'S CAVALRY (FRONTIER FORCE)

It was 1916 before the regiment arrived for service in Mesopotamia. It proceeded to attack the Turks at Ctesiphon, Tigris, Sharqat and finally to capture Baghdad. The following Sikh officers were awarded the Indian Distinguished Service Medal for their gallantry in their pursuit and defeat of Turks in Mesopotamia.

RESSAIDAR	HARNAM SINGH	1919	MESOPOTAMIA
RISALDAR	SUKHPAL SINGH	1919	MESOPOTAMIA

Indian Distinguished Service Medal, 1914 – 1921 (cont.)

23RD CAVALRY (FRONTIER FORCE)

During the First World War the regiment had arrived in Mesopotamia and was to take part in the advance to Baghdad and finally to capture Mosul. They chased a Turkish battalion, sabred 100 and captured 350. They fought at Sharqat on their advance to capture Mosul. The following Sikh soldiers were awarded the Indian Distinguished Service Medal for their gallantry in Mesopotamia as well as the cavalrymen who had volunteered to fight in France and East Africa.

DAFFADAR	SHER SINGH	1917	FRANCE
LANCE NAIK	BAHADUR SINGH	1918	EAST AFRICA
DAFFADAR	BHAGAT SINGH	1919	MESOPOTAMIA
DAFFADAR	HARDITT SINGH	1919	MESOPOTAMIA
DAFFADAR	SANT SINGH	1920	MESOPOTAMIA

25TH CAVALRY (FRONTIER FORCE)

During the First World War the 25TH Cavalry went to German East Africa and joined in the pursuit of the German general Von Lettow Voreck to the Mozambique border. They were withdrawn from cavalry operations in the face of the depredations of the tsetse fly on their horses. They were back at home in time for the Third Anglo-Afghan War, to face the Afghans across the North West Frontier of India. The following Sikh soldiers were awarded the Indian Distinguished Service Medal for their gallantry in East Africa and on the North West Frontier of India.

LANCE DAFFADAR	SOHAN SINGH	1915	EAST AFRICA
KOT DAFFADAR	SUBA SINGH	1915	EAST AFRICA
SOWAR	BUDH SINGH	1919	N. W. FRONTIER

30TH LANCERS (GORDON'S HORSE)

During the First World War the Regiment was part of the Ambala Cavalry Brigade, 1ST Indian Cavalry Division. They were sent to France for service on the Western Front where they at times would serve in the trenches as infantry. The Regiment stayed in France until March 1918, when the division was broken up and reformed in Egypt. Jemadar Kapur Singh was awarded the Indian Distinguished Service Medal for his conspicuous gallantry whilst fighting in the trenches.

JEMADAR	KAPUR SINGH	1916	FRANCE

Indian Distinguished Service Medal, 1914 – 1921 (cont.)

29TH LANCERS (DECCAN HORSE)

The 29TH Lancers with its sister regiment, the 20TH Deccan Horse, was sent to France for service on the Western Front and was part of the 9TH Cavalry Brigade of the 2ND Indian Cavalry Division. The cavalrymen would at times serve as infantry in the trenches. The regiment fought in the Battles of Givenchy, Somme, Bazentin, Devil Wood, Flers Courcelettes, and Cambrai, before being withdrawn for service in Palestine and Egypt. The following Sikh soldiers were awarded the Indian Distinguished Service Medal for their gallantry and leadership in battle.

RISALDAR	CHANDA SINGH	1917	FRANCE
JEMADAR	MAHAN SINGH	1917	FRANCE
SOWAR	HIRA SINGH	1917	FRANCE
JEMADAR	NATHA SINGH	1918	FRANCE
SOWAR	KHEM SINGH	1919	EGYPT
SOWAR	NIKA SINGH	1919	EGYPT

31ST DCO LANCERS

During the First World War, the 31ST remained on the North West Frontier of India. They fought in the Third Afghan War earning two gallantry awards in Waziristan. The regiment had also supplied volunteers to fight in Egypt. The following Sikh soldiers were awarded the Indian Distinguished Service Medal for their conspicuous gallantry.

RISALDAR	KABUL SINGH	1919	EGYPT
SOWAR	KARAM SINGH	1919	EGYPT
SOWAR	CHANAN SINGH	1919	EGYPT
SOWAR	SUNDAR SINGH	1919	EGYPT
RESSAIDAR	INDER SINGH	1919	WAZIRISTAN
LANCE DAFFADAR	UTTAM SINGH	1919	WAZIRISTAN

Indian Distinguished Service Medal, 1914 – 1921 (cont.)

32ND LANCERS

The 32ND Lancers went to Mesopotamia in 1916 and were the first Imperial troops to enter Baghdad. One wing of the 32ND Lancers, together with the 21ST Cavalry, during the course of the pursuit, charged a Turkish column and captured 1,000 prisoners. In 1917, they made their famous charge, coming against an entrenched Turkish position, charging without any hesitation and suffering heavy casualties. The following Sikh soldiers were awarded the Indian Distinguished Service Medal for their gallantry in Mesopotamia.

SOWAR	BAHADUR SINGH	1917	MESOPOTAMIA
LANCE DAFFADAR	TARA SINGH	1917	MESOPOTAMIA
RESSAIDAR	SUNDAR SINGH	1918	MESOPOTAMIA
DAFFADAR	JIWAN SINGH	1918	MESOPOTAMIA
JEMADAR	BACHITAR SINGH	1921	MESOPOTAMIA

33RD QVO LIGHT CAVALRY

The 33ND went to Mesopotamia in October 1914 to carry out reconnaissance and establish some standing patrols. One of the Patrols clashed with the Turks and lost an officer and a Sowar. The regiment was attacked while digging trenches by a force of 1,000 Arabs, which they repulsed without serious loss. After the abortive attempt to relieve Kut, the regiment returned to India to reinforce and refit. The following Sikh soldiers were awarded the Indian Distinguished Service Medal for their gallantry in Mesopotamia.

SOWAR	BUTA SINGH	1915	MESOPOTAMIA
SOWAR	MANGAL SINGH	1915	MESOPOTAMIA
LANCE DAFFADAR	KHARAK SINGH	1916	MESOPOTAMIA
DAFFADAR	DARBARA SINGH	1916	MESOPOTAMIA
DAFFADAR	MANGAL SINGH	1916	MESOPOTAMIA
KOT DAFFADAR	SHAM SINGH	1919	MESOPOTAMIA

Indian Distinguished Service Medal, 1914 – 1921 (cont.)

38TH KGO CENTRAL INDIA HORSE

The 38TH went to France in December 1914 as part of the Mhow Brigade of the 2ND Indian Cavalry Division. The regiment was involved in the first Battle of Ypres, in the first attacks at Neuve Chapelle and the Battles of the Somme, Festubert, Morval, and Cambrai. It had suffered 950 casualties before being withdrawn for service in Egypt and Palestine. The regiment finally returned to India in 1921 after further service in Syria, having spent more than six years abroad. The following Sikh soldiers were awarded the Indian Distinguished Service Medal for their gallantry and leadership.

JEMADAR	RAM SINGH	1917	FRANCE
LANCE DAFFADAR	MEHR SINGH	1917	FRANCE
SOWAR	DURBARA SINGH	1917	FRANCE
DAFFADAR	PARTAB SINGH	1918	FRANCE
DAFFADAR	SHER SINGH	1918	FRANCE
DAFFADAR	KHANDARA SINGH	1918	FRANCE
DAFFADAR	LABH SINGH	1918	FRANCE
DAFFADAR	ARJAN SINGH	1918	FRANCE
SOWAR	NAND SINGH	1918	FRANCE
LANCE DAFFADAR	UJAGGAR SINGH	1918	FRANCE
RISALDAR	NATHA SINGH	1918	FRANCE
DAFFADAR	SHAM SINGH	1918	FRANCE
LANCE DAFFADAR	TARA SINGH	1918	FRANCE
SOWAR	BISHAN SINGH	1919	EGYPT
R. MAJOR	AMAR SINGH	1920	EGYPT

ADEN TROOP

Aden Troop was a small cavalry unit specially raised in India for service in Aden. One of the least known reverses suffered by the British Army in the First World War was that happened at Lahej in early July 1915. The intense heat and insufficient preparations resulted in the repulse against the Turks. Lance Daffadar Hira Singh was awarded the Indian Distinguished Service Medal for his gallantry in this sorry affair.

| DAFFADAR | HIRA SINGH | 1915 | ADEN |

Indian Distinguished Service Medal, 1914 – 1921 (cont.)

ROYAL HORSE ARTILLERY

During the First World War, the Royal Horse Artillery was responsible for light, mobile guns that provided firepower in support of the cavalry and supplemented the Royal Field Artillery. In 1914 there was one battery to each Brigade of Cavalry. It served in France and Flanders until after the armistice. The following Sikh soldiers were awarded the Indian Distinguished Service Medal for their gallantry while serving the guns in France.

DRIVER	LEHNA SINGH	1918	FRANCE
LANCE NAIK	ARJAN SINGH	1918	FRANCE

ROYAL FIELD ARTILLERY

The Royal Field artillery were equipped with medium calibre guns and Howitzers and deployed close to the front lines. It served in France and Flanders until after the armistice. Many acts of heroism were performed by the men of the Royal Field artillery including the following Sikh soldiers who were awarded the Indian Distinguished Service Medal for their gallantry while serving the guns.

DRIVER	MAHARAJ SINGH	1919	FRANCE
DRIVER	NATHA SINGH	1919	FRANCE
H. MAJOR	PIARA SINGH	1919	FRANCE

INDIAN MOUNTAIN ARTILLERY BRIGADE

On 23RD October 1914, the Indian Mountain Artillery Brigade arrived off Bahrain Island in the Persian Gulf. The Brigade co-operated with the Navy in an immediate attack on Fao Peninsula to clear the Turks out of the Shatt al-Arab and was in continuous action to clear the Turks out of Mesopotamia. The following Sikh soldiers were awarded the Indian Distinguished Service Medal for their gallantry while serving the guns in Mesopotamia.

JEMADAR	PHAGA SINGH	1919	MESOPOTAMIA
JEMADAR	SAWAN SINGH	1919	MESOPOTAMIA
LANCE NAIK	GUNGA SINGH	1919	MESOPOTAMIA
LANCE NAIK	HAMEL SINGH	1919	MESOPOTAMIA

MOUNTAIN BATTERY, ROYAL GARRISON ARTILLERY

The Mountain Batteries of the Royal Garrison Artillery served in Salonika from November 1916 to May 1918, where Havildar Kala Singh was awarded the Indian Distinguished Service Medal for his conspicuous gallantry in action.

Indian Distinguished Service Medal, 1914 – 1921 (cont.)

1ST (KOHAT) BATTERY

The story of British and Indian operations in Persia (modern Iran) during the period 1914-20 is quite complicated. There were British-Indian operations against local tribes, military activities to protect supplies and trade routes from robber bands, actions against Army Mutineers and the constant threat (real or imagined) of German or Turkish involvement to stir up anti-British feeling. Major operations were undertaken including the occupation of the port of Bushire (and fighting in its hinterland) in 1915 and 1918. An attack was launched on the regiment at Resht on 20TH July by Jangali troops. The attack was beaten and the following Sikh soldiers were awarded the Indian Distinguished Service Medal for their conspicuous gallantry in this action.

HAVILDAR	JAGGAT SINGH	1919	SOUTH PERSIA
JEMADAR	MUNSHA SINGH	1919	SOUTH PERSIA
GUNNER	KISHEN SINGH	1919	SOUTH PERSIA

EGYPT

On the commencement of the First World War, the first artillery unit to embark from India was the 7TH Indian Mountain Artillery Brigade, comprising the 21ST (Kohat) and 26TH (Jacob's) Mountain batteries. The two mountain batteries took part in the defence of the Suez Canal and played a prominent part in repelling the Turkish attacks at Kantara and Ismailia. The following Sikh soldiers were awarded the Indian Distinguished Service Medal for their gallantry at Suez Canal.

DRIVER	BHOLA SINGH	1915	Suez Canal
GUNNER	GAZAN SINGH	1915	Suez Canal

6TH MOUNTAIN BATTERY

The following Sikh Gunners were awarded the Indian Distinguished Service Medal for their conspicuous gallantry in Mesopotamia.

LANCE NAIK	HARNAM SINGH	1919	MESOPOTAMIA
GUNNER	DALIP SINGH	1919	MESOPOTAMIA
DRIVER	HAZARA SINGH	1919	MESOPOTAMIA

Indian Distinguished Service Medal, 1914 - 1921 (cont.)

DRIVER NARYAN SINGH
21ST KOHAT MOUNTAIN BATTERY

The 21ST Mountain Battery landed at Gallipoli on 25TH April 1915, where the gunners worked closely in support of the Australian and New Zealand Corps. Driver Naryan Singh was awarded the Indian Distinguished Service Medal for many instances of bravery while mending telephone lines under fire. "The only other point worth mentioning before the Suvla Push is the communications. Owing to losses among signallers, and the battery being split up into three bits, each with a distant P.O. We were soon reduced to one signaller per phone who was on duty day and night, always sleeping with his instrument in his ear. The headquarters phone was run by the Mess Orderly, Pyara Singh, in addition to his other duties. We had one linesman only who managed to keep alive during the whole war in some wonderful way. He was always out repairing lines in dangerous places, and two or three times brought back chits from Australian Officers to say they had seen him repairing lines under heavy fire. His name was Naryan Singh and he got an Indian Distinguished Service Medal." *'Anzac, Gallipoli, 1915' by Col. A.C. Ferguson, 21st (Kohat) Mountain Battery.*

GALLIPOLI

During the eight months of fierce fighting the Sikh gunners won the admiration of the troops they supported. Even today greetings are exchanged between Indian Batteries and the Australian and New Zealand Corps on the Regimental Day. The following Sikh soldiers were awarded the Indian Distinguished Service Medal for their conspicuous gallantry at Gallipoli.

GUNNER HAVILDAR	GAJJAN SINGH	1915	GALLIPOLI
DRIVER	BHOLA SINGH	1915	GALLIPOLI
SUBEDAR	HEM SINGH	1915	GALLIPOLI
NAIK	NIKA SINGH	1915	GALLIPOLI

MESOPOTAMIA

From Gallipoli regiment proceeded to Mesopotamia, and on 19TH September 1916 took part in a punitive action to punish the Arabs at As Salihan. The regiment fired 438 rounds and had three gunners wounded. The Arabs had about 1,000 casualties compared to the Sikhs' 200. From November 1916, the regiment was divided between Ahwaz and Basra before proceeding to Baghdad in 1918. The following Sikh soldiers were awarded the Indian Distinguished Service Medal for their conspicuous gallantry while serving in Mesopotamia.

JEMADAR	AMAR SINGH	1918	MESOPOTAMIA
HAVILDAR	JAGGAT SINGH	1919	MESOPOTAMIA
GUNNER	KISHEN SINGH	1919	MESOPOTAMIA

Indian Distinguished Service Medal, 1914 - 1921 (cont.)

22ND DERAJAT MOUNTAIN BATTERY (FRONTIER FORCE)
EAST AFRICA

The 22ND Derajat Mountain Battery served in East Africa from 30TH November 1916 until 10TH December 1919. During January and February 1917, the battery suffered great hardships. For ten days men only received 16 ounces of food and the remainder of the time the allowance was 25 ounces. This, combined with the rains and the sodden nature of the country, caused a great deal of sickness amongst the men. The battery was constantly called upon to bombard the enemy positions to cover reconnaissance in force. It fought some sharp actions at Mtanda Wala, Mnindi, Nanyatim, Ndessa, Mtone Chini, and Ruangwa. On 30TH October a section under Subedar Santa Singh and Jemadar Jagat Singh marched to Nahungo and engaged the enemy at the Mbemkuru River, where Jagat Singh was shot in the chest. The towering figure of Santa Singh was awarded the Indian Distinguished Service Medal and commended by his commanding officer. "The Commanding Officera takes this opportunity on behalf of the battery of congratulating Lieutenant Santa Singh Bahadur Indian Distinguished Service Medal on account of the honours and rewards that have been lately been conferred on him in recognition of his splendid services to the battery and the state during the war."

23RD PESHAWAR MOUNAIN BATTERY (FRONTIER FORCE)
MESOPOTAMIA

On 3RD March 1915, the regiment fought a sharply contested action in the Karun Valley. An attack on Shaiba by the enemy, whose strength was estimated at 25,000 Turks and Arabs with twenty-four guns, was beaten off, pursued and defeated. The following Sikh Gunners were awarded the Indian Distinguished Service Medal for their conspicuous gallantry.

GUNNER	KISHEN SINGH	1915	MESOPOTAMIA
GUNNER	HARNAM SINGH	1915	MESOPOTAMIA
GUNNER	JWALA SINGH	1916	MESOPOTAMIA
GUNNER	MEHR SINGH	1916	MESOPOTAMIA

25TH MOUNTAIN BATTERY
MESOPOTAMIA

The following Sikh Gunners were awarded the Indian Distinguished Service Medal for their conspicuous gallantry Mesopotamia.

SUBEDAR	KISHEN SINGH	1919	MESOPOTAMIA
JEMADAR	RAM SINGH	1919	MESOPOTAMIA

Indian Distinguished Service Medal, 1914 - 1921 (cont.)

24TH HAZARA MOUNTAIN BATTERY (FRONTIER FORCE)
EAST AFRICA

The 24TH (Hazara) Indian Mountain Battery served in East Africa from 26TH April 1917. A typical extract from their War Diary reads : "Ndundwala 2nd July 1917.. one section came into action and fired 87 rounds shrapnel at enemy holding river crossing place at range 750 yards. Forward observer reported three direct hits on his breastworks." They returned to India in November 1918. The following Sikh Gunners were awarded the Indian Distinguished Service Medal for their conspicuous gallantry in East Africa.

GUNNER	GEHNA SINGH	1917	EAST AFRICA
GUNNER	RAM SINGH	1917	EAST AFRICA
GUNNER	NAR SINGH	1918	EAST AFRICA
SUBEDAR	SANT SINGH	1919	EAST AFRICA

27TH MOUNTAIN BATTERY
EAST AFRICA

The 27TH Indian Mountain Battery with 6 guns formed part of Indian Expeditionary Force 'C', from 27TH August 1914 to 2ND January 1918 in East Africa. The Mountain Battery was divided between the Magadi and Voi-Tsavo areas and spent a few months countering enemy raids on the railway. A succession of actions took place in which the regiment proved invaluable, but the enemy never stood to fight for any length of time. The following Sikh Gunners were awarded the Indian Distinguished Service Medal for their conspicuous gallantry.

gallantry.

HAVILDAR	BACHAN SINGH	1915	EAST AFRICA
NAIK	SUNDAR SINGH	1916	EAST AFRICA
HAVILDAR	BHAN SINGH	1916	EAST AFRICA
NAIK	NARAIN SINGH	1917	EAST AFRICA
HAVILDAR	NARAIN SINGH	1918	EAST AFRICA
NAIK	NATHA SINGH	1917	EAST AFRICA

Indian Distinguished Service Medal, 1914 - 1921 (cont.)

28TH MOUNTAIN BATTERY
EAST AFRICA

The 28TH Indian Mountain Battery with 6 guns arrived in German East Africa with Indian Expeditionary Force 'B' on the 30TH October 1914, returning to India in December 1916. The 28TH Battery's first engagement occurred with the guns tied to the deck of HM Transport ship Bharata, firing in support of the unsuccessful British attempt to capture Tanga, on the 3RD and 4TH November 1914. A succession of actions took place in which the regiment, with its sister regiment the 27TH, proved invaluable, including their actions in defending Jasin on the 18TH January 1915. The following Sikh Gunners were awarded the Indian Distinguished Service Medal for their conspicuous gallantry.

GUNNER	NARAIN SINGH	1917	EAST AFRICA
HAVILDAR	SANT SINGH	1917	EAST AFRICA
DRIVER	SANTOKH SINGH	1918	EAST AFRICA

30TH MOUNTAIN BATTERY
MESOPOTAMIA

SUBEDAR	DAYA SINGH	1915	MESOPOTAMIA
JEMADAR	KISHAN SINGH	1915	MESOPOTAMIA
GUNNER	PHUMAN SINGH	1916	MESOPOTAMIA
GUNNER	MOTA SINGH	1916	MESOPOTAMIA

32ND MOUNTAIN BATTERY
PALESTINE

The 32ND Mountain Battery mobilised at Maymo in April 1918 for service in Egypt and Palestine. The 32ND was the first to enlist Ahirs, as Jat Sikhs had been scarce since 1916, given their over-recruitment in all the teeth arms of the Indian Army. The battery claims to have been the first battery in action across the Turkish lines in the final advance of the Expeditionary Force. Lance Naik Sham Singh was awarded the Indian Distinguished Service Medal for his conspicuous gallantry in Palestine.

35TH PACK BATTERY
WAZIRISTAN

During 1920 the situation in Waziristan continued to deteriorate and a striking force that included the 35TH Pack Battery was launched on the Waziris with devastating effect. Jemadar Pakhar Singh was awarded the Indian Distinguished Service Medal for his conspicuous gallantry.

Indian Distinguished Service Medal, 1914 - 1921 (cont.)

HONG KONG AND SINGAPORE BATTERY
PALESTINE

No. 1 Mountain Battery, Hong Kong & Singapore, Royal Garrison Artillery added to the strength and mobility of the artillery in the Western Desert and Palestine. This battery was manned by British and Indian officers and Sikh and Punjabi Muslim other ranks. It was equipped with horses and mules when it fought in the Western Desert against the Senussi in the first half of 1916, but in June 1916 it was converted to camel transport. With the limited range of its guns, the battery had to fight from a position well forward in both attack and defence. Its personnel were highly regarded for their bravery in action and professionalism. Within the Brigade, the battery was affectionately known as the "Bing Boys" on account of the high-pitched plaintive noise made by the discharge of the mountain gun. Gunner Jinder Singh was awarded the Indian Distinguished Service Medal for his conspicuous gallantry in Palestine.

MACHINE-GUN CORPS
MESOPOTAMIA

Royal Warrant created the Machine Gun Corps on October 14TH 1915, with infantry, cavalry and motor branches. In early 1916 a heavy branch was added. The men were specialists trained in the use of machine guns, being issued with the new Lewis guns as they became available. 170,500 officers and men served in the Machine-Gun Corps with 62,049 becoming casualties and 12,498 being killed. The following Sikh soldiers of the Machine Gun Corps were awarded the Indian Distinguished Service Medal for their conspicuous gallantry in Mesopotamia.

JEMADAR	AMAR SINGH	1918	MESOPOTAMIA
NAIK	KISHEN SINGH	1919	MESOPOTAMIA

1ST KGO SAPPERS AND MINERS

During the First World War, the Sappers and Miners had not only served in France and Flanders 1914-15, but also in Palestine 1918, Aden, Mesopotamia 1915-18, Persia 1918, North West Frontier India 1915-17, and Baluchistan 1918.
In France the Bengal Sappers and Miners came into line with the Meerut Division on October 29TH 1914. At Festubert, the 3RD Company distinguished itself in filling in German saps under heavy fire and in bayonet fighting. In December and January the 4TH Company shared in heavy fighting near the northwest of Festubert and Havildar Sucha Singh was decorated for gallantry in mining operations. The Sappers and Miners in the sodden and desolate battlefields of France carried out many acts of gallantry in dropping their spades and grabbing the bayonet! The following Sikh soldiers were awarded the Indian Distinguished Service Medal for their conspicuous gallantry in France. Continued on next page.

Indian Distinguished Service Medal, 1914 - 1921 (cont.)

1ˢᵀ KGO SAPPERS AND MINERS (cont.)

SAPPER	SOBA SINGH	1915	FRANCE
SUBEDAR	SUNDAR SINGH	1915	FRANCE
HAVILDAR	SUCHA SINGH	1915	FRANCE
SAPPER	BASANT SINGH	1915	FRANCE
JEMADAR	BASANT SINGH	1915	FRANCE
`NAIK	MAGH SINGH	1916	FRANCE
NAIK	SAWAN SINGH	1916	FRANCE

MESOPOTAMIA

"Theirs was a busy life in Mesopotamia. In addition to making roads, bridging creeks, repairing buildings and installing water supplies, they converted river steamers into ironclads, mounted guns on ships and barges, laid a mine field, blew up wrecks, repaired a steam launch, electrified houses and even designed and erected gallows." At times they picked up rifles in support of the infantry. The following Sikh soldiers were awarded the Indian Distinguished Service Medal for their conspicuous gallantry in Mesopotamia.

JEMADAR	HARNAM SINGH	1916	MESOPOTAMIA
NAIK	KIRPAL SINGH	1916	MESOPOTAMIA
SAPPER	PALA SINGH	1917	MESOPOTAMIA
NAIK	BISHAN SINGH	1917	MESOPOTAMIA
LANCE NAIK	HARI SINGH	1917	MESOPOTAMIA
HAVILDAR	ISHAR SINGH	1917	MESOPOTAMIA
NAIK	KALA SINGH	1917	MESOPOTAMIA
SAPPER	PALA SINGH	1917	MESOPOTAMIA
JEMADAR	GUJAR SINGH	1918	MESOPOTAMIA
JEMADAR	BHOLA SINGH	1919	MESOPOTAMIA
JEMADAR	GURNAM SINGH	1919	MESOPOTAMIA
NAIK	HAZARA SINGH	1919	MESOPOTAMIA
HAVILDAR	NIKKA SINGH	1920	KUT AL AMARA

Indian Distinguished Service Medal, 1914 - 1921 (cont.)

1ST KGO SAPPERS AND MINERS (cont.)
PALESTINE

During the First World War, the 1ST KGO Sappers and Miners were part of the engineering troops, which assisted Allenby to break the Turkish front and sweep through Palestine and Syria. The following Sikh soldiers were awarded the Indian Distinguished Service Medal for their conspicuous gallantry in Palestine

| HAVILDAR | INDAR SINGH | 1919 | PALESTINE |
| NAIK | MALLA SINGH | 1919 | PALESTINE |

WAZIRISTAN

During the Waziristan operations the Sappers and Miners carried out their usual duties in the field. They demolished towers, fortified positions and posts, built roads and bridges; they even erected aerial ropeways in the Khaibar Pass. They also took up arms to repulse the wild tribesmen. The following Sikh soldiers were awarded the Indian Distinguished Service Medal for their conspicuous gallantry in Waziristan.

H. MAJOR	SANTA SINGH	1921	WAZIRISTAN
LANCE NAIK	JIT SINGH	1921	WAZIRISTAN
SAPPER	HIRA SINGH	1921	WAZIRISTAN

3RD SAPPERS AND MINERS
FRANCE

The Germans had gained a footing in the little village of Neuve Chapelle on October 26TH. They clung to it in spite of desperate counter attacks, culminating in and assault in which the Sappers and Miners co-operated with the 47TH Sikhs. The attack of the 47TH Sikhs with the two companies of Sappers and Miners on either side of them was carried out with great gallantry. The Sikhs and Sappers covering the seven hundred yards between them and Neuve Chapelle by rushes alternating with fire, as if on a training ground, they reached the ruins of the village and drove out the Germans, reported by prisoners to be three battalions by close hand-to-hand fighting.

The following Sikh soldiers were awarded the Indian Distinguished Service Medal for their conspicuous gallantry in France.

| LANCE NAIK | INDAR SINGH | 1915 | FRANCE |
| NAIK | HARNAM SINGH | 1916 | FRANCE |

Indian Distinguished Service Medal, 1914 - 1921 (cont.)

3RD SAPPERS AND MINERS (cont.)

" As per their sister regiment, 1st KGO Sappers and Miners, the 3TH Sappers and Miners had a busy life in Mesopotamia. In addition to making roads, bridging creeks, repairing buildings and installing water supplies, they converted river steamers into ironclads, mounted guns on ships and barges, laid a mine field, blew up wrecks, repaired a steam launch, electrified houses and even designed and erected gallows." At times picked up rifles in support of the Infantry. The following Sikh soldiers were awarded the Indian Distinguished Service Medal for their conspicuous gallantry in Mesopotamia.

LANCE NAIK	BAGHA SINGH	1916	MESOPOTAMIA
HAVILDAR	SAHIB SINGH	1916	MESOPOTAMIA
NAIK	GANDA SINGH	1916	MESOPOTAMIA
NAIK	JHANDA SINGH	1916	MESOPOTAMIA
HAVILDAR	CHANDA SINGH	1916	MESOPOTAMIA
SUBEDAR	BARYAM SINGH	1919	MESOPOTAMIA
JEMADAR	BIR SINGH	1919	MESOPOTAMIA

RAILWAY BATTALION, SAPPERS AND MINERS

HAVILDAR	PALA SINGH	1915	EAST AFRICA
JEMADAR	MANGAL SINGH	1918	EAST AFRICA

12TH PIONEERS
FRANCE

In 1914 12TH Pioneers were stationed at Quetta and comprised four companies of Jats and four of Lobana Sikhs. During the First World War they were ordered for service in France and Mesopotamia. Sepoy Sadhu Singh was awarded the Indian Distinguished Service Medal for his gallantry in France.

HAVILDAR ISHAR SINGH
9TH BHOPAL INFANTRY
MESOPOTAMIA

At Shaikh Saad on 7TH January1916, in an action in which the machine-gun officer and eleven men had been wounded, Havildar Ishar Singh had taken control of the machine gun detachment. With four men he had brought the guns into the firing line under heavy rifle fire and worked them with good effect. Under Havildar Ishar Singh's leadership, the whole detachment showed great daring in their attacks on the enemy. Havildar Ishar Singh was awarded the Indian Distinguished Service Medal for his conspicuous gallantry and leadership.

Indian Distinguished Service Medal, 1914 - 1921 (cont.)

9TH BHOPAL INFANTRY
MESOPOTAMIA

Lance Naik Maima Singh was awarded the Indian Distinguished Service Medal for consistent good work and devotion to duty in Mesopotamia since the outbreak of the war. He had been twice wounded in action. Regardless of his wounds he carried on killing the Turks.

SEPOY TEJA SINGH
9TH BHOPAL INFANTRY
MESOPOTAMIA

Sepoy Teja Singh was awarded the Indian Distinguished Service Medal for gallantry in action in Mesopotamia. During a withdrawal a wounded Indian officer who could not move had been left behind. He would have been captured and killed had not Sepoy Teja Singh dashed forward under heavy fire and carried him back to a place of safety, some 150 yards in the rear.

SUBEDAR MAJOR BHUR SINGH
9TH BHOPAL INFANTRY
FRANCE

Subedar Major Bhur Singh was awarded the Indian Distinguished Service Medal at Neuve Chapelle in France, on October 28TH 1914. He gallantly held on to his portion of trench under very heavy rifle and artillery fire, when the remainder of the Company had been killed. It was mainly due to Subedar Major Bhur Singh's fine example that the portion of the line entrusted to him remained intact.

HAVILDAR AMAR SINGH
9TH BHOPAL INFANTRY
FRANCE

Havildar Amar Singh was awarded the Indian Distinguished Service Medal at Neuve Chapelle in France, on October 28TH 1914. Throughout the day he showed conspicuous gallantry under heavy rifle and artillery fire. He led his section with ability and skill during the attacks on the enemy. At one time he became isolated but continued to hold the ground gained till dark, and only withdrew when ordered to do so by his company commander.

.

Indian Distinguished Service Medal, 1914 - 1921 (cont.)
14TH KGO FEROZEPORE SIKHS
EGYPT

The 14TH Sikhs arrived at the Suez Canal on the 2ND of December. The troops were employed in routine defence duties and in extending and improving the defences of the Canal. In the early morning of the 28TH of January about two hundred of the enemy attacked 14TH Sikhs' outpost line held by "E" Company. The Turks were repulsed, and suffered heavy casualties. They left number of killed and wounded on the field. The Sikhs captured some prisoners, who were in a sorry state after their march from Palestine across the Sinai Desert.

Although Qantara was not one of the enemy's principal objectives, a small force attacked it early on the morning of the 3RD of February. These attacks were all beaten back by the double companies of the 14TH Sikhs. The following Sikh soldiers were awarded the Indian Distinguished Service Medal for their conspicuous gallantry in Egypt.

LANCE NAIK	BHAG SINGH	1914	EGYPT
SEPOY	BISHAN SINGH	1914	EGYPT
SEPOY	BOGA SINGH	1914	EGYPT
SEPOY	DARBARA SINGH	1914	EGYPT
SEPOY	INDAR SINGH	1914	EGYPT
SEPOY	RAM SINGH	1914	EGYPT
DRUMMER	HARNAM SINGH	1914	EGYPT

GALLIPOLI

The Gallipoli peninsular in Turkey has been perennially important because of its strategic position. In First World War, Allied forces unsuccessfully stormed the Turkish front. In the battle, 14TH Sikhs lost three hundred and seventy-one officers and men killed or wounded. Never has any battalion displayed such courage and devotion to duty as were displayed by the 14TH Sikhs in the Third Battle of Krithia. Writing to the Commander-in-Chief in India a few weeks after the event, General Sir Ian Hamilton paid noble tribute to the heroism of all ranks. The following are some of the passages from his letter " In the highest sense of the word extreme gallantry has been shown by this fine Battalion. In spite of these tremendous losses there was not a sign of wavering all day. Not an inch of ground gained was given up and not a single straggler came back. The ends of the enemy's trenches leading into the ravine were found to be blocked with the bodies of Sikhs and of the enemy who died fighting at close quarters, and the glacis slope is thickly dotted with the bodies of these fine soldiers all lying on their faces as they fell in their steady advance on the enemy."

Continued on next page.

Indian Distinguished Service Medal, 1914 - 1921 (cont.)

14TH KGO FEROZEPORE SIKHS (cont.)

"The history of the Sikhs affords many instances of their value as soldiers, but it may be safely asserted that nothing finer than the grim valour and steady discipline displayed by them on the 4TH June has ever been done by soldiers of the Khalsa." The gallantry of the Regiment was also referred to by the Secretary of State for India (Mr. Austen Chamberlain) in a moving speech in the House of Commons. The following Sikh soldiers were awarded the Indian Distinguished Service Medal for their conspicuous gallantry in Gallipoli.

LANCE NAIK	BHAGWAN SINGH	1916	GALLIPOLI
HAVILDAR	BIR SINGH	1916	GALLIPOLI
W. ORDERLY	GURDIT SINGH	1916	GALLIPOLI
S. MAJOR	SHAM SINGH	1916	GALLIPOLI
LANCE NAIK	SUCHA SINGH	1916	GALLIPOLI
LANCE NAIK	AMAR SINGH	1916	GALLIPOLI
SEPOY	JAGAT SINGH	1916	GALLIPOLI
NAIK	KALA SINGH	1916	GALLIPOLI
SEPOY	CHAMAN SINGH	1916	GALLIPOLI
LANCE NAIK	JIWAN SINGH	1916	GALLIPOLI
NAIK	JOGINDER SINGH	1916	GALLIPOLI
LANCE NAIK	GAJJAN SINGH	1916	GALLIPOLI
SEPOY	LAL SINGH	1916	GALLIPOLI
SEPOY	BHOG SINGH	1916	GALLIPOLI
NAIK	CHANAN SINGH	1916	GALLIPOLI
SEPOY	SUNDAR SINGH	1916	GALLIPOLI
SEPOY	LAL SINGH	1916	GALLIPOLI
SEPOY	BHARPUR SINGH	1916	GALLIPOLI
DRUMMER	CHANDA SINGH	1916	GALLIPOLI
DRUMMER	INDAR SINGH	1916	GALLIPOLI
SEPOY	KALA SINGH	1916	GALLIPOLI
SEPOY	JIWAN SINGH	1916	GALLIPOLI
LANCE NAIK	HARNAM SINGH	1916	GALLIPOLI
SEPOY	PHUMAN SINGH	1916	GALLIPOLI
LANCE NAIK	SARMUKH SINGH	1916	GALLIPOLI

Indian Distinguished Service Medal, 1914 – 1921 (cont.)

14TH KGO FEROZEPORE SIKHS (cont.)

SEPOY	LIKAL SINGH	1916	GALLIPOLI
SEPOY	BACHAN SINGH	1916	GALLIPOLI
SEPOY	MANGAL SINGH	1916	GALLIPOLI
SEPOY	INDAR SINGH	1916	GALLIPOLI
SEPOY	GUJAR SINGH	1916	GALLIPOLI
SEPOY	CHAMAN SINGH	1916	GALLIPOLI
LANCE NAIK	RAM SINGH	1916	GALLIPOLI
SEPOY	GAJJAN SINGH	1916	GALLIPOLI
SEPOY	KHEM SINGH	1916	GALLIPOLI
SEPOY	MUNSHI SINGH	1916	GALLIPOLI
LANCE NAIK	BIR SINGH	1916	GALLIPOLI

MESOPOTAMIA

On evacuation from Gallipoli the battalion proceeded to Mesopotamia. It was involved in some fiercer fighting on the Tigres River in October 1918, where it suffered a total of 322 casualties, the heaviest amongst the units of 17TH Division. The following Sikh soldiers were awarded the Indian Distinguished Service Medal for their conspicuous gallantry in Mesopotamia.

SUBEDAR	JIWAN SINGH	1918	MESOPOTAMIA
JEMADAR	JASWANT SINGH	1918	MESOPOTAMIA
LANCE NAIK	WARYAM SINGH	1919	MESOPOTAMIA
SEPOY	PURAN SINGH	1919	MESOPOTAMIA
SUBEDAR	SANT SINGH	1919	MESOPOTAMIA
HAVILDAR	DIWAN SINGH	1919	MESOPOTAMIA
SEPOY	MOHAN SINGH	1919	MESOPOTAMIA
SEPOY	NATHA SINGH	1919	MESOPOTAMIA
SEPOY	RAUNAK SINGH	1919	MESOPOTAMIA

N. W. FRONTIER

Jemadar Sucha Singh and Naik Mangat Singh of the 14TH Sikhs were awarded the Indian Distinguished Service Medal for their conspicuous gallantry in the punitive expedition against the Waziris on the North West Frontier of India.

Indian Distinguished Service Medal, 1914 – 1921 (cont.)

15TH LUDHIANA SIKHS
FRANCE

The 15TH Ludhiana Sikhs first landed in Marseilles on 26TH September 1914. This was the first Indian contingent to land in Europe. "Unique stalwarts from the east" remarked the press. One of their most memorable events occurred on 28TH October 1914 when the regiment was detailed to capture the village of Neuve Chapelle, to which the advance lay across 800 yards under intense enemy fire. After bitter hand-to-hand combat the village was captured; of the 280 Sikhs who started assaulted only 58 survived.

The following soldiers were decorated for gallantry and devotion to duty whilst serving in France. They were a part of a party of ten men under Lieutenant Smyth who carried a consignment of bombs over 250 yards of open ground under shrapnel fire, having already watched two other groups fail in the attempt. Only two of the party reached the trench unhurt. Lieutenant Smyth was awarded the Victoria Cross, Lance Naik Mangal Singh the Indian Order Merit and the following soldiers the Indian Distinguished Service Medal for their conspicuous gallantry.

SUBEDAR	PHUMAN SINGH	1915	FRANCE
JEMADAR	WAZIR SINGH	1915	FRANCE
JEMADAR	BIR SINGH	1915	FRANCE
HAVILDAR	BISHAN SINGH	1915	FRANCE
HAVILDAR	BHAGWAN SINGH	1915	FRANCE
HAVILDAR	BACHAN SINGH	1915	FRANCE
HAVILDAR	BUDH SINGH	1915	FRANCE
NAIK	BHAGWAN SINGH	1915	FRANCE
SEPOY	DEWAN SINGH	1915	FRANCE
SEPOY	DAN SINGH	1915	FRANCE

Lieutenant Smyth and Naik Mangal Singh IOM

Indian Distinguished Service Medal, 1914 - 1921 (cont.)

15TH LUDHIANA SIKHS (cont.)
N. W. FRONTIER OF INDIA

Operations in the Third Afghan War ranged along much of the border area. Fighting occurred in Chitral, the Khyber Pass, through the Kurram Valley, the Tochi Valley, Waziristan and Baluchistan. The Afghans and their Pathan allies took the offensive at the outset on each front, except in Southern Baluchistan, where a pre-emptive British strike into Afghanistan forestalled any planned or potential Afghan incursions into India. The only other front on which the British conducted significant offensive operations was in the Khyber Pass, where British and Indian troops advanced into Afghanistan to seize the town of Dakka. The following Sikh soldiers were awarded the Indian Distinguished Service Medal for their conspicuous gallantry.

NAIK	HAZARA SINGH	1919	N. W. FRONTIER
SEPOY	INDAR SINGH	1919	N. W. FRONTIER
SEPOY	MAGH SINGH	1919	N. W. FRONTIER
SEPOY	SUNDAR SINGH	1919	N. W. FRONTIER
JEMADAR	SUCHA SINGH	1919	N. W. FRONTIER
NAIK	MANGAL SINGH	1919	N. W. FRONTIER

IRAQ

In the post-war carve-up of the Middle East, Britain was 'awarded' by the League of Nations a Class 'A' mandates over Iraq-colonialism with a different name. Throughout 1919 and 1920 there were constant uprisings in the north, spreading to the south especially in the Shiite cities of An-Najaf and Kabala. The British used warplanes to bomb and gas civilians. The rebellion lasted for over a year, at an enormous cost of lives and money: 10,000 Iraqi and 450 British dead. In an effort to disguise their land grab, in 1921 the British named one of Sharif Husayn's sons Faysal to be king of Iraq. Faysal had never before set foot in Iraq, but he was Arab and sufficiently pliant to British requests. He was a British puppet and his coronation was a strictly British affair. The following Sikh soldiers were awarded the Indian Distinguished Service Medal for their conspicuous gallantry in Iraq.

SUBEDAR	JAIMAL SINGH	1921	IRAQ
NAIK	DIWAN SINGH	1921	IRAQ
SUBEDAR	ATTAR SINGH	1923	IRAQ
SEPOY	BILA SINGH	1923	IRAQ
SEPOY	NARYAN SINGH	1923	IRAQ

Indian Distinguished Service Medal, 1914 - 1921 (cont.)
19TH PUNJABI RIFLES
FRANCE

The following Sikh soldiers of the 19TH Punjabi Rifles were awarded the Indian Distinguished Service Medal for their conspicuous gallantry in France.

NAIK	DULA SINGH	1915	FRANCE
SEPOY	SARIAN SINGH	1915	FRANCE
HAVILDAR	SUNDAR SINGH	1915	FRANCE
HAVILDAR	GANDA SINGH	1915	FRANCE
HAVILDAR	HARNAM SINGH	1915	FRANCE

TRANS-CASPIA

The British Army intervened in Persia almost from the outset of the war to prevent the loss of its oil supplies to pro-German factors in the Persian Government and, later, to the Turks. Following the collapse of the Russian Army after the 'October Revolution', the Turks increased pressure on the Caucasian front, heading towards Baku and the Caspian Sea. The British were already supporting 'White' Russian elements against the Bolsheviks in North and South Russia. So further intervention along the Persian frontier was pretty inevitable following the establishment of Bolshevik rule in Trans-Caspia early in 1918. On the 24TH July the Bolsheviks attacked and took the railway bridge over the Oxus at Charjui. The Trans-Caspian forces were routed and retreated all the way back to positions east of Bairam Ali. The Trans-Caspian government panicked and sent urgent requests to British for assistance. On 11TH August, a machine gun section of 19TH Punjabi Rifles was despatched to Bairam Ali to assist in its defence. The expected Bolshevik attack commenced early on the 13TH August and, despite sterling service by the two Punjabi machine gun teams, the Trans-Caspian forces were again defeated. The Punjabis covered their retreat back to Merv. The infantry counter-attack did not proceed well, with the Trans-Caspian infantry going to ground as soon as the Bolshevik artillery and machine guns opened fire, and the Turkmen disappearing altogether! The Punjabis, despite incurring heavy casualties fought their way into the town, capturing 16 machine-guns and 6 artillery pieces. During the early part of January, one company of the 19TH Punjabis was sent to reinforce two troops of 28TH Light Cavalry. A second company of the 19TH Punjabis was entrained at Bairam Ali to reinforce the front. The Trans-Caspian infantry was ordered to advance and soon met with the Bolsheviks who were supported by artillery fire. Despite fighting well for a change, the Trans-Caspian infantry were pushed back. They were greatly outnumbered and finally broke and ran. At this point it looked as if the whole position was being outflanked, but fortunately the train arrived from Bairam Ali carrying the second company of Punjabis

Continued on next page.

Indian Distinguished Service Medal, 1914 - 1921 (cont.)

19TH PUNJABI RIFLES (cont.)
TRANS-CASPIA (cont.)

They immediately detrained and advanced through the fog and attacked the Bolshevik right flank. The Bolsheviks suffered considerable casualties as they fled across the front of the original Punjabi company. The victorious Punjabis drove the remaining Bolsheviks into the desert. The following Sikh soldiers were awarded the Indian Distinguished Service Medal for their conspicuous gallantry in Trans-Caspia.

SEPOY	WARYAM SINGH	1920	TRANS-CASPIA
JEMADAR	NIHAL SINGH	1920	TRANS-CASPIA
HAVILDAR	ASA SINGH	1920	TRANS-CASPIA
NAIK	JOWALA SINGH	1920	TRANS-CASPIA
NAIK	KARAM SINGH	1920	TRANS-CASPIA
NAIK	SHER SINGH	1920	TRANS-CASPIA
LANCE NAIK	GURDIT SINGH	1920	TRANS-CASPIA
LANCE NAIK	SOHAN SINGH	1920	TRANS-CASPIA
LANCE NAIK	GIAN SINGH	1920	TRANS-CASPIA
LANCE NAIK	ASA SINGH	1920	TRANS-CASPIA
SEPOY	SURJAN SINGH	1920	TRANS-CASPIA
SEPOY	UDHAM SINGH	1920	TRANS-CASPIA
SEPOY	GANGA SINGH	1920	TRANS-CASPIA
SEPOY	BAL SINGH	1920	TRANS-CASPIA

THE 20TH DUKE OF CAMBRIDGE'S OWN INFANTRY
MESOPOTAMIA

The 20TH Duke of Cambridge's Own Infantry fought in Mesopotamia during the First World War. The regiment served with the 7TH Lahore Division in the advance through the Vale of Sharon, where it was engaged in some severe fighting. Sepoy Bachittar Singh was awarded Indian Distinguished Service Medal for gallantry while Naik Bhola Singh and Lance Naik Mehar Singh of the same regiment were awarded Gold and Silver medals respectively by H.M. The King of Serbia.

Indian Distinguished Service Medal, 1914 - 1921 (cont.)

21ST PUNJABIS

EGYPT

During the Great War, the regiment served in Egypt and Palestine. The following Sikh soldiers were awarded the Indian Distinguished Service Medal for their conspicuous gallantry in Egypt.

SEPOY	TEJA SINGH	EGYPT
JEMADAR	ISHAR SINGH	EGYPT
HAVILDAR	SHAM SINGH	EGYPT
LANCE NAIK	DHANA SINGH	EGYPT

22ND PUNJABIS

MESOPOTAMIA

During the Great War, the regiment served in Mesopotamia, Baluchistan and Persia. The following Sikh soldiers were awarded the Indian Distinguished Service Medal for their conspicuous gallantry.

SEPOY	MELA SINGH	1915	MESOPOTAMIA
HAVILDAR	RODA SINGH	1915	MESOPOTAMIA
HAVILDAR	GANGA SINGH	1916	MESOPOTAMIA
SEPOY	DALIP SINGH	1916	MESOPOTAMIA
HAVILDAR	JOWALA SINGH	1919	BALUCHISTAN
SEPOY	MANGAL SINGH	1919	BALUCHISTAN
SEPOY	JOGA SINGH	1919	BALUCHISTAN
SEPOY	PARTAB SINGH	1908	BALUCHISTAN
SEPOY	JAWALA SINGH	1908	BALUCHISTAN
SEPOY	JIWAN SINGH	1920	KUT AL AMARA
SEPOY	NARAYAN SINGH	1920	KUT AL AMARA
NAIK	SOLAKHAN SINGH	1920	KUT AL AMARA
HAVILDAR	HARI SINGH	1920	KUT AL AMARA
SEPOY	DHANA SINGH	1920	KUT AL AMARA

Indian Distinguished Service Medal, 1914 - 1921 (cont.)

23RD SIKH PIONEERS
EGYPT

In 1914, the 23RD were posted to a force that was being rushed towards Egypt. However, on their way they were ordered to destroy the fort of Sheikh Sayad. The fort lies at the end of a small peninsula of Arabia, whence the Red Sea traffic could be attacked. The Sikhs proceeded to attack the fort supported by the naval guns. They carried out demolitions at fort and guardhouses, which included the destruction of field guns. Twelve pioneers left to join the Somaliland Contingent as an explosion party, who after some arduous and waterless marching attacked and destroyed five forts at Shimber Berries and then rejoined the battalion at Aden. On January 18TH 1916 the 23RD proceeded to Egypt and Sinai. They joined the Desert Column, fought actions at Abu Zanena, El Arish and were the first unit to enter Palestine where they took over 850 German and Turkish prisoners including the commander of the Turkish 53RD Division. They shot down a German plane at El Arish. "One of them left their formation and with a view to machine- gunning us. They picked up their rifles and with the Machine guns we opened fire. We could see the splinters flying out of the plane and down he came about a mile away. It gave the Germans a shock and we were not molested again." After the success of Bir Sheba and the capture of Gaza the pioneers entered Jerusalem on December 9TH. "The history of the Sikh Pioneers henceforth in Egypt and Palestine is to a great extent, uneventful, save for the miracle of construction for which their name should long be famous in this phase of the World War". The following Sikh soldiers were awarded the Indian Distinguished Service Medal for their conspicuous gallantry in Egypt and Palestine.

SUBEDAR	HIRA SINGH	1916	EGYPT
LANCE NAIK	NATHA SINGH	1916	EGYPT
HAVILDAR MAJOR	FAUJA SINGH	1916	EGYPT
HAVILDAR	JAWAHIR SINGH	1916	EGYPT
JEMADAR	SADHU SINGH	1916	EGYPT
JEMADAR	ALA SINGH	1916	EGYPT
SUBEDAR	MOTA SINGH	1916	EGYPT

Indian Distinguished Service Medal, 1914 - 1921 (cont.)
23RD SIKH PIONEERS (cont.)
ASIA MINOR

" The 23RD leaving Alexandria on the 25TH February arrived at Constantinople on the 20TH of March, where they remained three days, and then made for Batoum across the Black Sea. They reached Batoum in ten days and were at once put to work on the Batoum-Tiflis-Baku railway. On April 7TH they reached Tiflis, and were at once ordered to Kars. Alexandropol and Kars had just been wrecked and burnt by Tartars out of vindictiveness. The Pioneers now proceeded to disarm the town, and re-establish order, remaining there till April 30TH, when more of the Armenians returned. By the 15TH May they were required to prepare a camp for the 27TH Division at Pendik. On June 29TH 1919 the Turkish peace was signed. The next duty for them was on the Hiader Pasha Ishmit portion of the Anatolian railway. This continued till the middle of November when the battalion arrived at Tuzla barracks en route for India." *Quoted from: THE HISTORY OF SIKH PIONEERS. BY MAJ.GEN. G.MACMUNN.* The following Sikh Pioneers were awarded the Indian Distinguished Service Medal for their conspicuous gallantry in Asia Minor.

HAVILDAR	PHUMAN SINGH	1921	ASIA MINOR
SUBEDAR	SUNDAR SINGH	1921	ASIA MINOR
SEPOY	LACHMAN SINGH	1921	ASIA MINOR
JEMADAR	WASAKHA SINGH	1921	ASIA MINOR
HAVILDAR MAJOR	KAKA SINGH	1921	ASIA MINOR
LANCE NAIK	SHAMIR SINGH	1921	ASIA MINOR

24TH PUNJABIS
MESOPOTAMIA

During the Great War, the regiment served in Mesopotamia, Russia and Greece. The following Sikh soldiers were awarded the Indian Distinguished Service Medal for their conspicuous gallantry in Mesopotamia.

LANCE NAIK	PAL SINGH	1915	MESOPOTAMIA
SEPOY	VIR SINGH	1915	MESOPOTAMIA
SEPOY	LABH SINGH	1915	MESOPOTAMIA
NAIK	LABH SINGH	1916	MESOPOTAMIA
NAIK	KHARAK SINGH	1915	MESOPOTAMIA
NAIK	KHAZAN SINGH	1915	MESOPOTAMIA
LANCE NAIK	GANDA SINGH	1919	MESOPOTAMIA
SEPOY	RAM SINGH	1915	MESOPOTAMIA

Indian Distinguished Service Medal, 1914 - 1921 (cont.)

24TH PUNJABIS (cont.)

SEPOY	JIWAN SINGH	1915	MESOPOTAMIA
SEPOY	THAKAR SINGH	1916	MESOPOTAMIA
HAVILDAR	BHAGWAN SINGH	1917	MESOPOTAMIA
SEPOY	KISHEN SINGH	1917	MESOPOTAMIA
SUBEDAR	UJAGAR SINGH	1919	MESOPOTAMIA
LANCE NAIK	LAL SINGH	1920	MESOPOTAMIA
HAVILDAR	MANGAL SINGH	1920	KUT AL AMARA
HAVILDAR	KESAR SINGH	1920	KUT AL AMARA
NAIK	BHAGAT SINGH	1920	KUT AL AMARA
NAIK	KHARAK SINGH	1920	KUT AL AMARA
SEPOY	PAL SINGH	1920	KUT AL AMARA
SEPOY	LAL SINGH	1920	KUT AL AMARA
SEPOY	AMAR SINGH	1920	KUT AL AMARA
SEPOY	KRISHEN SINGH	1920	KUT AL AMARA
NAIK	LACHMAN SINGH	1920	KUT AL AMARA
HAVILDAR	TAHL SINGH	1920	KUT AL AMARA
SEPOY	KARTAR SINGH	1920	KUT AL AMARA
SEPOY	LABH SINGH	1920	TURKEY

25TH PUNJABIS

During the First World War, the regiment served on the N.W. Frontier of India, in Mesopotamia, Salonika, Russia and Turkey. The following Sikh soldiers were awarded the Indian Distinguished Service Medal for their conspicuous gallantry.

HAVILDAR	SADHU SINGH	1907	N. W. FRONTIER
SUBEDAR	INDAR SINGH	1916	N. W. FRONTIER
LANCE NAIK	ARJAN SINGH	1917	MESOPOTAMIA
HAVILDAR	SAWAN SINGH	1918	MESOPOTAMIA
HAVILDAR	HARI SINGH	1921	WAZIRISTAN
LANCE NAIK	HARNAM SINGH	1921	WAZIRISTAN
JEMADAR	BHAGWAN SINGH	1922	WAZIRISTAN
SEPOY	BISHAN SINGH	1922	WAZIRISTAN

Indian Distinguished Service Medal, 1914 - 1921 (cont.)

26TH PUNJABIS

MESOPOTAMIA

During the First World War the regiment served in Mesopotamia, where the following Sikh soldiers were awarded the Indian Distinguished Service Medal for their conspicuous gallantry.

SEPOY	SHER SINGH	1916	MESOPOTAMIA
LANCE NAIK	CHANAN SINGH	1917	MESOPOTAMIA
LANCE NAIK	HAZARA SINGH	1917	MESOPOTAMIA
SEPOY	WARYAM SINGH	1919	MESOPOTAMIA

27TH PUNJABIS

MESOPOTAMIA

During the First World War the regiment served in France and Mesopotamia. The following Sikh soldiers were awarded the Indian Distinguished Service Medal for their conspicuous gallantry in Mesopotamia.

LANCE NAIK	NATHA SINGH	1916	MESOPOTAMIA
JEMADAR	BASAWA SINGH	1916	MESOPOTAMIA
HAVILDAR	HIRA SINGH	1916	MESOPOTAMIA
LANCE NAIK	SANTA SINGH	1916	MESOPOTAMIA
HAVILDAR	BELA SINGH	1917	MESOPOTAMIA
HAVILDAR	BHAGAT SINGH	1917	MESOPOTAMIA

28TH PUNJABIS

During the First World War the regiment served in Ceylon, Mesopotamia and Egypt. The following Sikh soldiers were awarded the Indian Distinguished Service Medal for their conspicuous gallantry in Egypt and Mesopotamia.

HAVILDAR	WADHAWA SINGH	1908	N.W.FRONTIER
JEMADAR	RAN SINGH	1917	MESOPOTAMIA
LANCE NAIK	LAL SINGH	1917	MESOPOTAMIA
SEPOY	MANSA SINGH	1917	MESOPOTAMIA
HAVILDAR	BASANT SINGH	1919	EGYPT
JEMADAR	SUNDER SINGH	1919	EGYPT
SEPOY	INDAR SINGH	1919	EGYPT

Indian Distinguished Service Medal, 1914 - 1921 (cont.)

29TH PUNJABIS

EAST AFRICA

During the First World War the regiment served in Palestine, Egypt and East Africa. The following Sikh soldiers were awarded the Indian Distinguished Service Medal for their conspicuous gallantry in East Africa.

JEMADAR	PALA SINGH	1915	EAST AFRICA
JEMADAR	BHAGWAN SINGH	1915	EAST AFRICA
SEPOY	PURAN SINGH	1917	EAST AFRICA
SUBADAR	UDHAM SINGH	1917	EAST AFRICA

30TH PUNJABIS

EAST AFRICA

The 30TH Punjabis arrived at Dar-es-Salaam in German East Africa on 11TH December 1916. They fought a major battle on the Rufiji River and suffered severe losses. In a desperate fought battle at Tandamuti Hill, the German Askaris cut one of the companies to pieces. The Askaris charged home again and again. In this desperate fighting 255 ranks and file were killed, wounded or missing. The following Sikh soldiers were awarded Indian Distinguished Service Medal for their conspicuous gallantry in Jungle fighting.

JEMADAR	HAKAM SINGH	1917	EAST AFRICA
HAVILDAR	LAL SINGH	1917	EAST AFRICA
SUBEDAR	THAKAR SINGH	1917	EAST AFRICA
HAVILDAR	GURDIT SINGH	1918	EAST AFRICA
HAVILDAR	DALEL SINGH	1921	EAST AFRICA

31ST PUNJABIS

MESOPOTAMIA

During the First World War on 15TH December 1915, the regiment disembarking at Basra at once moved to Kurna and then across the Hamar Lake to Hakika. Here the regiment made small expeditions to punish raiding lake tribes and was employed in escorting river steamers and convoys of lake Bellums between Nasiriyah and Kurna. The following Sikh soldiers were awarded the Indian Distinguished Service Medal for their conspicuous gallantry in patrolling the Lakes in Mesopotamia.

LANCE NAIK	LACHMAN SINGH	1916	MESOPOTAMIA
LANCE NAIK	PAKHAR SINGH	1916	MESOPOTAMIA
LANCE NAIK	GAJJAN SINGH	1917	MESOPOTAMIA

Indian Distinguished Service Medal, 1914 - 1921 (cont.)

32ND SIKH PIONEERS

The regiment was not called to arms till 1917. It had been continuously sending drafts to its sister regiments since 1914. In Mesopotamia it joined a Brigade advance on Ramadie. The regiment accompanied 'Tigris Corps' advancing on Tigris and then crossed the river and marched to Ain Nukhaila. They worked almost incessantly on the railway to Tekrit and after that on various duties. As soon as the Turks had evacuated the Fatha position, the 32ND were pushed on to work on the road through the Fatha Gorge on the right bank of the Tigris. The regiment moved on to Qalat Jabar then proceeded to Qalat-el-Bint. The day after the surrender the regiment was assembled at Sharqat for service against the Kurds and Arabs. The regiment had participated in taking 11,332 prisoners, fifty-one guns and 130 machine guns. All in a day's work for the Khalsa! The 2ND Battalion 32ND Regiment, raised at Sialkot in 1917, sailed for Bombay to Suez whence it arrived in the Palestine area at Ludd. It moved against the Turks at Bir Sheba, and then followed the advance to Damascus. The regiment returned to India in 1921. The following Sikh soldiers were awarded Indian Distinguished Service Medal for their conspicuous gallantry in Mesopotamia and Egypt.

JEMADAR	CHATTAR SINGH	1904	TIBET
SUBEDAR	SUNDAR SINGH	1912	ABOR
HAVILDAR	BUDH SINGH	1912	ABOR
HAVILDAR	ISHAR SINGH	1917	MESOPOTAMIA
SUBEDAR	ARJAN SINGH	1919	MESOPOTAMIA
HAVILDAR MAJOR	ARJAN SINGH	1921	MESOPOTAMIA
SEPOY	UDHAM SINGH	1921	MESOPOTAMIA
SUBEDAR MAJOR	HUKAM SINGH	1919	EGYPT
SUBEDAR	MAL SINGH	1918	EGYPT

33RD PUNJABIS

FRANCE

The regiment did not serve on the Western Front but sent a draft to fight in France. On September 25TH 1915 a section took part in the Battle of Loos, where they left their trenches and after a gallant struggle captured the German trenches immediately to their front, though sustaining heavy losses. Sepoy Lachman Singh was awarded the Indian Distinguished Service Medal for his conspicuous gallantry in France.

Indian Distinguished Service Medal, 1914 - 1921 (cont.)

33RD PUNJABIS (cont.)

EAST AFRICA

The 33RD Punjabis disembarked at Kilwe on 8TH May for service in German East Africa. One of the patrols advancing on Wungui was ambushed and wiped out. On 12TH June they suffered another catastrophe, when a patrol proceeding in the direction of Kilwe was ambushed suffering more casualties. After some small engagements, the regiment was engaged in heavy but successful battles at Kihunburu and Narugombe. The following Sikh officers were awarded Indian Distinguished Service Medal for their conspicuous gallantry in Africa.

SUBEDAR	AMAR SINGH	1918	EAST AFRICA
HAVILDAR	MEHR SINGH	1918	EAST AFRICA

34TH SIKH PIONEERS

FRANCE

The 34TH Sikh Pioneers first landed in Marseilles on 26 September 1914. On the 22ND October, a company took over an advanced post from the French at Festubert. It was attacked within the hour of relieving the French and all the British officers were wounded. Subedars Sher Singh and Natha Singh took over command and held the post very resolutely till the evening of the 26TH October. Sher Singh received an immediate Indian Distinguished Service Medal. In the trenches the battalion was under constant shelling and sniping and beat off two determined attacks by the Germans. On 23RD November the enemy attacked at dawn with a shower of bombs and hand grenades. The bombs fell fast and furious near the 34TH machine gun, and many men fell. Subedar Natha Singh at once took charge and kept the gun in action for some time against the enemy who had broken in. At last the only survivor of the gun crew, Havildar Nikka Singh, carried the gun out under heavy fire; both were awarded immediate gallantry awards. The 34TH had suffered heavy losses. Amongst the killed were Subedars Natha Singh, Ram Singh and Sundar Singh, with Subedar Sant Singh and Jemadars Pala Singh and Mit Singh wounded. The 34TH shared in the historic battles of Ypres and Festubert, where the companies had been distributed one to each brigade. After the intensive battle of Loos the battalion moved down to Marseilles and then eastwards for service in Mesopotamia. The following Sikh soldiers were awarded Indian Distinguished Service Medal for their conspicuous gallantry in France.

SUBEDAR	SHER SINGH	1916	FRANCE
SUBEDAR	MAGHAR SINGH	1916	FRANCE
HAVILDAR	PREM SINGH	1916	FRANCE
HAVILDAR	SUNDAR SINGH	1916	FRANCE
HAVILDAR	NARAYAN SINGH	1915	FRANCE

Indian Distinguished Service Medal, 1914 – 1921 (cont.)

34TH SIKH PIONEERS (cont.)

SEPOY	ISHAR SINGH	1916	FRANCE
SEPOY	SANT SINGH	1915	FRANCE
SEPOY	GOPAL SINGH	1915	FRANCE
SEPOY	KATHA SINGH	1915	FRANCE
SEPOY	ISHAR SINGH	1916	FRANCE
SUBEDAR	WASSAWA SINGH	1915	FRANCE

MESOPOTAMIA

On 17TH December 1915, the 34TH left Marseilles with the Lahore Division after 13 months arduous service in France. They landed at Basra on the 6TH January 1961, and joined the 3RD Division, which was already marching up the Tigris. They proceeded to Sheikh Saad and then to Wadi. At the fighting front the 34TH were busily employed in every sort of work from the front line redoubts to the light railway that was being made from Sheikh Saad towards Hai. The Pioneers were actively in support of all the battles in Mesopotamia culminating in the capture of Baghdad. The following Sikh soldiers were awarded Indian Distinguished Service Medal for their conspicuous gallantry in Mesopotamia.

HAVILDAR	SHAM SINGH	1916	MESOPOTAMIA
HAVILDAR	MANGAL SINGH	1916	MESOPOTAMIA
SEPOY	MAHTAB SINGH	1917	MESOPOTAMIA
SEPOY	MAL SINGH	1918	MESOPOTAMIA

WAZIRISTAN

At the conclusion of the Great War the 34TH went on to distinguish themselves in Waziristan. The campaign was fierce and bitter and ended in thorough pacification of the wild Waziris. The following Sikh soldiers were awarded Indian Distinguished Service Medal for their conspicuous gallantry in Waziristan.

HAV. MAJOR	KISHEN SINGH	1921	WAZIRISTAN
SUBEDAR	SOHAWA SINGH	1921	WAZIRISTAN
JEMADAR	SUNDAR SINGH	1921	WAZIRISTAN
HAVILDAR	JHANDA SINGH	1921	WAZIRISTAN
HAVILDAR	CHHUR SINGH	1921	WAZIRISTAN
LANCE NAIK	LABH SINGH	1921	WAZIRISTAN
LANCE NAIK	BHAG SINGH	1921	WAZIRISTAN

Indian Distinguished Service Medal, 1914 – 1921 (cont.)

35TH SIKHS

The 35TH Sikhs did not serve overseas during the Great War but sent significant drafts to the other Sikh regiments fighting on the Western Front, Egypt and Mesopotamia. However they participated in the Third Afghan War. Operations in the Third Afghan War ranged along much of the border area. Fighting occurred in Chitral, in the Khyber Pass, through the Kurram Valley, in the Tochi Valley, in Waziristan, and in Baluchistan. The following Sikh soldiers of the 35TH Sikhs were awarded Indian Distinguished Service Medal for their conspicuous gallantry.

SEPOY	ASA SINGH	1915	FRANCE
HAVILDAR	MULA SINGH	1916	FRANCE
JEMADAR	FAUJA SINGH	1916	FRANCE
SEPOY	BUDH SINGH	1916	MESOPOTAMIA
SEPOY	INDAR SINGH	1919	MESOPOTAMIA
LANCE NAIK	MUNSHA SINGH	1919	MESOPOTAMIA
HAVILDAR	TALOK SINGH	1919	N. W. FRONTIER
SEPOY	BAWA SINGH	1919	N. W. FRONTIER
BHISTI	BARA SINGH	1919	N. W. FRONTIER

36TH SIKHS

The regiment arrived at Basra in Mesopotamia on the 25TH February 1916, and was incorporated in the 37TH Division. On 12TH April they advanced through the marshes towards the enemy lines. The Turkish advance posts were driven in, but the advance was brought to a halt by very heavy machine gun and rifle fire. The regiment sustained very heavy casualties. Both the 36TH and 45TH Sikhs participated in the Battle of Hai River in early 1917. About 1,200 Turks held the position in very well prepared entrenchments. Both regiments assaulted; shoulder - to - shoulder in the face of heavy machine-gun fire. Although the first three trench lines were captured, casualties were very heavy during the course of the day. At one time, the 45TH was more or less isolated as the Turks launched enveloping counterattacks. These were eventually pushed back. The fierceness of the fighting can be judged by the fact that, at the end of the day, the 45TH was left with three British and three Indian officers and 200 men. The other battalion (the 36TH) also suffered heavily, and was led out the action by the Subedar Major, the lone survivor of the British and Indian officers who had taken part in the battle. On 22ND January 1918 they entrained for railhead under orders to join the North Persian Force.

Continued on next page

Indian Distinguished Service Medal, 1914 – 1921 (cont.)

36TH SIKHS (cont.)

The following Sikh soldiers of the 36TH Sikhs were awarded Indian Distinguished Service Medal for their conspicuous gallantry in Mesopotamia.

SUBEDAR	THAKUR SINGH	1916	MESOPOTAMIA
HAVILDAR	SUNDAR SINGH	1916	MESOPOTAMIA
HAVILDAR	DALL SINGH	1916	MESOPOTAMIA
HAVILDAR	NATHA SINGH	1916	MESOPOTAMIA
SEPOY	RALA SINGH	1916	MESOPOTAMIA
SEPOY	BISHEN SINGH	1916	MESOPOTAMIA
LANCE NAIK	INDAR SINGH	1916	MESOPOTAMIA
SEPOY	NAHAR SINGH	1916	MESOPOTAMIA
SEPOY	BAKSHISH SINGH	1916	MESOPOTAMIA
SEPOY	ATMA SINGH	1916	MESOPOTAMIA
SEPOY	BADHAWA SINGH	1917	MESOPOTAMIA
SEPOY	BANT SINGH	1917	MESOPOTAMIA
NAIK	KALA SINGH	1917	MESOPOTAMIA
SEPOY	KISHAN SINGH	1917	MESOPOTAMIA
LANCE NAIK	THAKUR SINGH	1917	MESOPOTAMIA
NAIK	RAM SINGH	1917	MESOPOTAMIA
SEPOY	NARYAN SINGH	1917	MESOPOTAMIA
SUBEDAR	PERTAB SINGH	1919	MESOPOTAMIA

Ressaidar Hardit Singh, I D S M
9TH Hodson's Horse. Killed in action in France
5TH December 1917, Age 25.

Jagjit S. Bhullar (Canada) sent *SikhSpectrum.com* this picture of his grandfather.

Indian Distinguished Service Medal, 1914 - 1921 (cont.)

45TH RATTRAY'S SIKHS

Prior to the Mesopotamian campaign the 45TH Sikhs sent volunteers to other Sikh regiments fighting at the Western Front, Egypt and Persia. The battalion was deployed in Mesopotamia in 1917. It was here on February 1ST 1917, on the banks of the Hai river, that the battalion displayed courage, unflinching valour and made supreme sacrifice, a feat always recalled with pride. The Hai River is an offshoot of the Tigris River and connects the former to the Euphrates. However, nothing could deter the Sikhs who at that time were led by second-generation commanding officer, Lt.Col. HB Rattrays. The Turks let loose a heavy barrage on the battalion at break neck speed. Despite that the Jawans of the Sikh Regiment crushed and crippled the Turkish defences. The victory became possible only with heavy casualties. Out of 8 British officers, 17 Indian officers and 562 other ranks who participated in the attack, 154 other ranks were killed and 280 wounded. The following Sikh soldiers of the 45TH Sikhs were awarded Indian Distinguished Service Medal for their conspicuous gallantry.

SEPOY	FATEH SINGH	1915	FRANCE
SEPOY	UJAGAR SINGH	1915	FRANCE
LANCE NAIK	KESAR SINGH	1916	FRANCE
JEMADAR	MEHAR SINGH	1916	N. W. FRONTIER
SEPOY	PURAN SINGH	1916	N. W. FRONTIER
SEPOY	SUNDAR SINGH	1916	GALLIPOLI
LANCE NAIK	BHAG SINGH	1916	GALLIPOLI
HAVILDAR	SARUP SINGH	1917	MESOPOTAMIA
HAVILDAR	KAKA SINGH	1917	MESOPOTAMIA
HAVILDAR	BAGGA SINGH	1917	MESOPOTAMIA
HAVILDAR	PREM SINGH	1919	MESOPOTAMIA
HAVILDAR	WAZIR SINGH	1919	MESOPOTAMIA
SEPOY	KALA SINGH	1919	MESOPOTAMIA
NAIK	INDAR SINGH	1919	MESOPOTAMIA
NAIK	BANTA SINGH	1919	MESOPOTAMIA
NAIK	BASANT SINGH	1919	MESOPOTAMIA
NAIK	GURDIT SINGH	1919	MESOPOTAMIA

Indian Distinguished Service Medal, 1914 - 1921 (cont.)

45TH RATTRAY'S SIKHS (cont.)

The following Sikh soldiers of the 45TH Sikhs were awarded Indian Distinguished Service Medal for their conspicuous gallantry in Mesopotamia.

NAIK	NARAIN SINGH	1919	MESOPOTAMIA
NAIK	RATTAN SINGH	1919	MESOPOTAMIA
NAIK	SURAIN SINGH	1919	MESOPOTAMIA
SUBEDAR	KESAR SINGH	1919	MESOPOTAMIA
HAVILDAR	ISHAR SINGH	1919	MESOPOTAMIA
HAVILDAR	JIWAN SINGH	1921	MESOPOTAMIA
NAIK	LAL SINGH	1921	MESOPOTAMIA
NAIK	JASWANT SINGH	1921	MESOPOTAMIA
NAIK	MAGHAR SINGH	1921	MESOPOTAMIA
NAIK	BAKHTAWAR SINGH	1921	MESOPOTAMIA
NAIK	TAHEL SINGH	1921	MESOPOTAMIA
NAIK	HAZARA SINGH	1921	MESOPOTAMIA
LANCE NAIK	CHATTAR SINGH	1921	MESOPOTAMIA
SEPOY	GANGA SINGH	1921	MESOPOTAMIA
SEPOY	BHAG SINGH	1921	MESOPOTAMIA
SEPOY	SEWA SINGH	1921	MESOPOTAMIA
SEPOY	SETA SINGH	1921	MESOPOTAMIA
SEPOY	INDAR SINGH	1921	MESOPOTAMIA
SEPOY	KISHAN SINGH	1921	MESOPOTAMIA
SEPOY	KEHAR SINGH	1921	MESOPOTAMIA
SEPOY	MUKAN SINGH	1921	MESOPOTAMIA
SEPOY	JIT SINGH	1921	MESOPOTAMIA
SEPOY	MEHAR SINGH	1921	MESOPOTAMIA
JEMADAR	KESAR SINGH	1921	MESOPOTAMIA

Indian Distinguished Service Medal, 1914 - 1921 (cont.)
46TH PUNJABIS
EGYPT

At the beginning of the First World War the regiment did not have the chance of going overseas in any of the Expeditionary Forces. Eventually in 1917 the 46TH obtained their desire and got away from India to join the Egyptian Expeditionary Force. Active operations in that area were then drawing to a close, and so they did not get an opportunity to prove their worth in the field. They did, however, distinguish themselves in the quelling of the serious riots in Cairo, for which the following soldiers were awarded the Indian Distinguished Service Medal for their gallantry.

SUBEDAR	JOTA SINGH	1917	EGYPT
NAIK	MAHNGA SINGH	1917	EGYPT
SEPOY	BHAGAT SINGH	1917	EGYPT

47TH SIKHS
FRANCE

The 47TH Sikhs first landed in Marseilles on 26 September 1914. They took part in the Battles of La Bassee, Armentieres, Givenchy, Neuve Chapelle, Ypres, Festubert and Aubers Ridge. The attack on La Bassee on October 28TH 1914 was memorable. Only two companies went into assault all by themselves, for orders to the other two on the flanks had been cancelled. This was carried out with great dash and daring in the face of heavy resistance and fierce hand-to-hand fighting developed. " When our men were about 100 yards from the outskirts of the village, the Germans in the front trenches began to bolt, pursued by the gallant Sikhs and Sappers with bayonet, a few being killed others captured. The Indians then tore into the village; Sikhs and Sappers mixed together, and worked in parties up the streets, under furious fire from the roots of the buildings. The blood of our men was up and nothing could stop them. After long and ferocious struggle, the whole of the main street was captured". Of the 280 men who went into the battle only 68 returned. " The 47TH were raised in 1901 and have no Battle Honours on their colours. Throughout its services in France this magnificent Regiment never failed to answer all calls. Its reputation would be secure and its right to fight shoulder to shoulder with our best troops would be established if based only on the record of Neuve Chapelle but this action was only of many in which the 47TH distinguished themselves. The History of the Indian Army contains few nobler pages than that of the 28TH October 1914". (*Quoted from; The Indian Corps in France.*) The battalion was mentioned in the British Parliament for its outstanding bravery and steadfastness during the assault.

Indian Distinguished Service Medal, 1914 - 1921 (cont.)

47TH SIKHS (cont.)

FRANCE

The following Sikh soldiers of the 47TH Sikhs were awarded Indian Distinguished Service Medal for their conspicuous gallantry in France.

HAVILDAR	BHOLA SINGH	1915	FRANCE
NAIK	JAGAT SINGH	1915	FRANCE
SEPOY	KESAR SINGH	1915	FRANCE
SEPOY	BHUTA SINGH	1915	FRANCE
HAVILDAR	BHAGAT SINGH	1915	FRANCE
NAIK	MOTA SINGH	1915	FRANCE
SEPOY	WARIAM SINGH	1915	FRANCE
NAIK	MIT SINGH	1915	FRANCE
SEPOY	KEHR SINGH	1915	FRANCE
HAVILDAR	LACHMAN SINGH	1915	FRANCE
NAIK	KISHEN SINGH	1916	FRANCE

MESOPOTAMIA

On 17TH December 1915, the 47TH Sikhs left Marseilles in France for Mesopotamia and landed at Basra on 7TH January 1916. During the next three years in Mesopotamia the Sikhs fought at Dujailah, Bait Aiesse, Kut al Amara, Kizail Rabat, Jebel Mamrin and Tekrit. At Dujailah, entirely isolated and unsupported they twice repulsed determined Turkish attacks. The letter to the regiment from General Keary included, "The attack on Dujailah was most gallantly carried out and its capture was a notable achievement. The withdrawal from it was a military necessity, which the 8TH Brigade could not have averted." The following Sikh soldiers of the 47TH Sikhs were awarded Indian Distinguished Service Medal for their conspicuous gallantry in Mesopotamia.

SUBEDAR	MIT SINGH	1916	MESOPOTAMIA
HAVILDAR	MAL SINGH	1916	MESOPOTAMIA
LANCE NAIK	AMAR SINGH	1916	MESOPOTAMIA
LANCE NAIK	KEHR SINGH	1916	MESOPOTAMIA
SEPOY	NIKKA SINGH	1916	MESOPOTAMIA

Indian Distinguished Service Medal, 1914 - 1921 (cont.)

47TH SIKHS (cont.)

NAIK	MASTAN SINGH	1916	MESOPOTAMIA
SEPOY	DIAL SINGH	1916	MESOPOTAMIA
SEPOY	JOWALA SINGH	1916	MESOPOTAMIA
NAIK	BHAGAT SINGH	1917	MESOPOTAMIA
HAVILDAR	BAKSHISH SINGH	1917	MESOPOTAMIA
NAIK	KISHEN SINGH	1917	MESOPOTAMIA
LANCE NAIK	SUNDAR SINGH	1917	MESOPOTAMIA
LANCE NAIK	ARJAN SINGH	1917	MESOPOTAMIA
SUBEDAR	MIT SINGH	1917	MESOPOTAMIA
NAIK	DALIP SINGH	1918	MESOPOTAMIA
SEPOY	HARDIT SINGH	1919	MESOPOTAMIA

48TH PIONEERS

MESOPOTAMIA

Shortly after the outbreak of First World War, the 48TH Pioneers were bound for Mesopotamia. Within couple of days of disembarking in mid-November 1914 they found themselves in action at Sahil. Thereafter they took a very active part in virtually all of the early battles in Mesopotamia. In November 1915, during a bloody engagement, the Pioneers lost 57% of its officers and men (8 British Officers, 9 Indian Officers, and 259 Other Ranks). Then they began the long match back down the Tigris to Kut al Amara where the 6TH Division was besieged from 4TH December 1915, until it surrendered on 29TH April 1916. Roughly three hundred and forty other ranks of the 48TH Pioneers were besieged in Kut, of which three hundred were taken Prisoner. The following Sikh soldiers of the 48TH Pioneers were awarded Indian Distinguished Service Medal for their conspicuous gallantry in Mesopotamia.

NAIK	NAND SINGH	1915	MESOPOTAMIA
JEMADAR	SAHIB SINGH	1915	MESOPOTAMIA
HAVILDAR	DIAL SINGH	1915	MESOPOTAMIA
HAVILDAR	DEWA SINGH	1915	MESOPOTAMIA
SUBEDAR	LEHNA SINGH	1915	KUT AL AMARA
SEPOY	HARI SINGH	1915	KUT AL AMARA
LANCE NAIK	DHANA SINGH	1915	KUT AL AMARA
NAIK	DIAL SINGH	1915	KUT AL AMARA

Indian Distinguished Service Medal, 1914 - 1921 (cont.)

51ST SIKHS (FRONTIER FORCE)
MESOPOTAMIA

During the First World War the regiment served in Aden, Egypt, and Mesopotamia. For their services in the Middle East, they were given the title: 51ST The Prince of Wales's Own Sikhs (Frontier Force). The following Sikh soldiers were awarded Indian Distinguished Service Medal for their conspicuous gallantry in Mesopotamia.

SEPOY	BHOLA SINGH	1916	MESOPOTAMIA
SUBEDAR	LABH SINGH	1916	MESOPOTAMIA
JEMADAR	SUNDAR SINGH	1916	MESOPOTAMIA
JEMADAR	PREM SINGH	1916	MESOPOTAMIA
SEPOY	SUNDAR SINGH	1916	MESOPOTAMIA
SEPOY	DALIP SINGH	1917	MESOPOTAMIA
LANCE NAIK	GURDIT SINGH	1917	MESOPOTAMIA
SEPOY	KISHAN SINGH	1917	MESOPOTAMIA
HAVILDAR	HIRA SINGH	1918	MESOPOTAMIA
NAIK	LABH SINGH	1918	MESOPOTAMIA
SEPOY	MANGAL SINGH	1918	MESOPOTAMIA
SUBEDAR	UJAGAR SINGH	1918	MESOPOTAMIA
SUBEDAR	ARJAN SINGH	1918	MESOPOTAMIA
LANCE NAIK	JOWALA SINGH	1918	MESOPOTAMIA
SEPOY	ISHAR SINGH	1918	MESOPOTAMIA
HAVILDAR	MANGAL SINGH	1918	MESOPOTAMIA

52ND SIKHS (FRONTIER FORCE)
MESOPOTAMIA

During the First World War the Regiment served in Mesopotamia and the following Sikh soldiers were awarded the Indian Distinguished Service Medal for their gallantry.

HAVILDAR	INDAR SINGH	1916	MESOPOTAMIA
HAVILDAR	MIT SINGH	1917	MESOPOTAMIA
NAIK	SUNDAR SINGH	1917	MESOPOTAMIA

Indian Distinguished Service Medal, 1914 - 1921 (cont.)

53RD SIKHS (FRONTIER FORCE)

One of the more memorable exploits of 53RD Sikhs was in the storming of the heights at Dargai during the Pathan Revolt of 1897- 8 on the North West Frontier of India. The 53RD Sikhs were right behind the Gordon Highlanders and shared the victory when the tribesmen were routed. In the First World War, they served in Aden, Egypt and Mesopotamia. The following Sikh soldiers were awarded Indian Distinguished Service Medal for their conspicuous gallantry in Egypt and Mesopotamia.

LANCE NAIK	BHOLA SINGH	1916	MESOPOTAMIA
LANCE NAIK	RAM SINGH	1916	MESOPOTAMIA
SEPOY	JOWAHIR SINGH	1916	MESOPOTAMIA
SEPOY	MEHR SINGH	1916	MESOPOTAMIA
HAVILDAR	HARNAM SINGH	1916	MESOPOTAMIA
HAVILDAR	ARJAN SINGH	1916	MESOPOTAMIA
SEPOY	JIWAN SINGH	1916	MESOPOTAMIA
HAVILDAR	HARI SINGH	1917	MESOPOTAMIA
JEMADAR	HAZARA SINGH	1917	MESOPOTAMIA
JEMADAR	GURDIAL SINGH	1918	EGYPT
LANCE NAIK	BAHADUR SINGH	1918	EGYPT
HAVILDAR	MANGAL SINGH	1918	EGYPT
SEPOY	PALA SINGH	1918	EGYPT

54TH SIKHS (FRONTIER FORCE)

The 54TH Sikhs gained fame at the time of the Sepoy Mutiny. They marched from Abbottabad to Delhi, a distance of 560 miles in 30 days in the June heat, going into action on their arrival. During the First World War, they served in France and Mesopotamia, moving on to Waziristan in 1918. The following Sikh soldiers of the 54TH Sikhs were awarded the Indian Distinguished Service Medal for their conspicuous gallantry.

SEPOY	DELAIR SINGH	1916	FRANCE
SEPOY	DARBARA SINGH	1916	FRANCE
SEPOY	JHANDA SINGH	1917	MESOPOTAMIA
SUBEDAR	KESAR SINGH	1918	WAZIRISTAN
HAVILDAR	BACHANT SINGH	1918	WAZIRISTAN

Indian Distinguished Service Medal, 1914 - 1921 (cont.)

55TH COKE'S RIFLES (FRONTIER FORCE)

The 55TH Rifles did not serve abroad during the First World War, but many men of the regiment did, however, see service abroad during the war, while attached to other units. For the duration of the war, the regiment saw active service in the North-West Frontier of India, fighting many of the numerous marauding tribes that populated the area. The following Sikh soldiers were awarded the Indian Distinguished Service Medal for their conspicuous gallantry.

SUBEDAR	HARDIT SINGH	1918	EAST AFRICA
SEPOY	ISHAR SINGH	1919	BUSHIRE
JEMADAR	MOTA SINGH	1919	BUSHIRE
HAVILDAR	CHANNAN SINGH	1917	WAZIRISTAN
SEPOY	BAGGA SINGH	1917	WAZIRISTAN
HAVILDAR	LALL SINGH	1920	WAZIRISTAN
JEMADAR	DALEL SINGH	1920	WAZIRISTAN
NAIK	FAUJA SINGH	1908	N. W. FRONTIER
SEPOY	BAGH SINGH	1908	N. W. FRONTIER
SEPOY	BELA SINGH	1908	N. W. FRONTIER

56TH PUNJABI RIFLES (FRONTIER FORCE)

During the First World War the regiment served in Egypt and Mesopotamia. The following Sikh soldiers were awarded the Indian Distinguished Service Medal for their conspicuous gallantry.

SUBEDAR	BAKSHISH SINGH	1916	MESOPOTAMIA
JEMADAR	INDAR SINGH	1916	MESOPOTAMIA
HAVILDAR	BUDH SINGH	1916	MESOPOTAMIA
NAIK	ATTAR SINGH	1916	MESOPOTAMIA
JEMADAR	WAZIR SINGH	1916	MESOPOTAMIA
HAVILDAR	MANGAL SINGH	1916	MESOPOTAMIA
LANCE NAIK	BISHAN SINGH	1916	MESOPOTAMIA
SEPOY	SUBA SINGH	1916	MESOPOTAMIA
SEPOY	BHAGA SINGH	1917	MESOPOTAMIA
LANCE NAIK	SUNDAR SINGH	1917	EGYPT
LANCE NAIK	BAL SINGH	1919	EGYPT

Indian Distinguished Service Medal, 1914 - 1921 (cont.)

57TH WILDE'S RIFLES (FRONTIER FORCE)

The Mohmand Expedition

In 1908 a punitive expedition was mounted against the Mohmands, on the North West Frontier of India, for their raids into the British territory. At the commencement of the operations the regiment was ordered to push forward and seize a hill on the front. This the regiment did with great dash and gallantry, turning the enemy out of several Sangars at the point of the bayonet. A series of actions were fought, as a result of which no more raiding was made across the border by the Mohmands. The following is an extract from the official dispatch: " Thus ended the Mohmand expedition of 1908, which, though short, was memorable for the many hardships and privations undergone in excessive heat under a fiery sun with a very limited amount of water. The choking dust and plagues of flies were a severe test of endurance by day, whilst at night the men were kept awake at their posts for hours together, owing to the constant fire kept up by the enemy, which would have proved even more costly than it did, but for the labour expended on the entrenchments, and which added considerably to the daily labour the troops were called on to perform."

The following officers and men of the 57TH Rifles were awarded the Indian Distinguished Service Medal for their gallantry during the Mohmand Expedition.

JEMADAR	BHAGAT SINGH	1908	N. W. FRONTIER
HAVILDAR	JAGAT SINGH	1908	N. W. FRONTIER
SEPOY	GIAN SINGH	1908	N. W. FRONTIER
SEPOY	MANGAL SINGH	1908	N. W. FRONTIER
SEPOY	NIHAL SINGH	1908	N. W. FRONTIER

FRANCE

The 57TH Rifles disembarked at Marseilles on 26TH September 1914 for service on the Western Front. From the first landing in France the weather remained bitterly cold. The troops from India were clothed in Khaki drill and it was some months before serge became available for them. During their service in France until December 1915, the regiment had fought at Oostaverne, Messines, Festubert and Givenchy. The Sikh company especially distinguished itself at Wytschaete. The following Sikh soldiers were awarded the Indian Distinguished Service Medal for their conspicuous gallantry in France.

NAIK	SOHAN SINGH	1915	FRANCE
HAVILDAR	BUR SINGH	1915	FRANCE

Indian Distinguished Service Medal, 1914 - 1921 (cont.)

57TH WILDE'S RIFLES (FRONTIER FORCE) (cont.)
EAST AFRICA

The East African Campaign was a series of battles and guerrilla actions, which started in German East Africa and ultimately, impacted portions of Mozambique, Northern Rhodesia, Kenya, Uganda, and the Belgian Congo. The 57TH Rifles were engaged in long months of hard trekking and stiff fighting against a determined enemy. The German colonial forces fought for the duration of World War One and surrendered only after that war had ended. The following officers and men of the 57TH Rifles were awarded the Indian Distinguished Service Medal for their gallantry during the East African Campaign.

HAVILDAR	KAPUR SINGH	1916	EAST AFRICA
HAVILDAR	BHAGWAN SINGH	1916	EAST AFRICA
HAVILDAR	UDHAM SINGH	1916	EAST AFRICA
HAVILDAR	SUNDAR SIINGH	1916	EAST AFRICA
JEMADAR	HIRA SINGH	1916	EAST AFRICA
NAIK	AMIR SIGNH	1916	EAST AFRICA
NAIK	AMAR SINGH	1916	EAST AFRICA

58TH VAUGHAN'S RIFLES (FRONTIER FORCE)
FRANCE

The 58TH Rifles landed in Marseilles on 11TH October 1914. On October 31ST as they rushed the German trenches the enemy bolted and the few who stood their ground fell before the bayonets of the regiment. On the 24TH at the Battle of Festubert, Havildar Indar Singh held the position against heavy enemy attacks, for which he was awarded an immediate Indian Order of Merit. On December 18TH very heavy fighting ensued, but the 58TH more than held it's own and succeeding in regaining portions of the lost trenches and preventing any breakthrough by the enemy. The last tour of duty of the 58TH in the trenches in France ended on October 29TH. The following Sikh soldiers were awarded the Indian Distinguished Service Medal for their conspicuous gallantry in France.

NAIK	DEWA SINGH	1915	FRANCE
SUBEDAR	INDAR SINGH M.C	1915	FRANCE
HAVILDAR	SUNDAR SINGH	1915	FRANCE
NAIK	DEWA SINGH	1915	FRANCE
SUBEDAR	PHUMAN SINGH	1915	FRANCE

Indian Distinguished Service Medal, 1914 - 1921 (cont.)

58TH VAUGHAN'S RIFLES (FRONTIER FORCE) (cont.)
PALESTINE

Disembarking at Port Said on December 14TH, the 58TH Rifles was sent at once to a camp at Suez, where it was fully occupied in working the defences of the Suez Canal. The regiment was then called upon to fight the Turks at the villages of Yasur, El Kustineh and Tel El Turmis in Palestine. The following Sikh soldiers were awarded the Indian Distinguished Service Medal for their conspicuous gallantry in Palestine.

LANCE NAIK	BHAG SINGH	1917	PALESTINE
LANCE NAIK	PRITAM SINGH	1917	PALESTINE
LANCE NAIK	DIWAN SINGH	1917	PALESTINE
SEPOY	BHOLA SIINGH	1917	PALESTINE
SEPOY	BARA SINGH	1917	PALESTINE
SEPOY	AMAR SINGH	1917	PALESTINE

WAZIRISTAN

At the conclusion of the First World War the 58TH Rifles proceeded to Waziristan on the North West Frontier of India. They carried out punitive expeditions against the Waziris right up to 1921, in which the following Sikh soldiers were awarded the Indian Distinguished Service Medal for their gallantry

| SUBEDAR | KEHAR SINGH | 1921 | WAZIRISTAN |
| HAVILDAR | LAL SINGH | 1921 | WAZIRISTAN |

59TH SCINDE RIFLES (FRONTIER FORCE)

The 59TH Rifles landed in Marseilles on 26TH 1914, and fought in the battles of Givenchy, Neuve Chapelle, Ypres and Loos, suffering heavy casualties in the trenches. A British officer reported: " On the right Captain Scale reached the German wire with a platoon of Sikhs. The wire was, of course, uncut and the platoon was wiped out by machine gun fire. Jemadar Mangal Singh and another Sikh platoon took and held a German sap; capturing a German officer and some men. They held it for twenty four hours until the Sappers dug out to them and relieved them." From France the 59TH Rifles proceeded to Mesopotamia on 4TH January 1916. They fought in the battle of Dujailah and the final attempt to relieve Kut. While in Mesopotamia the regiment pursued and constantly clashed against the Turks. The following Sikh soldiers were awarded the Indian Distinguished Service Medal for their conspicuous gallantry.

| SUBEDAR | BISHAN SINGH | 1916 | FRANCE |
| NAIK | PHUMAN SINGH | 1916 | MESOPOTAMIA |

Indian Distinguished Service Medal, 1914 - 1921 (cont.)

62ND PUNJABIS

MESOPOTAMIA

At the outbreak of the First World War the 62ND Punjabis proceeded to Egypt and were given the task of defending the Timash-Bitter Lake section of the Suez Canal. Early in January 1914, the Turks raided Kantara and supported by rifle and machine gun fire succeeded in approaching the west bank. The Punjabis distinguished themselves by rushing the Turks down the fire swept bank. The Turkish raiding party was successfully charged, killing or wounding all the occupants of the boat. The Turks continued their attacks and were repulsed and attacked, paying heavily for their persistence. Some six officers and two hundred men surrendered in the trenches facing the Punjabis. On July 9TH, the 62ND joined the 28TH Brigade and embarked for Aden. Sheikh Othman was recaptured on July 21ST. Operations to clear the mainland were undertaken by sending out columns to Fiyush and Waht. The enemy were attacked and chased out of the area. Havildar Bishan Singh won the Indian Distinguished Service Medal for exemplary courage in the operations of this day. On December 22ND, the 62ND embarked at Aden for Basra, Mesopotamia. During their service in Mesopotamia they fought at Dujailah, Bait Aiesse, Kut al Amara, Kizail Rabat, Jebel Mamrin, and Tekrit. During the Kut al Amara relief operations, the 28TH Infantry Brigade, which included the 62ND Punjabis, made a frontal attack on the Tigris. The Turks repulsed the attack, inflicting 1,600 casualties on the British Force. On the 21ST they participated in the costly frontal attack against the Turkish positions at Hanna. All attempts to advance were met by very heavy machine gun fire from the Turkish trenches and the attack failed to make any further progress. The British casualties were two thousand seven hundred and forty. In this grim battle the 62ND Punjabis had 372 casualties. On April 30TH 1916 news was received that the garrison of Kut had surrendered. The Kut relief operation had cost the British 23,500 casualties, the 62ND share being 560. Finally the regiment participated in the fighting at the Hai Salient where the Turks lost heavily and abandoned many rifles with much ammunition and equipment. The following Sikh soldiers were awarded the Indian Distinguished Service Medal for their conspicuous gallantry.

HAVILDAR	BISHAN SINGH	1916	ADEN
HAVILDAR	MAHEL SINGH	1916	MESOPOTAMIA
HAVILDAR	SUNDAR SINGH	1917	MESOPOTAMIA
HAVILDAR	SEWA SINGH	1919	MESOPOTAMIA
SEPOY	CHANNAN SINGH	1917	MESOPOTAMIA

Indian Distinguished Service Medal, 1914 - 1921 (cont.)

66TH PUNJABIS

MESOPOTAMIA

At the outbreak of the First World War, the 66TH Punjabis, then stationed in Burma, were mobilised and ordered to Mesopotamia. They arrived at Basra on 30TH March 1915. During the Turkish attack on Shaiba, which lasted three days, the 66TH protected the approaches to Basra against a large force of Turkish cavalry. On the 22ND November, when the Brigade attacked the Turkish entrenchments near Ctesiphon, the 66TH pushed in and with dahs (choppers), which they had brought from Burma, hacked down the wooden posts and forced their way into trenches, killing many of the enemy with their bayonets. In the words of the official history of the Great War, it "was a fine performance, well conceived and gallantly executed; the operation is one of which the attacking force may well be proud." The battalion had gone into battle the strongest unit in the force and finished the day just half strong. They had suffered 242 casualties. During the fighting many deeds of gallantry were performed. Jemadar Bishan Singh set an example of coolness to his men and led them with courage and resolution. Jemadar Bishan Singh and Mugh Singh were awarded the Indian Order of Merit for gallantry and outstanding leadership. The battalion was lost to the Turks at Kut Al Amara, and when re-formed proceeded to Waziristan. The following Sikh soldiers were awarded the Indian Distinguished Service Medal for their conspicuous gallantry in Mesopotamia.

SEPOY	DHIR SINGH	1915	MESOPOTAMIA
SEPOY	SANTA SINGH	1915	MESOPOTAMIA
HAVILDAR	MIT SINGH	1917	MESOPOTAMIA
LANCE NAIK	CHANNAN SINGH	1917	MESOPOTAMIA
SUBEDAR	DHARAM SINGH	1917	MESOPOTAMIA
HAVILDAR	HARBACHAN SINGH	1920	MESOPOTAMIA
JEMADAR	SUNDAR SINGH	1920	MESOPOTAMIA
HAVILDAR	GAJJAN SINGH	1920	MESOPOTAMIA
HAVILDAR	LAL SINGH	1920	MESOPOTAMIA
NAIK	INDAR SINGH	1920	MESOPOTAMIA
NAIK	GANGA SINGH	1920	MESOPOTAMIA
LANCE NAIK	LAL SINGH	1920	MESOPOTAMIA

Indian Distinguished Service Medal, 1914 - 1921 (cont.)

67TH PUNJABIS

MESOPOTAMIA

On 7TH March 1915, while in Loralai, the 67TH Punjabis received its orders to mobilize for overseas service to Mesopotamia. It soon proceeded east to Persia, where it took part in operations against Turkish regular army and hostile tribesmen around Ahwaz. Following this, the 67TH Punjabis with its Brigade were transferred to the Euphrates front to take part in the capture of Nasiriyah. After a stiff fight on the 24TH and 25TH July 1915, Nasiriyah was taken, although the 67TH suffered 31 killed and 36 wounded. In October 1915, the Battalion moved to the Tigris River, where it left detachments at Qalat Saleh and Ali-eh-Gharbi. Then moved to Ruz, and thence in March 1918 to Tawilah. On 10TH October 1918 the Punjabis embarked at Basra for service in Salonika. Eventually they arrived back in India on 1ST October 1920, after five and half years of overseas service. The following Sikh soldiers were awarded the Indian Distinguished Service Medal for their conspicuous gallantry in Mesopotamia.

HAVILDAR	INDAR SINGH	1915	MESOPOTAMIA
SUBEDAR	LACHMAN SINGH	1915	MESOPOTAMIA
JEMADAR	KHEM SINGH	1915	MESOPOTAMIA
HAVILDAR	MAHAN SINGH	1915	MESOPOTAMIA

69TH PUNJABIS

In 1914 the 69TH, on their way to Egypt, were ordered to destroy the fort of Sheikh Sayad at Aden. Subedar Labh Singh of the Machine Gun section was awarded an immediate Indian Distinguished Service Medal for his gallantry in this action. The 69TH for the next six months was engaged in the defence of the Suez Canal. Then after a short spell at Gallipoli embarked for France, after spending three months in the trenches and participating in the battle of Loos, the 69TH served in the Aden Field Force for three years. On 11TH September 1918, Lance Naik Prabhu Singh led a spirited charge and, although outnumbered three to one, drove off the Turks and recovered the bodies of fallen comrades. The following Sikh soldiers were awarded the Indian Distinguished Service Medal for their conspicuous gallantry.

NAIK	PUNNA SINGH	1915	FRANCE
HAVILDAR	GURDIT SINGH	1915	FRANCE
HAVILDAR	BHULLA SINGH	1915	FRANCE
LANCE NAIK	PRABHU SINGH	1918	ADEN
SUBEDAR	LABH SINGH	1914	ADEN

Indian Distinguished Service Medal, 1914 - 1921 (cont.)

72ND PUNJABIS

On the outbreak of the First World War in August 1914, the 72ND Punjabis were stationed in Peshawar, on the North West Frontier of India. While the 72ND had been engaged in various Frontier operations, it had also been called upon to supply trained personnel for new units that were being formed. They also supplied drafts to regular units serving in overseas theatres. Eventually the battalion was ordered for service overseas. The battalion disembarked at Suez on 10TH March 1918 and went into camp at Tel-el-Kebir. Then it proceeded to Palestine and was sent into the line immediately. On 28TH July the battalion was called upon to carry out a night raid on a ridge held by about 100 Turks with 3 machine guns. The raiding party consisted of 3 Indian officers and 140 Sikhs. When the raiding party was 150 yards from the enemy trenches it was caught in a barrage of artillery and machine gun fire. They gallantly pushed on with great determination; a few succeeded in getting through the enemy wire and right up to the enemy defences, but they were too few to be effective and eventfully aborted the raid. During the final operations against the Turks, the 72ND helped to capture El Tireh, a stoutly fortified village, where the enemy offered a determined resistance. On the conclusion of the First World War the battalion was employed on garrison duties until 1921, first in Palestine and afterwards in Egypt. The following Sikh soldiers were awarded the Indian Distinguished Service Medal for their conspicuous gallantry in Palestine.

SEPOY	HARI SINGH	1919	PALESTINE
SEPOY	GURDAS SINGH	1919	PALESTINE
LANCE NAIK	SOHAN SINGH	1919	PALESTINE
HAVILDAR	BHAGAT SINGH	1919	PALESTINE

74TH PUNJABIS

On the outbreak of war in August 1914, the 72ND Punjabis were stationed in Hong Kong. During 1915 and 1916 they remained at Hong Kong, from time to time providing drafts to other regiments on active service. A complete company went to join the 67TH Punjabis in Mesopotamia, where Subedar Wariam Singh was awarded the Indian Distinguished Service Medal for his conspicuous gallantry against the Turks. After a brief spell on the North West Frontier the regiment proceeded to Palestine. In Palestine they participated in the final breakthrough towards Damascus. They hotly pursued the Turks in the direction of Haifa, Aleppo, and Damascus and until 1920 they were employed on guard duties at a prisoner of war camp at Tel-el-Kebir, returning to Indian in January 1921.

| SUBEDAR | WARIAM SINGH | 1918 | MESOPOTAMIA |

Indian Distinguished Service Medal, 1914 - 1921 (cont.)

76TH PUNJABIS

MESOPOTAMIA

At the outbreak of the First World War, the 76TH Punjabis were mobilised and proceeded to Egypt to protect the Suez Canal. The Turks, after meeting a repulse, made no more attempts on the Suez Canal. The battalion then joined the 12TH Indian Brigade and landed in Basra in March 1915. As the battle at Shaiba raged on, the battalion's machine gun section was sent across to Shaiba. The Turks were subjected to devastating fire from the machine guns as they fled from the battlefield. Soon after the victory at Shaiba, the 76TH formed a part of the force for operations in Persian Arabistan, to restore the supply of oil, which had been interrupted by the Beni Turuf tribe. The battalion forded a river and attacked a fort, which was strongly held by the enemy. The Arabs fled when charged but were pursued and the majority of them killed. Then the battalion participated in the fighting at Akaika Channel, Nasiriyah, Ctesiphon, and finally fell to the Turks at Kut al Amara The battalion was re-formed after the war and proceeded to Waziristan. The following Sikh soldiers were awarded the Indian Distinguished Service Medal for their conspicuous gallantry.

JEMADAR	GULZARA SINGH	1916	MESOPOTAMIA
HAVILDAR	NARAIN SINGH	1916	MESOPOTAMIA
LANCE NAIK	MAJJA SINGH	1916	MESOPOTAMIA
LANCE NAIK	CHAJJA SINGH	1916	MESOPOTAMIA
LANCE NAIK	GANGA SINGH	1915	MESOPOTAMIA
SEPOY	THAKUR SINGH	1916	MESOPOTAMIA
SEPOY	ISHAR SINGH	1915	MESOPOTAMIA
SEPOY	RAHLA SINGH	1916	MESOPOTAMIA
SEPOY	BELA SINGH	1916	MESOPOTAMIA
SEPOY	DHARAM SINGH	1915	MESOPOTAMIA
HAVILDAR	BEANT SINGH	1920	KUT AL AMARA
HAVILDAR	BHOLA SINGH	1920	KUT AL AMARA
HAVILDAR	HUKAM SINGH	1920	KUT AL AMARA
NAIK	BATTAN SINGH	1920	KUT AL AMARA
SUBEDAR	NARAIN SINGH	1920	WAZIRISTAN
JEMADAR	PRITPAL SINGH	1920	WAZIRISTAN
HAVILDAR	PURAN SINGH	1920	WAZIRISTAN

Indian Distinguished Service Medal, 1914 - 1921 (cont.)

82ND PUNJABIS

Although the battalion did not get the opportunity of fighting against the Germans and the Turks during 1914 and 1915, many of its officers and men went as reinforcements to other units and fought in decisive battles in the various theatres of war. In December 1915, the Battalion mobilised and joined the Mesopotamia Expeditionary Force. During the bloody Battle of Dujaila, the Battalion suffered 233 casualties. In this action Sepoy Kesar Singh was awarded the Indian Order of Merit for his gallantry and initiative in leading his section under heavy fire after his section commander was killed, and for subsequently extricating the remaining men of the section from a difficult position though he himself was wounded. The Battalion saw further action at the Hai Salient and Tigres before proceeding to guard the Persian Border. The following Sikh soldiers were awarded the Indian Distinguished Service Medal for their conspicuous gallantry in Mesopotamia.

SUBEDAR	HIRA SINGH	1916	MESOPOTAOMIA
SUBEDAR	DALIP SINGH	1917	MESOPOTAOMIA

87TH PUNJABIS

The 87TH was at Jhelum when the First World War broke out in 1914. Almost immediately the Battalion was obliged to provide drafts for the 76TH Punjabis, which was sent to Mesopotamia, and to 10TH Jats and 47TH Sikhs in France. The Battalion also continued to provide reinforcements for Punjabi units in Mesopotamia. When the 87TH had sent away more than 1,400 men as drafts to other units, it was itself called upon to proceed to Mesopotamia in 1917. Following the fall of Baghdad the 87TH remained on garrison duties until the summer of 1918. In the autumn the 87TH participated in the attack on Jebel Hamrin, and pursued the Turks, in dogged actions until the last days of October when the Turks capitulated. The breakdown of Turkish authority inspired many sections of the local population to question British authority, especially in Kurdistan. Continuous operations were carried out in South Kurdistan, and the area was finally pacified. In July 1920 the 87TH was in the forefront during the Rumaitha operations and suffered 69 casualties. At last, in April 1921, after four years overseas service the Battalion moved back to India. The following Sikh soldiers were awarded the Indian Distinguished Service Medal for their conspicuous gallantry in Mesopotamia.

SEPOY	SOHAN SINGH	1917	MESOPOTAOMIA
SEPOY	BHAN SINGH	1921	MESOPOTAOMIA

Indian Distinguished Service Medal, 1914 - 1921 (cont.)

89TH PUNJABIS

In 1914, the 89TH were posted to a force that was being rushed towards Egypt. However, on their way they were ordered to destroy the fort of Sheikh Sayad. The fort lay at the end of a small peninsula of Arabia, whence the Red Sea traffic could be attacked. The 89TH proceeded to attack the fort, supported by the naval guns. The landing was made in the face of small-arms fire but resistance was soon overcome and the fort and surrounding high ground captured. After Sheikh Sayad the 89TH proceeded to Egypt, where it participated in repulsing an attempt by Turkish forces to seize control of the critical Suez Canal, then in British hands. After a short stay in the disastrous Gallipoli expedition, the 89TH proceeded to France and were posted to the Ferozepore Brigade. On the Western Front the 89TH fought actions at Neuve Chapelle and the second battle of Ypres, before being withdrawn and ordered to Mesopotamia. After the grim fighting in Mesopotamia the 89TH saw action in Greece and Russia. The following Sikh soldiers were awarded the Indian Distinguished Service Medal for their conspicuous gallantry.

HAVILDAR	HARNAM SINGH	FRANCE
HAVILDAR	NARYAN SINGH	FRANCE
JEMADAR	BAGGA SINGH	FRANCE
LANCE NAIK	BUTA SINGH	EGYPT
SEPOY	DASAUNDA SINGH	EGYPT
NAIK	INDAR SINGH	GALLIPOLI
HAVILDAR	GURDIT SINGH	MESOPOTAMIA
NAIK	KISHAN SINGH	MESOPOTAMIA
SEPOY	WARIAM SINGH	MESOPOTAMIA
LANCE NAIK	SANTA SINGH	MESOPOTAMIA
SEPOY	MIT SINGH	MESOPOTAMIA
LANCE NAIK	HAZURA SINGH	MESOPOTAMIA
SEPOY	GURDIT SINGH	MESOPOTAMIA
SEPOY	MEHR SINGH	MESOPOTAMIA

Indian Distinguished Service Medal, 1914 - 1921 (cont.)

MESOPOTAMIA OPERATIONS

Major-General Charles Townsend, who had taken over command of operations, found himself besieged in Kut al Amara. In April 1916 Townsend surrendered the town, along with 6,000 Indians and 2,070 British soldiers. A force of Indians under General Fenton Aylmer had tried repeatedly and unsuccessfully to relieve Kut al Amara and had suffered over 21,000 casualties. Nonetheless, by December 1916 the British renewed their advance up the Tigris with 166,000 men - over 100,000 of them Indians. On 11TH March 1917 they entered Baghdad. 1917-18 saw a continued Allied advance northwards through the rest of Mesopotamia, and on to the Caspian Sea and to the Mosul oilfields. These were taken over on 14TH November 1918, just before the end of the war, at which time there were reckoned to be 260,000 Indian soldiers in Mesopotamia, three times as many as the British contingent. It had taken the Allies four years and cost 80,000 casualties to drive the Turks out of the Mesopotamian oilfields. Altogether, some 675,000 Indian fighting troops saw service in Mesopotamia, as well as hundreds of thousands of auxiliary troops.

90TH PUNJABIS

MESOPOTAMIA

The regiment took part in the Second Afghan War and in 1914, at the start of First World War the regiment was in the Nasirabad Brigade, 5TH (Mhow) Division stationed in India until 1915, when they were transferred to the 12TH Brigade of 12TH Indian Division. They fought in the Battle of Shaiba, the Battle of Khafajiya and the Battle of Nasiriya in the Mesopotamia Campaign. When the 12TH Division was disbanded in 1916, they moved to the 15TH Indian Division. When attached to the 15TH they took part in the Action of As Sahilan, the Capture of Ramadi, the Occupation of Hit and the Action of Khan Baghdadi. The following Sikh soldiers were awarded the Indian Distinguished Service Medal for their conspicuous gallantry in Mesopotamia.

SUBEDAR	HARNAM SINGH	1916	MESOPOTAMIA
SEBEDAR	NARAYAN SINGH	1916	MESOPOTAMIA
JEMADAR	KISHAN SINGH	1916	MESOPOTAMIA
JEMADAR	SUNDAR SINGH	1916	MESOPOTAMIA
HAVILDAR	SOBHA SINGH	1916	MESOPOTAMIA
HAVILDAR	BISHAN SINGH	1916	MESOPOTAMIA
NAIK	PURAN SINGH	1916	MESOPOTAMIA
SEPOY	MANGAL SINGH	1916	MESOPOTAMIA
SEPOY	GURDIT SINGH	1916	MESOPOTAMIA
SEPOY	BHAGAT SINGH	1916	MESOPOTAMIA

Indian Distinguished Service Medal, 1914 - 1921 (cont.)

91ST PUNJABIS (LIGHT INFANTRY)

The following Sikh soldiers of the 91ST Punjabis were awarded the Indian Distinguished Service Medal for their conspicuous gallantry in Egypt and Mesopotamia.

SUBADAR	SUNDAR SINGH	1917	EGYPT
SEPOY	KISHEN SINGH	1917	EGYPT
LANCE NAIK	KISHAN SINGH	1919	MESOPOTAMIA
SEPOY	NARINJAN SINGH	1919	MESOPOTAMIA

92ND PUNJABIS

EGYPT

At the outbreak of the First World War the 92ND Punjabis proceeded to Egypt and were given the task of defending the Sarapeum section of the Suez Canal. Early in January, the Turks raided Kantara. Supported by rifle and machine gun fire they succeeded in approaching the Sarapeum. The 92ND successfully charged the attackers, taking many prisoners. The Turks did not give up. On the morning of the 4TH they were still in strength, entrenched on the East Bank of the Canal. The 92ND Punjabis were ordered to attack and round up the Turks in this position. This they did successfully. The Turks laid down their arms and surrendered to the Punjabis. In July the 92ND embarked for service in Mesopotamia. The following Sikh soldiers of the 92ND Punjabis were awarded the Indian Distinguished Service Medal for their conspicuous gallantry in Egypt.

NAIK	KARAM SINGH	1914	EGYPT
SEPOY	DHARAM SINGH	1914	EGYPT
SEPOY	JAGINDAR SINGH	1914	EGYPT
NAIK	DALIP SINGH	1914	EGYPT

Sikh officers sitting on captured Turkish tank in Gaza, 1918.

Indian Distinguished Service Medal, 1914 - 1921 (cont.)

92ND PUNJABIS (cont.)

MESOPOTAMIA

The following Sikh soldiers of the 92ND Punjabis were awarded the Indian Distinguished Service Medal for their conspicuous gallantry in Mesopotamia.

JEMADAR	KISHAN SINGH	1916	MESOPOTAMIA
HAVILDAR	SAPOORAN SINGH	1916	MESOPOTAMIA
HAVILDAR	WASAKHA SINGH	1916	MESOPOTAMIA
HAVILDAR	HARNAM SINGH	1916	MESOPOTAMIA
NAIK	HARI SINGH	1916	MESOPOTAMIA
NAIK	BASANT SINGH	1916	MESOPOTAMIA
NAIK	HARNAM SINGH	1916	MESOPOTAMIA
NAIK	CHANAN SINGH	1916	MESOPOTAMIA
LANCE NAIK	DALIP SINGH	1916	MESOPOTAMIA
SEPOY	SAMPOORAN SINGH	1916	MESOPOTAMIA
SEPOY	SOHAN SINGH	1916	MESOPOTAMIA
SEPOY	KISHAN SINGH	1916	MESOPOTAMIA
SEPOY	JHANDA SINGH	1916	MESOPOTAMIA

93RD BURMA INFANTRY

MESOPOTAMIA

At the outbreak of the First World War the 93RD Burma Infantry proceeded to Egypt and were given the task of defending a section of the Suez Canal. From Egypt the 93RD proceeded to France and became part of the Dehra Dun Brigade. In France the 93RD fought at the battle of Loos, in which Lance Naik Mihan Singh was awarded the Indian Distinguished Service Medal for his gallantry. From France the 93RD proceeded to Mesopotamia and took part in the abortive attempt at the relief of Kut, where it suffered badly, and eventually moved to serve in Burma. The following Sikh soldiers of the 93RD were awarded the Indian Distinguished Service Medal for their conspicuous gallantry in Mesopotamia.

LANCE NAIK	MIHAN SINGH	1915	FRANCE
LANCE NAIK	BHAN SINGH	1916	MESOPOTAMIA
HAVILDAR	SAHIB SINGH	1916	MESOPOTAMIA
SEPOY	BHAN SINGH	1916	MESOPOTAMIA

Indian Distinguished Service Medal, 1914 - 1921 (cont.)

107TH PIONEERS
FRANCE

At the outbreak of the First World War, the 107TH Pioneers were ordered to France. On the 24TH December, they attacked a German trench; in this sharp fight they lost 17 other ranks killed. Subadar Labh Singh and Havildar Singh were awarded an immediate Indian Distinguished Service Medal. From France the regiment proceeded to Mesopotamia and saw action at Basra, Sannaiyat, Tigres and finally Baghdad, before being ordered to Persia. The following Sikh soldiers of the 107TH Pioneers were awarded the Indian Distinguished Service Medal for their conspicuous gallantry in France..

SUBEDAR	LABH SINGH	1915	FRANCE
HAVILDAR	BHAGAT SINGH	1915	FRANCE
HAVILDAR	ACHHAR SINGH	1915	FRANCE
SEPOY	PHAGA SINGH	1915	FRANCE
LANCE NAIK	JITHA SINGH	1916	FRANCE

INDIAN SUBORDINATE MEDICAL DEPARTMENT

At the outbreak of the Great War, one and a half million volunteers came forward from the Indian subcontinent. Of these 140,000 saw active service on the Western Front in France and Belgium. 90,000 served in the front-line Corps, and some 50,000 in auxiliary battalions. Nearly 700,000 then served in the Middle East, fighting with great distinction against the Turks in the Mesopotamian campaign. They served on the Gallipoli peninsula, and went to East and West Africa, and even to China. The following Sikh officers of the Medical Department were awarded gallantry awards for their devout service in all these theatres of war.

ASS. SURGEON	KISHAN SINGH	1916	FRANCE
ASS. SURGEON	BISHAN SINGH	1916	MESOPOTAMIA
ASS. SURGEON	JASWANT SINGH	1916	MESOPOTAMIA
ASS. SURGEON	HARNAM SINGH	1916	MESOPOTAMIA
ASS. SURGEON	INDAR SINGH	1916	MESOPOTAMIA
ASS. SURGEON	CHANDA SINGH	1919	MESOPOTAMIA
ASS. SURGEON	UJAGAR SINGH	1919	TRANS-CASPIA
ASS. SURGEON	LEM SINGH	1919	ADEN
ASS. SURGEON	BIR SINGH	1918	EAST AFRICA
ASS. SURGEON	H.S.GILL	1920	MESOPOTAMIA

Indian Distinguished Service Medal, 1914 - 1921 (cont.)

BURMA MILITARY POLICE

The Burma Military Police Force was a paramilitary force. All the personnel were Indian Army volunteers. The Military Police Battalions were organized like regular army regiments; their duties were entirely military. The Burma Military Police included 3,937 Sikhs. They had extensive experience of military operations in the jungle covered mountainous frontier tracts of Burma, while keeping the peace amongst the turbulent tribes. During the First World War the Burma Police Battalions were milked dry of soldiers for service in the major theatres of war. They defended the Suez Canal and went on to serve in Mesopotamia. The following Sikh soldiers of the Burma Military Police were awarded the Indian Distinguished Service Medal for their conspicuous gallantry.

HAVILDAR	TRILOK SINGH	1918	BURMA
HAVILDAR	ARJAN SINGH	1918	BURMA
SUBEDAR	AMAR SINGH	1918	BURMA
SOWAR	RAGHBIR SINGH	1918	BURMA
SEPOY	INDER SINGH	1918	BURMA
SEPOY	MAL SINGH	1918	BURMA
SUBEDAR	ARJAN SINGH	1920	BURMA FRONTIER
JEMADAR	MOTA SINGH	1920	BURMA FRONTIER
SOWAR	JOWAHIR SINGH	1916	KACHIN HILLS
SOWAR	BHAGWAN SINGH	1916	KACHIN HILLS
SOWAR	MASTAN SINGH	1916	KACHIN HILLS
SOWAR	MEHR SINGH	1916	KACHIN HILLS
LANCE NAIK	CHET SINGH	1917	EGYPT
SEPOY	HARNAM SINGH	1917	EGYPT
LANCE NAIK	KIRPAL SINGH	1917	EGYPT
SEPOY	KAKA SINGH	1917	EGYPT
HAVILDAR	NAR SINGH	1919	MESOPOTAMIA
HAVILDAR	PALA SINGH	1919	MESOPOTAMIA
LANCE NAIK	MOHAN SINGH	1919	MESOPOTAMIA
SEPOY	KARTAR SINGH	1919	MESOPOTAMIA

Indian Distinguished Service Medal, 1914 - 1921 (cont.)

BURMA MOUNTED RIFLES

Sikhs and Punjabi Mussulmans of the Burma Police Battalions were bodily formed into three squadrons of Burma Mounted Rifles for service in Trans-Caspia in 1917. The British Army intervened in Persia almost from the outset of the war to prevent the loss of its oil supplies to pro-German factors in the Persian Government and, later, to the Turks. So further intervention along the Persian frontier was inevitable following the establishment of Bolshevik rule in Trans-Caspia. On 5TH July 1917 a troop of Burma Mounted Rifles under Jemadar Partab Singh effectively cleared several camps and drove the tribesmen into the hills. On 22ND January 1918, Burma Mounted Rifles encountered considerable opposition and, displaying dash and spirit, completely routed the robbers, killing about 80 of them. During their stay in South Persia the Burma Mounted Rifles mounted continuous punitive actions against the well-organised robber bands and Russian Bolsheviks. Major actions were fought at Gumun, Northern Fars, Ziarat, Kuh-I-Khan, Deh Shaik, and Shiraz. At Ahmadadbad on 16TH June, it is estimated that of about 3,200 tribesmen engaged, 200 had been killed and 300 wounded. General Malleson reported that Russian circles were filled with the greatest admiration for the part played by the Indian troops, whom they regarded as being equal to ten times the number of any of the other combatants. The following Sikh soldiers of the Burma Mounted Rifles were awarded the Indian Distinguished Service Medal for their conspicuous gallantry South Persia.

JEMADAR	PARTAB SINGH	1918	SOUTH PERSIA
DAFFADAR	CHANAN SINGH	1918	SOUTH PERSIA
JEMADAR	PERTAB SINGH	1918	SOUTH PERSIA
RISALDAR	GULZAR SINGH	1918	SOUTH PERSIA
DAFFADAR	WARIAM SINGH	1918	SOUTH PERSIA
SOWAR	SAUDAGAR SINGH	1918	SOUTH PERSIA
SOWAR	MAN SINGH	1918	SOUTH PERSIA
DAFFADAR	MOHAR SINGH	1919	SOUTH PERSIA
DAFFADAR	RALLA SINGH	1919	SOUTH PERSIA
SOWAR	UTTAM SINGH	1919	SOUTH PERSIA
DAFFADAR	HUKAM SINGH	1919	SOUTH PERSIA
JEMADAR	WARIAM SINGH	1919	BUSHIRE
LANCE DAFFADAR	BASTA SINGH	1919	BUSHIRE
LANCE DAFFADAR	MEJA SINGH	1919	BUSHIRE

Indian Distinguished Service Medal, 1914 - 1921 (cont.)

FARIDKOT SAPPERS AND MINERS

Faridkot was a Sikh Princely State in the Punjab. The ruler on the outbreak of war supplied a company of his Sappers and Miners for British use. The unit was about 130 men strong with over 90% of them being Jat Sikhs. They were despatched to British East Africa with Indian Expeditionary Force "B" in October 1914. Fewer than 25 died during the campaign, and this low figure is a tribute to the hardiness of Jat Sikhs. The unit was awarded the Battle Honours: Kilimanjaro, Behobeho, East Africa 1914-1918. The following Sikh soldiers of Faridkot Sappers and Miners were awarded the Indian Distinguished Service Medal for their conspicuous gallantry East Africa.

SUBEDAR	RAGHBIR SINGH	1917	EAST AFRICA
HAVILDAR	HARNAM SINGH	1917	EAST AFRICA
NAIK	SAWAN SINGH	1917	EAST AFRICA
LANCE NAIK	KISHEN SINGH	1917	EAST AFRICA
JEMADAR	MOTI SINGH	1918	EAST AFRICA
JEMADAR	CHET SINGH	1918	EAST AFRICA
NAIK	THANA SINGH	1918	EAST AFRICA

JIND INFANTRY

Jind was a Sikh Princely State in the Punjab. The ruler on the outbreak of war supplied a regiment of infantry about 130 strong for British use. They were despatched to British East Africa with Indian Expeditionary Force "B" in October 1914 and were on active service for three years. The Jind Infantry suffered particularly heavy casualties at the battle of Jasin. Among others the conduct of Major General Natha Singh was singled out for special commendation. The following Sikh soldiers of Jind Infantry were awarded the Indian Distinguished Service Medal for their conspicuous gallantry at the battle of Jasin.

HAVILDAR	GUJAR SINGH	1915	EAST AFRICA
SEPOY	SADHU SINGH	1915	EAST AFRICA
SEPOY	LAKHA SINGH	1915	EAST AFRICA
CAPTAIN	BIHARA SINGH	1915	EAST AFRICA
SEPOY	JAGTA SINGH	1915	EAST AFRICA
SEPOY	KHIWAN SINGH	1915	EAST AFRICA
SUBEDAR	BAHAL SINGH	1915	EAST AFRICA
SUBEDAR	BISHAN SINGH	1915	EAST AFRICA

Indian Distinguished Service Medal, 1914 - 1921 (cont.)

KAPURTHALA SERVICE INFANTRY

Jind was a Sikh Princely State in the Punjab. At the outbreak of the Great War in 1914 the ruler supplied a regiment of infantry for British use. The Kapurthala Service Infantry regiment was dispatched for active service in East Africa, where it remained for nearly four years and did excellent work. On 2ND November 1915, the East African Mounted Rifles and the Kapurthala Infantry launched a simultaneous frontal attack on the mountain positions at Longindo. Subedar Gurdit Singh was awarded the Indian Distinguished Service Medal for his conspicuous gallantry during this action.

PATIALA INFANTRY

Patiala was a Premier Sikh Princely State in the Punjab. At the outbreak of the Great War in 1914, the States forces were mobilised for service in the Middle East against the Axis Powers. The Battalion under the command of Colonel Gurbux Singh arrived at Suez on November 16TH 1914. It defended the portion of the Suez Canal from Tinch to Port Said during the Turkish attacks between January and February 1915. In September 1915 a company of the battalion reinforced the 14TH Sikhs at Gallipoli. The regiment remained on the Suez Canal defence duty from Ismailia to Sarapeum. From the beginning of 1916 to the middle of April 1917 the entire battalion remained on front line duty on various posts in Jordan, stretching from Kubri to Ayun Mussa, including Gabel Murr Post and Bir- Mubaik. It also saw action in the Jordan Valley. The following Sikh soldiers of Patiala Infantry were awarded the Indian Distinguished Service Medal for their conspicuous gallantry in Egypt.

NAIK	RATTAN SINGH	1916	EGYPT
SEPOY	SEWA SINGH	1916	EGYPT
JEMADAR	PARTAP SINGH	1916	EGYPT
CAPTAIN	GURDIAL SINGH	1916	EGYPT
LIEUTENANT	JASMER SINGH	1916	EGYPT
SEPOY	JAWALA SINGH	1916	EGYPT
LANCE DAFFADAR	ATTAR SINGH	1919	N. W. FRONTIER
JAMADAR	RAM SINGH	1919	N. W. FRONTIER

Indian Distinguished Service Medal, 1914 - 1921 (cont.)

MALAY STATES GUIDES

The Guides, Infantry and a battery of Artillery were raised in 1875, with class composition of Sikhs and Punjabi Mussulmans, being ex-Indian Army soldiers. During the First World War, the Battery and the Infantry joined the Aden Defence Force from October 1915 onwards. The Battery at the strength of 3 Indian officers, 54 Gunners, 50 Drivers and 5 followers, the Infantry numbering 788 all ranks, predominantly Sikhs. They continually clashed with the Turks and had a great deal of marching under very hot sun. Havildar Wir Singh of the Artillery and the following Infantry soldiers were awarded the Indian Distinguished Service Medal for their conspicuous gallantry in Aden.

NAIK	SANTA SINGH	1916	ADEN
JEMADAR	BOGH SINGH	1916	ADEN
HAVILDAR	BAGGA SINGH	1919	ADEN
SEPOY	SURIAN SINGH	1919	ADEN
SEPOY	LAL SINGH	1919	ADEN
HAVILDAR	WIR SINGH	1920	ADEN

INDIAN DISTINGUISHED SERVICE MEDAL
1922 – 1947

HAVILDAR LAL SINGH
INDIAN FIELD AMBULANCE

"Havildar Lal Singh was awarded the Indian Distinguished Service Medal for good service to duty at Chern March 1941, Teclesan March 1941, and Amba Alagi May 1941 in Ethiopia. He worked unceasingly under difficult circumstances and often under intensive fire rallying the stretcher-bearers and recovering the wounded from the danger zone. His conduct and influence was outstanding."

NAIK PALA SINGH
13TH FRONTIER FORCE REGIMENT

"Naik Pala Singh was awarded the Indian Distinguished Service Medal for conspicuous bravery and devotion to duty. On 8TH May 1941, in the attack on Castle Hill in the battle of Amba Alagi in Ethiopia. Naik Pala Singh and all his section were wounded by mortar fire. Inspite of his wound he kept his Bren gun in action giving valuable covering fire to the leading troops. He refused to leave his position to seek medical attention until the objective was captured. Naik Pala Singh has participated in every action in which the battalion has been engaged."

Indian Distinguished Service Medal, 1922 – 1947 (cont.)

SEPOY JASWANT SINGH
INDIAN FIELD AMBULANCE

"On the night of 22ND and 23RD March the Fort Hill in Ethiopia was under heavy and constant mortar and shellfire from 20.30 hrs to 0400 hrs. At about 0200 hrs. Ambulance Sepoys Abdul Wahid and Abdul Wahab were severely wounded. They were about 200 yards from the Advanced Dressing Station, under some rocks and both required help to reach the Advanced Dressing Station. Though they were plenty of other Ambulance Sepoys in the vicinity, no one went to the help of these two wounded men except Sepoy Jaswant Singh who went to their aid, and brought them to safety, carrying Abdul Wahid and supporting Abdul Wahab under heavy constant fire. For his gallantry and devotion to duty, Sepoy Jaswant Singh was awarded the Indian Distinguished Service Medal."

JEMADAR SANT SINGH
12TH FRONTIER FORCE REGIMENT

"On 8TH May 1941, during the battle for Amba Alagi in Ethiopia, Jemadar Sant Singh was ordered to make a night attack and capture Red Hill on which the enemy had established a well-entrenched and strongly held advanced position covering their main defences on the Falaga Pass. Jemadar Sant Singh's platoon succeeded in covering the approach to the objective over rough and stony ground in the dark with singularly little noise. The answer given to the enemy when they finally challenged was a bomb, which burst right on top of his position. The enemy at once started to bomb heavily the surrounding slopes at a rate, which they maintained constantly until the near end. During its ascent the platoon was met by rifle and machine gun fire on a fixed line from the enemy's main position. The flashes of exploding bombs revealed Jemadar Sant Singh's men steadily climbing the slope in well-controlled formation while they gave their Sikh battle cry. Throughout the action Jemadar Sant Singh, having been wounded by a piece of bomb in the face, remained quietly cool and could be heard encouraging his men to greater efforts and guided by the enemy rifle flashes, issuing clear directions for their advance. This continued until they were momentarily checked beneath the top of the hill by a high wall up to which he had personally led his men. Only then did he call out that he was held up and could discover no way round the dark. Opposition had practically ceased and the hill was virtually taken. The reserve platoon, which was lying quietly hidden close at hand, then came in on the enemy's flank and the position was captured three minutes later."
Jemadar Sant Singh was awarded the Indian Distinguished Service Medal for conspicuous bravery and devotion to duty.

Indian Distinguished Service Medal, 1922 – 1947 (cont.)

SIKH LIGHT INFANTRY

"The Sikh Light Infantry were an advance guard to 99TH Brigade in Burma. They had gone about eight miles from Meiktila, near the village of Pambhait, where they suddenly discovered a large concentration of Japanese in and around the village. A plan of attack was made and the battalion put in the attack with tanks in support. The enemy, though in large numbers, had little chance against the determined attack of Sikh Light Infantry, though it fought desperately the characteristic of Japanese soldiers. The men of Sikh Light Infantry as usual were terrific and showed tremendous dash and courage of a high order and so was their morale. As a result of single day's fierce hand- to -hand fighting, 254 dead bodies of Japanese were counted. In addition the battalion captured two 75 mm guns, two Medium Machine Guns, two 4-inch Mortars and a large quantity of small arms and equipment." The following Sikh soldiers were awarded the Indian Distinguished Service Medal for their conspicuous gallantry in this battle.

SEPOY	GINDER SINGH	1945	BURMA
LANCE NAIK	ISHAR SINGH	1945	BURMA

"The battle of Pyawbwe was the most decisive of the battle in Central Burma and it was here that Lt General Honda's army was shattered completely. The task of the Sikh Light Infantry in the battle of Pyawbwe was to take the high ground South-East of Pyawbwe and this high ground came to be known as "Pagoda Hill'. The objective was captured but the leading section under Havildar Bishan Singh was wiped out. Inspite of all efforts no further progress could be made to capture the second lump on which was the prized "Pagoda". The Japanese counter attacked to regain the position, but all their attacks were repulsed. Next day, under the command of the brave and inspiring second-in-command Major JD Maling MC the battalion put in an attack to capture the "Pagoda Hill" on which the enemy seemed to have been heavily lodged. The attack was successful and the enemy, leaving its dead, ran away. The next day about 200 enemy dead were counted in this area. Major Maling was wounded due to enemy shelling and had to be evacuated. He was awarded the DSO in this battle".

Naik Mehar Singh was awarded the Indian Distinguished Service Medal for his conspicuous gallantry in this battle.

Indian Distinguished Service Medal, 1922 – 1947 (cont.)

1ST PUNJAB REGIMENT
NORTH AFRICA

During the Second World War, the Battalions of the 1ST Punjab Regiment served in several theatres of war against the Japanese, Germans and Italians. At the outbreak of the war the 1ST Battalion was stationed in the Khyber Pass. In June 1941, it moved to Bombay and embarked for Iraq. In Iraq the Battalion helped to prepare defences against a possible German advance through the Caucasus. On November 21ST 1941, the Battalion set out on the long journey to North Africa and joined the 5TH Indian Infantry Brigade of the 4TH Indian Division. On February 3RD the Battalion had taken up defensive position at Tmimi. The Germans opened up a heavy artillery bombardment on this position and shortly afterwards launched a strong infantry attack supported by tanks. Neither the numerical superiority of the Germans nor their violent attacks could shake the determination of the men, who repulsed them with heavy losses. On July 19TH it went into battle on the vital Ruweisat Ridge. During this action the Battalion suffered some 140 casualties. For their courage during this fierce battle Naik Hazara Singh and Lance Naik Indar Singh were awarded immediate Indian Distinguished Service Medal. The great battle of El Alamein began on October 23RD. In this battle the Battalion was given the task of raiding enemy positions to the south of the Ridge and to kill as many of the garrison as possible. The Punjabi raiders suffered considerable casualties in these operations and the following Sikh soldiers were awarded Indian Distinguished Service Medal for their conspicuous gallantry in the Western Desert.

HAVILDAR	NATHA SINGH	1941	NORTH AFRICA
NAIK	SARDARA SINGH	1941	NORTH AFRICA
SEPOY	SARDARA SINGH	1941	NORTH AFRICA
HAVILDAR	SAPURAN SINGH	1941	NORTH AFRICA
SEPOY	KARAM SINGH	1941	NORTH AFRICA
NAIK	BACHAN SINGH	1941	NORTH AFRICA
LANCE NAIK	HARBANS SINGH	1941	NORTH AFRICA
SEPOY	BAKHTAWAR SINGH	1941	NORTH AFRICA
SEPOY	BAGHA SINGH	1941	NORTH AFRICA
LANCE NAIK	SURJAN SINGH	1942	NORTH AFRICA
NAIK	UJAGAR SINGH	1942	NORTH AFRICA
LANCE NAIK	UJAGAR SINGH	1942	NORTH AFRICA
HAVILDAR	JOGINDER SINGH	1943	NORTH AFRICA

Indian Distinguished Service Medal, 1922 – 1947 (cont.)

1ˢᵀ PUNJAB REGIMENT (cont.)

BURMA

In the middle of November 1942, the Battalion left the Western Desert for Iraq, to guard the oil pipeline. Eventually, towards the end of October 1943, it proceeded to take part in the Second Arakan Campaign in Burma. In January 1944, the Battalion was engaged in eliminating strong enemy posts north of Rehkat Chaung. They attacked strongly fortified defences known as the Razabil Fortress, although the attacks were repulsed, they inflicted large casualties on the Japanese. At Ahkaungbaukywa, Arakan, on the 25ᵀᴴ January 1944 Subedar Arjan Singh personally led an assault of ten men up the western slope of Four Tree Hill. In the face of intense machine-gun and grenade fire, they destroyed an enemy post consisting of a bunker covered by wire and flanked by foxholes. The Battalion fought actions at Kanyindan, Jatsoma, Kohima, Bishenpur-Silchar track, and the Irrawaddy Basin. They finally moved to Meiktila and joined in the race for Rangoon in pursuit of the Japanese, who surrendered on August 15ᵀᴴ 1945. The following Sikh soldiers were awarded Indian Distinguished Service Medal for their conspicuous gallantry in Burma.

NAIK	SHAMSHER SINGH	1943	BURMA
JEMADAR	KALA SINGH	1943	BURMA
SEPOY	MAN SINGH	1944	BURMA
LANCE HAVILDAR	SANTA SINGH	1945	BURMA

2ᴺᴰ PUNJAB REGIMENT

WAZIRISTAN

In 1936, a revolt broke out in Waziristan, a mountainous region inhabited by warlike tribes, an area that was part of North-West Frontier Province of India. A Muslim holy man, the Faqir of Ipi, led the Waziris against the occupying British-Indian regime. 2ᴺᴰ Punjab Regiment was part of the force, which put down the revolt, in which the following Sikh soldiers were awarded the Indian Distinguished Service Medal for their gallantry in action.

| LANCE NAIK | SADHU SINGH | 1936 | WAZIRISTAN |
| NAIK | MANGAL SINGH | 1937 | WAZIRISTAN |

SOMALILAN

During the Second World War, the Battalions of the Regiment served in several theatres of war against the Japanese, Germans and Italians. In June 1940, the 1ˢᵀ Battalion was ordered to Somaliland, where it reinforced the Somaliland Camel Corps and saw several actions against the Italians, for which Havildar Agar Singh and Sepoy Attar Singh were mentioned in dispatches.

Indian Distinguished Service Medal, 1922 – 1947 (cont.)

2ND PUNJAB REGIMENT (cont.)

MIDDLE EAST

In July 1941, the Battalion moved to Alexandria for service in the Western Desert. In its first full scale action in the forward area of Ruweisat Ridge the Battalion encountered and endured almost every possible military adversity, all crowded into brief period of time. For nearly two years following this action the Battalion did garrison and security duties in various parts of the eastern Mediterranean until 1944, when it was called upon to play its part in the northward advance through Italy. The following Sikh soldiers were awarded Indian Distinguished Service Medal for their conspicuous gallantry in the Western Desert.

LANCE NAIK	KISHAN SINGH	1942	MIDDLE EAST
HAVILDAR	GURCHARAN SINGH	1942	MIDDLE EAST
LANCE NAIK	TULSA SINGH	1942	MIDDLE EAST
LANCE NAIK	HARBANS SINGH	1942	MIDDLE EAST

ITALY

During its service in the Italian theatre, the Battalion fought series of actions at Ortona, Pratelle, Modina, Donato, Vignola, and Sogliano. The decorations awarded for operations included: a posthumous Indian Order Merit to Subedar Kehar Singh, Military Cross to Subedar Sunda Singh, and Military Medal to Lance Naik Rai Singh. On 27TH Jemadar Gurdit Singh took out a fighting patrol of about platoon strength, his orders being ' to raid known enemy positions in the Casa Nuova, to kill as many Germans as possible, and to secure identifications.' Covered by the bank of the Sillaro River, his patrol worked its way to within 50 yards of the enemy position before fire was opened on it. At this point another enemy party, estimated at about twenty strong, was seen moving down the Sillaro Ridge to take the Patrol in rear. The Jemadar successfully disengaged himself from the action to his front and engaged the new party threatening his rear, inflicting several casualties and causing it to withdraw in disorder. One of the most strenuous actions in the Battalions long history was fought in the 20TH and 21ST April 1945, on the banks of River Idice against crack German troops belonging to the 4TH Paratroop Division. After this battle there was no further organized resistance by the Germans in the Italian theatre. The following Sikh soldiers were awarded Indian Distinguished Service Medal for their conspicuous gallantry in Italy.

HAVILDAR	BALDEV SINGH	1945	ITALY
HAVILDAR	GURBUX SINGH	1945	ITALY

Indian Distinguished Service Medal, 1922 - 1947 (cont.)
8TH PUNJAB REGIMENT (cont.)
N. W. FRONTIER

A revolt broke out in Waziristan, a mountainous region inhabited by warlike tribes, an area that was part of North-West Frontier Province of India. A Muslim holy man, the Faqir of Ipi, led the Waziris against the occupying British-Indian regime. 8TH Punjab Regiment, with sister Regiment the 2ND Punjab, was part of the force, which put down the revolt, in which the following Sikh soldiers were awarded the Indian Distinguished Service Medal for their gallantry.

JEMADAR	BATTAN SINGH	1939	N. W. FRONTIER
JEMADAR	KARTAR SINGH	1939	N. W. FRONTIER
SEPOY	TARA SNGH	1939	N. W. FRONTIER

BURMA

During the Second World War, the Battalions of the Regiment served in several theatres of war against the Japanese, Germans and Italians. Four Battalions served in Burma and fought at Donbaik, North Arakan, The Shweli, Myitson, and Kama. Subedar Man Singh was awarded the Indian Distinguished Service Medal for his conspicuous gallantry in Burma.

3RD BATTALION, 8TH PUNJAB REGIMENT
ITALY

During the Second World War, the 3RD Battalion served in Persia, Egypt, and Italy. In Italy the Battalion fought actions at The Trigno, Perano, The Sangro. Villa Grande, Gustav Line, Monte Grande, and the Senio. Havildar Kuldip Singh was awarded the Indian Distinguished Service Medal for his conspicuous gallantry in Italy.

11TH SIKH REGIMENT
N. W. FRONTIER

On the North West Frontier of India, Faqir of Ipi with 10,000 followere started his self styled Jihad against the British government. He was joined by Haji of Turangzai with 1,400 Lashkars. They waged a highly effective guerrilla warfare against the British. The following Sikh soldiers were awarded the Indian Distinguished Service Medal for their conspicuous gallantry on the Frontier.

NAIK	HARCHAND SINGH	1930	N. W. FRONTIER
SEPOY	MALL SINGH	1930	N. W. FRONTIER
SEPOY	BAGH SINGH	1932	N. W. FRONTIER
SEPOY	JOWALA SINGH	1932	N. W. FRONTIER
LANCE NAIK	CHANNAN SINGH	1933	N. W. FRONTIER
JEMADAR	SUNDAR SINGH	1934	N. W. FRONTIER

Indian Distinguished Service Medal, 1922 - 1947 (cont.)

11TH SIKH REGIMENT (cont.)

HAVILDAR	SEWA SINGH	1937	N. W. FRONTIER
HAVILDAR	GURBACHAN SINGH	1937	N. W. FRONTIER
LANCE NAIK	NAND SINGH	1937	N. W. FRONTIER
LANCE NAIK	BHAGAT SINGH	1937	N. W. FRONTIER
NAIK	DHAN SINGH	1937	N. W. FRONTIER
SEPOY	JAGIR SINGH	1939	N. W. FRONTIER
SEPOY	BACHAN SINGH	1939	N. W. FRONTIER
SEPOY	JARNAIL SINGH	1939	N. W. FRONTIER
NAIK	KARTAR SINGH	1939	N. W. FRONTIER
NAIK	JAGIR SINGH	1942	N. W. FRONTIER
NAIK	NATHA SINGH	1942	N. W. FRONTIER

ERITREA

During the Second World War, all the Battalions of the Regiment served in several theatres of war against the Japanese, Germans and Italians. The 4TH Battalion was the first to be mobilised, and set sail for Egypt in September 1940. After a short spell at Siddi Barrani it joined the "Gazelle Force" for the drive into Eritrea. The Battalion kept in pursuit of the Italians at Kassala and Agordat, as they kept slipping away before the attack. Finally the Battalion was in the brigade attack on Aqua Col, a strongly held enemy feature, in early 1941.The fighting was so fierce, that the two companies that went into assault, one had 87 casualties. "Naik Ujjagar Singh, moving ahead of his section, attacked a machine gun post single handed. He shot down two of the enemy with his rifle, and then, after throwing grenades into the post, rushed to the position, bayoneted the remainder of the detachment, and captured the machine gun." On 15TH March, the Sikhs stormed The Samana Ridge of the Keren Hills. In this action, Naik Nasib Singh, who had six Italians to his score, won an Indian Distinguished Service Medal. Another Indian Distinguished Service Medal went to Naik Daulat Singh for fine and resolute leadership. On the 30TH November, the Battalion was involved, with the help of 1ST Punjab Regiment, in desperate fighting at Omars. They overran the garrison of 3,000 men, at a combined cost of 336 casualties and Jemadar Gurbaksh Singh was awarded a posthumous Indian Order of Merit for outstanding gallantry and an Indian Distinguished Service Medal was awarded to Havildar Karam Singh for great personal courage and leadership.

Indian Distinguished Service Medal, 1922 - 1947 (cont.)

11TH SIKH REGIMENT (cont.)
MIDDLE EAST

"The 4TH Battalion 11TH Sikh Regiment passed through the Royal Sussex, wheeled to the left at Martuba and, pushing through a defile, came within the sight of the long straight highway which leads between the Derna airfields to the edge of the escarpment. Five miles away airplanes could be seen landing and taking off constantly. The road itself was choked with transport. Two companies of Sikhs were dropped to block the road against forces retreating from the east, while the Bren gun carriers and the remainder of the Battalion scrambled down onto the plain. Then the carriers led the charge. The enemy columns were completely unprepared as the carriers and the lorried infantry swept down upon them shooting them up in Wild West fashion. Three hundred prisoners, five 88-mm. guns and many vehicles were captured. Such transport as escaped stampeded down the road toward the brink of the cliffs above Derna. The carriers poured onto the airfields, and riddled planes, large and small. Transport planes, bombers, fighters, gliders, all were destroyed or captured in the wild scrimmage. In the midst of this action, twelve large JU 52 troop carriers appeared overhead, circled and settled in. The Sikhs scarcely believing their luck, held their fire until the last plane glided down. Then all opened fire in on a single word of command. Rifles, machine guns, mortars, anti tank guns, field guns and even pistols were used to pour a storm of shot and shell into the Junkers. Eight of these large aircrafts were shot to pieces. Two got off the ground but crashed. Out of the dozen only two managed to get away. The escort of ME 110s turned up belatedly and raked the aerodrome but without result. The jubilant Sikhs found themselves in possession of tremendous booty. Halfaya and Bardia were being maintained from Derna and no less then 183 aircraft, both sound and damaged were captured on the landing grounds. Thousands of bombs were stacked round about, as well large quantities of petrol, wine and food. From contemplation of such and appetizing scene the Sikhs tore themselves away with reluctance, and by nightfall had reached the edge of the escarpment. Looking down they saw the snug town and port of Derna eight hundred feet below." (Quoted from: The Tiger Kills) The Battalion continued to be involved in some more fighting at Siddi Barrani, and Libija. They had a major reverse at El Alamein and were forced to disperse to the rear in small parties. The regiment was re-formed and after service in Lebanon and Syria was ordered to Italy in July 1944." The following Sikh soldiers were awarded the Indian Distinguished Service Medal for their conspicuous gallantry in the Middle East.

SEPOY	NASIB SINGH	1941	MIDDLE EAST
LANCE NAIK	DAULAT SINGH	1941	MIDDLE EAST
HAVILDAR	KARAM SINGH	1941	MIDDLE EAST
JEMADAR	KAPUR SINGH	1942	MIDDLE EAST

Indian Distinguished Service Medal, 1922 - 1947 (cont.)

11TH SIKH REGIMENT (cont.)

NAIK	JAGIR SINGH	1942	MIDDLE EAST
SEPOY	DALIP SINGH	1942	MIDDLE EAST
NAIK	RUR SINGH	1942	MIDDLE EAST
HAVILDAR	KARAM SINGH	1942	MIDDLE EAST
HAVILDAR	KISHAN SINGH	1942	MIDDLE EAST
HAVILDAR	DHIRTA SINGH	1943	MIDDLE EAST
LANCE NAIK	SOHAN SINGH	1943	MIDDLE EAST
LANCE NAIK	RAUNAK SINGH	1943	MIDDLE EAST
SEPOY	BACHAN SINGH	1943	MIDDLE EAST
HAVILDAR	SADHU SINGH	1943	MIDDLE EAST
NAIK	CHANAN SINGH	1943	MIDDLE EAST

ITALY

The 4TH Royal Battalion, 11TH Sikh Regiment, joined the 4TH Indian Division in central Italy in July 1944. On 30TH August 1944, the Battalion carried out an attack on the Gothic Line and quickly captured a pair of fortified farm areas. The advance was then carried out towards the fortified village of Monte Calvo. The troops moved with great dash, they killed and wounded many of the enemy and took forty-two prisoners. The Battalion had been sharing the fortunes with the 2ND Battalion, 11TH Sikh Regiment, in the hard and gradually successful fighting for the Gothic Line. At Coriano, the ridge across the Conca River had to be captured for making a breakthrough in the Po Valley possible. The Germans repulsed initial attacks on September 13TH, eventually after furious counter attacks the Ridge was captured by the 2ND Battalion, which went on to capture Poggio San Giovanni. The 4TH Battalion captured San Marino, this small independent republic within Italy on 24TH September 1944. Both Battalions were constantly engaged in succession of minor operations, until the 'cease fire' on the 29TH. The following Sikh soldiers were awarded the Indian Distinguished Service Medal for their conspicuous gallantry.

HAVILDAR	JAGIR SINGH	1945	ITALY
NAIK	RAM SINGH	1945	ITALY
LANCE NAIK	BALL SINGH	1945	ITALY
SEPOY	BABU SINGH	1945	ITALY
SEPOY	JAGAT SINGH	1945	ITALY
HAVILDAR	PALA SINGH	1945	ITALY

Indian Distinguished Service Medal, 1922 - 1947 (cont.)

11TH SIKH REGIMENT (cont.)
MALAYA

The 5TH Battalion, 11TH Sikh Regiment, was the first to reach Malaya in April 1941. As soon the operations commenced, the Japanese with their overwhelming superiority, overwhelmed the Indian forces. The Battalion fought an action at Kuantan, which had an airfield from 27TH December 1941 to 3RD January 1942. After fighting an action at Niyor on 25TH January, the Battalion destroyed the causeway connecting the peninsula to Singapore Island and was forced to disperse in small parties. Only about 200 of them were able to reach Singapore. With the fall of Singapore in February 1942, the remnants of the 5TH Battalion became prisoners of war. The Battalion was not reformed on repatriation. The following Sikh soldiers were awarded the Indian Distinguished Service Medal for their gallantry in Malaya.

NAIK	NATHA SINGH	1942	MALAYA
NAIK	GURDEV SINGH	1942	MALAYA
SEPOY	BHAG SINGH	1942	MALAYA
SEPOY	BHAG SINGH	1944	MALAYA

BURMA

The 1ST Battalion, Sikh Regiment landed in Rangoon in February 1942 and took part in some fierce fighting. The Japanese had built up their strength in the area and pushed the British forces to the Indian border. The battalion was rested and refitted and was back in the war zone on the Indo - Burma border. In early 1943 the Japanese attempted an invasion of India, beginning in the coastal strip of Arakan. There, a platoon of 1ST Battalion, Sikh Regiment was sent to mask a Japanese post and seize it if possible, which they did. They then fought off violent counter-attacks after which the position was surrounded, preventing re-supply. Asked by radio how long they could hold out, the platoon commander replied: 'Without food for 6 more days; without ammunition, as long as you like, we have bayonets.' It was no idle boast, as the Sikhs repeatedly proved. The attack resumed on 11 March as the Japanese fought a rearguard action, Naik Nand Singh of 1ST Battalion; won the Victoria Cross in this action.

"On March 11, 1943 the battalion was the advance party along the Maungdaw-Buthidaung road. The Japanese were holding a knife-edge hill feature and putting up stiff resistance. The only way to approach the hill was by means of a narrow track. On this track leading the attack was the section commanded by Naik Nand Singh. When the section reached the crest it came under heavy machinegun fire and every man in the section was killed or wounded. Naik Nand Singh dashed forward alone, he was wounded by a grenade as he neared the first Japanese trench. He took out his bayonet and killed the two occupants.
Continued on next page.

Indian Distinguished Service Medal, 1922 - 1947 (cont.)

11TH SIKH REGIMENT (cont.)

BURMA

Under heavy fire Nand Singh jumped up and charged the second trench, he was again wounded by a grenade and knocked down, but he got up and hurled himself into the trench again killing two Japanese with his bayonet. He then moved on to the third trench and captured it single-handed. With the capture of the third trench the enemy fire started to die away and the rest of the platoon charged the other Japanese positions, killing with bayonet and grenade thirty seven out of the forty Japanese holding it. Naik Nand Singh wounded six times in the assault literally carried the position single-handed. For his valour an immediate award of Victoria Cross was bestowed upon him. The company commander Major John Brough was awarded the DSO and the platoon commander Jemadar Mehr Singh the Indian Order of Merit."

The Battalions kept in pursuit of the Japanese and fought them at Buthidaung, Kanglatongbi, Shandatgyi, Kama, The Irrawaddy, and finally at Sittang on 15TH August. The Japanese surrendered on 16TH August 1944. The following Sikh soldiers were awarded the Indian Distinguished Service Medal for their gallantry in Burma.

HAVILDAR	GURNAM SINGH	1942	BURMA
HAVILDAR	JOTA SINGH	1943	BURMA
LANCE NAIK	HARCHAND SINGH	1944	BURMA
SEPOY	CHARAN SINGH	1944	BURMA
LANCE NAIK	DEWA SINGH	1944	BURMA
NAIK	NARANJAN SINGH	1944	BURMA
SEPOY	HAZARA SINGH	1944	BURMA
SEPOY	JAWAHIR SINGH	1945	BURMA
SEPOY	BHAG SINGH	1945	BURMA
NAIK	HUKMA SINGH	1945	BURMA
HAVILDAR	GURDAIL SINGH	1945	SPEC. OPERATIONS

Indian Distinguished Service Medal, 1922 - 1947 (cont.)

12TH FRONTIER FORCE REGIMENT

N. W. FRONTIER

On the North West Frontier of India, Faqir of Ipi with 10,000 followere started his self styled Jihad against the British government. He was joined by, the Haji of Turangzai and his sons, with 1,400 Lashkars They waged a highly effective guerrilla warfare throughout the 1930s and 1940s until the British departure in 1947. The following Sikh soldiers were awarded the Indian Distinguished Service Medal for their gallantry on the Frontier.

SUBEDAR	WARYAM SINGH	1924	N. W. FRONTIER
HAVILDAR	SADHU SINGH	1935	N. W. FRONTIER
LANCE NAIK	SARBUN SINGH	1935	N. W. FRONTIER

MIDDLE EAST

During the Second World War, the Battalions of the 12TH Frontier Force Regiment, served in several theatres of war against the Japanese, Germans and Italians. The 1ST and the 3RD Battalions served in North Africa, Syria, Iraq and Iran against the Axis forces. During September 1941, the 1ST battalion arrived in the Sudan and was moved to the frontier. On November 6TH, it joined a small mixed force and attacked the enemy position at Fort Gallabat. The Fort was captured after fierce hand-to-hand fighting, after this action the battalion was occupied in constant offensive patrolling, and causing further casualties to the enemy. From November 6TH to November 11TH an action was fought near Jebel Serobatib, some thirty miles northeast of Kassala, over very difficult rocky country. One company of the Battalion assisted in this attack in which 262 prisoners were taken and considerable damage inflicted. The Battalions were heavily involved in the fighting at Agordat, Keren, and Amba Alagi and then moved onto fight at Gazala, Bir Hacheim and El Adem. Finally the 1ST Battalion was ordered to Italy in 1943. The following Sikh soldiers were awarded the Indian Distinguished Service Medal for their gallantry in action in the Middle East.

NAIK	DALIP SINGH	1942	MIDDLE EAST
L. D.	CHANAN SINGH	1942	MIDDLE EAST
JEMADAR	SANT SINGH	1942	MIDDLE EAST

Indian Distinguished Service Medal, 1922 - 1947 (cont.)

12TH FRONTIER FORCE REGIMENT (cont.)
ITALY

The 1ST Battalion, 12TH Frontier Force Regiment, landed at Taranto harbour in Italy on September 19TH 1943. On November 27^{TH,} the Battalion was involved in a fierce firefight for the capture of Mozzagrogna. "Once again the bombardment held the enemy garrison in the deep dug-outs, and once again as it lifted the Germans rushed to their surface posts. Again the battle resolved into dozen of sudden deadly encounters in cellars, on rooftops, in alleys, and behind the angles of broken walls. In a crypt a number of Germans who had taken refuge in the vine vats were despatched. The hours of the night passed, and the grim game went on until the streak of dawn showed in the east. In the first light a roar from the south of the village drowned the chatter of small arms fire. The road to Sangro was open, and the British tanks were crowding through." On December 14TH 1st Battalion seized positions along the lateral road, which ran parallel to the Moro. An enemy force, which included flame–throwers charged the consolidation groups and cut off the Dogra Company. At dawn the Sikh and Dogra companies of Frontiersmen hurled back the enemy in headlong flight and captured the disabled tanks. Frontiersmen were formidable fighters and fought on at Sangro, Romagnoli, The Moro, Impossible bridge, Cassino, Pignataro, Advance to Florence, Campriano, Gothic line, Coriano, The Senio, Santerno Crossing. The following Sikh soldiers were awarded the Indian Distinguished Service Medal for their gallantry in action in Italy.

HAVILDAR	KULDIP SINGH	1944	ITALY
HAVILDAR	MEHAR SINGH	1944	ITALY
HAVILDAR	KARAM SINGH	1944	ITALY
SEPOY	AVTAR SINGH	1944	ITALY
NAIK	UJAGAR SINGH	1945	ITALY
HAVILDAR	DILWAR SINGH	1945	ITALY

BURMA

The feat of arms of the 4TH Battalion, 12TH Frontier Force Regiment are too numerous to be listed here. However the following Sikh soldiers were awarded the Indian Distinguished Service Medal for their gallantry in action in Burma.

HAVILDAR	NAJAR SINGH	1942	BURMA
DAFFADAR	GOBIND SINGH	1945	BURMA
NAIK	PRITAM SINGH	1945	BURMA
NAIK	SHER SINGH	1945	BURMA
NAIK	PURAN SINGH	1945	BURMA

Indian Distinguished Service Medal, 1922 - 1947 (cont.)
13TH FRONTIER FORCE RIFLES
N. W. FRONTIER

On the North West Frontier of India, Faqir of Ipi with 10,000 followere started his self styled Jihad against the British government. He was joined by, the Haji of Turangzai and his sons, with 1,400 Lashkars They waged a highly effective guerrilla warfare throughout the 1930s and 1940s until the British departure in 1947. The following Sikh soldiers were awarded the Indian Distinguished Service Medal for their gallantry on the Frontier.

LANCE NAIK	KAKA SINGH	1930	N. W. FRONTIER
JEMADAR	NIDHAN SINGH	1932	N. W. FRONTIER
NAIK	SHAM SINGH	1939	N. W. FRONTIER
HAVILDAR	LAL SINGH	1937	N. W. FRONTIER

MIDDLE EAST

During the Second World War, the Battalions of the Regiment served in several theatres of war against the Japanese, Germans and Italians. The 13TH Frontier Force Rifles served in North Africa, Egypt, Syria and Iraq. During September 1941, the 4TH Battalion arrived in the Sudan and became part of a special independed force to watch Kassala, and greatly distinguished itself both in the preliminary offensive patrolling and during the advance into Eritrea. This small body operated from Gash Delta. Small parties of the enemy were frequently captured, telephone lines were cut, and convoys of lorries bringing supplies were shot up. The battle for Barentu was a grim soldiers battle in which the better men won by sheer fighting ability. On January 21ST the 13TH Frontier Force Rifles evicted a Colonial Brigade from a strong position astride the road and the fighting continued for three days, the enemy resisting most stubbornly, and finally Barentu fell on February 2ND. Another position considered impregnable by the Italians was captured, after some hard fighting in which the 13TH Frontier Force Rifles particularly distinguished themselves. Finally the Italians fell back on Amba Alagi, it was a very strong position on a 3,350 metres high mastiff. After some fierce fight the Italians surrendered ceremonially on 19TH May 1941. After an incursion into Syria, where they captured Deir ez Zor and Raqqa, they were back in North Africa and fought at the battles of Gazala, Sidi Razegh, and Gambut Mersa Matruh. The resistance in North Africa came to an end on 12TH May. The following Sikh soldiers were awarded the Indian Distinguished Service Medal for their gallantry in action in the Middle East.

HAVILDAR	BABU SINGH	1941	MIDDLE EAST
NAIK	INDAR SINGH	1941	MIDDLE EAST
HAVILDAR	KEHR SINGH	1943	MIDDLE EAST
NAIK	NIKA SINGH	1941	MIDDLE EAST

Indian Distinguished Service Medal, 1922 - 1947 (cont.)
13TH FRONTIER FORCE RIFLES (cont.)
ITALY

On 19TH September 1943, 13TH Frontier Force Rifles, landed at Taranto harbour in Italy. As Jemadar Thakur Singh led his platoon forward to the south of San Angelo, his men spotted four self-propelled guns concealed under the foliage of trees. A burst of tracer gave the tank escorts the clue. They plastered the site with armour piercing shells as they closed in for the kill. Similarly when German armoured vehicles sallied out to deal with the Indian skirmishers, the tank men saw them first and smashed them. The enemy was unable to frustrate such efficient teamwork, and Panaccioni fell to the Frontier Force Rifles. With tank support they attacked Pignataro at twilight. The defenders fought fanatically but by dawn Pignataro was cleared of the enemy. In the four days of fierce fighting, approximately 1,000 Germans had been killed and captured in the San Angelo-Pignataro - Panaccioni Horseshoe. Frontiersmen were formidable fighters and fought on at Sangro, Romagnoli, The Moro, Impossible bridge, Cassino, Pignataro, Advance to Florence, Campriano, Gothic line, Coriano, The Senio, and Santerno Crossing. The following Sikh soldiers were awarded Indian Distinguished Service Medal for their gallantry in action.

NAIK	JOGINDER SINGH	1944	ITALY
NAIK	INDAR SINGH	1944	ITALY
HAVILDAR	PARTAB SINGH	1945	ITALY
HAVILDAR	ISHAR SINGH	1945	ITALY

BURMA

The following Sikh soldiers of 13TH Frontier Force Rifles, were awarded Indian Distinguished Service Medal for their gallantry in action in Burma'

NAIK	ASSA SINGH	1944	BURMA
NAIK	BACHAN SINGH	1944	BURMA
SEPOY	GURBACHAN SINGH	1944	BURMA
SEPOY	AMAR SINGH	1944	BURMA
NAIK	GULZAR SINGH	1944	BURMA
SEPOY	AMAR SINGH	1944	BURMA
HAVILDAR	SARBAN SINGH	1944	BURMA
SEPOY	SOHAN SINGH	1945	BURMA
SEPOY	CHANAN SINGH	1945	BURMA
NAIK	KARTAR SINGH	1945	BURMA
NAIK	TARA SINGH	1945	BURMA

Indian Distinguished Service Medal, 1922 - 1947 (cont.)

14TH PUNJAB REGIMENT

MIDDLE EAST

During the Second World War, the Battalions of the Regiment served in several theatres of war against the Japanese, Germans and Italians. They served in Egypt, Aden, Italian East Africa, Burma, Siam, Malaya and Hong Kong. The 3RD Battalion joined the 5TH Indian Division in North Africa and fought at battles of Agordat, Keren, Alam el Halfa, and the Defence of Alamein Line. The following Sikh soldiers were awarded the Indian Distinguished Service Medal for their gallantry in action in the Middle East.

HAVILDAR	SHAM SINGH	1936	MIDDLE EAST
NAIK	BELA SINGH	1937	MIDDLE EAST
SEPOY	PURAN SINGH	1942	MIDDLE EAST
SEPOY	TARA SINGH	1942	MIDDLE EAST

BURMA

In 1941, while serving in Malay, and having fought some rearguard actions against the Japanese, the 1ST Battalion was concentrated at Changlun on the Singora Road. The Battalion was directed to occupy a position at Asun. Now came a catastrophe. As the Punjabis were assembling to occupy their new position, a Japanese mechanized force headed by medium tanks broke through the rearguard and smashed through the Battalion. In the ensuing fighting the Japanese swarmed through the Punjabis. By the evening the 1ST Battalion ceased to exist as a fighting formation. However the 4TH, the 7TH and the 9TH Battalions fought with great distinction against the Japanese at the battles of The Yu, North Arakan, Buthidaung, Razabil, Maungdaw, Ngakyedauk Pass, Imphal, Shenam Pass, Nungshigum, Bishenpur, Kanglatongbi, Jessami, Naga Village, Mao Songsang, Monywa, Kyaukse, Nyaungu Bridgehead, Letse, Rangoon Road, Pegu, and Sittang. At Potsangbam, north of Ningthoukong, a murderous battle of attrition between the tanks and the village's defenders, could have given the Japanese a victory over the British armour, had not a daring patrol action by the 9TH Battalion succeeded in capturing three of the efficient 47 mm anti tank guns on 7TH May. The following Sikh soldiers were awarded the Indian Distinguished Service Medal for their gallantry in action in Burma.

HAVILDAR	FAQIR SINGH	1944	BURMA
NAIK	PURAN SINGH	1944	BURMA
NAIK	GURBAKSH SINGH	1944	BURMA
HAVILDAR	JOGINDER SINGH	1945	BURMA
SEPOY	JAIMAL SINGH	1945	BURMA

Indian Distinguished Service Medal, 1922 - 1947 (cont.)
15TH PUNJAB REGIMENT
MIDDLE EAST

During the Second World War, the Battalions of the Regiment served in several theatres of war against the Japanese, Germans and Italians. They served in Burma, Malaya, Singapore, Netherlands East Indies, Somaliland, Aden, Persia, Iraq, Syria and Italy. In the Middle East the 2ND Battalion fought at Suez Canal, Meggido, Sharon and Palestine. The following Sikh soldiers were awarded the Indian Distinguished Service Medal for their gallantry in action the Middle East.

SEPOY	PUNJAB SINGH	1937	MIDDLE EAST
SEPOY	BAKSHISH SINGH	1941	MIDDLE EAST

ITALY

In December 1944, the 2ND Battalion, 15TH Punjab Regiment, captured the town of Lanciano and received a rousing welcome from the liberated civilians. On December 8TH, they crossed the Moro to establish a bridgehead; and cleared a strong point with a bayonet. On December 22ND, the Battalion had thrown the enemy out of Vezzano. In the pursuit of the Germans the Battalion fought at the battles of Santro, Cassino, the Senio and smashing of the Gothic Line. The following Sikh soldiers were awarded the Indian Distinguished Service Medal for their gallantry in action in Italy.

SUBEDAR	ARJAN SINGH	1944	ITALY
LANCE NAIK	GURDAS SINGH	1944	ITALY
HAVILDAR	KARTAR SINGH	1945	ITALY

BURMA

The 1ST and the 4TH Battalions fought in Burma at the battles of; Rathedaung, North Arakan, Kohima, Jail Hill, Naga Village, Kyaukmyaung Bridgehead, Mandalay, Fort Dufferin, Meiktila, Nyaungu Bridgehead, Taungtha, The Irrawaddy, Yenaungyaung, Kama, Taungoo and Sittang. The following Sikh soldiers were awarded the Indian Distinguished Service Medal for their gallantry in action in Burma,

JEMADAR	CHANAN SINGH	1943	BURMA
JEMADAR	KARTAR SINGH	1932	BURMA
NAIK	AMAR SINGH	1944	BURMA
NAIK	SANTOKH SINGH	1945	BURMA
LANCE NAIK	DIWAN SINGH	1945	BURMA
NAIK	MEHNGA SINGH	1945	BURMA
SEPOY	GIAN SINGH	1946	BURMA

Indian Distinguished Service Medal, 1922 - 1947 (cont.)

16TH PUNJAB REGIMENT

N. W. FRONTIER

On the North West Frontier of India, Faqir of Ipi with 10,000 followere started his self styled Jihad against the British government. He was joined by, the Haji of Turangzai and his sons, with 1,400 Lashkars They waged a highly effective guerrilla warfare against the British throughout the 1930s and 1940s until the British departure in 1947. The following Sikh soldiers were awarded the Indian Distinguished Service Medal for their gallantry.

SEPOY	GURBAKSH SINGH	1937	N. W. FRONTIER
HAVILDAR	KEHAR SINGH	1937	N. W. FRONTIER

MIDDLE EAST

During the Second World War, 4TH Battalion, 16TH Punjab regiment joined the 4TH Indian Infantry Division in Egypt. From the Egyptian Frontier the Battalion advanced into Abyssinia and Eritrea against the predominately Italian forces. The advance continued through Elghena where the Battalion took 40 Italian prisoners. On 13TH March, the Battalion in a hard fought battle captured Engiahat and considerable amount of enemy material, which the hastily retreating enemy had abandoned. The Brigade then advanced on to capture the formidable fortifications of Massawa. After a short stay at Massawa, the Battalion embarked for the Western Desert on 23RD April. The main attack on the Omars took place on 22ND November. To quote from the Divisional diary: "As at Omar Nuovo, the spirit of the infantry prevailed. Dashing through the gaps in the wire, the Punjabis fell with the bayonet on the first trenches and cleared them. A brilliant operation followed in which platoons and sections, methodically stalking enemy weapon pits and strong points, destroyed post after post. Moving always to the flank and skirting resistance, the Indians quartered the ground like terriers, ferreting out the defenders. The Sepoys packed their pockets with captured Italian grenades. As in East Africa, these small light missiles proved excellent weapon. Hurling them high the Punjabis, under cover of their bursts, raced in with steel." The Battalion went on to fight at Sidi Barrani, Benghazi, El Alamein, Mareth, Akarit, Djebel Garci, and Tunis. The following Sikh soldiers were awarded the Indian Distinguished Service Medal for their gallantry in action in the Middle East.

NAIK	CHANAN SINGH	1943	MIDDLE EAST
LANCE NAIK	JASWANT SINGH	1942	MIDDLE EAST
SEPOY	HARBANS SINGH	1942	MIDDLE EAST
HAVILDAR	BHOLA SINGH	1943	MIDDLE EAST
JEMADAR	JAIMAL SINGH	1941	MIDDLE EAST

Indian Distinguished Service Medal, 1922 - 1947 (cont.)

16TH PUNJAB REGIMENT (cont.)

ITALY

In November the 4TH Battalion, 16TH Punjab regiment, headed south through the Sinai desert to Suez, to take a ship to Italy. The Battalion fought an action on the Adriatic Front in which the following Sikh N.C.O.'s were awarded the Indian Distinguished Service Medal. After spending six weeks on Monte Cassino, the Battalion was despatched to Burma.

NAIK	KARNAIL SINGH	1944	ITALY
NAIK	GURNAM SINGH	1944	ITALY

BURMA

The 1ST Battalion, 16TH Punjab regiment, early in 1943, joined the 23RD Indian Division and proceeded to Imphal, and then across the frontier into Burma at Tamu. The Battalion fought actions at Kaladan, Imphal, Tamu Road, Litan, and the Arakan Beaches. The following Sikh soldiers were awarded the Indian Distinguished Service Medal for their gallantry in action in Burma.

HAVILDAR	INDAR SINGH	1932	BURMA
HAVILDAR	ARJAN SINGH	1944	BURMA
SEPOY	NARANJAN SINGH	1942	BURMA
NAIK	PIARA SINGH	1945	BURMA

PATIALA INFANTRY

BURMA

1ST Patiala Infantry was an all Sikh Regiment, with Sikh officers and a Sikh Commanding Officer. The soldiers were handpicked stalwarts, not one of them less than six foot in height. In early April the Regiment, was sent hurriedly to Burma to join the newly raised 23RD Indian Division to stem the Japanese advance into India. In Burma the Regiment performed prodigal feats against the Japanese. Field Marshal Slim had this to say about the Patialas; "I want it conveyed to 1ST Patiala that if I had to pick one unit for any special task, it would be 1ST Patiala. I am sanctioning a special one month's leave to the whole unit at Shillong." The following Sikh soldiers were awarded the Indian Distinguished Service Medal for their gallantry in action in Burma.

JEMADAR	MANGAL SINGH	1943	BURMA
SEPOY	KAKA SINGH	1945	BURMA
NAIK	JAGIR SINGH	1945	BURMA
NAIK	ATMA SINGH	1945	BURMA

Indian Distinguished Service Medal, 1922 - 1947 (cont.)

NABHA AKAL INFANTRY

ITALY

Nabha Akal Infantry joined the 10TH Indian Infantry Division in March 1944, and was sent to Italy to join the Eighth Army on the Adriatic front. The division foughtin the rest of the Italian Campain, facing hard fighting northwards through Central Italy. Numerous mountain battles and river crossings followed with *Operation Olive* on the Gothic Line and then the spring 1945 offensive. The Nabha Akals suffered many casualties before final victory in Italy in May 1945. The following Sikh officers were awarded the Indian Distinguished Service Medal for their gallantry in action in Italy.

| HAVILDAR | BARA SINGH | 1945 | ITALY |
| HAVILDAR | INDER SINGH | 1945 | ITALY |

INDIAN ARMOURED CORPS

MIDDLE EAST

During the Second World War, eleven Indian armoured regiments served in West Asia, East Africa, the Western Desert and Italy. Two regiments fought in Italian East Africa, Three Indian armoured regiments took part in fighting in the Western Desert. One regiment fought the notable defensive battle against Rommel's panzers at El Mechili from 4TH to 8TH April 1941. Another regiment manned the defences at Tobruk against the Africa Corps. Risaldar Ranjit Singh was awarded the Indian Distinguished Service Medal for his conspicuous gallantry in the Western Desert.

ITALY

In June 1944, three Indian armoured regiments sailed for Italy and joined the 10TH Indian Division with which they fought the Germans until the end of the campaign. These regiments brought credit to Indian armour in the Italian campaign. The 6TH DCO Lancers crossed the Po river and was all set to race for Venice when their advance was stopped as General Clarke wanted an American unit to be the first to enter Venice. The following Sikh soldiers were awarded the Indian Distinguished Service Medal for their conspicuous gallantry in action in Italy.

LANCE DAFFADAR	KEHAR SINGH	1944	ITALY
S. D. M.	KIRPAL SINGH	1944	ITALY
A. L. D.	KEHR SINGH	1944	ITALY
DAFFADAR	MAKHAN SINGH	1944	ITALY
DAF. MAJOR	KIRPAL SINGH	1944	ITALY

Indian Distinguished Service Medal, 1922 - 1947 (cont.)

INDIAN ARTILLERY

N. W. FRONTIER

On 15TH August 1935, on the North West Frontier of India, the Haji of Turangzai and his sons, with 1,400 Lashkars, fostered an open revolt against the British rule. The Peshawar Brigade, which included two Mountain Batteries moved out to Pir Kala at the edge of British administered territory to suppress the revolt. The advance began on the 23RD, the objective being Dand, seven miles away. Strong opposition was met from the hills on the both flanks and both mountain batteries were in action, having to be reinforced by two field batteries before the infantry could go forward. The Peshawar Brigade, with the support of the field and mountain batteries, carried out several operations against the villages and to clear out nests of snipers, and always met with opposition. In one action the tribesmen were severely handled and lost about fifty killed. On 15TH October, receiving acceptance of the Government's terms, the Peshawar Brigade withdrew across the borders. The following Sikh Gunners were awarded the Indian Distinguished Service Medal for their conspicuous gallantry on the North West Frontier of India.

SUBEDAR	PAL SINGH	1936	N. W. FRONTIER
JEMADAR	THAKAR SINGH	1936	N. W. FRONTIER
LANCE NAIK	JAGRUP SINGH	1936	N. W. FRONTIER
HAVILDAR	MASTAN SINGH	1936	N. W. FRONTIER
DRIVER	HARI SINGH	1936	N. W. FRONTIER

MIDDLE EAST

2ND Indian Field and 1ST Indian Anti Tank Regiments took part in Libyan battles against Rommel, winning distinction at Bir Hacheim. Mr. Winston Churchill the primenister praised the performance of the Indian Artillery in the floor of the House of Commons of the British Parliament, on the day following the action at Bir Hacheim. The following Sikh Gunners were awarded the Indian Distinguished Service Medal for their conspicuous gallantry in the Middle East.

SIGNALLER	NARAIN SINGH	1941	MIDDLE EAST
LANCE NAIK	BAGGA SINGH	1941	MIDDLE EAST
HAVILDAR	PRITAM SINGH	1942	MIDDLE EAST
SIGNALMAN	AMAR SINGH	1942	MIDDLE EAST
NAIK	KEHAR SINGH	1942	MIDDLE EAST
HAVILDAR	SANTOKH SINGH	1942	MIDDLE EAST

Indian Distinguished Service Medal, 1922 - 1947 (cont.)

INDIAN ARTILLERY (cont.)

BURMA

The bitterest fighting experienced by the gunners was on the 600-yard wide bridgehead at Kyaukmyaung, 46 miles north of Mandalay. The battle raged for 20 days and 20 nights. The Japanese were thrown back eventually after the biggest concentration of artillery fired in the Burma campaign. The following Sikh Gunners were awarded the Indian Distinguished Service Medal for their conspicuous gallantry in Burma.

GUNNER	SHAMSHER SINGH	1943	BURMA
GUNNER	MEHNGA SINGH	1944	BURMA
GUNNER	HARI SINGH	1944	BURMA
H. MAJOR	DARSHAN SINGH	1945	BURMA
GUNNER	TEJA SINGH	1945	BURMA

INDIAN ENGINEERS

MIDDLE EAST

The heroic crossing of Wadi Zig Zaouw River in Egypt, the brilliant technical feat of forcing a track through the Matmata hills leading to the downfall of Rommel at Wadi Akarit were some of the achievements of the Indian engineers during this time. The following Sikh Sappers were awarded the Indian Distinguished Service Medal for their conspicuous gallantry in the Middle East.

JEMADAR	SAJJAN SINGH	1943	MIDDLE EAST
SAPPER	KARTAR SINGH	1941	MIDDLE EAST
JEMADAR	GURBACHAN SINGH	1942	MIDDLE EAST
LANCE NAIK	HARI SINGH	1942	MIDDLE EAST
JEMADAR	SAJJAN SINGH	1942	MIDDLE EAST
JEMADAR	NARINDER SINGH	1942	MIDDLE EAST

ITALY

"The Impossible Bridge" over the River Moro in Italy came to be a legend in the annals of combat engineering when the Indian Engineers crossed over to the enemy side and built a bridge in reverse direction, to overcome the technical difficulty arising out of lack of construction space on the home bank." The following Sikh NCOs were awarded the Indian Distinguished Service Medal for their conspicuous gallantry in Italy.

| NAIK | DAN SINGH | 1945 | ITALY |
| NAIK | JASWANT SINGH | 1944 | ITALY |

Indian Distinguished Service Medal, 1922 - 1947 (cont.)

INDIAN ENGINEERS (cont.)

BURMA

The Chindwin Bridge, the largest bridge built during the Second World War, was constructed by the Indian Engineers and played a crucial part in the defeat of the Japanese and their subsequent rout from Burma in 1945. The following Sikh Sappers were awarded the Indian Distinguished Service Medal for their conspicuous gallantry in Burma.

NAIK	MOHINDER SINGH	1944	BURMA
NAIK	BISHAN SINGH	1944	BURMA
HAVILDAR	SANTA SINGH	1945	BURMA
HAVILDAR	RANDHIR SINGH	1944	BURMA
SAPPER	DHAMAN SINGH	1944	BURMA
HAVILDAR	GURCHARAN SINGH	1947	SPEC. OPERATIONS

INDIAN SIGNAL CORPS

MIDDLE EAST

Many were the times when the battle hinged on a Punjabi signaller forcing those magic invisible waves through the ether by sheer will-power. The following Sikh Signallers were awarded the Indian Distinguished Service Medal for their conspicuous gallantry in the Middle East.

SIGNALMAN	BANTA SINGH	1941	MIDDLE EAST
NAIK	HAZARA SINGH	1941	MIDDLE EAST
SIGNALMAN	AMAR SINGH	1941	MIDDLE EAST
LANCE NAIK	GIRDHARA SINGH	1941	MIDDLE EAST
HAVILDAR	NARANJAN SINGH	1942	MIDDLE EAST
JEMADAR	FAUJA SINGH	1942	MIDDLE EAST
HAVILDAR	SANTOKH SINGH	1942	MIDDLE EAST
SIGNALMAN	JAGAT SINGH	1943	MIDDLE EAST
SIGNALMAN	PARTAB SINGH	1943	MIDDLE EAST
LANCE NAIK	RATTAN SINGH	1943	MIDDLE EAST
HAVILDAR	SARDAR SINGH	1943	MIDDLE EAST
SIGNALMAN	JOGINDAR SINGH	1943	MIDDLE EAST
NAIK	KARTAR SINGH	1943	MIDDLE EAST

Indian Distinguished Service Medal, 1922 - 1947 (cont.)

INDIAN ARMY SERVICE CORPS

First line transport, used by fighting units in battle, to carry weapons, ammunition, reconnaissance parties, commanders, was an integral part of each unit, maintained by the unit's own drivers. Second line transport, lorries carrying rations, water, petrol, ammunition unto battalion batteries, was the responsibility of the Royal Indian Army Service Corps. Each Brigade, and Divisional troops, included one transport company of Royal Indian Army Service Corps The following Sikh officers and drivers were awarded the Indian Distinguished Service Medal for their conspicuous gallantry in battle.

SUBEDAR	DALIP SINGH	1937	WAZIRISTAN
DRIVER	HARPAL SINGH	1937	N. W. FRONTIER
NAIK	SUCHA SINGH	1941	SYRIA
DRIVER	JOGINDER SINGH	1944	ITALY
LANCE NAIK	KEHAR SINGH	1944	ITALY
JEMADAR	RATTAN SINGH	1944	ITALY
JEMADAR	DYAL SINGH	1944	ITALY
DAF. MAJOR	KIRPAL SINGH	1944	ITALY

BURMA MILITARY POLICE

BURMA

The Burma Military Police Force was a paramilitary force. All the personnel were Indian Army volunteers. The Military Police Battalions were organized like regular army regiments; their duties were entirely military. The Burma Military Police included 3,937 Sikhs. They had extensive experience of military operations in the jungle covered mountainous frontier tracts of Burma while keeping the peace amongst the turbulent tribes. The following Sikh officers and men were awarded the Indian Distinguished Service Medal for their conspicuous gallantry in Burma.

SEPOY	INDER SINGH	1932	BURMA
SEPOY	MAL SINGH	1932	BURMA
SOWAR	RAGHBIR SINGH	1932	BURMA
SUBEDAR	AMAR SINGH	1934	BURMA
SUBEDAR	GANDA SINGH	1934	BURMA
HAVILDAR	TRILOK SINGH	1934	BURMA
HAVILDAR	ARJAN SINGH	1935	BURMA

Indian Distinguished Service Medal, 1922 - 1947 (cont.)

THE BURMA REGIMENT

The Burma Regiment was raised in India in September 1942 from mainly Indian former members of The Burma Rifles who had survived the retreat from Burma. In 1944 the Regiment supported 6TH Brigade's attack to clear Ardura Spur. It saw further action at Ukhrul, Maoku, Nyaungu Bridgement and Meiktila. After serving in Sumatra the Regiment was disbanded in 1947.

Naik Karam Singh was awarded the Indian Distinguished Service Medal for his conspicuous gallantry in Burma.

INDIAN MEDICAL SERVICE
MIDDLE EAST

Each regiment of cavalry, battalion of infantry, brigade of artillery, ammunition column, squadron or bridging train of engineers and certain supply trains has an officer of the Indian Medical Service attached to it, together with a small detachment of other ranks for technical charge of water carts and water supplies. Men of the regiment are placed under the Medical officer as stretcher-hearers; wounded are collected to a Regimental Aid Post, which is established by the medical officer in a shelter or protected spot near regimental headquarters. The following Sikh soldiers of the Indian Medical Service were awarded the Indian Distinguished Service Medal for his conspicuous gallantry in attending to the wounded while still under enemy fire.

NAIK	BASANT SINGH	1941	MIDDLE EAST
SEPOY	JASWANT SINGH	1941	MIDDLE EAST
HAVILDAR	LAL SINGH	1942	MIDDLE EAST

The Indian Armoured Corps in the Middle East, March 1944.

INDIAN DISTINGUISHED SERVICE MEDAL AND BAR

The following Indian officers were awarded a Bar to their Indian Distinguished Service Medal, that is, they won the IDSM again.

47TH SIKHS

SUBEDAR	MIT SINGH M.C.	MESOPOTAMIA 1916
		MESOPOTAMIA 1917

2ND LANCERS

LANCE DAFFADAR	SOBHA SINGH	FRANCE 1918
		FRANCE 1918

58TH RIFLES (FRONTIER FORCE)

SEPOY	DEWA SINGH	FRANCE 1915
		EGYPT 1918

6TH K.E.O CAVALRY

JEMADAR	AMIR SINGH	FRANCE 1917
		FRANCE 1918

BURMA MOUNTED RIFLES

JEMADAR	PARTAB SINGH	SOUTH PERSIA 1918
		SOUTH PERSIA 1918

55TH RIFLES (FRONTIER FORCE)

SUBEDAR	FAUJA SINGH	N.W.FRONTIER 1908
		EGYPT 1919

66TH PUNJABIS

JEMADAR	SUNDAR SINGH	MESOPOTAMIA 1917
		KUT AL AMARA 1920

INDIAN ARMY SERVICE CORPS

SUBEDAR	DALIP SINGH	BANGALORE 1933
		N. W. FRONTIER 1937

2ND PUNJAB REGIMENT

LANCE NAIK	KRISHAN SINGH	EAST AFRICA 1941
		MIDDLE EAST 1942

MILITARY MEDAL

Awarded to non-commissioned officers and men of the army for individual or associated acts of bravery brought to notice by recommendation of a commander-in-chief in the field.

INDIAN ARMOURED CORPS

L. DAFFADAR	BUDH SINGH	1945	BURMA
L. DAFFADAR	BABU SINGH	1945	BURMA
SOWAR	BHAG SINGH	1945	BURMA
SOWAR	DAIDAN SINGH	1945	BURMA
DAFFADAR	JAMEL SINGH	1946	BURMA
SOWAR	K. SINGH	1945	BURMA
NAIK	MOHINDAR SINGH	1945	BURMA
SOWAR	MOLLARA SINGH	1945	BURMA
SOWAR	NARANJAN SINGH	1944	BURMA
DAFFADAR	R. SINGH	1945	BURMA
L. DAFFADAR	RANBIR SINGH	1946	BURMA
DAFFADAR	SARUP SINGH	1946	BURMA
DAFFADAR	MUKAN SINGH	1946	FAR EAST
DAFFADAR	BALWANT SINGH	1945	ITALY
DAFFADAR	BADAN SINGH	1945	ITALY
SOWAR	CHANDAR SINGH	1945	ITALY
L. DAFFADAR	NARHAR SINGH	1945	ITALY
L. DAFFADAR	SULTAN SINGH	1944	ITALY
SOWAR	S. SINGH	1945	ITALY

Military Medal (cont.)

BOMBAY GRENADIERS

HAVILDAR	DALIP SINGH	1945	BURMA
SEPOY	HARPAL SINGH	1945	BURMA
LANCE NAIK	LACHMAN SINGH	1945	BURMA
SEPOY	PAHLAND SINGH	1945	BURMA
SEOY	RAM SINGH	1945	BURMA

INDIAN ARTILLERY

NAIK	BACHAN SINGH	1945	BURMA
DRIVER	BHARAT SINGH	1945	BURMA
GUNNER	BALDEV SINGH	1946	BURMA
LANCE NAIK	KAKA SINGH	1944	BURMA
LANCE NAIK	LALL SINGH	1944	BURMA
NAIK	RAM SINGH	1946	BURMA
HAVILDAR	SHER SINGH	1944	BURMA
LANCE NAIK	SUJJAN SINGH	1945	BURMA
GUNNER	TEJA SINGH	1944	BURMA
NAIK	TEJA SINGH	1944	BURMA

INDIAN SIGNALS

NAIK	BAKSHISH SINGH	1946	BURMA
SIGNALMAN	GURCHARAN SINGH	1944	BURMA
HAVILDAR	KARTAR SINGH	1945	BURMA
LANCE NAIK	M. SINGH	1945	BURMA
LANCE NAIK	MEHR SINGH	1945	BURMA
LANCE NAIK	MEHAR SINGH	1944	BURMA
HAVILDAR	PARTAP SINGH	1945	BURMA
LANCE NAIK	S. SINGH	1944	BURMA
LANCE NAIK	BAWA SINGH	1945	ITALY
LANCE NAIK	GURDIT SINGH	1945	ITALY

Military Medal (cont.)

INDIAN ARMY ENGINEERS

HAVILDAR	BANTA SINGH	1945	ITALY
HAVILDAR	B. SINGH	1944	ITALY
SAPPER	FAUJA SINGH	1945	ITALY
NAIK	GURMUKH SINGH	1945	ITALY
LANCE NAIK	HARBAX SINGH	1945	ITALY
NAIK	JAGIR SINGH	1945	ITALY
NAIK	KHEM SINGH	1945	ITALY
LANCE NAIK	NARANJAN SINGH	1945	ITALY
HAVILDAR	PIARA SINGH	1945	ITALY
LANCE NAIK	LALL SINGH	1945	ITALY
LANCE NAIK	S. SINGH	1945	ITALY
L. HAVILDAR	D. SINGH (BAR)	1946	FAR EAST
NAIK	BALDEV SINGH	1945	BURMA
LANCE NAIK	BABU SINGH	1945	BURMA
SAPPER	DALIP SINGH	1945	BURMA
NAIK	DALIP SINGH	1944	BURMA
HAVILDAR	GURNAM SINGH	1945	BURMA
NAIK	HAKIM SINGH	1945	BURMA
SAPPER	ISHAR SINGH	1945	BURMA
SAPPER	KARTAR SINGH	1945	BURMA
LANCE NAIK	NARANJAN SINGH	1945	BURMA
SAPPER	SARWAN SINGH	1944	BURMA
LANCE NAIK	UJAL SINGH	1946	BURMA
NAIK	SADHU SINGH	1944	BURMA

Military Medal (cont.)

1ˢᵀ PUNJAB REGIMENT

SEPOY	ALSI SINGH	1945	BURMA
SEPOY	BODHU SINGH	1945	BURMA
SEPOY	MAKHAN SINGH	1946	BURMA
SEPOY	RAGHBIR SINGH	1945	BURMA
SEPOY	SHER SINGH	1945	BURMA
NAIK	SADHU SINGH	1945	BURMA
SEPOY	RATTAN SINGH	1945	BURMA
NAIK	LADHU SINGH	1945	BURMA
SEPOY	KISHOR SINGH	1946	FAR EAST
NAIK	HIMAT SINGH	1945	ITALY
NAIK	SOHAN SINGH	1945	ITALY
SEPOY	NAHAR SINGH	1945	ITALY
LANCE NAIK	RAGHBIR SINGH	1945	ITALY

HONG KONG AND SINGAPORE ARTILLERY

LANCE NAIK	SANG SINGH	1946	HONG KONG
HAVILDAR	UDHAM SINGH	1946	HONG KONG

During the First World War the Hong Kong and Singapore Artillery proceeded to Egypt and saw extensive service with the Imperial Camel Corps in the Western Desert and Palestine.

During the Second World War the gunners made a gallant stand against the Japanese in Singapore. However 20 gunners were massacred at the San Wai Battery after they had surrendered.

Military Medal (cont.)

2ND PUNJAB REGIMENT

LANCE NAIK	BHUR SINGH	1945	ITALY
SEPOY	CHARAN SINGH	1945	ITALY
NAIK	D. SINGH	1944	ITALY
SEPOY	DHAN SINGH	1945	ITALY
HAVILDAR	G. SINGH IDSM	1944	ITALY
NAIK	HAZARA SINGH	1945	ITALY
HAVILDAR	KAZAN SINGH	1946	ITALY
LANCE NAIK	RAI SINGH	1945	ITALY
NAIK	S. SINGH	1946	FAR EAST
LANCE NAIK	AMAR SINGH	1945	BURMA
HAVILDAR	DESA SINGH	1945	BURMA
SEPOY	HOSHIAR SINGH	1944	BURMA
SEPOY	MAN SINGH	1944	BURMA
NAIK	SOHAN SINGH	1945	BURMA

8TH PUNJAB REGIMENT

SEPOY	JAGDISH SINGH	1945	ITALY
LANCE NAIK	KARTAR SINGH	1944	ITALY
SEPOY	S. SINGH	1945	ITALY
SEPOY	MOHAR SINGH	1946	FAR EAST
NAIK	THAKAR SINGH	1945	BURMA

SIKH LIGHT INFANTRY

SEPOY	INDAR SINGH	1945	BURMA
SEPOY	JOGINDER SINGH	1945	BURMA
NAIK	JAIPAL SINGH	1945	BURMA
SEPOY	JAWAHIR SINGH	1945	BURMA
SEPOY	KUNDAN SINGH	1945	BURMA
HAVILDAR	AJIT SINGH	1945	?

Military Medal (cont.)

11TH SIKH REGIMENT

HAVILDAR	AJIT SINGH	1945	BURMA
LANCE NAIK	ARJAN SINGH	1946	BURMA
SEPOY	ARJAN SINGH	1946	BURMA
LANCE NAIK	BACHINT SINGH	1945	BURMA
LANCE NAIK	BHAG SINGH	1945	BURMA
SEPOY	BHAN SINGH	1945	BURMA
SEPOY	BAWA SINGH	1946	BURMA
SEPOY	BASU SINGH	1946	BURMA
LANCE NAIK	DALWARA SINGH	1945	BURMA
SEPOY	GURDIAL SINGH	1945	BURMA
LANCE NAIK	INDAR SINGH	1945	BURMA
SEPOY	JOGINDER SINGH	1945	BURMA
NAIK	JAIPAL SINGH	1945	BURMA
SEPOY	KARAM SINGH	1945	BURMA
NAIK	KARTAR SINGH	1945	BURMA
SEPOY	KAPUR SINGH	1945	BURMA
SEPOY	KANDAN SINGH	1945	BURMA
SEPOY	MAGHAR SINGH	1944	BURMA
SEPOY	MEHAR SINGH	1944	BURMA
LANCE NAIK	MANSAL SINGH	1945	BURMA
SEPOY	MOTA SINGH	1947	?
SEPOY	NAZAR SINGH	1944	BURMA
SEPOY	PURAN SINGH	1944	BURMA
SEPOY	PARTAB SINGH	1945	BURMA
SEPOY	SAJJAN SINGH	1944	BURMA
SEPOY	SARWAN SINGH	1944	BURMA
NAIK	UJAGAR SINGH	1946	BURMA

Military Medal (cont.)

11TH SIKH REGIMENT (cont.)

HAVILDAR	ATMA SINGH	1945	ITALY
HAVILDAR	CHARAN SINGH	1945	ITALY
SEPOY	H. SINGH	1945	ITALY
SEPOY	M. SINGH	1945	ITALY
HAVILDAR	SHAM SINGH	1945	ITALY
SEPOY	NAND SINGH	1945	ITALY
NAIK	MOHAN SINGH	1945	ITALY
SEPOY	HARBANS SINGH	1945	ITALY
NAIK	MANGAL SINGH	1945	ITALY
SEPOY	MAGHAR SINGH	1945	BURMA
SEPOY	PIARA SINGH	1945	BURMA

12TH FRONTIER FORCE REGIMENT

NAIK	JHANDA SINGH	1945	ITALY
LANCE NAIK	JOGINDAR SINGH	1945	ITALY
HAVILDAR	SARWAN SINGH	1944	ITALY
SEPOY	SADHU SINGH	1945	ITALY
NAIK	AMAR SINGH	1945	BURMA
NAIK	BAKSHISHA SINGH	1945	BURMA
LANCE NAIK	CHANAN SINGH	1945	BURMA
SEPOY	DALIP SINGH	1945	BURMA
NAIK	DILBARA SINGH	1945	BURMA
SEPOY	GURBUX SINGH	1945	BURMA
SEPOY	JITAN SINGH	1946	BURMA
LANCE NAIK	LACHMAN SINGH	1945	BURMA
LANCE NAIK	MOHINDER SINGH	1944	BURMA
L. HAVILDAR	SHER SINGH IDSM	1945	BURMA
HAVILDAR	SUCHA SINGH	1945	BURMA
NAIK	TIRLOK SINGH	1945	BURMA
SEPOY	VAKIL SINGH	1945	BURMA

Military Medal (cont.)

13TH FRONTIER FORCE RIFLES

LANCE NAIK	BARKAT SINGH	1944	ITALY
SEPOY	DALIP SINGH	1945	ITALY
L. HAVILDAR	GLAN SINGH	1945	ITALY
SEPOY	GURDIAL SINGH	1945	ITALY
NAIK	JAGIR SINGH	1945	ITALY
LANCE NAIK	M. SINGH	1945	ITALY
SEPOY	SARWAN SINGH	1945	ITALY
NAIK	SANTA SINGH	1945	ITALY
NAIK	TEJA SINGH	1945	ITALY
SEPOY	BADHAWA SINGH	1944	BURMA
SEPOY	BEANT SINGH	1945	BURMA
NAIK	BACHAN SINGH	1945	BURMA
LANCE NAIK	DEWA SINGH	1944	BURMA
RIFLEMAN	HARNAM SINGH	1945	BURMA
LANCE NAIK	J. SINGH	1946	BURMA
NAIK	K. SINGH	1944	BURMA
SEPOY	NAND SINGH	1945	BURMA
C. H. M.	SARWAN SINGH	1944	BURMA
LANCE NAIK	SANTA SINGH	1945	BURMA
HAVILDAR	SADHU SINGH	1945	BURMA
SEPOY	SANGHERA SINGH	1945	BURMA
SEPOY	TARA SINGH	1945	BURMA
HAVILDAR	TEJPAL SINGH	1945	BURMA
NAIK	N. SINGH	1947	?
L. HAVILDAR	R. SINGH	1947	?

Military Medal (cont.)

14TH PUNJAB REGIMENT

HAVILDAR	BHAG SINGH	1945	BURMA
NAIK	BASANT SINGH	1944	BURMA
SEPOY	BHAN SINGH	1944	BURMA
SEPOY	DHARM SINGH	1945	BURMA
HAVILDAR	GURBAKH SINGH IDSM	1945	BURMA
NAIK	INDAR SINGH	1944	BURMA
LANCE NAIK	KEHR SINGH	1944	BURMA
SEPOY	KISHAN SINGH	1945	BURMA
NAIK	P. SINGH IDSM (BAR)	1944	BURMA
SEPOY	PREM SINGH	1944	BURMA
HAVILDAR	RANJIT SINGH	1944	BURMA

15TH PUNJAB REGIMENT

LANCE NAIK	BEANT SINGH	1947	MP42
LANCE NAIK	SANT SINGH	1947	MP42
C. H. M.	CHATTAR SINGH	1944	ITALY
SEPOY	S. SINGH	1945	ITALY
SEPOY	UJAGAR SINGH	1945	ITALY
SEPOY	BAWA SINGH	1945	BURMA
SEPOY	BABU SINGH	1945	BURMA
SEPOY	CHANAN SINGH	1945	BURMA
NAIK	DIDAR SINGH	1945	BURMA
LANCE NAIK	DIDAR SINGH	1946	BURMA
HAVILDAR	KAM SINGH	1945	BURMA
LANCE NAIK	MAHAN SINGH	1945	BURMA
SEPOY	MOHINDER SINGH	1946	BURMA
SEPOY	S. SINGH	1945	BURMA
SEPOY	SANTOKH SINGH	1945	BURMA

Military Medal (cont.)

16TH PUNJAB REGIMENT

LANCE NAIK	BHAG SINGH	1944	BURMA
SEPOY	DHAN SINGH	1945	BURMA
NAIK	JORA SINGH	1944	BURMA
NAIK	KESAR SINGH	1944	BURMA
LANCE NAIK	KARTAR SINGH	1944	BURMA
NAIK	LALL SINGH	1944	BURMA
NAIK	PRITAM SINGH	1944	BURMA
HAVILDAR	S. SINGH	1944	BURMA
NAIK	SARWAN SINGH	1944	BURMA
SEPOY	TEJA SINGH	1944	BURMA
SEPOY	WARYAM SINGH	1944	BURMA

INDIAN STATES FORCES

| LANCE NAIK | NAG SINGH | 1945 | BURMA |

NABHA AKAL INFANTRY

NAIK	BACHAN SINGH	1945	ITALY
SEPOY	DALIP SINGH	1945	ITALY
NAIK	GURBACHAN SINGH	1945	ITALY
NAIK	JOGINDER SINGH	1945	ITALY
SEPOY	LABH SINGH	1945	ITALY
HAVILDAR	NIKKA SINGH	1945	ITALY
HAVILDAR	PRITAM SINGH	1945	ITALY
SEPOY	RAM SINGH	1945	ITALY
HAVILDAR	SOBHA SINGH	1945	ITALY
HAVILDAR	SHER SINGH	1945	ITALY

Military Medal (cont.)

PATIALA INFANTRY

SEPOY	JANG SINGH	1944	BURMA
LANCE NAIK	JOGINDER SINGH	1945	BURMA
SEPOY	MALKIAT SINGH	1944	BURMA
HAVILDAR	MOHINDER SINGH	1945	BURMA
SEPOY	SUCHA SINGH	1944	BURMA
SUBEDAR	AJMER SINGH	44/46	BURMA
SUBEDAR	DARBARA SINGH	44/46	BURMA
SUBEDAR	CHARAN SINGH	44/46	BURMA
N. SUBEDAR	AMIR SINGH	44/46	BURMA
N. SUBEDAR	SARWAN SINGH	44/46	BURMA
NAIK	BIR SINGH	1946	FAR EAST
C. H. M.	G. SINGH	1946	FAR EAST
NAIK	G. SINGH	1946	FAR EAST
SEPOY	K. SINGH	1946	FAR EAST
BRIG.	SUKHDEV SINGH	44/46	FAR EAST
MAJOR	KULDIP SINGH	44/46	FAR EAST
MAJOR	BALDEV SINGH	44/46	FAR EAST
S. MAJOR	RAKHA SINGH	44/46	FAR EAST

Havildar Singh was awarded the IOM (Indian Order of Merit) for shooting a German officer and killing ten other ranks in France and Flanders in the First World War.

Military Medal (cont.)

INDIAN ARMY SERVICE CORPS

DRIVER	DARBARA SINGH	1945	ITALY
LANCE NAIK	GURDIAL SINGH	1944	ITALY
NAIK	GULA SINGH	1945	ITALY
DRIVER	GULZARA SINGH	1945	ITALY
LANCE NAIK	GHULA SINGH	1945	ITALY
LANCE NAIK	HARBANS SINGH	1944	ITALY
LANCE NAIK	KAKA SINGH	1944	ITALY
LANCE NAIK	KARTAR SINGH	1945	ITALY
LANCE NAIK	LACHMAN SINGH	1945	ITALY
DRIVER	PRITAM SINGH	1945	ITALY
HAVILDAR	RESHAM SINGH	1946	ITALY
DRIVER	UJAGAR SINGH	1945	ITALY
NAIK	NARIAN SINGH	1946	FAR EAST
HAVILDAR	GANGA SINGH	1946	BURMA

LANCE NAIK KARAM SINGH PVC MM
THE SIKH REGIMENT

Lance Naik Karam Singh is unique as the only recipient of both the PVC and MM. He was honoured with the highest wartime gallantry medal, Param Vir Chakra, for his outstanding role in the battle of Tithwal in 1948, and had previously been awarded the Military Medal for bravery in Burma during the Second World War.

DISTINGUISHED FLYING CROSS

The Distinguished Flying Cross is a military decoration awarded to personnel of the United Kingdom's Royal Air Force, and formerly to officers of other Commonwealth countries, for "an act or acts of valour, courage or devotion to duty whilst flying in active operations against the enemy".

WING COMMANDER KARTAR SINGH TAUNQUE, DFC

Wing Commander Kartar Singh Taunque, then Hawai Sepoy 1st Class, became the first ever personnel of Indian Air force (then Royal Indian Air force) to win a gallantry award. He won this award for a successful bombing raid during "Operations in Waziristan 1937-38". This daring bombing sortie required tremendous courage and presence of mind on the part of Taunque for calculating terminal velocity, feeding speed and heading on the compass on the fly, and releasing 112-1b RL bombs at the enemy targets over the Pir of Ipi's fortress with pinpoint accuracy and devastating impact. He was awarded the Distinguished Flying Cross and later also served in Mesopotamia.

SQUADRON LEADER MAHENDER SINGH PUJJI, DFC

Squadron Leader Mohinder Singh Fuji flew in a combat role from emblematic RAF stations in the British Isles such as Kenly, putting his life on the line to defend the British mainland. He flew in some of the Allies' first offensive operations over Occupied France. He later flew briefly in the North African theatre, as well as extensively in the China / Burma / including the North West Frontier Province of India. He is one of very few Indian pilots in the Second World War to have seen service in, and to wear the campaign stars of, all three theatres of war. He was awarded the Distinguished Flying Cross in 1945.

MARSHAL OF THE AIR FORCE ARJAN SINGH, DFC

Marshal of the Air Force Arjan Singh, DFC is the only officer of the Indian Air Force to be promoted to five star rank, equal to a Field Marshal, to which he was promoted in 2002. He entered the RAF College Cromwell in 1938 and was commissioned as a Pilot Officer in December 1939. He led No.1 Squadron, Indian Air Force into command during the Arakan Campaign in 1944. He was awarded the Distinguished Flying Cross in 1944. Marshal of the Air Force Arjan Singh retired in 1969 at the age of 50. He was appointed Ambassador to Switzerland in 1971. He was also concurrently the Ambassador to the court of Pope Paul VI at the Vatican. Arjan Singh went on to serve as a High Commissioner to Kenya in 1974. While in Kenya, he was also High Commissioner to Seychelles.

MEDAILLE MILITAIRE (FRANCE)

The Medaille Militaire is issued to any non-commissioned officer or enlisted personnel who distinguishes himself by acts of bravery in action against an enemy force.

2ND LANCERS (GARDNER'S HORSE)
KOT DAFFADAR   SANT SINGH   FRANCE

21ST CAVALRY (FRONTIER FORCE)
DAFFADAR   SANTOKH SINGH   FRANCE

1ST KING GEORGE'S OWN SAPPERS AND MINERS
HAVILDAR   HARDIT SINGH   MESOPOTAMIA

SIKH (UNIT UNTRACEABLE)
SEPOY   PURAN SINGH   EAST AFRICA

PUNJABIS (UNIT UNTRACEABLE)
BUGLER   SIKHAN SINGH   EAST AFRICA

14TH KING GEORGE'S OWN FEROZEPORE SIKHS
SUBADAR MAJOR   SHAM SINGH   GALLIPOLI

24TH PUNJABIS
HAVILDAR   SAWAN SINGH   GALLIPOLI

34TH SIKH PIONEERS
HAVILDAR   MANGAL SINGH   FRANCE

45TH RATTRAY'S SIKHS
NAIK   SHAM SINGH   MESOPOTAMIA

52ND SIKHS (FRONTIER FORCE)
HAVILDAR   SAWAN SINGH   MESOPOTAMIA

INDIAN SUBORDINATE MEDICAL DEPARTMENT
ASSISTANT SURGEON   HIRA SINGH I.D.S.M   EAST AFRICA

MALAY STATES GUIDES INFANTRY
HAVILDAR   KEHAR SINGH   ADEN

THE LEGION OF HONOUR

Created in 1802 by Napoleon Bonaparte, the Legion of Honour is the highest award given by the French Republic for outstanding service to France, regardless of the social status or the nationality of the recipients. The President of the Republic is the Grand Master of the Order of the Legion of Honour.

HARDIT SINGH MALIK

Hardit Singh Malik was the first Sikh to fly in action. Born on 23RD November 1894, Hardit was educated at a public school, Eastbourne College, and went on to Balliol College, Oxford. When the First World War broke out in 1914 he volunteered to join the Royal Flying Corps, the first Sikh or Indian ever to do so. Hardit wore a specially designed helmet over his turban, and he went 'solo' in a Cauldron after just two and half hours of instruction, and got his wings in under a month. Under the command of Major Barkar, Hardit fought against the legendary 'Red Baron' Manfred von Richthofen's Staffel. He was one of the most popular officers at Biggin Hill and was a fighter ace with 9 victories. He was recalled to India in 1944 to become Prime Minister of the predominantly Sikh state of Patiala. He later became India's first High Commissioner to Canada and then Ambassador to Paris. In 1952 he was awarded the Legion D'Honneur, which was personally presented by president Coty of France.

THE PURPLE HEART

The Purple Heart is a United States military decoration awarded in the name of the President to those who have been wounded or killed while serving on or after April 5TH 1917 with the U.S. military. The National Purple Heart Hall of Honor is located in New Windsor, New York The original idea for the Purple Heart (the Badge of Military Merit) is the oldest symbol and award that is still given to members of the U.S. military, surpassed in history only by the long obsolete Fidelity Medallion.

SERGEANT UDAY SINGH TAUNQUE

Sergeant Uday Singh Taunque (1982-2003) was the first soldier of Indian origin to die fighting in the Iraq war as part of US army. He was born in Jaipur, India on 23 April 1982. In June 2000 he left for the US with his father and sister and decided to join the US Army. Uday enlisted in the army on 28TH August 2000 and on termination of initial training at Fort Knox was assigned to Charlie Company 1ST Battalion, 34TH Armor Regiment, based at Fort Riley, Kansas, USA. Uday's unit was deployed to Iraq in September 2003. On 1ST December, Uday was in the lead Humvee of his platoon as a gunner while out on reconnaissance in Habbaniyah, when the platoon came under fire. Uday was the first to return fire, and kept the insurgents pinned down until reinforcements arrived. However, in the continuing fire fight he was hit with a gunshot to his head and subsequently died whilst being transported to the hospital. The mission led to the capture of a number of terrorists and large cache of weapons. Uday was awarded with the Bronze Star and Purple Heart for his bravery and ultimate sacrifice.

Uday's ashes are buried at Arlington National Cemetery, Arlington (near Washington D.C.) Section 60 Gravesite No 8122. Also, a memorial for perpetuating his memory is established at his home in Chandigarh. Illinois General Assembly also paid homage to Sereant Uday's bravery and martyrdom by passing a Senate Resolution. It is also noteworthy that Sergeant Uday came from a distinguished militay family and his grandfather, Wing Commander Kartar Singh Taunque, was the first ever personnel of Indian Airforce, then Royal Indian Airforce, to win a gallantry award for Operations in Waziristan during World War II.

SILVER STAR

The Silver Star is the third highest award given for valour that can be awarded to a member of any branch of the United States Armed Forces. It is awarded to any person who distinguishes him or herself by extraordinary heroism in action against an enemy of the United States, or while engaged in military operations involving conflict with an opposing foreign force, or while serving with friendly foreign forces engaged in an armed conflict against an opposing armed force in which the United States is not a belligerent party.

LANCE NAIK HARNAM SINGH
2ND PUNJAB REGIMENT

Citation for Silver Star: "For gallantry in action in Italy on 20TH April 1945. Lance Naik Harnam Singh commanded a section of the 1ST Battalion in the assault on the Idice River, and personally led his section in a charge through intense enemy fire and established their first objective on the riverbank. Later he again led his section in a charge across the River Idice through water against withering machine-gun fire from well-prepared positions. When most of his section had been killed or wounded, Lance Naik Harnam Singh himself attacked the German pillboxes, and continued to silence German positions until he became unconscious from the wounds he had received. The personal leadership and gallantry of Lance Naik Harnam Singh were outstanding and his actions an inspiration to all with whom he served."

JEMADAR GURNAM SINGH,
12TH FRONTIER FORCE REGIMENT

Citation for Silver Star: "For gallantry in action in Italy on 11TH April 1945. During the assault operations on the Santerno River defences, the platoon commanded by Jemadar Gurnam Singh was assigned to clear the enemy defences beyond the river and establish the bridgehead. As his Platoon moved forward they were subjected to intense and accurate shelling, and mines disabled the leading "Kangaroos". Dismounting his platoon, Jemadar Gurnam Singh, with complete coolness, led his men through the heavy shelling and minefields, across the stream to the far flood-bank. Without further orders he personally led his men in a series of attacks against enemy strong points situated in houses and field defences. His platoon was far ahead of the remainder of the company and engaged from all sides at close quarters. With continued coolness he held off superior numbers of the enemy until the arrival of the remainder of the company. Jemadar Gurnam Singh's gallant and cool-headed leadership in a most difficult situation had set an example, which his men could not fail to follow, and resulted in their taking many prisoners and inflicting heavy casualties. The enemy, forced back from his counter-attack line, was unable to rally, and the bridgehead was firmly secured."

BRONZE STAR

The Bronze Star Medal was instituted in February 1944 to be awarded to personnel, male or female, serving in any capacity with the Army, Navy, Marine Corps or Coast Guard of the USA, who 'on or after 7 December 1941 shall have distinguished themselves by heroic or meritorious military achievements, or service in connection with military operations.'

SAPPER ATMA SINGH,
BENGAL SAPPERS AND MINERS

Citation for Bronze Star: " For Meritorious Service in support of combat operations against the enemy during the period 18TH August 1944 to 18TH December 1944. During the period his conduct has been exemplary and has been characterized by his direct and courageous approach to all the problems faced by his platoon, with complete and utter disregard for his personal safety. His inspiring and competent handling of enemy mines has been beyond praise. On one occasion he single-handedly lifted over 200 mines of all types and later leading a party to rescue a wounded comrade from a heavily mined area. Sapper Atma Singh was instrumental in maintaining ammunition supplies to the forward infantry in Baffadi area in November 1944 by repairing an aerial ropeway that was three times cut by sell-fire, and his fearless behaviour under enemy fire had consistently been outstanding example to his comrades."

LANCE NAIK MEHR SINGH,
INDIAN SERVICE CORPS

Citation for Bronze Star: "During the early part of the Cassino operations Lance Naik Mehr Singh was on duty at Caira Signal Centre for a period of over a week during which time the signal centre itself and the line to 7TH Brigade and to 4TH Indian Division were frequently under heavy fire from guns and mortars. Naik Mehr Singh never failed or hesitated in his task of repairing lines under heavy enemy fire. At that time his lines were being cut by shelling hourly throughout the day and night, and by his devotion to duty and calm courage he maintained the communications of the Division at a vital period, setting and example to all those who were with him."

Bronze Star (cont.)

SEPOY BISHAN SINGH, 15TH PUNJAB REGIMENT

Citation for Bronze Star: " On 15TH September 1944 Sepoy Bishan Singh was acting as orderly to the officer commanding 'C' Coy during the breaching of the Gothic Line of Borgo San Lorenzo in Italy. Sepoy Bishan Singh most gallantly volunteered to make a most difficult and dangerous journey back over steep and shell torn ground to fetch up ammunition. At the time enemy counter attack was developing and the company was dangerously short of ammunition; an attempt had been made to get ammunition by mule and had been found impossible. Inspite of the great personal danger from the heavy and accurate enemy shelling and mortaring, Sepoy Bishan Singh not only made a successful journey back carrying 80 Lb box of ammunition up a precipitous slope, but also immediately started off a second time on this hazardous journey. Again he was successful, and with the ammunition thus available, and inspired by Sepoy Bishan Singh's magnificent courage and devotion to duty, the company successfully beat off the enemy attack and established itself firmly in position".

BURMA GALLANTRY MEDAL

The Governor of Burma awarded the Burma Gallantry Medal to officers, NCOs and men of the Burma forces for acts of conspicuous gallantry in the performance of their duties. Following Sikh soldiers of the Burma Regiment were awarded the Burma Gallantry Medal for their gallantry against the Japanese in Burma.

THE BURMA REGIMENT

JEMADAR	GHUR SINGH	1943	BURMA
SEPOY	KEHAR SINGH	1944	BURMA
LANCE NAIK	INDAR SINGH	1944	BURMA
LANCE NAIK	KARNAIL SINGH	1944	BURMA
SEPOY	NAND SINGH	1944	BURMA
NAIK	PARTAB SINGH	1944	BURMA

Burma Gallantry Medal (cont.)

THE BURMA REGIMENT (cont.)

SEPOY	ARJAN SINGH	1945	BURMA
HAVILDAR	NIKKA SINGH	1945	BURMA
SEPOY	SARDAR SINGH	1945	BURMA
SEPOY	PHUMAN SINGH	1945	BURMA
SEPOY	TARA SINGH	1945	BURMA
SEPOY	SARDARA SINGH	1945	BURMA
JEMADAR	JAMAN SINGH	1945	BURMA
JEMADAR	TRILOK SINGH	1946	BURMA

THE GEORGE CROSS

The George Cross (GC) is the highest civil decoration of the Commonwealth of Nations. The George Cross is the civilian counterpart of the Victoria Cross and the highest gallantry award for civilians as well as for military personnel in actions which are not in the face of the enemy or for which purely military honours would not normally be granted.

RAGHBIR SINGH
CORPS OF INDIAN ENGINEERS, CEYLON

On 19TH October, 1944, Jemadar Raghbir Singh was in command of a craft at Guide Pier, Colombo. The craft had completed fueling and, on starting the engine, an explosion took place and fire broke out in the engine room. Two of the crew who were in the engine room were engulfed in flames when Jemadar Raghbir Singh went to their assistance. He dragged them from the burning room and extinguished the flames, and then proceeded to extinguish the fire in the craft. This Jemadar's complete disregard for personal danger, devotion to duty and gallant action resulted in the craft being saved from complete destruction, but unfortunately the two men whom he had rescued from the burning engine room died of their injuries. Jemadar Raghbir Singh was awarded the George Cross for his gallant actions.

THE EMPIRE GALLANTRY MEDAL

The Empire Gallantry Medal was introduced on 29TH December 1922. It was intended to recognize specific acts of gallantry, and was replaced by the George Cross in September 1940. When the George Cross was introduced, living recipients of the EGM could return their EGM and receive the George Cross.

HAVILDAR MAJOR KARTAR SINGH
THE PUNJAB REGIMENT

"On the 5TH October 1944, Company Havildar Major Kartar Singh was carrying out rifle grenade practice with the other men his Company, when an explosion occurred as one of the men was firing a grenade. The fragments of the discharger cup struck one of the men, badly injuring him. Company Havildar Major Kartar Singh, was just behind the injured man, went forward to help him and whilst doing so noticed that the grenade which had been loaded into the injured man's rifle had fallen out of the discharger cup and was lying on the ground smoking a short distance away. Without hesitation Company Havildar Major Kartar Singh dashed forward, picked up the smoking grenade and hurled it away, where it exploded. Company Havildar Kartar Singh quick presence of mind and disregard for personal safety, without doubt saved the lives of three of his comrades."

SAPPER AJMER SINGH
THE CORPS OF INDIAN ENGINEERS

"At Goppe Bazaar, Arakan in Burma on the 22ND July 1944, an extremely heavy rainfall had caused a chaung to rise very rapidly and flood a Supply Depot to such a depth that large quantities of rations were in danger of being swept away. All the available troops in the area were called on to salvage supplies, which necessitated wading through a raging torrent. During these operations Sapper Ajmer Singh, seeing a man in great difficulties, immediately went through the torrent of water to his aid and succeeded in helping him to the shore in time to be revived. Some twenty minutes later a man was seen to be on the verge of drowning and being swept away by the strong current. Without hesitation, Sapper Ajmer Singh swam after him and managed, with difficulty, bring him to safety in a semi-conscious condition. Later yet another man seen floundering in mid-stream. For the third time Sapper Ajmer Singh, exhibiting a tenacious disregard for his own safety, went to the rescue and brought this man to safety. By his prompt action in effecting these three rescues, all within the period of one hour, Sapper Ajmer Singh showed gallantry and devotion to duty of a very high order."

The Empire Gallantry Medal (cont.)

SAPPER BHAG SINGH
INDIAN ENGINEERS

On 20TH February 1945, a platoon of 81ST Indian Field Company was employed in clearing elephant grass on the south bank of the Divisional Bridgehead. While the Sappers were burning grass, an explosion caused a lane in which petrol was being laid to ignite. A Sapper was trapped in the flames and Sapper Bhag Singh with other men attempted to reach him. Sapper Bhag Singh succeeded in dragging the body clear but the trapped man died from his injuries. Sapper Bhag Singh afterwards returned into the flames in order to ascertain that no another man of his section had been left trapped in the fire. During the whole time there was danger of further undetected enemy ammunition exploding. Sapper Bhag Singh himself suffered some injuries, and was awarded the Empire Gallantry Medal for his gallantry unmindful of personal danger.

HAVILDAR PURAN SINGH
PUNJAB REGIMENT

On the night of 16th 17th June 1944, a number of tribesmen, which included a notorious man called Pappu, committed a robbery in a house in a village in the Meerut district of India. Pappu and three of his accomplices were armed with guns. After the robbery Pappu and two other men made their way to the unit lines and were stopped and questioned by a Sepoy on duty, who asked them what they wanted. One of the men replied that they wished to see a soldier named Ram Harian. Knowing that no such man lived in the unit lines the Sepoy became suspicious and caught hold of one of the thieves, but was pushed to side by Pappu. When the Sepoy held on to the second man, and shouted for help, Pappu and the other man ran away. It was whilst these two men were being chased by another Indian soldier, who pointed an empty rifle at them that Havildar Puran Singh arrived upon the scene. Noticing that the two men were being chased and would not stop, he ran between them and the soldier with the rifle, whereupon the notorious Pappu drew out a double-barrelled gun and levelling, it at Havildar Puran Singh fired two cartridges, which, fortunately, misfired. Havildar Puran Singh stood his ground and with the help he received from a number of other soldiers who had arrived upon the scene, succeeding overpowering Pappu and the other man. Havildar Puran Singh displayed great bravery and was instrumental in the capture of two very dangerous men. Havildar Puran Singh was awarded the Empire Gallantry Medal for his extreme bravery.

GEORGE MEDAL

The George Medal was instituted, together with the George Cross, on 24TH September 1940. At that time there was a particular need to reward a great many people in all walks of life. However, it was the intention of the authorities that the George Cross should stand supreme and that the award of larger numbers should not undermine its position as the 'civilian Victoria Cross'. The result was that the George Medal, or GM, was introduced as a 'junior' to the George Cross.

CAPTAIN SARTAJ SINGH, INDIAN ARTILLERY

"At base camp on 24TH April 1943, Captain Sartaj Singh displayed outstanding initiative and disregard of personal danger when he affected the arrest of a soldier of his Battery who had just fired at and killed his Battery Commander. The soldier was armed with a rifle and was obviously prepared to resist arrest. Captain Sartaj Singh, who was unarmed, closed with the soldier, who fired several rounds at him at close range, wounding him twice, in the arm and the groin. Notwithstanding, Captain Sartaj Singh closed and held the soldier until assistance arrived. He then organised the restoration of the situation before allowing medical assistance to be rendered. His brave and prompt action understandably prevented the soldier form causing further injury to personnel."

AL VALORE MILITARE (ITALY)

The Medal Al Valore Militare was awarded to officers and men of the armed forces for gallantry in action against the enemy.

36TH SIKHS
NAIK	KALA SINGH	MESOPOTAMIA

45TH RATTRAY'S SIKHS
LANCE NAIK	FATEH SINGH	MESOPOTAMIA

47TH SIKHS
HAVILDAR	MAL SINGH	MESOPOTAMIA

7TH WILDE'S RIFLES, FRONTIER FORCE
LANCE NAIK	YAR SINGH	EAST AFRICA

THE DISTINGUISHED SERVICE ORDER

The Distinguished Service Order is a military decoration awarded for distinguished leadership during active operations against the enemy.

MAJOR GURBAKSH SINGH
INDIAN MEDICAL SERVICE

"During the attack on M Di Buffalo in Italy, on the 6TH and 7TH October 1944, the Regimental Aid Post in which Major Gurbaksh Singh was tending his wounded came under heavy enemy shelling on many occasions. Twice the Regimental Aid Post was hit, but this unit Medical Officer continued on imperturbably treating the wounded with complete disregard of his own personal danger. His only thought was to attend to the casualties and he only moved his Regimental Aid Post on the order of the Commanding Officer. Throughout this action Major Gurbaksh Singh, inspite of 47 years of age, with his courage and determination was instrumental in maintaining a very high standard of morale." Major Gurbaksh Singh was awarded an immediate Military Cross followed by the DSO on 21ST November 1944.

MAJOR SARBJIT SINGH KALHA
1ST PUNJAB REGIMENT

"On the 21ST and 22ND February 1944 in the operations to clear the Ngakyedauk Pass in Burma, Major Kalha was commanding 2ND Battalion 1ST Punjab Regiment, and was ordered to attack and capture the feature 1070 and Sugar Loaf respectively of the above dates. The execution of this task, on which the success of the whole operations depended, called for careful planning and bold execution. That it was carried out with complete success reflects great credit on Major Sarbjit Singh Kalha. He displayed military skill and determination and a willing ness to take risks to achieve his object unusual in such young officer and the success o the operation was largely due to his vigorous action." Major Sarbjit Singh Kalha was especially recommended and awarded the DSO, as his leadership and skill undoubtedly were the main factors in re-opening the Pass when the others had failed.

Lt.Col. Kalha died Java in course of restoring the country to their previous overlords the Dutch, on the behest of Winston Churchill.

" Many a fine soldier died in this quarrel which had nothing to do with them, men who had fought in East Africa, the Desert the Arakan, Assam and Burma. Amongst these was one of the finest soldiers in the Indian Army, Lieutenant Colonel Sarbjit Singh Kalha, and DSO and Bar, just the sort of officer that his country now most needed" Quoted from The Indian Army by Charles Chenevix Trench.

The Distinguished Service Order (cont.)

COLONEL BALWANT SINGH SIDHU
1ST PATIALA REGIMENT

"Colonel Balwant Singh Sidhu was in command of the 1ST Patiala during the operations from March to August 1944, in Burma. During the whole of this period his Battalion did extremely well in all different phases of warfare they were called upon to and there is no doubt at all that their continued and conspicuous successes were due in the greatest measure to the leadership of Colonel Balwant Singh, which was at all times of the highest order. His strong personality, his tactical skill, his intimate knowledge of the Japanese and of Japanese tactics again and again proved invaluable and enabled his battalion to carry out their task with maximum casualties to the enemy and minimum casualties to his own troops. This is concrete proof of his skilful leadership. In action his personal example undoubtedly had a great and most beneficial effect on all ranks in his battalion as had also his inspiring leadership. On many occasions his personal knowledge of the country over which the Brigade was to operate was of the greatest assistance to Brigade Command, and enabled plans to be made with certainty that could never have been done from maps or air photographs. Colonel Balwant Singh has undoubtedly proved himself to be and outstanding Commander and great leader of men." Colonel Balwant Singh Sidhu was awarded the DSO on 13TH October 1944.

CBE

Colonel Balwant Singh Sidhu was also awarded the CBE, which denotes a Commander in The Most Excellent Order of the British Empire.

"Since arrival on the Burma Border in April 1942, Colonel Balwant Singh with his Battalion has borne large share of the patrolling along the frontier and into Burma under most adverse weather conditions. Throughout this period Colonel Balwant Singh has displayed high standard of determination, initiative and physical endurance. Under appalling weather conditions he visited all his posts on the edge of the Kabaw Valley scattered along a front of more than 30 Miles. On another occasion he personally led a large raiding party on Mawlaik. The party was actually out for 22 days and covered 331 Miles. Weather conditions could hardly have been worse as it rained almost continuously for 12 days, which brought down all the mountain streams in spate and flooded the rivers in the Valley. For over 80 Miles the party had to cut its way through jungle and had to cross several rivers in flood. The determination and initiative shown by Colonel Balwant Singh in the conduct of this Raiding party was of a high order". Colonel Balwant Singh was awarded the CBE on 16TH December 1943.

The Distinguished Service Order (cont.)

MAJOR HARBANS SINGH VIRK
4TH ROYAL BATTALION (SIKHS)
12TH FRONTIER FORCE REGIMENT

"On the 8TH March 1945, Major Virk was in command of 'C Coy.' and with Royal Deccan Horse in support, was ordered to attack and capture the village of Sadaung, in Burma, which was known to contain a strong force of the enemy with 75mm guns, Medium Machine guns and Mortars. He went in from the North at 1315 hrs, and inspite of heavy enemy fire, had secured a firm base well inside the village. At 1430 hours however his company was held up by heavy mortar fire from somewhere to the South of the village, and very accurate Medium Machine Gun fire from the front and a pagoda to the left flank. Discharger Grenades were also being showered in to his position. Nothing daunted, this gallant officer, filled with determination to exterminate the enemy, left the platoon in what cover was available, and extricated his other two, with the object of putting in and attack from the Eastern Flank. The country here was very boggy, and two tanks at once sank into the mud, but relying on swift and decisive action to achieve success he ordered the tanks away to high ground on the left to give covering fire and act as long stop, and formed his men, up for the attack. At 1600 hrs, he rose, and with great shout to his men dashed into the centre of the enemy position, which was quickly overrun. He then his men on in a further magnificent charge, to clear the southern portion of the village, and finally reported at 1700 hrs that the enemy were beaten and running. The tanks then came to their own and demoralized and running Japanese. The enemy killed by Major Virk and his company on this afternoon, amounted to over one hundred and the booty included two 75mm guns, five Medium Machine Guns, two 81 mm Mortars and quantities of small arms and equipment, at the cost of comparatively light casualties to our men. This victory was solely due to the high courage and initiative of this lion-hearted officer. Throughout the action, under extremely heavy fire, he was ubiquitous, climbing on to the tanks to give orders under hail of bullets, and so inspiring his men with his indomitable spirit, that when he gave the order for the --- charge, they followed him with the utmost dash, and the battle was won. This officer has shown highest qualities of courage and leadership throughout the present operations, and has led and inspired his men on the victory on several previous occasions. It was the faith in their leader, inspired and bred from previous actions that gave the great impetus to the company to achieve what they did on this day. He personally killed considerable amount of Japanese soldiers. I cannot praise the fighting qualities of this officer too highly." Major Harbans Singh Virk was awarded an immediate Military Cross followed by the DSO on 27TH May 1945.

The Distinguished Service Order (cont.)
LIEUTENANT COLONEL GURBAKSH SINGH
JIND INFANTRY

"Throughout the operations in Malaya, this officer commanded a battalion, which was responsible for the ground defence of two main aerodromes in Singapore. These areas were regularly and heavily bombed, and later dive-bombed and machine-gunned. Lieutenant Colonel Gurbaksh Singh was most successful in avoiding heavy casualties in his unit by skill and resource in the dispositions of his command. He maintained a very high standard of morale and efficiency, for which his own gallant bearing under fire and his determined personality were responsible. In the later stages of the fighting when the forward troops withdrew in the Tengah area, leaving the flanks of the aerodrome unprotected, the battalion defended their position on 10TH and 11TH February with commendable tenacity, inflicting heavy casualties on the enemy. The battalion eventually withdrew in good order, having suffered considerable loss after the action of which and Indian State Force Unit should well be proud. Subsequently Lieutenant Colonel Gurbaksh Singh took a prominent part in the defence of the outskirts of Singapore, where he again displayed a high degree of courage and leadership under continuous shelling and mortar machine gun fire". Lieutenant Colonel Gurbaksh Singh was awarded the DSO on 13TH December 1945.

Lieutenant Colonel Gurbaksh Singh was also awarded 'Order of the British Empire'. See page 316.

Brigadier Gurbaksh Singh (1952). He was elder brother of Lieutenant General Harbaksh Singh.

BRITISH EMPIRE MEDAL

This is the Medal of the Most Excellent Order of the British Empire for Meritorious Service.

STAFF SERGEANT GURBAX SINGH
15TH BATTALION RAOC

"Sergeant Gurbax Singh has served 23 years with Colours and has and exemplary record of conduct. He is honest, extremely loyal and hardworking Warrant Officer who stands out amongst his contemporaries by virtue of his character and overall contribution to the Army and Corps. Sergeant Gurbax Singh has served in Aden, BAOR, Northern Ireland and United Kingdom, during which time he served with MRF and Intelligence. In the rank of Sergeant, while posted to JATE as Chief Clerk, he was tasked with the reorganisation of the Headquarters. This involved a complete change of organisation and procedures which required high degree of man management and professionalism, particularly due to its being a Tri - Service establishment. In addition he set up a Conference Hall for use by NATO and Commonwealth forces. In 1987 as a WO2 he was posted to the newly established Directorate of Exams and Courses, again as Chief Clerk. Here his duties included the setting up of the administration for the newly formed Directorate. He also had the task of organising the printing, security and distribution of all course, study and examination material for the new JCSC package. His posting to the Battalion in September 1988 was at short notice, only two days before he was due to start his terminal leave and was specifically to sort out problems left by his unfortunate predecessor who had acute welfare problems compounded by a nervous breakdown. The situation was retrieved in a remarkably short time and was achieved by his motivating his staff, whose morale at that time was at a very low ebb and by the fact that he spared himself not at all. In short, his performance and effort far exceeded that which one reasonably expect, especially as by this time he was serving on continuance, having reverted to the substantive rank of Staff Sergeant with the local rank of Warrant Officer Class 11. Staff Sergeant Singh's loyalty and integrity are bywords. The example he sets professionally, and the pastoral care he take over his staff and on the sporting field considering his age, he enlisted at the age of twenty six, and the fact that his is a diabetic, make him conspicuous amongst his contemporaries." Sergeant Gurbax Singh was awarded the BEM on 31ST October 1989.

British Empire Medal (Cont.)

HAVILDAR SHER SINGH
13ᵀᴴ FRONTIER FORCE RIFLES

"Havildar Sher Singh was captured in the Tobruk area in June 1942, and eventually taken to Benghazi Prisoner of War Camp. There were 24,000 Prisoners of War in the camp - of all kinds. The conditions were appalling and had a demoralizing effect on the men. Also, most of them had been captured at Tobruk, so at first the morale was very low. These men were, therefore, extremely difficult to handle. Havildar Sher Singh was the Havildar Major in 'B' Camp (India Camp). This camp was a 'small Indian' containing several thousand Indians. Havildar Sher Singh worked under very trying conditions, often at danger to his life, and maintained the only possible order in the circumstances. When pro-Axis Indians were introduced into the camp to win over the Indian Prisoners of War, he was of very great assistance to the Officer in Charge in carrying out his anti Axis propaganda activities."

THE WAR OFFICE
LONDON, S.W.1.
23ᴿᴰ July 1944

Sir Robert Knox, K.C.V., D.S.O.

Dear Knox,

Included is a list of recommendations submitted by the Commander-in-Chief, Middle East in 1943 with the recommendation for the award of the Indian Distinguished Service Medal in respect of Havildar Sher Singh, 13ᵀᴴ Frontier Force Rifles in recognition of his services whilst a Prisoner of War. This recommendation was placed in the Prisoner of War Pool at the War Office until verification had been received that Havildar Sher Singh had been repatriated. The Viceroy of India who recommends the award of the British Empire Medal, a recommendation that I support, has submitted the recommendation to His Excellency. The relative citation for this award is herewith attached. Will you kindly let me know if this recommendation may be submitted for His Majesty's approval.

Yours Sincerely.

(Sgd.) H. C. B. Wemmays

British Empire Medal (Cont.)

HAVILDAR GURCHARAN SINGH
ROYAL INDIAN ENGINEERS

"Havildar Gurcharan Singh remained staunch and loyal in spite of heavy pressure by the Indian National Army and the Japanese to go over to them. Being educated and of somewhat better class than the average Sepoy Gurcharan Singh had particularly hard time. He was looked upon as one of the leaders of the resistance movement and suffered much in consequence. As ninety nine percent of the Sikhs had gone over to the Indian National Army, it was particularly awkward and difficult for this young Non Commissioned Officer to resist their overtures and later coercion. On this account Gurcharan Singh's conduct is deserving of high praise, especially as he succeeded in keeping out of the movement and influenced other sections of the unit who throughout leant heavily upon him. Throughout captivity Gurcharan Singh, remained an example of discipline and loyalty to his superiors and as such had a most salutary effect upon other men in his camp. Havildar Gurcharan Singh was always cheerful and maintained high morale throughout some very trying periods. He used to disseminate the pro-allied war news among the men and organise relief and benefits for the sick and invalids, He did some very useful work in the camp Poultry Farm, often at the risk of being beaten up by the Japanese supervising personnel."

HAVILDAR PRITAM SINGH
INDIAN SIGNAL CORPS

"Havildar Pritam Singh is and outstanding efficient and zealous Subedar, His encouragement on the one hand and his fair yet strict sense of discipline have made him a shining example to the Junior Non Commissioned Officers and men .He has served with this unit for a year during which time he saw service in the Arakan until the end of the Burma Campaign. It was during this period that his qualities of courage, cheerfulness and industry came to the fore. He was always to be found where men were in the greatest difficulties, helping and inspiring them with confidence in action. On many occasions as a result of these self-imposed tasks over and above his normal duties, communications have been provided in time when circumstances appeared against their completion. His tireless energy and his exemplary turnout in the worst conditions are by-words in the unit. No praise is too high for the leadership of Havildar Gurcharan Singh."

British Empire Medal (Cont.)

HAVILDAR LACHMAN SINGH
INDIAN ENGINEERS

"Havildar Lachman Singh has been in command of troops engaged in numerous bomb disposal operations in Assam and Burma from January 1943 to September 1945. At all times he has shown a high standard of leadership and by his enthusiasm and example had maintained the morale of his men at a very high level whilst they were engaged in their dangerous tasks. Particular work was done by Havildar Lachman Singh during the period May to August 1945 in clearing bombs, mines and booby-traps from Rangoon and Southern Burma."

HAVILDAR MAJOR JOHAR SINGH
ROYAL INDIAN ARMY SERVICE CORPS

"During the period September to December 1944, while his Company was employed as Divisional Ammunition Coy at Vaccihio and Creapino in Italy, Havildar Major Johar Singh was outstanding for his selfless devotion to duty, turning out at all times both by day and night to organise ammunition convoys, and to direct the recovery of vehicles which had become bogged in the heavy mud, in addition to hi normal duties. His personal example, initiative, and cheerful willingness contributed t a large extent to the smooth flow of ammunition t the guns and forward ammunition points during a period when heavy rains and bad roads made replenishment extremely difficult". Havildar Major Johar Singh was awarded the B.E.M. on 28TH June 1945.

NAIK SODAGHAR SINGH
ROYAL INDIAN ARMY SERVICE CORPS

"During the period September and December 1944, Naik Sodaghar Singh was a block Commander in a Motor Transport Platoon engaged in carrying ammunition to the forward gun positions. He at all times lead his men with zeal and efficiency and showed great devotion to duty under most circumstances. Special mention must be made of his work on the night of 22/25TH December 1944. The Division AP in Faenza came under heavy shellfire and a 3-ton lorry containing 25 PDR cartridge and shells caught fire. The vehicle was standing among some 300 tons of other arms. Naik Sodaghar Singh and his Platoon officer distinguished themselves by towing the vehicle away to a safe area. The Division AP was thus saved from a serious fire, which might easily have caused and explosion of the gravest consequence." Naik Sodaghar Singh was awarded the B.E.M. on 13TH April 1945.

British Empire Medal (Cont.)

HAVILDAR SUJAN SINGH
ROYAL INDIAN ARMY SERVICE CORPS

"During the six months this Company has been engaged on the "Aid to Russia", Havildar Sujan Singh has constantly performed his duties in praiseworthy manner. On one occasion in February 1944, when some of the vehicles of the Convey were caught on the top of Shah Pass in a blizzard and the Platoon office remained behind, he brought remainder of the Convey safely 200 miles to the Company Lines. By his own cheerfulness and personal example he has maintained discipline and morale among the men in spite of the serious conditions experienced on the "Aid to Russia" route." Havildar Sujan Singh was awarded the BEM on 11TH May 1944.

HAVILDAR FITTER KARAM SINGH
INDIAN ELECTRICAL AND MECHANICAL ENGINEERS

"Havildar Karam Singh had served with 5 Indian Infantry Brigade workshops for over three and half years. During the period under review he was the senior Indian Non Commissioned Officer in the Divisional Gun Repair Section. In addition to his normal duties as fitter NC.O, he carried out all the machining work of the Section, and by his skill and ingenuity manufactured parts for Field and Anti Tank Guns which enabled these equipments to function when thy were most required. During the Cassino Battle, he cheerfully worked 18-20 hours a day in order to put the Guns back into action. His magnificent and devotion to duty inspired the craftsmen working under him, and during the period the small section turned out over 70 repaired Guns. It was largely due to Havildar Karam Singh's efforts that every gun was back into action in the minimum possible time." Havildar Karam Singh was awarded the BEM on 7TH October 1944.

A Sikh obervation officer in Italy.

ORDER OF THE BRITISH EMPIRE

The Most Excellent Order of the British Empire is a British order of chivalry established on 4TH June 1917 by King George V for those who have played a distinguished role in any field in their region or country. Appointments are made on the advice of the governments of the United Kingdom and some Commonwealth realms.

OFFICERS OF THE ORDER OF THE BRITISH EMPIRE (OBE)

In February 1942, Singapore fell and the Japanese took many Indian soldiers as prisoners. They were separated from the rest of the POWs and subjected to propaganda to join the Indian National Army, which at that stage was fighting alongside the Japanese. It seems that "up to 30,000 Indian soldiers joined the INA either willingly or under duress" and the rest, called "non-volunteers" were immediately taken to a concentration camp and subjected to varying degrees of torture. Notwithstanding torture some officers coaxed their soldiers to refrain from joining the Japanese. The following Sikh officers were awarded OBEs (Order of the British Empire) for playing a distinguished role as prisoners of the Japanese.

MAJOR LAKHINDER SINGH
2ND PUNJAB REGIMENT

Major Lakhinder Singh was a D.A.Q.M.G. in the absence of the Sub Area Commander. With two staff officers he moved up to Tehran to take charge of the Polish evacuation, and took upon himself the whole work administering the Sub Area as well the routine work in the Ahwaz itself. During this period and extreme hot weather, he not only showed outstanding ability, and exercised great power of endurance, but also carried out most of the duties obtaining to the administration of the Sub Area in such a meritorious manner as to preclude any chance of a complete breakdown which might otherwise have been the case. The period covered by this officer's meritious service is 21ST March 1942 to 18TH August 1942. Major Lakhinder Singh was awarded The Most Excellent Order Of The British Empire.

Order of the British Empire (Cont.)

JEMADAR SADHU SINGH
INDIAN STATES FORCES

"During the period 7TH to 30TH September 1946, Jemadar Sadhu Singh, as the commander of a Platoon detachment at Bogale (Pyapon District), during the civilian Police strike, maintained law and order in the town of 7,000 inhabitants. Just after the arrival of his Platoon in the town, Decoits became active and wholesale looting began. Within a week Jemadar Sadhu Singh with his men not only had stopped the looting but also had driven the dacoits into the hinterland. On several occasions, although surrounded and outnumbered, he handled the situation fearlessly and his outstanding courage won the admiration of all the civilians. The conduct and personality of Jemadar Sadhu Singh inspired the greatest confidence in the minds of the townsfolk who regarded his presence as a guarantee of protection against dacoit activities". Jemadar Sadhu Singh was awarded The Most Excellent Order Of The British Empire.

LT. COL. NARAIN SINGH
JAMMU AND KAHSMIR INFANTRY

" During the period under review, May to August 1945, 4TH Battalion J and K infantry has been employed rounding up Japanese deserters and strays, and dealing with number of bands of very well armed dacoits and the collection of hidden arms and ammunition. The work has been carried out in very bad monsoon weather, on almost non-existent tracks often in dense jungle particularly in the Allaneyo and Thayetic areas. The results achieved had been beyond expectation; the dacoit in the area has practically ceased, larger quantities of arms recovered and confidence restored. This is attributed in no small measure to the personal energy and determination of the Colonel of the Battalion Lt.Col, Narain Singh. With his Battalion extended over several hundreds of square miles of territory he has had a most difficult task in very adverse weather conditions." Lt.Col, Narain Singh was awarded The Most Excellent Order Of The British Empire.

Order of the British Empire (Cont.)

LT.COL. GURBAKSH SINGH DSO
JIND INFANTRY

"For his outstanding loyalty, leadership and personal example whilst in captivity. From February 1942 to December 1942, he resisted all efforts to force him and his men especially the Sikhs to join the Indian National Army. Despite the personal intervention of the then leader of the I.N.A the majority of his Sikhs and many those of other units were dissuaded by him from wavering from their allegiance. Some months later, he with all his Sikh officers called before Subash Chandra Bose. After half an hour of the subtlest persuasion ending in vile threats, this splendid officer rose and said: " I am a man of principle, if I could betray one Master I could betray another." This remark spoken with such dignity and strength appeared to receive the actual approval of Subash Chandra Bose, the conversation ended and the party was sent back to their camp at Kluang. Thereafter they were never again worried or threatened nor any attempts made to renew their efforts to shake their loyalty. From that time to the end of his captivity Lt. Col. Gurbaksh Singh concentrated his efforts on the welfare his men. He organised and gave lectures on village uplift, agriculture and education. During this period he also wrote and staged no fewer than 29 Indian Dramas to keep up the spirits and moral of the Camp. At the end he brought back to India his complete Regiment, loyal almost to a man. By his wonderful example and leadership and the faith placed in him by all, he has earned and deserves the highest possible praise and distinction". Lt. Col. Gurbaksh Singh was awarded: The Most Excellent Order Of The British Empire.

LT.COL PREM SINGH GYANI
ROYAL INDIAN ARTILLERY

"Lt.Col Prem Singh Gyani has commanded 2 Indian Field Regiment, Indian Artillery, throughout the 1945 Burma campaign with great skill and determination. This Regiment first supported the 11TH East African Division during their advance down the Kabaw valley to Kalewa and it was mainly due to this officer that it successfully overcame the very great difficulties of terrain and bad weather. As an Army Field Regiment it then supported 7TH Indian Division in their attack across the Irrawaddy and subsequent advance to Prome. In particular during the battle north of Prome occasioned by the breakout of the Japanese Arakan force across the Irraawaddy. Lt.Col Prem Singh Gyani displayed great gallantry, drive and initiative in organizing and directing his artillery fire, which caused very heavy casualties. This officer has throughout shown the powers of leadership, devotion to duty and personal disregard of danger and fatigue of a very high order, which definitely merits recognition." Lt.Col Prem Singh Gyani Singh was awarded: The Most Excellent Order Of The British Empire.

Order of the British Empire (Cont.)

MEMBERS OF THE ORDER OF THE BRITISH EMPIRE (MBE)

SUBEDAR	JOGINDER SINGH	1941	MIDDLE EAST
SUBEDAR	RATTEN SINGH	1941	MIDDLE EAST
LIEUTENANT	MAKHAN SINGH	1942	MIDDLE EAST
W. OFFICER	BHAG SINGH	1943	MIDDLE EAST
LIEUTENANT	RUR SINGH	1943	MIDDLE EAST
CAPTAIN	GURDIAL SINGH	1943	MIDDLE EAST
SUBEDAR	PARTAP SINGH	1944	MIDDLE EAST
CAPTAIN	ATMA SINGH	1944	ITALY
SUBEDAR	TARA SINGH	1944	ITALY
SUBEDAR MAJOR	BABU SINGH	1945	ITALY
SUBEDAR	NAGINDAR SINGH	1945	ITALY
CAPTAIN	RALLA SINGH	1945	ITALY
CAPTAIN	CHANDAN SINGH	1945	ITALY
SUBEDAR	GURBUX SINGH	1945	ITALY
RISALDAR	SURJAN SINGH	1945	ITALY
MISTER	J. SINGH AHLUWALIA	1943	BURMA
CAPTAIN	SANT S. SABHERWAL	1943	BURMA
LIEUTENANT	SEWA SINGH	1943	BURMA
MAJOR	SURJAN SINGH	1945	BURMA
CAPTAIN	S. SINGH GREWAL	1945	BURMA
LIEUTENANT	AJIT SINGH	1945	BURMA
LIEUTENANT	DHIAN SINGH	1945	BURMA
SUBEDAR MAJOR	SULAKHAN SINGH	1945	BURMA
SUBEDAR	JAGIR SINGH	1945	BURMA
JEMADAR	UJAGAR SINGH	1945	BURMA
MAJOR	BUDH SINGH	1946	BURMA
MAJOR	BHAG SINGH	1946	BURMA

Order of the British Empire (Cont.)

Members of the Order of the British Empire (MBE) (Cont.)

MAJOR	BALWANT SINGH	1946	BURMA
MAJOR	BHAGAT SINGH	1946	BURMA
CAPTAIN	P. JAGJIT SINGH	1946	BURMA
SUBEDAR MAJOR	RANJIT SINGH	1946	BURMA
SUBEDAR	BUDH SINGH	1946	BURMA
JEMADAR	PARTAP SINGH	1946	BURMA
JEMADAR	HARNAM SINGH	1946	BURMA
RISALDAR MAJOR	UJAGAR SINGH	1946	BURMA
JEMADAR	SHER SINGH	1945	ESCAPE AND EVASION
LIEUTENANT	BAKHTAWAR SINGH	1943	ESCAPE AND EVASION
SUBEDAR MAJOR	MAHINDER SINGH	1946	P. O. W.
RISALDAR	JASWANT SINGH	1946	P. O. W.

CROIX DE GUERRE (FRANCE)

The Croix de Guerre is bestowed on individuals who distinguish themselves by acts of heroism involving combat with enemy forces.

6TH KEO CAVALRY
DAFFADAR   NAND SINGH   FRANCE

20TH DECCAN HORSE
DAFFADAR   SARDARA SINGH   FRANCE

21ST MOUNTAIN BATTERY
JEMADAR   PURAN SINGH   MESOPOTAMIA

GUIDES FRONTIER FORCE
HAVILDAR   KISHAN SINGH   MESOPOTAMIA

1ST BATTALION, 22ND PUNJABIS
SUBEDAR   BADAN SINGH   KUT AL AMARA

1ST BATTALION, 23RD SIKH PIONEERS
SUBEDAR MAJOR   MAN SINGH   EGYPT

47TH SIKHS
HAVILDAR   DEWDA SINGH IDSM   MESOPOTAMIA

48TH PIONEERS
SUBEDAR   LEHNA SINGH IDSM   FRANCE

66TH PUNJABIS
SUBEDAR MAJOR   BISHEN SINGH   EAST AFRICA

BURMA MILITARY POLICE
SOWAR   KAKA SINGH IOM   MESOPOTAMIA

9TH PUNJABIS
SEPOY   NIHAL SINGH IOMD   FRANCE

FARIDKOT SAPPERS
JEMADAR   MOTI SINGH IDSM   EAST AFRICA

JHIND INFANTRY
CAPTAIN   SUNDAR SINGH   EAST AFRICA

CROIX DE GUERRE (BELGIUM)

The Croix de Guerre is bestowed on individuals who distinguish themselves by acts of heroism involving combat with enemy forces.

9TH HODSON'S HORSE
LANCE DAFFADAR   SORAIN SINGH   FRANCE

13TH LANCERS
LANCE DAFFADAR   HAZURA SINGH   FRANCE

16TH CAVALRY
KOT DAFFADAR   JASWANT SINGH   FRANCE

18TH KGO LANCERS
DAFFADAR   JAIMAL SINGH   FRANCE

29TH LANCERS
RESSAIDAR   DAYA SINGH   FRANCE
DAFFADAR   PURAN SINGH   FRANCE

31ST DCO LANCERS
LANCE DAFFADAR   HAZURA SINGH   FRANCE

36TH JACOB'S HORSE
DAFFADAR   KARTAR SINGH   FRANCE

Unveiling of the monument for Indian soldiers fallen in Belgium during the First World War
(Hollebeke, Belgium, 3RD April 1999)

Picture: Johan Meire
http://www.sikhspectrum.com

CROSS-OF ST. GEORGE (RUSSIA)

Established in the Russian Empire in 1807, being Imperial Russia's highest military award for gallantry in the face of enemy, it held the same value and honour as the British Victoria Cross, US Medal of Honor, French Legion of Honor, and Indian Param Vir Chakra.

16TH CAVALRY
LANCE DAFFADAR   NARAIN SINGH   CROSS OF ST. GEORGE

3RD SAPPERS AND MINERS
JEMADAR   GURMUKH SINGH   CROSS OF ST. GEORGE
HAVILDAR   DALIP SINGH IOM   CROSS OF ST. GEORGE

35TH SIKHS
HAVILDAR   BIR SINGH   CROSS OF ST. GEORGE

JACOB'S MOUNTAIN BATTERY
HAVILDAR   LACHMAN SINGH   CROSS OF ST. GEORGE

12TH PIONEERS
SEPOY   SUNDAR SINGH   CROSS OF ST. GEORGE

14TH SIKHS
NAIK   DILWARA SINGH   CROSS OF ST. GEORGE
NAIK   SHER SINGH   CROSS OF ST. GEORGE

29TH PUNJABIS
HAVILDAR   RAM SINGH   CROSS OF ST. GEORGE

34TH SIKH PIONEERS
HAVILDAR   SHAM SINGH   CROSS OF ST GEORGE

36TH SIKHS
HAVILDAR   BADAN SINGH   CROSS OF ST. GEORGE

47TH SIKHS
JEMADAR   MOTA SINGH   CROSS OF ST. GEORGE

48TH PIONEERS
LANCE NAIK   MAHAN SINGH   CROSS OF ST. GEORGE

51ST SIKHS, FRONTIER FORCE
SEPOY   DALIP SINGH   CROSS OF ST. GEORGE

JHIND INFANTRY
NAIK   SUCHA SINGH   CROSS OF ST. GEORGE

THE GUIDES

DEFENCE OF THE KABUL RESIDENCY

The British Residency was in the Bala Hissar, an ancient fortress located in Kabul, Afghanistan. On the 3RD September 1879, without warning, Afghan soldiers attacked the Residency and were joined by the civilian population. British officers and Indian troops of the Queen's Own Corps of Guides faced countless thousands of Afghan soldiers and civilians. Soon all the British officers were dead. The Guides fought desperately, even charging out of the Residency to bayonet the crews of artillery brought against them. The Residency was set on fire and the buildings started to collapse. All day the Afghans called upon the Guides to surrender, promising them their lives. The Guides rejected this offer and after 12 hours of fighting the few remaining men commanded by a Sikh Jemadar, Jewand Singh, fixed bayonets and charged out to their deaths. Over 600 Afghan dead bore witness to the heroic resistance of this small force.

KABUL MEMORIAL

This memorial has been erected to perpetuate the remembrance of the conspicuous gallantry of the Officers, Non-Commissioned Officers and men of the Queen's Own Corps of Guides who, when escort to major Sir Louis Cavagnari KCSI, fell in the defence of the Residency of Kabul on September 3RD 1879.

The annals of no army and no regiment can show a brighter record of devoted bravery than has been achieved by this small band of Guides, by their deeds they have conferred undying honours not only on the Regiment to which they belong but on the whole British army.

The following Sikh soldiers sacrificed their lives in the defence of the Residency of Kabul, on 3RD September 1879, and in Kabul itself.

GUIDES CAVALRY KILLED AT KABUL RESIDENCY

JEMADAR	JEWAND SINGH	KILLED 3 SEPT. 1879
DAFFADAR	HIRA SINGH	KILLED 3 SEPT. 1879
SOWAR	AMAR SINGH	KILLED 3 SEPT. 1879
SOWAR	WAZIR SINGH	KILLED 3 SEPT. 1879
SOWAR	RATAN SINGH	KILLED 3 SEPT. 1879

The Guides (cont.)

GUIDES CAVALRY KILLED AT KABUL RESIDENCY (cont.)

SOWAR	MUL SINGH	KILLED 3 SEPT. 1879
SOWAR	JIWAN SINGH	KILLED 3 SEPT. 1879
SOWAR	HARMAN SINGH	KILLED 3 SEPT. 1879
SOWAR	THAKUR SINGH	KILLED 3 SEPT. 1879
SOWAR	DEVA SINGH	KILLED 3 SEPT. 1879

GUIDES INFANTRY KILLED AT KABUL RESIDENCY

JEMADAR	MEHTAB SINGH	KILLED 3 SEPT. 1879
HAVILDAR	KHARAK SINGH	KILLED 3 SEPT. 1879
HAVILDAR	HAZARA SINGH	KILLED 3 SEPT. 1879
HAVILDAR	DEVI SINGH	KILLED 3 SEPT. 1879
SEPOY	JAI SINGH	KILLED 3 SEPT. 1879
SEPOY	AMAR SINGH	KILLED 3 SEPT. 1879
SEPOY	FATTEH SINGH	KILLED 3 SEPT. 1879
SEPOY	WARIAM SINGH	KILLED 3 SEPT. 1879
SEPOY	MITH SINGH	KILLED 3 SEPT. 1879
SEPOY	HIRA SINGH	KILLED 3 SEPT. 1879
SEPOY	CHANDA SINGH	KILLED 3 SEPT. 1879
SEPOY	GURDIT SINGH	KILLED 3 SEPT. 1879
SEPOY	GAJA SINGH	KILLED 3 SEPT. 1879
SEPOY	WARIAM SINGH	KILLED 3 SEPT. 1879
SEPOY	NIDHAM SINGH	KILLED 3 SEPT. 1879
SEPOY	TAHIL SINGH	KILLED 3 SEPT. 1879
SEPOY	RANJU SINGH	KILLED 3 SEPT. 1879
SEPOY	BHAGAT SINGH	KILLED 3 SEPT. 1879
SEPOY	ESA SINGH	KILLED 3 SEPT. 1879
SEPOY	NARAIN SINGH	KILLED 3 SEPT. 1879
SEPOY	HARI SINGH	KILLED 3 SEPT. 1879
SEPOY	OODHAM SINGH	KILLED 3 SEPT. 1879
SEPOY	GURDIT SINGH	KILLED 3 SEPT. 1879

The Guides (cont.)

GUIDES CAVALRY KILLED AT KABUL

KOT DAFFADAR	ATAR SINGH	KILLED 2 APRIL 1879
SOWAR	SHAMUR SINGH	KILLED 2 APRIL 1879
SOWAR	BUDH SINGH	KILLED 13 DEC. 1879
SOWAR	CHOGAT SINGH	KILLED 13 DEC. 1879
SOWAR	JUGGUT SINGH	KILLED 13 DEC. 1879
SOWAR	CHET SINGH	KILLED 23 DEC. 1879

GUDIES INFANTRY KILLED AT KABUL

SUBEDAR	JOWALA SINGH	KILLED 14 DEC. 1879
SEPOY	KHARAK SINGH	KILLED 14 DEC. 1879
HAVILDAR	NARAIN SINGH	KILLED 14 DEC. 1879
SUBEDAR	RUP SINGH	KILLED 14 DEC. 1879
HAVILDAR	TAHIL SINGH	KILLED 14 DEC. 1879
SEPOY	GURDIT SINGH	KILLED 14 DEC. 1879
SEPOY	FATEH SINGH	KILLED 14 DEC. 1879
SEPOY	JETHA SINGH	KILLED 14 DEC. 1879

THE KABUL RESIDENCY

DIVISION OF THE ARMY AFTER INDEPENDENCE

Following reorganisation of the Indian armed forces in 1922, the cavalry regiments were amalgamated in pairs to form new regiments. In the Infantry the regiments were converted into the battalions of one large regiment consisting of four or five active battalions plus a training unit for the regiment.

Infantry Regiments

Regiment	Remarks
1ST Punjab Regiment	To Pakistan, August 1947
2ND Punjab Regiment	To India, August 1947
8TH Punjab Regiment	To Pakistan, August 1947
11TH Sikh Regiment	To India, August 1947
12TH Frontier Force Regiment	To Pakistan, August 1947
13TH Frontier Force Rifles	To Pakistan, August 1947
14TH Punjab Regiment	To Pakistan, August 1947
15TH Punjab Regiment	To Pakistan, August 1947
16TH Punjab Regiment	To Pakistan, August 1947
The Sikh Light Infantry	To India, August 1947

The Engineers

Partition 1947: Pakistan received 34 Engineer units while India received 61 Engineer units. All the Muslim Sappers opted for Pakistan and the Sikhs for India.

Artillery

Following the 2.1 split of the twenty-eight regiments on Partition, Indian received eighteen and a half whilst Pakistan received nine and a half. All Muslim Gunners opted for Pakistan and the Sikhs for India.

Division of the Army after Independence (cont.)

Cavalry Regiments

Regiment	Remarks
1ST Skinner's Horse	To India, August 1947
2ND Lancers	To India, August 1947.
3RD Cavalry	To India, August 1947.
4TH Hodson's Horse	To India, August 1947
5TH Probyn's Horse	To Pakistan, August 1947.
6TH DCO Lancers	To Pakistan, August 1947.
7TH Light Cavalry	To India, August 1947
8TH Light Cavalry	To India, August 1947.
9TH Horse	To India, August 1947
10TH The Guides	To Pakistan, August 1947.
11TH Frontier Force	To Pakistan, August 1947.
12TH Frontier Force	To Pakistan, August 1947.
13TH DCO Lancers	To Pakistan, August 1947.
14TH Scinde Horse	To India, August 1947
15TH Lancers	To Pakistan, August 1947.
16TH Light Cavalry	To India, August 1947
17TH Poona Horse	To India, August 1947.
18TH KEO Cavalry	To India, August 1947
19TH KGO Lancers	To Pakistan, August 1947.
21ST Central India Horse	To India, August 1947
20TH Lancers	To India, August 1947

Division of the Army after Independence (cont.)

Faridkot Sappers and Miners)

Both Field companies of Faridkot Sappers and Miners were absorbed into the Indian Army in 1948 and re-designated:

2ND Faridkot Field Co. became 94TH Field. Co. (Faridkot) Bengal Group.

1ST Field Co. became 368TH Field. Co. (Faridkot) Bengal Group.

Jind Infantry

Jind Infantry Battalions were absorbed into the Indian Army in 1951 and re-designated:

13TH (Jind) Bn. Punjab Regiment.

Nabha Akal Infantry

Nabha Infantry Battalion was absorbed into the Indian Army in 1954 and re-designated:

14TH (Nabha) Bn. The Punjab Regiment.

Patiala Infantry

Patiala Infantry Battalions were absorbed into the Indian Army in 1954 and re-designated:

15TH (Patiala) Bn. The Punjab Regiment.

16TH (Patiala) Bn. The Punjab Regiment.

Malaya States Guides

The Malay States Guides, Infantry and Artillery, were disbanded in 1926.

Burma Military Police
Burma Mounted Rifles

Burma Mounted Rifles and Burma Military Police Battalions were merged into various Burma Regiments and fought against the Japanese in Burma during the Second World War. At the end of the Second World War and the Independence of Burma the Sikh soldiers of Burma Regiments were absorbed into the Indian Army.

PARAM VIR CHAKRA

The Param Vir Chakra (PVC) is the highest gallantry award given to the Indian armed forces, for the highest degree of valour in the presence of the enemy. The PVC is the post-Independence equivalent of the Victoria Cross. Since Independence only 21 awards were made, as many as 14 of these are posthumous awards.

Param Vir Chakra (cont.)

LANCE NAIK KARAM SINGH PVC

"During the Jammu and Kashmir operations against the Pakistan Army in the summer of 1948, the Indian Army made substantial gains in the Tithwal sector. This led to the capture of Tithwal on 23RD May 1948. The battle of Tithwal went on for months. The enemy could not, however, make a dent on the Indian defences. On October 13TH, they launched a desperate attack in Brigade strength to evict the Indian Army from their strongly held positions. The objective was to recapture Richhmar Gali to the south of Tithwal and to outflank the Indian Army by marching on to Nastachur Pass to the east of Tithwal. Both attempts failed. During this attack, some bitter fighting took place in the Richhmar Gali area on the night of October 13TH. The attack commenced with heavy shelling of guns and mortar. The fire was so devastating that nearly all bunkers in the platoon's area were damaged. In this action the 1ST Battalion, Sikh Regiment played a very important role in beating back the enemy onslaught. Lance Naik Karam Singh was commanding a forward outpost when the enemy, in vastly superior strength, attacked his post eight times. The Sikhs repulsed the enemy every time. When ammunition ran short, Lance Naik Karam Singh joined the main company position, knowing full well that due to the heavy enemy shelling, no help would be forthcoming. Although wounded, he brought back two injured comrades with the help of a third Jawan.

Ringed by enemy fire, it was almost impossible for them to break out. Ignoring all dangers, he crawled from place to place encouraging his men to keep up the fight. Often he beat back the enemy with grenades. Twice wounded, he refused evacuation and continued to hold on to the first-line trenches. The fifth enemy attack was very intense. Two enemy soldiers came so close to his position that he could not engage them without hitting his men. Lance Naik Karam Singh, jumped out of his trench and bayoneted the two intruders to death. This bold action so demoralized the enemy that they broke off the attack. Karam Singh and his men also repulsed three more enemy attacks."

Lance Naik Karam Singh was honoured with the highest wartime gallantry medal, Param Vir Chakra, for his outstanding role in the battle of Tithwal.
Lance Naik Karam Singh also earned a Military Medal in the Second World War.

Param Vir Chakra (cont.)

NAIB SUBEDAR BANA SINGH PVC

Naib Subedar Bana Singh was born in Kadyal, Jammu on 6TH January 1949. He was enrolled in the Indian Army on 6TH January 1969 into the Jammu and Kashmir Light Infantry (Jak Li). During June 1987, the 8TH Jak Li was deployed in the Siachen area. It was found that a large number of Pakistani infiltrators had intruded in the Siachen Glacier. The ejection of these infiltrators was considered difficult but necessary and a special task force was constituted for the purpose. Naib Subedar Singh volunteered to join this force.
His award citation states:

"Naib Subedar Bana Singh volunteered to be a member of a task force constituted in June 1987 to clear an intrusion by an adversary in the Siachen Glacier area at an altitude of 21,000 feet. The post was virtually an impregnable glacier fortress with ice walls, 1,500 feet high, on both sides. Naib Subedar Bana Singh led his men through an extremely difficult and hazardous route. He inspired them by his indomitable courage and leadership. The brave Naib Subedar and his men crawled and closed in on the adversary. Moving from trench to trench, lobbing hand grenades, and charging with the bayonet, he cleared the post of all intruders."

Naib Subedar Bana Singh was awarded the Param Vir Chakra, the highest wartime gallantry medal, for conspicuous bravery and leadership under most adverse conditions.

Maharajah Dulip Singh. (1838-1893)
The last sovereign of the Sikh Empire.

Param Vir Chakra (cont.)

SUBEDAR JOGINDER SINGH PVC

"On 28TH September 1936 Subedar Joginder Singh enrolled in the 1ST Battalion, Sikh Regiment. During the 1962 Indo-China War, Subedar Joginder Singh commanded a platoon in the Tawang sector of NEFA (North East Frontier Agency). While holding a defensive position on a ridge in Tongpeng La area on Bum La axis, the platoon noticed heavy enemy concentration across the McMohan Line on October 20TH. This was indeed preparatory to the Chinese advance on Bum La axis on October 23RD.

At 0530 hours on October 23RD, the Chinese launched a heavy attack on the Bum La axis. The intention was to achieve a breakthrough to Tawang. The enemy attacked the Ridge in three waves, each about 200 strong. The attack was supported by artillery and mortar fire, besides other weapons. The fierce resistance of the Sikh Platoon, however, compelled the enemy to fall back with heavy losses. He regrouped quickly and launched a fresh attack under the cover of an artillery barrage. However, Subedar Joginder Singh and his platoon stood firm like a rock before the advancing enemy. In this fierce action, the platoon lost half of its men but not the will to fight. Subedar Joginder Singh, despite a wound in the thigh, refused evacuation. His platoon also refused to yield any ground to the enemy. The last wave of the Chinese attack, which was more determined and more forceful, followed next. Now the platoon had very few men left to fight. Subedar Joginder Singh, therefore, manned a light machine-gun and killed a large number of the enemy, but he could not stem the tide of the enemy advance single-handedly. The Chinese Army continued advancing with little concern for their casualties. By now all Subedar Joginder Singh's platoon's ammunition had been exhausted. With the situation desperate, Subedar Joginder Singh and his men emerged from their position with fixed bayonets, shouting the Sikh battle cry, "Wahe Guruji ka Khalsa, Wahe Guruji ki Fateh." They fell upon the advancing enemy and bayoneted many to death. Finally better weapons and numerical superiority of the enemy prevailed and Subedar Singh was killed in this epic battle. For his inspiring leadership, courage and devotion to duty, Subedar Joginder Singh was awarded the highest wartime gallantry medal, the Param Vir Chakra, posthumously".

Subedar Joginder Singh was born on 26TH September 1921, in Faridkot, Punjab.

Param Vir Chakra (cont.)

FLYING OFFICER NIRMAL JIT SINGH SEKHON PVC

"Fg. Off. Nirmal Jit Singh Sekhon was commissioned into the Indian Air Force on 4TH June 1967. During the 1971 Indo-Pak conflict, Fg. Off. Sekhon was with the 18TH "Flying Bullets" Squadron flying the Folland Gnat Fighter based at Srinagar. In accordance with the international agreement dating back to 1948, no air defence aircraft were based at Srinagar. This changed with the outbreak of hostilities with Pakistan in 1971. Fg. Off. Sekhon was, therefore, unfamiliar with the terrain and was not acclimatized to the altitude of Srinagar, especially with the bitter cold and biting winds of the Kashmir winter. Nevertheless, from the onset of the war, he and his colleagues fought successive waves of intruding Pakistani aircraft with valour and determination, maintaining the high reputation of the Gnat aircraft.

Early morning on the 14TH of December 1971, Srinagar Airfield was attacked by a wave of six enemy Sabre aircraft. Flying Officer Sekhon was on readiness duty at the time. However, he could not take off at once because of the clouds of dust raised by another aircraft, which had just taken off. By the time the runway was fit for take off, no fewer than six enemy aircraft were overhead, and strafing of the airfield was in progress. Nevertheless, in spite of the mortal danger of attempting to take off during an attack, and in spite of the odds against him, Flying Officer Sekhon took off and immediately engaged a pair of the attacking Sabres. He succeeded in damaging two of the enemy aircraft. In the fight that followed, at tree top height, he all but held his own, but was eventually overcome by sheer weight of numbers. His aircraft crashed and he was killed.

In thus sacrificing himself for the defence of Srinagar, Flying Officer Sekhon achieved his objective, for the enemy aircraft fled from the scene of the battle without pressing home their attack against the town and the airfield. The sublime heroism, supreme gallantry, flying skill and determination above and beyond the call of duty, displayed by Flying Officer Sekhon in the face of certain death, set new heights to Air Force traditions."

Nirmal Jit Singh Sekhon was the only officer of the Indian Air Force to be awarded the Param Vir Chakra.

Nirmal Jit Singh Sekhon was born on 17TH July 1943, in Ludhiana, Punjab.

ASHOKA CHAKRA

India's highest military decoration awarded for valour, courageous action or self-sacrifice away from the battlefield. It is the peace time equivalent of the Param Vir Chakra and is awarded for the "most conspicuous bravery or some daring or pre-eminent valour or self-sacrifice."

SUBEDAR SURINDER SINGH
THE SIKH REGIMENT

"Subedar Surinder Singh of the 3RD Battalion, The Sikh Regiment heroically gunned down four Pakistani terrorists single-handedly, before succumbing to his injuries in a fierce encounter in counter-insurgency operations, while commanding a platoon on the Line of Control in the Rajouri sector of Jammu on March 3RD, 2002. In all, six terrorists were killed in this operation. Subedar Singh was posthumously awarded the Ashoka Chakra, the country's highest peacetime gallantry award for displaying most conspicuous bravery beyond the call of duty and making the supreme sacrifice".

HAVILDAR BACHITTAR SINGH (POSTHUMOUS)
THE SIKH REGIMENT

"In 1948, Battalions of the Sikh Regiment were involved in the 'Hyderabad Police Action', the operation that ended the rule of the Nizam and led to the integration of the princely state of Hyderabad into the Indian Union. During the operation, in spite of the withering fire, Havildar Bachittar Singh, succeeded in capturing two vehicles and their militant escorts. Later in the day separatists attacked the Sikhs from a well-entrenched position. As Havildar Bachittar Singh led a charge on the entrenched position he was mortally wounded, but crawled forward and silenced the enemy with grenades. Refusing any medical help, he kept encouraging his men till the end." He was posthumously awarded the Ashoka Chakra, becoming the first Indian soldier to receive this gallantry award.

Ashoka Chakra (cont.)

NAIB SUBEDAR GURNAM SINGH (POSTHUMOUS)
BOMBAY ENGINEERING GROUP

"On 23RD September 1973, the College of Military Engineering, Pune, arranged a demonstration for visiting staff and student officers of the Defence Services Staff College, Wellington. One of the items was the actual firing of the Charge Line Mine Clearing, an explosive device for clearing enemy minefields. Naib Subedar Gurnam Singh, being an eminent expert instructor in mine clearing, was detailed to fire an explosive charge under simulated battle conditions. Seven Sappers assisted him in this task. While Naib Subedar Gurnam Singh was in the process of setting up and preparing the Charge Line Mine Clearing for firing, the tail initiator of the charge was prematurely activated. He at once realized that the entire explosive was likely to blow up within a matter of seconds. Realizing the danger to the men under his command, he immediately ordered them to run to a safe distance, and in utter disregard for his personal safety set upon the hazardous task of uncoupling the activated tail initiator to render the Charge Line Mine Clearing completely safe, to ensure the safety of the equipment and also to avoid the upsetting of the proceeding of the demonstration. But unfortunately, in spite of his best efforts and determination, he was not able to prevent the explosion within the time available at his disposal. There was a terrific explosion and Naib Subedar Gurnam Singh was blown to pieces. Thus in order to save the lives of the men under his command, Naib Subedar Gurnam Singh made the supreme self-sacrifice. Through his action, he displayed the most conspicuous gallantry, leadership and devotion to duty in the highest tradition of the Indian Armed Forces. In appreciation of the conspicuous bravery of Naib Subedar Gurnam Singh, the President of India awarded him with "Ashoka Chakra" posthumously on 26TH January 1974, which was received by Smt Jagir Kaur, widow of Naib Subedar Gurnam Singh at the Republic Day Parade"

Ashoka Chakra (cont.)

HAVILDAR JOGINDER SINGH (POSTHUMOUS)
THE SIKH REGIMENT

"On 24TH April 1956, The Sikh Regiment was employed in restoring law and order in Naga Hills and Havildar Joginder Singh was acting as an escort commander of a small convoy of three jeeps carrying important stores for the forward post in Phake. He was sitting in the leading jeep armed with a sten gun. As the jeep was negotiating a bend on the road, hostiles suddenly opened Light Machine-gun fire on him from a hillock nearby. He was wounded in the right leg but leaving his jeep, ran forward to attack the hostile post. During the advance he was wounded again in the right shoulder. This did not deter him and he continued his charge followed by six members of his party, who inspired by his leadership left their vehicle to join him in the assault. When Havildar Joginder Singh was about 25 yards from the hostiles, a Light Machine-gun burst hit him in the stomach and he fell down. Despite his wounds, he continued to crawl forward and threw two grenades on the hostile Light Machine-gun post and silenced it. Havildar Joginder Singh refused to allow any one to dress his wounds but urged his men to continue their advance and capture the objective, which they soon did. A few minutes later he breathed his last. Because of his inspiring example and gallant leadership, Havildar Joginder Singh's men were able to destroy the hostiles Light Machine-Gun post that blocked the road and the much-needed stores were able to reach the forward company in time. His inspiration to duty will remain an inspiration to all." Havildar Joginder Singh was awarded a posthumous Ashoka Chakra.

Ashoka Chakra (cont.)

SEPOY MEWA SINGH
THE SIKH REGIMENT

"On 27TH April 1956, whilst a battalion of The Sikh Regiment was employed in restoring law and order in Naga Hills, Sepoy Mewa Singh was a member of a temporary protective post. Just as the post was about to withdraw under orders, a gang of about 10-armed hostiles appeared on the scene and opened fire on the post. Sepoy Mewa Singh at once brought his light machine-gun into action from his hip. Then along with the other members of the post charged forward to the hostile gang, killing one and wounding two more. The remaining hostiles fled into the jungle leaving behind two rifles, which Sepoy Mewa Singh captured. The success of this assault was due entirely to the dash and gallant action of Sepoy Mewa Singh.

Again on 5TH May 1956, he was member of a section that was sent out to patrol the area around milestone 25 on Kohima-Phake Road. Just as the patrol reached the area, a gang of hostiles suddenly opened fired on it. Sepoy Mewa Singh who was in the leading section was ordered to give covering fire with his light machine-gun from flank to enable the patrol to charge the hostiles. He brought his gun into action immediately. A minute later he was wounded in the neck but withstanding his serious wounds, continued firing his light machine- gun until the patrol cleared the hostile position, killing one and wounding two hostiles. This second success was also largely due the determined and fearless action of Sepoy Mewa Singh. The aggressive spirit and determination on both occasions of this youthful soldier was very commendable." Sepoy Mewa Singh was awarded the Ashoka Chakra for his gallantry.

Ashoka Chakra (cont.)

NAIK LAL SINGH
THE SIKH REGIMENT

In May 1957, whilst a battalion of The Sikh Regiment was employed in restoring law and order in Naga Hills, Naik Lal Singh was in command of Patrol party, which was patrolling the Merema area. The hostiles ambushed the Patrol party at a strategic place where there were two adjacent knolls in the front and another at the back, which could effectively block the withdrawal of the party. The hostiles opened fire with automatic rifles, covering the return route of the Patrol. Without getting unnerved and with complete disregard to his own safety, Naik Lal Singh led his men in the hazardous task of attacking and occupying one of the front knolls, which allowed them a better tactical position to attack the rest of the hostiles. Realizing the danger the hostiles took to the bush and disappeared." Naik Lal Singh exhibited courageous leadership and gallantry of a high order in this action for which he was awarded the Ashoka Chakra.

LANCE NAIK GIAN SINGH
JAMMU AND KASKHMIR MILITIA

"The Indo-Pakistani War of 1947, was fought over the region of Kashmir from 1947 to 1948. On 25TH November 1948, Lance Naik Gian Singh was in the foremost section of a column, which, having already captured a nearby ridge was advancing on a hill feature at Poonch in Kashmir. The enemy had retreated to a new position and was firing heavily from it with automatic weapons. Advance towards the enemy position lay over a narrow ridge with a deep fall on either side and there was enemy light machine-gun which covered the route. For the column to move forward it was imperative that this gun should be put out of action. Lance Naik Gian Singh who was the Bren gunner of the forward section, with complete disregard for his personal safety, jumped forward and took a position right in front of the enemy gun, despite the shower of bullets; and with lightning speed opened fire thus silencing the enemy. This spontaneous act of great courage enabled the column to pierce the enemy's defences." Lance Naik Gian Singh displayed gallantry of a high order in this action for which he was awarded the Ashoka Chakra.

MAHAVIR CHAKRA

The Mahavir Chakra is the second highest military decoration in India and is awarded for acts of conspicuous gallantry in the presence of the enemy.

JEMADAR NAND SINGH, VICORIA CROSS
THE SIKH REGIMENT

"During the Indo-Pakistani War of 1947, some 4,000-6,000 raiders had entered the Uri sector of Jammu and Kashmir. On December 12TH, the 1ST Battalion, The Sikh Regiment marched out from Uri to remove this threat. They quickly overcame the opposition on the way and reached the main enemy position where they encountered a strong enemy force, and a fierce hand-to-hand fight ensued. In this encounter, "B" and "D" Companies suffered heavy casualties and were ordered to withdraw. The enemy did not allow the Sikhs a smooth withdrawal. From well dug positions, they wounded 15 Sikh soldiers who lay within ten metres of the enemy position. The Sikh counter-attack on the enemy bunkers resulted in more causalities. "D" Company was then ordered to attack the enemy from the left flank. At this juncture, Jemadar Nand Singh was commanding a forward platoon of "D" Company. He led his platoon into the attack like a band of Trojans. The enemy's intense fire, however, brought down many Sikhs. Nand Singh pressed on despite an injured leg. His men, shouting cries of 'Jo Bole So Nihaal, Sat Sri Akal', closed in on the enemy. In the hand-to-hand fighting that followed, Jemadar Nand Singh was the first to draw his bayonet and killed five enemy soldiers. His men now were inspired to frenzy and, acting like fiends, bayoneted the enemy right and left. The enemy broke and tried to flee, but not many escaped. Jemadar Nand Singh had done his duty and captured the objective, but as he stood on top of the bunker, a burst of light machine-gun fire hit him in the chest, killing him on the spot."

In the words of the Battalion Commander, "The valour, leadership and selfless devotion to duty displayed by this son of India in this little action was something that cannot be described, much less matched."

This extraordinary performance won him Mahavir Chakra, posthumously. Jemadar Nand Singh is the only Indian soldier to have the combination of Mahavir Chakra and the Victoria Cross gallantry awards.

Mahavir Chakra (cont.)

SEPOY AMAR SINGH
1ST PATIALA INFANTRY

"During the Indo-Pakistani War of 1947-1948, Sepoy Amar Singh was manning a light machine-gun at Zoji La Pass in Srinagar, when the enemy opened fire with machine-guns and began advancing down the ridge towards the piquet. The surprise attack knocked out a third of the soldiers manning the post. Amar Singh was wounded in the head but with a sheer effort of will hung on to consciousness and continued firing. Time and again that morning, the enemy made determined attempts to overrun the post but the Sepoys deadly fire drove them away and held them at bay. Hours later when reinforcements arrived, the snow covered ground on which the Sepoy was lying was drenched with his blood but he insisted on remaining at his post. He was finally evacuated during the night." Sepoy Amar Singh was awarded the Mahavir Chakra for exceptional gallantry.

MAJOR MALKAIT SINGH BRAR (POSTHUMOUS)
PARACHUTE REGIMENT

"During the Indo-Pakistani War of 1947-1948, a forward post manned by Indian soldiers in Kashmir came under heavy fire and suffered heavy casualties. Eventually only two men were left to hold the position. As they braced themselves for the enemy's final charge, Major Malkait Singh Brar of the 1ST (Para) Kumaon Regiment came running to their aid. He did not stop when he reached the post but carried on, firing at the enemy with his Bren gun. The enemy, caught by surprise, was forced to shelter behind rocks. Then the major, though wounded, supervised the evacuation of the wounded soldiers from the forward post. He had just finished doing this when a mortar bomb exploded close to him dealing him a mortal blow." Major Brar was posthumously awarded the Mahavir Chakra for exceptional gallantry.

MAJOR GURDIAL SINGH
RAJPUT REGIMENT

"During the Indo-Chinese conflict of 1962, a battalion of the Rajput Regiment was entrusted with the task of defending the Namkhachu River area. The Chinese attacked on the 20TH October with heavy artillery and mortar fire. Quickly overrunning the outer defences, they began to close in on the Battalion Headquarters from all sides. Seeing them come, the second-in-command, Major Gurdial Singh realized that only a swift and bold manoeuvre could avert a total rout. Rallying the survivors, he led a charge on the advancing enemy, taking them by surprise. Many Chinese were killed and the rest fell back, giving some of the Indian soldiers, who had been trapped in vulnerable positions, time to withdraw to safer ground." Major Gurdial Singh was awarded the Mahavir Chakra for conspicuous gallantry.

Mahavir Chakra (cont.)

LIEUTENANT COLONEL MADAN MOHAN SINGH BAKSHI
ARMOURED CORPS

"During the Indo-Pakistani War of 1965, Lieutenant Colonel Bakshi, Commanding the 4TH Horse Squadron, noticed a squadron of enemy Patton tanks on the Libbe-Phillora road in the Sialkot sector of Punjab. Immediately he attacked and knocked out two tanks. Then he charged through the enemy tanks though his tank was hit twice. He knocked out a third tank and continued to charge ahead and crossed the Libbe-Phillora road. His tank caught fire when it was hit for the fourth time. As his crew bailed out they came under heavy enemy machine-gun fire. Colonel Bakshi led his men to take shelter in a sugarcane field. At their rescue he resumed command of his regiment and inflicted heavy losses on the enemy tanks, as some fled in panic." Lt. Col, Bakshi was awarded the Mahavir Chakra for his leadership, initiative and courage.

LIEUTENANT COLONEL RANJIT SINGH
THE PUNJAB REGIMENT

"During 1965 Indo-Pakistani War, to stop Pakistani infiltrators entering Kashmir, the Haji Pir pass had to be captured. The 19TH Punjab Regiment had to first capture Bedori, located en-route to the Pass. There were two enemy companies and four machine-guns guarding Bedori. Despite this Lieutenant Colonel Ranjit Singh and his men attacked the superior Pakistani force and forced it to withdraw. After establishing a link with Haji Pir Pass it became imperative to secure the Kahuta Bridge. The Indians already held a forward position on the bridge, but the road to it was infested with Pakistani soldiers. Lieutenant Colonel Singh's mission was to secure the bridge and ensure a link-up between the base and the Indian forward camp. On the evening of 9TH September, Lieutenant Colonel Singh and his men charged the Pakistanis, who fled away in panic". For his gallant actions Ranjit Singh was awarded the Mahavir Chakra.

SUBEDAR AJIT SINGH (POSTHUMOUS)
THE SIKH REGIMENT

"During the 1965 Indo-Pakistani War, the 4TH Battalion, The Sikh Regiment was assigned the task of capturing the village of Barkhi in Pakistan. As Subedar Ajit Singh and his section launched their assault on Barkhi, a well-positioned Pakistani machine-gun held up their advance. Subedar Ajit Singh was given the responsibility for destroying the gun. As he charged at the enemy position, a burst of machine-gun fire wounded him in the chest. He carried on defiantly and went near enough to throw a grenade that effectively silenced the gun. His gallantry inspired his comrades and they routed the enemy but the Subedar succumbed to his injuries." He was posthumously honoured with the Mahavir Chakra.

Mahavir Chakra (cont.)

MAJOR GENERAL MOHINDER SINGH
INFANTRY DIVISION

"During the 1965 Indo-Pakistani War, the 115TH Infantry Division was deployed in the Lahore area of the Punjab. Major General Mohinder Singh assumed command of the division on the 15TH of September. Commissioned in the army in 1940, the Major General was already a decorated soldier. He had been awarded the Military Cross for bravery during the Second World War. As head of the Infantry division, one of the first responsibilities he was entrusted with was the capture of Ichhogil Canal. Major General Singh planned the operation well. As the assault commenced, disregarding the risk to his own life, he moved from one formation to the other, exhorting and inspiring his men to their best. The bridge was successfully captured. For his able leadership and sound operational planning, he was decorated with the Mahavir Chakra."

BRIGADIER KHEM KARAN SINGH
ARMOURED BRIGADE

"During the 1965 Indo-Pakistani War, Brigadier Khem Karan Singh, Commander of 1ST Armoured Brigade at Sialkot in the Punjab, was assigned the task of destroying the enemy armoured division. The enemy tank force was larger and technically superior. Brigadier Singh moved his forces at night, covering a vast area, and surprised the enemy by launching a well-planned attack from the rear the next morning. The sudden attack caught the enemy off guard and unnerved him. In the first three days of the battle, 75 enemy tanks were destroyed and the enemy command thoroughly demoralized. The Indian losses were minimal. At the end of the battle, the Indians had gained control of Phillora, a vital communications point in Sialkot. For his unflagging sense of duty and leadership, Brigadier Singh was duly awarded the Mahavir Chakra."

LIEUTENANT COLONEL GURBANS SINGH SANGHA
THE MAHAR REGIMENT

"During the 1965 Indo-Pakistani War, the 3RD Battalion, The Mahar Regiment, commanded by Lieutenant Colonel Gurbans Singh Sangha, was deployed in Jammu and Kashmir. When the Information that Pakistani infiltrators were sneaking into the State reached the unit, it commenced search operations in the Dewa and Chhamb-Jaurian sectors. During these operations the Pakistanis attacked them in great force. Colonel Sangha and his men fought back spiritedly and not only drove the enemy back, but also managed to recapture some Indian posts lost earlier. Stung by the defeat, the Pakistanis launched a massive attack backed by artillery on 1ST September. The Indians had neither artillery nor air support, but Colonel Sangha marshalled his resources and fought back so well that the enemy could make no headway and eventually had to give up the attack." Colonel Sangha was awarded the Mahavir Chakra for his astute leadership.

Mahavir Chakra (cont.)

MAJOR BALJIT SINGH RANDHAWA (POSTHUMOUS)
THE RAJPUT REGIMENT

"During the 1965 Indo-Pakistani War, Major Baljit Singh Randhawa commanding 4TH Battalion, The Rajput Regiment was assigned the task of recapturing positions lost to Pakistani infiltrators at Kargil and securing other posts in the area to prevent future encroachments. Kargil was strategic for it overlooked Indian positions. The Pakistani posts were strongly defended with machine-guns and mortars. The terrain was extremely steep with precipitous slopes. The two-pronged attack began with temperatures below freezing point while a cold, gusty wind raged. As Major Singh led his company up the slope, they were subjected to mortar and machine-gun fire. Realizing that his troops were an easy target for the enemy, Major Singh ordered them to take cover, and then moving cautiously up with a few men, wrested one post from the enemy. An enemy machine-gun deterred further advance. Relentlessly Major Singh continued the attack, but was hit by a burst of rifle fire and fell down mortally wounded. He exhorted his men to continue the advance, steadfastly resisting all the attempts to assist him. Major Singh did not live long but the mission he led was a complete success." He was posthumously awarded the Mahavir Chakra.

MAJOR KULDIP SINGH CHANDPURI
THE PUNJAB REGIMENT

"Major Kuldip Singh Chandpuri who, with his small band of men of The Punjab Regiment, held fast to the Indian base at Longewal, despite several Pakistani attacks to dislodge them. The Battle of Longewala was one of the first major engagements during the Indo-Pakistani War of 1971, fought between assaulting Pakistani forces and Indian defenders at the Indian border post of Longewala, in the Thar Desert of the Rajasthan state in India. The Battle goes down in the annals of military history as a classic case of human resolve and motivation in the face of extremely heavy odds. In this battle a handful of troops, numbering approximately 100 of The Punjab Regiment, not only faced a brigade attack supported by a regiment and a squadron of tanks but successfully stalled the same after incurring heavy losses on the enemy at the cost of negligible casualty to the defenders. In addition, as a result of the subsequent combined Army-Air Force effort, the enemy suffered more casualties thereby turning the tides against the superior force of the attackers During the battle, Major Chandpuri's men had completely destroyed 12 enemy tanks and the Indian Air Force accounted for 25 tanks and a railway train. The Pakistani retreating force was seen moving with only eight functional tanks out of a totally 59 tanks All through the operations the Major kept up his men's morale, moving from bunker to bunker, urging them to hold on and fight back." His dynamic leadership and gallantry won Major Kuldip Singh the Mahavir Chakra.

Mahavir Chakra (cont.)

SUBEDAR GURDIAL SINGH
THE SIKH REGIMENT

"In the 1971 Indo-Pak War the East Pakistan towns of Khulna, Chaugacha, Durinda, Makapur and Siramani were the scenes of battle victories by the Sikhs. In the western sector, in the battle of Chhamb, 27 men of 5TH Battalion laid down their lives as they withstood three well-coordinated enemy attacks with tanks and earned the regiment a crucial time of 30 hours." Subedar Gurdial Singh was awarded the Mahavir Chakra for his astute leadership and gallantry at the battle of Chhamb.

SUBEDAR MALKIAT SINGH (POSTHUMOUS)
THE PUNJAB REGIMENT

"The 14TH Battalion, The Punjab Regiment, was deployed near Garibpur on the eastern front during the 1971 Indo-Pak War. As Pakistani activities increased across the border, the Regiment was asked to capture Garibpur in the early hours of 21ST November. The pitched battle for Garibpur lasted till the next day as the regiment took all Pakistani positions. In the Pakistani counter attack Subedar Malkiat Singh defended a position that was under constant and fierce enemy infantry and armoured attacks. Undaunted, he crawled forward and took on the advancing enemy soldiers, killing two machine-gunners. He was hit twice by rifle fire, but carried on the enemy until a tank shell struck him, killing him instantly." For his courageous act of gallantry, Subedar Singh was posthumously awarded the Mahavir Chakra.

MAJOR JASBIR SINGH
THE SIKH REGIMENT

"The Sikh Regiment was deployed in Chhamb sector on the western front during the 1971 Indo-Pakistani War. Major Jasbir Singh's Company of the The Sikh Regiment was in possession of the crucial Phagia Ridge position. The enemy began the first of its offensives to dislodge the Indian forces there. The first attack was successfully repulsed, but the Pakistani troops returned with a stronger force the next day. They broke through the Indian defence and soon bitter hand-to-hand fighting ensued in which the Pakistanis were hurled back for the second time with a loss of twelve lives. The fighting was at its fiercest on December 5TH. The Sikh Company suffered heavy casualties, but led by a determined Major Jasbir Singh, they not only repulsed the advance but also recaptured a post on the Ridge lost earlier". Major Jasbir Singh was awarded the Mahavir Chakra for his exemplary leadership.

Mahavir Chakra (cont.)

LIEUTENANT COLONEL INDERBAL SINGH BAWA (POSTHUMOUS)
5TH GORKHA RIFLES

"Lieutenant Colonel Inderbal Singh Bawa commanded 4TH Battalion, 5TH Gorkha Rifles during operations in Sri Lanka in 1988. The battalion was entrusted with the task of clearing the enemy in the axis of Vasavilan, Urgmpurai and Jaffna Fort. These were well-defended militant strongholds. Lieutenant Colonel Bawa inflicted heavy casualties on the enemy along the way to capture these strongholds. In early October by marching through heavily fortified enemy territory Lieutenant Colonel Bawa successfully extricated stranded Indian soldiers from the militant's strongholds. Towards the end of the operations, a suicide squad sprayed him with bullets, killing him instantly." Lieutenant Colonel Inderbal Singh Bawa was posthumously honoured with Mahavir Chakra for his supreme sacrifice.

MAJOR AMARJIT SINGH BAL
ARMOURED CORPS

"During the 1971 Indo-Pakistani War, Major Bal was in command of a squadron at Jarpal, overlooking the Basant River. It was a position most vulnerable to enemy attack. Sure enough, the Pakistani forces began shelling the area heavily. The Indian troops foiled these attempts repeatedly, killing several enemy troops. The Pakistanis persisted and launched several counter-attacks over the next two days. The Indians were heavily outnumbered, but Major Bal was able to inspire his men to repel several enemy attacks. As many as 27 Pakistani M-48 tanks were destroyed". For his inspirational leadership and able manoeuvring of his troops in battle, Major Bal was awarded the Mahavir Chakra.

MAJOR DALJIT SINGH NARANG (POSTHUMOUS)
ARMOURED CORPS

"Even before the 1971 Indo-Pakistani War had officially begun in December 1971, there were innumerable skirmishes in the Eastern sector between Indian and Pakistani forces. At this time, Major Daljit Singh Narang commanded the 'C' Squadron of the Deccan Horse in Jessore. To prevent enemy encroachments, the Squadron set up effective roadblocks around Garibpur on the 20TH of November. The very next day, two Infantry Battalions attacked the Squadron's position. The battles raged long and furious, for both sides were evenly matched. Major Narang stood in the turret of his tank, directing the operations. Bolstered by his presence, his men fought back gallantly, inflicting severe casualities on the enemy. During the fighting Indian forces destroyed ten Pakistani tanks, losing three of their own. However, Major Narang was targeted by the enemy and struck down fatally by a barrage of machine-gun fire. His indomitable courage had, however, ensured a hard-fought victory for the Indian Squadron." The Nation duly honoured this gallant soldier, who was posthumously awarded the Mahavir Chakra.

Mahavir Chakra (cont.)

SECOND LIEUTENANT SHAMSHER SINGH SAMRA (POSTHUMOUS)
THE GUARDS

"During the 1971 Indo-Pakistani War, Second Lieutenant Samsher Singh Samra and the 8TH Battalion, The Guards were deployed to capture Hilly Complex in the east. The mountainous complex was well defended by the Pakistanis, who had constructed concrete shelters by burrowing through the hills. A company of the The Guards was ordered to advance and capture Uthali, a strongly defended Pakistani position. Halfway towards its objective, the company came under heavy fire from a machine-gun and could not proceed. The Guards in this region fought several pitched battles. It was by his heroism in one such battle that Second Lieutenant Samra covered himself with glory. Accurate enemy firing had stalled the advance of the Guards. Second Lieutenant Samra intervened at this juncture and exhorted his men to advance along the left flank. As Lieutenant Samra moved to within 25 metres of the enemy position, under heavy machine-gun fire a bullet stuck him. Ignoring the pain, he charged at the machine-gun bunker and destroyed it by hurling an accurately aimed grenade. He then charged towards another bunker, but he was hit a second time, this time fatally. He fell to the ground, the grenade still in his hand". For his awe-inspiring bravery, Second Lieutenant Samra was decorated with the Mahavir Chakra.

SUBEDAR MOHINDER SINGH
THE PUNJAB REGIMENT

"During the 1971 Indo-Pakistani War, the 21ST Battalion, The Punjab Regiment, including Subedar Mohinder Singh, were deployed at the Kargil sector in the north overlooks the critically vital Srinagar-Leh highway. The deployment was to prevent Pakistani encroachments in the area. Close by lay the heavily fortified enemy position at Hathi Matha, from where, it was believed, that further Pakistani offensives would commence. To prevent this, the 21ST Battalion was asked to capture Brachil pass, as it was an important vantage point. The attack commenced early on 7TH December, and in a short while they had reached the left shoulder of the pass where they were held up by heavy enemy fire. Subedar Mohinder Singh, commanding a platoon, charged forward and engaged the enemy in close combat. His men, inspired by his daring, fought ferociously and forced the Pakistanis to retreat. This victory was a morale-booster and led to many other successes in this area." For his gallantry and leadership Subedar Mohinder Singh was awarded the Mahavir Chakra.

Mahavir Chakra (cont.)

LIEUTENANT COLONEL K. S. PANNU
THE PARACHUTE REGIMENT

"During the 1971 Indo-Pakistani War, Lieutenant Colonel K. S. Pannu was commanding 2ND Para (Maratha) Regiment. Lieutenant Colonel Pannu is most famous for having led the 2nd Para in the famous Tangail Airdrop to capture the Poongli Bridge over the River Jamuna on 11 December 1971, during the Bangladesh Liberation war. The battalion was airdropped near Tangail (now in Bangladesh) and tasked to cut off the 93 Brigade of Pakistani Army which was retreating from the north to defend Dacca and its approaches. For his conspicuous gallantry and leadership, Lt Col Pannu was awarded the Mahavir Chakra."

WING COMMANDER HARCHARAN SINGH MANGAT
INDIAN AIR FORCE

"During the 1971 Indo-Pakistani War, Wing Commander Harcharan Singh Mangat, who commanded a fighter-bomber squadron on an airfield at the western front, swiftly retaliated against Pakistani raids into Indian Territory. On the 4TH December, his squadron took off to attack enemy targets. The Wing Commander led a formation of four aircraft, and his aircraft was hit three times, but continued on his way unperturbed, 200 kilometres deep into enemy territory. As another aircraft suffered a direct hit and was badly damaged, Wing commander Mangat immediately ordered a pull out and with some adroit manoeuvring led it back to base, despite the damage sustained by the aircraft. Wing Commander Mangat continued with his missions into Pakistan inflicting immense damage to their forces." Wing Commander Harcharan Singh was awarded the Mahavir Chakra for his gallant actions against the enemy.

LIEUTENANT COLONEL NARINDER SINGH SANDHU
THE DOGRA REGIMENT

"During the 1971 Indo-Pakistani War, the Pakistani Army held the vitally strategic bridge over the River Ravi at Dhera Baba in Punjab. Lieutenant Colonel Narinder Singh Sandhu was asked to lead the 10TH Battalion, The Dogra Regiment to secure the eastern end of the bridge. In readiness, however, Pakistanis had already set in place several fortified shelters and machine-gun positions. As Lieutenant Colonel Sandhu began his attack his tanks immediately got stuck in the marshes bordering the river. His men then dismounted and began the five-kilometre march to the bridge. When they were 15 metres away from the bridge, they sprang out at the enemy with the cry "Durga Mata Ki Jay". Lieutenant Colonel Sandhu remained in the forefront all through this fierce engagement, despite being wounded in the leg. His mere presence inspired his men and they emerged victorious." Lieutenant Colonel Sandhu was decorated with the Mahavir Chakra for his gallantry and skilful leadership.

Mahavir Chakra (cont.)

LIEUTENANT COLONEL SUKHJIT SINGH
ARMOURED CORPS

"During the 1971 Indo-Pakistani War, The Scinde Horse Regiment, commanded by Lieutenant Colonel Sukhjit Singh, crossed into enemy territory and established itself near Nainakot. On 10TH December, Pakistani forces made a powerful armoured attack to dislodge the Indians from this position. Lieutenant Colonel Sukhjit put up a determined resistance. Leading from the front, he directed his tanks with great skill and courage. The enemy, having lost one of its tanks, retreated. The next day he led an operation to capture enemy tanks at Malakpur. During this move his forces came under heavy artillery and mortar fire, but an unruffled Lieutenant Colonel surged ahead. In the ensuing operation, eight tanks and some Pakistani officers were captured. Not only did the Lieutenant Colonel win a Mahavir Chakra for his inspirational leadership, his regiment earned several battle honours for its exceptional courage."

SECOND LIEUTENANT RANJEEV SINGH SANDHU (POSTHUMOUS)
THE ASSAM REGIMENT

"During the operations in Sri Lanka in 1988, as Second Lieutenant Sandhu was leading a convoy back from Mangani, militants launched a sudden attack on the convoy and Sandhu was grievously wounded. Though bleeding heavily he crawled out, carbine in hand to prevent the militants from capturing jeep's weapons and ammunition. As a militant approached the jeep, Lieutenant Sandhu sprayed him with bullets, instantly killing Kumaran, a prominent militant leader. Sandhu continued firing till his very last breath, thwarting all militant attempts to approach the jeep." For his supreme sacrifice, Second Lieutenant Sandhu was posthumously awarded the Mahavir Chakra.

BRIGADIER SANT SINGH, MVC and BAR
THE PUNJAB REGIMENT

"Brigadier Sant Singh was a much-distinguished soldier decorated with the Mahavir Chakra during the 1965 Indo-Pak War. Commanding the Punjab Regiment in the eastern sector during the 1971 war with Pakistan, Brigadier Singh was entrusted with the task of capturing Mymensingh, a well-defended enemy stronghold. Pakistanis were aware of an impeding Indian attack, and had deployed a strong force to hold back any Indian advance. The experienced Brigadier, however, foiled their plans by his tactics and resourcefulness and easily captured Mymensingh. He then marched ahead another 60 kilometers to capture Madhopur, a vital town on the road to Dhaka. His gallantry encouraged the Indians to advance rapidly, despite strong Pakistani resistance. For his inspiring leadership, the Brigadier was awarded the Bar to his Mahavir Chakra."

Mahavir Chakra (cont.)

BRIGADIER MANJIT SINGH
INFANTRY BRIGADE

"In October 1987, Brigadier Manjit Singh assumed command of the 41ST Infantry Brigade, deployed in Sri Lanka as part of India's peacekeeping forces. One of the Brigade's first tasks was to clear the Jaffna terrorist stronghold, and to establish a link with the Maratha Light Infantry in Jaffna port. All the approach roads were heavily mined and the Brigadier, on arriving at Palali Airfield, found several Indian troops facing stiff resistance at Anna Collai and Manipal. Brigadier Manjit Singh by deploying just two companies of the Rajasthan Rifles was able to break the militant cordon and secure a link with forces at Jaffna fort" Brigadier Singh was honoured with Mahavir Chakra for his leadership.

BRIGADIER HARBHAJAN SINGH (POSTHUMOUS)
THE RAJPUT REGIMENT

"Despite the unilateral cease-fire declared by the Chinese after the 1962 war, tensions still remained high all along the Sikkim-Tibet border. In September 1967 the 70TH Field Company Engineers were deployed to lay a wire fence along the disputed border area of Nathu La to end the frequent skirmishes between Indian and Chinese forces. The 18TH Battalion, The Rajput Regiment, led by Brigadier Harbhajan Singh, took up positions to provide protection to the Engineers. No sooner had the work commenced than the Chinese opened fire on the Indians from the front and from the flanks. Harbhajan Singh led the charge at the attackers. He bayoneted three Chinese soldiers and then turned his attention to an enemy light machine-gun. Even as he hurled a grenade at the gunner, bullets ripped through his body, killing him instantly." Major Harbhajan Singh was posthumously awarded the Mahavir Chakra

AIR COMMODORE MEHAR SINGH
INDIAN AIR FORCE

"Air Commodore Mehar Singh was the Air Officer Commanding No.1 Group of the Indian Air Force during 1947-48 Jammu and Kashmir operations. He carried out a bombing-cum supply mission in a Dakota with great effectiveness. The innovation enabled the Indian Air Force to send supplies to the Poonch in its armed Dakotas. In May 1948, a besieged Leh was desperately in need of reinforcements. By flying a Dakota to the Leh airstrip, the Air Commodore accomplished a mission till then considered impossible. Inspired by Mehar Singh's extraordinary flight, the Indian Air Force began regular supplies to Leh, saving it from capitulation. Air Commodore Mehar Singh was awarded the Mahavir Chakra for his daring operations." Tragically he died in a flying accident.

Mahavir Chakra (cont.)

MAJOR BHUPINDER SINGH (POSTHUMOUS)
ARMOURED CORPS

"During the 1965 Indo-Pakistani War. Major Bhupinder Singh commanded the 'B' squadron of the 4TH Horse. On the 11TH September he successfully led his squadron in cutting off the enemy retreat along the Gadgor-Phillora road. In the battle of Sadoke that followed, Major Singh took over the command of the Regiment after the Commander was forced to abandon his tank. Inspired by this gallantry, the Regiment fought valiantly and destroyed several enemy tanks. Nine days later the Major led his men in the battle of Sodreke. His tank, targeted by the enemy, caught fire after it was struck several times. The Major continued fighting even when all but two of his tanks were disabled. However, he sustained severe burns when he was finally compelled to abandon his burning vehicle, and died soon after." He was posthumously honoured with the Mahavir Chakra for his awe-inspiring courage and gallantry.

LIEUTENANT COLONEL INDERJIT SINGH BUTALIA (POSTHUMOUS)
THE DOGRA REGIMENT

"During the operations in Jammu and Kashmir in 1947-1948, Indian forces captured Naushera and then advance on Jhangar was the next objective. However, the ring of enemy positions around Naushera made a breakthrough impossible. Early on 22ND February Lieutenant Colonel Inderjit Singh Butalia with The Dogra Regiment embarked on a reconnaissance mission in the surrounding areas. On their return, however, they fought a sharp action against the Pakistanis in which Colonel Butalia was mortally wounded. Despite his grave injuries he refused evacuation, insisting that the enemy attack should repulsed, which the Dogras did successfully." For his supreme sacrifice Colonel Butalia was posthumously honoured with the Mahavir Chakra."

HAVILDAR SARUP SINGH (POSTHUMOUS)
THE JAMMU AND KASHMIR MILITIA

"During the 1962 Indo-China War, the 14TH Battalion, The Jammu and Kashmir Militia were deployed in the Ladakh sector. Havildar Sarup Singh was the second-in-command at the post at Bhujang. The Chinese, armed with automatic weapons and mortars, mounted a massive attack on the post on the night of 19TH October. The few Indian defenders of this post were ill equipped to resist this furious Chinese onslaught. The Chinese came in waves and seemed unstoppable, but, inspired by the Havildar, the Indians fought gallantly, inflicting heavy casualties on the enemy. The Havildar was finally overpowered and killed." For his act of courage and supreme gallantry Havildar Sarup Singh was posthumously honoured with the Mahavir Chakra.

Mahavir Chakra (cont.)

CAPTAIN GURJINDER SINGH SURI (POSTHUMOUS)
ARMY ORDNANCE CORPS

"Captain Gurjinder Singh Suri commanded a military Post at Faulad situated at a height of 11,200 ft in the Gulmarg sector of Jammu and Kashmir. On November 9TH 1999, the enemy launched an attack on the post, which was successfully repulsed. Captain Gurjinder Singh Suri immediately deployed his support group to take care of any reinforcement interference, and set out to clear the enemy bunkers, one by one. During the operations when Captain Suri saw a fire from a bunker seriously injured a comrade, he quickly moved on to clear the bunker. He killed two enemy soldiers with his AK rifle and silenced the machine-gun. However, he got a burst in his left arm in the process. Unmindful of his injury, he continued to lead his men. He then lobbed two hand-grenades into another bunker and entered inside spraying bullets, and killed one enemy soldier. At this point, he was hit by a rocket-propelled grenade and was critically wounded. He refused to be evacuated and continued to exhort his men till he breathed his last. Captain Suri displayed extraordinary leadership, inspired by which the Ghataks (platoon) fell upon the enemy with vengeance and annihilated them. Captain Gurjinder Singh Suri thus displayed conspicuous bravery and leadership of the highest order in the face of the enemy, and made the supreme sacrifice in the highest traditions of the Indian Army." Captain Gurjinder Singh Suri was posthumously honoured with the Mahavir Chakra.

LIEUTENANT COLONEL HARBANS SINGH VIRK
THE PARACHUTE REGIMENT

"During 1948 Indo-Pakistani conflict, Lieutenant Colonel Harbans Singh Virk led the 3RD (Para) Maratha Light Infantry with great success against the Pakistani forces at Naushahra. His tactical skills not only led to several successful attacks on the enemy but also saved the Indian garrison at Naushera during the famous battle of 'Kala Gosh Galla'. His most notable achievement however was the recapture of Jhangar. During the advance on Jhangar the Maratha Battalion was held up at Phir Thil Naka and suffered heavy casualties. But Lieutenant Colonel Harbans Singh surprised the enemy by launching a counter-attack at dawn The Indians advanced steadily despite the heavy mortar and small arms fire. The onslaught continued into the next day and by afternoon Jhangar had been secured. From Jhangar, the Marathas advanced yet again and captured the hill feature overlooking the valley." Lieutenant Colonel Harbans Singh Virk was honoured with the Mahavir Chakra in recognition of his outstanding leadership.

Mahavir Chakra (cont.)

MAJOR GENERAL RAJINDAR SINGH, MVC & BAR
ARMOURED CORPS

Major General Rajindar Singh was the first soldier to receive the Mahavir Chakra non–posthumously and also Bar to the Mahavir Chakra.

"In 1948, Lieutenant Colonel. Rajindar Singh was in command of the 7TH Light Cavalry in Jammu and Kashmir. His bold and imaginative employment of tanks materially changed the course of events in that theatre, earning him the Mahavir Chakra. During the 1965 Indo-Pakistani War, Major General Rajindar Singh led his formation into battle against numerically superior and better-equipped armoured forces in the Sialkot Sector. Inspired by his tactical ability and leadership, his troops inflicted heavy tank casualties on the enemy armoured forces. By his presence in the thick of the battle, in utter disregard for his personal safety, Major General Rajindar Singh inspired the tank crews to engage the enemy forces closely. He commanded the highly complex armoured formation in an outstanding manner, and established such moral ascendancy over the enemy that in the latter stages of the campaign the enemy tanks avoided battle and had to be sought out to be destroyed." Throughout these operations, Maj. Gen. Rajindar Singh displayed conspicuous bravery and leadership of a very high order in the best traditions of the Indian Army for which he was awarded the Bar to his Mahavir Chakra.

NAIK SHANGARA SINGH (POSTHUMOUS)
THE SIKH REGIMENT

"During the 1971 Indo-Pakistani War, The Sikh Regiment attacked Pun Kanjiri a strong enemy held position in the Punjab. During the attack on Pun Kanjiri, enemy fire had pinned down the platoon in which Lance Naik Shangara Singh was second in command. In utter disregard for personal safety, Lance Naik Shangara Singh made a dash through the minefield towards the first machine gun post and hurled a grenade inside the bunker successfully silencing the gun. Then he charged the second machine gun post, leapt over the loophole and succeeded in physically snatching the gun. In doing so, he received a burst of fire in his abdomen, but undeterred he continued to hold the machine gun. The enemy was completely unnerved and fled from the bunker leaving the machine gun in Lance Naik Shangara Singh's hands. In this heroic action, Lance Naik Shangara Singh displayed conspicuous gallantry and exemplary dedication to duty in the face of the enemy and made the supreme sacrifice in the highest traditions of the Army." Naik Shangara Singh was posthumously honoured with the Mahavir Chakra.

Mahavir Chakra (cont.)

SEPOY HARI SINGH
1ST PATIALA INFANTRY

"During 1947-1948 Indo-Pakistani conflict, Sepoy Hari Singh was a rifleman in the leading company of 1st Patiala Infantry during its advance on Jhangar in Jammu and Kashmir. During the advance his section came under heavy fire during the assault and was pinned down by fire from a bunker. Sepoy Hari Singh attacked the bunker with a grenade and killed the defenders inside with a Sten gun. He then came under fire from another bunker and got wounded in the knee. Still not deterred, he threw another grenade at the second bunker, killing one of the enemy soldiers, while the second one fled for his life. When the rest of his company joined him, they engaged an enemy section led by an officer. Sepoy Hari Singh, rushing 20 yards ahead of his section, managed to kill the officer. Sepoy Hari Singh, by his individual actions, was responsible for destroying two enemy bunkers and killing numerous enemies including an officer." Sepoy Hari Singh for his gallantry was awarded the Mahavir Chakra on 17TH March 1948."

BRIGADIER JOGINDER SINGH BAKSHI
MOUNTAIN BRIGADE

"During the 1971 Indo-Pakistani War, Brigadier Joginder Singh Bakshi was commanding a Mountain Brigade during the operations against Pakistan on the eastern front. The Brigade, under his leadership, launched a series of successful attacks and captured a number of well-prepared enemy localities, culminating in the capture of Bogra. Brigadier Bakshi displayed professional competence of a high order and by his daring execution outwitted the opposing forces, breaking their resistance and capturing a large number of men and equipment, including the Commander of 205TH Brigade of the Pakistan Army." Throughout the operations Brigadier Bakshi displayed conspicuous gallantry, determination and skill for which he was honoured with Mahavir Chakra.

JEMADAR SAPURAN SINGH
1ST PATIALA INFANTRY

"During 1948 Indo-Pakistani conflict, Jemadar Sapuran Singh was in command of a Platoon piquet at Gumri in Jammu and Kashmir. The enemy attacked this piquet with two companies supported by guns and three-inch mortars. Jemadar Sapuran Singh rushed forward with his men to the outpost, crossing some 800 yards of heavily blitzed area and repulsed and completely defeated the enemy attack. Later the enemy launched his biggest attack, only to be pushed back with heavier losses. With sheer guts and determination, Jemadar Sapuran Singh completely overwhelmed the superior enemy causing him at least 600 casualties. This officer showed the most inspiring leadership and indomitable courage over a long period under most trying conditions, commanding the complete confidence of the men under his command." For his conspicuous gallantry and leadership Jemadar Sapuran Singh was honoured with Mahavir Chakra.

Mahavir Chakra (cont.)

AIR VICE MARSHAL PREM PAL SINGH
INDIAN AIR FORCE

"During the 1965 Indo-Pakistani War, Wing Commander Prem Pal Singh was the Commanding Officer of an operational Bomber Squadron. He undertook six major offensive and tactical close-support operations which included: reconnaissance over the Sargodha Airfield complex; Dab, Akwal and Murid Airfields; marking of Peshawar Airfield; and bombing of Pakistan troop and armour concentrations in various sectors. Disregarding personal safety in these very dangerous operations in the face of heavy enemy anti-aircraft fire, he led a number of bombing and reconnaissance missions with courage, determination and tenacity. Throughout the operations, Wing Commander Singh displayed a high sense of duty, professional skill and gallantry in the best traditions of the Indian Air Force for which he was awarded the Mahavir Chakra"

GROUP CAPTAIN MAN MOHAN BIR SINGH TALWAR
INDIAN AIR FORCE

"During the 1971 Indo-Pakistani War, Wing Commander Talwar, Commanding Officer of a Bomber Squadron, lead five day and night-bombing missions against very heavily defended enemy targets within the first 10 days of operations. He inflicted severe damage to the Pakistani Air Force installations at Sargodha. In a daylight mission in the Chhamb area, in support of the Army, he attacked four heavily defended gun positions near the Munawar Tawi River and effectively silenced three of them, facilitating the advance of troops in difficult terrain. The bold leadership, tenacity of purpose, flying skill and conspicuous gallantry displayed by Wing Commander Talwar were largely responsible for the many successes of his squadron for which he was awarded the Mahavir Chakra."

NAIK CHAND SINGH (POSTHUMOUS)
THE SIKH REGIMENT

"During 1948 Indo-Pakistani conflict, the Pakistanis attacked an Indian piquet across the Jhelum in Punjab. Naik Chand Singh was in command of the Platoon defending the piquet. Three times he came out of his trench to hurl grenades at the enemy, and was wounded in the left forearm. When the enemy brought a three-inch mortar gun into action it became imperative to silence it. Naik Chand Singh and three other volunteers crawled up to a few yards from the mortar position and, after hurling grenades, charged the enemy. One of the crew manning the gun was killed. The others ran away. On returning to his piquet, Naik Chand Singh found the enemy entrenched on his left flank. With great daring he came out of cover to throw grenades at the enemy position but was killed instantly by machine-gun fire. However, the loss of the mortar demoralized the enemy and he withdrew under the cover of darkness". Naik Chand Singh was posthumously awarded the Mahavir Chakra.

Mahavir Chakra (cont.)

JUNIOR COMMISSIONED OFFICER LAL SINGH
1ST PATIALA INFANTRY

"During 1947-1948 Indo-Pakistani conflict, the Indian attempt to recapture Dras and Kargil from Pakistani forces became possible after tanks had cleared the way at Zoji La. JCO Lal Singh led the attack on a strongly defended enemy post on the way to Dras. Despite the incessant fire he crawled towards the enemy post and was hit several times. The firing also damaged his wireless set, cutting off communication with the company headquarters. Though bleeding profusely he held on grimly to his position till reinforced, then putting himself at the head of his troops, he charged the enemy, killed several of them, and recaptured the feature." Junior Commissioned Officer Lal Singh was decorated with the Mahavir Chakra for his conspicuous gallantry.

JEMADAR HARDEV SINGH (POSTHUMOUS)
1ST PATIALA INFANTRY

"During 1947-1948 Indo-Pakistani conflict, a platoon under the command of Jemadar Hardev Singh was sent to investigate the condition of the bridge reported damaged by Pakistani troops. When the Patrol was nearing a hill feature near Machoi, astride the track, it came under heavy fire from the hillside. The Pakistanis were approximately a Company in strength and were firing on the patrol with two medium machine-guns, four light machine-guns and two-inch Mortars. Due to heavy snow all around, the troops could not take secure positions quickly and suffered heavy casualties. Jemadar Hardev Singh collected his men towards the hillside in the west, where he kept the enemy engaged, and got hit twice in the process; he continued his efforts to organize the men until killed by a machine-gun burst". He was posthumously honoured with the Mahavir Chakra for his conspicuous gallantry.

NAIK PRITAM SINGH
1ST PATIALA INFANTRY

"At Gumri in Jammu and Kashmir during 1947-1948 Indo-Pakistani conflict, Naik Pritam Singh was in charge of a Signal Detachment when enemy shelling cut all line communications and made movement impossible. He volunteered to go and repair the lines. Escaping sure death right under the noses of the enemy, he mended the wires and got back under the hail of machine-gun fire. He repeated the ordeal through heavy fire twice in the afternoon. Once he repaired the line to another piquet and next he replaced a broken-down wireless set of yet another piquet. Naik Pritam Singh showed exemplary fortitude, courage and devotion to duty throughout the nerve-shattering and most trying operations. He was fearless and tenacious in his conduct." He was decorated with the Mahavir Chakra for his conspicuous gallantry.

Mahavir Chakra (cont.)

MAJOR GENERAL GURBAKSH SINGH
MOUNTAIN DIVISION

"During the 1965 Indo-Pakistani War, Gurbaksh Singh, General Officer Commanding a Mountain Division was responsible for operations against Pakistan in the Khem Karan Sector. His formation captured its initial objectives on the first day but was forced to fall back to better tactical positions owing to attacks by an overwhelmingly superior enemy armoured force. Three enemy armoured groups, followed by an Infantry Division, later launched an attack. Although the enemy force was numerically superior, the troops under the command of Gurbaksh Singh not only held their position, but also practically eliminated one-and-a-half enemy tank regiments. Early next morning the remnants of this attacking tank force were forced to surrender. By personal example he inspired his troops to face overwhelming odds successfully and inflict heavy losses on a well-equipped enemy force for which he was awarded the Mahavir Chakra."

SEPOY KEWAL SINGH (POSTHUMOUS)
THE SIKH REGIMENT

"Sepoy Kewal Singh was a member of 4TH Battalion, Sikh Regiment deployed in Walong sector during the Indo-China conflict in 1962. The Chinese first attacked on 24TH October, but met with fierce resistance. The second attack followed on 27TH October and posed a severe threat to the Regiment's defences. At the Chinese advance Sepoy Kewal Singh charged at them with his bayonet. Then in the hand-to-hand fighting that followed he killed a few but was fatally wounded. He carried on nevertheless till he expired". For his single-minded courage and daring, Sepoy Kewal Singh was posthumously awarded the Mahavir Chakra.

BRIGADIER HARDEV SINGH KLER
MOUNTAIN BRIGADE

"Brigadier Hardev Singh Kler commanded a Mountain Brigade during the 1971 Indo-Pakistani War. The Brigade had to move along the Kamalpur-Turang River and clear enemy positions at several places on the way, including Kamalpur, Bakshigunj, Jamalpur, Tangail and Turang. The Brigadier led the advance from the front, directing the operations with great skill, disregarding the dangers to his life. It was at the battle of Jamalpur that he proved his mettle. The inspiring presence of the Brigadier helped his troops lay siege behind the enemy positions south of Jamalpur. The enemy was successfully halted; even their subsequent efforts to recapture the position were foiled by the Brigadier's astute strategy. The Pakistanis suffered heavy losses and a heavy cache of arms and ammunition fell into Indian hands." Brigadier Kler was decorated with the Mahavir Chakra for his inspiring leadership and gallantry.

Mahavir Chakra (cont.)

SUBEDAR GURDIAL SINGH
1ST PATIALA INFANTRY

"During 1947-1948 Indo-Pakistani conflict, Subedar Gurdial Singh was the leading platoon commander in a Battalion of 1ST Patiala Infantry. The platoon manned a piquet in Jammu and Kashmir, which was attacked by the Pakistani forces. An enemy mortar knocked out the leading section. Without being downhearted or waiting for any orders Subedar Gurdial Singh rushed towards the enemy with his two sections. He threw a grenade at one bunker from 20 yards while the enemy was still firing ceaselessly, and led a bayonet charge that killed two of the enemy. His courageous action filled the men with invincible spirit and demoralized the whole enemy party. He led yet another bayonet charge firing from his hip and accounted for two enemies in a bunker. On 18TH March, during the advance on Jhangar, while attacking feature Ring Contour, he led his men with such skill that the enemy, though in a very commanding position, was thrown out and ran for their lives leaving behind a lot of equipment. He successfully captured a difficult objective without any loss to his platoon. In both these actions Subedar Gurdial Singh's leadership, personal bravery, an utter fearlessness not only caused great damage to the enemy, but also proved a source of lasting inspiration to all the men in his unit. He worthily earned the respect of all ranks of his company and the award of Mahavir Chakra."

The 15TH Punjab Regiment (1ST Patiala) is the only unit of the Army awarded Eight Mahavir Chakras in a single operation: Battle of Zoji La in 1948.

MAJOR AJIT SINGH
THE JAT REGIMENT

"During the 1962 Indo-China War, with the overwhelming Chinese build-up and the post at Nulla Junction having fallen to them, Major Ajit Singh was asked to fall back to Tsogsalu to organise a more coordinated defence there. He, however, asked that he and his men be given an opportunity to fight and retake the post at Nullah Junction. This was agreed to and his men reoccupied the Nulla Junction. The Hot sprint Post was also thus defended and continued under their control. It was only when he was subsequently ordered to withdraw from these posts in view of the continued heavy enemy build-up opposite Hot spring and reports of enemy infiltration into Marsmikla that Major Ajit Singh withdrew to take up defensive position in the rear. Major Ajit Singh displayed great courage and leadership during these operations for which he was awarded the Mahavir Chakra"

Mahavir Chakra (cont.)

SUBEDAR BISHAN SINGH, OBI, MC. (POSTHUMOUS)
THE SIKH REGIMENT

"During the 1965 Indo-Pakistani War, a battalion of the Sikh Regiment was on patrol at Uri in Kashmir when it bumped into and overwhelming Pakistani force, and fierce hand-to-hand fight took place. Subsequently during the withdrawal, Subedar Bishan Singh was Second in Command of a Company, when a fierce hand-to-hand fight again took place and the company was compelled to withdraw. Subedar Bishan Singh with what was left of his small company organised a counter attack. Although wounded in the right arm, he personally led his company and bayoneted two of the enemy to death. During another wave of the enemy attack Subedar Bishan Singh was wounded for the second time, but with utter contempt for his life he led his men on to the enemy. He killed another couple of the enemy with his bayonet. This so demoralized the enemy that they fled in all directions. Subedar Bishan Singh was then chasing the fleeing enemy, shouting Sikh war cries of "Sat Sri Akal". It was then that this brave officer paid the highest price for his outstanding gallantry. A bullet in the chest killed him. As an act of cool courage, inspiring leadership and dogged determination against heavy odds, this outstanding example would find few to surpass it. This gallant action fought by this brave officer to death enabled the battalion to evacuate all its casualties to safety and gave the enemy a bloody wound to lick." Subedar Bishan Singh was decorated with the Mahavir Chakra for his inspiring leadership and gallantry.

NAIK DARSHAN SINGH (POSTHUMOUS)
THE SIKH LIGHT INFANTRY

"During the 1965 Indo-Pakistani War, Naik Darshan Singh was commanding the leading section of a company of The Sikh Light Infantry, which was ordered to clear a heavily defended bunker in the Mendhar Sector of Jammu and Kashmir. His approach lay over a most difficult and steep terrain, which was extensively mined, and completely dominated by small arms fire. As he led his men in a charge on the enemy, his left leg was blown off by a mine but he continued crawling forward and exhorting his men to carry on with the charge. Whilst cutting wire obstacles, another mine exploded wounding him severely. Unmindful of his wounds, he dragged himself forward to an enemy bunker and threw a grenade into it. Encouraged by his action, the few remaining men of his section charged and destroyed the bunker. By this time, his entire section had become casualties; the men had cleared the way for the success of their company in these operations. Naik Darshan Singh died shouting to the follow - up echelon to come by the route, which had been cleared of mines by the charge of his section. He made the supreme sacrifice of his life for the success of his company." Naik Darshan Singh was posthumously honoured with the Mahavir Chakra for his conspicuous gallantry.

Mahavir Chakra (cont.)

BRIGADIER JOGINDER SINGH GHARAYA
INFANTRY BRIGADE

"During the 1971 Indo-Pakistani War. Brigadier J.S.Gharaya was commanding an infantry brigade in the Eastern Front in the Jessore Sector. His brigade was attacked on four successive occasions and despite heavy casualties, his troops stood their ground largely to his excellent tactical handling, outstanding courage, constant presence and guidance. During the subsequent offensive operations, Brigadier Gharaya was with the leading troops when he was severely wounded. He refused to be evacuated till he had seen the attack through. Throughout this operation, Brigadier Gharaya conducted himself with extraordinary courage and through his personal example inspired such spirit and confidence among troops that lead to the complete success of the difficult operations." For his extraordinary courage and leadership he was awarded the Mahavir Chakra.

LIEUTENANT COLONEL SAMPURAN SINGH, Vr.C.
THE PUNJAB REGIMENT

"During the 1965 Indo-Pakistani War, in the advance to Haji Pir Pass it was essential to capture Bedori as this feature overlooked the entire area. The approaches this important tactical feature was precipitous and extremely difficult. The enemy was holding this massive feature with two companies and was covering the approaches with medium machine-gun and light machine-guns. On 28TH August, the 19TH Battalion, The Punjab Regiment was ordered to capture this important feature with utmost speed. Heavy enemy fire soon pinned down the advance of the leading companies. It appeared that Bedori was invincible. It was at this crucial moment that Lieutenant Colonel Sampuran Singh decided to lead his men to the objective. Without showing any regards for his personal safety Colonel Sampuran Singh led the charge that captured Bedori and forced the enemy to run away. The success was entirely due to his outstanding leadership, courage and devotion to duty." Lieutenant Colonel Sampuran Singh was honoured with the Mahavir Chakra for his courage and outstanding leadership.

MAJOR SARDUL SINGH RANDHAWA
LADAKH SCOUTS

"On 22ND December 1962, Major Sardul Singh Randhawa was in command of a Sub Sector in the area of Karakoram Pass in Northern Ladakh, when nearby posts were overrun by numerically superior Chinese forces. Major Randhawa proved himself to be a fearless and gallant leader as he systematically withdrew his troops and casualties in spite of danger to his own life." Major Randhawa displayed courage and leadership of a highest order for which he was awarded the Mahavir Chakra.

Mahavir Chakra (cont.)

MAJOR SHER PRATAP SINGH SHRIKENT
GORKHA RIFLES

"Major Shrikent was the adjutant of a battalion of Gorkha Rifles in North East Frontier Agency when on 20TH October 1962 the Chinese surrounded the battalion headquarters. Major Shrikent, finding the situation desperate, snatched a Sten gun from an orderly, rallied the few survivors of the Battalion Headquarters, gallantly charged the enemy with complete disregard for his personal safety and inflicted heavy losses on the advancing Chinese forcing them to withdraw. Major Shrikent displayed courage and leadership of a highest order, for which he was awarded the Mahavir Chakra.

MAJOR RANJIT SINGH DYAL
PARACHUTE REGIMENT

"During the 1965 Indo-Pakistani War, Major R.S.Dayal led an assault on Sank in Jammu and Kashmir Sector. The assault was stalled by heavy Pakistani fire. On the following night he again led an assault that captured Sank. He pursued the enemy relentlessly and fighting with great zeal captured Ledwali Gali on 27TH August. Thereafter, marching by night through very difficult terrain, he took the enemy by surprise and captured Haji Pir Pass. In this action, a Pakistani officer and 11 soldiers were taken prisoners. On the following morning, Major Dyal deployed a platoon to capture another feature. Seeing that the Patrol had come under heavy enemy fire, he immediately went to help it with another platoon. In the face of heavy enemy machine gun and mortar fire, he led his two platoons in a lightning attack as a result of which the enemy fled in confusion. Throughout this operation, Major Ranjit Singh Dyal displayed outstanding leadership and courage of a very high order in the best traditions of the Indian Army." For his courage and leadership Major Dyal was awarded the Mahavir Chakra

LIEUTENANT COLONEL RANJIT SINGH DYAL
THE PUNJAB REGIMENT

"During the 1965 Indo-Pakistani War, to stop Pakistani infiltrators entering Kashmir, the Haji Pir pass had to be captured. The 19TH Battalion, The Punjab Regiment had to first capture Bedouri, located en-route to the Pass. There were two enemy companies and four machine-guns guarding Bedori. Despite this Colonel Dyal and his men attacked, and the Pakistani soldiers were forced to withdraw, and a link with Haji Pir Pass was established. It then became imperative to secure the Kahuta Bridge. The Indians already held a forward position on the bridge, but the road to it was infested with Pakistani soldiers. Colonel Dyal Singh's mission was to secure the bridge and ensure a link-up between the base and the Indian forward camp. On the evening of 9TH September, Colonel Dyal Singh and his men charged the Pakistanis and drove them away. For his gallant actions Ranjit Singh was awarded the Mahavir Chakra."

Mahavir Chakra (cont.)

LIEUTENANT COLONEL SANT SINGH
THE SIKH LIGHT INFANTRY

"During the 1965 Indo-Pakistani War, Lieutenant Colonel Sant Singh was given the task of clearing an objective, which notwithstanding the ceasefire had been encroached by Pakistan forces. This was a difficult feature and strongly defended by the enemy. Despite enemy mines and artillery fire, Lieutenant Colonel Sant Singh moved forward with his men, charged the enemy and, after a bitter hand-to-hand fight, cleared the objective. Later taking advantage of his position, Lieutenant Colonel Sant Singh moved from bunker to bunker in the face of artillery and automatic fire encouraging his men and cleared another objective, which had been also encroached by Pakistani forces. Throughout Colonel Sant Singh displayed conspicuous gallantry and leadership of a high order for which he was awarded the Mahavir Chakra."

BRIGADIER SANT SINGH, MVC and BAR
THE SIKH LIGHT INFANTRY

"During the 1971 Indo-Pakistani War, Brigadier Sant Singh, while commanding a sector on the Eastern Front, achieved spectacular results with a mixed force, having one regular battalion, advancing 38 miles almost on foot, to secure Mymensingh and Madhopur in eight days. During the advance, in spite of stiff opposition from the enemy, he cleared heavily defended positions at several places. Throughout these actions, Brigadier Sant Singh personally led and directed the troops, exposing himself to enemy medium machine gun fire and shelling. His personal gallantry, leadership, skilful handling of meagre resources, audacity, improvisation and maximum use of local resources were responsible for the successful and rapid advance against much stronger enemy in well prepared defensive positions. Throughout Brigadier Sant Singh displayed conspicuous gallantry and inspiring leadership for which he was awarded a Bar to his Mahavir Chakra."

Brigadier Sant Singh

VIR CHAKRA

Vir Chakra is a gallantry award presented for acts of bravery in the battlefield. It is third in precedence in the wartime gallantry awards and comes after the Param Vir Chakra and Mahavir Chakra.

SEPOY SAMPURAN SINGH
THE SIKH REGIMENT

"During the 1971 Indo-Pakistani War, Sepoy Sampuran Singh was in a listening post deployed ahead of a defended locality in an area in Jammu and Kashmir in December 1971. When the enemy approached this defended locality in battalion strength, Sepoy Sampuran Singh held on to the listening post engaging the enemy with the light machine gun for two hours. Despite his having been severely wounded, Sepoy Sampuran Singh kept on firing till he fell unconscious."

SEPOY DYAL SINGH
THE SIKH REGIMENT

"During 1947-1948 Indo-Pakistani conflict, a company of 1ST Battalion, The Sikh Regiment was pursuing a band of raiders in the Handwara area. The raiders escaped over the bridge at Kapwara. They also set fire to it to prevent our troops using it in for pursuit. They had covered the burning bridge with effective automatic rifles. Volunteers were asked for to extinguish the fire while the company took up position covering the bridge. Sepoy Dyal Singh was the first to volunteer. Under heavy fire, he skilfully led the party of two other volunteers to the burning bridge and started extinguishing the fire. While so engaged he was hit in the leg by a burst of Light Machine Gun, but nothing daunted him, having dressed up his wound, he continued to carry on the task and refused to leave his post until the fire was completely put out. By now the enemy had withdrawn from the covering position and hastily retreated. But for Sepoy Dyal Singh's courage, tenacity of purpose and devotion to duty under difficult conditions, the bridge at Kapwara which was so vital for the pursuit of the enemy the next day could not have been saved."

Vir Chakra (cont.)

SUBEDAR GURCHARAN SINGH
THE SIKH REGIMENT

"During 1947-1948 Indo-Pakistani conflict, in the Uri area of Kashmir, Subedar Gurcharan Singh was ordered to launch an attack on the Pakistanis, who were found to be deploying their forces to in an attempt to encircle the Sikh Battalion's positions. Subedar Gurcharan Singh attacked the enemy, but being outnumbered and sustaining heavy casualties, had to withdraw. On the commander's decision to withdraw his forces, the responsibility of guarding the rear fell on Subedar Gurcharan Singh, who with his men bore the brunt of the enemy's fire bravely till all troops withdrew safely. Subedar Gurcharan Singh displayed sincere devotion to duty with utmost courage and spirit of sacrifice."

SEPOY GURBACHAN SINGH (POSTHUMOUS)
THE SIKH REGIMENT

"During 1947-1948 Indo-Pakistani conflict, Sepoy Gurbachan Singh was Bren Gunner with a platoon of "C" Company of the 1ST Battalion, The Sikh Regiment in Tithwal area of Jammu and Kashmir. On 13TH October 1948, his platoon was rushed to reinforce "A" Company, which had suffered heavy casualties as a result of continuous heavy attacks by the enemy. Sepoy Gurbachan Singh was wounded on his way to "A" Company position but declined to stay behind and reached the "A" Company position with his platoon. On reaching "A" Company position, be brought his Bren gun into action under heavy enemy shelling. When most of the "A" Company bunkers had been destroyed, he kept his gun firing and was instrumental in beating off enemy attacks. He was again hit and wounded but stuck to his Bren gun and refused evacuation. Inspired by his courage and determination, his comrades who were in critical position, stood to their posts and put up a brave fight. In the meantime, Sepoy Gurbachan Singh got a direct hit and gave his life manning his gun. Sepoy Gurbachan Singh displayed courage of the highest order and in the best tradition of the Indian Army."

SEPOY MAGHAR SINGH
THE SIKH REGIMENT

"During 1947-1948 Indo-Pakistani conflict, in Tithwal area of Jammu and Kashmir, an enemy attack resulted in the telephone line being cut off, and there was only wireless communication which was not very satisfactory. Sepoy Maghar Singh had gone forward alone under heavy shelling and had repaired the line. The line was again cut off and once again Sepoy Maghar Singh repaired the line very quickly. Throughout the day, Sepoy Maghar Singh stayed with the Company, going up and down, repairing the line whenever it was damaged which was quite often. Sepoy Maghar Singh set an example of devotion to duty at the risk of his own life."

Vir Chakra (cont.)

SEPOY ZAIL SINGH (POSTHUMOUS)
THE SIKH REGIMENT

"During 1947-1948 Indo-Pakistani conflict, Pakistanis attacked No 2 Platoon of "A" Company of 1ST Battalion, The Sikh Regiment while in operations against tribesmen in Kashmir Valley. The enemy with two strong companies and with support from guns, mortars and Medium Machine Guns put in a murderous and fierce assault and managed to come within 20 yards of the forward Sikh positions. Sepoy Zail Singh firing his Bren gun from the hip went forward to deal with the forward elements of the enemy. While in this act he received a burst of rifle fire and was seriously wounded in the left thigh but kept on advancing towards the enemy. This so disconcerted the enemy that he withdrew on Sepoy Zail Singh's front. While retiring the enemy shot Sepoy Zail Singh in the head, which instantly killed this gallant soldier. His act of bravery, utter disregard for life and devotion to duty was not only an outstanding example to all ranks of the Platoon but also responsible for the final defeat of the enemy."

SEPOY KABAL SINGH (POSTHUMOUS)
THE SIKH REGIMENT

"During 1947-1948 Indo-Pakistani conflict, Sepoy Kabal Singh was No. 2 Bren Gunner positioned to the side from which the enemy launched its attack on "A" Company of 1ST Battalion, The Sikh Regiment. Heavy firing preceded the attack and most of the bunkers had collapsed due to direct firing of the enemy 3.7 Howitzer gun. Sepoy Kabal Singh faced the enemy onslaught and killed nearly two sections of the enemy with his Bren gun. Though wounded, he refused to be evacuated and stuck to his Bren gun and repulsed the enemy attack. The enemy then launched yet another attack and Sepoy Kabal Singh again inflicted heavy casualties on them but was again wounded in the attack. Many of his comrades had also become casualties, but he did not loose courage and stayed at his post repelling the enemy attacks. When the enemy failed in its fourth attack, it started firing heavy guns on the trench of Sepoy Kabal Singh and killed him at his post. Sepoy Kabal Singh's courage and devotion to duty was and inspiration to all his comrades."

Sepoy Kabal Singh

Vir Chakra (cont.)

JEMADAR KARNAIL SINGH
THE SIKH REGIMENT

"During 1947-1948 Indo-Pakistani conflict, when his company advanced to village of Keri in Jammu and Kashmir, Jemadar Karnail Singh was in command of the leading platoon. He led his platoon to the top of a spur and engaged the enemy. The enemy suddenly appeared on all the features surrounding the spur and brought heavy rifle and automatic fire to bear upon the platoon. Four of his men were killed, two of who were the Bren gunners. Jemadar Karnail Singh now took over one Bren gun himself and engaged the enemy but was wounded twice. Though badly wounded and in great pain, he continued to fire the gun. By now out of a total of 22 men of his platoon, six had been killed and seven, including Jemadar Karnail Singh himself wounded. Jemadar Karnail Singh fought on until he was ordered by his company commander to withdraw."

MAJOR KEHAR SINGH
THE SIKH REGIMENT

"During 1947-1948 Indo-Pakistani conflict, 1ST Battalion, The Sikh Regiment was given the task of securing the strongly held Richmar Gali ridge near Tithwal in Jammu and Kashmir. This feature was vital for the defence of Tithwal. The approaches to Richmar Gali were very step and covered with thick forest. Major Kehar Singh commanding the battalion conducted this attack by encircling the enemy from their left flanks with one company. This move completely surprised the enemy, who fled in haste. But the enemy soon counter attacked his left flank. Major Kehar Singh directed the battle and the enemy attack was beaten back with heavy casualties. A Company, which pursued the retreating enemy, met with heavy resistance. Major Kehar Singh again went to direct the attack. After a fierce battle the enemy retreated leaving behind many dead, and large number of arms and ammunition. It was the inspiring leadership, great personal courage and dogged determination on the part of Major Kehar Singh that carried the day."

NAIK GURJANT SINGH (POSTHUMOUS)
THE SIKH REGIMENT

"During the 1971 Indo-Pakistani War, Naik Gurjant Singh was a section commander of one of the assaulting Platoons of The Sikh Regiment. The Platoon attacked Parbat Ali in the Rajasthan Sector on the night of 12TH December 1971. After his platoon had captured the objective, the enemy was seen forming up for a counter-attack. His platoon was ordered to charge the enemy and break up their assault. Naik Gurjant Singh led his section in the attack and in the hand-to-hand fighting bayoneted seven enemy soldiers to death. Naik Gurjant Singh was mortally wounded during the fighting and succumbed to his injuries."

Vir Chakra (cont.)
CAPTAIN JAGIR SINGH KOKRI
THE SIKH REGIMENT

"During 1947-1948 Indo-Pakistani conflict, Captain Jagir Singh Kokri was in command of a leading company of 7TH Battalion, The Sikh Regiment and was assigned to capture a strongly held feature overlooking Tarehgam village. It was a vital feature for the Indian troops to capture as it led to army's forward garrisons at Shulur in the Kashmir Valley. Marching all night through thick jungle and under constant threat of enemy ambush, Captain Kokri attacked the enemy forward outpost the following morning and put them to flight. Leading his men from the front against heavy enemy fire, he continued to repulse the enemy counter-attacks. Both sides were fighting on a narrow ridge covered with thick forest and having sheer drop on each side. That made the flank attack near impossible. Even the two-inch mortar support was out of question. Taking advantage of their numerical superiority, the enemy launched a determined counter-attack but Captain Kokri countered it in a bayonet charge. After a fierce fight the enemy fled, leaving seven of their dead behind. It was Captain Jagir Singh Kokri's courage and leadership that drove away the enemy and brought the entire feature under control of Indian troops."

NAIB SUBEDAR GURCHARAN SINGH
THE SIKH REGIMENT

"During the 1971 Indo-Pakistani War, Naib Subedar Gurcharan Singh was a platoon commander of The Sikh Regiment occupying a defensive area in the Eastern Sector. Two enemy platoons supported by medium machine guns established themselves between two Sikh company-defended locations and brought down heavy and accurate fire on his company. Naib Subedar Gurcharan Singh led his platoon in a lightning counter attack but was pinned down by rifle fire. He skilfully moved one of his light machine guns to an advantageous position for neutralizing the enemy's weapons. Crawling from man to man, he inspired and exhorted his troops to get up and attack the enemy. Undeterred by the enemy fire and with complete disregard for his own safety, he got up and led the assault. Unnerved by this determined attack, the enemy hastily withdrew. In this action, Naib Subedar Gurcharan Singh displayed gallantry, leadership and determination of high order."

Naib Subedar Gurcharan Singh

Vir Chakra (cont.)
JEMADAR MALL SINGH
THE SIKH REGIMENT

"During 1947-1948 Indo-Pakistani conflict, 1ST Battalion, The Sikh Regiment was sent on a fighting patrol against tribesmen operating in Uri Sector of Jammu and Kashmir when it came into contact with the enemy in great strength. A patrol commanded by Jemadar Mall Singh was ordered to and competed with the enemy to occupy a high feature. Just before the platoon got on to its objective, it came under heavy enemy automatic fire. However Jemadar Mall Singh bravely led his platoon up the hill and occupied it. In the process, he lost three of his men while another four were wounded. He himself was wounded in the jaw by a grenade splinter. Despite his wound, he continued to lead his platoon and give directions. When the enemy attacked his position, Jemadar Mall Singh with two sections of his platoon counter attacked the enemy and repulsed the attack, thus saving the hill feature from falling to the enemy. He refused to be evacuated and volunteered to lead his platoon again. In spite of his wound, he stayed in command of his platoon throughout the operation."

LANCE NAIK PRITAM SINGH (POSTHUMOUS)
THE SIKH REGIMENT

"During the 1965 Indo-Pakistani war, at Burki in the Lahore sector of Punjab, Lance Naik Pritam Singh showed great courage and utter disregard for personal life when he wiped out an enemy Machine-Gun post. With only a handful of soldiers, he rushed at the post and, firing a Sten gun, killed the enemy gunner. In skirmish that followed, he bayoneted the other two members of the post, and in the process was mortally wounded. Without caring for his wounds, he led a charge to the next bunker where he collapsed and died of his wounds."

SEPOY GURMEL SINGH (POSTHUMOUS)
THE SIKH REGIMENT

"During the 1965 Indo-Pakistani war, in a bid to seal off routes of infiltrations for the Pakistanis in Jammu and Kashmir, 1ST Battalion, The Sikh Regiment who was in the Tithwal sector attacked Pakistani positions. A company captured Richhmar Ridge and then attacked and captured the Pir Sahiba feature. A platoon attack on an enemy position was held up as Medium Machine Gun and Light Machine Gun fire of the enemy covered its only approach route. Sepoy Gurmel Singh, who was in the forward section, rushed forward, charged straight for the enemy Light Machine Gun, and holding it by the barrel, pulled it out; but while doing so he got a burst from enemy Light Machine Gun and was instantly killed. Sepoy Gurmel Singh displayed exemplary courage and determination in the best traditions of the Indian Army." Through out September, Pakistani troops tried hard to recapture this feature but were unsuccessful.

Vir Chakra (cont.)

SEPOY SHINGARA SINGH
THE SIKH REGIMENT

"During 1947-1948 Indo-Pakistani conflict, in the Tithwal Sector of Jammu and Kashmir, the forward Company of The Sikh Regiment was attacked and suffered very heavy casualties. Sepoy Shingara Singh succeeded in reaching the Company and started collecting casualties. As the shelling continued and most of the casualties were buried under collapsed bunkers, Sepoy Shingara Singh had to dig them out and bring them to Medical Officer. The job was very dangerous and there was little cover to move about. At one time, Sepoy Shingara Singh was himself half buried under a bunker out of which he was trying to get a casualty out, and which got direct hit. But this brave soldier not only got himself out but succeeding in rescuing the other three comrades buried in the bunker."

LANCE HAVILDAR GURDEV SINGH
THE SIKH REGIMENT

"During the 1965 Indo-Pakistani War, a company of the Sikh Battalion was ordered to capture an important objective in Tithwal Sector in Jammu and Kashmir, for which it was necessary to clear a Pakistani military post. When the forward platoon closed on the enemy post and severe hand-to-hand fighting developed; Havildar Gurdev Singh was ordered to strengthen the assault with his section. While charging the enemy Havildar Gurdev Singh was severely wounded in the left arm. In spite of his injury, he pressed forward, bayoneting and shooting at the enemy with one hand. Thereafter, on the commencement of the main attack on the objective, he refused to be evacuated and improvised a sling for his wounded arm and joined the main attack. By firing Sten gun with his right hand and throwing grenades with his wounded left arm, he cleared three enemy bunkers almost single handedly. Subsequently, deploying his section on the captured position, he joined the reserve platoon, which was then attacking other localities of the enemy and bravely joined in the attack. He refused to be evacuated till the entire company reorganization was complete. Havildar Gurdev Singh's complete disregard of his own safety in the face of the enemy and his unflinching devotion to duty were a source of great inspiration to his men."

Lance Havildar Gurdev Singh

Vir Chakra (cont.)

LANCE NAIK RAM SINGH
THE SIKH REGIMENT

"During 1947-1948 Indo-Pakistani conflict, when 1ST Battalion, The Sikh Regiment was advancing on the Srinagar-Baramulla Road, Lance Naik Ram Singh was commanding the leading section. When held up by the enemy fire, without any regard for his own safety, Lance Naik Ram Singh rushed up, threw two hand grenades on the enemy position, killing seven raiders and capturing six rifles and some ammunition. Having advanced a little, he again destroyed another enemy position and captured two rifles and some grenades. Lance Naik Ram Singh displayed bravery and never hesitated in taking personal risks, thus setting a fine example to his men."

MAJOR SAMPURAN SIGNH
THE SIKH REGIMENT

"During 1947-1948 Indo-Pakistani conflict, Major Sampuran Singh led a patrol of four platoons of The Sikh Regiment in Uri Sector of Jammu and Kashmir and captured an enemy outpost. The enemy attacked the outpost with very heavy fire. Major Sampuran Singh, exhibiting the highest qualities of ability and leadership, successfully extricated the patrol, suffering only one causality in the entire action. On 14TH October and enemy force of about 300 advanced on a position which was commanded by Major Sampuran Singh, and managed to get within 30 yards of the post and attempted to overrun it. Major Sampuran Singh personally took a platoon forward to reinforce the post. A fierce engagement ensued at the end of which the enemy withdrew in disorder having suffered heavy casualties. Major Sampuran Singh displayed outstanding leadership, personal example of courage and devotion to duty."

HAVILDAR AJMER SINGH
THE SIKH REGIMENT

"During the 1965 Indo-Pakistani War, as a platoon of The Sikh Regiment mounted and attack on Burki in Pakistan, Havildar Ajmer Singh found his platoon pinned down by rapid medium machine-gun fire of the enemy. With great presence of mind, he crawled towards the enemy bunker, although hit by rifle fire, he continued to advance on the enemy. Inspired by his example, his platoon rushed forward and completely destroyed the enemy position. The leadership and courage displayed by Havildar Ajmer Singh in this action in the best traditions of the Indian Army."

Vir Chakra (cont.)

MAJOR SARDARA SINGH
THE SIKH REGIMENT

"During 1947-1948 Indo-Pakistani conflict, Pakistanis attacked a Company position of The Sikh Regiment in Tithwal Sector of Jammu and Kashmir. Major Sardara Singh was in command of this company. The Pakistani attack was supported by heavy concentration of 25 pounders, 3.7(How) and Mortar fire. This did not deter Major Sardara Singh who went from place to place encouraging his men till the attack was beaten off. Due to shelling most of the forward bunkers had collapsed and there were a lot of casualties. Major Sardara Singh went from place to place, ordering the evacuation of serious wounded cases and organising the defence again. He also directed fire of the supporting weapons on to the enemy concentration, which was preparing for another attack. Throughout the day the enemy put in eight attacks and fired about 2 to 3 thousand shells and bombs. Major Sardara Singh re-organised his defences and directed supporting fire on to the enemy, resulting in the repulse of the enemy with very heavy losses. Throughout Major Sardara Singh was an example of coolness under very trying conditions. But for the lead given by this officer and his right appreciation of the situation, the position would have been over-run by the enemy."

HAVILDAR SARJAN SINGH
THE SIKH REGIMENT

"During 1947-1948 Indo-Pakistani conflict, when a company of 1^{St} Battalion, The Sikh Regiment was in position on the Srinagar-Baramulla Road, Sepoy Sarjan Singh was No. 1 of the Bren gun. The tribesmen attacked the position and got a footing on the bridge, which Sepoy Sarjan Singh was covering with his Bren gun. The enemy tried to cut the wire across the bridge as an obstacle. On hearing this, Sepoy Sarjan Singh without regard for his life crawled forward with grenades and dealt with the enemy. Next morning four bodies of the enemy were found near the wire. This act of bravery not only inspired his comrades but also helped in saving the bridge."

NAIK NAIB SINGH (POSTHUMOUS)
THE SIKH REGIMENT

"During the 1971 Indo-Pakistani war, Naik Naib Singh with The Sikh Regiment was in a defended locality in the Western Sector. On the night of 3RD December 1971, the enemy launched an attack in strength on his post. Naik Naib Singh enthused his men and directed their fire. When his own ammunition was exhausted, he resorted to hand-to-hand fighting and killed an enemy soldier with his bayonet. In the encounter he was mortally wounded and died of his injuries."

Vir Chakra (cont.)

SEPOY SARUP SINGH
THE SIKH REGIMENT

"During 1947-1948 Indo-Pakistani conflict, "D" Company of The Sikh Regiment attacked a hill feature in Jammu and Kashmir, which was occupied by a Pakistani infantry company with automatic rifles. As the enemy fire held up the leading platoon, Sepoy Sarup Singh climbed a tree under heavy enemy fire and started sniping effectively the enemy whose bunkers were visible to him. This helped the leading platoon to advance further. The advance of this platoon was again held up when the Bren gunner of this platoon got seriously wounded in the leg as the section advanced close to the enemy bunker. Seeing danger from the enemy, Sepoy Sarup Singh climbed down from the tree and with the help of hand grenades was able to dislodge the enemy. The enemy was on a commanding position and having lost it, was forced to give up one flank of his position.

On 22ND May 1948, the Company in Uri Sector was ordered to capture a hill feature during a night attack and ran into an enemy ambush and came under heavy Medium Machine Gun and Light automatic fire. The leading platoon had to withdraw on own side of the Nullah as it was night and the company had run into an enemy ambush. One of the Sepoys of the leading platoon was killed on the enemy side of the Nullah. Sepoy Sarup Singh under enemy small fire brought the dead body of his companion with his arms and equipment to his own side of the Nullah, He then supported the withdrawal of his own troops across the Nullah. Though wounded in the hands he continued firing and pinned down the enemy. After sometime he was wounded again, this time in the face and was evacuated. In the above mentioned two different actions Sepoy Sarup Singh set fine example of devotion to duty, courage and personal bravery of high order."

HAVILDAR GURDEV SINGH
THE SIKH REGIMENT

"During the 1971 Indo-Pakistani War, Havildar Gurdev Singh was a platoon Havildar of a platoon of The Sikh Regiment deployed in an area in the Western Sector. On 3RD December 1971, the enemy in overwhelming strength, supported by heavy and accurate artillery fire, attacked his company position. Havildar Gurdev Singh moved from bunker to bunker encouraging and inspiring his men. It was due largely due to him that the attack was repulsed. Throughout, Havildar Gurdev Singh displayed gallantry, determination, leadership and devotion to duty of a high order."

Vir Chakra (cont.)

SEPOY SARWAN SINGH (POSTHUMOUS)
THE SIKH REGIMENT

"During 1947-1948 Indo-Pakistani conflict, Sepoy Sarwan Singh was No. 2 of the forward Bren gun section of 'A' Company of 1ST Battalion, The Sikh Regiment deployed in the Tithwal Sector of Jammu and Kashmir. On 13TH October 1948 the enemy attacked the Company after a heavy concentration of supporting arms fire. Sepoy Sarwan Singh was supplying ammunition to his No. 1 Bren gunner and also engaging the enemy with his rifle fire. During this engagement, his No.1 gunner was hit by a bullet and killed. Sepoy Sarwan Singh took over the gun and kept it firing till the attack was beaten off. However he along with many others of his platoon was wounded and the strength of the platoon had considerably decreased. Refusing to be evacuated he held on to his position during another three attacks of the enemy until he was mortally wounded and died. Sepoy Sarwan Singh showed great devotion to duty and cool courage under the most trying conditions. It was due to his exemplary courage that eight determined attacks of the enemy were repulsed and position was saved from being over-run."

HAVILDAR SEWA SINGH
THE SIKH REGIMENT

"During 1947-1948 Indo-Pakistani conflict, whilst advancing on Urie-Domel Road in Jammu and Kashmir, The Sikh Regiment came under heavy enemy fire. The leading platoon of the company was only 40 yards from the enemy bunker and the rest of the platoon was pinned down in a nullah under the incessant mortar and Light Machine Gun fire. The communication between the Platoon and Company Headquarters broke down. As it became imperative for the forward platoon to withdraw and, in the pitch dark no signalling was possible, Sepoy Sewa Singh went forward from his Company Headquarters under intensive fire and communicated the orders to the Platoon. He not only carried out his mission successfully but also brought back severely wounded Sepoy from the forward line. Again on 24TH August 1948, Sepoy Sewa Singh was the leading scout of the patrol, which made a close contact with the enemy and came under heavy fire. Three men of his patrol were wounded straightaway, but the patrol continued their advance on the enemy as Sepoy Sewa Singh attacked them with grenades. The deadly grenade throwing of Sepoy Sewa Singh was largely responsible for enemy's hasty retreat. This gallant Sepoy, though exposed to enemy fire, disregarding any risk of personal safety, went around and collected the casualties and brought them back. Sepoy Sewa Singh's courageous and gallant action set an excellent example of devotion to duty."

Vir Chakra (cont.)

SEPOY SHER SINGH (POSTHUMOUS)
THE SIKH REGIMENT

"During 1947-1948 Indo-Pakistani conflict, Sepoy Sher Singh was Bren gunner No.2 of his platoon which was rushed to the Tithwal areas of Jammu and Kashmir, to reinforce 'A' Company of The Sikh Regiment after the latter had come under heavy enemy attack and suffered many casualties. The enemy had also blocked the track leading to the 'A' Company position by continuous shelling. Defying death, Sepoy Sher Singh kept on advancing towards the position and also simultaneously feeding his No. 1 Bren gunner. When a bullet hit his No. 1 Bren gunner, Sepoy Sher Singh started manning the gun single-handedly and inflicted heavy casualties on the enemy. He was chiefly responsible for repulsing the enemy attack. He kept his Bren gun in action in spite of heavy shelling by the enemy. During the action Sepoy Sher Singh was mortally wounded and succumbed to his injuries. He had shown remarkable courage and devotion to duty during the fighting."

NAIK SOWARN SINGH (POSTHUMOUS)
THE SIKH REGIMENT

"During 1947-1948 Indo-Pakistani conflict, Naik Sowarn Singh was a Section Commander of a leading section of The Sikh Regiment. In December 1948 his section was sent out on a fighting patrol in Jundwara area of Kashmir Valley. The area was a difficult terrain and deeply snow bound. When the Patrol reached the village of Koralpur, it ran into an enemy ambush. The Pakistanis opened up with heavy automatic fire thus pinning the patrol to the ground. Another enemy party, some 80 men strong, tried to attack the leading section from the flank shouting war cries: "Maro Nara Haidri-Pakistan Zindabad". Naik Sowarn Singh ordered his section to turn to his flank and rushed to his Light Machine Gun group. Taking the gun himself, he started spraying bullets from his hip and shouting the Sikh war cry of: "Bole So Nihal-Sat Sri Akal". His section mowed down the enemy who had taken up positions over an open stretch of deep snow. The enemy tried to flee in all directions but was caught in the deep snow. Hardly anyone could escape. Suddenly Naik Sowarn Singh was hit in the head by a bullet. He fell down shouting, "Kill them, Die here but do not let them go back alive." This inspired his men and they stood their ground in spite of having lost their leader. Naik Sowarn Singh's great courage, leadership and devotion to duty was instrumental in inflicting shattering defeat on the enemy which was ten times the number of his section. His gallant action has been source of great inspiration to the men in his company who now have a saying "if you have to die, die like Sowarn Singh"."

Vir Chakra (cont.)

SEPOY UJAGAR SINGH
THE SIKH REGIMENT

"During 1947-1948 Indo-Pakistani conflict, 1ST Battalion, The Sikh Regiment, was holding Mirkalsi Bridge in Kashmir Valley at Tithwal. At dawn the enemy, of two company strong well supported by 3.7 gun hows, mortars and medium machine-guns put in a heavy attack on a Sikh platoon. Sepoy Ujagar Singh was mortar No. 1 of his platoon. One Bren gunner of the enemy stubbornly advanced within 10 yards of Sepoy Ujagar Singh. While supporting his platoons with his mortar, Sepoy Ujagar Singh at the same time engaged the enemy Bren gunner at point blank range with his mortar, but it seemed to have little effect on the enemy. He then snatched the rifle of his mortar No.2 and closed in with the enemy Bren gunner. Shooting the gunner dead, he captured the Bren gun with its ammunition, went back to his position and carried on with his 2-inch mortar support of his platoon. The gallant action was instrumental in demoralizing the enemy and had a marked effect on the course of the battle. As inspiration to all ranks of his platoon, this brave man's courage, devotion to duty and total disregard of life and were an outstanding example to his Company."

MAJOR AMRIK SINGH
THE SIKH REGIMENT

"During the 1971 Indo-Pakistani War, Major Amrik Singh was commanding a company in a battalion of The Sikh Regiment in the Rajasthan Sector. After attacking and capturing and enemy screen position on the night of 10TH December 1971, he volunteered to lead the assault on another position. A company of Pakistani regular soldiers, well fortified and protected, held the objective minefield 600 metres deep. Major Amrik Singh led the assault and under his inspiring leadership his company charged through minefield and captured the objective after fierce hand-to-hand fighting. During the assault, Major Amrik Singh was seriously wounded hut continued to direct his men and repulsed the enemy's counter-attack. In this action, Major Amrik Singh displayed gallantry, determination and leadership of a high order."

NAIK PRITAM SINGH AND
LANCE NAIK SARWAN SINGH

"During the 1962 Indo-China War, the Chinese forces attacked Gurung Hill in overwhelming strength. Naik Pritam Singh and Lance Sarwan Singh formed part of artillery Observation Post that controlled and conducted the defensive fire from the guns. They continued to perform their duties with great courage in the face of heavy enemy fire. This enabled the Observation Post to bring down effective artillery fire on the attacking enemy. During this action Naik Pritam Singh and Lance Sarwan Singh displayed courage and devotion to duty of a higher order. Both were awarded the Vir Chakra."

Vir Chakra (cont.)

NAIK CHAND SINGH
THE SIKH REGIMENT

"During the 1965 Indo-Pakistani War, Naik Chand Singh of "B" Company, The Sikh Regiment, was the leading Section Commander in an assault on Raja Piquet, a well-fortified defended locality of the enemy, across the Cease Fire Line in Poonch sector. In face of heavy automatic fire, the battalion closed in on the objective. The leading troops of 'A', 'B' and 'C' Companies were now within 50 yards of the objective when the entire battalion was pinned down by heavy automatic fire. From this proximity many brave assaults were made but the Pakistani medium machine-guns and grenades accounted for every brave soldier who moved forward. The casualties especially those of "A" Company began to rises at an alarming rate. It was at this time that Naik Chand Singh, seeing his comrades being decimated before him, dashed forward under the heavy medium machine-gun fire and lobbed grenades into the nearest bunker. He crawled back, got more grenades and again went forward. By those repeated assaults on the bunker he silenced the medium machine-gun and established a foothold in the enemy post. From there he led the assault upon the other bunkers and cleared no less than ten bunkers by is dash and disregard for life. By this act of extreme gallantry Naik Chand Singh stopped the mounting loss of lives. His individual action inspired all those around him, and was largely instrumental in helping the battalion in capturing its objective."

NAIB SUBEDAR GIAN SINGH (POSTHUMOUS)
THE SIKH REGIMENT

"During the 1965 Indo-Pakistani War, Naib Subedar Gian Singh was on a patrol in the Amritsar Sector. The enemy opened up with heavy automatic and small arms fire. In utter disregard of his personal safety, he rushed forward and started returning the fire from behind the cover of a raised bund. He kept changing his position stealthily and continued to engage the enemy with great determination, grit and presence of mind in spite of being surrounded from three sides by the enemy. He drew maximum enemy fire on himself, which enabled the rest of the patrol to take cover and deal with the situation. In this gallant act, he was hit by and enemy Medium Machine Gun burst, but he continued to engage the enemy till he succumbed to his injuries. In this action, Naib Subedar Gian Singh displayed gallantry, determination and leadership of a high order".

Vir Chakra (cont.)

SUBEDAR MASSA SINGH (POSTHUMOUS)
THE SIKH REGIMENT

"During the 1965 Indo-Pakistani War, Subedar Massa Singh was commanding a platoon of 'C' Company of The Sikh Regiment during the night of 10/11 September 1965. His Company was given the task of assisting the tanks in overcoming any tank obstacle on way to Burki. When the leading tank reached near the far end of village of Burki, it went over a mine and was disabled. Two more tanks were disabled due to the enemy mines and the advance was held up. Subedar Massa Singh and his men were very near the disabled tanks and came under heavy small arms fire from the eastern bank of the Ichhogil Canal. It was very difficult to evacuate the casualties unless the enemy's small arms fire was eliminated. Subedar Massa Singh, realizing that any delay in eliminating enemy's small arms fire would mean mores casualties to his men, immediately decided to assault the enemy position. His platoon had already suffered heavy casualties due to enemy shelling and was reduced to only a handful. Despite that he decided to assault the enemy position with whatever men he had. During the assault he was fatally wounded, but continued to exhort his men to the objective. The enemy position was over run and the small arms fires eliminated. Subedar Massa Singh showed great courage and bold leadership in taking such spontaneous action. But for him the evacuation of own casualties would not have been possible. Subedar Massa Singh gave his life that the life of others, who were already wounded, could be saved."

LANCE NAIK HARBHAJAN SINGH
THE SIKH REGIMENT

"During the 1971 Indo-Pakistani War, Lance Naik Harbhajan Singh was commander of the leading section of his company of The Sikh Regiment, which was given the task of attacking the positions occupied by the Pakistanis in the Eastern Sector. His company came under intense and accurate small arms fire when it was only 300 yards short of enemy-held positions. As Lance Naik Harbhajan Singh handling the light machine gun, advanced on the enemy, he was hit by a burst from a machine gun; he continued to crawl forward when he was hit by another burst. Still undeterred, he continued to crawl forward and taking up a suitable position destroyed the enemy pillbox. Unmindful of his injuries, he deployed his section in defence and ensured that his men had dug in completely as they repulsed Pakistani counter charges on the positions captured. In this action, Lance Naik Harbhajan Singh displayed gallantry, leadership and determination of a high order."

Vir Chakra (cont.)

SEPOY BHAG SINGH
THE SIKH REGIMENT

"During 1947-1948 Indo-Pakistani conflict, on the night of 22ND / 23RD November 1947, in operations against tribesmen at Uri, in the Kashmir Valley, the enemy about 600 strong attacked a hill feature. The feature was occupied by a weak platoon of 'D' Company of The Sikh Regiment under the command of Subedar Gurcharan Singh. Sepoy Bhag Singh was No. 1 of the light machine-gun of the forward sections, which were only 6 strong. When the attack started, the section came under very heavy automatic and rifle fire and the main attack fell on them. The section held off their fire until the enemy was within 20-30 yards of their position and then opened up at once. Sepoy Bhag Singh used his light machine-gun with great skill and under the accurate fire of his light machine-gun and the effect of the hand grenades, the enemy was checked and forced to withdraw some distance behind boulders and bushes. The enemy's first attempt to capture the feature was thus foiled. The Pakistanis put in another attack supported by heavy mortar fire. When the section commander Lance Naik Bachittar Singh was wounded, Sepoy Bhag Singh took complete control of the situation and spraying with his light machine–gun and shouting Sikh war cries of "Bole So Nihal-Sat Sri Akal" enjoined his men to fight on to the last. His men by spirited action forced the enemy to withdraw behind cover again. Sepoy Bhag Singh inspired great confidence in his men and held on to his section post against heavy odds. The enemy's second attempt to capture the platoon position having thus failed, he started withdrawing and pulling out his dead and wounded under heavy covering fire. During the attack on this most vital feature, Sepoy Bhag Singh displayed great personal courage and determination. Although young and inexperienced, he faced very difficult situation with confidence and skill. Which inspired only three remaining men of his section to hold on to their post against very heavy odds".

HAVILDAR MALKIAT SINGH
THE SIKH REGIMENT

"During the 1962 Indo-China War, Havildar Malkiat Singh was platoon Havildar of a battalion of Sikh Regiment deployed in an area in the Western Sector. He was assigned the task of capturing an enemy light machine gun, which had been firing at the troops, and inflicting casualties. Havildar Malkiat Singh led a section with courage and speed and he assaulted the enemy machine gun inflicting casualties on the enemy and silencing the gun. In this action, Havildar Malkiat Singh displayed commendable courage, determination, leadership and devotion to duty of a high order."

Vir Chakra (cont.)

SEPOY MOHAN SINGH
THE SIKH REGIMENT

"During the 1971 Indo-Pakistani War, Sepoy Mohan Singh was with the assaulting company of The Sikh Regiment during an attack on an enemy feature in Rajasthan Sector on 13TH December 1971. When his platoon reached near the objective, it came under intense and accurate fire from an enemy heavy machine gun located on the flank. Sepoy Mohan Singh charged the enemy machine gun post with utter disregard for his personal safety. He was seriously wounded in his left leg by a Medium Machine Gun burst. Unmindful of his injuries he crawled to the enemy bunker and silenced the medium machine gun. This enabled the Company to capture the objective. In this action, Sepoy Mohan Singh displayed gallantry, determination and devotion to duty of a high order."

SEPOY RACHHPAL SINGH
THE SIKH REGIMENT

"During the 1971 Indo-Pakistani War, Sepoy Rachhpal Singh was a member of crew of a recoilless gun detachment deployed in a company locality of The Sikh Regiment, holding the Phagha ridge in the chhamb sector. On 5TH December 1971, the enemy launched a determined attack and managed to penetrate the defended locality. Eight Pakistani soldiers charged the gun detachment in a bid to destroy it. Sepoy Rachhpal Singh was one of the men involved in hand-to-hand fight with the enemy. He shot and bayoneted three Pakistani soldiers and captured one light machine gun and two rifles. The enemy consequently withdrew in disorder. In this action Sepoy Rachhpal Singh displayed gallantry, determination and devotion to duty of a high order."

NAIB SUBEDAR NIRMAL SINGH (POSTHUMOUS)
THE SIKH REGIMENT

The Kargil War, an armed conflict between India and Pakistan took place between May and July 1999 in the Kargil district of Kashmir. The cause of the war was the infiltration of Pakistani soldiers and Kashmiri militants into positions on the Indian side of the Line of Control. "Operation Vijay" was a name of the successful Indian operation to push back the Pakistani infiltrators from the Kargil Sector." On 5TH July 1999, Subedar Nirmal Singh was leading a small team to establish a foothold on an objective in Drass sub-sector as part of 'Operation Vijay'. While advancing, Subedar Singh noticed enemy movement. Before enemy could react, he directed fire of automatic weapons on enemy and inflicted heavy casualties. The enemy was forced to retreat. Subedar Karnail Singh quickly reached on the objective and captured it. Rest of the company followed up next day and reorganized defences. Subedar Nirmal Singh was mortally wounded on the slope of Helmet and made a supreme sacrifice for the nation."

Vir Chakra (cont.)

LANCE NAIK MOHINDER SINGH (POSTHUMOUS)
THE SIKH REGIMENT

"On 23RD July 1988, "Bravo" and "Delta" Companies of 16TH Battalion, The Sikh Regiment were tasked to search and destroy the militants in an area in Sri Lanka. As the Companies advanced they came under heavy fire from militants. "Delta" Company closing in on the enemy bunker from the east came under heavy rifle fire and the company commander decided to launch a counter attack. One General Purpose Machine Gun was taking a heavy toll of the assaulting troops. Lance Naik Mohinder Singh, Light Machine Gun number 1, fired at the bunker from the hip position. He realised that his fire made little impact on small loopholes. So he dashed towards the General Purpose Machine Gun and caught it by the barrel and received the full burst of fire and died on the spot, his act silenced the militant's General Purpose Machine Gun. The enemy gunners fled in apprehension of being charged by the Sikhs. This made it possible for the assaulting company to move forward and capture the hideout. Lance Naik Mohinder Singh's personal example of courage inspired his comrades to rush forward and capture the camp. Lance Naik Mohinder Singh displayed conspicuous courage and valour against the militants."

MAJOR DEVINDERJIT SINGH PANNU (POSTHUMOUS)
THE SIKH REGIMENT

" During the 1971 Indo-Pakistani War, Major Devinderjit Singh Pannu was commanding a company of The Sikh Regiment occupying a key position for the defence of Chhamb when the enemy launched an attack on it on night of December 1971. Major Pannu immediately rushed to one of his platoons occupying a position at a border outpost and held out against heavy attacks throughout the night and thereafter for sixteen hours while the position had virtually been surrounded. He then withdrew to his main position where the enemy subjected his company to a battalion strength attacks on two successive nights. Major Pannu repeatedly exposed himself to enemy small arms and artillery fire while moving from one locality to another, inspiring his men to beat back the enemy. Realizing the importance of this position, the enemy launched another battalion attack on 5TH morning, preceded by heavy artillery fire. While moving from trench to trench, encouraging his men, Major Pannu was mortally wounded by a shell and died at his post. Throughout, Major Devinderjit Singh Pannu displayed gallantry, determination and leadership of a high order."

Vir Chakra (cont.)

NAIB SUBEDAR KARNAIL SINGH (POSTHUMOUS)
THE SIKH REGIMENT

'Operation Vijay' was a name of the successful Indian operation to push back the Pakistani infiltrators from the Kargil Sector.'

"During 'Operation Vijay' Naib Subedar Karnail Singh and five soldiers of 8TH Battalion, The Sikh Regiment was deployed on the reverse slope of area Helmet in the Kargil Sector of Kashmir. This small section came under heavy enemy fire on 6TH July 1999. The enemy opened heavy fire from three directions and followed it up with an attack with 15 intruders on the position held by Naib Subedar Karnail Singh, who directed the fire of automatic weapons on the approaching enemy. Naib Subedar Karnail Singh kept fighting the enemy with extreme bravery till in the hand-to-hand fighting the attack was repulsed. Karnail Singh was seriously wounded during the fighting. Soon the enemy launched a counter-attack with 40 to 50 intruders. Despite being seriously wounded Naib Subedar Karnail Singh challenged the enemy and charged at them with his men inflicting heavy casualties on them in close combat. He killed four enemy intruders and injured many more, forcing them to flee. He along with his men kept the enemy at bay till they all succumbed to their fatal injuries. Displaying conspicuous courage, bravery and exceptional devotion to duty, Naib Subedar Karnail Singh made a supreme sacrifice of his life."

SEPOY SATPAL SINGH
THE SIKH REGIMENT

"Sepoy Satpal Singh along with his section was deployed in the Drass sector during' Operation Vijay' on 6TH July 1999. The enemy launched an attack with 15 to 16 intruders and intense fire fighting ensued between Sepoy Satpal Singh and the intruders. While repulsing the attack, Sepoy Satpal Singh got seriously wounded. Showing utter disregard to his personal safety he kept firing incessantly, inflicting heavy casualties on the enemy. He did not allow the enemy to come closer and beat back the counter attack. The enemy launched second counter attack with 40 to 45 intruders. He boldly confronted them again. Though suffering from multiple gunshot wounds, he kept engaging the intruders and killed four of them. Many more intruders were injured and this finally forced the enemy to flee. He held on to his post and kept motivating his comrades to fight till the last. Displaying extreme bravery and courage, Sepoy Satpal Singh single handedly took on the enemy face-to-face at close quarters that motivated the troops around him and subsequently repulsed the fierce counter attack. Sepoy Satpal Singh was mortally wounded during the fighting and succumbed to his injuries."

Vir Chakra (cont.)

SEPOY BOOTA SINGH
THE SIKH LIGHT INFANTRY

"During the 1971 Indo-Pakistani War, Sepoy Boota Singh was with a company of a battalion of The Sikh Light Infantry, which was deployed in an area in the Western Sector. The company after capturing an area was in the process of reorganisation when the enemy launched a counter-attack supported by artillery and mortar fire. Sepoy Boota Singh noticed two enemy soldiers at close quarters. With complete disregard for his safety, he came out of his trench and started firing from the hip. He got one of the enemy soldiers and bayoneted the other to death. Seeing this gallant action, other men of his section came out of the trenches and charged at the assaulting enemy causing heavy casualties on the enemy and breaking up the assault. In this action, Sepoy Boota Singh displayed gallantry and devotion to duty of a high order."

SEPOY DHARAM SINGH
THE SIKH LIGHT INFANTRY

"During the 1965 Indo-Pakistani War, a company of The Sikh Light Infantry, in which Sepoy Dharam Singh was serving, was ordered to clear an encroachment on a feature near Kalidhar in Jammu and Kashmir, which had been made by Pakistani forces notwithstanding the cease-fire. When its advance was held up due to a minefield, which was covered by enemy medium machine gunfire and shelling. Sepoy Dharam Singh volunteered and crossed the minefield to give a lead to the others. His gallant act inspired them in achieving the objective in time. Subsequently, during the counter-attack launched by the enemy, he killed two enemy soldiers who closed in on him. In this action Sepoy Dharam Singh displayed commendable courage and devotion to duty."

SEPOY KARNAIL SINGH (POSTHUMOUS)
THE SIKH LIGHT INFANTRY

"During the 1971 Indo-Pakistani War, Sepoy Karnail Singh was with a Commando Company during the operations in Vera-Burj area in the Western Sector a scene of bitter fighting. On 9TH December 1971, the commando company was ordered to reinforce these localities. The Pakistanis launched an attack in strength to recapture these positions. During the attack, an enemy medium machine gun opened up for from a well-entrenched position on a flank inflicting heavy casualties on the troops. In utter disregard of his personal safety, Sepoy Karnail Singh charged the bunker and succeeded in killing the enemy. In the process, an enemy grenade fatally wounded him. In this action Sepoy Karnail Singh displayed gallantry of a high order."

Vir Chakra (cont.)

SEPOY KULDIP SINGH (POSTHUMOUS)
THE SIKH LIGHT INFANTRY

"During the operations in Sri Lanka in 1987-1988, 13TH Battalion, The Sikh Light Infantry t was assigned the mission to conduct heliborne operations on the night of 11TH October 1987 and capture the university. The operations commenced as per the time schedule. "Delta" Company was to move in two waves from Ml-8 helicopters after 10 Para Commando team had secured the landing zone. Only one platoon of the "Delta" Company was able to land since all the available helicopters were severely hit by the enemy fire. Thus the platoon of "Delta" Company lay deep inside enemy territory, totally isolated with Sepoy Kuldip Singh as one of its members. The link-up on foot was delayed owing to unusual enemy opposition. The beleaguered platoon with Sepoy Kuldip Singh fought valiantly till the last man and last round and set a glowing example of courage, bravery and devotion to duty. Sepoy Kuldip Singh died fighting."

SUBEDAR PIARA SINGH (POSTHUMOUS)
THE SIKH LIGHT INFANTRY

" During the 1965 Indo-Pakistani War, on the night of 2ND November 1965, Subedar Piara Singh was commanding a platoon in a battalion of The Sikh Light Infantry. The Battalion was ordered to clear a feature in the Mendhar Sector in Jammu and Kashmir, which had been encroached upon by Pakistani forces, notwithstanding the cease-fire. He led the assault through the minefield in the course of which he lost 25 men to mines and artillery fire. Undaunted by the losses and with total disregard for his own safety, he led the charge on an enemy bunker from where a light machine gun was enfilading another platoon of his company. After silencing the light machine gun, he proceeded to the next hunker from where one 83mm rocket launcher was firing and holding up furthers advance. As he threw grenades into the bunker, both his legs were blown off by 83mm rocket, but the grenade he threw kill the occupant of the bunker. A few minutes later he also died, but only after capturing his objective and exhorting his few remaining men to exploit further. In this mission Subedar Piara Singh displayed leadership and indomitable courage and made the supreme sacrifice in the best traditions of the Indian Army."

Subedar Piara Singh

Vir Chakra (cont.)

HAVILDAR PIARA SINGH
THE SIKH LIGHT INFANTRY

"During the 1971 Indo-Pakistani War, Havildar Piara Singh was a Platoon Havildar of the leading platoon of a Battalion of The Sikh Light Infantry advancing in an area in the Rajasthan Sector. On 8TH December 1971, the Pakistanis counter-attacked this platoon in force. Deploying one of its sections to give fire support, the platoon charged the assaulting enemy. The light machine gunner in the supporting section of the platoon was hit and rendered ineffective. Havildar Sarup Singh rushed to this machine gun and started firing it at the enemy. He was hit in his right shoulder from a light machine gun burst, but unmindful of his severe injury he stuck to his post providing effective fire support to his platoon. Thus the enemy counter-attack was repulsed. In this action, Havildar Piara Singh displayed commendable courage, initiative and leadership."

SUBEDAR PRITAM SINGH (POSTHUMOUS)
THE SIKH LIGHT INFANTRY

"During the 1971 Indo-Pakistani War, Subedar Pritam Singh was the senior JCO of a company of The Sikh Light Infantry during the operations in the Shakargarh Sector. A platoon under Subedar Pritam Singh was ordered to clear the villager Pila Dogran. The platoon came under accurate enemy fire, resulting in five casualties, including one of the light machine gun teams. Realizing the gravity of the situation, Subedar Pritam Singh quickly got hold of the light machine gun, regrouped the platoon and pressed home the attack. The fire from his light machine gun silenced one of the medium machine guns of enemy. At this stage he was seriously wounded but refused to be evacuated. He kept up at his task till he succumbed to his injuries."

SUBEDAR SAMPURAN SINGH (POSTHUMOUS)
THE SIKH LIGHT INFANTRY

"During the operations in Sri Lanka in 1988, Subedar Sampuran Singh of The Sikh Light Infantry was a platoon commander with the heliborne force, which dropped in the heart of Jaffna Town to destroy the militant's headquarters as part of IPKF operations in Sri Lanka. Due to poor flying and navigational error, the force was dropped west of the designated location zone. Soon militants who effectively engaged the force from all directions surrounded it. Seeing no way out, Subedar Sampuran Singh motivated his men to give their best till the last man and last round. The entire force–one officer, one junior commissioned officer and 28 men fought till the end and inflicted heavy casualties on militants but in the process made the supreme sacrifice in the highest tradition of their service. Subedar Sampuran Singh displayed conspicuous courage and valiant leadership in the face of militants."

Vir Chakra (cont.)

SEPOY SUKHWANT SINGH (POSTHUMOUS)
THE SIKH LIGHT INFANTRY

"During the operations in Sri Lanka in 1988, 13TH Battalion, The Sikh Light Infantry was asked to undertake a heliborne operation and capture the Jaffna University Campus. The heliborne operation had to be called off since all the available helicopters had been severely hit by enemy fire. The operation then had to be carried out on foot. On their advance to the Jaffna University an unexpected large force ambushed the Sikhs. The gallant platoon of "Delta" Company continued to resist the enemy till the last man and the last round. Sepoy Sukhwant Singh set a glowing example of tenacity, courage and boldness in the face of the enemy and made the supreme sacrifice."

SEPOY SWARAN SINGH
THE SIKH LIGHT INFANTRY

"During the 1971 Indo-Pakistani War, Sepoy Swaran Singh was with a company of The Sikh Light Infantry during their attack on an enemy position in the Western Sector. The company assault was held up due to heavy and accurate medium machine gun fire from an enemy bunker located on a flank. Sepoy Swaran Singh, with complete disregard for his safety, crawled up to the medium machine gun post and silenced it with a grenade. Immediately after this, an enemy soldier charged him. Sepoy Swaran Singh killed the enemy with his bayonet. In this action, Sepoy Swaran Singh displayed gallantry of high order."

SECOND LIEUTENANT VIRENDRA PRATAP SINGH
SIKH LIGHT INFANTRY REGIMENT

"On 7TH September during the 1965 Indo-Pakistani War, Second Lieutenant Virendra Pratap Singh was platoon commander in a company of The Sikh Light Infantry, which was ordered to attack the Pakistani post at Kundanpur. Although wounded, he continued to lead his men in the face of intense artillery and small arms fire. Later, finding that his Company Commander was missing, he took over command. Leading the company, he over - ran the enemy position and captured a number of prisoners, a tank gun and two Medium Machine Guns. In this action, Second Lieutenant Virendra Pratap Singh displayed cool courage, initiative and determinate of high order."

Vir Chakra (cont.)

LANCE NAIK PHUMAN SINGH
15TH (PATIALA) BN. THE PUNJAB REGIMENT

"On 10TH December during 1947-1948 Indo-Pakistani conflict, during the attack on Mandiala in Jammu and Kashmir, Lance Havildar Phuman Singh was in command of a section of the left forward platoon which was held up by accurate fire from two enemy snipers, from well protected and concealed positions. Lance Naik Phuman Singh, utter regardless of the intense fire, stalked alone within grenade throwing distance and killed both the snipers, thus clearing the way for hi platoon for further advance. Another sniper shot at him from 10yards. He escaped narrowly, but this only infuriated him. With amazing speed he put his bayonet through the sniper. In these two actions he displayed remarkable grit and set a fine example of selfless devotion to duty, individual gallantry and high skill at arms."

HAVILDAR GURDIAL SINGH
15TH (PATIALA) BN. THE PUNJAB REGIMENT

"During 1947-1948 Indo-Pakistani conflict, in Jammu and Kashmir State, Havildar Gurdial Singh of The Punjab Regiment was commander of a section of the leading platoon which was ordered to attack and destroy enemy bunkers. The route to objective lay over a bare narrow spur to pass some 300 yards below and then another 300 yards uphill, all in full view of the enemy in well dug bunkers. His platoon had hardly advanced 30 yards when most of his section became casualties. Without looking back Havildar Gurdial Singh pushed on to his objective. After advancing some 200 yards the platoon came under accurate fire from hidden enemy position, which both sections, after short brilliant charge neutralized it. Havildar Gurdial Singh was soon at the head of his section shouting Sikh war cries of "Bole So Nihal-Sat Sri Akal", and firing accurately form hip with his Sten gun. From here onwards, it was an advance over a very naked spur to the enemy bunkers. His left forward group came under intense rifle and grenade fire from a well-camouflaged bunker. He moved to the pinned down group and then charged the bunker and was wounded by a grenade, which shattered his right thigh completely. Two Pakistanis, one rifleman and the other swordsman counter attacked his left forward group. The rifleman was killed by one of his groups and when the swordsman was about to deliver blow, Gurdial Singh rolled over to his side and killed him with his Sten gun and thus saved the man from certain death. Although severely wounded and profusely bleeding, he refused to be carried back and to be attended to until the objective was captured. Right through this action, Havildar Gurdial Singh demonstrated leadership, individual bravery and toughness of a rare variety. He has made a name for himself and commands respect amongst the men for his outstanding conduct in that action."

Vir Chakra (cont.)

HAVILDAR SEWA SINGH
15TH (PATIALA) BN. THE PUNJAB REGIMENT

"During 1947-1948 Indo-Pakistani conflict, Havildar Sewa Singh was in command of a forward platoon of The Punjab Regiment during flanking movement to the east of Chhamb. As his platoon was being heavily sniped at, he went to the foremost man of his platoon and carried out useful reconnaissance from a completely exposed position, showing utter disregard for his personal safety. Having located the enemy resistance point, without waiting for orders he led the platoon, charged into the forward enemy line and encouraged his men to blitz through. The men responded splendidly to his inspiring call and the enemy position was charged by bayonets and captured after a fierce hand-to-hand fighting. Havildar Sewa Singh displayed an outstanding will to win."

MAJOR JOGINDER SINGH
15TH (PATIALA) BN. THE PUNJAB REGIMENT

"During 1947-1948 Indo-Pakistani conflict, an attack on a strong enemy position in Jammu and Kashmir, the whole of the leading section of the company commanded by Major Joginder Singh was wiped out by the enemy. Major Joginder Singh pushed another platoon forward and led a charge without losing any moment, killed and wounded 12 enemy soldiers at that spot. Men intoxicated by the good bag and having been inspired to a frenzy by their leader ran up the slopes to the bunker and delivered a cold blooded bayonet charge and routed the Pakistanis. Again during the advance on Jhangar, he attacked the enemy with just one platoon and out manoeuvred the enemy. He enthused his troops with an indomitable will to win and the men followed him cheerfully giving their very best. Throughout this short and brilliant action, Major Joginder Singh exhibited outstanding courage and leadership."

NAIK MEHAR SINGH
15TH (PATIALA) BN. THE PUNJAB REGIMENT

"During 1947-1948 Indo-Pakistani conflict, Naik Mehar Singh was leading a section of The Punjab Regiment on an advance on Jhangar and attack on Pir Thil Nakka. During the assault, the Pakistani Light Machine Gun and grenades attack on his section wounded two of his men. Naik Mehar Singh pushed on the attack, throwing grenades in front of him and charged the enemy and accounted for two enemies killed in the trenches. Without waiting for the rest of the platoon to catch up, he charged with his men, all-firing from hip and secured a foothold on the enemy positions. In both these actions, Naik Mehar Singh displayed outstanding initiative and daring which filled everyone in his company with enthusiasm and high spirits. Throughout the long hour of action, he set an example of leadership, tenacity of purpose and devotion to duty."

Vir Chakra (cont.)

LANCE NAIK NAURANG SINGH
15TH (PATIALA) BN. THE PUNJAB REGIMENT

"Lance Naik Naurang Singh was commanding a section of The Punjab Regiment on their attack on Pir Thil Nakka. The enemy was very active on his front and the going was particularly difficult. He ordered the whole of his section to throw a grenade each and then led an assault through the inferno of fire, capturing the enemy post in a fast charge. He then pressed on to an enemy position in the rear, which was still active, completely overrunning it without any loss to his men. At this stage another enemy post on the flank was spotted. After firing some rifle grenades at the post, he closed on it and destroyed it. By these isolated individual actions on his own initiative, he gained for his company very advantageous ground, which was responsible for routing the well-entrenched enemy in that sector. All throughout the action, he did not consider his own safety for a minute and exhibited fearless dash, which made his men follow him cheerfully through very tough action."

SUBEDAR SANT SINGH (POSTHUMOUS)
15TH (PATIALA) BN. THE PUNJAB REGIMENT

"During 1947-1948 Indo-Pakistani conflict, Jemadar Sant Singh was in command of a leading platoon in Jammu and Kashmir, and was ordered to capture a feature at Machhoi. The advance lay over 2,000 yards of heavily snow covered ground in full view of the enemy. Any outflanking move was out of question because of heavy snow and sheer climb. Right from the star line, his platoon came under Medium Machine Gun fire halting the advance. He kept moving from section to section inspiring his men to carry on without caring for personal safety. His men responded promptly and unfalteringly. He continued the assault under heavy fire with himself in the frontline with such dash that the enemy fled leaving behind 12 dead. His fearless and vigorous drive contributed chiefly to the success of the attack. In this long and difficult action, Jemadar Sant Singh showed leadership, courage and tenacity of purpose of a high calibre."

SEPOY JAGJIT SINGH (POSTHUMOUS)
THE PUNJAB REGIMENT

"During the 1971 Indo-Pakistani War, the Pakistanis launched an attack in strength with infantry and armour on the defences occupied by a battalion of Punjab Regiment in the Rajasthan Sector. Sepoy Jagjit Singh was manning a light machine gun post in the forward defended locality. During the attack, his bunker was badly damaged by enemy fire. Realizing the importance of maintaining a heavy volume of fire against the enemy, with utter disregard for his personal safety, came out in the open and kept firing his gun and was mortally wounded and killed by enemy fire. Sepoy Jagjit Singh made a supreme sacrifice for his country.

Vir Chakra (cont.)

NAIB SUBEDAR BALWANT SINGH
15TH (PATIALA) BN. THE PUNJAB REGIMENT

"During 1947-1948 Indo-Pakistani conflict, Subedar Balwant Singh was in command of a platoon at Zojila Pass in Jammu and Kashmir. He was detailed to bypass an enemy post and occupy a hill feature adjacent to it. There was 200 yards of detour, involving climbing on heavily snow-covered hills in close proximity to the enemy. Subedar Balwant Singh, without caring for darkness and snow that stood in his way, reached the top of the hill in four hours and encircled on enemy post hardly 200 yards below. With his platoon he lay there for the whole night and at dawn, realizing that the enemy was hiding below in curved caves and might escape, he did not wait for orders, led out two sections and systematically charged one cave after another with automatics rifles. Throughout this vital engagement, Subedar Balwant Singh displayed consistent superb courage, utter fearlessness and most invigorating leadership."

HAVILDAR MUKAND SINGH
15TH (PATIALA) BN. THE PUNJAB REGIMENT

"During 1947-1948 Indo-Pakistani conflict, Havildar Mukand Singh was a platoon Havildar of the company of The Punjab Regiment, and was detailed to destroy an enemy resistance pocket at Zojila Pass. He manoeuvred round the enemy position, while the rest of his platoon gave covering fire. Every inch of a distance of about 200 yards from the enemy position was covered by heavy enemy automatic fire. Havildar Mukand Singh was the leading man of the section and by his dauntless action persuaded every man to follow him fearlessly over the area heavily swept by enemy fire. Two of his men were seriously wounded. Leading five remaining men, he blitzed the enemy position with grenades, killing five of the enemy and capturing two. In addition he captured a Bren gun, a collection of arms and a large quantity of ammunition equipment and documents. Throughout this operation, Havildar Mukand Singh showed leadership, courage and determination of a very high order."

HAVILDAR DILBAG SINGH (POSTHUMOUS)
THE PUNJAB REGIMENT

"During the 1971 Indo-Pakistani War. Lance Havildar Dilbagh Singh was a section commander in a pioneer platoon of Punjab Regiment during operations in the Shakargarh Sector of Kashmir. After the capture of Shabazpour position, Lance Havildar Dilbagh Singh was given the task of making a safe lane through the minefield 600 yards deep. Notwithstanding intense enemy fire, he kept on prodding the removing enemy mines in complete disregard of his personal safety. The safe lane was almost complete when Lance Havildar Dilbagh Singh was blown up while neutralizing and anti-tank mine."

Vir Chakra (cont.)

LANCE NAIK SAJJAN SINGH
15TH (PATIALA) BN. THE PUNJAB REGIMENT
"15TH (PATIALA) BN. THE PUNJAB REGIMENT

"During 1947-1948 Indo-Pakistani conflict, at Machhoi in Jammu and Kashmir while attacking a feature, Lance Naik Sajjan Singh was in command of a forward section platoon of The Punjab Regiment. During the assault his section was subjected to particularly heavy fire from enemy 2-inch mortars and grenades, killing two of his men and temporarily halting his section. He went from man to man, cheering and directing them, taking no notice whatever of the intense fires all rounds him, filling his men with complete confidence and air of superiority. From here he blitzed the enemy position and was responsible for killing two with his Sten gun and grenade. All through the action by his utter fearlessness and disregard for his personal safety, he made the men willingly go through terribly tough and dangerous time and was always in complete control of the situation. Lance Naik Sajjan Singh exhibited leadership, courage and vigorous dash which command spontaneous respect from his men."

LANCE NAIK CHAND SINGH (POSTHUMOUS)
15TH (PATIALA) BN. THE PUNJAB REGIMENT

"During 1947-1948 Indo-Pakistani conflict, Lance Naik Chand Singh was in command of leading section of a patrol at Machhoi in Jammu and Kashmir. His platoon came under heavy and accurate Medium Machine Gun and automatic fire, killing and wounding half of his section straightaway. He collected the Light Machine Gun and 2 inch mortar bomb (to be used as grenades) from his dead comrades with a view to reorganizing his section and containing the enemy to prevent him from taking away his wounded comrades. From about 12 noon to about 5.30 p.m., when reinforcements arrived, he so directed the fire of his party that the enemy, in spite of continuous and frantic efforts, was unable to move. The enemy concentrated all his efforts on Lance Naik Chand Singh's little hideout causing two casualties to his party of five. But he held on. At 5.30 p.m. when an attack was put in by his company on the enemy occupied hill feature, he got out of his hideout with his party and joined the battle, silencing an enemy sniper post. This superb gallant action of Naik Chand Singh was largely responsible for saving nine of his comrades and the whole of platoon equipment. In an all-day battle, he displayed the highest qualities of leadership, personal bravery and selfless devotion to duty."

Vir Chakra (cont.)

SEPOY GAJJAN SINGH (POSTHUMOUS)
15TH (PATIALA) BN. THE PUNJAB REGIMENT

"During 1947-1948 Indo-Pakistani conflict, Sepoy Gajjan Singh was Bren gun No.1 At Zojila Pass piquet in Kashmir. After stand down, he was away from his position when the enemy opened up heavy Medium Machine Gun and Light Machine Gun fire on the piquet. He rushed back to the piquet position under very accurate and close fire to man his Medium Machine Gun and was hit in the leg. Undeterred by his wound and determined to reach his Light Machine Gun, he crawled forward in full view of the enemy not caring for his personal safety. Having got his Light Machine Gun he was not satisfied with his position and crept forward to another place and was again wounded, this time in the shoulder; but managed to engage the enemy from his new position. His well-aimed fire was responsible for killing and wounding at least five Pakistani soldiers and temporarily slowing down the their attack. At this stage he was caught by an Medium Machine Gun burst which instantly killed him"

SEPOY HAZURA SINGH (POSTHUMOUS)
15TH (PATIALA) BN. THE PUNJAB REGIMENT

"During 1947-1948 Indo-Pakistani conflict, Sepoy Hazura Singh was doing LMF No.1 duty in a section outpost at Gumri in Jammu and Kashmir State. The enemy put in a two-company attack supported by mortars and Medium Machine Gun and managed to reach within 200 yards of the outpost. Although head covers and stone Sangars had collapsed because of enemy mortar fire, Sepoy Hazura Singh fired his weapon with extreme accuracy, causing serous losses to the enemy. He thus became the chief target for all enemy weapons. Though wounded in the left shoulder, he kept on using his weapon with deadly effect. The enemy, unable to over-run this outpost, tried a small detour. On his own initiative, Hazura Singh crawled some 15 yards to a new advantageous position but was hit again in the leg and thigh. Although feeling feeble from profuse bleeding he kept on engaging the enemy with great skill and accuracy, halting the new enemy move. He was caught by and Medium Machine Gun burst in the head, which killed him instantaneously. In making the supreme sacrifice, Sepoy Hazura Singh by his outstanding courage and skill at arms, caused heavy losses to the enemy, definitely breaking the tempo of the enemy attack."

Vir Chakra (cont.)

SEPOY TEJA SINGH (POSTHUMOUS)
15TH (PATIALA) BN. THE PUNJAB REGIMENT

"During 1947-1948 Indo-Pakistani conflict, Sepoy Teja Singh was wireless operator of a section piquet at Machhoi in Jammu and Kashmir, when the enemy put an attack. A direct mortar hit put his set out of commission and was wounded in the left arm. There being no other communication with the commander, he volunteered to go out some 300 yards to the main telephone line with his telephone to pass information the commander. He moved in full view of the enemy and under intense enemy Medium Machine Gun fire and was again hit this time in the thigh but managed to tap the line and send the message. Then he dashed back to join the battle, although bleeding heavily. When only some 20 yards from the piquet he was hit by a Medium Machine Gun burst in the chest and died. This young signaller displayed supreme courage and determination to carrying out his duties."

SEPOY ZAILA SINGH (POSTHUMOUS)
15TH (PATIALA) BN. THE PUNJAB REGIMENT

"During 1947-1948 Indo-Pakistani conflict, Sepoy Zaila Singh was No 2 of an Light Machine Gun outpost at Gumri in Jammu and Kashmir State. The enemy attacked the piquet with two companies with Medium Machine Gun and 2-inch mortar support and reached some 400 yards from the piquet. As his Light Machine Gunner No 1 got seriously wounded, Sepoy Zaila Singh at once took over the gun, killing or wounding at least three enemies. Under barrage of 2 inch mortar and heavy concentration of Medium Machine Gun cross fire, the enemy advanced to within 200 yards of this outposts, but Zaila Singh used his weapon with such devastating effect that the advance of the enemy was temporarily halted. His piquet commander ordered him back to the main position. Knowing that he was causing heavy losses to the enemy, he stuck to his position saying that he was more useful there. The enemy, unable to advance without overrunning this outpost, furiously engaged this one-man outpost with all the weapons he had, mortally wounding Sepoy Zaila Singh. This brave man by his selfless gallant stand and devotion to duty and his individual skilful action on the piquet made the supreme sacrifice for the safety of his comrades."

Vir Chakra (cont.)

SEPOY BACHAN SINGH
15ᵀᴴ (PATIALA) BN. THE PUNJAB REGIMENT

"During 1947-1948 Indo-Pakistani conflict, at Machhoi in Jammu and Kashmir, Sepoy Bachan Singh was a rifleman in the leading section of a platoon of The Punjab Regiment, which was heavily engaged by enemy Medium Machine Gun and Light Machine Gun fire from a hill feature. Sepoy Bachan Singh was hit by a burst in the leg shattering it completely. By skilful field craft and sheer guts he dragged himself a distance of 300 yards to where his section commander had signalled him. All the way to this place he was constantly under close automatic fire, missing him by inches. This did not deter the tough and tenacious soldier from carrying on to join his section. Having joined his section and after a little dressing to his wounds, he volunteered to be allowed to fire his rifle, although feeling very weak from loss of blood. He kept on shooting at the enemy for over eight hours lying on one side only till he was carried back. His personal valour and dogged determination, while being seriously wounded, set an inspiring example for comrades."

NAIK CHET SINGH
15ᵀᴴ (PATIALA) BN. THE PUNJAB REGIMENT

"During 1947-1948 Indo-Pakistani conflict, immediately around the Zojila Pass in Jammu and Kashmir, Naik Chet Singh was holding a piquet with 13 men when attacked by the Pakistanis with mortars and machine guns. Eight of his comrades were wounded. He battled for seven hours with such extraordinary determination and skill that the raiders broke off the attack, leaving behind 36 of their own dead. Naik Chet Singh was subsequently awarded a Vr.C. in this battle for his heroic act."

BRIGADIER SUKHDEV SINGH Vr.C. MC.
COMMANDING OFFICER
15ᵀᴴ (PATIALA) BN. THE PUNJAB REGIMENT

SUBEDAR RATTAN SINGH
THE PUNJAB REGIMENT

"During the 1971 Indo-Pakistani War, Subedar Rattan Singh was commanding a platoon of a company deployed in the Western Sector. On 5ᵀᴴ December 1971, the enemy attacked this position in strength. Subedar Rattan Singh moved from trench to trench and by his personal example infused courage and enthusiasm in his men and was of great help to his company commander in holding the post and repulsing enemy attacks. Throughout, Subedar Rattan Singh displayed gallantry and determination of a high order."

Vir Chakra (cont.)

SUBEDAR SOHAN SINGH (POSTHUMOUS)
THE PUNJAB REGIMENT

"On April 1, 1957, Subedar Sohan Singh of the Punjab Regiment, while heading a platoon on road protection duties between Khonoma and Dzulake in the Naga Hills, Tuensang area, encountered nearly 300 hostiles dug - in well-camouflaged positions and armed with light machine-guns, Tommy-guns and other weapons. While climbing a spur the leading section was fired upon from point-blank range, but it engaged the hostiles by throwing hand-grenades. As the heavy hostile fire continued, it had to be withdrawn behind the cover of smoke. Subedar Sohan Singh ordered his platoon to take up defensive positions, as fire poured from all directions. Cool and confident, Sohan Singh told the platoon not to be deterred and undertook to direct three-inch mortar fire on the hostiles. While doing so, he was hit by a Tommy gun burst, the platoon itself suffering heavy casualties. Thereupon, he decided to make a frontal charge on the hostiles on the spur to break the ring closing round the platoon. Bleeding profusely from severe wound he received, he crawled to his section to console the wounded and exhorted all personal to charge the hostile position with fixed bayonets. In the words of the only survivor of this encounter, Subedar Sohan Singh told his men that there would be no withdrawal and everyone should come up to the expectorations of Sikh chivalry and heroism. He led the charge till he was hit by another gun-burst which killed him instantly. The platoon was ultimately overpowered by the hostiles in a grim hand-t- hand fight, but not before it had inflicted heavy casualties on them. It was the bold and courageous leadership of Subedar Sohan Singh and his calm and fearless demeanour in the face of heavy odds which commanded the unflinching loyalty of his men, all of whom showed valour of a high order and literally fought to the last man and to the last round."

SEPOY AVTAR SINGH (POSTHUMOUS)
THE PUNJAB REGIMENT

"During the 1971 Indo-Pakistani War, on the night of 10TH December 1971, Sepoy Avtar Singh of Punjab Regiment was with a force attacking the right shoulder of Nangi Tekri in the Jammu and Kashmir Sector. This was a well-fortified position held in strength by the Pakistan army. During the attack, the assaulting troops were subjected to intense artillery and medium machine gun fire as a result of which Sepoy Avtar Singh lost one of his legs. Undaunted, he crawled up to a medium machine gun post in a bid to destroy it and while hurling himself at the gun was hit by a burst of automatic fire as a result of which he died. In this action, Sepoy Avtar Singh displayed gallantry and determination of a high order."

Vir Chakra (cont.)

HAVILDAR MALKIAT SINGH (POSTHUMOUS)
THE PUNJAB REGIMENT

"During the 1962 Indo-China War, Havildar Malkiat Singh was commanding a section post on high ground at Karpola, north of Tsengzong in North East Frontier Agency. On 10TH October 1962, when the Chinese launched a massive attack against the platoon's post at Tsengzong, Havildar Malkiat Singh brought intense and accurate fire to bear on the enemy. His section post did no have any overhead shelter, and he was quite aware that if their position was disclosed, it would be subjected to heavy shelling. Undaunted by any danger, and in complete disregard of his own safety, Havildar Malkiat Singh continued to bring down maximum fire on the enemy.

During subsequent attack on the Tsengzong position the same day, the section post of Havildar Malkiat Singh was subjected to intense mortar fire. He personally manned the gun position and continued accurate fire on the enemy until the post ran short of ammunition. By this time, the enemy had occupied his route of withdrawal to the South of Nyamkaachju and Havildar Malkiat Singh and his men were forced to withdraw through the thick jungle to the West. He then led his men by a circuitous and difficult route and reached Tsangdhar after about 48 hours. The party had no rations and had to carry a wounded soldier.

On 18TH October, 1962, learning that ammunition and other essential stores were urgently needed by the troops at Tsangle, three days march from Tsangdhar, Havildar Malkiat Singh volunteered to carry the stores. Twenty others rank of his platoon, following his example, volunteered to go with him. However, on the way to Tsangle, the party encountered a column of approximately twelve hundred Chinese. Undaunted by the enemy's overwhelming superiority in numbers, Havildar Malkiat Singh and his twenty brave men took up a position, brought down heavy fire on the enemy and put up a gallant fight in which he was killed. Throughout these operations, Havildar Malkiat Singh displayed consistent enthusiasm, exceptional bravery and gallant leadership."

LIEUTENANT MAHJIT SINGH BUTTAR
THE PUNJAB REGIMENT

"During the 1965 Indo-Pakistani War, on 21ST September 1965, Lieutenant Mahjit Singh Buttar was commanding a company of The Punjab Regiment on the Ichhogil Canal Bank in the Punjab. He exposed himself to enemy small arms, mortar and artillery fire in order to retain observation over the enemy on the far bank and to direct fire on the enemy. His efficient and gallant performance resulted in the destruction of an enemy tank and in raising the morale of his company. Lieutenant Buttar displayed courage and determination of a high order."

Vir Chakra (cont.)

LIEUTENANT COLONEL SAMPURAN SINGH, MVC
THE PUNJAB REGIMENT

"During the 1965 Indo-Pakistani War, Lieutenant Colonel Sampuran Singh was commanding 19TH Battalion, The Punjab in Jammu and Kashmir. In their advance to Haji Pir Pass it was essential to capture Bedori as this feature overlooked the entire area. The approaches to this important tactical feature were precipitous and extremely difficult. Two attempts to secure Bedori on the 26TH and 27TH August 1965 proved abortive. The enemy was holding this massive feature with two companies and was covering the approaches with Medium Machine-Gun and Light Machine-Guns. On 28TH August, the 19TH Battalion was ordered to capture this important feature with utmost speed so that they could resume the advance to Haji Pir. Two companies of the battalion advanced at 2100 hours but were soon pinned down by heavy enemy fire. For the moment it appeared that Bedori was invincible. It was at this crucial moment that Lieutenant Colonel Sampuran Singh decided to give a lead to his men to the objective. Without showing any regards for his personal safety, he continued to lead the advance and by first light next morning had captured Bedori and the enemy had been forced to run away. The success of the operation was entirely due to the outstanding leadership, courage and devotion to duty of Lieutenant Colonel Sampuran Singh."

SEPOY BACHITTAR SINGH (POSTHUMOUS)
THE PUNJAB REGIMENT

"During the operations in Sri Lanka in 1987-1988, Sepoy Bachittar Singh was detailed to form part of the patrol of The Punjab Regiment responsible for opening and clearing of Road Trincomalee-Nilaveli up to Traoposcatter. When the patrol reached the wooden bridge at 0645 hours, approximately 25 militants ambushed it. Sepoy Bachittar Singh was hit by a burst of light machine gun fire. With disregard to personal safety, and unmindful of his injury, Sepoy Bachittar Singh immediately charged the militants. He was fired upon at point blank range and was hit in the stomach by a burst of light machine gun. Though seriously injured and bleeding profusely, he fired at the militants and bayoneted them, killing one of them. As he was charging a party of the enemy, a militant threw a hand grenade at him. The grenade burst close to Sepoy Bachittar Singh and killed him instantly. His daring action inspired other patrol members to charge the enemy. Three militants, including the leader of the ambush party, were killed in a counter ambush. Sepoy Bachittar Singh displayed exceptional courage, initiative and dedication to duty, true to the traditions of the Indian Army. He went beyond the call of duty, in assaulting the militants, even having been seriously wounded."

Vir Chakra (cont.)

CAPTAIN GURMUKH SINGH GILL
THE PUNJAB REGIMENT

"During the 1965 Indo-Pakistani War, when Pakistani infantry and tanks concentrated an attack on Indian troops, Captain Gurmukh Singh Gill led a patrol of The Punjab Regiment to provide protection to Artillery Observation Post Officer, who was assigned the task of directing artillery fire in engaging and destroying the enemy. The patrol was within fifty yard of the enemy concentration where two infantry battalions with a squadron of tanks had formed up for an assault. Captain Gill took up a protective position as the observation post officer directed and brought down heavy and accurate fire, which forced the enemy infantry and tanks to break up in panic and confusion. Enemy tanks thereafter charged the protective patrol. In the process the Artillery Observation Post Officer was seriously wounded. Captain Gill, after administering first aid to the officer, carried him on his shoulders and fought his way back to safety. In this action, Captain Gill displayed gallantry, initiative and devotion to duty of a high order."

HAVILDAR JASSA SINGH
THE PUNJAB REGIMENT

"During the 1965 Indo-Pakistani War, Havildar Jassa Singh's company was holding defences along the Fazilka-Sulaimanke road. When the enemy mounted sudden attack in battalion strength and reached the company position, Havildar Jassa Singh charged the enemy with Browning machine gun and then fought single-handedly with an enemy section and killed or wounded at least seven enemy soldiers. Though wounded in the encounter, he kept on fighting with his men and repulsed the attack, inflicting heavy casualties on the enemy. In this encounter, Havildar Jassa Singh displayed gallantry and determination of a high order."

SECOND LIEUTENANT JOGINDER SINGH JASWAL
THE PUNJAB REGIMENT

"During the 1971 Indo-Pakistani War, Lieutenant Jaswal commanded a section which held a position in the Western Sector. The position was subjected to heavy and accurate shelling and attacked by the enemy. With complete disregard for his personal safety, he moved from one post to another to inspire his men. He brought heavy volume of fire on the enemy and repulsed their attack. The enemy attacked the position twice and on both occasions the attacks were repulsed. On 5TH December, he led a patrol to silence an enemy medium machine gun. In the process, he was hit by a medium machine gun burst in the neck. In spite of the wound, he brought back a wounded Naik who was with him. Throughout the fighting, Second Lieutenant Joginder Singh Jaswal displayed gallantry, leadership and devotion to duty of a high order."

Vir Chakra (cont.)

GUNNER AJIT SINGH
REGIMENT OF ARITLLERY

"During the 1971 Indo-Pakistani War, Gunner Ajit Singh was a radio operator with forward observation officer's party during the attack on an enemy position in the Fazilka Sector of the Punjab. During the assault, he was struck by a shell splinter and was seriously wounded. Unmindful of his injuries, he continued to operate the radio set transmitting the orders as a result of which accurate artillery fire was brought down on the enemy. In this action, Gunner Ajit Singh displayed gallantry, determination and devotion to duty of a high order while seriously injured."

HAVILDAR AJMER SINGH
REGIMENT OF ARITLLERY

"During the 1971 Indo-Pakistani War, Havildar Ajmer Singh while commanding a detachment of an air defence battery deployed for the protection of Amritsar airfield, directed the fire of his gun accurately and shot down one of the two Pakistani Star fighter aircraft raiding the airfield. In this action, Havildar Ajmer Singh displayed gallantry and professional skill of a high order."

SECOND LIEUTENANT GURJEET SINGH BAJWA
REGIMENT OF ARITLLERY

"During the 1971 Indo-Pakistani War, Second Lieutenant Gurjeet Singh Bajwa was the forward observation officer attached to a battalion of Kumaon Regiment. The battalion of Kumaon Regiment attacked an enemy border post in the Rajasthan Sector. During the attack, the Pakistanis subjected the Kumaon's to sustained and accurate fire from automatic weapons inflicting heavy causalities. With complete disregard for personal safety and unmindful of the heavy small arms fire and shelling, Second Lieutenant Bajwa continued to bring down accurate artillery fire on the enemy locality there by contributing to the success of the operations. In this action, Second Lieutenant Gurjeet Singh Bajwa displayed gallantry and determination of a high order."

MAJOR MANJIT SINGH DUGAL
REGIMENT OF ARITLLERY

"During the 1971 Indo-Pakistani War, Major Manjit Singh Dugal was a battery commander attached to The Dogra Regiment during the operations in the Eastern Sector. Throughout the operations, he provided effective artillery support and repeatedly exposed himself to enemy small arms and mortar fire to direct artillery fire on enemy targets. His conduct was source of inspiration to others and was instrumental in the success of the operations undertaken by The Dogra Regiment. In this action, Major Dugal displayed gallantry, determination and leadership of a high order."

Vir Chakra (cont.)

GUNNER GURDIP SINGH (POSTHUMOUS)
THE REGIMENT OF ARTILLERY

"During the 1962 Indo-China War, as the Chinese forces attacked Gurung Hill in Chushul Area in Ladakh, the artillery Observation Post commander was seriously wounded in the action and became unconscious. Technical Assistant Gurdip Singh, though wounded, took over command of the Post and continued to direct the fire of the artillery on the enemy, thereby inflicting heavy casualties on them. In this action Technical Assistant Gurdip Singh displayed great initiative and courage of a high order."

MAJOR SARVJIT SINGH RATRA
THE REGIMENT OF ARTILLERY

"During the 1965 Indo-Pakistani War, Major Sarvjit Singh Ratra performed the duties of Air Observation Post in Lahore Sector of the Punjab. In order to gain vital information and direct accurate fire on the Pakistani tank concentrations, bridges and crossing sites over the Ichhogil Canal, he had to undertake a number of flights over enemy piquets. With great courage, he carried out these extremely dangerous missions in an unarmed aircraft. Based on his information, Indian aircraft destroyed an important enemy bridge and thus cut off the enemy's armour exit route. He was responsible for the destruction of five enemy tanks and several vehicles. On numerous occasions, while flying low, he was fired upon by enemy medium machine gun. On the 17TH September 1965, three enemy fighters F-86 attacked him, and on the 21st September 1965, he encircled by three enemy F-86 fighters, which fired thrice; but on these occasions, he kept his composure and came back safely. His daring performance and willingness to face grave risks was a shining example to all his men."

CAPTAIN LACHMAN SINGH
THE REGIMENT OF ARTILLERY

"During 1947-1948 Indo-Pakistani conflict, Captain Lachman Singh was the Forward Observation Officer on Jhangar front in Kashmir valley as part of 50TH Para Brigade. He directed accurate and timely artillery fire on enemy positions under most trying conditions. On 15TH March, he was responsible for extricating a company of 3RD battalion Maratha Light Infantry, which had been pinned down by the enemy with automatic weapons and mortars. He continued to direct artillery fire on the enemy for eight hours from more or less an open position without caring for his personal safety, continuously exposing himself to enemy sniper and mortar fire. Again on 16TH March, during the battle of Thil, the decisive battle for Jhangar, he successfully directed accurate and timely artillery fire on enemy positions which supported 3RD Battalion, Maratha Light Infantry on to their objective."

Vir Chakra (cont.)

MAJOR ATMA SINGH HANSRA
THE REGIMENT OF ARTILLERY

"During the 1971 Indo-Pakistani War, on 5TH December, the enemy attacked Longewala in the Rajasthan Sector in overwhelming strength with armour and infantry. During the battle, which lasted up to 11TH December, Major Atma Singh Hansra of an Air Observation Post Flight, unmindful of the enemy fire, was continuously in the air spotting enemy moves and concentration of troops and armour and directing own artillery fire against them. He also brought back valuable information. During one of the flights when he had to force land, he brought the aircraft to a safe area, got it repaired and was on vigilance mission again."

CAPTAIN SUKHWANT SINGH GILL
THE REGIMENT OF ARTILLERY

"During the 1971 Indo-Pakistani War, Captain Sukhwant Singh Gill was battery commander attached to The Sikh Regiment in the Chhamb Sector. The Pakistanis launched a series of massive attacks supported by armour, artillery and mortar fire on the Indian positions. Captain Gill's accurate and effective control of the artillery fire was responsible to a large extent in inflicting heavy casualties and breaking up the enemy assault. On 6TH December as the Sikhs counter-attacked, Captain Gill, acting also as the Observation Post Officer, brought down heavy artillery and automatic fire on the enemy. Undeterred by heavy enemy artillery and automatic fire, he came out in the open to observe and direct the artillery fire, thereby contributing to the success of the attack."

MAJOR JAGDISH SINGH
THE REGIMENT OF ARTILLERY

"During the 1965 Indo-Pakistani War, Major Jagdish Singh was battery commander with an Infantry company, which launched an attack on an objective in the Poonch Sector. The company came under heavy enemy fire and Major Jagdish Singh was wounded. Undaunted, he accompanied the battalion commander right up to the objective and personally directed artillery fire accurately. He was thus able to reduce the number of casualties of the troops."

LIEUTENANT KARTAR SINGH SANDHU
THE REGIMENT OF ARTILLERY

"During 1947-1948 Indo-Pakistani conflict, Lieutenant Kartar Singh Sandhu was a Forward Observation Officer attached to 4TH Battalion, The Dogra Regiment during the Rajauri operations. In spite of being exposed to heavy enemy fire during the battle, which decided the fate of Rajauri, he continued pounding the enemy with accurate artillery fire and thereby completely demoralized them. Lieutenant Sandhu showed exemplary courage and devotion to duty."

Vir Chakra (cont.)

CAPTAIN HARBANT SINGH KAHLON
THE REGIMENT OF ARTILLERY

"During the 1971 Indo-Pakistani War, Captain Harbant Singh Kahlon was the Observation Post Officer with the Ranian position in the Western Sector. The Pakistanis launched seven attacks on this position between 3RD and 4TH December in overwhelming strength under heavy artillery support. Captain Kahlon, with complete disregard for his personal safety, moved from one position to another despite heavy shelling, observing and directing fire on enemy concentrations. With exceptional competence, he brought down own artillery fire as close as twenty yards from his own position to break up the enemy assault. The defensive battle of Ranian is attributable largely to Captain Kahlon's tireless, determined and bold efforts."

SECOND LIEUTENANT ARJUN SINGH KHANNA
THE REGIMENT OF ARTILLERY

"During the 1965 Indo-Pakistani War, Second Lieutenant Arjun Singh Khanna was the artillery Forward Observation Officer of a Parachute Field Regiment at Biar Bet during the operations against Pakistani intruders in the Kutch area. On 15TH April 1965, the intruders attacked Biar Bet, supported by artillery and tanks. Lieutenant Khanna engaged the intruders with accurate artillery fire and repulsed the attack. The intruders launched a fresh and determined attack with infantry, overwhelmingly superior in numbers, supported by artillery and tanks. Despite accurate shelling and direct fire from tanks, Lieutenant Khanna continued to direct effective fire towards the intruders and slowed down their advance. At one stage, when a shell fired from a tank demolished the overhead cover of his bunker, he shifted to a nearby trench and stuck to his duties until ordered to withdraw. In this action he had directed heavy artillery fire, which inflicted heavy casualties on the intruders. Under his artillery protection the troops were able to withdraw without leaving a single man or any equipment behind."

CAPTAIN SURJIT SINGH PARMAR
THE REGIMENT OF ARTILLERY

"During the 1971 Indo-Pakistani War, on 13TH December 1971, Captain Surjit Singh Parma was Observation Post Officer with a company of 11TH Battalion, Gorkha Rifles, which was assigned the task of attacking enemy entrenchments in the Eastern Sector. As the attack progressed, the enemy brought down accurate and effective machine gun and artillery fire. During the assault, Captain Parma's radio operator was wounded. Undaunted by this, he took over the radio set and carrying it himself continued to direct fire most effectively. Though hit by a bullet in the arm and by a splinter in the neck, he remained with the troops till the objective was captured."

Vir Chakra (cont.)

CAPTAIN PRITHVI PAL SINGH SANGHA
THE REGIMENT OF ARTILLERY

"During the 1971 Indo-Pakistani War, on 5TH December, the enemy attacked Longewala in the Rajasthan Sector with armour and infantry in overwhelming strength. Captain Sangha of an Air Observation Post flight was ordered to be airborne to direct tank and artillery fires against enemy tanks and troops concentrations. Throughout, this action from 5TH to 11TH December with complete disregard for his personal safety, he spent most of the time carrying out airborne missions of observing enemy movements and sending back valuable information and directing attacks."

CAPTAIN GURBAKSH SINGH SIHOTA
THE REGIMENT OF ARTILLERY

"During the 1971 Indo-Pakistani War, on 9TH, Captain Sihota of an Air Observation Post was ordered to carry a reconnaissance for the selection of a suitable landing site for helicopter borne operations in the Eastern Sector. Skilfully piloting his helicopter, he penetrated deep behind the enemy occupied territory. During this reconnaissance, the helicopter was fired upon and hit by enemy small arms fire. Captain Sihota, however, brought the damaged aircraft back to forward helipad. Although his helicopter was damaged, he undertook a mission to evacuate two serious casualties. Later, the same afternoon and in the same damaged helicopter, he led the first wave of the helicopter-borne operations and directed other helicopters to a safe landing."

LIEUTENANT RAVINDER SINGH BEDI
ARMOURED CORPS

"During the 1965 Indo-Pakistani War, Lieutenant Ravinder Singh Bedi's troop was ordered to move through the built-up area of Jhuggian and engage enemy bunkers, recoilless guns and tanks in Dograi and South of Dograi in Pakistan. To carry out his task, Lieutenant Bedi had to position his troop further West of Jhuggian, which was well within the enemy's tank and recoilless gun range. His troop engaged the enemy's soft vehicles, a recoilless gun and tanks South of Dograi. In this engagement he destroyed 3 by 3 ton vehicles of the enemy. When his tank was fired at by an enemy's recoilless gun and was hit, Lieutenant Bedi was seriously wounded. Undaunted, he continued to fight in his tank and lead his troop and did not abandon his tank until such time it started to fume and the ammunition started exploding. When this happened, Lieutenant Bedi, though wounded, and under heavy artillery and mortar shelling, helped the other tank casualties to get out of the burning tank and lead them to safety. This act of leadership and courage was a great source of inspiration to his men in carrying out the difficult task assigned to them."

Vir Chakra (cont.)

CAPTAIN GRUMEET SINGH PUNIA
THE REGIMENT OF ARTILLERY

"During 1947-1948 Indo-Pakistani conflict, and the Indian thrust towards Shakargarh Sector in Jammu and Kashmir, Captain Gurmeet Singh Punia was ordered to register targets deep inside the enemy defences. Despite enemy small arms and artillery fires directed at him, he remained airborne directing the artillery fire on enemy targets. During this mission, he spotted three enemy Sabre aircraft in the area. Undeterred, he remained airborne to complete his task. When attacked by enemy aircraft, he displayed great presence of mind and kept flying with great skill, evading the initial attack. The enemy ultimately shot his aircraft. Though badly burnt, he nursed his aircraft back to base."

NAIB RISALDAR MOHAN SINGH
ARMOURED CORPS

"During 1947-1948 Indo-Pakistani conflict, Naib Risaldar Mohan Singh was the leader of a troop of 17TH Horse in the Shakargarh Sector of Jammu and Kashmir. On 13TH December the regiment was ordered to link up with infantry by crossing a minefield. Naib Risaldar Mohan Singh rushed through the minefield despite the fact that it had not been breached and cleared of mines. Later, on 16TH December, a squadron of the regiment was counter–attacked thrice by a regiment of Patton tanks. Though heavily outnumbered in these engagements, Naib Risaldar Mohan Singh directed steadfast fire of the squadron and broke the enemy's assault. The troop commanded by Naib Risaldar Mohan Singh knocked out eight enemy tanks."

SECOND LIEUTENANT HAR IQBAL SINGH
ARMOURED CORPS

"During the 1965 Indo-Pakistani War, on 8TH September, as the troop leader of the vanguard Squadron of the Poona Horse, Second Lieutenant Har Iqbal Singh Dhaliwal was leading the advance of his troop in Sialkot Sector in Pakistan. His first contact was made with five Pakistani Patton tanks on the north of Phillora crossroads. As he ordered his troops into firing positions, his tank was hit by direct fire from enemy tanks and burst into flames. He baled out with his crew and led them in the safety of a ditch. He saw that his driver had fallen down near the burning tank and was badly injured. With complete disregard of his personal safety, Lieutenant Dhaliwal ran forward under direct enemy fire, picked up the driver and brought him to safety. Then he led his full crew back to the rear of the Squadron position. In this action, Lieutenant Dhaliwal displayed exceptional courage and presence of mind and was a source of inspiration to all men under his command."

Vir Chakra (cont.)

NAIB RISALDAR BASTA SINGH
ARMOURED CORPS

"During the 1971 Indo-Pakistani War, Naib Risaldar Basta Singh was a troop leader in the 69TH Armoured Regiment during the operations in an area in the Eastern Sector. During the operations his troop came under heavy tank, artillery and anti-tank fire from the enemy position. With exceptional skill Naib Risaldar Basta Singh maneuvered his tank and knocked out an enemy tank and a 150-millimeter gun. Despite intense anti-tank, artillery and tank fire, Naib Risaldar Basta Singh was in the leading tank during the assault. When his tank was blown up he got into another tank and with total disregard for his safety, kept the leading the assault. The enemy was completely demoralized and abandoned the position in confusion and panic leaving behind many dead and a large quantity of equipment, ammunition and vehicles."

LIEUTENANT RAJVINDER SINGH CHEEMA
ARMOURED CORPS

"During the 1971 Indo-Pakistani War, Lieutenant Rajvinder Singh Cheema led his troop for the capture o certain areas in the Western Sector. He showed great skill and determination in crossing a bund and, undeterred by enemy fire, captured and enemy post. Even when isolated at night, he stuck to his position and repulsed enemy counter-attacks."

RISALDAR ACHHAR SINGH
ARMOURED CORPS

"During the 1965 Indo-Pakistani War, Risaldar Achhar Singh commanded a troop of Deccan Horse in the Punjab. When Deccan Horse took part in an attack on the Rohi Bund near Khem Karan, on Indian-Pakistan border, Risaldar Achhar Singh handled his troops with tact and courage. This resulted in the destruction of the enemy Regiment and made the operation a great success."

Risaldar Achhar Singh

Vir Chakra (cont.)

SECOND LIEUTENANT KANWARJIT SINGH (POSTHUMOUS)
ARMOURED CORPS

"During the 1971 Indo-Pakistani War, Second Lieutenant Kanwarjit Singh was commanding troops of Scinde Horse in the Shakargarh Sector. The squadron was ordered to attack the enemy holding Chakra crossing near the river Bein. Second Lieutenant Kanwarjit Singh closed in with the enemy positions despite stiff opposition and accurate anti-tank and artillery fire. In the fight he manoeuvred and handled his troop effectively and thus enabled the rest the squadron to locate and engage the enemy and inflicting considerable damage. He personally engaged and knocked out two enemy emplacements and a tank missile-launching site. While leading his troop, his tank became the target of concentrated fire. Undaunted, he remained in the open cupola of his tank directing operations and correcting the fire of his own tank when he was mortally wounded."

LANCE DAFADAR TARLOK SINGH
ARMOURED CORPS

"During the 1965 Indo-Pakistani War, Lance Dafadar Tarlok Singh destroyed four enemy tanks and one recoilless gun during an attack by 'A' squadron of the Deccan Horse in the Khem Karan Sector of the Punjab. On 12TH September, when his squadron was assaulting the enemy position on the Khem Karan distributaries, an enemy tank and gun were bringing down accurate fire on his squadron. Lance Dafadar Tarlok Singh attacked and destroyed the tank and the gun and thus enabled his squadron to send two tanks across the distributary."

SOWAR MOHAN SINGH
ARMOURED CORPS

"During the 1971 Indo-Pakistani War, Sowar Mohan Singh was gunner of a tank of 17TH Horse in the battle of the Basantar River in the Shakargarh Sector of Kashmir. On 16TH December 1971, the enemy armour put in a determined and fierce counter-attack. Sowar Mohan Singh, despite heavy odds, engaged numerous enemy tanks and personally accounted for five of them."

SQUADRON LEADER CHANDAN SINGH
INDIAN AIR FORCE

"During the 1962 Indo-China War, Squadron Leader Chandan Singh was detailed to carry out supply dropping in Chipchap area in Ladakh. On reaching the dropping area, he noticed that the outposts were under heavy fire from Chinese forces. He successfully dropped vital supplies to the garrison, although his aircraft was hit 19 times by enemy ground fire. Squadron Leader Chandan Singh displayed courage and devotion to duty in carrying out the task in complete disregard of his personal safety."

Vir Chakra (cont.)

MAJOR MALVINDER SINGH SHERGILL
ARMOURED CORPS

"During the 1971 Indo-Pakistani War, Major Malvinder Singh Shergill was commanding a squadron of 7th Cavalry in the Shakargarh Sector. On 8th December 1971, he was ordered to capture a railhead, which was held in strength by enemy infantry and armour. During the assault, he moved swiftly and captured the railhead despite heavy opposition and continued to hold the same till the infantry battalion moved forward and occupied it. During the period 7th to 12th December he led two missions against enemy armour and destroyed two tanks. On 13th December, his squadron was instrumental in throwing back elements of 20th Lancers and 33rd Cavalry of the Pakistani forces."

NAIB RISALDAR DAYAL SINGH
ARMOURED CORPS

"During the 1971 Indo-Pakistani War, Naib Risaldar Dyal Singh was a troop leader of Scinde Horse operating in Shakargarh Sector of Kashmir. His troop participated in the assault on an enemy position. Despite stiff enemy resistance he led the attack with courage and personally destroyed two enemy tanks. His bold action resulted in the capture of the objective."

RISALDAR KARTAR SINGH (POSTHUMOUS)
ARMOURED CORPS

"During the 1965 Indo-Pakistani War, Risaldar Kartar Singh commanded a troop of Poona Horse. On 11th September 1965, during the battle for the capture of Phillora in Pakistan, Risaldar Kartar Singh was the point troop leader when one of his tanks was suddenly hit and set on fire by enemy tanks at a range of approximately 600 yards. Risaldar Kartar Singh quickly appreciated that he was in an enemy ambush of tanks of approximately one squadron and recoilless guns. Disregarding his personal safety, he charged forward in his tank and shot and destroyed three Pakistani Patton tanks, thereby creating panic and confusion among enemy troops. When his tank was hit, he jumped out of the burning tank and under heavy enemy tank and artillery fire, rescued the injured crew and resumed his advance on the enemy with the two remaining tanks. While going in for the assault on Phillora ridge, the squadron came under recoilless gunfire from the flank. Risaldar Kartar Singh instantly changed direction and charged the recoilless gun position and silenced it. On 14th September, in the assault on Wazirwali, he repeated his earlier performance of rescuing the crew of a tank, which had been set ablaze by enemy fire. Throughout the action, he was subjected to intense small arms, mortar, and tank and artillery fire. Having rescued the crew he was mortally wounded when re-entering his tank."

Vir Chakra (cont.)

LANCE NAIK SARDAR SINGH (POSTHUMOUS)
THE GRENADIERS

"During the 1962 Indo-China War, on 20TH October, a Battalion of The Grenadiers was ordered to withdraw from a forward post in North East Frontier Agency. Lance Naik Sardar Singh was second- in -command of a section, which was deployed on the extreme flank of a Company. The Chinese troops, approximately a Company strong, had established themselves on the opposite bank of the Namkhachu River and had cut the withdrawal route by dominating the track leading back to Nathungla Pass. Lance Naik Sardar Singh's platoon was given the task of guarding the flank of the battalion position so as to prevent enemy interference with the withdrawal. Being in the forward most section, he ensured that the Section kept on firing at the enemy. He himself remained in the position till the whole Company had collected and withdrawn. While keeping the Chinese at bay he was mortally wounded. Lance Naik Sardar Singh made the supreme sacrifice for the safety of his comrades."

LIEUTENANT TEJA SINGH
THE JAMMU AND KASHMIR RIFLES

"During the 1965 Indo-Pakistani War, Lieutenant Tej Singh was in command of a Company of The Jammu and Kashmir Rifles in Khem Karan Sector of Indian-Pakistan border. On 6TH and 7TH September, in the face of heavy enemy ground and air shelling, he held on to his position and repulsed repeated enemy attacks. Running short of ammunition and water and in the absence of communication with his battalion headquarters, Lieutenant Tej Singh amidst heavy enemy shelling withdrew his men to safety. In this operation he displayed courage and leadership of a high order."

SECOND LIEUTENANT SURINDER PAL SINGH SEKHON
(POSTHUMOUS)
THE RAJPUTANA RIFLES

"During the 1965 Indo-Pakistani War, Lieutenant Surinder Pal Singh commanded a Company of The Rajputana Rifles. After a battalion of The Rajputana Rifles captured the bridge over river Ravi near Dera Baba Nanak on India-Pakistan border, the positions came under extremely heavy artillery fire as a result of which some men were wounded. During the shelling, 2ND Lieutenant Surinder Pal Singh Sekhon showed great courage and went round helping and dressing the wounded soldiers in his Company. While dressing one of the wounded soldiers, he was mortally wounded and died of his wounds. In this action, 2nd Lieutenant Sekhon showed exemplary devotion to duty and utmost concern for the men under his command, and thus upheld the highest traditions of the Indian Army."

Vir Chakra (cont.)

LIEUTENANT COLONEL AMRJEET SINGH BRAR
THE RAJPUTANA RIFLES

"During the 1971 Indo-Pakistani War, Lieutenant Colonel Amrjeet Singh Brar, was commanding a battalion of Rajputana Rifles, and was given the task of capturing important enemy position in Eastern Sector. Against heavy odds the attack was successfully carried out and the position held against fierce enemy counter-attacks. On 6TH December, the battalion surprised the enemy and captured all their troops without firing a single round, enabling the neighbouring formation to occupy that position. Again on 9TH December, Lieutenant Colonel Amrjeet Singh Brar led the battalion and captured the formidable Mynamati defences and held on against fierce enemy counter-attacks which were supported by tanks."

MAJOR PIARA SINGH
THE RAJPUT REGIMENT

"During 1947-1948 Indo-Pakistani conflict Major Piara Singh was in command of a Company of The Rajput Regiment. The Company was ordered to attack a very difficult hill feature on Kaman Gosha Dhar near Naushera, which was strongly held by the enemy. The attack was carried out with great dash and determination but it could not reach the top of the objective. The company suffered very heavily in casualties. Major Piara Singh, realizing the gravity of the situation, at once withdrew his company to 100 yards away from the objective. After reorganizing under the very nose of the enemy, he started to hit back with all the firepower of his company and was thus able to bring in the casualties from exposed ground. When the chance came for his Company to attack for the second time, Major Piara Singh personally led the attack and though hit by a bullet in the leg, went on leading his men to capture their objective. After the capture of the objective, he still refused to be evacuated until he was ordered to so by his commanding officer."

CAPTAIN GURCHARAN SINGH BHATIA
THE RAJPUT REGIMENT

"During the 1962 Indo-China War, Captain Gurcharan Singh Bhatia commanded a mortar section of The Rajput Regiment in Dhola area. On 20TH October, the mortar position of the battalion came under heavy artillery fire of the Chinese. Captain Gurcharan Singh Bhatia rushed to the mortar position and got the mortar section into action. The enemy was closing in under cover of artillery fire. When a shell landed close to one of the mortar pits and wounded the crew, he started firing the mortar himself. His cool courage and personal example were a source of inspiration to the men handling the mortars. Captain Bhatia continued firing until a barrage of enemy shells silenced the mortars."

Vir Chakra (cont.)

MAJOR MUKHTAR SINGH KHAIRA
THE DOGRA REGIMENT

"Major Mukhtiar Singh Khaira was in command of a reconnaissance patrol on the cease-fire line in Jammu and Kashmir. On 13TH December 1964, after negotiating a cliff, the patrol came upon a light machine gun position of the enemy. With complete disregard for his personal safety, Major Khaira, with one of his men crawled closer and threw two hand grenades on the gun. Almost simultaneously the machine gun fired three long busts towards the patrol party. Then the grenade exploded, and the machine gun stopped firing. Major Khaira and his companion, firing their Sten guns, charged the Pakistani Light Machine Gun. Six or seven Pakistani soldiers opened Sten gun and rifle fire on them. Undeterred by the numerical superiority of the enemy, Major Khaira and his companion threw two more grenades and fired at the Pakistani troops. The patrol captured the Pakistani Light Machine Gun and withdrew."

MAJOR DARSHAN SINGH LALLI (POSTHUMOUS)
THE DOGRA REGIMENT

"During the 1965 Indo-Pakistani War, Major Darshan Singh Lalli commanded a Company of The Dogra Regiment. During an advance on Haji Pir Pass on 20TH September, Major Darshan Singh Lalli was told to capture a feature defended by more than two enemy platoons. Despite heavy shelling and casualties, Major Lalli led a gallant charge and captured the objective and thereafter reorganized his position to bcat back any counter-attacks. The position was counter-attacked by nearly 250 personnel, supported by heavy artillery and Medium Machine Guns, but Major Lalli repulsed the attack with only 60 personnel, he himself going from bunker to bunker to encourage his men. One again when he was reorganizing his defences after Pakistani counter-attacks, he was killed by a burst of enemy Medium Machine Gun's fire."

SECOND LIEUTENANT PREMJIT SINGH CHIMA (POSTHUMOUS)
CORPS OF ENGINEERS

"During the 1965 Indo-Pakistani War, Second Lieutenant Premjit Singh Chima was with a field company in support of an infantry brigade group in Naya Chor area in the Rajasthan Sector. During the advance to Naya Choir, the tracks of a tank were damaged by anti-tank mine. Second Lieutenant Chima was ordered to make a safe lane in the minefield to retrieve the damaged tank. With complete disregard for his personal safety, he led his party for clearance of the lane. The enemy subjected the minefield clearance party to heavy machine gun and rifle fire. Undeterred Second Lieutenant Chima continued with the work and completed the task retrieving the tank. Subsequently while clearing another minefield near Parbat Ali, he was killed by a mine explosion.

Vir Chakra (cont.)

MAJOR BALJIT SINGH RANDHAWA (POSTHUMOUS)
THE RAJPUT REGIMENT

"During the 1965 Indo-Pakistani War, Major Baljit Singh Randhawa commanded a company of the Rajput Regiment in Kargil Sector. The company was ordered to attack a strongly held Pakistani position. As the company attacked it came under Heavy Mortar, Light Machine Gun and small arms fire. Without any regard for own safety, Major Randhawa led handful of men and succeeded in capturing the peak of the feature. While trying to destroy a Light Machine Gun Post, which was holding up further advance, he was mortally wounded by enemy fire. Even then he kept on encouraging his men to move forward."

LIEUTENANT JASBIR SINGH
THE GARHWAL RIFLES

"During the 1965 Indo-Pakistani War, Lieutenant Jasbir Singh was commanding a company of The Garhwal Rifles, which was ordered to clear an area in Rajasthan where the enemy had intruded after the cease-fire. After carrying out a nightlong march, the battalion reached a point behind the objective and assaulted the enemy position. Despite heavy enemy small arms and automatic fire, Lieutenant Jasbir Singh moved forward and continued fighting till the objective was cleared of intruders."

LIEUTENANT COLONEL KULDIP SINGH BRAR
THE MARATHA LIGHT INFANTRY

"During the 1971 Indo-Pakistani War, Lieutenant Colonel Kuldip Singh Brar was commanding a battalion of Maratha Light Infantry during the operation on the Eastern Front. His battalion was in the lead from 4TH to 16TH December 1971 and took major part in the liberation of Jamalpur. During the attack on Jamalpur on the night of 10TH December, Lieutenant Colonel Kuldip Singh Brar inspired his men to capture the objective. In the subsequent counter-attacks, he moved from one company locality to another, unmindful of his personal safety, encouraging his men to stand fast and beat back the enemy attacks. The enemy attacked six times but al these attacks were repulsed with heavy losses to the enemy in men and equipment."

MAJOR DAVINDER PAL SINGH
THE BIHAR REGIMENT

"During the 1971 Indo-Pakistani War, Major Davinder Pal Singh, commanding a company of Bihar Regiment, was assigned the task o capturing an enemy strong point in Eastern Sector. Despite intense shelling and small arms fires Major Davinder Pal Singh, with utter disregard for his safety, led his men and after fierce fighting captured the objective and a 105 medium machine gun."

Vir Chakra (cont.)

MAJOR HARPAL SINGH GREWAL (POSTHUMOUS)
THE BIHAR REGIMENT

"During the 1971 Indo-Pakistani War, Major Harpal Singh Grewal, officer commanding of a company of Bihar Regiment, was given the task of liquidating a well-fortified enemy post, which was held in great strength. During the assault his company came under heavy fire, but Major Grewal inspired his men to press home the attack. While leading the attack, Major Grewal was wounded by a burst from a machine gun. He, however, continued to lead the charge and liquidated the post. After the capture of the objective he succumbed to his injuries."

MAJOR HARDEV SINGH GREWAL (POSTHUMOUS)
THE JAT REGIMENT

"On 7TH December 1971, Major Hardev Singh Grewal was commanding a company of Jat Regiment deployed in a defensive position in the Chhamb Sector in Jammu and Kashmir. The enemy attacked and managed to get a foothold on one of his localities. He immediately launched a counter-attack and succeeded in restoring the situation and inflicting heavy casualties on the enemy. On 9TH December, the enemy again launched concerted infantry and armour assaults. Moving in the open in utter disregard if his safety, he encouraged his men and repulsed the attacks with heavy casualties to the enemy. On 10TH December, though wounded in the thigh, he continued to direct the operations. He was hit by and enemy machine gun bursts as a result of which he died."

COLONEL UMESH SINGH BAWA
THE JAT REGIMENT

Operation Vijay' was a name of the successful Indian operation to push back the Pakistani infiltrators from the Kargil Sector in 1999 Kargil war.

"During 'Operation Vijay', the Jats were asked to capture Pimple complex, a most dominating feature in the Mushkoh Valley. Colonel Bawa, the commanding officer of the unit planned an attack along the least expected and difficult approaches to surprise the enemy. Colonel Bawa led the attack from the front in a rare display of command and leadership qualities, motivated his men to achieve a near impossible military task against heavy odds. Under heavy enemy artillery, mortar and small arms fire. He took charge of the assaulting columns and personally supervised capture of four enemy positions that led to crumbling of enemy defences. The Jats, under his inspiring leadership also successfully repulsed the enemy counter attacks and capture of Pimple complex and another feature named Whaleback. The unit also recovered thirty-five weapons and twenty-two enemy dead bodies including that of an officer. Colonel Bawa displayed exemplary courage while leading from the front in the face of the enemy."

Vir Chakra (cont.)

SECOND LIEUTENANT BALJIT SINGH GILL
THE JAT REGIMENT

"During the 1971 Indo-Pakistani War, Second Lieutenant Baljit Singh Gill was in charge of a party of The Jat Regiment detailed to lay an ambush in Eastern Sector. He led his party by night and organised the ambush with professional competence. At dawn three enemy boats were sighted. Second Lieutenant Gill engaged the boats with accurate and effective fire and destroyed them. One officer and nine other ranks of the enemy were killed in the ambush."

MAJOR SARDUL SINGH RANDHAWA
THE LADAKH SCOUTS

"During the 1962 Indo-China War, on 17TH October when reports of a heavy Chinese concentration opposite post Chandni started coming in, Major Sardul Singh Randhawa was in command of Sub-Sector HQ in the area of Karakoram Pass and Chip Chap River in Northern Ladakh. He moved from one post to another in the face of enemy fire, inspiring confidence in his men and conducting operations credibly against overwhelming Chinese forces."

MAJOR SARLEJEET SINGH AHLUWALIA
THE LADAKH SCOUTS

"During the 1971 Indo-Pakistani War, Major Sarlejeet Singh Ahluwalia was commanding a company of Ladakh Scouts during the attack on enemy posts in an area in Western Sector. He led his company in an attack on an enemy post but came under intense enemy small arms fire and shelling. Despite all efforts, the attack failed to make progress. With fifteen other ranks, Major Ahluwalia moved across the fire - swept terrain and launched an attack from an unexpected direction and captured the objective, inflicting heavy casualties on the enemy."

MAJOR DALJEET SINGH SRA
THE MAHAR REGIMENT

"During the 1971 Indo-Pakistani War, Major Daljeet Singh Sra, commanding a company of Mahar Regiment, was detailed to establish a roadblock behind an enemy defensive position in an area in the Western Sector. Soon after the company column entered the enemy held territory, the leading platoon was fired at by an enemy machine gun. Major Sra ordered the other two platoons to get into firing position and he moved up to the area where the enemy fire held up the leading troops. At great personal risk he reformed his column and proceeded on his mission taking a different route. The timely and courageous action of Major Sra led to this successful establishment of the roadblocks, which inflicted heavy casualties on the enemy and resulted in capture of 12 Pakistani soldiers."

Vir Chakra (cont.)

LIEUTENANT COLONEL MANORANJAN SINGH
THE MAHAR REGIMENT

"Lieutenant Colonel Manoranjan Singh, commanding The Mahar Regiment, as part of Indian Peace Keeping Force in Sri Lanka, was tasked to capture Kopia North, a citadel of the militants from 13TH October onwards. His battalion made repeated attempts to capture this strongly held fortified militant's position, but met with strong resistance. Undaunted by the odds against him, Lieutenant Colonel Singh personally led the attack by his battalion on 18TH October 1987 and, after prolonged and bloody encounter, captured the prestigious stronghold. The battalion also captured intact factory of the militants for making explosive devices, 1000 Kilos of explosives were also seized."

SUB INSPECTOR AJIT SINGH
BORDER SECURITY FORCE

"During the 1971 Indo-Pakistani War, Sub-Inspector Ajit Singh was with the assaulting troops during an attack on a Pakistani position in the Western Sector. Medium machine guns fired at almost point-blank range on the advancing troops. Without regard to his safety, Ajit Singh rushed at one of the medium machine gun positions and grabbed the weapon from the enemy's hands and killed him. By his timely action in knocking out the medium machine gun, Ajit Singh ensured the success of the attack."

DEPUTY COMMANDANT JOGINDER SINGH (POSTHUMOUS)
BORDER SECURITY FORCE

"Deputy Commandant Joginder Singh was in charge of a post of the Border Security Force in Rajasthan Sector. On 17TH December 1971, he was assigned the task of organising fore support of the units taking up defensive positions west of Virawah. After reconnaissance, as his party was returning to Virawah, the enemy opened up from close range with heavy machine gun and mortar fire. He immediately jumped out of his vehicle and marshalling his small party, assaulted the enemy. Though hit by machine gun burst, he led his troops, fighting hand-to-hand till he succumbed to his injuries."

HEAD CONSTABLE MOHINDER SINGH (POSTHUMOUS)
BORDER SECURITY FORCE

"Head Constable Mohinder Singh was commanding a section post in the Western Sector. On 3RD December 1971, the enemy attacked the post with two rifle companies supported by divisional artillery. The enemy reached the wire obstacles surrounding his post. Undaunted and with utter disregard for his personal safety, he ran out of his trench and rallying his men charged at the enemy, killing four of them with his Sten gun. He continued to fight till he was seriously wounded by enemy LMG fire as a result of which he died."

Vir Chakra (cont.)

CAPTAIN RAVINDER SINGH CHOPRA
THE MADRAS REGIMENT

"During the operations in Sri Lanka in 1988, on 21ST April, Captain Ravinder Singh Chopra volunteered to accompany his Commanding Officer to intercept the militants at Urithirapuram. As they and their two platoons neared the target area, the militants fired upon them. In order to cover the move of his column, and also to pre-empt any attempt by the militants to escape, Captain Chopra along with his party manoeuvred to a flank in the face of intense automatic fire. He spotted a militant firing at the troops and with an accurate aim shot the militant dead. At this moment, the Commanding Officer was hit and collapsed, Captain Chopra rushed to the help of his Commanding Officer and in the process was himself hit by three or four bullets in his thighs, a graze across the chin and also a direct hit on his right hand, which shattered his right thumb and detached it from the hand. He also sustained two punctures on the front portion of his chest, despite these injuries, he continued to fire from his own weapon and to pass order to the platoon commanders directing their fire and movement. The militants eventually broke off action and withdrew. Captain Ravinder Singh Chopra reorganized his platoons and returned to the base, from where he was evacuated to hospital."

LIEUTENANT COLONEL ABJIT SINGH SEKHON (POSTHUMOUS)
THE MADRAS REGIMENT

"Lieutenant Colonel Abjit Singh Sekhon, Commanding Officer 7TH Madras Regiment, was deployed in Sri Lanka as part of the Indian Peace Keeping Force. On 13TH April 1988, he received information about location of an arms cache at a place called Vannerkulam and also the presence of some hard-core militants. He exercised imagination and calculated risk and approached to target areas in vehicles along a hitherto unmapped and sparsely used tract. He reached his target areas undetected and completely surprised the militants. In this action, Lieutenant Colonel Sekhon who was guiding the column killed two hard-core militants one of whom was found to be the Area Leader. Again on 21ST April 1988, when information was received about presence of 10 to 14 militants in village of Urithirapuran, he gathered two platoons and along with another officer, personally led the column to the site of the militants. The party came under intense fire from the militants. He jumped out of his vehicle and despite intense militant fire, organised his party and returned the fire. He personally shot dead one militant and wounded another. It was at this stage of encounter that Lieutenant Colonel Sekhon was hit by a militant's bullet through the chest and died on spot."

Vir Chakra (cont.)

SQUADRON LEADER GURSARAN SINGH AHLUWALIA
INDIAN AIR FORCE

"During the 1971 Indo-Pakistani War, Squadron Leader Gursaran Singh Ahluwalia was the senior flight commander of a bomber squadron. He was largely responsible for the planning, tactics, weapon delivery system and overall super supervision in the conduct of bomber operations of the unit. His planning and execution, which included leading seven missions into enemy territory and successfully completing them inspite of his aircraft being damaged on three missions due to heavy flak, acted as a source of inspiration to the air and ground crew."

FLIGHT LIEUTENANT APRAMJEET SINGH (POSTHUMOUS)
INDIAN AIR FORCE

"During the 1971 Indo-Pakistani War, Flight Lieutenant Apramjeet Singh flew 21 operational sorties consisting of escort and sweep missions deep inside enemy territory. On 4TH December 1971, he was detailed as No.2 on tactical reconnaissance mission in the Naya Chor-Umarkot-Dhornaro area. Near Naya Chor, he observed enemy vehicle convoys moving towards Dhornaro railway station. He immediately went in for as front gun attack and scored direct hits on the vehicles. His mission then flew over Dhornaro railway station and once again he attacked a goods train despite concentrated ground fire and caused considerable damage to the wagons. He pressed on with his third attack but while pulling up, his aircraft was damaged by ground fire. He brought the damaged aircraft under control and headed for base, which was about 100 miles away. Under compelling circumstances, he had to abandon the aircraft. In this operation, he made the supreme sacrifice."

FLIGHT LIEUTENANT SHIVINDER SINGH BAINS

During the 1971 Indo-Pakistani War, as a pilot in a fighter squadron, Flight Lieutenant Shivinder Singh Bains flew fourteen operational missions in the Poonch, Uri and Kargil Sectors in close support of the ground forces. He led missions deep into enemy territory in the face of heavy enemy ground opposition. He destroyed two enemy convoys of trucks in the Haji Pir Bulge. In one of the missions in the Poonch Sector, his aircraft hit the ground but he brought the aircraft back to base safely."

Vir Chakra (cont.)

SQUADRON LEADER IQBAL SINGH BINDRA
INDIAN AIR FORCE

" During the 1971 Indo-Pakistani War, Squadron Leader Iqbal Singh Bindra was commanding a detachment of a fighter-bomber squadron at a forward airfield. On 17TH December, while on a combat air patrol, he spotted one enemy F 104 approaching the airfield. He engaged it before it could launch an attack on the airfield. Finding tough opposition, the enemy aircraft abandoned the mission and attempted to escape but Squadron Leader Bindra pursued the aircraft and shot it down. In addition to carrying operational duties, he also ensured a high rate of aircraft serviceability."

SQUADRON LEADER CHARANJIT SINGH
INDIAN AIR FORCE

"During the 1971 Indo-Pakistani War, Squadron Leader Charanjit Singh undertook a large number of missions over the enemy territory and brought back very valuable information on enemy targets and dispositions. This greatly helped the planning and execution of operations. With full knowledge of the dangers involved, he volunteered and undertook these missions cheerfully. In these missions, he penetrated deep into enemy territory fearlessly during daytime."

FLIGHT LIEUTENANT MANJIT SINGH DHILLON
INDIAN AIR FORCE

"During the 1971 Indo-Pakistani War, Flight Lieutenant Manjit Singh Dhillon flew 50 sorties in the Chhamb, Shakargarh and Poonch Sectors. On 7TH December, he had to take off from Udhampur airfield when the enemy aircraft were in the vicinity. He skillfully manoeuvred the helicopter at very low height and achieved the mission successfully. On 10TH December, he undertook a sector reconnaissance flight and completed the task assigned to him despite heavy enemy fire. On the dame day, he evacuated 15 casualties and on 11TH December, he evacuated eight casualties from the Shakargarh Sector."

FLYING OFFICER SUKHDEV SINGH DHILLON

During the 1971 Indo-Pakistani War, Flying Officer Sukhdev Singh Dhillon flew as a pilot in a helicopter unit and single- handedly evacuated 87 battle casualties from the most difficult and hazardous terrain of the Kargil Sector in complete disregard of his personal safety. He carried out these evacuation missions in the face of heavy ground and air opposition."

Vir Chakra (cont.)

WING COMMANDER HARSER SINGH GILL (POSTHUMOUS)
INDIAN AIR FORCE

"During the 1971 Indo-Pakistani War, Wing Commander Harser Singh Gill led several operational missions on air defence, close support, and counter air operations during the period from 3RD to 13TH December. His squadron shot down one enemy F-194 aircraft over Jamnagar and hit another F 104 on 12TH December. Disregarding his personal safety, and with great courage and skill, he undertook strike missions over the Badin Signals unit complex in the face of intense enemy anti-aircraft fire. On 13TH December, he undertook another strike mission on the same target. During this attack his aircraft was shot down by enemy fire."

SQUADRON LEADER PREET PAL SINGH GILL

"During the 1971 Indo-Pakistani War, Squadron Leader Preet Pal Singh Gill carried out a number of successful night bombing missions over vital and heavily defended targets deep inside enemy territory, and caused severe damage to enemy installations notwithstanding heavy enemy opposition."

SQUADRON LEADER TEJ PRAKASH SINGH GILL
INDIAN AIR FORCE

"During the 1965 Indo-Pakistani War, Squadron Leader Tej Prakash Singh Gill led missions in support of the ground forces in the Sialkot, Chhamb, Lahore and Kasur Sectors. He took part in was many as 21 ground attacks. On 21ST September 1965, he encountered as very heavy barrage of anti-aircraft fire. Instead of breaking off the attack he pressed it home defiantly in utter disregard o his personal safety sand destroyed considerable number of enemy armour and field guns."

FLIGHT LIEUTENANT PERMINDER SINGH HARBANS
INDIAN AIR FORCE

"During the 1971 Indo-Pakistani War, Flight Lieutenant Perminder Singh Harbans was serving with a bomber squadron. On 5TH December, he was detailed on mission to raid an enemy airfield involving deep penetration into enemy territory, which had adequate radar coverage. The target was well defended by enemy fighters and anti-aircraft guns. Despite this he reached the target and bombed it with accuracy. He also successfully completed six other missions."

Vir Chakra (cont.)

FLIGHT LIEUTENANT LAL SINGH GREWAL
INDIAN AIR FORCE

"During 1947-1948 Indo-Pakistani conflict, Flight Lieutenant Lal Singh Grewal made a number of landings by day and night at Poonch while it was under enemy fire. He also dropped supplies of ammunition and rations in inclement weather to the garrisons in Kotli and Mirpur when these places were subjected to heavy enemy fire. He also captained aircraft during night bomb sorties. On 21ST March 1948, when Poonch was being shelled heavily by the enemy, he made two hazardous landings there, one by day and another by night, without any landing aids to deliver urgently required heavy guns and ammunition to the troops. He also flew in regularly the much-needed supplies to Leh."

SQUADRON LEADER JASBEER SINGH (POSTHUMOUS)
INDIAN AIR FORCE

"During the 1965 Indo-Pakistani War, Squadron Leader Jasbeer Singh was a Flight Commander in a fighter squadron operating in the Western Sector during the operations against Pakistan. On 7TH September 1965, he led a strike mission against a high-powered Pakistani radar unit near the Gujranwala airfield, which was greatly hampering air operations. As his formation was about to attack, he observed four enemy Sabre jets approaching in their flying formation. He immediately warned the formation but undaunted by the intercepting enemy aircraft of superior performance and intense ground fire, he pressed home his attack and inflicted severe damage to the radar station. In this final attack, when he had to approach the target very low, his aircraft was hit by ground fire and crashed near the target."

SQUADRON LEADER JASBIR SINGH
INDIAN AIR FORCE

"During the 1971 Indo-Pakistani War, Squadron Leader Jasbir Singh was a senior pilot of a fighter-bomber squadron. On 6TH December, he carried out a tactical reconnaissance mission deep behind the enemy lines in the Longewala area and brought back exhaustive information of vital importance, which altered the course of the battle in the area to advantage. Later on the same day he destroyed a tank and a large number of support vehicles in that area. Again on 9TH December, after carrying out another tactical reconnaissance, he attacked and destroyed four tanks despite heavy ground fire. His mission contributed significantly in neutralizing the enemy thrust in the area."

Vir Chakra (cont.)

SQUADRON LEADER JIWA SINGH (POSTHUMOUS)
INDIAN AIR FORCE

"During the 1971 Indo-Pakistani War, Squadron Leader Jiwa Singh led a formation to search and strike enemy tanks and troops, which were engaging the ground forces. He successfully located the hidden tank position and pressed home his attacks even though four enemy aircraft encircled his section. He engaged an enemy F-104 in and aerial combat so that his No.2 could get away to safety. In the combat, his aircraft was shot at low level as a result of which he was killed."

SQUADRON LEADER AJIT SINGH LAMBA
INDIAN AIR FORCE

"During the 1965 Indo-Pakistani War, as a Hunter pilot, Squadron Leader Ajit Singh Lamba flew total of 15 operational sorties, 11 in close support of the army in the Kasur and Lahore Sectors. He showed great skill and determination in seeking out enemy targets and pressing home his attacks in spite of intense ground fire and the presence of enemy interceptor aircraft. He successfully destroyed several enemy tanks and vehicles. His achievement in the destruction of enemy guns and armour near Harbanspura railway station was especially noteworthy because of the heavy defences surrounding these locations. Throughout the operations, Squadron Leader Ajit Singh Lamba showed marked keenness for action and was always an immediate and ready volunteer for any mission."

FLIGHT LIEUTENANT AMARJEET SINGH KULLAR
INDIAN AIR FORCE

" During the 1965 Indo-Pakistani War, Flight Lieutenant Amarjeet Singh Kullar flew in a four-aircraft formation, which destroyed a supply train at Raiwind railway station. The train was carrying badly needed supplies by the enemy forces in the Kasur region. The denial of this vital supply was a major factor in causing the withdrawal of enemy armour with very heavy losses. During seven other operational sorties, Flight Lieutenant Kullar destroyed or damaged at least six enemy tanks, armoured vehicles and gun emplacements. He carried out his attacks fearlessly against heavily defended enemy positions and his aircraft was hit by ground fire on three different occasions."

Vir Chakra (cont.)

FLIGHT LIEUTENANT PARMINDER PAUL SINGH KWATRA
INDIAN AIR FORCE

"During the 1971 Indo-Pakistani War, Flight Lieutenant Parminder Paul Singh Kwatra was attached to a fighter squadron. He flew several missions including three as mission leader in Poonch, Uri, Tithwal and Kargil Sectors, and successfully completed his missions. On 15TH and 16TH December, while engaged in attacks on the enemy posts, his aircraft engines flamed out but he continued the attack after relighting the engines. On 15TH December during and enemy raid on one of our airfields, the camouflage net covering a blast pen caught fire. He rushed to the spot and extinguished the fire."

FLIGHT LIEUTENANT HAMIR SINGH MANGAT
INDIAN AIR FORCE

"During the 1971 Indo-Pakistani War, Flight Lieutenant Hamir Singh Mangat, a Navigator in an Operational Bomber Squadron, successfully navigated by day and night a number of leader and marker aircraft on hazardous offensive and tactical close support mission deep into the Pakistan territory. Despite intense enemy fire and grave danger to his personal safety, he stuck to his post with cool courage and firm determination and accurately navigated the aircraft to their targets to carry out their vital missions. The courage and devotion to duty of Squadron Leader Sandhu are in the best traditions of the Indian Air Force."

SQUADRON LEADER INDERJEET SINGH PARMAR
INDIAN AIR FORCE

"During the 1965 Indo-Pakistani War, Squadron Leader Inderjeet Singh Parmar carried out 16 operational sorties, of which seven were low-level reconnaissance over enemy concentrations. During these missions, he operated at the extreme limits of the aircraft's radius of action. On the night of 14TH September he flew four combat sorties in quick succession. Single-handedly he succeeded in obstructing enemy bombers and putting them off bombing our airfield and vital radar installations. In two cases he chased the enemy bombers away before they could drop their bombs."

LIEUTENANT MOHAN SINGH
ASSAM REGIMENT

"During the 1971 Indo-Pakistani War, Lieutenant Mohan Singh was assigned the task of capturing an enemy medium machine gun post in the Amritsar Sector. In spite of intense enemy fire, Lieutenant Mohan Singh led his men to successful completion of the task in utter disregard for his own safety. He was personally responsible for silencing the Medium Machine Gun by lobbying a grenade into the post. In this action, Lieutenant Mohan Singh displayed gallantry, leadership and devotion to duty of a high order."

Vir Chakra (cont.)

WING COMMANDER MANMOHAN SINGH
INDIAN AIR FORCE

"During the 1971 Indo-Pakistani War, Wing Commander Manmohan Singh was in command of an operational fighter squadron in the Eastern Sector. He personally led 19 sorties and successfully engaged enemy defence positions, gunboats and ships despite heavy ground fire. His squadron provided very effective air cover for the successful completion of the task. In addition the squadron provided close support to the Army."

SQUADRON LEADER KIRPAL SINGH
INDIAN AIR FORCE

"During the 1971 Indo-Pakistani War, Squadron Leader Kirpal Singh, with utter disregard for his safety, carried out 9 successful operational sorties in the face of stiff enemy air and ground opposition. The information obtained from these sorties proved of great value to our air and ground forces in taking swift action to deal with enemy concentrations."

FLIGHT LIEUTENANT MANBIR SINGH
INDIAN AIR FORCE

"During the 1971 Indo-Pakistani War, Flight Lieutenant Manbir Singh, served with and operational squadron in Eastern Sector. He flew 20 sorties in counter air and offensive support missions over Bangladesh. He engaged enemy aircraft successfully forcing them to break off their attacks on the main formation. He executed bombing missions against heavily defended airfields and bomb strikes against a variety of targets. Guns of varying calibre protected these targets, and on more than one occasion his aircraft was hit by ground fire."

FLIGHT LIEUTENANT GURDEV SINGH RAI (POSTHUMOUS)
INDIAN AIR FORCE

"During the 1971 Indo-Pakistani War, Flight Lieutenant Gurdev Singh Rai was serving with as fighter-bomber squadron in the Western Sector. On 4TH December, he successfully carried out a strike mission on the Sakesar Signals unit's complex. The next day, he was detailed leader of the repeat strike mission. He exhibited conspicuous courage and determination in the face of strong enemy opposition and succeeded in damaging the radar unit to the extent that it went off the air completely. But unfortunately he could not be contacted thereafter."

Vir Chakra (cont.)

SQUADRON LEADER JASJIT SINGH

"During the 1971 Indo-Pakistani War, Squadron Leader Jasjit Singh flew a number of operational missions over heavily defended enemy areas. In spite of heavy ground opposition, he pressed on his attacks and destroyed a number of enemy tanks, gun positions and bunkers."

SQUADRON LEADER RAJBIR SINGH
INDIAN AIR FORCE

"Squadron Leader Rajbir Singh was with the Indian Air Force of the Indian Peace Keeping Force in Sri Lanka. On 3RD November 1987, Squadron Leader Singh was detailed to strike the militant's strongholds, which were impeding the advance of a Para Commando Regiment towards Mulai. On reaching the area he was directed to attack a stronghold, which was heavily defended with heavy machine guns. In spite of heavy ground fire, he carried out repeated front gun attacks with deadly accuracy. During this third attack on as machine gun nest, the aircraft was hit by ground fire. After pulling out of the attack, he noticed that the left engine was damaged and had heavy oil leak. He immediately switched off the left engine and established flight on a single engine to avoid engine fire. Though the aircraft was heavily loaded with ammunition he decided not to jettison the much-needed armament stores. Squadron Leader Rajbir Singh realised that he was flying over a very hostile area and a forced landing would result in captures by the militants. He kept absolutely calm, and nursed the aircraft back in a very professional manner. He tried to contact base Radio Telephony but the radio set also had been damaged by ground fire. In spite of heavy traffic over base, he landed the aircraft on as single engine, without causing any damage to the aircraft."

FLIGHT LIEUTENANT KULDEEP SINGH SAHOTA
INDIAN AIR FORCE

"During the 1971 Indo-Pakistani War, as a pilot of a fighter-bomber squadron, Flight Lieutenant Kuldeep Singh Sahota flew thirteen missions in support of the ground forces. He destroyed four enemy tanks and a few heavy guns. On two occasions, information brought by him about enemy tank concentrations in the Chhamb-Jaurian Sector resulted in planning of subsequent missions, which destroyed theses enemy tanks."

Vir Chakra (cont.)

SQUADRON LEADER AMAR JIT SINGH SANDHU
INDIAN AIR FORCE

"During the 1965 Indo-Pakistani War, Squadron Leader Amar Jit Singh Sandhu was the Flight Commander of an Operational Squadron which was assigned the task of establishing our air superiority over Pathankot region during the operations against Pakistan. He flew repeated missions in the Chhamb Sector and over Pasrur and Lahore areas, all the time seeking out enemy aircraft and engaging them. On 18TH September 1965, in a thrilling encounter against enemy aircraft he was able to outmanoeuvre the enemy with admirable skill, courage and judgment, and shot down a Sabre-jet. The courage and devotion to duty of Squadron Leader Sandhu are in the best traditions of the Indian Air Force."

FLIGHT LIEUTENANT CHARANJIT SINGH SANDHU
INDIAN AIR FORCE

"During the 1971 Indo-Pakistani War, Flight Lieutenant Charanjit Singh Sandhu was in command of a helicopter unit. On 7TH December, he personally led a special heliborne operation deep behind the enemy position in the Eastern Sector. During the first mission his force came under enemy fire but he successfully carried out the landing of his force. The same night, he flew and additional five similar missions. During the operations, he led a total of 34 such hazardous missions."

FLIGHT LIEUTENANT MOHINDER SINGH SANDHU
INDIAN AIR FORCE

"During the 1971 Indo-Pakistani War, Flight Lieutenant Mohinder Singh Sandhu flew a number of operational reconnaissance missions over enemy territory. On 4TH December he was detailed for an air mission over Sargodha at night. He carried out this mission successfully, causing extensive damage to enemy installations."

FLIGHT LIEUTENANT HAMIR SINGH MANGAT
INDIAN AIR FORCE

"During the 1971 Indo-Pakistani War, Flight Lieutenant Hamir Singh Mangat, a Navigator in an Operational Bomber Squadron, successfully navigated by day and night a number of leader and marker aircraft on hazardous offensive and tactical close-support mission deep in the enemy territory. Despite intense enemy fire and grave danger to his personal safety, he stuck to his post with cool courage and firm determination and accurately navigated the aircraft to their targets to carry out their vital missions. The courage and devotion to duty of Squadron Leader Sandhu are in the best traditions of the Indian Air Force."

Vir Chakra (cont.)

FLIGHT LIEUTENANT MANJIT SINGH SEKHON
INDIAN AIRFORCE

"During the 1971 Indo-Pakistani War, Flight Lieutenant Manjit Singh Sekhon was commanding a detachment of a frontline fighter squadron. He flew 14 missions at a low height in very difficult terrain of Jammu and Kashmir and caused extensive damage to several enemy bunkers, vehicles, guns mortar position, petrol and ammunition dumps. He carried out these missions in the face of heavy ground fire. He substantially contributed to the success of the ground forces in Kargil, Tithwal, Poonch, and Uri Sectors."

FLIGHT LIEUTENANT TRILOCHAN SINGH
INDIAN AIR FORCE

"During the 1971 Indo-Pakistani War Flight Lieutenant Trilochan Singh was Deputy Flight Commander in an Operational Squadron, flew 14 operational sorties against Pakistan. He carried out his mission in the face of heavy enemy ground fires and air opposition, and succeeded in destroying a considerable number of camouflaged enemy tanks and heavy guns. He gave effective air support to the ground forces and carried out successfully air strikes on the any armour, troop concentration and convoys. Throughout the operations, Flight Lieutenant Trilochan Singh displayed courage, determination and professional skill of a high order."

COMMANDER RAJINDER SINGH GREWAL
INDIAN NAVY

"During the 1971 Indo-Pakistani War, Commander Rajinder Singh Grewal was the commander in charge of all flying operations from INS Vikrant. The wind off Bangladesh during these operations was such that it made the taking off of aircraft from the Vikrant very difficult. Commander Grewal, however, continued to fly fighter-bombers and anti-submarine aircraft from this ship regularly. It was largely due to him that the two aircraft shot down by the enemy were recovered despite the fact that the wind conditions for recovery were extremely hazardous."

LIEUTENANT RAMINDER SINGH SODHI
INDIAN NAVY

"During the 1971 Indo-Pakistani War Lieutenant Raminder Singh Sodhi was the pilot of an Indian Naval Aircraft, which carried out repeated strikes on enemy ports in Bangladesh. He carried out eight strikes on the heavily defended ports of Chittagong, Khulna and Mongla. Although his aircraft was hit by enemy fire he continued his attack and led his section until one enemy ship and port oil installations were set on fire. On 11TH December he was with the force, which attacked Chittagong harbour. Despite heavy enemy anti-aircraft fire, he destroyed two oil tanks and shore installations."

KIRTI CHAKRA

Kirti Chakra is a military decoration awarded for self-sacrifice and gallantry away from the battlefield and comes after Ashok Chakra.

MAJOR INDERJEET SINGH BABBAR (POSTHUMOUS)

"In June 2003, Major Inderjeet Singh Babbar commanded troops of Red Horns Division, to seek-and-destroy militant separatists of 'United Liberation Front of Asom' in the state of Assam of India. Sentries were placed on the escape routes and a search party under Major Babbar approached a village to search a specific house. As the search party approached the house, it came under heavy automatic fire from the house. Major Babbar, in a swift action, charged into the house from where the militants had opened fire. In the ensuing encounter he sustained grievous injuries to his abdomen as he shot dead the militant. Meanwhile another militant from the adjacent house opened fire at Major Babbar. Undaunted and in complete disregard for his personal safety he continued to engage the militants, and killed the second militant. In spite of his critical injuries and profuse bleeding, Major Babbar, in the highest traditions of the Indian Army, refused to be evacuated and continued to systematically destroy the militant hideout. The third militant, who tried to flee while firing, was also injured by Major Babbar and later shot dead by one of the sentries. The dead militants were identified as self-styled lieutenant Ajit Saikia alias Kausher Ali, and Bhairab Deka. In this unparalleled act of raw courage Major Babbar killed two hardcore militants and succeeded in destroying the their hideout. In a search of the area the Army recovered one 7.62 mm universal machine gun with one box cylindrical magazine, one rifle AK-56 with three magazine, 290 live rounds, 109 rounds of fired cases, one Chinese grenade, three detonators with safety fuse, a large quantity of medicines, and four rucksacks with personal belongings. Major Babbar made the supreme sacrifice as he succumbed to his injuries."

'The United Liberation Front of Asom' is a separatist group from Assam in Northeast of India. It seeks to establish a sovereign Assam state via an armed struggle. The Government of India banned the organization in 1990 and classifies it as a terrorist group.

Kirti Chakra (cont.)

HAVILDAR MANJIT SINGH
16TH BATTALION, SIKH REGIMENT

"On 29TH June 2006, Havildar Manjit Singh was commander of an ambush party comprising four soldiers at a grid point in Northern Sector of India. At approximately 1915 hours movement of terrorists was observed near Line of Control. The ambush was re-sited to cover the likely route of infiltration. The weather was bad and visibility was very poor. On 30TH June the ambush party waited patiently for the infiltrating terrorists to come into the killing ground. At 0020 hours when the terrorists advanced, Havildar Manjit Singh opened fire. The terrorists retaliated with a heavy volume of fire and tried to escape. Havildar Manjit Singh had laid improvised obstacles to trap the terrorists. He immediately asked for illumination and engaged the fleeing terrorists. He exercised strict fire control and personally killed five terrorists."

NAIB SUBEDAR TRILOK SINGH
RASHTRIYA RIFLES

On the 12TH March 2003, Naib Subedar Trilok Singh was awarded the Kirti Chakra for his exemplary gallantry against the militants in Jammu and Kashmir.

LIEUTENANT KANAVDEEP SINGH (POSTHUMOUS)
10TH BATTALION, THE SIKH REGIMENT

"Lt Kanavdeep Singh led his platoon to the rescue of an ambushed patrol party but was pinned down by fire from another group of terrorists in an inaccessible position. The officer, who had managed to kill one hostile, ignored his considerable injuries to crawl over to and operate the rocket launcher to kill one and injure the third terrorist, before succumbing to his injuries." Lt Kanavdeep Singh was posthumously awarded the Kirti Chakra.

MR. SWARN SINGH BOPARAI
INDIAN ADMINISTRATIVE SERVICE

Mr. Swarn Singh Boparai was decorated with the most prestigious National awards, the Kirti Chakra and Padma Shri. During his long stint in the Indian Administrative Service he held many eminent positions, beginning with Deputy Commissioner of Patiala and later of Ferozepore. It was as Deputy Commissioner of Ferozepore that Mr. Boparai received the Padma Shri award for distinguished service during 1971 Indo-Pak War. Soon thereafter, in 1975, he was decorated with Kirti Chakra for acts of conspicuous gallantry in a serious law-and-order situation created by Lal Kurti Dal in Ferozepore District in November 1973. The outlaws had killed fifteen persons and injured thirteen others and torched the village of Alamgarh. The action of Mr. Boparai resulted in a bloodless arrest of the culprits, 158 in number, armed with a deadly arsenal comprising hand grenades, firearms, swords, axes, etc.

Kirti Chakra (cont.)

NAIK MUKHTIAR SINGH
4TH JAMMU AND KASHMIR INFANTRY

"On the night of 18TH/19TH March 1956, the position occupied by Indian troops on the Bela at Hussainiwala Head works, near Ferozepore on the Indo-Pakistani Border, was attacked. The attackers managed to secure a foothold on the Bela from the left flank. Naik Mukhtiar Singh personally led his section through heavy automatic fire to the threatened flank and stem the enemy advance. He killed two attackers, captured their rifles and led his section to secure the Bela. Whilst his section was securing the Bela, a hand grenade landed near him in the midst of his section. In order to save his section, he lifted the grenade with his left hand and tried to throw it back on the attackers. The grenade exploded and his left elbow was blown off. Though seriously wounded, he continued to exhort his men to fight on and refused to be evacuated. Naik Mukhtiar Singh, by his high example of personal leadership, courage and complete disregard for his personal safety, averted a disaster to his section and to the Bela Position." Naik Mukhtiar Singh was awarded the Kirti Chakra for his conspicuous gallantry in action.

COLONEL GURBIR SINGH SARNA (POSTHUMOUS)
RASHTRIYA RIFLES

"Colonel Gurbir Singh Sarna was Commanding Officer of a Rashtriya Rifles unit and led from the front during operation Chak Behrampura. On December 23RD 2006, he personally led to the elimination of hardcore terrorists in the Patan District of Jammu and Kashmir. Based on hard intelligence regarding the presence of four terrorists in a village, Colonel Sarna reached the spot along with his team of officers and cordoned off the targeted house. While the search was on, Colonel Sarna personally broke open the hideout and challenged the terrorists. He was the first to sight the terrorists in the hideout. The firefight between the officer and the terrorist started at very close range and resulted in the killing of one terrorist and injuring another. However, in the process, Colonel Sarna received multiple bullet injuries. Though bleeding profusely, he shouted to his men to leave him and passed instructions to continue the operation, which led to the elimination of other terrorists. He later succumbed to his injuries." Colonel Sarna was posthumously awarded the Kirti Chakra

NAIB SUBEDAR JAGROOP SINGH
28TH BATTALION, THE PUNJAB REGIMENT

On the 14TH August 1999 Naib Subedar Jagroop Singh of the 28TH Battalion, The Punjab Regiment was conferred the Kirti Chakra posthumously for taking part in the series of counter-insurgency operations in Jammu and Kashmir.

Kirti Chakra (cont.)

MAJOR JOGINDER SINGH TANWAR
RIFLE COMPANY

"Major Joginder Singh Tanwar, commanding a Rifle Company deployed in the Kalaruch Valley in Kupwara District in Jammu and Kashmir, had developed a very effective intelligence network in his area. On August 12TH 1999, a seek-and-destroy mission was launched in the Rangat forest. On August 13TH, while carrying out a search, Major Tanwar noticed a group of militants. He immediately opened fire, killing one militant on the spot. The panic-stricken militants started fleeing with Major Tanwar and his group in hot pursuit. Braving the rain of bullets, Major Tanwar kept firing. One more militant was killed during a firefight, which lasted almost one hour. Keeping track of militants in his area, Major Tanwar killed another militant on August 20TH. The operation was planned and coordinated so well that the troops did not suffer any casualty and arms and ammunition were also recovered from the militants. On September 8TH, Major Tanwar was tasked to lead a small team to seek and destroy militants likely to be hiding in Buinar. At about 1100 hours four militants opened heavy fire from a dominating position at close range, injuring Major Tanwar's left hand. Unmindful of his grievous injury, he took position behind a boulder and opened heavy and accurate fire with his right hand, killing three militants on the spot." Major Joginder Singh Tanwar thus displayed conspicuous gallantry, outstanding courage, dogged determination and exceptional leadership in fighting the militants for which he was awarded the Kirti Chakra.

CAPTAIN SAJJAN SINGH MALIK (POSTHUMOUS)
10TH PARA (SPECIAL FORCES)

Captain Sajjan Singh Malik of the 10TH Para (Special Forces) was posthumously awarded the Kirti Chakra. He was killed while battling terrorists in Gundpura village of Bandipur Tehsil in Baramulla, Jammu and Kashmir. He killed three terrorists in the encounter, before being killed himself.

The citation states: "Skillfully tracking the movement of a group of terrorists for a month, he laid a trap in Gundpura village in Baramulla District on the night of July 7TH. As the terrorists were leaving the village in the early hours the next day, he sprang the ambush. In the firefight he personally killed two terrorists in the narrow by-lanes of the village but in the process received three bullet injuries. Ignoring his injuries, he motivated his troops to surround and prevent the third terrorist from escaping. Lobbing grenades and with tremendous effort he closed in on the third terrorist, killing him at close quarters. He, however, succumbed to his injuries, sacrificing his life in the best traditions of the Indian Army."

Kirti Chakra (cont.)

SUBEDAR NASIB SINGH
THE SIKH LIGHT INFANTRY

"On 23RD May 1956, 'A' Company, 3RD Battalion, The Sikh Light Infantry, was given the task to clear Sihama Village in Nagaland, where the hostiles had established a camp. The village was located on a ridge, which had a very steep gradient. Subedar Nasib Singh was leading No. 2 Platoon of the Company for the operation. As they advanced along a narrow path surrounded by jungle about 500 yards short of the village they came under heavy fire from the hostiles from a close quarter, wounding the Section Commander. The section was pinned down and hostiles were causing further casualties. Subedar Nasib Singh, realizing the gravity of the situation, decided to lead the attack from a flank, hacking his way through the jungle. He was severely wounded in the leg but unmindful of his injury, charged the hostile position killing one and wounding another. He finally cleared the position by throwing a grenade and injuring one more hostile. The other hostiles withdrew to the village or melted away in the jungle. Subedar Nasib Singh's courageous action heartened his platoon, which went through the area, cleared the village from where the hostiles were still sniping, and recovered a large quantity of arms and ammunition." Subedar Nasib Singh, by his daring leadership and inspiring action, despite being severely wounded, displayed an excellent example of gallantry and courage for which he was awarded the Kirti Chakra"

CAPTAIN MEHTA SINGH (POSTHUMOUS)
THE SIKH LIGHT INFANTRY

"On 25TH August 1956, 'C' Company 3RD Battalion, The Sikh Light Infantry under Captain Mehta Singh was sent to secure Khonama in Nagaland, where the hostiles were holding the highest point of the village in strength. The company, by sheer dauntless courage, held on to the lower half of the village for nearly a month. It was surrounded by the hostiles and it was a problem even getting drinking water. Realizing the mounting pressure against the company, 17TH Rajput Regiment was ordered to relieve it. On 28TH August 1956, the hostiles, seeing the concentration of Rajputs, tried to inch near 'D' company with a view of making the relief impossible. Captain Mehta Singh, realizing the threat to his company and to the relieving unit, mounted a counter-attack to clear the company. The men of 'D' Company, after the month-long siege, continuous sniping by the hostiles, and irregular supply, had almost reached the point of exhaustion. Captain Mehta Singh, by his cool courage and fearlessness, led his company in a daring assault in which hand-to-hand fighting ensued and the hostiles were pushed back. The brave Mehta Singh, often called the "Hero of Kohima", fell mortally wounded in the stomach by a burst of machine-gun fire while leading the assault." Captain Mehta Singh was posthumously awarded the Kirti Chakra.

Kirti Chakra (cont.)

SEPOY SATNAM SINGH (POSTHUMOUS)
THE SIKH LIGHT INFANTRY

"On the night of $12^{TH}/13^{TH}$ March 1992, 7TH Battalion, Sikh Light Infantry was tasked to launch a major cordon and search operation in the area of Kakrali in the Ropar District of Punjab. Sepoy Satnam Singh was a member of the combing party led by Naib Subedar Bakshish Singh. On 13TH March, while the combing party was approaching a tube well, six militants armed with AK-47 rifles engaged them at a very close range. The combing party immediately returned the fire. The militants, while firing, attempted to escape by dashing towards nearby sugarcane fields. On seeing this, Sepoy Satnam Singh leapt forward and closed in with the militants, killing one of them and was injured in the ensuing close quarter battle. However, with utter disregard to his personal safety and profusely bleeding, he kept fighting and came face to face with the militant leader, the self-styled Lieutenant General Jarnail Singh alias Jaila, and shot him dead. He then lobbed a grenade, inflicting injuries on the escaping militants. However, at that very moment, he received a burst of AK-47 fire on his forehead killing him instantly. Due to this act of gallantry and the subsequent actions of the search party, an A-grade hard-core terrorist and five of his gang were eliminated. Three AK-47 rifles, three pistols, a revolver and a large quantity of ammunition were recovered. The dreaded gang of the Khalistan Liberation Force led by Jarnail Singh was responsible for killing nearly 150 people in the District. The elimination of this dreaded gang brought peace and normalcy to Ropar District. Sepoy Satnam Singh displayed conspicuous bravery and pre-eminent valour while making the supreme sacrifice." Sepoy Satnam Singh was posthumously awarded the Kirti Chakra.

SEPOY BALBIR SINGH (POSTHUMOUS)
22ND BATTALION, THE PUNJAB REGIMENT

On 14TH August 1999 Sepoy Balbir Singh was posthumously awarded Kirti Chakra for exemplary leadership and personal valour. He was killed fighting the terrorists in the operations in Jammu and Kashmir.

CAPTAIN SUKHWINDER JEET SINGH RANDHAWA (POSTHUMOUS)
167TH FIELD REGIMENT

Capt. Sukhwinder Jeet Singh Randhawa, an Army Officer of 167 Fd. Regt. made the supreme sacrifice of his life while combating militants in Jammu and Kashmir. He was awarded Kirti Chakra for displaying exemplary courage and an indomitable fighting spirit.

Kirti Chakra (cont.)

SEPOY MOHINDER SINGH
THE SIKH LIGHT INFANTRY

"On 4TH April 1956, the Naga insurgents had surrounded a patrol of 3RD Battalion, The Sikh Light Infantry. Two companies were tasked to break the cordon and establish contact with the patrol. As they attacked the insurgents and Hand-to-hand fighting then ensued, Sepoy Mohinder Singh saw two Nagas running away with a light machine-gun. Not caring for his own safety, he chased and killed them both single handedly with his bayonet." Sepoy Mohinder Singh displayed dauntless courage of the highest order for which he was awarded the Kirti Chakra.

SEPOY CHUHAR SINGH
THE SIKH LIGHT INFANTRY

"On 31ST May 1960, Sepoy Chuhar Singh, of 4TH Battalion, The Sikh Light Infantry, was proceeding on duty in the Naga Hills Tuensang Area, accompanied by two other soldiers, when his jeep was ambushed by about 40 hostiles and he was wounded in the stomach and forehead. Although bleeding profusely, he took up position with another soldier and returned fire. Later, he sent the second soldier to liase for help and continued to man his gun, keeping the hostiles at bay until reinforcements arrived. His vehicle was riddled with 37 bullet-holes. In this encounter, Sepoy Chuhar Singh saved the lives of his comrades, his vehicle and a large quantity of arms and ammunition." For his sustained bravery, cool courage and utter disregard of his personal safety he was awarded the Kirti Chakra.

WING COMMANDER DALJIT SINGH MINHAS (POSTHUMOUS)
INDIAN AIR FORCE

"On 5TH April 1988, Wing Commander Minhas was piloting a Hawker Hunter fighter when he experienced an engine flameout just 200 feet above the ground. He guided the aircraft away from a village and stayed with the aircraft to make sure it did not cause any loss of life on ground. He ejected from the Hunter at a very low level, as a result of which his parachute did not open and he died in the crash." Wing Commander Minhas was posthumously awarded Kirti Chakra.

COMMANDO SURJAN SINGH

National Security Guard Commando Surjan Singh was awarded the Kirti Chakra for his role in the Akshardham shoot-out, suffering grievous injuries during the operation.

(After lying in a coma for 600 days, Surjan Singh died on May 19, 2004.)

At least 33 persons were killed and 76 injured in an attack by Pakistan-based terrorists on the famous Akshardham temple on September 24, 2002. The National Security Guard commandos gunned down all the terrorists in a nightlong battle.

Kirti Chakra (cont.)

LIEUTENANT COLONEL JASWANT SINGH
RAJPUT REGIMENT

"Early in August 1955, Lieutenant Colonel Jaswant Singh was ordered to restore law and order at Khikya in the South Tuensang Frontier Division of the North-East Frontier Agency, where the hostiles had entrenched themselves into a strong base. By forced marches on three successive nights, Colonel Jaswant Singh, led his patrols in non-stop heavy rain along steep hills, covered by and impregnable jungle. The hostiles had laid Punjis (a covered pit with bamboo spikes sharpened to a needle point) up to two miles in front of the main positions and built stone stockades covering all the approaches. Twice the patrols ran into ambushes, and on both occasions Lieutenant Colonel Jaswant Singh personally led the charge against the hostiles and succeeded in getting his party out without suffering any casualties. He once fell into a punji and was injured but continued to lead his patrols. These courageous actions of the Commanding Officer were a source of inspiration to his men, who, though weary without sleep or proper food for three days, followed him cheerfully. When stiff opposition temporarily halted his troops, Lieutenant Colonel Jaswant Singh was found among the leading company, exhorting his men in the face of heavy automatic fire. In this action, 35 hostiles were killed and a similar number wounded, and the entire area was cleared of the hostiles." For his leadership and conspicuous gallantry Lieutenant Colonel Jaswant Singh Jaswant Singh was awarded the Kirti Chakra.

FLIGHT LIEUTENANT KARAN SHER SINGH KALSIA
(POSTHUMOUS)
INDIAN AIR FORCE

"On 19th January 1961, while on a training flight, Flight Lieutenant Kalsia found that the engine of his aircraft had flamed out. The aircraft was heading towards Jamnagar city and had he bailed out and abandoned the aircraft, it would have crashed in the city, causing extensive damage to life and property. Realising this, Flight Lieutenant Kalsia turned his aircraft away from the populated area and in doing so lost valuable height. He then attempted a force landing as he was left with no other option and was killed in the attempt. Flight Lieutenant Kalsia displayed courage of a very high order and gave his own life to avoid an accident, which might have resulted in the loss of several other lives. His gallant action was in the highest traditions of the Air Force." Flight Lieutenant Kalsia was posthumously awarded Kirti Chakra

Kirti Chakra (cont.)

JEMADAR KULWANT SINGH (POSTHUMOUS)
THE SIKH REGIMENT

"On 24TH June 1956, Jemadar Kulwant Singh was in command of a platoon engaged in clearing hostiles from Jotsoma Village in the Naga Hills District. His platoon was acting in defence of one of their troops flanks. The hostiles having already infiltrated along the flanks, had presented serious threat to the rear. This JCO on his own readjusted his platoon to foil their attempt. The hostiles reached close by and engaged the platoon with Sten gun and rifle fire, taking advantage of heavy under-growth and low visibility. Jemadar Kulwant Singh spotted two hostiles in their hideout and killed one of them with his sten gun while wounding the other. During the hostiles attack the JCO went round to each man, despite intense sniping and close automatic fire, warning them all to be watchful of the flanks where more hostiles had appeared. While doing so he was hit in the chest by a Tommy gun burst. Despite his grievous injury he continued to encourager his men to clear the hostile-infested area, which he succeeded in doing, before he expired. Jemadar Kulwant Singh demonstrated cool courage, dynamic leadership and unflinching devotion to duty while leading his men under most difficult conditions. He made the supreme sacrifice in the best traditions of the Army." Jemadar Kulwant Singh was posthumously awarded Kirti Chakra

SEPOY SEWA SINGH
THE SIKH REGIMENT

"During 1947-1948 Indo-Pakistani conflict, on 1^H September 1948, Sepoy Sewa Singh was ordered to assault a dug-in position which was protecting a 25 Pounder gun at Jalkot on the Indo-Pakistan borders. His section was held up by heavy light machine-gunfire. Sepoy Sewa Singh, entirely on his own initiative crawled forward and threw two grenades into the trench, thus silencing the light machine-gun. He then dashed forward and bayoneted three of the light machine-gun crew in the post. This bold action of his helped the advance of his section and enabled them to carry out their task successfully and without any casualties. Sepoy Sewa Singh, the youngest soldier in his platoon, thus displayed great offensive spirit and determination and set and example to all."

Kirti Chakra (cont.)

NAIK HARDIAL SINGH (POSTHUMOUS)
THE SIKH REGIMENT

"On 3RD November 1948, the Union Circle Inspector reported the presence of six notorious decoits fully armed in a nearby village. Naik Hardial Singh who was Section Commander in the platoon was ordered to capture these decoits. The platoon was guided to a nullah in an area covered with high grass, trees and thick shrubs. Placing two sections on the flanks the platoon commander ordered Naik Hardial Singh's section to comb the suspected area. When Naik Hardial Singh was hardly 30 yards from the dacoit's position he was fired upon and sustained a severe wound in his right thigh. Although he was offered field dressing, he refused to accept it and rushed towards the position, firing his Sten gun killing 3 dacoits. Two dacoits, however, retreated to take up a new position. Naik Hardial Singh chased them and threw a grenade at them. This killed one and wounded the other. The wounded dacoit fired a burst from his Thomson sub machine-gun and a bullet hit Naik Hardial Singh in the neck killing him on the spot. Naik Hardial Singh showed exemplary courage, leadership throughout this operation." Naik Hardial Singh was posthumously awarded Kirti Chakra.

CAPTAIN SAMPURAN SINGH GREWAL
INDIAN AIR FORCE

"When his aircraft was nearly 150 miles from Delhi and flying at an altitude of 19,000 feet, it suddenly encountered severe hailstorm. The impact of the hailstones was so great that one panel of the shatterproof glass of the pilot's windscreen was knocked out while the other panels were rendered opaque. Fragments from the glass from the windscreen lacerated Captain Grewal's head and face resulting in profuse bleeding. The damage to the aircraft and its controls and loss of pressurization with the consequent loss of oxygen to the crew and passengers, produced an extremely serious situation. In this emergency, Captain Grewal displayed great presence of mind, courage and skill in retaining control of the aircraft, negotiating it through the storm and landing safely at Palam Airport despite his own injuries and the damage sustained by the aircraft His outstanding performance ranks high in the annals of aviation and will serve as an inspiration to other pilots." Captain Grewal was awarded Kirti Chakra for his outstanding performance in an extremely dangerous situation.

Kirti Chakra (cont.)

NAIK KARNAIL SINGH (POSTHUMOUS)
THE PUNJAB REGIMENT

" On April 1^{St} 1957, the platoon to which Naik Karnail Singh belonged was sent on road protection duty from Zhulake to mile 17 on the Khonoma-Zhulake Road in Naga Hills. Near mile 18 they encountered nearly 3000 hostiles dug in well camouflaged trenches and armed with light machine-guns, rifles and muzzle loading guns. The leading section of the platoon was fired upon from point-blank range and suffered some casualties. When firing started, the hostiles came out of the jungle and engaged Karnail Singh's section and occupied the northern portion of a spur, which was in its possession. Naik Karnail Singh did not loose his nerve and directed fire on the hostiles, who, though suffering casualties, were in large numbers that they rapidly closed around his section. Naik Karnail Singh, picking up a dead comrade's rifle and bayonet, led his section to charge the hostile position. There was a bitter hand-to-hand fight in which all the hostiles were overpowered and bayoneted to death. Later after the engagement the body of Naik Karnail Singh was found still clutching at the shreds of hostiles clothes.

Naik Karnail Singh's complete disregard of personal safety and great devotion to duty was in the best traditions of the Army" Naik Karnail Singh was posthumously awarded Kirti Chakra.

Gallant soldiers of The Punjab Regiment performing bhangra on a captured Pakistani T-59 tank at Longewala. Major Kuldip Singh Chandpuri, who was the commander of the post, is standing with his back to camera.

Kirti Chakra (cont.)

I have been unable to trace the Kirti Chakra Citations of the following soldiers.

THE SIKH REGIMENT

1 SUBEDAR DHIAN SINGH

2 NAIK NAWAB SINGH TOMAR (POSTHUMOUS)

3 LANCE NAIK JAGJIT SINGH

4 HAVILDAR LASHKAR SINGH (POSTHUMOUS)

THE PUNJAB REGIMENT

HAVILDAR AMAR SINGH

SUBEDAR SOHAN SINGH (POSTHUMOUS)

NAIK KARNAIL SINGH (POSTHUMOUS)

MAJOR SUKHDEV SINGH (POSTHUMOUS)

LANCE NAIK CHARAN SINGH

MAJOR MOHINDE SINGH PATHANIA

SEPOY GURTEJ SINGH

SEPOY BALBIR SINGH

THE JAT REGIMENT

CAPTAIN HARIPAL SINGH AHLUWALIA

THE RAJPUT REGIMENT

LT. COL. JASWANT SINGH

THE ASSAM RIFLES

CAPTAIN HARBANS SINGH

THE ENGINEERS

NAIK AJIT SINGH

THE BIHAR REGIMENT

CAPTAIN AJIT SINGH

THE GARHWAL RIFLES

LT.COL. TEJINDER SINGH

THE MECHANISED INFANTRY REGIMENT

CAPTAIN HARDEV SINGH

THE GUARDS

HAVILDAR SARWAN SINGH

SHAURYA CHAKRA

Shaurya Chakra is an Indian military decoration awarded for valor, **Shaurya Chakra** action or self-sacrifice while not engaged in direct action with the enemy. It is the peacetime equivalent of the Vir Chakra It is generally awarded for counter-insurgency operations and actions against the enemy during peace-time.

The list of the Shaurya Chakra winners is incomplete as full data is unavailable.

Bibi Amrik Kaur, "lioness of the border area", was awarded the Shaurya Chakra for her fight against militants at her house in 1990.

Shaurya Chakra (cont.)

HAVILDAR BHAG SINGH
THE SIKH REGIMENT

"On November 2ND 1962, Havildar Bhag Singh was sent with a patrol to capture a notorious hostile leader in a village in the disturbed areas of Manipur. The patrol encircled the hostiles who ran in two directions firing at the patrol. Havildar Bhag Singh split his patrol for chasing both the hostile groups. A hostile threw a grenade, which narrowly missed Havildar Bhag Singh. He fired and wounded the leader of the gang who jumped down a deep ravine. Havildar Bhag Singh also jumped down, grappled with the leader and captured him. Some arms, ammunition were recovered from the hostiles." Havildar Bhag Singh was awarded the Shaurya Chakra for his courageous actions against the hostiles.

NAIK KEHAR SINGH
THE SIKH LIGHT INFANTRY

"Naik Kehar Singh was commanding the leading section of a patrol which set out on the 6TH December 1960, to locate and apprehend the hostiles in their hide-out in the area of Tophema and Gariphema in Nagaland. Over hazardous terrain and in complete darkness, Naik Kehar Singh led his patrol to the hostile camp and had it surrounded. Realizing that they were about to be trapped, the hostiles opened heavy small arms fire on the leading section. Firing his Sten gun from the hip, Naik Kehar Singh rushed undauntedly towards the hostile fire. He wounded three hostiles. His bold and determined action forced he hostiles to abandon their position and escape into thick jungle leaving behind three rifles, four muzzle loading guns and some ammunition." The courage, leadership and devotion to duty displayed by Naik Kehar Singh earned him the Shaurya Chakra.

SEPOY HARBANS SINGH (POSTHUMOUS)
THE SIKH REGIMENT

"On 10TH February 1964, Sepoy Harbans Singh was the leading scout of the rifle platoon which formed part of a column that set out to raid hostile hide-outs in Nagaland. While on the move Sepoy Harbans Singh gallantly charged a hostile position firing his rifle from his hip position, thereby wounding the hostiles who fled leaving behind rifles and ammunition. Harbans Singh once again took the position of a scout and led his section into thick jungle against persistent hostile small arms fire. Harbans Singh was wounded in the leg, yet continued firing from the hip as he advanced. Meanwhile a hostile light machine-gun opened fire on him and he sustained another bullet injury in the chest, which proved fatal. The gallant actions of Sepoy Harbans Singh inspired his comrades tremendously, who lead a determined assault on the hostiles and eliminated their fire." Sepoy Harbans Singh was posthumously awarded Shaurya Chakra.

Shaurya Chakra (cont.)

JEMADAR DALIP SINGH
THE SIKH REGIMENT

"On 19TH April 1956, in Naga Hills, Jemadar Dalip Singh volunteered with 7 other ranks to go to the aid of a patrol ambushed by the hostiles near the village of Lazaphemi. On arrival he found the patrol still busy clearing the hostile ambush. He promptly decided to cut off the hostiles retreat by occupying a dominating ridge behind them. While ascending along a steep gradient, well-concealed hostiles opened heavy fire at close range on the party, holding up their advance. Jemadar Dalip Singh took the only grenade-firing rifle in the party and attacked the hostiles with grenades, thereby dislodging them from their position. Although wounded in the process, he rushed forward single-handedly and charged the hostile post, taking advantage of the temporary confusion caused among the hostile ranks as a result of the explosion of rifle grenades. He shot dead two hostiles in his daring attack while others fled as they saw the charging Jemadar closely followed by his men. Again on 28TH April, as Jemadar Dalip Singh led the assault on Zulhami feature the hostiles opened heavy light machine-gun fire and one of the leading sections of his platoon got held up in a thick row of Punjis. Jemadar Dalip Singh rushed forward to cut a lane through the Punjis, to enable the advance to continue. Thus the momentum of the assault was kept at its highest pitch despite heavy fire. The platoon soon got on to its objective where again the Jemadar personally charged the fleeing hostiles, killing six and capturing their two rifles. On both these occasions, Jemadar Dalip Singh displayed leadership of a very high order." For his leadership and gallantry Jemadar Dalip Singh was awarded the Shaurya Chakra.

SEPOY RANJIT SINGH (POSTHUMOUS)
THE SIKH REGIMENT

"On 29TH April 1956, while restoring law and order in Naga Hills, Sepoy Ranjit Singh's battalion was engaged in capturing strong hostile hide-out at Zulhami. On capture of the objective, a small gang of hostiles emerged from the rear of the column and opened fire with rifles and Sten guns. The section was immediately ordered to assault the hostile party. Sepoy Ranjit Singh dashed ahead of his section and bayoneted one of the hostiles to death. He had hardly pulled the Bayonet out, when suddenly another hostile threw grenade at him, as a result of which Sepoy Ranjit Singh dropped down. Despite the serious chest wound, he tried to crawl forward, but due to the profuse bleeding his struggle could not last long and he expired within few seconds. His bold action had already facilitated the advance of his section, which successfully liquidated the hostile opposition." Sepoy Ranjit Singh was posthumously awarded the Shaurya Chakra.

Shaurya Chakra (cont.)

LANCE HAVILDAR BALWANT SINGH
THE SIKH REGIMENT

"During 1947-1948 Indo-Pakistani conflict, a train escort of The Sikh Regiment was detailed to escort a refugee train carrying approximately 3,000 Hindu refugees from Samerial Camp to Ravi Bridge near Dera Baba Nanak, on 29TH September 1947. When the train was about two miles away from Sialkot it was forced to halt by a block on railway line put up by local Muslims. Approximately 1,000 Muslims had taken up positions on either side of the railway line and were well armed, some with automatic rifles. As soon the train stopped, it was fired upon from both sides, as a result of which twelve refugees were wounded which caused great panic among them. Lance Havildar Balwant Singh realizing the gravity of the situation, on his own initiative come out of his compartment and took up position and opened fire on the mob with his Bren gun. He only partially succeeded in checking the advance of the mob that was heading for the train and were bent on annihilating the Hindu refugees. When the situation was getting out of hand, Balwant Singh crawled forward under heavy fire and threw hand grenades from close quarters at the mob and prevented the mob from coming near the train. His action enabled the front guard to remove the block thus allowing the train to proceed safely. Lance Havildar Balwant Singh's devotion to duty at the risk of his own life, his determination, initiative, courage and steadfastness displayed for the safety of approximately 3,000 Hindu refugee in the face of heavy odds are an act of gallantry worthy of highest praise." For his conspicuous gallantry Lance Havildar Balwant Singh was awarded the Shaurya Chakra.

MAJOR BALWANT SINGH
ASSAM RIFLES

"On 14TH May 1960, while restoring law and order in Naga Hills, Major Balwant Singh received information about the location of two hostile camps. He immediately decided to find the camps and leaving his bade after midnight with two platoons under his command land ambushers in the jungle and succeeded in capturing two hostile runners with documents and killing one. During subsequent operations, he personally led a platoon, which was ambushed by a strong hostile party. Unperturbed, he successfully brought his troops out of the ambush, in the process inflicting casualties on the hostile party. For the next three weeks he laid a number of ambushes in which some hostiles were killed and several wounded. With determination, untiring effort and persistence. He continued to comb the area and located and destroyed at least five major camps. His action completely demoralized the hostiles and forced them to abandon their strong bold. Major Balwant Singh's dogged perseverance, courage and leadership were source of inspiration to his men in these operations which were conducted in difficult terrain and severe monsoon conditions."

Shaurya Chakra (cont.)

SUBEDAR MOHAR SINGH
THE SIKH REGIMENT

"Subedar Mohar Singh was in command of a strong platoon garrison at Phek in Naga Hills, while rest of his company was engaged elsewhere. Knowing the reduced strength of the post, some 300 hostiles armed with light machine-guns and rifles surrounded the post on 29TH April 1956. Taking advantage of bad weather and darkness, the hostiles approached within 100 yards of the post, firing intensely and raising Naga war cries. Subedar Mohar Singh went around the post, directing fire and exhorting his men to stand firm, quite unmindful of bullets flying all around him from close range. The hostiles stopped their fire in the early hours and an assault appeared imminent. But Subedar Mohar Singh's skilful use of weapons and inspiring leadership held the hostiles at bay, thus breaking up a determined night attack by superior numbers.

Next morning the hostiles mustered their strength and re-emerged for assault. Subedar Mohar Singh held his fire until the hostiles had come within 200 yards and then he suddenly opened up with all his weapons with devasting effect. The assault was repulsed with 8 hostiles dead and many more wounded. Exploiting this success Mohar Singh personally lead an attack on a hostile position, which had seized the water point. This night attack was conducted with such daring and dash that the hostile position was cleared, killing 6 more and capturing some ammunition. Subedar Mohar Singh was wounded while leading this attack but though bleeding, he did not disclose this to anyone till the threat to his garrison was removed. Throughout this action he showed leadership, fearlessness and tactical skill of a high order, which made a deep impression on his men who responded magnificently." Subedar Mohar Singh's conspicuous gallantry earned him the Shaurya Chakra.

JEMADAR MOHINDER SINGH
THE SIKH LIGHT INFANTRY

"The Sikh Light Infantry were employed in restoring law and order in Naga Hills. Jemadar Mohinder Singh was commanding the leading platoon of his company that was ordered to clear Jotsoma Village on 21ST June 1956. His section was met with intense automatic and rifle fire from prepared positions. Jemadar Mohinder Singh appreciated the situation and charged forward with his men. He was seriously wounded in the chest and the platoon was halted. Quite unmindful of personal danger and despite his serious injury, he quickly reorganized the platoon, arranged support and evacuated the casualties. This was accomplished in the face of heavy odds. His leadership and cool courage enabled his platoon to get out of a critical situation. The soldierly qualities displayed by him while himself badly wounded were worthy of the highest commendation." For which Jemadar Mohinder Singh was awarded the Shaurya Chakra.

Shaurya Chakra (cont.)

THE SIKH REGIMENT

SEPOY HARCHAND SINGH
LANCE HAVILDAR BALWANT SINGH
SUBEDAR MOHAR SINGH
JEMADAR MOHINDER SINGH
SEPOY RANJIT SINGH (POSTHUMOUS)
JEMADAR DALIP SINGH
SEPOY HARBANS SINGH (POSTHUMOUS)
LANCE HAVILDAR PIARA SINGH
SEPOY SURJIT SINGH (POSTHUMOUS)
SEPOY JASWANT SINGH
HAVILDAR SUKHVIJNDER SINGH (POSTHUMOUS)
SEPOY NIRBHAY SINGH (POSTHUMOUS)
SEPOY DALJIT SINGH
NAIK BALBIR SINGH (POSTHUMOUS)
SEPOY IKBAL SINGH (POSTHUMOUS)
LANCE NAIK SATNAM SINGH (POSTHUMOUS)
SUBEDAR JASHPAL SINGH
SEPOY GURTEJ SINGH (POSTHUMOUS)
SUBEDAR SUKHAIN SINGH
SEPOY HARVINDER SINGH
HAVILDAR SHER SINGH
HAVILDAR GURCHARAN SINGH
HAVILDAR BHAG SINGH
SEPOY SUKHBIR SINGH (POSTHMOUS)
LT JOGA SINGH (POSTHMOUS)
SEPOY PARAMJI SINGH (POSTHMOUS)
C. H. M. SARBJIT SINGH
SEPOY JASBIR SINGH
NAIK GUJRANT SINGH (POSTHMOUS)

Shaurya Chakra (cont.)

THE PUNJAB REGIMENT

SUBEDAR KARTAR SINGH MC
LANCE NAIK MILKHA SINGH
LANCE NAIK BISHAN SINGH
NAIK HARDIAL SINGH (POSTHUMOUS)
SEPOY GURBHAN SINGH
SEPOY MEGH SINGH
JEMADAR PIRTHI SINGH
HAVILDAR BALWANT SINGH
NAIK KESAR SINGH
2ND LT HARDIP SINGH GUMAN
MAJOR KANWAL JIT SINGH
SEPOY MANJIT SINGH (POSTHUMOUS)
SEPOY JASWINDER SINGH
SEPOY RANJODH SINGH
SEPOY LAKHA SINGH
SUBEDAR NAIB SINGH
SUBEDAR AVTAR SINGH (POSTHUMOUS)
LANCE NAIK SADHU SINGH
HAVILDAR LAKHVINDER SINGH (POSTHUMOUS)
LT COL BACHITTAR SINGH (POSTHUMOUS)
NAIB SUBEDAR AJIT SINGH
SUBEDAR SUKHWINDER SINGH
NAIK PIARA SINGH
SEPOY RAJINDER SINGH (POSTHMOUS)
SEPOY SUKHRAJ SINGH
NAIK SUBEDAR AJIT SINGH
SEPOY RANJIT SINGH

THE SIGNALS

LANCE NAIK JAGBEER SINGH

Shaurya Chakra (cont.)

INDIAN AIR FORCE

WATCHMAN AMAR SINGH
ASST. ST. MASTER APAR SINGH CHEEMA
CORPORAL SARMUKH SINGH
CORPORAL GURDIP SINGH DEOL
CORPORAL DARSHAN SINGH BRAR
SERGEANT SHER SINGH KADIAN
SERGEANT JAGMEL SINGH
FLT. LT.RAJDEEP SINGH MANN
FLT. CPT. MOHINDER JEET SINGH BAINS
SQN. LEADER.GURCHARAN SINGH MADAN
SQN. LEADER TEJWANT SINGH
SQN. LEADERR AJINDER PAL SINGH DHILLON
SQN. LEADER MANJIT SINGH SEKHON
SQN. LEADER DAVINDER SINGH SANT
SQN. LEADERSUKHMANDER SINGH SIDHU
SQN. LEADER GULZARINDER SINGH BRAICH
SQN. LEADERN ARINDER SINGH
SQN. LEADER TEJINDER PAL SINGH CHIMA
WNG. CMDR. JASMINDER SINGH KAHLON
WNG. CMDR. BALJIT SINGH CHOKKER
WNG. CMDR. AJIT SINGH SAICH
WNG. CMDR. HARPAL SINGH NATT
WNG. CMDR. RAVINDER SINGH MANN
MAJOR GUR IQBAL SINGH DHODI

THE BORDER SCOUTS
SCOUT SAUDAGAR SINGH

THE BIHAR REGIMENT
CAPTAIN GS GREWAL

Shaurya Chakra (cont.)

REGIMENT OF ARTILLERY

SUBEDAR MAJOR DHAN SINGH
BRIGADIE RAJINDER SINGH VSM
MAJOR GURMUKH SINGH DHILLON
CAPTAIN GURJEET SINGH BAJWA
SUBEDAR MOHAN SINGH
MAJOR JASWINDER PAL SINGH
COL MALKIAT SINGH DULLAT
MAJOR HARBUX SINGH GILL
SUBEDAR SINGARA SINGH
SUBEDAR BALWANT SINGH
GUNNER RANJIT SINGH
MAJOR GURTEJ SINGH GREWAL

THE PARACHUTE REGIMENT

MAJOR MANPREET SINGH BAINS
PRIVATE SATPAL SINGH
PRIVATE GIAN SINGH (POSTHMOUS)
CAPTAIN R. SINGH MANN
NAIK SUBEDAR SOMVIR SINGH
HAVILDAR SAHIB SINGH
PRIVATE BHUPINDER SINGH
LT. AMARJIT SINGH
HAVILDAR MANJIT SINGH
JEMADAR BALBIR SINGH
LT COL SURIJNDER SINGH BAJWA
NAIB SUBEDAR SURJIT SINGH
CAPTAIN RAMVINDER SINGH GILL
LANCE NAIK JASBIR SINGH
2ND LT PARMJIT SINGH BAJWA
PRIVATE DALIP SINGH

Shaurya Chakra (cont.)

JAMMU AND KASHMIR RIFLES
HAVILDAR SEWA SINGH
SUBEDAR SANTOKH SINGH

THE DOGRA REGIMENT
MAJOR KULDIP SINGH

THE JAT REGIMENT
CAPTAIN MANJINDER SINGH

SIKH LIGHT INFANTRY
LANCE NAIK TIRATH SINGH (POSTHUMOUS)
SEPOY DARA SINGH (POSTHUMOUS)
NAIK KEHAR SINGH
LANCE HAVILDAR MAKHAN SINGH
SEPOY NISHAN SINGH
LANCE NAIK JOGINDER SINGH
SEPOY SURJIT SINGH
SEPOY RAUNAK SINGH
LANCE NAIK HARMAL SINGH
CHM SARBJIT SINGH
SUBEDAR JAGDEV SINGH (POSTHUMOUS)

THE ENGINEERS
SAPPER GIAN SINGH
NAIB SUBEDAR LAHORA SINGH
LANCE HAVILDAR MUKHTIAR SINGH
SUBEDAR SEWA SINGH
SAPPER HARBANS SINGH (POSTHUMOUS)
LANCE NAIK PURAN SINGH (POSTHUMOUS)
LANCE NAIK DHIABN SINGH
MAJOR BHUPINDER SINGH
SAPPER BALBIR SINGH (POSTHUMOUS)
MAJOR HS SIDHU (POSTHUMOUS)

Shaurya Chakra (cont.)

THE GUARDS

NAIK LACHMAN SINGH
GUARDSMAN TEJ SINGH
GUARDMAN SURJAN SINGH
NAIB SUBEDAR HARNAM SINGH
HAVILDAR HARMINDER SINGH
LANCE NAIK MAJOR SINGH
LANCE NAIK MANROOP SINGH
MAJOR SANDHU HARINDER PAL SINGH
NAIK TEJ SINGH
GUARDSMAN KARNAIL SINGH (POSTHUMOUS)

GENERAL RESERVE ENGINEER FORCE

MECH TARCHAN SINGH
DME BAHADUR SINGH
PIONEER BALBIR SINGH (POSTHUMOUS)
DME JOGINDER SINGH
DRIVER KARTAR SINGH (POSTHUMOUS)
QEM BIR SINGH (POSTHUMOUS)
AE KEHAR SINGH CHIMA
QEM MOHINDER SINGH
SURDT MOHAN SINGH
DME IQBAL SINGH

THE MECHANISED INFANTRY REGIMENT

NAIB SUBEDAR JASWANT SINGH (POSTHUMOUS)
HAVILDAR KAN SINGH
COL AJIT SINGH
MAJOR PARMVIR SINGH JAMWAL

RAJ RIF

MAJOR JAGROOP SINGH BRAR
COL RAJ PAL SINGH SHERGIL

Shaurya Chakra (cont.)

THE ARMOURED REGIMENT
NAIN SUBEDAR MOHAR SINGH (POSTHUMOUS)
DAFADAR TASVIR SINGH (POSTHUMOUS)
MAJOR AMANPREET SINGH LEGHA
DAFADAR HARBHAJAN SINGH (POSTHUMOUS)
SOWAR SULTAN SINGH

THE GARHWAL RIFLES
MAJOR PARMINDER SINGH BHINDER

THE ASSAM REGIMENT
CAPTAIN HARBINDER SINGH GILL
SUBEDAR KEHAR SINGH
MAJOR SUKHMEET SINGH

THE RAJPUT REGIMENT
LT HARJINDER PAL SINGH DHAMI

INFANTRY BATTALIONS (TA)
GDR ARJAN SINGH
SUBEDAR DALIP SINGH (POSTHUMOUS)
LANCE NAIK RANJODH SINGH
MAJOR BHUPINDER SINGH
SEPOY SAHIB SINGH
SEPOY AMRIK SINGH
HAVILDAR SHER SINGH

INDIAN NAVY
ABLE SEAMAN J. S. BAWA
ORD. SEAMAN BACHAN SINGH
ABLE SEAMAN TEJA SINGH
L. S. CMDR. DILBAG SINGH SIDHU
LT. CMDR. K. S. SANDHU
LT. CMDR. R. S. GILL
LT. CMDR. KAMAL SINGH

ABOUT THIS BOOK

Since ancient times soldiers have been honoured for gallantry in battle. Over the years and in different societies such honours have taken many forms, but since the 1850's specific acts of bravery 'in the face of the enemy' have been recognised by the award of a range of wearable decorations.

These provide a visible indication both of the bravery of the recipient and of its recognition by the government and nation.

Guru Nanak laid the foundation of a new religion in the fifteenth century. His followers called themselves Sikhs or disciples. To combat the Mohammedan's persecution Guru Gobind Singh transformed the Sikhs from a religious into a military body. He demanded brave deeds and zealous devotion to the cause as proof of faith until religious fervour was entirely eclipsed by military zeal.

This collection of the gallantry awards endeavours to celebrate the heroic Sikh military traditions of individual bravery, of undying loyalty, of courage and dedication to duty in virtually every field of battle.

Narindar Singh Dhesi was born in 1940 at Eldoret in Kenya, where his father, Waryam Singh, an Akali freedom fighter, had migrated from the Punjab. He moved to England in 1957 and joined the British Army. After leaving the armed forces in 1964 he went into the building and construction industry. He is married with four children and is living in retirement at Southend on Sea, England.

A companion volume by the same author, *Sikh Soldier Battle Honours* is also available.

www.ingramcontent.com/pod-product-compliance
Lightning Source LLC
Chambersburg PA
CBHW080632230426
43663CB00016B/2845